W9-CMT-578

STUDIES ON THE CIVILIZATION AND CULTURE OF NUZI AND THE HURRIANS

Volume 6

STUDIES ON THE CIVILIZATION AND CULTURE OF NUZI AND THE HURRIANS

Edited by

David I. Owen

TWO HUNDRED NUZI TEXTS FROM THE ORIENTAL INSTITUTE OF THE UNIVERSITY OF CHICAGO

Part I

DS
70.5
.N9S88
v. 6
seab

By
M. P. Maidman

CDL Press
Bethesda, Maryland

THE UNITED LIBRARY
2121 Sheridan Road
Evanston, Illinois 60201

© 1994.

All rights reserved. This book may not be reproduced, in whole or in part, in any form (beyond that copying permitted by Sections 107 and 108 of the U.S. Copyright Law and except by reviewers for the public press), without written permission from the publisher.

Cover Design by Ellen Maidman. Drawing based on a figurine of Ishtar found at Nuzi.
Published by CDL Press, POB 34454, Bethesda, MD 20827.
Printed by Bookcrafters, Fredericksburg, Virginia.

ISBN 1-883053-05-6

Library of Congress Cataloging-in-Publication Data

Two hundred Nuzi texts from the Oriental Institute of the University of Chicago / [translated and edited by] M.P. Maidman.
v. <1 > cm. — (Studies in the civilization and culture of Nuzi and the Hurrians ; v. 6)
Texts in Akkadian (romanized); translation and commentary in English.
Includes bibliographical references and index.
ISBN 1-883053-05-6 : $50.00
1. Akkadian language—Texts. 2. Nuzi (Extinct city)—Economic conditions—Sources. I. Maidman, M. P. II. University of Chicago. Oriental Institute. III. Title: 200 Nuzi texts from the Oriental Institute of the University of Chicago. IV. Series.
PJ3870.T86 1994
492′.1—dc20 94-16989
CIP

To Ellen

CONTENTS

FOREWORD

In his introduction to *JEN* VII (SCCNH 3, p. 1), Maynard P. Maidman promised a companion commentary consisting of *Two Hundred Texts from the Oriental Institute of the University of Chicago* (=*THNT*). Less than five years later we are pleased to publish here the first half of that major effort reflecting the meticulous research that has gone into his project. Although this substantial volume represents only half of the commentary (*JEN* 674-774), it nevertheless includes all collations to the two hundred *JEN* VII texts (below, Appendix: Additions to *JEN* VII) and numerous references throughout to the forthcoming part II. It can be said that no study of Nuzi texts to date has contained as extensive and detailed commentary on so many texts. Each of the *JEN* VII documents has been collated sign by sign. The texts have been matched with others in the various Nuzi publications. Witness lists have been established and clarified. Individual participants in these archives have been highlighted and their careers augmented through detailed analyses. Numerous corrections to previous readings in dictionaries and in secondary studies have been offered as have many improvements in the interpretation of these and related documents (see, for example, comments to *JEN* 699 on the *ilku*-tax; 718 on *sassukku;* 763 on *peniḫuru* and 764 on *ḫararnu*).

Indeed, Maidman's work sets a standard against which future work on the Nuzi texts will have to be measured. He has demonstrated once again the need to guard against uncritical textual emendations and reconstructions, the need for repeated collations and, most of all, the required mastery of the archives. He has also shown how valuable the contributions of Lacheman and Gelb have been to the interpretation of these texts as revealed by his careful scrutiny of the Lacheman papers and the *CAD* files. His addition of specialized indexes that relate these documents to others in the archives will assure the use of this volume for future research by anyone working with Nuzi sources. And, most of all, his work reflects the richness and vitality of Nuzi textual data for our understanding of Hurrian society and culture in the fifteenth and fourteenth centuries B.C.E.

There remains a great deal more work to be completed with respect to the Oriental Institute Nuzi holdings. As outlined below in Maidman's Introduction, hundreds of texts and fragments remain to be edited in addition to the remaining *JEN* VII texts. Maidman's work is much advanced on all levels and we can look forward to the appearance of additional volumes and secondary studies in this series that will reflect the results of his efforts.

Working with him to bring the Nuzi texts to full publication has been a particularly rewarding experience. Maynard's dedication to Nuzi research is exceptional. It will be through this dedication that the Chicago tablets and fragments will finally see the light of publication.

Finally, I would like to thank Dr. Mark E. Cohen and the CDL Press for the care expended in the composition of this complex manuscript and Ellen Maidman for the handsome new cover design marking the move to CDL Press.

* * *

The appearance of Volume 6 of SCCNH represents a transition between the substantial volumes which have characterized this series and the beginning of the publication of an annual which will be considerably smaller. I began this series with the *Lacheman AV* (=SCCNH 1) and with the cordial help and cooperation of Professor Martha A. Morrison with whom I co-edited volumes 1-4. She played a significant role on the editorial level and was a major contributor to the volumes themselves. I am most grateful for all her input over the years. The current volume also marks a change in publishers. I have moved from a long and cordial association with James E. Eisenbraun at Eisenbrauns to Dr. Mark E. Cohen at CDL Press. The reason for this change lies primarily in my desire to turn the series into an annual so as to facilitate not only the study and publication of the outstanding Nuzi texts, but also to make the results of the interpretation of these tablets available more expeditiously. Furthermore, after discussions with Professor Gernot Wilhelm, we decided to join efforts to expand the scope of the series by increasing the focus on Hurrian studies. Thanks to the discovery of the Boğazköy bilingual and other new Hurrian finds, this area of research has become increasingly more productive.

Volume 7 of SCCNH will appear in January 1995 and the annual will be co-edited by Professor Gernot Wilhelm and myself. It and subsequent volumes will consist ca. 150-175 pages, appearing in January every year. The editors will consider articles submitted on historical, philological, archaeological and art historical topics relating to the general topics of Nuzi, Hurrians, Hurrian and Hurro-Akkadian in their widest contexts. Manuscripts in Europe may be sent directly to Professor Gernot Wilhelm, Institut für Orientalische Philologie der Julius-Maximilians-Universität Würzburg, Ludwigstraße 6, D-97070 Würzburg, Germany. Those from North America and Asia should be sent to Professor David I. Owen, Near Eastern Studies, Rockefeller Hall 360, Cornell University, Ithaca, NY 14853-2502 USA. Inquiries may also be made by electronic mail to DIO1@CORNELL.EDU or by facsimile to (USA) 607-255-1345 or (Germany) 049-931-57-22-61. Preferably, manuscripts should be submitted in electronic form (IBM or MAC format with the name and version of the word processor used) along with a printed copy. Closing date for manuscripts each year will be July 15th.

Volumes 1-5 may be obtained directly from Eisenbrauns, POB 275, Winona Lake, IN 46590 USA. Volume 6 and following may be obtained directly from CDL Press, P.O. Box 34454, Bethesda, MD 20827 USA. Subscriptions may be ordered from either publisher.

David I. Owen
Ithaca, New York
1 April 1994

PREFACE

The present volume contains editions and indices to half of the 200 Nuzi texts published in *Joint Expedition with the Iraq Museum at Nuzi, VII: Miscellaneous Texts* (=*SCCNH* 3). Editions of the remaining *JEN* VII texts are to appear in a forthcoming volume. These two volumes represent, together with *JEN* VII itself, the completion of the first stage of a project which has engaged my attention for years: the publication of the remaining Nuzi texts housed (or once housed) in the Oriental Institute of the University of Chicago. There remain to be published some 110 relatively complete tablets and major fragments, a further 458 significant fragments (i.e., fragments where continuous context can be discerned and where up to one-third of the original context remains), and about 1300 more small (sometimes very informative) pieces. Work on all this material has reached an advanced stage. In many cases, it has been completed. An exhaustive catalogue of the Oriental Institute Nuzi collection is also largely completed and should neatly cap the Chicago phase of the Nuzi text publication project.

The story of the Nuzi texts of Chicago is a complex one (see *JEN* VII, pp. 1-3). It involves study and examination of a good number of these tablets by many individuals over several decades. Definitive edition of these texts demands scrutiny, where possible, of these previous attempts to understand this material.

The first and most systematic attempt to treat these Nuzi texts appears as the Nuzi file of the *Chicago Assyrian Dictionary*. At the *Dictionary*'s offices, located down the hall from the Nuzi tablets themselves, several file drawers of cards contain transliterations of hundreds of texts. This store of data is the work of I.J. Gelb, P.M. Purves, E.R. Lacheman, and others. For access to, and unlimited use of, these files, I thank Erica Reiner, Editor-in-Charge of the *CAD*. Her cooperation in this project has been unfailing.

Thanks are also due to Edith Porada. With great generosity, she made available to me her extensive dissertation notes. These notes contain copies of seal impressions from many of the texts from the Oriental Institute and elsewhere. Her study further includes notes on the legends associated with these impressions, witness sequences, and archaeological provenience.

Ernest R. Lacheman studied much of the Chicago material. His unpublished notes—mostly transliterations—appear in a bewildering array of forms and formats. For allowing me to explore and to use the Lacheman manuscripts, I am indebted to David I. Owen, Lacheman's literary executor.

I owe David much more. He has been a constant source of encouragement and advice in this endeavor, and the outcome has benefited greatly for his influence.

Of course, the most valuable resource in editing these texts remains the tablets themselves. J.A. Brinkman, Curator of the Tablet Collection of the Oriental Institute has continued to facilitate my use of the Nuzi documents. From the very outset of the project, Brinkman has appreciated keenly the significance of the texts and the importance of their publication.

I am once again happily in the debt of the Social Sciences and Humanities Research Council of Canada for its generous support. The financial burden of my research on the Nuzi texts as been largely borne by the Council. An SSHRC Research Time Stipend for 1988-89 gave me the time to complete the lion's share of the manuscript of this book. Most recently, an SSHRC Research Grant gave me the time and money to complete the volume.

York University and my home within the University, the Department of History, have continued to facilitate my work. A York University Faculty of Arts Fellowship has materially aided in me in my research and successive chairmen of the Department, especially Professors Russell Chace and Richard Hoffmann, have done all they could to find me the time and other resources I require for the project. I also thank Professor John Warkentin of York's Department of Geography for discussing with me matters of topography.

I dedicate this volume to Ellen, my wife. Her burden has been heavy; her help, in many ways, indispensable. I thank her for all this and especially for our continuing adventure.

M.P. Maidman
Washington, D.C.
4 October 1993

ABBREVIATIONS

Abbreviations follow Borger (1967, 661-72) with the following additions.

AAN	Cassin, E., and J.-J. Glassner. 1977. *Anthroponymie et Anthropologie de Nuzi*. Vol. 1, *Les Anthroponymes*. Malibu: Undena.
AHw	von Soden, W. 1965-81. *Akkadisches Handwörterbuch*. Wiesbaden: Otto Harrassowitz.
AOAT	Alter Orient und Altes Testament.
C	Texts published by G. Contenau (1931).
CTN	Cuneiform Texts from Nimrud.
EN	*Excavations at Nuzi*.
EN 9/1	Texts published by E.R. Lacheman, D.I. Owen, *et al.* (1987).
G	Texts published by C.J. Gadd (1926).
HSS, V	Texts published by E. Chiera (1929).
HSS, IX	Texts published by R.H. Pfeiffer (1932).
HSS, XIII	Texts published by R.H. Pfeiffer and E.R. Lacheman (1942).
HSS, XIV	Texts published by E.R. Lacheman (1950).
HSS, XV	Texts published by E.R. Lacheman (1955).
HSS, XVI	Texts published by E.R. Lacheman (1958).
HSS, XIX	Texts published by E.R. Lacheman (1962).
JEN	Texts published by E. Chiera (1927, 1930, 1931, 1934a, 1934b), by E.R. Lacheman (1939b), and by E.R. Lacheman and M.P. Maidman (1989).
LG	Texts published by E.R. Lacheman (1967).
L-O	Texts published by E.R. Lacheman and D.I. Owen (1981).
NPN	Gelb, I.J., P.M. Purves, and A.A. MacRae. 1943. *Nuzi Personal Names*. OIP, 57. Chicago: Univ. of Chicago Press.
OA	*Oriens Antiquus*.
Po	Followed by a number, this siglum is employed by Lacheman to indicate seal impressions published by Porada (1947).
P-S	Texts published by R.H. Pfeiffer and E.A. Speiser (1936).
SCCNH	*Studies on the Civilization and Culture of Nuzi and the Hurrians*.

THNT	*Two Hundred Nuzi Texts from the Oriental Institute of the University of Chicago, Part I.*
UF	*Ugarit-Forschungen.*
YNER	Yale Near Eastern Researches.

INTRODUCTION

The purpose of this volume is to make available editions of half of the two hundred texts published as *JEN* VII by Lacheman and Maidman (1989). The edition of each of these texts consists of transliteration, translation, comments, and notes. Several indices to the texts catalogue their registration numbers (this index alone precedes the text editions), the personal names, geographical names, and occupations attested in the documents, unusual or otherwise significant lexemes treated in the editions, witness sequences standard in certain contracts, and text series of which the tablets under study are part. A few partial transliterations of texts from the second half of *JEN* VII and a bibliography of works cited conclude the volume.

The prototype for volumes of this type is the pioneering work of Pfeiffer and Speiser (1936). That volume served both to publish and edit Nuzi texts. It quickly became a standard in the field and influenced subsequent, similar efforts (Cassin 1938; H. Lewy 1942; Wilhelm 1980, 1985). As the present work also traces its ancestry back to that of Pfeiffer and Speiser, so the title of the present volume recalls, deliberately, that of the earlier effort: *One Hundred New Selected Nuzi Texts*.

Two Hundred Nuzi Texts .... (hereafter *THNT*), like *One Hundred ... Nuzi Texts*, sets out to establish text by means of transliteration, to translate these texts, and to give appropriate comments and notes to the text. That is, the scope of the edition is limited: elucidation of the plain sense of the text with notes confined mostly to justifying the readings proposed, especially where the text has deteriorated—almost always the case.[1] Given that the present volume is dependent in concept upon Pfeiffer and Speiser (1936) and given the relative brevity of the earlier work, how is it that this work, treating one hundred texts like the earlier book and purporting to note only problems of establishing the text, is so much longer than its model?[2]

First, when it comes to the Nuzi texts, there is an especially keenly felt need to establish text thoroughly, conservatively, and inductively. The history of Nuzi text interpretation and study has often been lurid, as alleged Nuzi data have served masters as distant from each other as "J" and Marx. From the 1920s to the present, the texts have often suffered from superficial

[1] See pp. 7-8 below for further delineation of the scope of the notes.

[2] Brevity needs no justification; length does.

"philology" as well as from superficial secondary treatment. This is ironic, given the uniquely full record afforded by these documents. Texts were located in archives from all over Nuzi and represent its major social and economic institutions over a period of a century and a half. The abuse of this material through willful ignorance of its local context is therefore especially galling. Thus solid foundation needs to be laid for students of Nuzi and even more so, perhaps, for "outsiders." With its textual breadth and depth properly appreciated, Nuzi ought to be at the head of all those Late Bronze Age archival collections now emerging from all over Mesopotamia. These text editions aim to correct, in part, the former abuse.[3] And that requires lengthy treatment.

Furthermore, since these documents are so tightly integrated in archival complexes, major text restoration can often be undertaken because of an extensive network of documentary interconnections. Thus, the careful student of the corpus can work wonders with but little material. The weaving of this network emerging from the single text takes considerable space to accomplish.[4]

Thus for reasons both extrinsic and intrinsic to the corpus of the Nuzi texts, establishment of model text editions is a lengthier task than is usually the case. For this reason, the editions of the second one hundred texts of *JEN* VII require a separate volume.[5]

Aside from the self-evident reasons for producing text editions and those additional reasons peculiar to the Nuzi corpus, *THNT* can serve the student as a general introduction to the Nuzi texts and Nuzi society. In this capacity, *THNT* strives to follow Gadd (1926). Only those of us who have plowed the fields of Nuzi studies can fully appreciate the utility and wealth of information (in 1926!) of that publication and how effective an introduction it constituted to Nuzi studies in general. Through text and observations on the text, the reader is plunged into this world and emerges prepared for more specialized study. That work and its later imitators have long been out of print and out of date. May *THNT* prove a worthy successor to Gadd's monograph.

To the same end, the bibliography employed in *THNT*, and summarized at its conclusion, should prove a useful tool to novice students of the Nuzi texts.[6]

---

[3] The sound and meticulous work of Gernot Wilhelm has already made caricaturing the Nuzi texts more difficult than has previously been the case.

[4] These advances in restoration on the "lower," textual, level result in advances at the "higher" level of social and economic history. Thus, the extensive notes offer to the new student of Nuzi (and others) an entrée into the material whereby the isolated document can be juxtaposed with the corpus of which it is part.

[5] For the convenience of the reader of *JEN* VII, lines from the second hundred texts (775-881) which are not represented in the hand copies are found here in an appendix.

[6] Extensive, practically exhaustive, bibliography on Nuziana up to 1972 is contained in Dietrich, Loretz, and Mayer (1972). Additional bibliography up to and including 1983 appears in Fadhil (1983, 346-50). Many books and other studies on Nuzi have appeared since 1983, and an additional update is needed.

The following remarks pertain to the four elements of the text editions in this volume: transliteration, translation, comments, and notes.

The Transliterations

At the heart of the text editions, of course, lie the transliterations which are not, in the case of these texts, a simple matter. A variety of sources has been employed to establish accurate readings.

The foundation of the transliteration, where possible, is the tablet itself rather than the published copy. The copies themselves, although reliable for the most part, suffer from a number of peculiarities (see Lacheman and Maidman [1989, 3-10] for details). Divergences of the copy from the tablet are, where significant, always noted. Except where such notes appear, the reader may assume that the copy reflects the artifact faithfully.

An important source of information for what appears—or once appeared—on these tablets are the transliterations and other personal notes of E.R. Lacheman. These papers are based on careful and repeated study of many of the Chicago Nuzi tablets. Lacheman's papers are cited only when helpful or crucial to understanding the tablet or his hand copy. I do not cite them when he is clearly wrong: these are, after all, private, preliminary notes, not a finished product submitted for public scrutiny. And they should not be carelessly reproduced. All references in these editions to Lacheman, without further specificity, are to these private, unpublished papers.

In fact, the Lacheman papers result in a good deal of modification both in the copy and the transliteration. These contributions are acknowledged in every instance. Where collation corroborates Lacheman's notes, this is indicated. Furthermore, where these papers contain solutions to problems or other interesting suggestions (regardless of whether I agree or disagree with them), I forward those thoughts in Lacheman's name.[7]

It is frequently the case that Lacheman's papers (and the *CAD* Nuzi file, as well) contain signs no longer present on the tablet. The reader should be cautioned that these "fuller" readings of text now effaced may, in fact, be illusory. Often, these readings are only careless omissions of square brackets. However, others are certainly correct.

Substantial help in the reconstruction of text comes from the *CAD* Nuzi file. These cards, compiled in the 1930s and 1940s, contain transliterations of most of the major Nuzi tablets housed in the Oriental Institute.[8] Organized to facilitate word retrieval for the *Dictionary*, this file (like the Lacheman papers) frequently captures the text from tablets which have suffered subse-

---

[7] Conversely, solutions and suggestions *not* acknowledged are based on my own work, regardless of what is contained in these papers.

[8] The file also contains transliterations of published Nuzi texts from Harvard and elsewhere available at the time to the *Dictionary* workers.

quent deterioration.[9] The transliterations and marginal comments by their authors and other *Dictionary* workers thus constitute a valuable source for the reconstruction of the text of these documents. As stated above, some of the "fuller" readings of the *CAD* Nuzi file represent inadvertent failure to add square brackets where needed.[10]

As is the case with the Lacheman papers, the evidence of the *CAD* Nuzi file is selectively used. Restorations based on the *CAD* Nuzi file are always noted where helpful. New data are similarly noted.[11] It is clear that much material, especially among the marginalia, is off-the-cuff speculation, unsupported, and wrong. These items are not noted, for, as with the Lacheman papers, this material was not meant for publication.

A complicating factor in the use of the Lacheman papers and the *CAD* Nuzi file is that Lacheman both contributed to the creation of the file[12] and derived information from it for his own research. Although the existence of a relationship between the *CAD* Nuzi file cards and the Lacheman papers is often clear, the direction of that relationship is sometimes obscure. It is definitely inconsistent. Wherever possible, priority of contribution is noted at the appropriate point.

The reconstruction of personal names is a yet more complicated instance of this process. Sometimes the *CAD* Nuzi file, Lacheman's papers, and Gelb, Purves, and MacRae (1943; hereafter, *NPN*) derive from each other. Sometimes not. Therefore, *unless otherwise indicated,* all are cited independently. No judgment is implied by this procedure. I cite neutrally and with no implicit approval of the reconstruction.

Another independent source of information on these texts as they appeared in the 1940s comes from the card files compiled by Edith Porada for her doctoral dissertation. In addition to drawings of seal impressions for these texts, Porada noted the names of the "sealers" as they were then preserved, archaeological provenance of the tablets, and other data. This information sometimes differs from or adds to that derived from the other sources. Wherever this takes place, acknowledgment is there given to Miss Porada. Once again, I wish to express my gratitude for her cooperation and generosity in allowing me access to her files.

---

[9] *JEN* 745 is an excellent example. The tablet has deteriorated badly since the *CAD* Nuzi file transliteration was made. Consequently, the file data become crucial in restoring this text.

[10] It is clear that some restorations were simply made without use of square brackets at all.

[11] As is the case with the Lacheman papers (see above, note 7), the *CAD* Nuzi file reconstructions are not noted as such where they merely agree with conclusions independently reached.

[12] For example, Lacheman authored the *CAD* Nuzi file cards for *JEN* 721, 752, 755, 757, 758, 761, as well as other texts.

Nuzi tablets from the Oriental Institute which remain unpublished (i.e., *JENu* texts) occasionally contribute to text restoration.[13]

The use of so many different "sources" for a single tablet in the transliterating of that tablet inevitably leads to a dilemma. If one wishes to present maximum text—and I do—how does one acknowledge the contributions of sources other than the artifact, how does one indicate deterioration of the artifact, and so on?[14] The solution adopted here depends on *ad hoc* diacritics for the affected signs. Using the copies in *JEN* VII as the starting point for reading the text, signs lacking these diacritics indicate that the copy faithfully renders the artifact at that point. The sources of signs restored in square brackets are indicated in the appropriate note.

* to the upper left of a sign = sign obliterated since copy was made, i.e., it is no longer visible.

• to the upper left of a sign = sign partially obliterated since copy was made, i.e., less is now visible.

\+ to the upper left of a sign = sign present but not copied by Lacheman *or* more of sign visible than copied by Lacheman.[15]

Apropos of "+", I have already noted elsewhere (Lacheman and Maidman 1989, 4-7) that I have effected a *Verbesserung* of Lacheman's copies with the augmentation of very many minor and some major additions and corrections to signs copied by him. This improvement of existing signs and addition of new signs was undertaken where the visual disruption of Lacheman's original copy could be kept to a minimum. *In such cases, no "+" signs appear at these points in the transliteration.* Only where the existing signs could not be augmented easily and where new signs could not conveniently be inserted does the transliteration reflect this by the presence of "+".

\+ preceding a line number = the whole line has been omitted in Lacheman's copy, e.g., *JEN* 694:25, 26. Such lines were indicated in *JEN* VII with the notation, "Additional text; see *THNT*."[16]

The result of this procedure is a maximum "transliteratable" text: signs with • or * are transliterated according to the collated copy. Signs with "+" are transliterated according to my collation alone. In this sense, it is a composite text which does not exist..

Additional sigla used in the transliterations are:

---

[13] See, for example, *JEN* 736, comments and note to line 19.

[14] It seems silly to set up a standard critical apparatus or score for "exemplars" of a single tablet.

[15] +*ma* = *ma* is complete; +⸢*ma*⸣ = *ma* is not complete but more is there than depicted in the copy.

[16] For the convenience of the user of *JEN* VII, such whole line additions to the *second* hundred texts published in that volume are included as an appendix to the present volume.

{ } = scribal plus

< > = scribal omission

[( )] = possible, but not necessary, restoration

[(?)] = possible missing signs, but not necessarily so

S.I. = seal impression[17]

Po # = Lacheman's way of indicating impressions published by Edith Porada (1947). In most cases, it is tentatively assumed that these numbers are correct.[18] Except where noted,[19] they have not been checked.

n

.

. = gap of missing line(s)

.

n+1

GÍN = the logogram for *šiqil* (<*šiqlu*) is rendered GÍN, not SU.[20] This is in agreement with *AHw* (1248a: "'SU' lies GÍN!") and against Lacheman (1937). SU for *šiqlu* probably never existed.

Also regarding transliteration, the following two items should be noted.

Horizontal and vertical lines in the transliteration which separate lines of text reflect scribal lines on the tablet itself. For the most part, these lines are also placed at the appropriate spot of the translation.[21]

The order of lines at the end of texts is the order of scribal intent as I perceive it. No explicit justification is given and, therefore, my conclusions are open to dispute.

---

[17] In the copies in *JEN* VII, "S.I." or "seal impression" upside down means that the impression is upside down with respect to the main body of the text. "S.I." or "seal impression" right side up means *all* other cases, including indeterminate cases.

[18] Sporadic collation of seal impressions with the Po numbers assigned to them by Lacheman reveals a sizable number of errors. He often confused seal impressions containing similar iconographic motifs. Scholars focusing on seal usage in these texts must check the impressions on the tablets (or casts) themselves to confirm that they are correctly identified.

[19] See, for example, notes to *JEN* 745:29; 753:18-21; 767:20-21; and 768:22.

[20] See *JEN* 701:10; 729:7; 730:[13]; 733:[9]; 734:<6>.

[21] Exceptions to this practice are: *JEN* 750:19-20 where the horizontal line appears arbitrarily placed. The horizontal lines in *JEN* 733 and 754 are ignored in the translation. These are "old" texts where the lines are regularly present and, therefore, fail to have contextually significant meaning.

The Translations

The translations strive to be literal without doing violence to English usage. The unit of translation is the clause or contextual unit rather than the line.

Personal names in translation are "normalized" to *NPN* rubric form or as close to it as possible.[22] *ad loc.* spellings are rejected as far as possible.

! after a translated word indicates what the Akkadian was meant to represent rather than what it actually says.

sic after a translated word indicates what the Akkadian actually says, regardless of the resulting illogic.

The Comments

The comments describe, where appropriate, the physical state of the tablet, especially in cases where the object has deteriorated further since the original copy was made. This section also defines the number of lines missing from the text, their location, and, where prudent, their contents. Furthermore, where the text is not typical, the general contents and structure of the document are here defined. Previous treatments of the tablet are also noted in this section. Beyond this, "Comments" contains other, general, observations elucidating the contents of the text. Where none of these elements comes into play, no comments are made.

The Notes

The notes to the lines deal with three types of issue: justifying the transliteration, supplying topographic and toponymic context, and describing scribal patterns and peculiarities. There are few instances of "secondary" notes, that is, attempts, *per se*, at establishing the context (archival or otherwise) of a document. Problems of content are rarely noted, much less wrestled with. And other problems are ignored as well.[23] Why this preoccupation with a relatively humble notational horizon? To learn the answer, one has only to recall the history of arbitrary restorations in Nuzi texts by those wishing to advance assorted historiographic and other agendas.

---

[22] For example, the translation of *JEN* 733 contains the form, "Lu-nanna" (cf. *NPN*, 94b), to represent the PN *Nu-la-a*[*n*]-*n*[*a*] (line 22).

[23] The odd secondary problem is addressed. See, for example, *JEN* 764:5, second note. I intend dealing elsewhere with broader implications of many of these texts. These include treatment of individual, isolated texts. See already Maidman (1987a) and my treatment of other documents such as *JEN* 699, where stages of an ongoing phenomenon may be traced in more than one tablet.

The first burden of these notes, explicit justification of the transliteration, is by far the most important and occupies the most space.[24] Accordingly, very many notes are devoted to explaining the filling in of lacunae, i.e., transliterations within square brackets. In broad terms, verbal and other forms within gaps are filled in, where possible, on the basis of forms from elsewhere in the text or from other texts (parallel texts where possible) written by the same scribe. Many other notes in this category are devoted to correcting the copy.[25]

The second type of note, emphasizing and defining local topography and toponymy is, in essence, a subset of the first type since these items aid in establishing the text.[26] However, textual restoration, in these cases, is not just limited to specifying particular place names: by establishing place names, local scribal practices become clear and other, non-toponymic, text restoration can be made.

The third type of note, dealing with scribal practice, accomplishes several ends. First, clarification of scribal peculiarities aids in the understanding of the plain sense of the text (and thus also serves to establish the text). Second, such notes serve to elicit the "logic" of the Nuzi scribes and act as a counterweight to a general misapprehension: Nuzi scribes were arbitrary in language and practice. Finally, through this vehicle, the practice of Nuzi scribes may be compared with that of practitioners of this profession elsewhere.[27]

A full list of those notes involving scribal practice is found below in the list of terms treated under the heading "scribal errors and peculiarities."

---

[24] In a sense, this task comprehends the following two as well, since "primary interpretation" (see the definition of Gelb [1967, 3-4]) is facilitated in all three ways.

[25] See, for example, *JEN* 762:11 second note.

[26] The text, of course, can aid in defining the place. See, for example, the notes to *JEN* 732:17-23 and 774:5-6. *JEN* 771 *passim* contains perhaps the most extensive notes in this category amongst these texts.

[27] Nuzi scribal errors have occasionally been examined in the past. See, for example, Grosz (1988, 90-91). Scribal errors occurring elsewhere are noted throughout the scholarly literature. Note, for example, Tadmor (1961, 144: Kurkh monolith; and note 8: Amarna tablets); and especially Delitzsch (1920, v-vii). A recent contribution is Zawadski (1987, 15-21). He describes Neo-Babylonian scribal practice and the *modus operandi* employed when the scribe had made a mistake and then tried to correct it, focusing on the effects of attempted scratching out of incorrect signs. (This phenomenon is relatively rare in the *THNT* texts.)

Zawadski describes (1987, 21) a situation where scribes would write a great deal on a single day. The later it got, the more tired they became and the more errors they made. This phenomenon may well be attested among the Nuzi texts as well. See below, the note to *JEN* 716:3. Another similarity to a Nuzi scribal quirk, this time among the Middle Babylonian scribes of Nippur, was pointed out to me by Joachim Oelsner. See below, *JEN* 728:7, second note.

REGISTER OF TABLETS

This is a two way register. The second, *JENu* → *JEN*, register is useful since the catalogue numbers found in Lacheman and Maidman (1989, 15-17, 22-43) have undergone some slight change. (See already, Lacheman and Maidman 1989, 17, n. 1.) These revisions are based on the now complete, exhaustive catalogue (Maidman forthcoming) of the Nuzi texts housed in the Oriental Institute. (The numbers employed in this complete catalogue have already been used by Maidman [1989, 1990] to identify tablets.) This catalogue has resulted in two kinds of changes. These are: (1) slight changes in text numbers (e.g., by the addition of "a," "b," etc. after the number), due to the identification of more than one tablet or fragment in a single storage box; (2) addition of material due to joins. Regarding the latter, note that the *JEN* numbers of *JEN* VII remain unchanged in this volume despite the newly joined material. The new joins affect six texts (the last two not treated in this volume):

JEN 680 = *JENu* 847+1141g
JEN 720 = *JENu* 555(+)1076a
JEN 739 = *JENu* 225a+1141aj
JEN 756 = *JENu* 297+1167d
JEN 776 = *JENu* 92+1127d+1173+1174
JEN 846 = *JENu* 648+1143o

Note that data regarding room numbers of these tablets are to be found in Lacheman and Maidman (1989, 22-43).

JEN	*JENu*
674	727a
675	590a
676	101a
677	610
678	564
679	1007a
680	847+1141g
681	977
682	985a
683	356
684	605
685	569
686	173
687	362a
688	981
689	880a
690	363a+363b
691	804
692	235
693	628
694	104a
695	1144
696	578a
697	397
698	81
699	65
700	96a
701	485a
702	285a
703	244a
704	346
705	698
706	223
707	941a
708	435
709	986
710	289a
711	299
712	See *JEN* 753
713	1044a
714	300+1142
715	523a
716	313
717	399
718	604
719	367a+367b+367c+367d
720	555(+)1076a
721	752a
722	760
723	790a
724	827a
725	917 (=A11963)
726	806a
727	514
728	686a
729	615
730	539
731	583
732	351
733	737
734	412
735	396
736	634+690
737	1030a
738	183
739	225a+1141aj
740	734
741	625
742	517c+519
743	916
744	782a
745	311
746	883
747	414
748	621a
749	421a
750	240a
751	624a
752	807a
753	258
754	678a
755	654
756	297+1167d
757	885
758	597a
759	305a
760	448
761	963
762	611+731j
763	221 (=A11907)
764	1029
765	613a
766	568a
767	319
768	783a
769	383
770	89
771	862a
772	820
773	826a
774	398

JENu	*JEN*
65	699
81	698
89	770
96a	700
101a	676
104a	694
173	686
183	738
221 (=A11907)	763
223	706 (=*JEN* 793)
225a+	
1141aj	739
235	692
258	753
240a	750
244a	703
285a	702
289a	710
297+	
1167d	756
299	711
300+	
1142	714
305a	759
311	745
313	716
319	767
346	704
351	732
356	683
362a	687
363a+	
363b	690
363b+	
363a	690
367a+	
367b+	
367c+	
367d	719
367b+	
367a+	
367c+	

JENu	*JEN*
367d	719
367c+	
367a+	
367b+	
367d	719
367d+	
367a+	
367b+	
367c	719
383	769
396	735
397	697
398	774
399	717
412	734
414	747
421a	749
435	708
448	760
485a	701
514	727
517c+	
519	742
519+	
517c	742
523a	715
539	730
555(+)	
1076a	720
564	678
568a	766
569	685
578a	696
583	731
590a	675
597a	758
604	718
605	684
610	677
611+	
731j	762
613a	765
615	729
621a	748

JENu	*JEN*
624a	751
625	741
628	693
634+	
690	736
654	755
678a	754
686a	728
690+	
634	736
698	705
727a	674
731j+	
611	762
734	740
737	733
752a	721
760	722
782a	744
783a	768
790a	723
804	691
806a	726
807a	752
820	772
826a	773
827a	724
847+	
1141g	680
862a	771
880a	689
883	746
885	757
916	743
917 (=A11963)	725
941a	707
963	761
977	681
981	688
985a	682
986	709
1007a	679
1029	764

JENu	*JEN*
1030a	737
1044a	713
1076a(+) 555	720
1141g+ 847	680
1141aj+ 225a	739
1142+ 300	714
1144	695
1167d+ 297	756

TEXT EDITIONS:

JEN 674 — *JEN* 774

JEN 674

OBVERSE

1 ṭup-pí ma-+r[u-ti +š]a
2 ^{m}Ku-uš-ši-+y[a ša ^{m}A-ri]-+pa!-+pu
3 ù ša ^{m}Te-[ḫi-pa-pu DUMU.MEŠ X-x?]-+uz-+z[i]
4 ^{m}Te-ḫi-ip-til-l[a DUMU Pu-ḫi-še-en-ni]
5 a-na m[a-r]u-t[i i-te-ep-šu-šu-ma]
6 2 ANŠ[E A.Š]À ši-[qa/qú]
7 ša A[N.ZA.KÀ]R Ku-n[a-tù]
8 ki-m[a ḪA.L]A-šu a-⸢na ^{m}⸣Te-ḫi-ip-[til-la]
9 i[t-ta-a]d-nu ù ^{m}⸢Te-ḫi⸣-[ip-til]-⸢la⸣
10 [16? ANŠE?] ŠE.MEŠ a-na ^{m}Ku-u[š-ši-y]a a-⸢na ^{m}⸣[A-ri-pa-pu]
11 [ù a-n]a ^{m}Te-ḫi-pa-pu k[i-ma] NÍG.BA-šu-nu ⸢SUM⸣-aš?-[šu-nu-ti]
12 [šum-ma A.+Š]À di-na TUK-ši ^{m}Ku-uš-ši-ya ^{m}A-ri-pa+-
:+pu
13 [ù ^{m}T]e-ḫi-pa-pu ú-za-ak-ku-ma
14 [a-na ^{m}T]e-ḫi-ip-til-la i+na-an-dì-nu
15 [šum-ma ^{m}K]u-uš-ši-ya ù ^{m}Te-ḫi-pa-pu ⸢ù⸣ [^{m}A-ri-pa-pu]
16 [KI.BAL-t]u 2 MA.NA KÙ.+⸢SIG$_{17}$⸣
17 [a-na $^{m+}$T]e-ḫi-ip-til-la ⸢ú⸣-[ma]-al-[lu]-ú

---

18 IGI Muš-te-šup DUMU ⸢Ar-na⸣-+pu
19 IGI Na-aš-wi DUMU ⸢Ka⸣-lu-li
20 IGI Wa-an-ti-ya DUMU ⸢Na⸣-ḫi-a-šu
21 IGI Šum-m[i-y]a DUMU A-ri-ka$_4$-⸢na⸣-[ri]
22 IGI Muš-+te-+⸢ya +DUMU +Ar-še⸣-[ni]
23 IGI A-tal-te-šup DUMU Šu[m-mi-ya]
24 [I]GI Pu-i-ta-e DUMU *N[u-uz-za]

LOWER EDGE

25 IGI Ur-ḫi-ya DUMU •Ar-*š[a-tù-ya]
26 IGI En-na-šúk-rù DUMU T[a-a-a]

REVERSE

27 [an-nu]-⸢ti⸣ ši-⸢bu-ti⸣ [ša U]RU Nu-[zi]
28 [IGI Š]úk-ra-pu DUMU Tù-u[n-t]ù-•y[a]
29 [IGI Š]a-ka$_4$-⸢ra-a-a⸣ DUMU Ta-an-ta-•ú-[a]
30 +[IG]I +A-be-ya [D]UMU Pa-az-+[z]i-y[a]
31 +[I]GI Ik-ki-y[a D]UMU Ni-nu-a-tal
32 +[IG]I Ar-+zi-[iz]-+⸢za⸣ DUMU Ni-ki
33 [IGI] Al-pu-ya DUMU Ḫa-ši-ya
34 [IGI] •⸢Ti⸣-in-ti-ya DUMU A-ka$_4$-a-a
35 [IGI Šu-+u]l-mi-ya DUMU Pu-⸢ya⸣
36 [IGI Ta]-⸢a-a⸣ +D[UMU A]-+⸢pil⸣-X[XX DU]B.⸢SAR⸣

37 [*an-nu-*+*t*]*i* +*ši*-+*bu*-+*t*[*ù ša* U]RU ⸢*A*⸣!-[*pè-na-aš*] ⸢*ù*⸣! ⸢*šu*⸣-*nu*-[*ma* NIGIN-*ú* A.ŠÀ]

+S.I.

+38 ⸢^{NA_4} KIŠIB⸣ *Muš-te-šup* DUMU *A*[*r-na-pu*]

+S.I.

+39 ⸢^{NA_4} KIŠIB *Na*⸣-*aš-wi* DU[MU *Ka-lu-li*]

.

.

.

LEFT EDGE

[S.I.]

40 ^{NA_4} KIŠIB *Ti-<in>-ti-ya ši-bi*

41 +[*š*]*a* URU *A-pè-na-aš*

TRANSLATION

(1-5) Tablet of adoption of Kuššiya, [of] Arip-apu, and of Teḫip-apu [sons of] ...-uzzi. [They] adopted Teḫip-tilla [son of Puḫi-šenni].

(6-9) They gave to Teḫip-tilla as his inheritance share a 2 homer irrigated field, ... of the *dimtu* of Kunatu.

(9-11) And Teḫip-tilla gave to Kuššiya, to [Arip-apu, and] to Teḫip-apu as their gift [16? homers?] of barley.

(12-14) [Should] the field have a case (against it), Kuššiya, Arip-apu, [and] Teḫip-apu shall clear (the field) and give (it) [to] Teḫip-tilla.

(15-17) [Should] Kuššiya, Teḫip-apu, and [Arip-apu] abrogate (this contract), they shall pay [to] Teḫip-tilla 2 minas of gold.

(18-27) Before Muš-tešup son of Arn-apu; before Našwi son of Kaluli; before Wantiya son of Naḫi-ašu; before Šummiya son of Arik-kanari; before Muš-teya son of Ar-šenni; before Atal-tešup son of Šummiya; before Pui-tae son of Nuzza; before Urḫiya son of Ar-šatuya; before En-šukru son of Taya. These are the witnesses [of] the town of Nuzi.

(28-37) [Before] Šukr-apu son of Tuntuya; [before] Šakaraya son of Tantawa; before Abeya son of Pazziya; before Ikkiya son of Ninu-atal; before Ar-zizza son of Niki; before Alpuya son of Ḫašiya; [before] Tintiya son of Akaya; before Šulmiya son of Puya; [before] Taya son of Apil-sin, the scribe. These are the witnesses [of] the town of Apena [and], as well, they are the [measurers of the field].

(38-41) (*seal impression*) seal impression of Muš-tešup son of Arn-apu; (*seal impression*) seal impression of Našwi son of [Kaluli]; [(*seal impression*)] seal impression of Tintiya, witness of the town of Apena.

NOTES

l. 1. The added signs at the ends of ll. 1-3 appear on the reverse after a break at the edge. It should be noted that they appear, at first glance, to supply the ends of ll. 2-4 respectively.

l. 3: ᵐ*Te-*[*ḫi-pa-pu*]. Restored from l. 11.

l. 5: [*i-te-ep-šu-šu-ma*]. Or the like. Cf. *JEN* 67:6, written by the scribe who wrote this text.

l. 7: A[N.ZA.KÀ]R *Ku-n*[*a-tù*]. This text deals with real estate almost certainly in Apena. The standard Nuzi-Apena witness sequence is present (see note to l. 23, below), a characteristic feature of Teḫip-tilla real estate adoptions involving Apena land. Cf. also l. 41. The *dimtu* of Kunatu, located in Apena (cf. *JEN* 81:6-7; 679:5-6), is the only known toponym consistent with the extant traces.

l. 10: [16? ANŠE?]. This restoration is reasonable, based as it is on other, similar Apena texts with 8:1 ratio of price per unit of land. This assumes, of course, that the full price was actually paid. On the uniform ratio in a series of "Apena" texts, see Weeks (1972, 202). See further, below, note to l. 23.

l. 11: ⸢SUM⸣-*aš*?-[*šu-nu-ti*]. Cf. the similar *JEN* 67:14.

l. 15. The order of the PNs here differs from that of ll. 2-3, 10-11, and 12-13.

l. 15: [*ri-pa-pu*]. Lacheman records these signs as preserved.

l. 23: *Šu*[*m-mi-ya*]. There are no traces after *Š*[*um*]. The traces copied by Lacheman belong with l. 22, and are clearly ⸢*Ar-še*⸣.

The restoration, *Šu*[*m-mi-ya*], as indeed all the witness PN restorations in this text, is based on the standard Nuzi-Apena witness sequence in Teḫip-tilla real estate adoption tablets. This group of texts, with nearly identical witness lists and other common characteristics, is discussed by Lacheman (1967, 6-8, 20 n. to 1:17); Weeks (1972, 202-3); and Fadhil (1983, 12, 15-17). The texts of this group are: *JEN* 5, 71, 81, 94, 96, 202, 418, 580, 674-680, and *LG* 1. For further on this group, see above, note to l. 10, and below, note to *JEN* 675:47.

l. 27. This line starts the reverse. No lines are effaced between l. 26 and l. 27.

l. 32: [*iz*]. Lacheman records this sign as partially preserved.

l. 37: *ši-bu-t*[*ù*]. The traces favor *tù* rather than *ti* as expected (cf. l. 27). For this alternation, cf. *JEN* 5:25, 35.

l. 37: [*ša* U]RU ⸢*A*⸣!-[*pè-na-aš*] ⸢*ù*⸣! ⸢*šu*⸣-*nu*-[*ma* NIGIN-*ú* A.ŠÀ]. Or the like. The restoration is based on analogous formulations in closely related texts such as *JEN* 678:34.

l. 38. Lacheman identifies the seal impression above this line as Po 391. See, further, below, note to l. 39.

l. 38: [*na-pu*]. Lacheman once saw the former sign as partially preserved and the latter as completely preserved.

l. 39. Lacheman identifies the seal impression above this line, as well as that above l. 38, as Po 391. This could well be the case. Some implications of multiple use of the same seal in the same document are discussed below, note to *JEN* 675:45.

Below this line, Lacheman reads for the upper edge, NA$_4$ ^{m}[x x x]. If so, [*Ša-ka$_4$-ra-a-a*] is a plausible restoration, conforming to the standard Apena sealing sequence. See below, note to *JEN* 675:47.

JEN 675

OBVERSE

1 [*ṭup-pí ma-ru*]-*ti ša*
2 [^{m}*A-be-ya* DUMU *Ki-pa*]-•⸢*a*⸣-*pu*
3 [*ša* ^{m} -*ya* DUMU •*Ḫ*]*a-na-a-a*
4 [*ša* ^{m}*Šu-um-mi-ya*? •D]UMU *Ḫa-na-a-a-ma*
5 [*ša* ^{m}*E-te-eš-še-ni*] DUMU $^{+}$*Z*[*i*]/$^{+}$*K*[*é*]-[*x*]-⸢*x*⸣-*a-a*
6 [*ù ša* ^{m}*Ur*?- DUMU] *Wa-an-t*[*i*-]
7 •^{m}•*Te*-*⸢*ḫi*⸣-[*ip-til-la* DUMU *P*]*u-ḫi-še-e*[*n-ni*]
8 *a-na ma-r*[*u-ti i-te-ep-šu*]-*šu-ma*
9 1 ANŠE 5 ^{GI}[^{Š} APIN A.ŠÀ *ši*?-*qa*?/-*qú*?]
10 AŠ AN.ZA.KÀR š[a $^{m?}$*Šu*?-*ul*?-*mi*?-*y*]*a*?
11 AŠ URU *A-pè-n*[*a-aš ki-ma* ḪA.L]A-*šu*
12 *a-na* ^{m}*Te-ḫi-ip*-[*til-la it-ta-a*]*d-nu*
13 *ù* ^{m}*Te-ḫi*-•*ip*-[*til-la* 12? ANŠE?] ŠE.MEŠ
14 *a-na* ^{m}*A-be-y*[*a a-na* ^{m}]-*ya*
15 *a-na* ^{m}*Šu-um-mi*-[*ya*? *a*-$^{+}$*n*]*a* ⸢$^{+m+}$*E*⸣*te-eš-še-ni*
16 ⸢*ù a*⸣-[*na*] $^{m?}$[*Ur*?- $^{+}$*k*]*i*-$^{+}$*ma* NÍG.BA-*šu-nu id-din*
17 •*šum-m*[*a* A.Š]À *di-na* TUK-*ši*]
18 *⸢3⸣+[2 ŠEŠ.MEŠ *an-nu*-**t*]*i* *⸢*ú*⸣-**za-ak-ku-ma*
19 [*a-na* ^{m}*Te-ḫi-ip-til-la*] *i-na-an-dì-nu*
20 [*šum-ma* 5 ŠEŠ.MEŠ **a*]*n*-**nu-ti*
21 [KI.BAL-*tu* 2 MA.*N]A KÙ.SIG$_{17}$
22 [*a-na* ^{m}*Te-ḫi-ip-til*-•*l*]*a* SI.A-*ú*
23 [IGI *Muš-te*-•*šu*]*p* DUMU *Ar-na-pu*
24 [IGI *Na-aš-w*]*i* ⸢DUMU⸣ *Ka$_4$-lu*-⸢*li*⸣

LOWER EDGE

25 [IGI] $^{+}$*Wa*-$^{+}$*an-ti-ya* DUMU *Na*-⸢*ḫi*⸣-*a-šu*
26 •IGI *A-tal-te-šup* DUMU *Šu*[*m-m*]*i-ya*

REVERSE

27 •IGI *Pu-i-ta-e* DUMU *Nu-*⁺⸢*uz*⸣*-za*

28 ⸢IGI⸣ *Šum-mi-ya* DUMU *A-ri-ka*$_4$*-na-ri*

29 [IGI]⸢*Muš*⸣*-te-šup* DUMU *Ar-še-ni*

30 IGI *U*[*r-*•*ḫ*]*i-ya* DUMU *Ar-ša-tù-ya*

31 [I]GI *E*[*n-na-š*]*úk-rù* DUMU *Ta-a-a*

32 •IGI *Šúk-*•*r*[*a-p*]*u* DUMU *Tù-un-tù-ya*

33 IGI *Ša-ka*$_4$*-*[*ra-a*]*-*•*a* DUMU *Ta-an-ta-ú-a*

34 IGI *A-*⁺⸢*be*⸣*-ya* DU[MU *Pa-a*]*z-zi-ya*

35 IG[I *I*]*k-ki-ya* DUM[U *N*]*i-nu-a-tal*

36 IGI *Ar-zi-iz-za* D[UM]U *Ni-ki*

37 IGI *Al-pu-ya* DUMU *Ḫa-*⸢*ši*⸣*-ya*

38 IGI *Ti-in-ti-ya* DUMU *A-*[*k*]*a*$_4$*-a-a*

39 IGI *Šu-ul-mi-ya* DUMU *Pu-*•*ya*

40 IGI *Pa-ak-la-pí-ti* DUMU *K*[*a*$_4$*-n*]*i*

41 •IGI *Ta-a-a* DUB.⸢SAR⸣

42 *an-nu-ti* IGI.MEŠ *ù mu-še-*•⸢*el*⸣*-mu-ú*

S.I. Po 314

43 ^{NA_4} KIŠIB ^{m}*Muš-te-šup* DUMU *Ar-na-pu*

S.I. Po 391

44 [^{NA_4} KIŠIB] •^{m}•*Na-aš-wi* •DUMU •*Ka*$_4$*-lu-li*

UPPER EDGE

S.I. Po 580

45 [^{NA_4} KIŠIB? ^{m}*Pu-i*]*-ta-e* DUMU

⁺46 [*Nu*]*-*⸢*uz*⸣*-za*

LEFT EDGE

S.I. Po 580

47 NA$_4$ ^{m}*Ša-ka*$_4$*-*⁺*ra-*⁺*a-*⁺⸢*a*⸣

48 *ša* URU *A-pè-na-*<*aš*>

•S.I. Po 580

NA$_4$ ^{m}*T*[*i-in-ti-ya*]

•*ša* *URU [*A-pè-na-aš*]

S.I.

49 ^{NA_4} KIŠIB [^{m}]

50 **ša* *URU[ ]

TRANSLATION

(1-8) Tablet of adoption of [Abeya son of] Kip-apu, [of] ...-ya [son of] Ḫanaya, [of Šummi-ya?] also son of Ḫanaya, [of Eteš-šenni] son of Zi-/Ke-...a-a, [and of Ur?-... son of] Wanti-... . [They] adopted Teḫip-tilla son of Puḫi-šenni.

(9-12) They gave to Teḫip-tilla [as] his inheritance share a 1.5 homer [irrigated? field] in the *dimtu* of [Šulmiy]a(?), in the town of Apena.

(13-16) And Teḫip-tilla gave to Abeya, [to] ...-ya, to Šummi-[ya?], to Eteš-šenni, and to [Ur?-...] as their gift [12? homers?] of barley.

(17-19) Should [the field have a case (against it)], these 5 "brothers" shall clear (the field) and give (it) [to Teḫip-tilla].

(20-22) [Should] these [5 "brothers" abrogate (this contract)], they shall pay [to] Teḫip-tilla [2] minas of gold.

(23-42) [Before] Muš-tešup son of Arn-apu; [before] Našwi son of Kaluli; [before] Wantiya son of Naḫi-ašu; before Atal-tešup son of Šummiya; before Pui-tae son of Nuzza; before Šummiya son of Arik-kanari; [before] Muš-tešup son of Ar-šenni; before Urḫiya son of Ar-šatuya; before En-šukru son of Taya; before Šukr-apu son of Tuntuya; before Šakaraya son of Tantawa; before Abeya son of Pazziya; before Ikkiya son of Ninu-atal; before Ar-zizza son of Niki; before Alpuya son of Ḫašiya; before Tintiya son of Akaya; before Šulmiya son of Puya; before Pakla-piti son of Kani; before Taya, the scribe. These are the witnesses and the (field) measurers.

(43-50) (*seal impression*) seal impression of Muš-tešup son of Arn-apu; (*seal impression*) seal impression of Našwi son of [Kaluli]; (*seal impression*) [seal impression of] Pui-tae son of Nuzza; (*seal impression*) seal impression of Šakaraya of the town of Apena; (*seal impression*) seal impression of Tintiya of the town of Apena; (*seal impression*) seal impression of ... of the town of ... .

COMMENTS

This tablet has deteriorated slightly since the copy was made. Also, a small fragment (which bears no separate number) has since been joined to the tablet, adding to the text of lines 15 and 16, *q.v.*

On the tablet, the last seal impression and lines 49-50 appear on the left edge, below and facing the opposite direction from lines 47-48 and their associated seal impressions. This positioning is not clearly depicted in the copy of this text.

NOTES

l. 2. This line has been restored from l. 14 and from *JEN* 658:2, a related context. Cf. also *JEN* 367:8.

l. 3: [*-ya*]. Restored from l. 14.

l. 4: [^{m}*Šu-um-mi-ya*?]. *Šum-mi* is restored from l. 15. *ya*? follows the lead of *NPN*, 138a *sub* ŠUMMIJA 3), 52b *sub* ḪANAJA 48).

l. 5: [^{m}*E-te-eš-še-ni*]. Restored from l. 15.

l. 5: *Z*[*i*]/*K*[*é*]. The end of the sign has traces of three wedges, not the single one copied.

l. 6: [^{m}*Ur*?]. For this restoration, see note to l. 16.

l. 9: 5. The number is definitely 5 (so too Lacheman), not 6 (as copied) or 7 (cf. *CAD* Nuzi file: ⸢7⸣; and *JEN* 658:3, 7, perhaps relating to the same land).

This amount of land represents one-half homer; i.e., 1 *awiḫaru* = 1/10 homer. For the literature on this aspect of Nuzi metrology, see Maidman (1976, 365, n.401).

l. 10: [m?*Šu?-ul?-mi?-y*]*a*?. Known Apena *dimtu* names consistent with these meager traces are: Sulae (cf. *JEN* 5:6) and Šulmiya (cf. *JEN* 71:8). The latter is more probable in this line since Taya (son of Apil-sin), the scribe of this tablet (l. 41), never uses *ša* in describing the former GN but often employs it in noting the latter (e.g., *JEN* 418:6); and *ša* is partially preserved in this line.

l. 13: [12? ANŠE?]. For the rationale for these restorations, see note to *JEN* 674:10.

l. 16: m?[*Ur*?]. Lacheman apparently once saw at this point: m*Ur*-[ ].

l. 17: [*ši*]. Lacheman once saw this sign as preserved.

l. 18: [ŠEŠ.MEŠ]. This restoration, rather than [LÚ.MEŠ], is based on *JEN* 71:15, 17; 580:15, 17. All three texts were written by the same scribe.

l. 20: [ŠEŠ.MEŠ]. See note to l. 18.

l. 24. This line is part of the obverse.

ll. 25-26. These lines appear on the lower edge.

l. 27. This line begins the reverse.

l. 29: *šup*. This seems to be a scribal error for *ya*. The witness, Muš-te*ya* son of Ar-šenni, appears in all other texts of this series but *JEN* 71, where the key part of his name is effaced.

l. 37: *Al*. The sign is written perfectly normally.

ll. 45-48. Note that seal Po 580 "identifies" three individuals in this text. (See already the analogous instances cited by Porada [1947, 128 (re ## 116, 154, 188), 130 (re # 336), and *passim*]. See also the note to *JEN* 717:21. Regarding Po 580, however, cf. the notes to JEN 677:39; 678:39; 680:37, 40.)

This is significant. It means that the sealing with accompanying legend, ^{NA_4} KIŠIB PN, does not serve to identify that PN as the owner of the seal whose impression appears on the tablet. Rather, here and in analogous Nuzi texts, the legend identifies the person who performed the act of sealing (or even an individual who was merely present at the sealing; see below, note to *JEN* 752:37-38). The *procedure* of sealing—irrespective of the seal employed—is part of the drawing up of written Nuzi real estate adoption contracts and other documents. To the extent that the same seal was used by different sealers, sealing appears *not* to have represented the equivalent to our (identifying) signature on a legal document. In this sense, the seal impression in these Nuzi contracts is perfectly equivalent to a fingernail or textile impression. (The act of sealing appears to serve as an additional [especially solemn?] indication of the presence of a witnessing individual at a transaction.)

This type of usage has several implications. To name but two, "^{NA_4} KIŠIB PN" should be rendered "(stone) seal impression of PN" and not "impression of the (stone) seal of PN." Second and more important, in the Nuzi texts, the *isolated* impression with accompanying legend usually may *not* be employed as evidence for establishing seal ownership. An analogous phenomenon occurs in a Neo-Babylonian context, where the fingernail marks of witnesses to a contract turn out to be nothing more than forgeries. The impressions are made by the scribe's stylus. See Frame (1982, 161 with n. 8).

For further details and examples of the sharing or borrowing of seals at Nuzi, see Stein (1987, 238); and, below, notes to *JEN* 676:38, 40; 717:21; 752:37-38; 762:22-23; 768:22.

l. 47: ^{m}*T*[*i-in-ti-ya*]. Though not quite as copied, the trace is consistent with *T*[*i*]. The restoration is based on the standard Apena sealing sequence. Cf., for example, *JEN* 96:37-42, especially l. 41.

ll. 49-50. These lines are copied by Lacheman together with the obverse. As indicated above, comments, these lines (and their associated sealing) are upside down with respect to ll. 47-48 and their sealings. This last sealing has been collated and is not Po 580.

l. 49: [^{m}]. But for the identification of this person as hailing from the town of [ ] (note, however, that *ša* URU is no longer visible on the tablet), one would have expected [^{m}*Ta-a-a* DUB.SAR] or the like, in accordance with the standard Apena sealing sequence (see above, note to l. 47).

JEN 676

OBVERSE

1 *ṭup-pí ma-ru-ti ša*
2 ^{m}*Še-né-ya* DUMU *Tu-ra-ri*
(erasure)
3 ^{m}*Te-ḫi-ip-*$^{\bullet}$*til-*$^{\bullet}$*la* $^{+}$⸢DUMU⸣ *Pu-ḫi-š*[*e-en-ni*]
4 *a-na ma-*[*r*]*u-ti* DÙ-$^{+}$⸢*ma*⸣
5 1 ANŠE ⸢A.ŠÀ⸣ *ši-qa i-na* AN.ZA.$^{\bullet}$K[ÀR *ša*]
6 *Šu-ul-mi-ya* AŠ URU *A-pè-*[*na-aš*]
7 *ki-ma* ḪA.LA-*šu a-na* ^{m}*Te-ḫi-*[*ip-til-la i*]*t-*$^{+}$*ta-ad-nu*
8 *ù* ⸢^{m}*Te*⸣*-ḫi-ip-*⸢*til*⸣*-la* 6[+2? ANŠE? ŠE.MEŠ]
9 *ki-*⸢*ma* NÍG⸣.BA-*š*[*u*] *a-na* ^{m}*Še-*[*né-ya it?-t*]*a?-*[*din*]
(erasure)
10 *šum-ma* A.ŠÀ *di-na* [T]UK-*ši* $^{+}$⸢^{m}⸣[*Še-n*]*é-*$^{+}$⸢*ya*⸣
11 (erasure) *ú-za-ak-*ka_4*-m*[*a*]
12 *a-na* ^{m}*Te-ḫi-ip-til-*[*l*]*a i+na-an-din*

13 ⸢*šum*⸣-*ma* ^{m}*Še-né-ya* ⸢KI⸣.BAL-*at*
14 [2] MA.NA KÙ.SIG$_{17}$ *a-na* ^{m}*Te-ḫi-ip-til-la*
15 ⸢*ú*⸣-*ma-al-la*

---

16 $^{+}$[IG]I *Muš-te-šup* DUMU *Ar-na-pu*
17 [IG]I *Na-aš-wi* DUMU *Ka*$_{4}$*-lu-li*
18 IGI *Wa-an-ti-ya* DUMU *Na-ḫi-a-*[*šu*]
19 IGI *Šu-um-mi-ya* DUMU *A-ri-ka*$_{4}$-[*na-ri*]
20 IGI *Muš-te-ya* DUMU *Ar-še-*[*ni*]
21 IGI *A-tal-te-šup* DUMU *Šum-mi-*•*y*[*a*]
22 IGI *Pu-i-ta-e* DUMU *Nu-*[*uz-za*]

LOWER EDGE

23 IGI *Ur-ḫi-ya* DUMU *Ar-*•*ša-tù-y*[*a*]
24 IGI *En-na-šúk-rù* DUMU *Ta-a-a*

REVERSE

25 IGI *Šúk-ra-pu* DUMU *Tù-un-tù-ya*
26 IGI *Ša-ka*$_{4}$*-ra-a-a* DUMU *Ta-an-ta-ú-*[*a*]
27 IGI *A-be-ya* DUMU *Pa-az-zi-ya*
28 IGI *Ik-ki-ya* DUMU *Ni-nu-a-tal*
29 IGI *Ar-zi-iz-za* $^{+}$DUMU [*N*]*i-ki*
30 IGI *Al-pu-ya* DUMU ⸢*Ḫa*⸣*-ši-ya*
31 IGI *Ti-in-ti-ya* DUMU *A-ka*$_{4}$-$^{+}$*a*-$^{+}$*a*
32 IGI *Šu-ul-mi-ya* DUMU *Pu-*$^{+}$*ya*
33 IGI *Pa-ak-la-pí-ti* DUMU *Ka*$_{4}$*-ni*
34 IGI *Ta-a-a* DUB.SAR *an-nu-ti* ⸢*ša*⸣ $^{+}$URU [*A*]-$^{+}$*pè*-$^{+}$*na*-$^{+}$*aš*
35 *an-nu-ti* IGI.MEŠ *ù* A.ŠÀ *šu-nu-ma* NIGIN.MEŠ

S.I. Po 314

36 ⸢^{NA_4} KIŠIB ^{m}*Muš*⸣-*te*-$^{+}$⸢*šup*⸣ DUMU [*A*]*r-na-pu*

S.I. Po 391

37 ⸢^{NA_4}⸣ KIŠIB ^{m}*Na-aš-wi* DUMU *Ka*$_{4}$*-lu-li*

S.I. Po 580

38 $^{[N]A_4}$ KIŠIB ^{m}*Pu-i-ta-e* DUMU *Nu-uz!-za*

UPPER EDGE

S.I. Po 179

39 ^{NA_4} KIŠIB ^{m}*Ta-a-a* $^{+}$D[UB.$^{+}$S]AR

LEFT EDGE

S.I. Po 76	S.I. Po 580
40 ^{NA_4} KIŠIB ^{m}*Ti-i*[*n-ti-y*]*a*	⸢^{NA_4}⸣K[IŠIB] $^{+}$⸢^{m}⸣*Ša-ka*$_{4}$*-ra-a-a ši-bi*
41 *ša* [URU *A-pè-na-aš*]	⸢*ša*⸣ URU *A-pè-na-aš*

TRANSLATION

(1-4) Tablet of adoption of Šenneya son of Turari. He adopted Teḫip-tilla son of Puḫi-šenni.

(5-7) They (*sic*) gave to Teḫip-tilla as his inheritance share a 1 homer irrigated field in the *dimtu* [of] Šulmiya, in the town of Apena.

(8-9) And Teḫip-tilla gave to Šenneya as his gift 6[+2? homers? of barley].

(10-12) Should the field have a case (against it), Šenneya shall clear (the field) and give (it) to Teḫip-tilla.

(13-15) Should Šenneya abrogate (this contract), he shall pay to Teḫip-Tilla [2] minas of gold.

(16-35) Before Muš-tešup son of Arn-apu; before Našwi son of Kaluli; before Wantiya son of Naḫi-ašu; before Šummiya son of Arik-kanari; before Muš-teya son of Ar-šenni; before Atal-tešup son of Šummiya; before Pui-tae son of Nuzza; before Urḫiya son of Ar-šatuya; before En-šukru son of Taya; before Šukr-apu son of Tuntuya; before Šakaraya son of Tantawa; before Abeya son of Pazziya; before Ikkiya son of Ninu-atal; before Ar-zizza son of Niki; before Alpuya son of Ḫašiya; before Tintiya son of Akaya; before Šulmiya son of Puya; before Pakla-piti son of Kani; before Taya, the scribe. These are from the town of Apena. These are the witnesses and, as well, they measured the field.

(36-41) (*seal impression*) seal impression of Muš-tešup son of Arn-apu; (*seal impression*) seal impression of Našwi son of Kaluli; (*seal impression*) seal impression of Pui-tae son of Nuzza; (*seal impression*) seal impression of Taya, the scribe; (*seal impression*) seal impression of Tintiya of [the town of Apena]; (*seal impression*) seal impression of Šakaraya of the town of Apena.

COMMENTS

This text was collated from a pair of very good casts. The tablet had deteriorated slightly between the time the copy was made and the time the casts were taken.

Contrary to the impression of the copy, the ends of lines 31-32, 39 are not at all damaged or cracked.

NOTES

l. 6: *Šu-ul-mi-ya*. Lacheman elsewhere reads the masculine determinative before this name. This is to be expected for the scribe of this tablet, Taya. Cf. *JEN* 71:8.

l. 7: *i*]*t-ta-ad-nu*. Lacheman accidentally omitted the *ta* from the copy. It is perfectly preserved.

There is a single adopter and *it-ta-din* is expected. Cf., for example, *JEN* 96:8. However, this apparent error of plural for singular may be linked to three other anomalies in this text. Erasures follow lines 2 and 9 and a third erasure begins line 11. A single conjecture would account for all four peculiarities: the scribe wrote this text as if there were two adopters until just before he wrote *uzakkama* (l. 11), at which point he realized or learned that there was only one. A second PN would have appeared after lines 2 and 9. These he now erased. This same PN would have appeared in line 11, after a copula, had the scribe continued, oblivious of his misapprehension. Apparently, he got only a bit past the copula before correcting himself. (Note the clear remains of *ù* at the start of the erased line following line 9 and at the start of line 11 [the *CAD* Nuzi file notes the erasure of *ù* before *uzzakama;* Lacheman judges two signs to have been erased at the start of line 11].) Although careful to erase the PNs after lines 2 and 9 and at the start of line 11, the scribe failed to alter the incorrect plural verb form of line 7—by oversight or, more likely, because leaving it alone would have made no substantive difference in the text (cf. below, note to *JEN* 703:6). After realizing his error, the scribe put all subsequent verbs in the singular. And, there are no further erasures.

One seeming difficulty with this speculation is the presence of the verb *ittadin* (or the like) after *Šenneya* in line 9, implying but one adopter. In fact, on the cast, the trace is unclear.

The singular pronominal suffix in NÍG.BA-*š*[*u*] in line 9 probably refers to Teḫip-tilla. Cf. *JEN* 680:9 and the note thereto.

l. 8: ⸢*til*⸣. The last part of the sign is a *Winkelhaken,* not as copied.

l. 8: 6[+2? ANŠE?]. Eight homers of barley would be the expected full price for this amount of land at this location. See above, note to *JEN* 674:10.

l. 9: [*it*?-*t*]*a*?-[*din*]. On the dubious interpretation of the trace, see above, note to l. 7.

l. 11. On the indentation of the text at this point, see above, note to l. 7.

l. 19. For the NA which appears in the copy at the end of this line, see below, note to l. 34.

l. 34: *an-nu-ti* ⸢*ša*⸣ URU [*A*]-*pè-na-aš*. This is a scribal afterthought; in any case, the clause does not fit on the reverse proper. Cf. *JEN* 674:36-37, where the scribe accomplished in a more orderly fashion that which he attempted here in ll. 34-35; and *JEN* 675:41-42, where he simply omitted the thought altogether.

The NA of the copy at the end of l. 19 represents the *na* of [*A*]-*pè-na-aš*.

ll. 38, 40. As already noted regarding *JEN* 675:45-48, the same seal would here too appear to be used by more than one person. It should further be noted that Tintiya here uses seal Po 76, whereas, in *JEN* 675:47, he

employes seal Po 580. That is, the same person employs different seals, for no apparent reason other than convenience.

JEN 677

OBVERSE

1 ṭup-pí ma-$^{+}$ ⸢ru⸣-[ti] š[a]
2 ^{m}Tup-ka$_4$-a-$^{+}$pu D[UMU] ⸢Ar⸣?-[ ]
3 ^{m}Te-ḫi-ip-$^{+}$ til-$^{+}$ la D[UMU!] *P[u-ḫi-še-en-ni]
4 a-⸢na •ma-ru-ti⸣ •DÙ-$^{+}$ [s]ú-[ma]
5 ⸢1? ANŠE⸣ 5 ^{GIŠ}APIN ⸢A.$^{+}$ŠÀ⸣ [ši-qú]
6 AŠ AN.ZA.KÀR ⸢Sú⸣-la-e [AŠ UR]U [A-pè-•n]a-aš
7 ki-ma ḪA.LA-šu a-na ^{m}[T]e-ḫi-i[p-til]-•la
8 it-ta-din ⸢ù⸣ $^{m•}$Te-[ḫi]-ip-[til-la]
9 12 ANŠE ŠE.M[EŠ k]i-[ma NÍG].BA-[šu]
10 a-na ^{m}Tup-ka$_4$-⸢a⸣-[pu] i[t-ta-di]n
11 šum-ma A.ŠÀ di-⸢na⸣ [T]UK-š[i]
12 ^{m}Tup-ka$_4$-a-pu ⸢ú⸣-[za-ak-ka$_4$-ma]
13 a-na ^{m}Te-ḫi-•ip-[til-la i-na-an-d]in
14 šum-ma ^{m}Tup-ka$_4$-a-⸢pu⸣ KI.⸢BAL⸣-[a]t
15 2 MA.NA KÙ.SIG$_{17}$ a-na
16 ^{m}Te-ḫi-ip-til-la ú-ma-al-[l]a
17 IGI Muš-te-šup DUMU Ar-na-pu
18 IGI Na-aš-wi DUMU Ka$_4$-lu-li
19 IGI Wa-an-ti-ya ⸢DUMU⸣ [N]a-ḫi-a-š[u]
20 IGI Pu-i-ta-e ⸢DUMU⸣ *[N]u-uz-z[a]

LOWER EDGE

21 IGI A-tal-te-šup DUMU •[Š]um-mi-y[a]
22 IGI Muš-te-ya ⸢DUMU⸣ •Ar-•še-ni
23 IGI Šum-mi-ya DUMU ⸢A⸣-ri-•ka$_4$-na-r[i]

REVERSE

24 IGI Ur-ḫi-ya DUMU Ar-ša-tù-a
25 IGI En-na-šúk-rù DUMU Ta-a-a
26 IGI Šúk-ra-pu DUMU T[ù-u]n-tù-ya
27 IGI Ša-ka$_4$-ra-a-a DUMU Ta-ta-ú-a
28 IGI A-be-ya DUMU Pa-az-zi-ya
29 IGI Ik-ki-ya DUMU Ni-nu-a-tal
30 IGI Ar-zi-iz-za DUMU Ni-ki
31 IGI Al-pu-ya DUMU Ḫa-ši-ya
32 IGI Ti-in-ti-ya DUMU A-ka$_4$-a-a
33 IGI Šu-ul-mi-ya DUMU Pu-ya

34 *an-nu-tù-ma* A.ŠÀ NIGIN *ù* IGI.ME[Š]

S.I. Po 314

35 ^{NA_4} KIŠIB ^{m}*Muš-te-šup* DUMU ⌈*Ar*⌉*-na-pu*

S.I. Po 391

36 ^{NA_4} KIŠIB ^{m}*Na-aš-•wi* [DUMU *Ka$_4$-lu-li*]

S.I. Po 580

37 ^{NA_4} KIŠIB ^{m}*Pu-i-•*⌈*ta*⌉*-e* [DUMU? *Nu?-uz?-za?*]

UPPER EDGE

S.I. Po 179

38 NA$_4$ ^{m}*Ta-a-a* •DU[B.SAR]

LEFT EDGE

	S.I. Po 580	S.I. Po 76
39	NA$_4$ ^{m}*Ša-[ka$_4$]-ra-a-a*	NA$_4$ ^{m}*Ti-in-ti-ya*
40	*ša* •URU *A-pè-na-aš*	

TRANSLATION

(1-4) Tablet of adoption of Tupk-apu son of Ar(?)-... . He adopted Teḫip-tilla son of Puḫi-šenni.

(5-8) He gave to Teḫip-tilla as his inheritance share a 1(?).5 homer [irrigated] field in the *dimtu* of Sulae, [in] the town of Apena.

(8-10) And Teḫip-tilla gave to Tupk-apu as [his] gift 12 homers of barley.

(11-13) Should the field have a case (against it), Tupk-apu shall clear (the field) [and] give (it) to Teḫip-tilla.

(14-16) Should Tupk-apu abrogate (this contract), he shall pay to Teḫip-tilla 2 minas of gold.

(17-34) Before Muš-tešup son of Arn-apu; before Našwi son of Kaluli; before Wantiya son of Naḫi-ašu; before Pui-tae son of Nuzza; before Atal-tešup son of Šummiya; before Muš-teya son of Ar-šenni; before Šummiya son of Arik-kanari; before Urḫiya son of Ar-šatuya; before En-šukru son of Taya; before Šukr-apu son of Tuntuya; before Šakaraya son of Tantawa; before Abeya son of Pazziya; before Ikkiya son of Ninu-atal; before Ar-zizza son of Niki; before Alpuya son of Ḫašiya; before Tintiya son of Akaya; before Šulmiya son of Puya. And these (are the ones who) measured the field and are witnesses.

(35-40) (*seal impression*) seal impression of Muš-tešup son of Arn-apu; (*seal impression*) seal impression of Našwi [son of Kaluli]; (*seal impression*) seal impression of Pui-tae [son? of? Nuzza?]; (*seal impression*) seal impression of Taya, the scribe; (*seal impression*) seal impression of Šakaraya of the town of Apena; (*seal impression*) seal impression of Tintiya.

COMMENTS

This tablet has deteriorated slightly since the copy was made. Also, two chips from the tablet were subsequently joined to the main piece, yielding more text for lines 1-3, 10-12. In the latter case only were the signs added to Lacheman's hand copy. All additions, of course, are represented in the edition.

NOTES

l. 2: ⸢*Ar*⸣?. The *CAD* Nuzi file, *NPN* (158a, *sub* TUPK-APU 2), and Lacheman concur that the sign represented is AR.

l. 4. No sign appears between *ti* and DÙ; the line is mostly intact.

l. 5: ⸢1⸣?. The vertical wedge is difficult to discern. However, the full price for 1.5 homers of land in this location should amount to 12 homers of barley (see note to *JEN* 674:10), and this figure does appear in line 9.

l. 5: [*ši-qú*]. These signs are represented as preserved in the *CAD* Nuzi file and Lacheman's records.

l. 6: ⸢*Sú*⸣. ⸢*Su*⸣ is also possible (if perhaps less likely) since the scribe of this text employs both writings for this GN: *Sú*: *JEN* 5:6; 678:5; *LG* 1:6. *Su*: *JEN* 94:6.

l. 19: [*N*]*a*. This sign has the usual form. It is not as copied.

l. 37: [DUMU? *Nu*?-*uz*?-*za*?]. Although this restoration is reasonable (cf., for example, *JEN* 676:38), one wonders if there is enough space for all these signs.

l. 39. Lacheman identifies at least one of the sealings above this line as Po 76. Cf. *JEN* 676:40. Collation confirms this identification for the right-hand seal impression (above "Tintiya"). Lacheman and Maidman (1989, 51) is to be corrected accordingly. The left-hand seal impression is indistinct.

Cf. the notes to *JEN* 678:39; 680:37, 40.

JEN 678

OBVERSE

1 *ṭup-pí* $^{+}$*m*[*a-ru-ti ša*]

2 ^{m}*Ta-a-a* $^{+}$DU[MU *A*]*k-ku-le-en-ni*

3 ^{m}*Te-ḫi-ip-ti*[*l-l*]*a* DUMU *Pu-ḫi-še-ni*

4 *a-na ma-ru-***t*[*i*] DÙ-*ma*

5 2 $^{+}$ANŠE ⸢A.ŠÀ⸣ [*ši*]-*qa i+na* AN.ZA.KÀR *Sú-la-e*

6 AŠ URU *A-pè-n*[*a-a*]*š ki-ma* ḪA.LA-*šu*

7 *a-na* ^{m}*Te-*$^{•}$*ḫ*[*i-i*]*p-til-la it-ta-din*

8 *ù* ^{m}*Te-[ḫi-i]p-til-la* ⸢16⸣ ANŠE ŠE.MEŠ
9 *ki-ma* NÍG.[BA-*š*]*u a-na* ^{m}*Ta-a-*⸢*a*⸣ *it-ta-ad-*⸢*na*⸣*-aš-*⸢*šu*⸣
10 *šum-ma* A.Š[À *di-n*]*a*! TUK-*ši* ^{m}*Ta-a-a*
11 *ú-za-a*[*k-ka*$_4$*-m*]*a a-na* ^{m}*Te-ḫi-ip-til-la i+na-an-din*
12 •*šum-***m*[*a* ^{m}*T*]*a-a-a* KI.BAL-*at*
13 2 [MA].N[A KÙ].SIG$_{17}$ *a-na* ^{m}*Te-ḫi-ip-til-la*
14 ⸢*ú-ma-al*⸣*-la*
15 IGI *Muš-*⸢*te-šup*⸣ DUMU ⸢*Ar*⸣*-na-pu*
16 IGI *Na-aš-*[*w*]*i* DUMU ⸢*Ka*⸣!*-lu-***l*[*i*]
17 IGI *Wa-an-*⸢*ti*⸣*-ya* DUMU *Na-ḫi-*•⸢*a*⸣*-*[*šu*]
18 IGI *Šum-mi-*[*y*]*a* DUMU *A-ri-k*[*a*$_4$*-na-ri*]
19 IGI *Muš-t*[*e-y*]*a* DUMU *Ar-še-*[*ni*]
20 IGI *A-tal-te-*[*š*]*up* DUMU *Šum-mi-*[*ya*]
21 IGI *Pu-i-*•*ta-*⸢*e* •DUMU *Nu*⸣*-***u*[*z-za*]
22 IGI *Ur-ḫi-ya* [DUMU *Ar-š*]*a-*[*tù-ya*]
23 IGI ⸢*En-na*⸣*-*[*šúk-rù*] DUMU *Ta-a-a*

LOWER EDGE

24 [*an-nu-t*]*i ši-bu-ti ša* URU *Nu-zi*
25 [IGI *Šúk-r*]*a-pu* DUMU *Tù-*•*un-tù-*⸢*ya*⸣
26 [IGI *Ša*]*-*•*ka*$_4$*-ra-a-a* DUMU *Ta-an-*⸢*ta-ú*⸣*-a*
27 [IGI *A-be*]*-*⸢*ya*⸣ DUMU *Pa-az-zi-y*[*a*]

REVERSE

28 [IGI *Ik-ki-*$^{+}$*y*]*a* DUMU *Ni-nu-a-*•⸢*tal*⸣
29 ⸢IGI *Ar*⸣*-*[*z*]*i-iz-za* DUMU *Ni-ki*
30 IGI *Al-pu-ya* DUMU *Ḫa-*•*ši-ya*
31 IGI *Ti-in-t*[*i-ya* D]UMU *A-*[*ka*$_4$]*-a-a*
32 IGI *Šu-ul-mi-*[*ya* DUMU *Pu-y*]*a*
33 IGI *Ta-a-a* DUB.S[AR-*r*]*ù*

---

34 *an-nu-ti ši-*⸢*bu*⸣*-t*[*i*] *ša* URU ⸢*A-pè*⸣*-na-aš ù šu-nu-ma* NIGIN-*ú* A.ŠÀ

S.I. Po 314

35 $^{[N]A_4}$ KIŠIB ^{m}⸢*Muš*⸣*-*[*te-šu*]*p* DUMU *Ar-n*[*a-pu*]

S.I. Po 391

36 ^{NA_4} KIŠIB [^{m}*N*]*a-*⸢*aš-wi*⸣ [DUMU *Ka*]*-lu-li*

S.I. Po 580

37 $^{N[A_4}$ KIŠIB ^{m}*P*]*u-i*!*-ta-e* DUMU *Nu-uz-za*

S.I. Po 179

38 [^{NA_4} KIŠIB ^{m}*Ta-a*]*-a* DUB.SAR

LEFT EDGE

S.I.	S.I. Po 76
39 $^{+}$NA$_4$ [^{m}*Š*]*a-ka*$_4$*-ra-a-a ši-bi*	[N]A$_4$ ^{m}*Ti-in-ti-ya ši-*[*bi*]
40 ⸢*ša*⸣ URU *A-pè-na-aš*	[*ša* U]RU *A-pè-na-aš*

TRANSLATION

(1-4) Tablet of adoption [of] Taya son of Akkul-enni. He adopted Teḫip-tilla son of Puḫi-šenni.

(5-7) He gave to Teḫip-tilla as his inheritance share a 2 homer irrigated field in the *dimtu* of Sulae, in the town of Apena.

(8-9) And Teḫip-tilla gave to Taya as his gift 16 homers of barley.

(10-11) Should the field have a case (against it), Taya shall clear (the field) and give (it) to Teḫip-tilla.

(12-14) Should Taya abrogate (this contract), he shall pay to Teḫip-tilla 2 minas of gold.

(15-24) Before Muš-tešup son of Arn-apu; before Našwi son of Kaluli; before Wantiya son of Naḫi-ašu; before Šummiya son of Arik-kanari; before Muš-teya son of Ar-šenni; before Atal-tešup son of Šummiya; before Pui-tae son of Nuzza; before Urḫiya son of Ar-šatuya; before En-šukru son of Taya. These are the witnesses of the town of Nuzi.

(25-34) [Before] Šukr-apu son of Tuntuya; [before] Šakaraya son of Tantawa; [before] Abeya son of Pazziya; [before] Ikkiya son of Ninu-atal; before Ar-zizza son of Niki; before Alpuya son of Ḫašiya; before Tintiya son of Akaya; before Šulmiya son of Puya; before Taya, the scribe.

These are the witnesses of the town of Apena and, as well, they are the measurers of the field.

(35-40) (*seal impression*) seal impression of Muš-tešup son of Arn-apu; (*seal impression*) seal impression of Našwi [son of] Kaluli; (*seal impression*) seal impression of Pui-tae son of Nuzza; (*seal impression*) seal impression of Taya, the scribe; (*seal impression*) seal impression of Šakaraya, witness of the town of Apena; (*seal impression*) seal impression of Tintiya, witness [of] the town of Apena.

COMMENT

This tablet has deteriorated slightly since the copy was made.

NOTES

l. 5: ANŠE. This sign is more fully developed than the copy indicates. It is virtually identical to ANŠE in line 8.

l. 10: [*di-n*]*a*!. This reading is to be preferred to [*pí-ir*]-*qa*. Wherever this clause is sufficiently preserved in the Apena series of texts (see note to *JEN* 674:23), *di-na* is always present.

l. 16: ⸢*Ka*⸣!. The sign is preserved on the tablet as copied.

l. 22: [*Ar-š*]*a*-[*tù-ya*]. The name is restored (as are all comparably damaged witness PNs in this text) from the standard Nuzi-Apena witness sequence. See note to *JEN* 674:23.

l. 34: NIGIN-*ú* A.ŠÀ. These signs follow immediately after *šu-nu-ma*. They are not written on the following line. ":" (Lacheman and Maidman [1989, 53]) finds no counterpart on the tablet.

l. 39. In his notes, Lacheman suggests that the first sealing is not part of the Po corpus and that the second sealing equals Po 76. Collation confirms both that the right-hand sealing is Po 76 and that the left-hand sealing is not Po 580. Lacheman and Maidman (1989, 53) is to be corrected accordingly. The left-hand sealing is the same as the first sealing over *JEN* 680:40. Cf. the notes to *JEN* 677:39; 680:37, 40.

JEN 679

OBVERSE

1 [*ù ša* ^{m}*Ma?-* DUMU •*Ḫ*]*u-ti-ya-ma*
2 [^{m}*Te-ḫi*]-*⸢*ip*⸣-[*til-la* DUMU *Pu-ḫi*]-*še-ni*
3 [*a-na*] *ma-ru*-*[*t*]*i* [DÙ-*šu-m*]*a*
4 [AN]ŠE 4 ^{GIŠ}•API[N A.ŠÀ *ši*-*[*q*]*ú i+na*
5 [*šu-p*]*a-al* AN.[ZA].K[ÀR *ša*] **Ku-na-tù*
6 [AŠ] •URU *A-pè-n*[*a*]*-aš* •*ki*-•⸢*ma*⸣ Ḫ[A].•LA-*šu*
7 [*a-n*]*a* ^{m}•*Te*-⸢*ḫi-ip*⸣-**til*-•*la* •*it*-[*ta-a*]*d-nu*
8 •⸢*ù*⸣ ^{m}⸢*Te*-**ḫi*⸣-*[*i*]*p*-**til*-*[*l*[*a* ANŠ]E ŠE.MEŠ
9 [*ki-ma*] *NÍG.*BA-**š*[*u-nu a-na* ^{m}*Me*-•*l*]*e-ya*
10 [*ù a-na*] *⸢m⸣?[*Ma?-* *it-ta-din*]
11 *[*šu*]*m*-*⸢*ma* *A⸣.[ŠÀ *di-na* TUK-*ši* ^{m}*Me-le-ya*]
12 *⸢*ù*⸣ *m*⸢*Ma*⸣?-[*ú-za-ak-ku-ma*]
13 [*a*-•*n*]*a* •m•*Te*-**ḫi*-*⸢*ip*⸣-**ti*[*l*]-*[*l*[*a i-na-an-din*]
14 [*šum*]-•*ma* •m•*Me*-**le*!-**ya* *⸢*ù*⸣ [^{m}*Ma?-*]
15 KI.BAL-**tù* 2 M[A.NA KÙ].⸢SIG$_{17}$⸣!?
16 *a-na* ^{m}*Te*-•*ḫi*-•*ip-til-la* [*ú-m*]*a-al*-•*lu-ú*
17 IGI *Muš-te-šup* DUMU [*Ar-n*]*a-pu*
18 IGI *Na-aš-wi* DUMU **K*[*a$_{4}$-lu-l*]*i*
19 IGI *Wa-an-ti*-•*ya* [DUMU •*N*]*a-ḫi-a-šu*
20 IGI *A-tal-te*-•*šup* [DUMU *Šum*]-•⸢*mi*⸣-*ya*
21 IGI *Pu*-•*i*-**ta*-[*e* DUMU *Nu-uz*]-*za*

LOWER EDGE

22 •IGI *Šum-mi-ya* DUMU ⸢*A*⸣-*ri-ka$_{4}$-na-ri*
23 IGI •*Muš-te*-•*ya* •DU[MU •*A*]*r*-•*še-ni*

REVERSE

24 IGI *Ur-ḫi-[y]a* DUM[U] *Ar-ša-tù-ya*

25 IGI *En-na-šúk-rù* DUMU *Ta-a-a*

26 IGI *Šúk-ra-pu* DUMU *Tù-un-tù-ya*

27 IGI *Ša-⸢ka*$_4$*⸣-ra-a-a* DUMU *Ta-an-ta-ú-a*

28 IGI *A-[b]e-ya* DUMU *Pa-az-zi-ya*

29 ⸢IGI⸣ •*Ik-ki-ya* DUMU *Ni-nu-a-tal*

30 IGI *Ar-zi-iz-za* DUMU *Ni-ki*

31 IGI *Al-pu-ya* DUMU *Ḫa-ši-ya*

32 IGI *Ti-in-•ti-ya* [D]UMU *A-ka*$_4$*-a-a*

33 IGI *Šu-ul-[m]i-ya* DUMU *Pu-ya*

34 [IG]I *Ta-•⸢a⸣-•a* ⸢DUB⸣.SAR

35 [*an-nu-ti*] *ši-bu-ti* +⸢*ù*⸣ •*š[u-+n]u-+ma* NIGI[N!-*ú* A.ŠÀ]

36 [IGI *Pa-ak-l]a-[p]í-t[i* DUM]U *Ka*$_4$*-ni*

S.I. Po 314

37 $^{[N]A_4}$ KI[ŠI]B ⸢^{m}*Muš*⸣-[*t*]*e-šup* DUMU *Ar-na-pu*

S.I. Po 391

38 [^{NA_4} K]I[ŠIB] ^{m}*Na-aš-wi* DUMU *Ka*$_4$*-lu-li*

S.I. Po 580

39 [^{NA_4} KIŠIB ^{m}•*P]u-i-ta-e* DUMU *Nu-uz-za*

LEFT EDGE

S.I. Po 580

40 NA$_4$ ^{m}*Ša-ka*$_4$*-•ra-[a-a ši?-bi?]*

41 *ša* URU •*A-[pè-na-aš]*

TRANSLATION

....

(1-3) [and of Ma?-...] also [the son of] Ḫutiya. [They] adopted Teḫip-tilla son of Puḫi-šenni.

(4-7) They gave to Teḫip-tilla as his inheritance share a(n) x.4 homer irrigated [field] to the west of the *dimtu* [of] Kunatu, [in] the town of Apena.

(8-10) And Teḫip-tilla [gave to Meleya and to Ma?-... as] their gift x homer(s) of barley.

(11-13) Should the field [have a case (against it), Meleya] and Ma(?)-... [shall clear (the field) and give (it)] to Teḫip-tilla].

(14-16) Should Meleya and [Ma?-...] abrogate (this contract), they shall pay to Teḫip-tilla 2 minas of gold.

(17-36) Before Muš-tešup son of Arn-apu; before Našwi son of Kaluli; before Wantiya [son of] Naḫi-ašu; before Atal-tešup [son of] Šummiya; before Pui-tae [son of] Nuzza; before Šummiya son of Arik-kanari; before Muš-teya son of Ar-šenni; before Urḫiya son of Ar-šatuya; before En-šukru son of Taya; before Šukr-apu son of Tuntuya; before Šakaraya son of

Tantawa; before Abeya son of Pazziya; before Ikkiya son of Ninu-atal; before Ar-zizza son of Niki; before Alpuya son of Ḫašiya; before Tintiya son of Akaya; before Šulmiya son of Puya; before Taya, the scribe. These are the witnesses and, as well, they are the measurers [of the field]. Before Pakla-piti son of Kani.

(37-41) (*seal impression*) seal impression of Muš-tešup son of Arn-apu; (*seal impression*) seal impression of Našwi son of Kaluli; (*seal impression*) seal impression of Pui-tae son of Nuzza; (*seal impression*) seal impression of Šakaraya, [witness?] of the town of Apena.

COMMENTS

This tablet has suffered considerable deterioration since Lacheman's copy was made. Note, for example, that nothing at all remains of lines 10-12. Interpretation is further hampered due to a downward slant of the first lines, a slant hard to follow owing to the destruction of the middle portion of these lines.

Preceding line 1, one line (only) is entirely effaced. This line may be restored with confidence because of the following factors. Plural verbs (lines 7, 15, 16) indicate more than one adopter. Line 14 identifies the first of these as Meleya. The enclitic *-ma* following the patronymic in line 1 indicates that the two adopters share the same father. (This construction is similar to *JEN* 675:3-4; cf. already Gelb's recognition of this principle [*NPN*, 8].) Therefore, the missing first line will have read: *ṭup-pí ma-ru-ti ša* ^{m}*Me-le-ya* DUMU *Ḫu-ti-ya*.

NOTES

l. 1: [^{m}*Ma*?-]. The second adopter's PN is preserved only in a small trace in line 12.

l. 3: [DÙ-*šu-m*]*a*. Or the like. Cf. *JEN* 580:7. For an alternative restoration, see, for example, note to *JEN* 674:5.

l. 5: *Ku-na-tù*. This *dimtu* name lacks the masculine determinative in two other documents written by the scribe of this text (the only other places—as far as I know—to mention this *dimtu* at all): *JEN* 81:6; 674:7. Therefore, the determinative is not restored here.

l. 15: ⌜SIG_{17}⌝!?. The last trace is a single vertical, not a double vertical as copied.

ll. 22-23. These lines appear on the lower edge.

l. 24. This line begins the reverse.

l. 35: *ši-bu-ti*. The *ši* is a normal one, not as copied.

l. 35: ⌜*ù*⌝ *š*[*u-n*]*u-ma* NIGI[N!-*ú* A.ŠÀ]. Lacheman interpreted these signs as (and his copy reflects): [*š*]*a* KÙ.BA[BBAR] *na-din-*[ ]. (An unpublished paper of his accords with this as well.) However, collation reveals ⌜*ù*⌝

followed by four horizontal wedges (the bottom one longest) ending in a break. After the break, NU is nearly complete and MA is entirely preserved. The resultant text and restoration of this line is very close to *JEN* 678:34. Cf., above, note to *JEN* 674:37: [*ša* U]RU ⸢*A*⸣!-[*pè-na-aš*] ⸢*ù*⸣! ⸢*šu*⸣-*nu*-[*ma* NIGIN-*ú* A.ŠÀ].

l. 36: [*Pa-ak-l*]*a*-[*p*]*í-t*[*i*]. For the restoration of this name, cf., for example, *JEN* 675: 40; 676:33. The scribe has here backtracked to include a name inadvertently omitted before l. 34.

JEN 680

OBVERSE

[ṭup-pí]*⸢ma-ru-ti⸣ ša
+⸢^{m}+E-+pu-•zi⸣ DUMU Ḫa-na-ak-ka$_{4}$ •ù [ša ^{m}Še-eš-wa-a-a DUMU]
+^{m}+Te-+ḫi-+⸢ip⸣-til-⸢la⸣ DUMU Pu-ḫi-še-en-ni
+a-+na +ma-[ru]-⸢ti⸣ +DÙ-+⸢uš⸣-ma
1 +⸢ANŠE A.ŠÀ +ši-qa⸣ •i+*na *AN.•ZA.KÀR
ša Šu-ul-+m[i-ya] •AŠ •URU •A-pè-na-aš
ki-ma ḪA.LA-šu [a-n]a ^{m}Te-ḫ[i-i]p-til-la it-+ta-+a[d-nu]
ù ^{m}Te-ḫi-[ip]-til-la 6 [+2?] •ANŠE ŠE.MEŠ
ki-ma NÍG.BA-[šu] a-na ^{m}E-⸢pu⸣-zi ù a-na ^{m}Še-[eš-wa]-•a-a
it-ta-a[d-n]a-aš-šu-nu-⸢ti⸣
šum-ma A.ŠÀ [di-n]a TUK-ši ^{m}⸢E⸣-pu-⸢zi⸣ ù ^{m}Še-e[š-w]a-a-a
ú-za-ak-ku-[m]a a-na ^{m}Te-[ḫi-i]p-til-l[a i-n]a-an-[dì-n]u
šum-ma ^{m}E-p[u-z]i ⸢ù ^{m}⸣Še-e[š-wa]-a-⸢a KI.BAL⸣-+tu
2 MA.NA K[Ù.SIG$_{17}$ a-n]a ^{m}Te-ḫi-i[p-til-la]
ú-ma-al-[lu-ú]
+ ____

IGI Muš-te-[šup DUM]U ⸢Ar-na⸣-p[u]
IGI Na-aš-wi [DUMU] Ka$_{4}$-lu-li
IGI Wa-an-ti-[y]a DUMU Na-ḫi-•a-•šu
IGI Šum-•mi-y[a DUM]U A-r[i-ka$_{4}$-na]-⸢ri⸣
IGI Mu[š]-⸢te⸣-[y]a DUMU [Ar]-še-ni
IGI A-⸢tal⸣-te-šup •DUMU [Šu]m-mi-[ya]
IGI •Pu-i-ta-⸢e⸣ [DU]MU Nu-uz-za
+IGI +⸢Ur⸣-ḫi-ya [DUM]U Ar-ša-tù-ya

LOWER EDGE

+IGI En-šúk-rù [DUMU] Ta-a-a
[IGI Šúk-ra-pu DUMU Tù-u]n-tù-ya
[IGI Ša-ka$_{4}$-ra-a-a DUMU Ta-an]-ta-ú-a

REVERSE

27 [IGI _A-be-y_]_a_ *⸢DUMU⸣ [_Pa-az-_•_z_]_i-ya_

28 •IGI •⸢_Ik_⸣-*_ki-_•_ya_ DUMU _N_[_i-nu-a-_•_t_]_al_

29 IGI •_Ar-_•_zi-iz-za_ DUMU _N_[_i-_•_k_]_i_

30 IGI _Al-_⸢_pu_⸣_-ya_ DUMU _Ḫa-š_[_i-y_]_a_

31 IGI _Ti-in-ti-ya_ DUMU _A-ka_$_4$_-a-a_

32 IGI _Šu-ul-mi-ya_ DUMU _Pu-ya_

33 IGI _Ta-a-_•_a_ +[DU]MU _A-pil_-XXX DUB.SAR

34 _an-nu-ti š_[_i-b_]_u-ti ša_ URU _A-pè-na-aš ù šu-nu-ma_

: _mu-še-el-mu-_[_ú_]

: _ša_ A.ŠÀ

S.I. Po 314

35 ⸢^{NA_4}⸣ •KIŠIB $^{m+}$_M_[_uš-te-š_]_up_ ⸢DUMU _Ar_⸣_-na-pu_

S.I. Po 391

36 ^{NA_4} •KIŠIB •^{m}•_Na-aš-wi_ DUMU _Ka_$_4$_-lu-li_

S.I.

37 [^{NA_4} KIŠIB ^{m}]•_Pu-i-t_[_a-e_]

38 [DUMU •_N_]_u-uz-za_

UPPER EDGE

S.I.

39 [^{NA_4} KIŠIB ^{m}*_T_]_a-_*_a-_*_a_ DUB.+SA[R]

LEFT EDGE

	S.I.	S.I. Po 76
40	[NA$_4$ ^{m}_Ša-ka_$_4$]-•_ra-a-a ši-_⸢_bi ša_	NA$_4$⸣ ^{m}•_Ti-_•_in-_•_ti-y_[_a_ (_ši-bi_) _ša_]
41	[URU] •_A-pè-na-_[_aš_]	[URU] •_A-pè-na-aš_

TRANSLATION

(1-4) [Tablet of] adoption of Epuzi son of Ḫanakka and [of Šešwaya son of ...]. They adopted Teḫip-tilla son of Puḫi-šenni.

(5-7) They gave to Teḫip-tilla as his inheritance share a 1 homer irrigated field in the _dimtu_ of Šulmiya, in the town of Apena.

(8-9) And Teḫip-tilla gave to Epuzi and to Šešwaya as his gift 6 [+2?] homers of barley.

(10-12) Should the field have a case (against it), Epuzi and Šešwaya shall clear (the field) and give (it) to Teḫip-tilla.

(13-14) Should Epuzi and Šešwaya abrogate (this contract), they shall pay to Teḫip-tilla 2 minas of gold.

(15-34) Before Muš-tešup son of Arn-apu; before Našwi son of Kaluli; before Wantiya son of Naḫi-ašu; before Šummiya son of Arik-kanari; before Muš-teya son of Ar-šenni; before Atal-tešup son of Šummiya; before Pui-tae son of Nuzza; before Urḫiya son of Ar-šatuya; before En-šukru son of Taya; [before Šukr-apu son of] Tuntuya; [before Šakaraya son of] Tantawa;

[before] Abeya son of Pazziya; [before] Ikkiya son of Ninu-atal; before Arzizza son of Niki; before Alpuya son of Ḫašiya; before Tintiya son of Akaya; before Šulmiya son of Puya; before Taya son of Apil-sin, the scribe. These are the witnesses of the town of Apena and, as well, they are the measurers of the field.

(35-40) (*seal impression*) seal impression of Muš-tešup son of Arn-apu; (*seal impression*) seal impression of Našwi son of Kaluli; (*seal impression*) seal impression of Pui-tae son of Nuzza; (*seal impression*) seal impression of Taya, the scribe; (*seal impression*) seal impression of Šakaraya, witness of the town of Apena; (*seal impression*) seal impression of Tintiya, [witness? of] the town of Apena.

COMMENTS

This tablet appears to have suffered deterioration since the copy was made. The copy was collated against casts, the original being unavailable. The casts, however, seem excellent. A small fragment (*JENu* 1141g) has recently been identified as belonging to this text; the joined piece contributes to the beginnings of lines 2-5.

Collation shows a horizontal line made by the scribe after line 15.

NOTES

l. 2: [^{m}*Še-eš-wa-a-a*]. Restored from l. 11.

l. 8: 6 [+2?]. The amount of land sold is one homer (l. 5; assured by the recent join). Therefore, eight homers of barley represents the usual price for this amount of land in this location. See note to *JEN* 674:10. The *CAD* Nuzi file for this text records nine homers of barley.

l. 9: [*šu*]. There does not seem to be enough room for [*šu-nu*]. Thus, the pronominal suffix would appear to refer to Teḫip-tilla, the donor of the gift. Usually, the suffix refers to the recipient(s) of the gift, as exemplified by *JEN* 674:11; 675:16; 722:12. (By the same token, the pronominal suffix attached to ḪA.LA, "inheritance share," refers to the recipient, not the donor[s], as shown, for example, by *JEN* 674:8; 675:11.)

l. 11: [*n*]*a*. The horizontal lines are shorter than copied and represent a normal *na*.

l. 24. This line begins the lower edge.

l. 25: [*Šúk-ra-pu* DUMU *Tù-u*]*n-tù-ya*. Restored (as are all comparably damaged witness PNs in this text) from the standard Nuzi-Apena witness sequence. See note to *JEN* 674:23.

l. 36. This line curves up to avoid the ends of lines originating on the obverse.

l. 37. In his notes, Lacheman asserts that the seal impression above this line is not to be found in Porada (1947). Collation confirms that this sealing is not Po 580. Lacheman and Maidman (1989, 57) is to be corrected accordingly. Cf. the notes to *JEN* 677:39; 678:39.

l. 39: SA[R]. The traces form a more typical SAR than the copy indicates.

l. 40. In his notes, Lacheman asserts that the first seal impression above this line is not to be found in Porada (1947). He identifies the second impression as Po 76. Collation confirms both that the right-hand sealing is Po 76 and that the left-hand sealing is not Po 580. Lacheman and Maidman (1989, 57) is to be corrected accordingly. The left-hand sealing is the same as the first sealing over *JEN* 678:39. Cf. the notes to *JEN* 677:39; 678:39.

JEN 681

OBVERSE

1 [^{m}I]n-ni-ki DUMU [Ḫa-ši-ya]
2 ^{m}T[e]-ḫi-•ip-til-la DUMU P[u-ḫi-še-en-ni]
3 a-na ma-ru-t[i] DÙ-s[ú?-ma]
4 1 ANŠE A.ŠÀ ⸢i⸣+na e-⸢le⸣-[en]
5 ù i+na [š]u-pa-al AN.[ZA.KÀR]
6 ša +T[a-an]-na-taš-ši [ki-ma ḪA.LA-šu]
7 +⸢a⸣-+n[a ^{m}Te-*ḫ]i-ip-til-la i[t-ta-din]
8 [ù ^{m}Te]-ḫi-ip-til-la ⸢4⸣ [+? ANŠE ŠE.MEŠ]
9 +k[i-ma NÍG].BA-šu a-na ^{m}In-[ni-ki]
10 i[t-ta-ad-na]-aš-šu šum-ma A.ŠÀ d[i?-na TUK-ši]
11 +^{m}+I[n-ni]-•ki ú-za-ak-ka$_{4}$-[ma]
12 a-n[a ^{m}Te-ḫi]-ip-til-la i+na-a[n-din]
13 +šum-[ma ^{m}In-ni]-ki KI.BAL-[a]t
14 2 [MA.N]A KÙ.SIG$_{17}$ ⸢a-na⸣ $^{[m]}$Te-ḫ[i]-ip-til-+la
15 •⸢ú⸣-[m]a-al-la ⸢il⸣-ka$_{4}$ ša A.ŠÀ
16 [^{m}I]n-ni-ki-ma na-ši

---

17 [IGI M]uš-te-šup DUMU +⸢Ar⸣-na-pu
18 [IGI Ki]p-ta-e DUMU En-⸢na⸣-ma-ti
19 [IGI P]í-ru DUMU Na-iš-ké-el-pè
20 [IGI Š]i-mi-ka$_{4}$-tal DUMU +⸢Ta⸣-ku
21 [IGI Ut]-⸢ḫap-ta-•e⸣ •DUMU +[Z]i-ké
22 [IGI A?-ri?-ké?-na?-ri? DUMU M]il-ka$_{4}$-pu

LOWER EDGE

+23 [IGI Ar-ša-lim DUMU Tam]-pu-uš-til
24 [IGI Te-e]š-šu-⸢ya⸣

25 [DUMU] •*Ki-in-•ni-*⌜*ya*⌝

REVERSE

26 I[GI *Ḫ*]*a-ši-pár-al-la*

27 ⁺D[UM]U *Pa-li-ya*

28 IGI *T*[*a*]*-a-a* DUB.SAR

29 IGI *P*[*u*]*-•un-•ni-ya* DUMU *Nu-uz-za*

S.I. Po 314

30 [$^{\mathrm{NA}_4}$ KIŠIB ^{m}]*M*[*uš-te*]*-šup* DUMU *Ar-na-pu*

S.I. Po 637

31 $^{\mathrm{NA}_4}$ KIŠIB ^{m}*Pí-ru*

S.I. Po 564

32 $^{\mathrm{NA}_4}$ KIŠIB ^{m}⌜*Pu*⌝*-•un-ni-ya* DUMU *Nu-uz-*⌜*za*⌝

LEFT EDGE

S.I. Po 179

33 ^{N}[$^{\mathrm{A}_4}$ KIŠI]B ^{m}*Ta-a-a* D[UB.SAR-*r*]*i*

TRANSLATION

....

(1-3) Inniki son of Ḫašiya. He adopted Teḫip-tilla son of Puḫi-šenni.

(4-7) He gave to Teḫip-tilla [as his inheritance share] a 1 homer field to the east and to the west of the *dimtu* of Tanna-tašši.

(8-10) [And] Teḫip-tilla gave to Inniki as his gift 4 [+? homers of barley].

(10-12) Should the field [have] a ca[se? (against it)], Inniki shall clear (the field) and give (it) to Teḫip-tilla.

(13-15) Should Inniki abrogate (this contract), he shall pay to Teḫip-tilla 2 minas of gold.

(15-16) Inniki shall furthermore bear the *ilku* of the field.

(17-29) [Before] Muš-tešup son of Arn-apu; [before] Kip-tae son of Enna-mati; [before] Piru son of Naiš-kelpe; [before] Šimika-atal son of Takku; [before] Utḫap-tae son of Zike; [before Arik-kanari? son of] Milk-apu; [before Ar-šalim son of] Tampuštil; [before] Teššuya [son of] Kinniya; before Ḫašip-paralla son of Paliya; before Taya, the scribe; before Punniya son of Nuzza.

(30-33) (*seal impression*) [seal impression of] Muš-tešup son of Arn-apu; (*seal impression*) seal impression of Piru; (*seal impression*) seal impression of Punniya son of Nuzza; (*seal impression*) seal impression of Taya, the scribe.

COMMENTS

There are a few signs of deterioration in the tablet since the copy was made. Also, it seems that deterioration occurred between the time the *CAD*

Nuzi file transliteration was made and the time of Lacheman's copy. See especially below, notes to lines 22 and 23.

Only one line is missing at the start. It will have read: *ṭup-pí ma-ru-ti ša*.

JEN 681 has close links to *JEN* 683. Some of these are described below in the notes to lines 1, 5 and 6.

NOTES

l. 1: [*Ḫa-ši-ya*]. Restored from *JEN* 683:2. According to *JEN* 683, Inniki son of Ḫašiya cedes land to Teḫip-tilla son of Puḫi-šenni, which, as in this text, adjoins land associated with Tanna-tašši (here, the PN is qualified by the term, *dimtu*; in *JEN* 683:7, it is not). These are the only two Nuzi texts to my knowledge where this GN appears. The two Innikis, therefore, most likely represent the same person, and so "Ḫašiya" may be restored with some confidence.

l. 5: AN.[ZA.KÀR]. In an unpublished note, Lacheman reads: AN.[ZA.KÀR *Na-ni-ya* AŠ (<*le*?-*et*?>—M.P.M.) *mi-iṣ-ri*], making this line parallel to *JEN* 683:6-7. However, there appears to be insufficient room for such a restoration.

l. 6: *T*[*a-an*]-*na-taš-ši*. The restoration is assured by *JEN* 683:7.

The town with which this *dimtu* (l. 6) / land (*JEN* 683:7) is to be linked is not known for certain. The witnesses to these two transactions are associated, for the most part, with Nuzi itself.

There is some circumstantial evidence, though, linking this land with the town of Turša:

(a) Tanna-tašši is a rare PN. One Taya son of Tanna-tašši (*JEN* 79:15) is witness to a Teḫip-tilla transaction involving Turša land (*JEN* 79:6).

(b) Ilu-êriš son of Tanna-tašši (*JEN* 552:18) is witness to a contract whereby Teḫip-tilla's father, Puḫi-šenni, obtains land in Natmani (*JEN* 552:11). This town may have been especially close to Turša. See, for example, *JEN* 68, 297, 415, 603. The real estate strategy of the Teḫip-tilla Family in general is marked by proximity of family holdings and, to this extent, these texts argue for the proximity of the two towns. See also H. Lewy (1968, 154-56). The same Ilu-êriš is witness to another real estate text (*JEN* 404:28-29). However, the location of the property involved cannot be determined with precision (*JEN* 404:8).

(c) The *dimtu* of Naniya mentioned in *JEN* 683:6 (and there alone) as being adjacent to the land of Tanna-tašši may possibly be linked to the person after whom the structures of Naniya of *JEN* 272:13 were named. This real estate is located in Turša (*JEN* 272:6) and, it is implied, may have been obtained by Teḫip-Tilla.

l. 7: *i*[*t-ta-din*]. Or the like.

l. 8: ⸢4⸣ [+?]. The *CAD* Nuzi file transliteration implies a total of 4 homers.

l. 13: *šum-*[*ma*]. The first sign is complete and typical, not as copied. Lacheman records the second sign as partially preserved.

l. 14: [MA]. Lacheman records the start of this sign as preserved.

l. 22. This is the bottom line of the obverse, not as depicted.

The *CAD* Nuzi file and *NPN*, 97b (*sub* MILK-APU 3)) read, in effect, [IGI]-*ké-na-ri* DUMU *Mil-ka*$_4$*-pu*. This implies (a) a tablet better preserved than when Lacheman made his copy; and (b) the missing PN is Arik-kanari (cf. *NPN*, 26a).

l. 23: [*Ar-ša-lim* DUMU *Tam*]-*pu-uš-til*. The last three signs are clearly preserved, though not copied. Tampuštil is certainly the patronymic. Ar-šalim is the likely PN of the witness since this son of Tampuštil is a ubiquitous witness in Teḫip-tilla texts (see *NPN*, 146b; there is only one other attested son of a Tampuštil, Utḫap-tae [see Cassin and Glassner 1977, hereafter *AAN*, 139a]). The *CAD* Nuzi file transliteration actually preserves, in effect, [*Ar*]-*ša-lim*.

The reading *Ar-ša-lim* rather than *Ar-ša-lì* (see *NPN*, 31b) seems now to be confirmed by the spelling *Ar-šá-li-im* in *EN* 9/1, 41:27.

l. 25. This line appears at the bottom of the lower edge.

JEN 682

OBVERSE

1 $^{+}$˹EME˺-[š]*u*? [*ša* ^{m}]*Zi-li-y*[*a*]

2 DUMU *Te-•en!-˹te-ya a-na˺! pa-ni* $^{˹•\mathrm{LÚ}˺.[\mathrm{MEŠ}]}$

3 *ḫal-ṣú-uḫ*$_5$*-le-e •ù ˹a-na pa-ni˺*

4 $^{˹\mathrm{LÚ}˺.\mathrm{ME[Š]}}$ DI.KU$_5$.MEŠ *ki-na-*an-*[*na iq-ta-bi*]

5 18 ANŠE •A.•ŠÀ *ši-i-•qà* [*i?-na? mi?-in?-da?-ti?* / *ta?-a?-a?-ri?*]

6 *š*[*a?*] •˹*e*˺?-•*kál-•li* AŠ ŠÀ! A.˹GÀR˺!? URU *Nu*!?-[*zi?*]

7 *a-˹na* ^{m}˺*T*[*e-ḫ*]*i!-ip-til-la ad-din-ma •a-*[*n*]*a*

8 *ma-ru-•ti ˹e˺-pu-us-sú ù*

9 ^{m}*Te-ḫi-•ip-*[*til-l*]*a a-na ya-ši* 40 ˹ANŠE˺ •ŠE

10 *ki-ma* NÍG.B[A-*y*]*a id-dì-na-am*

11 *šum-ma* A.ŠÀ.M[EŠ] ˹*di*˺-[*n*]*a i-ra-aš-šu-ú*

12 *ú-za-ak-k*[*a*$_4$*-m*]*a a-na* ^{m}˹*Te*˺*-ḫi-˹ip˺-til-la*

13 *a-na-an-˹dì˺-*[*in*] ˹*iš*˺*-t*[*u*] ˹*u*$_4$*-mi*˺

14 *an-ni-ti aš-šu*[*m* A.ŠÀ] •*an-nu-•ti*

15 AŠ EGIR ^{m}*Te-*[*ḫi-i*]*p-til-la*

16 *la i-ša-˹as˺-sí*

LOWER EDGE

17 ŠU ^{m}TI.LA-[KU]R DUMU

: *A-pil*-XXX DUB.⌜SAR⌝

REVERSE

S.I. Po 492

18 ^{NA_4} KIŠI[B ^{m}*Tar-m*]*i*-⌜*te-šup*⌝ DUMU

:*E*[*ḫ-l*]*i-te-šup*

S.I. Po 924

19 NA$_4$ ^{m}*Tar-mi-ya* DUMU *Ú-na*

:*-ap-ta-e*

S.I. Po 663

20 NA$_4$ ^{m}*Te-ḫi-ip-til-la*

21 •DUMU [*Pu*]-*ḫ*[*i*]-*še*-⌜*en-ni*⌝

TRANSLATION

(1-4) Declaration [of] Ziliya son of Tenteya before lands officer[s] and before judges; [he spoke] as follows:

(5-13) "I have given to Teḫip-tilla an irrigated field, 18 homers [by?] the palace(?) [standard?], in the heart of the *ugāru*(?) of the town of Nuzi(?) and have adopted him. And Teḫip-tilla has given to me as my gift 40 homers of barley. Should the field have a case (against it), I shall clear (the field) and give it to Teḫip-tilla."

(13-16) From this day forward, he shall not hail Teḫip-tilla (into court) over the [field].

(17) The hand of Balṭu-kašid son of Apil-sin, the scribe.

(18-21) (*seal impression*) seal impression of Tarmi-tešup son of Eḫli-tešup; (*seal impression*) seal impression of Tarmiya son of Unap-tae; (*seal impression*) seal impression of Teḫip-tilla son of Puḫi-šenni.

COMMENTS

This tablet is somewhat difficult to read owing to a glaze from a virtual bath in a glue- or varnish-like substance. The tablet has also suffered slight deterioration since the copy was made.

NOTES

l. 1: [*ša*]. Lacheman records this sign as partially preserved.

l. 2: *en*!. Though no longer complete, the sign appears correct as copied.

l. 2: [MEŠ]. This restoration is supported by the same scribe's practice in *JEN* 170:3; 173:2; 187:2. There is a seeming difficulty in this: only Teḫip-tilla son of Puḫi-šenni (ll. 20-21) is a lands officer in this text. The two other sealers (ll. 18-19) are judges. For these identifications and an evaluation of a related difficulty, see Maidman (1981, 237-38, n. 17). It appears

that judges in contexts such as the present one act as virtual lands officers and, perhaps through scribal carelessness, are so identified.

l. 3: *uḫ*$_5$. The sign is clearly A', not AḪ as copied.

l. 5: [*i?-na? mi?-in?-da?-ti?* / *ta?-a?-a?-ri?*]. After *ši-i-qà*, nothing is visible. Lacheman once read: [x]-*na* [x x]. This may have some bearing on the interpretation of the difficult next line. At the least, it is consistent with the proposed reconstruction. It should be emphasized that this restoration is purely speculative, and it supports an interpretation of line 6 which itself is largely speculative.

l. 6. Interpretation of this line is vexing. The signs not broken away are faint. The first preserved sign after the break currently lacks the lower right vertical. All that remains of the second sign is the top of the vertical wedge. The first two wedges of the third sign are also missing. Indeed, URU is the only clear sign on this line.

Bearing this in mind, we may tentatively interpret the first half of the line (together with the missing end of the previous line!) as a typical Nuzi formula indicating the standard of measurement employed. However, syllabic spellings of *ekallu* at Nuzi are rare and, it appears, confined to *ekallu* with a meaning other than "palace," "royal" (see *CAD*, E, 60b).

The latter part of the line should indicate the location of the land; AŠ and URU confirm this. The signs between, however, are unclear and the first of these, at least, is not accurately copied. It actually appears as  .

Lacheman interprets these signs as ŠÀ A.ŠÀ. Although ŠÀ-*bi* is the expected form for *libbi*, we may accept ŠÀ, if not with enthusiasm. A.ŠÀ, however, is to be rejected. Though the traces do not contradict this interpretation, the resultant meaning ("amid the land of the town of ...") is jejune. Rather, we might opt, though the traces now become a problem, for A.⌜GÀR⌝. The term *ugāru* is frequently used in the location of plots of land (see below for an example). It was a specific area most usually associated with one of several particular towns in the Nuzi texts. See Maidman (1976, 147) and below, note to *JEN* 685:5. (Cf. Zaccagnini [1979c, 28-29] for another view, though one not affecting the present argument. See also Wilhelm [1983, 312-13].) One of the towns with an *ugāru* was Nuzi itself (see, for example, *JEN* 126:9) and the sign after URU has been interpreted by Lacheman and the *CAD* Nuzi file as *Nu*-[*zi*]. This too represents a difficulty since the trace, though faint, is essentially as copied. It does not look like NU.

Nevertheless, a Nuzi location for this land *is* supported by independent, circumstantial evidence. The same adopter and adoptee reappear in *JEN* 69. There, Ziliya cedes real estate by the Sara(e) Canal, itself elsewhere defined as located in Nuzi (*HSS*, V, 56:6-7 and perhaps *JEN* 9:5-6 [where, be it noted, the *ugāru* is again mentioned]). If, as seems likely (and by analogy to other, less ambiguous cases [e.g. the case of

Tauḫḫe son of Teḫiya in *C* 3 and *L-O* 15), Ziliya transfers land in the same area twice to Teḫip-tilla, then the 18 homers of irrigated land (irrigated by the Sara(e) Canal?) here at stake are to be located in Nuzi.

(The Teḫip-tilla of this text is the same individual who is adopted in *JEN* 69. See, below, note to l. 7.)

l. 7: ⸢^{m}⸣*T[e-ḫ]i!-ip-til-la*. That the adoptee is Teḫip-tilla *son of Puḫi-šenni* is rendered all but certain by (a) the findspot of this tablet, room 16, a Teḫip-tilla Family context; (b) the fact that this son of Puḫi-šenni is explicitly the recipient of Ziliya's land in *JEN* 69 (l. 3), also from room 16; and (c) the fact that this son of Puḫi-šenni may have disposed of land of Ziliya son of Tenteya in a real estate exchange agreement (*JEN* 791, *q.v.*) involving another party.

Note that Teḫip-tilla's patronymic in l. 21 of the present text does not constitute proof. He seals this text in his capacity as *ḫalṣuḫlu* (cf. l. 3), not as principal party (see Maidman [1981, 237-38, n. 17]).

l. 11: ⸢*di*⸣*-[n]a*. This reading, as opposed, say, to *[pí]-i[r-q]a*, is supported by the same scribe's choice of terminology elsewhere. See, for example, *JEN* 148:9; 173:13.

JEN 683

OBVERSE

1 *ṭup-pí ma-ru-ti š[a]*
2 ^{m}*In-ni-ki* DUMU *Ḫa-ši-ya*
3 ^{m}*Te-ḫi-ip-til-la* DUMU •*Pu-ḫi-še-en-ni*
4 *a-na ma-ru-ti* DÙ-*sú-ma*
5 4 ANŠE A.Š[À] *ši-qa i-na e-le-en*
6 AN.ZA.KÀR *ša* ⸢^{m}⸣*Na-ni-ya* •*i-na*
7 *[l]e-et mi-iṣ-ri ša Ta-an-na-taš-ši*
8 ⸢*ki*⸣*-ma* ḪA.LA-*šu a-na* ^{m}*Te-ḫi-ip-til-la*
9 *it-ta-dì-[i]n ù* ^{m}*Te-ḫi-ip-til-la*
10 $^{+}$15 ANŠE ⸢ŠE⸣.M[EŠ] ⸢*ù*⸣ 30 [+20?] MA.NA ⸢URUDU⸣.MEŠ
11 *ki-ma* NÍG.BA-*š[u]* ⸢*a*⸣*-na* ^{m}⸢*In*⸣*-[ni]-*$^{+}$⸢*ki*⸣
12 ⸢*it*⸣*-ta-ad-n[a-a]š-šu šu[m-ma]*
13 A.ŠÀ *pa-qí-ra-[n]a i-r[a]-aš-[š]i*
14 ^{m}*In-ni-ki ú-za-ak-*⸢*ka*$_{4}$⸣*-ma*
15 *a-*•*n[a* ^{m}*]Te-ḫi-ip-Ti[l-l]a i+na-an-din*
16 *šu[m-ma* ^{m}*]In-ni-[ki]* KI.BAL-*at*
17 ⸢2⸣[(?)] •⸢MA⸣.•NA [KÙ.BABBAR 2] •MA.NA KÙ.SIG$_{17}$
18 *⸢*a-*na⸣ [^{m}*Te-ḫi-ip-til-la*]
19 ⸢*ú-ma-al-la*⸣

+ ____

20 *IGI *Mu-ša-pu* DUMU *Ḫa-ši-ip-[a-pu]*

21 IGI *E-mu-ya* DUMU *Ip-ša-*•*ḫ[a-lu]*

LOWER EDGE

22 •IGI *Še-el-la-pa-*•*i* [DUMU *Ar-ta-e*]

+23 [IGI] *ta?/uš?*[ ]⸢x⸣[ ]

+24 [IGI] DUMU AN?[ ]

REVERSE

25 •IGI **Šu*!-•*pa-a-a* DUMU *Ar-ta-*•*tal*

26 •IGI ⸢*Ka*⸣*-ta-a-a* DUMU *Ar-na-*•*pu*

27 *IGI •*Še-*$^{+}$⸢*eḫ*⸣*-li-ya* DUMU *Zu-zu*

28 IGI *Ké-eš-ḫa-a-a* DUMU ⸢*Ki-in*⸣*-ni-ya*

29 IGI ÌR-[DINGIR-*šu* DUMU BÀD-LUGAL-*r*]*u*?

30 IGI *Ta-ú-ka*$_4$ D[UMU] ⸢*A-ri*⸣*-ip-ú-ra-***aš-*[*še*]

31 ⸢IGI⸣ •*Kip-ta-*⸢*e*⸣ [D]UMU *En-na-m*[*a-ti*]

32 [IG]I *Ta-an-te-*[*y*]*a* DUMU *A-ka*$_4$*-a-*⸢*a*⸣

33 IGI *Mu-uš-*[*t*]*e-šup* DUMU *Ar-na-*[*p*]*u*

34 IGI *Ta-*⸢*a-a*⸣ DUMU IBILA-XXX DUB.S[AR]

S.I. Po 996

35 $^{[N]A_4}$ KIŠIB ^{m} ⸢ÌR⸣-DINGIR-*šu* DUMU BÀD-LUGAL

S.I. Po 314

36 •$^{⸢NA_4⸣}$ KIŠIB ^{m}*Mu-uš-te-šup*! DUMU *Ar-*•*na-*•*pu*

UPPER EDGE

S.I. Po 301

37 •^{NA_4} KIŠIB ^{m}*E-*•*mu-ya*

38 DUMU ⸢*Ip*⸣*-ša-ḫa-lu*

LEFT EDGE

S.I.

39 •^{NA_4} •KIŠIB ^{m}*Ta-a-a* DUB.•SAR

TRANSLATION

(1-4) Tablet of adoption of Inniki son of Ḫašiya. He adopted Teḫip-tilla son of Puḫi-šenni.

(5-9) He gave to Teḫip-tilla as his inheritance share a 4 homer irrigated field to the east of the *dimtu* of Naniya, adjacent to the border of (the *dimtu* of?) Tanna-tašši.

(9-12) And Teḫip-tilla gave to Inniki as his gift 15 homers of barley and 30 [+20?] minas of copper.

(12-15) Should the field have claimants, Inniki shall clear (the field) and give (it) to Teḫip-tilla.

(16-19) Should Inniki abrogate (this contract), he shall pay to Teḫip-tilla 2 minas [...? of silver and 2] minas of gold.

(20-34) Before Muš-apu son of Ḫašip-apu; before Emuya son of Ipša-ḫalu; before Šellapai [son of Ar-tae]; [before] ... ta(?)/uš(?) ...; [before] ... son of AN-...; before Šupaya son of Arta-atal; before Kataya son of Arn-apu; before Šeḫliya son of Zuzu; before Kešḫaya son of Kinniya; before Ward-ilišu [son of] Dûr-šarru; before Tauka son of Arip-urašše; before Kip-tae son of Enna-mati; before Tanteya son of Akaya; before Muš-tešup son of Arn-apu; before Taya son of Apil-sin, the scribe.

(35-39) (*seal impression*) seal impression of Ward-ilišu son of Dûr-šarru; (*seal impression*) seal impression of Muš-tešup son of Arn-apu; (*seal impression*) seal impression of Emuya son of Ipša-ḫalu; (*seal impression*) seal impression of Taya, the scribe.

COMMENTS

A few signs show marks of deterioration since the copy was made.

For further comments on this text, see comments and notes to *JEN* 681 whose transaction is related to the one described in this text.

NOTES

l. 10: 15. Though slightly effaced, the figure is more clearly preserved than the copy indicates.

l. 10: 30 [+20?]. The lower half of the line is broken away at this point as is the space immediately to the right of the three wedges. Two additional wedges may have stood originally where the lacuna now appears.

ll. 19-20. Between these lines there is a tablet-wide horizontal line made by the scribe.

l. 20: *Ḫa-ši-ip-*[*a-pu*]. The last preserved sign is a clear *ip*, not *ya* as copied. The patronymic is restored on the basis of *JEN* 20:25, the only attested Muš-apu son of a Ḫašip-... . The context of that name in *JEN* 20 does not pose difficulties for its appearance here.

l. 21: *mu*. This sign is clear. The PU of the copy is incorrect.

l. 22: [DUMU *Ar-ta-e*]. Lacheman and *NPN*, 33a, 129b see these signs as preserved. No traces of these signs survive.

ll. 23-24. These last lines of the lower edge are badly scarred. Only scattered traces of signs are discernible, as implied by the transliteration. The ⌜x⌝ of l. 23 is:

The *CAD* Nuzi file transliteration, apparently made when this tablet was in slightly better condition, reflects for l. 24: [IGI x x]-*a* DUMU $^{d?}$[AK-DINGIR].RA. No l. 23 is acknowledged.

As with l. 22, Lacheman maintains readings for these lines not reflected in his own copy and certainly not now visible. These are:

23 [IGI *T*]*a-e* DUMU *Na-e-ké-a*

24 [IGI] *E-te-ya* DUMU *Na-ip-*[*šur-ra*]

Cf. *NPN*, 141b *sub* 16), 49a *sub* ETEJA 2) respectively for these individuals. Lacheman's readings are certainly capable of being reconciled with the traces visible at the time of the most recent collation.

l. 27: *Zu-zu*. The last sign of the copy, *ya*, is not there. The tablet is well preserved at this point.

l. 29. This line is restored on the basis of l. 35.

l. 29: [*r*]*u*?. The traces point more easily to [*r*]*i*. However, the latter form of this name is nowhere else attested at Nuzi.

l. 36. In his notes, Lacheman identifies the seal impression above this line as Po 917.

l. 36: *šup*!. Correct as copied.

ll. 37-38. These lines and the sealing above it are all on the upper edge.

l. 39. In his notes, Lacheman identifies the seal impression above this line as Po 304.

JEN 684

OBVERSE

1 ⸢*ṭup*⸣-*pí ma-ru-ti ša*

2 ^{m}*Ta-i-še-en-ni* DUMU *A-*⸢*x*⸣-[ ]-°*šu*

3 ^{m}*Te-ḫi-ip-til-la* DUMU *Pu-*[*ḫi-še-en-ni*]

4 *a-na ma-r*[*u-t*]*i* DÙ-*m*[*a*]

5 1 ANŠE 3 ⸢^{GIŠ}APIN A⸣.[ŠÀ] DIŠ?

6 *i+na a-*⸢*aḫ*⸣ *a-tap-*[*pí*] ⸢*x-el*⸣-*ḫu-e*

7 *i+na* URU *Ši-ni-na* [*k*]*i-ma*

8 ḪA.LA-*šu a-na* ^{m}*Te-ḫ*[*i*]-*ip-til-la*

9 *it-ta-din ù* ^{m}⸢*Te*⸣-*ḫi-ip-*[*ti*]*l-la*

10 14 ANŠE ŠE.MEŠ *ki-ma* NÍG.$^{+}$B[A-*šu*]

11 *a-na* ^{m}*Ta-i-še-en-ni i*[*t-ta-din*]

12 *šum-ma* A.ŠÀ *di-na i-ra-aš-*[*ši*]

13 ^{m}*Ta-i-še*!-[*e*]*n-ni ú-za-a*[*k-*ka_4*-ma*]

14 *a-na* ^{m}*Te-ḫi-ip-til-la i+na-*[*an-din*]

15 *šum-ma* ^{m}*Ta-i-še-en-ni* KI.[BAL-*at*]

16 2 MA.NA KÙ.[S]IG_{17}

17 ⸢*a-na*⸣ ^{m}⸢*Te*⸣-*ḫi-ip-til-la ú-*[*ma-al-la*]

18 IGI *Mu-uš-*⸢*te-šup* DUMU *Ar*⸣-[*na-pu*]

19 IGI *Pí-ru* [DUMU *Na-iš-ké-el-pè*]

20 IGI *Te-*[*ḫi-ya* DUMU *A-ka$_4$-a-a*]

.

.

.

REVERSE

21 [IG]I *A-wi-•iš-*[*uš-še* DUMU]

22 *Pa-l*[*i*]-⸢*ya*⸣

23 IGI *A-kip*-LUGAL DUMU *Ar-•zi-*[*iz-za*]

24 IGI *Šur-ki-til-la* DUMU NÍG.BA-[*ya*]

25 IGI *Pu-ḫi-še-ni* <DUMU> KI.MIN

26 IGI *Nu-la-za-ḫi* DUMU *E-ri-*[*iš-x-x*]

27 IGI *Ik-ki-ú* DUMU *Ḫa-pí-r*[*a*]

28 IGI *Ḫa-aš-ši-mi-•ka$_4$* •DUMU *Ša!-t*[*ù-ké-x*]

29 5 ⸢LÚ⸣.MEŠ *ši-bu-*[*t*]*i ša* URU ⸢*A*⸣?-[*pè?-na?-aš?*]

30 IGI *Ta-a-a* DUMU *A-pil*-XXX [DUB.SAR-*rù*]

31 *ù* A.ŠÀ *an-nu-ti-ma* L[Ú.MEŠ *ši-bu-ti*]

32 *ša pí-i ṭup-*⸢*pí*⸣ *mu-*[*še-el-mu*]*-ú*

S.I. Po 605

.

.

.

S.I. Po 723

UPPER EDGE

33 ^{NA_4} KIŠIB ^{m}*Šur-ki-til-•la*

34 +DUMU NÍG.BA-*ya*

LEFT EDGE

S.I. Po 10 S.I. Po 637

35 NA$_4$ ^{m}*Ta-a-a* DUB.SAR ^{NA_4} KIŠIB ^{m}*Pí-*[*ru*]

TRANSLATION

(1-4) Tablet of adoption of Tai-šenni son of A-x-...-šu. He adopted Teḫip-tilla son of Puḫi-šenni.

(5-9) He gave to Teḫip-tilla as his inheritance share a 1.3 homer ... field on the bank of the X-elḫue Canal, in the town of Šinina.

(9-11) And Teḫip-tilla gave to Tai-šenni as [his] gift 14 homers of barley.

(12-14) Should the field have a case (against it), Tai-šenni shall clear (the field) [and] give (it) to Teḫip-tilla.

(15-17) Should Tai-šenni abrogate (this contract), he shall pay to Teḫip-tilla 2 minas of gold.

(18-32) Before Muš-Tešup son of Arn-apu; before Piru son of Naiš-kelpe; before Teḫiya [son of Akaya]; before Awiš-ušše [son of] Paliya; before Akip-šarri son of Ar-zizza; before Šurki-tilla son of Qîšteya; before Puḫi-

šenni <son of> the same; before Nula-zaḫi son of Êriš-...; before Ikkiu son of Ḫapira; before Ḫaš-šimika son of Šatuke-...—(these) 5 men are the witnesses of the town of Apena(?)—before Taya son of Apil-sin, [the scribe]. And, (regarding) this field, (all) these are furthermore, the [witnesses] (who), as per the tablet, are measurers.

(33-39) (*seal impression*) ...; (*seal impression*) seal impression of Šurki-tilla son of Qîšteya; (*seal impression*) seal impression of Taya, the scribe; (*seal impression*) seal impression of Piru.

COMMENT

This tablet appears virtually as copied.

NOTES

l. 2: *A*-⌜*x*⌝-[ ]-*šu*. Lacheman proposes the reading, *A-k*[*ap-tùk-k*]*e*, based on *JEN* 718:3 where Tai-šenni son of Akap-tukke adopts Teḫip-tilla son of Puḫi-šenni. However, there seems to be no other contextual link between *JEN* 718 and 684. Thus the assertion of identity for these two adopters is questionable.

l. 6: ⌜*x-el*⌝-*ḫu-e*. These signs appear as copied. Lacheman proposes, in effect, ⌜*né-el*⌝-*ḫu-e*. If one reads *a-t*[*a-ap-p*]*í*, then *el-ḫu-e* results. I cannot make sense of ⌜*x-el*⌝-*ḫu-e* or ⌜*né-el*⌝-*ḫu-e* or *el-ḫu-e*.

l. 10: 14. The number is clearly preserved and correct as copied. The *CAD* Nuzi file reads 15.

l. 11: ᵐ*Ta-i-še-en-ni*. The I sign is clear and typical, not the "DUMU" of the copy.

l. 11: *i*[*t-ta-din*]. Or the like.

l. 18: ⌜*Ar*⌝-[*na-pu*]. This restoration, as well as other witness PN restorations in this text, is based on a largely standard Nuzi-Šinina witness sequence common to *JEN* 21, 74, 684, 685, and 766. See already Cassin (1938, 75) for the first two of these texts; Weeks (1972, 203) for the first four of these texts (see below, comments to *JEN* 766 on the inclusion of the fifth text in this series); and Fadhil (1983, 153-54), likewise for the first four of these texts.

For other features common to the first four of these texts and other observations on this cluster, see Weeks (1972, 303-4).

l. 21. Before the resumption of the text at this point, Lacheman reads, in effect:

LOWER EDGE
IGI *Š*[*e-el-wi-ya* DUMU *Ar-zi-ka*$_4$*-ri*]
IGI *Ḫ*[*a-ra-pa-tal* DUMU *A-kip*-LUGAL]
IGI *Tú*[*r-še-en-ni* DUMU *A-ri-pa-ap-ni*]

Although the indicated traces are no longer discernible, the restorations are almost certainly correct (except that *A-kip*-LUGAL should be *A-rip*-LUGAL), based, as they are, on the standard Nuzi-Šinina witness sequence (see above, note to l. 18). Cf. *JEN* 21:19-21; 74:23-25; 685:20-22; 766:15-16.

l. 25: <DUMU>. The surface of the tablet is undamaged between *ni* and KI. A scribal lapse is assumed based on the "correct" *JEN* 685:26. Yet, note that *JEN* 74:29 is identical to this line, i.e., lacking DUMU.

l. 26: *E-ri-*[*iš-x-x*]. This PN is restored according to *JEN* 685:27. See the comment to that line.

l. 29: 5. The number is clear. No sign is effaced.

l. 29: URU ⸢*A*⸣?-[*pè?-na?-aš?*]. The last, partially preserved, sign appears as copied. One could force a reading, *Š*[*i!-ni-na*], based on the clear parallel with *JEN* 21:29 and 74:33. Cf. also *JEN* 766:20. However, ⸢*A*⸣-[*pè-na-aš*] more easily fits the traces and seems to find a parallel in *JEN* 685:30. See further, note to *JEN* 685:30.

(Below S.I. Po 605). The *CAD* Nuzi file reads, at this point: [^{NA_4} KIŠIB ^{m}*Mu-uš-te*]-*šup* DUMU *Ar-na-pu*.

In an unpublished note stemming, apparently, from a later date, Lacheman reads: [^{NA_4} KIŠIB ^{m}*Mu-uš-te-šup*] DUMU ⸢*Ar*⸣-*na-pu*. (In this same note, Lacheman identifies the sealing as Po 314.)

Although nothing of this line remains legible (this is reflected in the copy), these "readings" are consistent with *JEN* 21:33; 74:37; and 685:34-35.

l. 33: ^{m}*Šur-ki-til-la*. ŠUR appears clearly and not as the PUR of the copy.

l. 34: DUMU. Though faint, the sign is complete.

l. 35. Collation confirms that Taya's sealing above this line is Po 10. (Lacheman once asserted it was not.)

l. 35: KIŠIB ^{m}. The number of vertical wedges is correct as copied.

JEN 685

OBVERSE

1 [^{m}]⸢*Ṭá-ab*⸣-*til-*⸢*la* DUMU⸣ *Šúk-ri-**⸢*ya*⸣

2 [^{m}*T*]*e-ḫi-ip-til-*[*l*]*a* DUMU *Pu-ḫi-še-e*[*n-ni*]

3 [*a-n*]*a ma-ru-t*[*i*] DÙ-*ma*

4 ⸢9⸣ ^{GIŠ}[APIN] +⸢A.+ŠÀ *ši*⸣?-*qa a-ša*[*r*]

5 *i+na le-*[*et* A?.ŠÀ? *ša?*] ⸢^{m}⸣?*Ka*$_4$-•*an*-•*ku*

6 AŠ URU *Ši-*[*ni*]-*na* ⸢*ki*⸣-*ma* ḪA.⸢LA⸣-[*šu*]

7 *a-na* ^{m}*Te-ḫi-*[*i*]*p-til-la i*[*t-ta-din*]

8 *ù* ^{m}*T*[*e*]-*ḫi-ip-til-la* ⸢*a-na*⸣

9 ^{m}*Ṭá-ab-til-la* 10 ANŠE ŠE.MEŠ
10 *ki-ma* NÍG.BA-*šu it-ta-d*[*in*]
11 *šum-ma* A.ŠÀ *di-na i-ra-***aš*-[*ši*]
12 ^{m}*Ṭá-ab-til-la ú-za-ak*-[*ka*$_4$-*ma*]
13 *a*-[*n*]*a* ^{m}*Te-ḫi-ip-til-la i+na-a*[*n-din*]
14 [*šum*]-*ma* ^{m}*Ṭá-ab-til-la* KI.B[AL-*at*]
15 ⸢2⸣ MA.NA KÙ.SIG$_{17}$ *a-na* ^{m}*Te-ḫi*-[*ip-Til-la*]
16 *ú*-⸢*ma*⸣-*al-la*

---

17 IGI ⸢*Mu-uš-te-šup*⸣ DUMU *Ar*-[*na-pu*]
18 IGI *Pí-r*[*u* DUMU *Na*]-⸢*iš*⸣-*ké-e*[*l-pè*]
19 IGI •*Te*-[*ḫ*]*i*-⸢*ya* DUMU *A*⸣-*ka*$_4$-*a-a*
20 IGI [*Še*]-*el-wi-ya* DU[MU] *Ar-z*[*i-ka*$_4$-*ri*]

LOWER EDGE

21 IGI *Ḫ*[*a-ra*]-*pa-tal* DUMU *A*-⸢*rip*⸣-LUGAL
22 IGI +⸢*Túr*⸣-*še-ni* DUMU *A-ri*-[*pa-ap-ni*]

REVERSE

23 IGI *A-w*[*i*]-•*šu-uš*-•*še* DUMU *Pa-li*-**y*[*a*]
24 IGI *A-kip*-⸢LUGAL⸣ [D]UMU *Ar-zi-i*[*z-za*]
25 IGI *Šur-ki-ti*[*l-la* DUM]U NÍG.BA-*ya*
26 IGI *Pu-ḫi-š*[*e-ni*] DUMU ⸢KI.MIN⸣
27 IGI *Nu-la-za-ḫi* [DUMU] •⸢*E*⸣-*ri*-+⸢*iš*⸣-*x*-⸢*x*⸣
28 IGI KALAG.GA-•KA-*šu* DUMU •⸢X-*x*⸣-AN
29 IGI *Ḫu-ti-ya* DUMU *Ul-lu-ya*
30 5 *ši*-⸢*bu*⸣-*ti an-nu-ti ša* URU *A*-**pè*-**na*-[*aš*]
31 [IGI] *Ta-a-a* DUB.SAR-*rù*
32 14 $^{LÚ.MEŠ}$ *ši-bu-ti an-nu-ti*
33 *ù šu*-•*nu-ma* A.ŠÀ *ú-še-el-w*[*u-ú*]

S.I. Po 314

34 ^{NA_4} KIŠIB ^{m}*Mu-uš-te*-•*šup*
35 DUMU *Ar-na-pu*

S.I. Po 637

36 $^{[N]A_4}$ KIŠIB ^{m}*Pí*-•*ru*

S.I.

37 *NA$_4$ *^{m}**T*[*úr*-**š*]*e-ni*

RIGHT EDGE

38 *DUMU **A*-[*ri-pa-ap*]-*ni*

UPPER EDGE

S.I.

.

.

.

LEFT EDGE

	S.I.	S.I.
39	[$^{\text{NA}_4}$ KI]ŠIB ^{m}*Šur-ki-til-la*	$^{\text{NA}_4}$ KIŠIB ^{m}[*T*]*a-a-a* DUB.$^{+}$SAR
40	DUMU NÍG.BA-*ya*	

TRANSLATION

....

(1-3) Ṭâb-Tilla son of Šukriya. He adopted Teḫip-tilla son of Puḫi-šenni.

(4-7) He gave to Teḫip-tilla as [his] inheritance share a 0.9 homer irrigated(?) field at ..., adjacent to [the field? of?] Kakku, in the town of Šinina.

(8-10) And Teḫip-tilla gave to Ṭâb-tilla as his gift 10 homers of barley.

(11-13) Should the field have a case (against it), Ṭâb-tilla shall clear (the field) [and] give (it) to Teḫip-tilla.

(14-16) Should Ṭâb-tilla abrogate (this contract), he shall pay to Teḫip-tilla 2 minas of gold.

(17-33) Before Muš-tešup son of Arn-apu; before Piru [son of] Naiš-kelpe; before Teḫiya son of Akaya; before Šelwiya son of Ar-zikari; before Ḫarap-atal son of Arip-šarri; before Tur-šenni son of Arip-papni; before Awiš-ušše son of Paliya; before Akip-šarri son of Ar-zizza; before Šurki-tilla son of Qîšteya; before Puḫi-šenni son of the same; before Nula-zaḫi [son of] Êriš-...; before Dan-rigimšu son of ...-AN; before Ḫutiya son of Ulluya—these 5 witnesses are of the town of Apena—before Taya the scribe. These are the 14 witnesses and, as well, they measured the field.

(34-39) (*seal impression*) seal impression of Muš-tešup son of Arn-apu; (*seal impression*) seal impression of Piru; (*seal impression*) seal impression of Tur-šenni son of Arip-papni; (*seal impression*) ...; (*seal impression*) seal impression of Šurki-tilla son of Qîšteya; (*seal impression*) seal impression of Taya, the scribe.

COMMENTS

This tablet was in a slightly more damaged state when collated than when copied. Furthermore, the copy itself reflects a stage of deterioration more advanced than when the tablet was first examined. Lacheman's papers record readings even fuller than his (later) copy justifies. For example, in line 4, where the copy indicates ^{GIŠ}[APIN], Lacheman reads ^{GIŠ}A[PI]N. Recognizing the discrepancy, he noted at such junctures: "based on readings made before break occurred." There is no further elaboration of this comment.

Before line 1, one line is entirely effaced. This line will have read: *ṭup-pí ma-ru-ti ša*.

NOTES

l. 4: [APIN]. See above, comments to this text.

l. 4: ⌜A.ŠÀ *ši*⌝?-*qa*. This reconstruction is plausible, though the spacing seems overly generous (perhaps [MEŠ] followed ⌜A.ŠÀ⌝) and the traces of *ši* are not as unambiguous as one might wish. Nevertheless, at one point, Lacheman did espouse the interpretation offered here. An alternative reading, tentatively proposed in the *CAD* Nuzi file and by Lacheman, is ⌜A.ŠÀ *i*⌝-*na*. However, the resulting combination, *ina ašar* (GN), is, at best, rare at Nuzi and probably should be avoided.

l. 4: *a-ša*[*r*]. In an unpublished note (not from his paper alluded to above, in the comments to this text), Lacheman reads: *a-*⌜*šar* AN.ZA.KÀR *Tup-ki-te*⌝-[*šup*]. This *dimtu* seems nowhere else attested at Nuzi.

l. 5: *le*-[*et* A?.ŠÀ? *ša*?] ⌜m⌝?*Ka*$_4$-*an-ku*. "Based on readings made before break occurred," Lacheman once read: *le*-[*et* A.GÀR *š*]*a* m*Ka*$_4$-*an-ku*. This reading, without brackets, reappears in the *CAD* Nuzi file, modified by: m*Ka*$_4$-*an-ku*-[ ]. (In this connection, note that a PN, Kankuzi, is attested; see *AAN*, 76b *sub* KANKUZI. However, this name is extremely rare.)

This interpretation is difficult. *ugāru* in the Nuzi texts is most usually identified by town names, less frequently by *dimtu* names. (See already above, note to *JEN* 682:6.) Nowhere (but here) is an *ugāru* identified by the name of an individual. If the last part of the line is indeed a PN, then [A.ŠÀ *ša*] should probably be restored.

l. 16: *ú-*⌜*ma*⌝*-al-la*. The bottom horizontal of the second sign is broken, not as copied.

l. 20: *Ar-z*[*i-ka*$_4$*-ri*]. This restoration, as well as other witness PN restorations in this text, is based on the Nuzi-Šinina witness sequence. For further details, see note to *JEN* 684:18.

l. 21: *A-*⌜*rip*⌝-LUGAL. The traces can support *A-*⌜*kip*⌝-LUGAL as well. Confusion in similar circumstances is noted in *NPN*, 55b, *sub* ḪARAP-ATAL.

l. 23. This line, not line 24, begins the reverse.

l. 23: *A-w*[*i*]*-šu-uš-še*. Of the sign, ŠU, only the head of a vertical stroke remains. A spelling, *A-wi-iš-uš-še*, is thus also possible.

l. 27: ⌜*E*⌝*-ri-*⌜*iš*⌝*-x-*⌜*x*⌝. The decipherment of this name is difficult. *A-ri-li-ya*, *E-ri-li-ya*, *E-ri-iš-x*, *E-ri-iš-x-x*, and *E-ri-x-ya* have all been proposed. The first sign is mostly effaced but, amongst the traces, an initial horizontal points definitely to E rather than to A. The third sign does not appear as copied but is a clear, if slightly damaged, IŠ. The last wedges do not represent YA, as copied. Rather, they represent two signs, one complete and one partial. The rendering of these signs in *NPN*, 48a (*sub* ÊRIŠ…), 108a (*sub* NULA-ZAḪI 2)) is close to the mark except for the bottom horizontal of the first sign. *NPN* exaggerates it so that the sign appears (incorrectly) to resemble KÙ.

l. 28: KALAG.GA-KA-*šu* DUMU ⸢X-*x*⸣-AN. The rendering of the first name, i.e., Dan-rigimšu, follows Fadhil (1983, 153b). Cf. *NPN*, 78b, *sub* KAL.GA-*ka-šu* (*JEN* 21:27 should be added to *NPN*'s reference to the present text). However, the GA could as easily be a BI. Although the end of the next sign is effaced, the interpretation, KA, seems secure.

The first two signs of the patronymic might easily be ⸢MA⸣-[N]A, although the vertical of the MA is now gone. However, no known Nuzi PN results. Nothing appears after AN. Yet, *NPN*, *ibid.*, suggests lost wedges at this point. The *CAD* Nuzi file indeed has *-an-nu* as the end of the PN.

l. 30: URU *A-pè-na-*[*aš*]. URU is clear and typical in shape, not as copied. After this sign, only A remains. But this sign appears quite clearly as copied. A problem arises since the sign sequence, *Ši-ni-na*, is expected after URU, as pointed out above, in the note to *JEN* 684:29: URU. Indeed, at one point, Lacheman suggested the ingenious reading: URU *Šini*(=MIN)*-n*[*a*]*-ma*, an idea he subsequently rejected. (Again, it should be noted that A is clear.) On the evidence of both his copy and papers, Lacheman settled on URU *A-pè-na-*[*aš*] as the interpretation of this sequence of wedges.

To complicate matters, after the A, there do appear indentations in the clay, shaped as follows: .

If this shape represents the BE of Lacheman's copy, then the copy is idealized and the scribe wrote a uniquely poor BE. It may be, however, that the sign is effaced and that the shape is part of the pitting of the tablet surface.

That these signs are no longer visible is particularly to be regretted. Since the real estate involved is located in Šinina (l. 6) and since the witness sequence is the standard Nuzi-Šinina series (see note to l. 20), to have these witnesses identified here (and their counterparts, perhaps, in *JEN* 684:29) as hailing from Apena rather than Šinina would be intriguing.

Before elaborating, it should be stressed that the following comments *depend* on the reading, URU *A-pè-na-*[*aš*], in this line and are consequently speculative. Those comments do not constitute evidence for reading that GN.

If, then, the reading here and in *JEN* 684:29, "URU *Apenaš*," prove correct, then this might suggest geographical proximity of the towns of Apena and Šinina (see already, Weeks [1972, 203] for this possibility). Apena and Šinina represent, respectively, the fifth and sixth most important foci of real estate acquisition for Teḫip-tilla son of Puḫi-šenni (Maidman 1976, 205). Only in Apena and Šinina among the seven chief towns of Teḫip-tilla's real estate activities is acquisition achieved by real estate adoption to the total exclusion of real estate exchange (i.e., the device of *šupe''ultu*). Teḫip-tilla's holdings in both towns were mainly inherited by Teḫip-tilla's second son, Šurki-tilla (Maidman 1976, 509),

though some Apena real estate was inherited by Teḫip-tilla's eldest son, Enna-mati.

In more general terms, if Apena and Šinina were indeed neighboring towns, then the clear Teḫip-tilla real estate strategy of concentrated acquisition of nearby (if not contiguous) plots of land in a few, carefully delineated areas, acquires a new characteristic. That is, not only were land acquisitions limited to the area of a few towns but, in at least one instance (i.e., Apena and Šinina), those towns were themselves geographically linked. (For a possible parallel linkage of the towns of Artiḫi and Ḫušri, see Maidman (1976, 194, 407f., n. 706.) This led to intense activity, a common mode of acquisition which was unusual (i.e., real estate adoption with no exchange activity), and even a single patrimonial holding for one of Teḫip-tilla's sons.

If only the evidence were clearer.

l. 33: *w[u]*. If correctly interpreted, the sign is unusual; the scribe of this text habitually uses MU in this environment.

l. 37. The seal impression of Tur-šenni, above this line, is identified by Lacheman as not appearing in Porada (1947).

ll. 37-38: *T[úr-š]e-ni* // DUMU *A-[ri-pa-ap]-ni*. The restoration of these names, despite the paltry surviving traces, is assured by the common ending, *-ni*, in the names of son and father. Only Tur-šenni (l. 22) fulfills these conditions.

(Upper Edge). Below the seal impression which straddles the bottom of the reverse and the top of the upper edge, Lacheman read, at one point: [$^{\text{NA}_4}$ KIŠIB ^{m}]X-[ ]. Lacheman did not note the shape of the trace.

l. 39. Lacheman identifies the first of the sealings above this line as Po 723 and the second one as not appearing in Porada (1947).

JEN 686

OBVERSE

1 *⸢ṭup⸣-pí ma-ru-t[i] ⸢ša⸣ ^{m}Šu-mu-li*
2 DUMU *A-ri-pè-en-ni ^{m}Te-ḫi-ip-til-la*
3 DUMU *Pu-ḫi-še-en-ni a-⸢na⸣ ma-⸢ru⸣-ti i-pu-us-sú*
4 1 ANŠE A.ŠÀ AŠ ^{GIŠ}*ta-a-a-r[i]* GAL *ša* É.GAL
5 •AŠ *le-et I-a-ar-ru* ⁺*a*-⁺*na e-le-nu* AŠ ^{GIŠ}*ta-a-a-ri* GAL
: *ša* É.GAL *a-na*
6 ^{m}*Te-ḫi-ip-til-la ki-ma* ⁺⸢ḪA⸣.LA *i-d[i]-in*
7 *ù ^{m}Te-ḫi-ip-til-la* 10 •A[N]ŠE ŠE
8 •*a-na ^{m}Šu-mu-li* <*ki-ma*> NÍG.BA *i+di!-in*
9 *⸢il⸣-ka$_4$ ša* A.ŠÀ *šu-ma na-a-ši*

10 [*šu*]*m-ma* A.ŠÀ *pa-qí-ra-na*
11 ⸢*ì*⸣*-ra-aš-ši* ^{m}*Šu-mu-li*
12 *ú-za-ak-kà a-na* ^{m}*Te-ḫi-ip-til-la*
13 *i-na-di-in*
14 [*šum*]*-ma!* ^{m}*Šu-•mu-•li i-*⸢*bala-kat*⸣
15 [10 M]A.NA ⸢KÙ.SIG$_{17}$ *ú*⸣*-ma-al-la*

---

16 [IGI] ⸢*A-kip*⸣*-til-la* •DUMU *Tù-ra-ri*
17 [IGI *Wu*]*-•ur-tù-ru-uk* DUMU *Ma-li-ya*
18 [IGI *Ša-t*]*ù-ša* DUMU *Tù-•ra-•ri*
19 [IGI *Ut-ḫi-i*]*p-til-la* DUMU •⸢*Tup-•ki*⸣*-ya*

LOWER EDGE

20 [4 LÚ.ME]Š *mu-še-el-•wu* ⸢*ša*⸣ A.ŠÀ
21 [*ù na*]*-di-•na-nu š*[*a* ŠE.MEŠ]
22 [IGI]*⸢x⸣[DUMU]

REVERSE

23 *IGI [*Ar-te-šup* DUMU *It*]*-ḫi-iš-ta*
24 IGI [*Pu-ḫi-še-en-ni* DUMU] ⸢*A*⸣*-ta-a-te*
25 IGI [*Tar-mi*]*-*⸢*te-šup* DUMU⸣ *Ar-te-ya*
26 IGI *Te-šu-up-er-wi* DUMU *Šúk-ri-ya*
27 IGI *Ḫa-ni-a-aš-ḫa-ri* DUMU *A-ri-ya*
28 IGI *A-ri-ḫa-*⸢*ar*⸣*-me* DUMU *E-en-<na>-mil-ki*
29 IGI *Ki-ip-*⸢*ta*⸣*-li-li* ŠEŠ-*šú*
30 IGI *Tar-mi-ya* DUMU *Ma-ša-an-te*
31 IGI *It-ḫa-*[*p*]*í-ḫe* DUB.SAR DUMU *Ta-a-a*

\+

---

32 IGI *Ša-aš-ta-e* DUMU *E-*⸢*eḫ-li-ya*⸣

\+

---

33 •IGI *Ur-⁺ḫ*[*i-y*]*a* DUMU *A-ru-pa*$_{12}$

S.I. Po 636

34 ⸢^{NA_4}⸣ KIŠIB ^{m}*Ur-ḫi-ya* DUMU •*Ar-ru-<pa*$_{12}$*?>*

S.I. Po 720

35 ^{NA_4} ⸢KIŠIB⸣ ^{m}*Tar-mi-te-*⸢*šup*⸣
36 DUMU ⸢*Ar-te-⁺ya*⸣

RIGHT EDGE

S.I. Po 265

37 ^{NA_4} KIŠIB ^{m}*Te-šu-u*[*p*]*-er-wi* AŠ?

LEFT EDGE

S.I. Po 691

38 [^{NA_4} KIŠIB?] DUB.SAR

TRANSLATION

(1-3) Tablet of adoption of Šumuli son of Arip-enni. He adopted Teḫip-tilla son of Puḫi-šenni.

(4-6) He gave to Teḫip-tilla as an inheritance share a field, 1 homer by the large standard of the palace, adjacent to Yarru, to the east, by the large standard of the palace.

(7-8) And Teḫip-tilla gave to Šumuli <as> a gift 10 homers of barley.

(9) And he shall bear the *ilku* of the field.

(10-13) Should the field have claimants, Šumuli shall clear (the field); he shall give (it) to Teḫip-tilla.

(14-15) Should Šumuli abrogate (this contract), he shall pay 10 minas of gold.

(16-33) [Before] Akip-tilla son of Turari; [before] Wur-turuk son of Maliya; [before] Šatuša son of Turari; [before] Itḫip-tilla son of Tupkiya [(These) 4] men are the measurers of the field [and] the distributors of [the barley. Before] ... [son of] ...; before [Ar-Tešup son of] Itḫišta; before [Puḫi-šenni son of] Adatteya; before Tarmi-tešup son of Ar-teya; before Tešup-erwi son of Šukriya; before Ḫaniašḫari son of Ariya; before Ariḫ-ḫarpa son of Enna-milki; before Kip-talili, his brother; before Tarmiya son of Mašante; before Itḫ-apiḫe, the scribe, son of Taya;

---

before Šaš-tae son of Eḫliya;

---

before Urḫiya son of Arrumpa.

(34-38) (*seal impression*) seal impression of Urḫiya son of Arrumpa; (*seal impression*) seal impression of Tarmi-tešup son of Ar-teya; (*seal impression*) seal impression of Tešup-erwi x(?); (*seal impression*) [seal impression of] the scribe.

COMMENT

This tablet has deteriorated slightly since the copy was made.

NOTES

l. 5: *I-a-ar-ru*. I A is to be preferred to YA. The space between the two signs is clear and pronounced, not as copied.

That this land is defined as "adjacent to Yarru" is sufficient to locate the real estate in the vicinity of the town of Artiḫi. Whatever Yarru is, it has toponymic force and its attestations are closely linked to Artiḫi. It is very likely not a common noun with merely general topographic significance.

Both Akkadian dictionaries consider the term, *yarru*, to be a substantive meaning "pond" or "pool." The word is to be identified with *yarḫu* with the same meaning. See *AHw*, 412a; and *CAD*, I/J, 326a. Note, however, *CAD*, E, 85b *sub* "*elēnu* 1. d)" where the term is translated "stream." See also Lacheman (1939a, 531); and Chiera-Lacheman *apud* Hayden (1962, 209, n. 220) who translate the term as "river." *AHw*, 412a, judges *yarru* to be of unknown linguistic provenience while H. Lewy (1968, 157, n. 57) considers it Hurrian for "water."

The identification of *yarru* with *yarḫu* is itself undemonstrated. Furthermore, since *yarru* is apparently only attested once each in Old and Neo-Babylonian contexts and four times in Nuzi, it may even be questioned whether the Nuzi lexeme is to be linked to the Old and Neo-Babylonian examples.

The Nuzi citations are *JEN* 400:9; 483:4; 686:5 (our passage); and 720:5. According to these texts, land is located respectively "on the 'bank' [i.e., *šapat*] of the route of/to *ya-ru*," "on the bank of *ya-ar-ru*," "adjacent to *i-a-ar-ru*," and "adjacent to *ya-ar-ru*." The designation "adjacent to" (i.e., *ina lēt*) regularly appears with names of routes (qualified normally by KASKAL). The phrase, "on the bank of," though common in contexts dealing with canals (Cassin 1938, 117), also describes the sides of roads (see *JEN* 106:8; 236:12; 407:7; 488:13; 691:8; etc.) and other topographical features (e.g. tels: *JEN* 483:7; buildings: *JEN* 236:13). And *JEN* 400:9, of course, explicitly refers to the *šaptu* of a route. Cf. *AHw*, 1176b, *s.v. šaptu* B 6 and B 7.

There is, then, no evidence whatever of an association of Yarru with water. Its connection with a route, in much the same manner as town names are connected with routes, led Oppenheim (1938, 144) to consider Yarru a GN, linked by road with Artiḫi.

It is reasonable to assume, then, that Yarru is indeed a toponym of sorts, though whether or not it is a town remains to be determined. It never appears prefixed by URU.

Regarding the relationship of Yarru and Artiḫi, their association is very strong. As noted above, there are four pertinent texts: *JEN* 400, 483, 686, 720 (cf. Fadhil 1983, 41a).

JEN 400:6-9 makes this relationship explicit.

JEN 483, an exchange transaction of Teḫip-Tilla, suggests that Yarru (l. 4) is located in the vicinity of Tīl Papante (l. 7; geographical proximity of plots of land involved in Teḫip-Tilla exchange transactions is the rule). Tīl Papante itself lies close by the town of Ḫušri (*JEN* 654:7-8). In turn, this town has close links with Artiḫi. (For the Artiḫi-Ḫušri connection, see above, note to *JEN* 685:30.)

JEN 686, the present text, is linked to Artiḫi as well, if somewhat indirectly. The witnesses to this text constitute a witness sequence common to several texts: *JEN* 419, 686, 710, 716, 728. (These texts share other features in common as well [Weeks 1972, 205]. *JEN* 728 should be added to Weeks's list; in his notes to *JEN* 710, Lacheman recognized the

place of *JEN* 728 in this cluster of texts.) *JEN* 419, at least, deals explicitly with Artiḫi real estate (ll. 5-6). Some of the witnesses have clear Artiḫi links through still other texts.

JEN 720, the last "Yarru" text, also has indirect Artiḫi links. It shares a witness sequence with *JEN* 22 and 409 (see below, comments to *JEN* 720). Now *JEN* 409 deals with land of one Ar-zizza son of Milkuya (l. 5). This person, in turn, appears as a witness in a text dealing explicitly with Artiḫi real estate (*JEN* 400:28, 7). The cluster of texts of which *JEN* 720 is part has other prosopographical ties to Artiḫi as well.

l. 5: *a-na*. Although *i-na* is perhaps expected, both signs are clear and complete.

ll. 5-6: AŠ ^{GIŠ}*ta-a-a-ri* GAL / / : *ša* É.GAL *a-na*. The ends of these lines are correct as copied.

The peculiar text here may be explained as follows. At some point after having written *i-di-in* in line 6, the scribe realized he forgot the preposition *a-na* before ^{m}*Te-ḫi-ip-til-la* at the start of the same line. He mistakenly thought he had also omitted any statement regarding the standard of measurement employed. In fact, he had already given that information in line 4. Thus, the hypercorrection appears before the legitimate correction at the ends of lines 5 and 6.

This text is marked by perhaps three uncorrected scribal omissions in ll. 8, 28, 34.

l. 15: [10]. This restoration and others further on in this text (PNs and other terms alike) are based on parallel passages in *JEN* 419, 710, 716, and/or 728, contexts which, in other ways, closely parallel the present one. See above, note to l. 5: *I-a-ar-ru*.

l. 22. See below, note to *JEN* 710:24.

l. 32. Above and below this line appear horizontal lines. These are not indicated in the copy. If these scribal lines are meant to bracket or emphasize the witness PN thereby enclosed, the following bears notice. Of the five texts marked by closely related witness sequences (see above, note to l.5: *I-a-ar-ru*), only here does Šaš-tae son of Eḫliya appear. The only other known intruder into this extraordinarily stable sequence is Šukriya son of x-liya in *JEN* 710:31 and 728:28.

It is tempting to link this exceptional witness to the exceptional lines surrounding his name.

ll. 33-34. The patronymic of this witness is Arrumpa. Note the unambiguous spelling *Ar-ru-um-pa* in *JEN* 461:9, 18; 716:33; *HSS*, XIII, 6:18; XVI, 366:11. Assimilation of /m/ is reflected in the *Ar-ru-pa* of *JEN* 419:31, 32; 716:36 (cf. l.33); 728:32 (probably). Therefore, when the same patronymic appears as *A-ru-um*-PI in *JEN* 707:23 (cf. l.20) and as *A-ru*-PI in *JEN* 686:33 (our passage) and 710:35, it appears that the sign PI can bear the value pa_{12} in the Nuzi texts. Furthermore, the writing, *Ar-ru* (l. 34) appears to be

an error for *Ar-ru-<pa$_{12}$>*. For further observations on values of PI in these texts, see below, note to *JEN* 707:6.

l. 38: [^{NA_4} KIŠIB?]. Cf. below, note to *JEN* 716:40.

JEN 687

OBVERSE

1 [*ṭu*]*p-pí ma-ru-ti ša* ^{m}*Pu-i-ta-e*

2 DU[MU] *E-te-še-en-ni*

3 ^{m}*Te-ḫi-ip-til-la* DUMU *Pu-ḫi-še-*[*en-n*]*i*

4 [*a-n*]*a ma-*⸢*ru*⸣*-ti i-pu-sú*

5 [1? A]NŠE •A.$^{+}$⸢ŠÀ $^{+}$*i-*$^{+}$*na*⸣ *le-*⸢*et*⸣

6 [ ] •⸢*li*⸣? •*zi lu ur* ⸢x x⸣? URU *Ar-ti*$_4$*-*⸢*ḫi*⸣

7 [*ki-m*]*u* ⸢ḪA⸣.LA-*šú a-na* ^{m}*Te-ḫi-ip-til-la* [*i-din*]

8 *ù* ^{m}*Te-ḫi-ip-til-la* 4 ANŠE 8 S[ILA$_3$ ŠE]

9 3 DAL Ì.X *a-na* ^{m}[*P*]*u-i-***ta-e*

10 *ki-mu* NÍG.BA *i-din*

11 *šum-ma* A.ŠÀ *pa-qí-ra-***n*[*a*]

12 *i-ra-aš-ši* ^{m}•*Pu-*[*i-ta*]*-*⸢*e*⸣

13 *ú-za-ak-kà il-ka*$_4$ *ša* A.ŠÀ

14 *šu-ú-ma na-a-ši*

15 *šum-ma* ^{m}*Pu-i-ta-e*

16 *i-bala-ka*$_4$*-at* 10 MA.NA KÙ.SIG$_{17}$

17 *ú-ma-al-la*

18 IGI *A-kip-til-la* DUMU *Tù-ra-ri*

19 IGI *Pí-ri-ku* DUMU *I-ip-pa-ri*

LOWER EDGE

20 IGI *Ut-ḫi-ip-til-la* DUMU *Tup-ki-ya*

21 *an-nu-tu*$_4$ IGI.MEŠ-*ti mu-še-el-wu*

REVERSE

22 *ša* A.ŠÀ *ù na-di-na-nu* AŠ?

23 *ša* KÙ.BABBAR (erasure)

24 IGI *Mu-ḫu-ur-sú* DUMU *Mil-ku-ya*

25 IGI *A-ta-a-a* DUMU *Wa-ti*$_4$*-mu-ša*

26 IGI *Ša-ma-ḫul* DUMU *Mil-ku-ya*

27 IGI *Te-ḫi-ip-til-la* DUMU *Ḫa-ši-ya*

28 IGI *A-ri-*⸢*pa*⸣*-a-pu* DUMU *Ké-en-ni*

29 IGI *Zi-***l*[*i*]*-*•*ip*-LUGAL DUMU *E-en-na-mil-ki*

30 IGI *It-ḫa-pí-ḫe* [DU]B.SAR

\+ ______

S.I.

31 ^{NA_4} KIŠIB *A-ta-*⌜*a-a*⌝ DUMU *Wa-*ti_4*-mu-*$^{+}$⌜*ša*⌝

S.I. Po 932A

32 ^{NA_4} KIŠIB *Te-ḫi-i*[*p-ti*]*l-la*

33 DUMU $^{+}$⌜*Ḫa*⌝-[*ši*]-*ya*

LEFT EDGE

S.I. Po 349 S.I.

34 ^{NA_4} KIŠIB ^{m} *Zi-li-ip-*LUGAL

35 [^{NA_4} KIŠIB *It*]-*⌜*ḫa*⌝-°*pí-ḫe* D[UB].SAR

TRANSLATION

(1-4) Tablet of adoption of Pui-tae son of Eteš-šenni. He adopted Teḫip-tilla son of Puḫi-šenni.

(5-7) [He gave] to Teḫip-tilla as his inheritance share a [1?] homer field adjacent to ..., in(?) the town of Artiḫi.

(8-10) And Teḫip-tilla gave to Pui-tae as a gift 4.1 homers [of barley] (and) 3 *tallū* of x-oil/-fat.

(11-13) Should the field have claimants, Pui-tae shall clear (it).

(13-14) He shall furthermore bear the *ilku* of the field.

(15-17) Should Pui-tae abrogate (this contract), he shall pay 10 minas of gold.

(18-30) Before Akip-tilla son of Turari; before Piriku son of Ippari; before Itḫip-tilla son of Tupkiya. These witnesses are the measurers of the field and the distributors x(?) of the money (lit. "silver"). Before Muḫur-sin son of Milkuya; before Ataya son of Wanti-muša; before Šamaḫul son of Milkuya; before Teḫip-tilla son of Ḫašiya; before Arip-apu son of Kenni; before Zilip-šarri son of Enna-milki; before Itḫ-apiḫe, the scribe.

(31-35) (*seal impression*) seal impression of Ataya son of Wanti-muša; (*seal impression*) seal impression of Teḫip-tilla son of Ḫašiya; (*seal impression*) seal impression of Zilip-šarri; (*seal impression*) [seal impression of] Itḫ-apiḫe, the scribe.

COMMENTS

When collated, this tablet was virtually in the same condition as it was when copied.

On the close connection of this text to *JEN* 15, 37, and 705 (particularly close), see below, note to *JEN* 705:15.

NOTES

l. 5: [1? A]NŠE. The *CAD* Nuzi file and Lacheman both read, at this point: 1 ANŠE.

l. 5: *le*-⌜*et*⌝. Despite the appearance of the tablet, Lacheman indicates that there are up to three effaced signs after this word.

l. 6: [ ] ⌜*li*⌝? *zi lu ur* ⌜x x⌝?. A toponym should be represented by this part of the text. Lacheman once read: *ti-li* [*ša*] *Zi-lu-ur-ḫé i-na*. (The *CAD* Nuzi file apparently reads the last two traces as *i-na* also. Cf. *JEN* 419:6; on the relevance of that text, see this note, further below.) If this idea is at all to be retained, it must be modified to: [*ti*]-*li* [m?]*Zi-lu-ur*-⌜*x*⌝ AŠ. If correct, this recalls another possible Artiḫi toponym, [*t*]*i*?-*li-i ša zi-li*-UR-*ki+i* (*JEN* 710:6-7; cf. Fadhil 1983, 43a). However, the reading of that passage is not without problems of its own. See below, note to *JEN* 710:7: *zi-li*-UR-*ki+i*.

Be it noted that in *JEN* 419, a similar transaction involving the same two principal parties, another rare term, *alupatḫi*, occurs in a position parallel to these signs (l. 6). (See Fadhil [1983, 41b-42a] for a somewhat forced attempt to explain *alupatḫi*.)

l. 6: *Ar-ti₄*-⌜*ḫi*⌝. The DI is clear and typical, not the KI of the copy.

l. 8: 4. Lacheman reads "5" and the copy appears slightly broken at this point. However, the number is clear and typical, resembling ZA rather closely.

l. 8: 8 S[ILA₃ ŠE]. The *CAD* Nuzi file reads the last two signs as if they were completely preserved.

This quantity represents 1/10 homer, dry capacity. (One wonders why "1 BÁN" [=8 SILA₃] is not written. On this aspect of the Nuzi metrology, see Wilhelm [1980, 26-27, 120].)

l. 9: X. This sign seems to be only slightly effaced. The shape is essentially as copied with two exceptions. The upper right wedge of the "ŠE" element is all but invisible and three "stacks" of two verticals, not two stacks, are clearly visible.

The sign no doubt represents an ideogram for an oil/fat product. Ì.ŠAḪ! and Ì.NUN! seem the best of essentially unattractive alternatives. The former, in fact, is accepted by Lacheman and *CAD*, N/1, 143a (although none of the other Nuzi examples offered by the *CAD* closely resembles the sign present here). The signs do *not* permit a restoration, Ì.KUR.⌜RA⌝.

l. 20. This line, not line 19, starts the lower edge.

l. 21: *-wu*. This last sign appears 90° counterclockwise to the rest of the signs on this line.

l. 22. This line, not line 23, begins the reverse.

l. 23: KÙ.BABBAR. "Money," not "silver," is the appropriate translation here since the commodities involved clearly do not include silver. See below, note to *JEN* 715:27.

l. 30. Below this line, the scribe has drawn a tablet-long horizontal line. This is not indicated in the copy.

JEN 688

OBVERSE

1 [*a*]-*mi*-•*ḫa*-•*ri* A.ŠÀ *i+na* ZAG KASKAL
2 [*ša*]⸢*x*⸣-*li-ya i+na* URU *Nu-zi*
3 [^{m}*Wa-an-ti*]-*ya* DUMU *Tu-ur-mar-ti*
4 ⸢*a*⸣-[*na* ^{m}*Te*-*ḫ*]*i*!-**ip*-•*til-la* DUMU *Pu-ḫi*-⸢*še*⸣-*en-ni*
5 *k*[*i-ma* NÍG.B]A!-⸢*šu*⸣ *id*-⸢*dì*⸣-*in*-<*na*>-*aš-šu*
6 *š*[*um-ma* A.ŠÀ] *pa-q*[*í*]-*ra-na ir-ta-ši*
7 ⸢*ù*⸣ [^{m}*Wa*]-*an-ti-ya ú-za-ak*-⸢*ka*$_4$⸣-*ma*
8 **a*-•*na* *^{m}•*Te-ḫi-ip-til-la* ⸢*i-na*⸣-*an-d*[*in*]
9 **šum*-**ma* *^{m}**Wa*-•*an-ti-ya* KI.•BAL-*ma*
10 •A.•ŠÀ [ ] •*i*?-*ri-iš* 2 MA.NA KÙ.•SIG$_{17}$
11 •⸢*a*-•*na*⸣ •^{m}•⸢*Te*⸣-*ḫi-ip-til-la ú-ma-al-la*

---

12 IGI *Mu-u*[*š-t*]*e-šup* DUMU *Ḫa-ši*-⸢*ya*⸣
13 IGI *Pí*-[*ru*] DUMU *Na-iš-ké*-⸢*el*⸣-+*pè*
14 *IGI **Zi*-[*k*]*a*$_4$-*a-a* DUMU *El*-⸢*ḫi*⸣-*ip*-LUGAL
15 •IGI ⸢*Šu-um*⸣-*mì*-•*ya* DUMU *A-ri-ka*$_4$-*na-ri*

LOWER EDGE

16 *IGI •*It*-•*ḫi*-•*iš*-•*ta* •DUMU *Ar-ta-e*
17 •IGI *Ta-a*-•*a* D[UMU (*Še*?-)**e*]*ḫ-li-ya*
18 *IGI *En*-•*n*[*a-ma-ti*] DUMU •*Ḫa*-•*ni-ku-ya*

REVERSE

19 IGI •*Te*-**ḫu*-[*u*]*p-še-en-ni* DUMU *Pí-ru*
20 IGI *Ḫu-iš-ša* DUMU *Ḫur-pí-še-en-ni*
21 IGI *Ar-tu-ki* DUMU SILIM-*pa-li-iḫ*-*^{d}•⸢IM⸣
22 IGI *Ta-a-a* DUMU IBILA-^{d}XXX DUB.SAR-*rù*

S.I. Po 28

23 [^{NA_4} K]IŠIB ^{m}*Wa-an-ti-ya* DUMU *Túr-mar-ti*

S.I. Po 917

24 •⸢^{NA_4}⸣•KIŠIB ^{m}*Mu*-⸢*uš*⸣-[*Te*-+*š*]*up* +DUMU ⸢*Ḫa*⸣-*ši*!-*ya*

UPPER EDGE

S.I. Po 184

25 •^{NA_4} •KIŠIB ^{m}*Ta-a-a* DUB.SAR-*ri*

TRANSLATION

(1-5) Wantiya son of Tur-marti gave to Teḫip-tilla son of Puḫi-šenni as his gift a(n) (x).x homer field to the right of the route [of the] ...[of] ...-liya, in the town of Nuzi.

(6-8) Should [the field] have claimants, Wantiya shall clear (the field) and give (it) to Teḫip-tilla.

(9-11) Should Wantiya abrogate (this contract) and demand (the return of the field), he shall pay 2 minas of gold to Teḫip-tilla.

(12-22) Before Muš-tešup son of Ḫašiya; before Piru son of Naiš-kelpe; before Zikaya son of Elḫip-šarri; before Šummiya son of Arik-kanari; before Itḫišta son of Ar-tae; before Taya son of (Š?)eḫliya; before Enna-mati son of Ḫanikuya; before Teḫup-šenni son of Piru; before Ḫuišša son of Ḫurpi-šenni; before Ar-tuki son of Šalim-pāliḫ-adad; before Taya son of Apil-sin, the scribe.

(23-25) (*seal impression*) seal impression of Wantiya son of Tur-marti; (*seal impression*) seal impression of Muš-tešup son of Ḫašiya; (*seal impression*) seal impression of Taya, the scribe.

COMMENTS

This tablet has apparently suffered deterioration since the copy was made. Many signs, especially on the left side of the obverse and the lower edge are no longer present to the extent they once were. The remaining signs are difficult to read owing to a fractured tablet surface and the encrustation of the surface with a glue- or varnish-like substance.

At first glance, this text appears to be a typical real estate adoption contract with the first four lines broken away:

ṭuppi mārūti ša
ᵐWantiya mār Tur-marti
ᵐTeḫip-tilla mār Puḫi-šenni
ana mārūti ītepušma

However, this document belongs to a rare, but clearly attested, genre, the *qīštu* text. *JEN* 283, 530, 556 are other examples from the archive of Teḫip-tilla son of Puḫi-šenni (Maidman 1976, 131, 336-37, nn. 208-13, for a general description of, and literature on, this text type; the literature there cited should have included H. Lewy 1942, 37, 304-5 [thanks to Carlo Zaccagnini for the reference]; add now Zaccagnini 1984, 83).

Compared to the standard real estate adoption, the text seems to start *in medias res* with a description of the real estate ceded, omitting the introductory clause entirely. Yet this is deliberate since (a) other texts of this genre share this characteristic; (b) the beginning of the obverse is broken in none of these texts; and (c) the patronymics of the principal parties are present in lines 3 and 4, a means of identification usually confined to the

initial appearance of principal PNs in a text. Also peculiar, the cession of real estate is called *qīštu* (l. 5; hence the modern designation of this genre). Other unusual, though not unique, features of the text include failure to mention purchase price (so too *JEN* 530; however, in both instances, there may have been no purchase price if the ceder were in debt to the purchaser), definition of what constitutes abrogation of the agreement (l. 10; so too *JEN* 530:9-10), and the sealing of the document by the ceder (l. 23; so too *JEN* 283:24; 530:22; 556:26). Elsewhere, in cases where the ceder does seal the document, he is usually identified as *bēl eqli*, whereas in these texts, the patronymic reappears (see, e.g., *JEN* 10:26; 592:29; however, cf., e.g., *JEN* 689:28; 729:27-28).

NOTES

l. 2: [ ]⌜*x*⌝-*li-ya*. Lacheman speculates and restores, in effect, [AN.ZA.KÀR *E*]*ḫ-li-ya*.

l. 5: [NÍG.B]A!. As noted in the introductory comments, this text bears close similarities to other *qīštu* texts. Although [ḪA.L]A is perhaps an easier reading to defend, the result would be a (unique) text genre, probably a type of truncated adoption contract. This would be too great a burden to place on a single, broken sign. The *CAD* Nuzi file has, in effect: [*ki-ma* NÍG.BA⌝ (*sic*), perhaps supporting the present reconstruction.

l. 10: A.ŠÀ [ ] *i?-ri-iš*. The *CAD* Nuzi file reads at this point: A.ŠÀ-*šu i-ri-iš*. (Cf., *JEN* 530:9-10). Lacheman's copy suggests *e-ri-iš*. The surviving traces before RI could support the reading I or E. Only two horizontals are visible, not three as copied.

Abrogation of the agreement is here defined as future *demand* for the alienated real estate, not future (illegal) *cultivation* of that land. This idea is more clearly stated (i.e., using another verb) in, for example, *JEN* 252:20-22; 741:16-20; 743:17-21; 744:18-22; 761:18-22.

See also, below, first note to *JEN* 689:14.

l. 5: *id-*⌜*dì*⌝*-in-<na>-aš-šu*. On this spelling, see below, note to *JEN* 692:13.

l. 17: [(*Še?-*)**e*]*ḫ-li-ya*. That "Eḫliya" is the patronym here is maintained by Lacheman and *NPN*, 41a (*sub* EḪLIỊA 29)) and 142b (*sub* TAỊA 18)). This individual is witness to a real estate adoption of Teḫip-tilla son of Puḫi-šenni (*JEN* 217:19). Yet, as Carlo Zaccagnini kindly points out to me, Taya son of Šeḫliya is witness to both a Teḫip-tilla *qīštu* text and a Teḫip-tilla personal antichretic loan (*JEN* 283:21; 489:22).

l. 18: *En-n*[*a-ma-ti*]. This is the only plausible reconstruction. See *NPN*, p. 54a, *sub* HANIKUỊA.

l. 25. After this line, on the left edge, Lacheman once read: NA_4 *Pí-ru*.

JEN 689

OBVERSE

1 [*ṭup-pí ma-ru*]-*ti ša*

2 [^{m}*Ta-i-še*]-*en-ni* •DUMU •*A-ḫu-ši-na*

3 [^{m}*Te-ḫi-ip-til*]-⌜*la*⌝ [DUMU *P*]*u-ḫi-še-•en-•ni*

4 [*a-na ma-ru-ti i-te-pu-*$^{+}$*u*]*š*?

5 [ ]⌜*ni*⌝?[AN?].$^{+}$⌜ZA?.$^{+}$KÀR⌝?[ ]

6 [ ]⌜x⌝ *ra a* [ ] *eš* ⌜x⌝ *i*

7 [x?]⌜x x⌝[*ki*]-*ma* ḪA.LA-[*šu* ^{m}*Ta*]-$^{+}$*i*-$^{+}$*še-en-ni*

8 [*a-n*]*a*! ^{m}*T*[*e-ḫi*]-*ip-Til-•la* ⌜*it*⌝-*t*[*a-din*]

9 [*šum*]-*ma* A.Š[À] *ù* G[EME$_2$] *nu* ⌜*um*⌝ ? [ ]⌜x⌝ x *ú*/*sa* ⌜x⌝ AŠ

10 [*pa-q*]*í-ra-na* •⌜*i*⌝-•[*r*]*a-aš*-⌜*šu*⌝

11 [^{m}*T*]*a-i*-$^{+}$[*š*]*e*-$^{+}$*e*[*n-ni*] *ú-za-ak*-[*ka*$_4$-*ma*]

12 [*a-na* ^{m}]*Te-ḫi-i*[*p-til*]-*la i+na-an*-[*din*]

13 [*šum-ma*] ^{m}•*Ta-i-še-•en-ni* KI.⌜BAL⌝[-*at*?]

14 [A.Š]À *ù* GEME$_2$-*sú i*-⌜*le-eq*⌝-*qè*

15 [*ù*? 1 MA.N]A KÙ.BABBAR 1 MA.NA KÙ.SIG$_{17}$

16 [*a-na*] ⌜^{m}⌝*Te-ḫi-•ip-•til-•la ú*-⌜*ma-al*⌝-*la*

\+ ____

17 [IGI] *Mu-uš-te-šup* DUMU *Ḫa-ši-y*[*a*]

18 [IGI] *It-ḫi-iš-ta* DUMU ⌜*Ar*⌝-[*ta-e*]

19 [IGI] *Te-ḫi-ya* DUMU *A-ka*$_4$-*a*-[*a*]

LOWER EDGE

20 [IGI] *Ar-te-ya* DUMU *Ar-t*[*a-e*]

21 [IGI] *Te-ḫi-ya* DUMU *A-ku-še-e*[*n-ni*]

22 ^{LÚ}*sà-sí-in-nu*

REVERSE

23 [IGI *W*]*a-an-ti-ya* DUMU *Ku-uš*-$^{+}$*ši*-[*ya*]

24 [IGI ^{d}*Ak*]-•*dingir-ra* DUMU ^{d}XXX-*na-ap*-[*šìr*]

25 [IGI *Ḫa-ma*]-*an-na* DUMU *Šu-ru-uk-ka*$_4$

26 [IGI *Pí-r*]*u* DUMU *Na-iš-ké-el-pè*

27 [IGI *Ta-a*]-*a* [DUM]U! **A-pil*-^{d}XXX DUB.SAR

S.I. Po 108

28 [NA$_4$] ^{m}*Ta-i-še-en-ni* DUMU *A-ḫu-ši-na*

S.I. Po 917

29 [NA$_4$ ^{m}*Mu-uš*]-•*te-šup* DUMU *Ḫa*-[*ši-ya*]

S.I.

30 [NA$_4$ ^{m} DU]MU? •*Ḫa*-⌜*ip*⌝?-[LUGAL?]

TRANSLATION

(1-4) [Tablet of] adoption of Tai-šenni son of Aḫušina. He adopted Teḫip-tilla son of Puḫi-šenni.

(5-8) Tai-šenni gave to Teḫip-tilla as [his] inheritance share ... *dimtu*(?) .... .

(9-12) Should the field and ... female slave have claimants, Tai-šenni shall clear (the field and female slave) [and] give (them) [to] Teḫip-tilla.

(13-16) [Should] Tai-šenni abrogate (this contract), by (re)taking the field and female slave, he shall pay [to] Teḫip-tilla [1] mina of silver (and) 1 mina of gold.

(17-27) [Before] Muš-Tešup son of Ḫašiya; [before] Itḫišta son of Artae; [before] Teḫiya son of Akaya; [before] Ar-teya son of Ar-tae; [before] Teḫiya son of Aku-šenni, the maker of bows and arrows; [before] Wantiya son of Kuššiya; [before] Akkadingirra son of Sin-napšir; [before] Ḫamanna son of Šurukka; [before] Piru son of Naiš-kelpe; [before] Taya son of Apil-sin, the scribe.

(28-30) (*seal impression*) [seal impression of] Tai-šenni son of Aḫušina; (*seal impression*) [seal impression of] Muš-tešup son of Ḫašiya; (*seal impression*) [seal impression of] ... son of(?) Ḫaip(?)-[šarri?].

COMMENTS

This tablet has suffered considerable damage, especially on the obverse. However, little of this damage has occurred since the copy was made. Despite the damaged first line, there seems little doubt that this is a tablet of real estate adoption, albeit with a new wrinkle: a female slave is also transferred (ll. 9, 14). To be sure, no price is mentioned for the commodities ceded. Yet this is not decisive negative evidence. By contrast, elements of the typical adoption phraseology are present. These include mention of the inheritance share (l. 7), the clear title clause (ll. 9-12), and the penalty clause (ll. 13-16).

NOTES

l. 4: [-*u*]*š*?. The trace of the sole surviving sign from this line is not as copied. Rather, it appears as:

The trace is certainly consistent with the restoration of the line as a whole and that restoration, in turn, is reasonable if the first three lines are restored correctly. There is some doubt, though, whether this trace ends the line immediately following line 3. Lacheman considers this to be line 5. The spacing allows for either possibility. If Lacheman is

correct, then (a) the content of line 4 is essentially correct as restored but is entirely effaced; (b) line 5 would consist of [-*u*]*š*? alone; and (c) all subsequent line numbers would be raised by one.

l. 5: ⸢ZA?.KÀR⸣?. These two signs are not as copied (i.e., as PA AŠ). Rather, they appear as:

l. 7: [x?]⸢x x⸣. Lacheman restores the start of this line as follows: [*an-nu-ti ki*]-*ma*. If correct, the traces at the start of the line might represent: [*an*]-⸢*nu-ti*⸣.

l. 9. The last part of this line should more closely define the identity of the female slave, e.g., by PN or land of origin. Carlo Zaccagnini (personal communication) interprets these signs as É *ú*-⸢*ba*⸣-*rù*. The context remains elusive.

l. 9: x. The fourth last sign is not as copied. It appears as:

l. 9: *ú*/*sa*. This sign is not precisely as copied. It could represent Ú or SA equally well.

l. 14. This line is unusual in that it defines what constitutes an abrogation of the contract on the part of the ceder of property. The definition itself is also unusual. Where defined at all, the abrogation is usually cast in terms of a demand for the property. For details, see above, note to *JEN* 688:10. Here, the abrogation consists of illegal seizure.

l. 14: [A.Š]À. This restoration follows Lacheman.

l. 14: GEME$_2$. This sign is correct as copied.

l. 16. Below this line, the scribe has drawn a horizontal line. This is not indicated in the copy.

l. 18: ⸢*Ar*⸣-[*ta-e*]. This is the most plausible reconstruction. See *NPN*, 76b *sub* ITḪIŠTA 1) -10).

l. 19. This is the last line of the obverse.

l. 20. This line, not line 19 as indicated in the copy, begins the lower edge.

l. 22: ^{LÚ}*sà-sí-in-nu*. The ZA is perfectly clear, as copied. Accordingly, correct *NPN*, 151a *sub* TEḪIḬA 4).

l. 23: *Ku-uš-ši*-[*ya*]. This is the most plausible reconstruction. See *NPN*, 170b *sub* WANTIḬA 14).

l. 24: [*Ak*]-*dingir-ra*. That these signs should be rendered phonetically follows from such spellings as "^{d}AK.KA.DINGIR.RA" and "AQ.QA.DINGIR. RA," i.e., nos. (3) and (6) in *NPN*, 17a *sub* ^{d}AK.DINGIR.RA; and "AK.KA. DINGIR.RA" in al-Rawi (1977, 451, text IM 70801 [=TF$_1$ 159]:"33"; cf. p. 309). Another example of "AQ.QA.DINGIR.RA" is to be found in *EN*, 9/1, 139:18.

l. 24: ^{d}XXX-*na-ap-*[*šìr*]. The restoration follows *NPN*, 17a *sub* ^{d}AK.DINGIR.RA 1); and 121a *sub* SIN-NAPŠIR 4). Lacheman reads ^{d}XXX-*na-ap-ši-ir*.

l. 25: [*Ḫa-ma*]-*an-na*. This is the most plausible reconstruction. See *NPN*, 140b *sub* ŠURUKKA 3) -6).

l. 30: *Ḫa-*⸢*ip*⸣?-[LUGAL?]. Of all the "Ḫaip-" names, this one represents the most attractive alternative here. See *NPN*, 50a. Cf., also, *AAN*, 48a.

JEN 690

OBVERSE

1 [*ṭup-pí*] •*ma-*•ru-•⸢*ti*⸣ *ša*
2 [^{m}*Pa-li*]-*ya* DU[MU]-⸢x-x⸣-[ ]
3 [^{m}*Te-ḫi*]-*i*[*p-til-la* DUMU *P*]*u-ḫi-še-en-ni*
4 [*a-na ma-ru-ti i-p*]*u-us-sú-ma*
5 [É?.ḪÁ? *ku?-up?-pa?-ti? ù?* A.ŠÀ] **pa-i-ḫu*
6 [*i?-na? le?-et?* A?.ŠÀ? *ša? šar?-ra?*]-•*ti i+na* •*lìb!?-bi-šu ep?-šu*
7 [x? x? ^{m}*Pa-li*]-*y*[*a*] *ki-ma* ḪA.LA-*šu*
8 [*a-na* ^{m}*Te-ḫi-ip-til-l*]*a it-ta-din*
9 [*ù* ^{m}*Te*]-*ḫ*[*i-ip-ti*]*l-*⸢*la*⸣ 7 ANŠE ŠE.MEŠ
10 [*ki-ma* NÍG].B[A-*šu a-n*]*a* ^{m}*Pa-li-ya it-ta-din*
11 [*šum-ma* É?.Ḫ]Á? •*ku-up-pa-ti* ⸢*ù*⸣ A.ŠÀ *pa-i-ḫu an-nu-ú*
12 [*di-na* TUK-š]*i* ^{m}*Pa-li-ya* •*ú-za-ak-*ka_4*-ma*
13 [*a-na* ^{m}*Te-ḫi-i*]*p-til-la* *⸢*i*⸣-[*n*]*a-an-din*
14 [*šum-ma* ^{m}*Pa-*•*l*]*i-ya* KI.BAL-*at* 2 MA.NA KÙ. SIG_{17}
15 [*a-na* ^{m}*Te-ḫ*]*i-ip-til-la ú-ma-al-la*
16 [IGI *Pí-ru*] DUMU *Na-iš-ké-el-pè*
17 [IGI *Ḫa-ši-pár*]*-al-la* DUMU *Pa-li-ya*
18 [IGI *A-tal-te*]*-šup* DUMU *Šum-mi-ya*
19 [IGI *Šum-mi-y*]*a* DUMU *A-ri-*ka_4*-na-ri*
20 [IGI *Muš-te-*•*y*]*a* DUMU *Ar-še-ni*
21 [IGI *It-ḫi-iš-t*]*a* DUMU *Ta-mar-ta-e*
22 [IGI *Ḫu-ti-pu-kùr*] DUMU *Ni-iš-ḫu-ḫa*
23 [IGI *A-ri-ké-ya*] DUMU *A-ri-ya*

.
.
.

REVERSE

24 [ ]⸢x⸣ *ša* [ ]
25 [ ] •*an-ni-im ù* [*š*]*u-nu-*⸢*ma*⸣ *mu-še-*⸢*el*⸣-
:*mu-ú*

S.I. Po 290

26 [$^{\text{NA}_4}$ KIŠIB ^{m}]*Ḫa-ši-pár-al-la* DUMU *Pa-li-ya*

S.I. Po 637

27 $^{\text{[N]A}_4}$ KIŠIB ^{m}*Pí-⸢ru⸣* DUMU *Na-iš-•ké-el-pè*

S.I. Po 179

28 [$^{\text{NA}_4}$ KIŠIB ^{m}*T*]*a-a-a* DUB.SAR-*ri*

S.I. Po 44

29 ⸢$^{\text{NA}_4}$⸣ KIŠIB ^{m}*It-ḫi-iš-ta* ⸢DUMU⸣ *Ta-mar-ta-e*

TRANSLATION

(1-4) [Tablet of] adoption of Paliya son of .... He adopted Teḫip-tilla son of Puḫi-šenni.

(5-8) Paliya gave [to] Teḫip-tilla as his inheritance share [*kuppu*?-structures? and] *paiḫu*[-land adjacent? to? the? land? of? the? quee]n(?), (the buildings) built up in its (i.e., the *paiḫu*-land's) midst.

(9-10) [And] Teḫip-tilla gave to Paliya [as his] gift 7 homers of barley.

(11-13) [Should] the *kuppu*-structures(?) and this *paiḫu*-land have [a case (against them)], Paliya shall clear (them) and give (them) [to] Teḫip-tilla.

(14-15) [Should] Paliya abrogate (this contract), he shall pay [to] Teḫip-tilla 2 minas of gold.

(16-25) [Before Piru] son of Naiš-kelpe; [before] Ḫašip-paralla son of Paliya; [before] Atal-tešup son of Šummiya; [before] Šummiya son of Arik-kanari; [before] Muš-teya son of Ar-šenni; [before] Itḫišta son of Tamar-tae; [before Ḫutip-ukur] son of Niš-ḫuḫa; [before Arik-keya] son of Ariya .... this ... and, as well, they are the measurers.

(26-29) (*seal impression*) [seal impression of] Ḫašip-paralla son of Paliya; (*seal impression*) seal impression of Piru son of Naiš-kelpe; (*seal impression*) [seal impression of] Taya, the scribe; (*seal impression*) seal impression of Itḫišta son of Tamar-tae.

COMMENT

This tablet has suffered some deterioration since the copy was made.

NOTES

l. 2: ⸢x-x⸣. Lacheman interprets these traces as *Ip-*.

ll. 5-6. The real estate described in these lines is almost certainly to be located in the town of Unap-še. See below, note to l. 18.

The interpretation of these two lines depends, unfortunately, upon three sets of variables. The first set consists of three alternative restorations of the first halves of lines 5 and 6. These alternatives are:

(A) [É.ḪÁ *ku-up-pa-ti ù* A.ŠÀ] *pa-i-ḫu* [ ]-*ti*

(B) [A.ŠÀ] *pa-i-ḫu* [(*ù*) É.ḪÁ *ku-up-pa*]-*ti*

(C) [É.ḪÁ *ku-up-pa-ti ù* A.ŠÀ] *pa-i-ḫu* [*i-na le-et* A.ŠÀ *ša šar-ra*]-*ti*

The second set of variables involves the problem of whether to read the second last word of line 6 (D) *ṭuppišu* or (E) *libbišu* (see below, note to l. 6: *lìb!?-bi-šu*).

Finally, the last word may be interpreted either as (F) *ibšû* or as (G) *epšū* (see below, note to l. 6: *ep?-šu*).

In theory, there result twelve possible interpretations to these lines. In fact, some of these are difficult if not totally out of the question. Without going into extensive detail regarding the alternatives, one possibility, C-E-G, yields the best sense while doing the least violence to the expected syntax. Other solutions are possible and one of those may be the correct one.

In delineating the first set of alternatives, it should be noted first that *ti* (l. 6) is partially effaced. It appears as: 

Each of the three alternatives, (A), (B), and (C), seems plausible. "É.ḪÁ *ku-up-pa-ti*" is restored in any case on the basis of line 11. (Although the relevant part of that line is itself partially restored, the basic sense of the segment is not in doubt.)

(For the meaning of *kuppu* and *paiḫu*, see, for the moment, Maidman [1976, 376, n. 479; and 376-78, n. 480 respectively].)

(A) commends itself as perhaps cleaving most closely to the formulation of line 11. However, the first half of line 6 is left unexplained. (B), advocated by Weeks (1972, 186-87), addresses the weakness of (A) by filling the gap in line 6 and making sense of the *ti* on that line. However, this is achieved at the cost both of a gap starting line 5 (the amount of the *paiḫu*-land would probably not fill this gap; *paiḫu*-land is rarely described by area or by dimensions where that information precedes the word *paiḫu*; see *JEN* 19:5; 46:5-7; 101:4; 255:8; 592:6; *G* 31:4-6; 50:11; *L-O* 15:5, 8-9; etc.; however, cf. *JEN* 242:4-5) and of an order of items diverging from that of line 11.

(C) combines the strengths of (A) and (B) and avoids their weaknesses. The order of line 11 is maintained, no gaps remain, and the isolated *ti* is explained. However, (C) is a solution requiring maximum restoration. Usually, restoration should be kept at a minimum. However, in this case, (C) appears attractive and relatively safe. The restoration of line 5 is based, as already noted, on the probable text of line 11. The restoration of l. 6 is grounded in the following facts. *JEN* 690 is part of a series of 12 texts sharing a common witness sequence and (wherever sufficiently preserved) other features as well. See below, note to l. 18. These texts would appear to have been written on a single occasion and to have dealt with land in the same vicinity. Now of the remaining 11 texts, 7

preserve description of the real estate transferred. In 4 of those 7, the real estate is located adjacent to A.ŠÀ.MEŠ/ḪÁ (*-ti*) *ša šar-ra-ti* (*JEN* 51:5-6; 408:6-7; 581:7; 582:5; only the first example may locate the land *within* this territory). Thus the restoration of line 6 in (C) becomes plausible.

l. 5: *pa-i-ḫu*. The last sign on this line is a typical ḪU, not as copied. The tablet is well preserved at this point.

l. 6: *lìb*!?-*bi-šu*. The question of which of two words is represented by these signs constitutes the second of the three sets of variables noted above. The first sign is partially effaced. It appears as: 

Lacheman copied the sign as if it were a clear *ṭup*. However, his notes indicate that an initial interpretation of *ṭup* was subsequently changed to *lìb* (other notes of his, though, reflect an unambiguous *ṭup*). This indicates, at the least, that the sign was not fully preserved at a time when Lacheman was still working on the Chicago tablets. The *CAD* Nuzi file has, in effect, *lìb*. The trace can support either *ṭup* or *lìb*, albeit uneasily.

Both interpretations yield sense. *ṭuppišu* might well refer to a document (e.g., a deed) of Paliya wherein was described the real estate to be alienated. The sense would then be that the buildings are "... built (*epšū*) (as stated) in his tablet" or, more likely, that the real estate is "(as) attested (*ibšû*) in his tablet." (The latter is essentially the position of Weeks [1972, 187]; see below, note to l. 6: *ep*?-*šu*, on the implications of *epšū* vs. *ibšû*.) For similar contexts (though phrased differently) in which the contents of tablets are referred to in subsequent contracts or other situations, see, for example, *JEN* 102:18-19, 28-29; 108:21.

libbišu too would make sense, referring to the location of real estate within a larger geographical horizon. Here it would be buildings upon (thus "in the midst of") the *paiḫu*-land.

The buildings are either *built* (*epšū*) in the midst (of the *paiḫu*-land) or the buildings, *such as they are* (*ibšû*), in the midst (of the *paiḫu*-land), ... (Alternately: the buildings and *paiḫu*-land, [the former] built / such as they are, in the midst of the land of the queen .... .) For similar formulations with **libbu*, see *JEN* 101:5-6 and 788:4-5 (cf. Lacheman's restoration in *HSS*, XIII, 161:4-5). Those contexts might be construed to argue for *epšū* rather than *ibšû*. See below, next note.

l. 6: *ep*?-*šu*. Some slight ambiguity exists regarding this word. In the choice between two alternatives lies the third set of variables contained in lines 5 and 6. Is it to be construed as *ibšû* (G preterite 3MP [subjunctive] of *bašû*) or *epšū* (G stative 3MP of *epēšu*)?

In favor of *ibšû* (the interpretation of Weeks [1972, 187]) is the fact that, given the right combination of restorations and interpretations of lines 5 and 6, acceptable contextual sense results, i.e., "... (such as) is attested in his tablet" or "... (such as) exist in its midst." Against *ibšû* is the fact

that, for the "acceptable contextual sense" to be achieved, a present-future or stative form, not a preterite, of *bašû* is expected. Neither dictionary recognizes *ibšû* in a context such as this one.

An interpretation of the word as *epšū* yields good contextual sense, i.e., "... built in its midst," less likely, ".... built (as stated) in his tablet," a sense consonant with the stative form of *epēšu* as given. Cf. the very similar *JEN* 101:5 (there, *ibšû* would seem to be precluded). Although neither dictionary recognizes this verbal form in Nuzi contexts such as this, both note *epšu* as a verbal adjective associated with buildings throughout the orbit of Akkadian usage (*AHw*, 231a; *CAD*, E, 246b-247a). To the examples there adduced (*HSS*, XIII, 161:4; *SMN* 3491:5 [to be published as *EN*, 9/3, 56:5]) there may now be added *JEN* 788:4.

l. 11: [*šum-ma* É?.Ḫ]Á?. The restoration can fit the lacuna, some 19 mm. in length.

l. 12: [*di-na*]. This restoration is based on a common pattern of a series of texts of which *JEN* 690 is one. See below, note to l. 18.

l. 14. After this line, there may appear a horizontal line on the tablet.

l. 16: [*Pí-ru*]. Cf., below, l. 27, for this restoration.

l. 17: [*Ḫa-ši-pár*]-*al-la*. Cf., below, l. 26, for this restoration.

l. 18: [*A-tal-te*]-*šup*. This restoration, as well as other witness PN restorations in this text, is based on a practically identical standard Nuzi -Unap-še witness sequence in Teḫip-tilla real estate adoption tablets. Some of these texts and their common features are noted by Cassin (1938, 99) and discussed by Weeks (1972, 208-9) and Fadhil (1983, 296, 298-99). The texts of this group are: *JEN* 44, 51, 58, 70, 408, 581, 582, 690, 756, *JENu* 140a, 716a(+)716d, *SMN* 1721. The two *JENu* items are unpublished. The *SMN* text is published in Maidman (1987c). *SMN* 1721 may have come from the same tablet as *JEN* 756 or *JENu* 140a (not both) or from neither of these. Eight of these twelve texts identify the real estate as located in the town of Unap-še: *JEN* 44:5; 51:6; 58:6; 70:7; 408:7; 581:6; 582:6; *JENu* 716a(+)716d:6. Of the remaining four texts, in all but *JEN* 690 the pertinent clause is destroyed.

l. 23. In accordance with the witness sequence noted immediately above, some nine or ten lines are effaced between lines 23 and 24.

ll. 24-25. Lacheman restores these two lines and the immediately preceding line as follows:

[LÚ.MEŠ *an-nu-ti* IGI.MEŠ]
[É.ḪÁ] *ù* [A.ŠÀ *pa-i-ḫu*]
[*ša ṭup-pí*] *an-ni-im* etc.

JEN 44:31-32; 51:33-34; 582:34-35; and 756:18-19 suggest another basis for reconstructing these lines. Accordingly, the lines may be interpreted as follows:

[*an-nu-ti š*]*a ša-*[*aṭ-ru*]
[*i-na ṭup-pí*] *an-ni-im* etc.

JEN 691

OBVERSE

1 [*ṭup*]-*pí ma-ru-ti ša* ^{m}⸢*Ša*⸣-[*l*]*i*-•[*p*]*u-ti*$_5$
2 [DUMU/*ù*] $^{+}$⸢*x*⸣-*un-na-an-ni* ^{m}*Te-ḫi-ip-til-*[*l*]*a*
3 [DUMU *Pu-ḫi-š*]*e-en-ni a-na ma-ru-*⸢*ti*⸣
4 [*i-te-pu-u*]*š-ma* ⸢10? ANŠE? A.ŠÀ⸣ [ ]
5 [*i-na* ^{GIŠ}*ta*]-⸢*a*⸣-*a-ri ma-an-du*$_4$ [(?)]
6 [ ] ḪA.LA-*ni i+na le-e*[*t*?]
7 [*š*]*a* ^{m}*A-kip-ta-še-en-*•*ni* [ ]
8 [*i-na ša*]-*pá-at* KASKAL-*ni* ⸢*ša*⸣
9 [URU *A*]-*pè-na-aš ki-ma* ḪA.LA-*šu*
10 [*a-na* $^{m+}$*T*]*e-*$^{+}$*ḫi-ip-til-la* SUM-*din-n*[*a-aš-šu*]
11 [*ù* ^{m}]*Te-ḫi-ip-til-*⸢*la* 8⸣ ANŠE [ŠE?(.MEŠ)]
12 [*ki-ma* $^{+}$N]ÍG.BA-*šu a-na* ^{m}*Ša-li-*⸢*pu*⸣-*ti*$_5$
13 [*it-ta*]-⸢*ad*⸣-*na-aš-š*[*u*] *il-ka*
14 [*ša* A.ŠÀ] ^{m}*Ša-li-*[*pu*]-*ti*$_5$-*ma na-a-ši*
15 [*šum-ma* A.Š]À *pa-qí-ra-na ir-ta-a-*⸢*ši*⸣
16 [^{m}*Ša-l*]*i-pu-ti*$_5$ *ú-za-ak-ka*$_4$-*m*[*a*]
17 [*a-na* ^{m}*T*]*e-ḫi-ip-til-la i+na-an-*[*din*]
18 [*ma-an-nu*] *ša i+na bi*$_4$-*ri-šu-*[*nu*]
19 [(*ša*) KI.BAL]-*tu*$_4$ 1 MA.NA KÙ.BABBAR
20 [1 MA.NA K]Ù.SIG$_{17}$ *ú-ma-al-la*

\+ ———

21 [IGI] ⸢DUMU? *x-ki*⸣?-*ya*
22 [IGI DUMU] *Ke-en*$_6$-*ni*

LOWER EDGE

23 [IGI DUMU] ⸢x⸣-[ ]
24 [IGI] $^{+}$DUMU ⸢*Ni*⸣-[ ]-⸢x⸣-[ ]
$^{+}$25 [IGI DUMU] ⸢x-x-x-x⸣

REVERSE

26 [IGI DUMU]-*li-*⸢*x*⸣
27 [IGI DUMU] *Zi-ka*$_4$-*a-a*
28 [IGI *Pí-ru* D]UMU *Na-*•*iš-*•*ké-*•*él-p*[*è*]
29 [IGI -*y*]*a*?/-⸢*e*⸣? DUMU *Zi*!-*ri-ra*
30 [IGI DINGIR-*ni-š*]*u* DUB.SAR DUMU ^{d}•XXX-*nap-*$^{+}$*šì*[*r*]
31 [IGI ÌR-DINGIR-š]*u* DUMU BÀD-•LUGAL

S.I.

32 $^{+⸢NA_4}$ $^{+}$KIŠIB $^{+m⸣\bullet}$*Ké-li-ya*

S.I.

33 [^{NA_4} KIŠIB ^{m}Z]*i-ka$_4$-a-a*

S.I.

34 [^{NA_4} KIŠIB ^{m}*É*]*ḫ-ḫe-él-te-šup*

35 [^{NA_4} KIŠIB ^{m}DINGIR]-*ni-š*⸢*u*⸣ DUB.SAR-*ri*

UPPER EDGE

S.I.

TRANSLATION

(1-4) Tablet of adoption of Šalim-pûti [son of/and] ...-unnanni. He adopted Teḫip-tilla [son of] Puḫi-šenni.

(4-10) He gave [to] Teḫip-tilla as his inheritance share a ...(?) field 10(?) homers(?) [by] the large standard ..., our inheritance share adjacent(?) to the ... of Akip-tašenni ...(?), abutting the road to [the town of] Apena.

(11-13) [And] Teḫip-tilla gave to Šalim-pûti [as] his gift 8 homers of [barley?].

(13-14) And Šalim-pûti shall bear the *ilku* [of the field].

(15-17) [Should] the field have claimants, Šalim-pûti shall clear (it) and give (it) [to] Teḫip-tilla.

(18-20 [Whichever] amongst them abrogates (this contract) shall pay 1 mina of silver (and) [1 mina] of gold.

(21-31) [Before ...] son(?) of ...-kiya; [before ... son of] Kenni; [before ... son of] ...; [before ...] son of Ni-...; [before ... son of] ...; [before ... son of] ...-li-...; [before ... son of] Zikaya; [before Piru] son of Naiš-kelpe; before ...-ya(?)/-e(?) son of Ziriraš; [before] Ila-nîšū, the scribe, son of Sin-napšir; [before] Ward-ilišu son of Dûr-šarru.

(32-35) (*seal impression*) seal impression of Keliya; (*seal impression*) [seal impression of] Zikaya; (*seal impression*) [seal impression of] Eḫli-tešup; [seal impression of] Ila-nîšū, the scribe (*seal impression*).

COMMENT

The tablet has suffered only slight deterioration since the copy was made.

NOTES

l. 2: [DUMU/*ù*]. The first of these alternatives is probably correct. All verbal and pronominal forms but one in this text indicate a single adopter. Furthermore, indication of the patronymic of the adopter or some notation of his status appears to be obligatory in these contracts.

Yet, if the third sign, indicating the plural pronominal suffix, in ḪA.LA-*ni* (l. 5) is not a scribal error, then perhaps ...-unnanni is a second adopter. (A further difficulty: "ḪA.LA-*ni*" would represent a rare, if not unique, shift from indirect to direct discourse in tablets of adoption.)

l. 2: ⌜*x*⌝. Two vertical wedges (MIN-like) are preserved.

l. 4. The restoration of this line follows that of the *CAD* Nuzi file.

l. 5. Cf. *JEN* 11:4, written by the same scribe. For another translation of GAL, in what is usually written, *ina tayyāri* GAL, see *JEN* 201:5.

ll. 8-9: [*i-na ša*]-*pá-at* KASKAL-*ni* ⌜*ša*⌝ // [URU *A*]-*pè-na-aš*. This description narrows the number of possible locations of the real estate at stake. In the Nuzi texts, the "road to Apena" is located in Artiḫi (*JEN* 274:4-5 [partially restored]), Nuzi (e.g., *JEN* 14:4-6), Unap-še (*P-S* 67:4-7, 9), and Zizza (*HSS*, XIII, 417:1, 7). (Cf. Maidman 1976, 146 and notes thereto.)

These possibilities are not further narrowed by the additional description of this land as *ina lēt*? [ ] *ša* ᵐ*Akip-tašenni* (ll. 6-7). In the extant Teḫip-tilla Family corpus of real estate texts, the designation, "Akip-tašenni," could refer to any of three locations. An Akip-tašenni Canal is located in the town of Zizza (e.g., *JEN* 93:5-6; cf. *JEN* 244:5-6) and, in fact, Lacheman suggests that *atappi* be supplied here. However, though land is located "*ina šapat*" (e.g., *JEN* 93:5) or "*ina aḫ*" (*JEN* 692:6) this canal, it is never "*ina lēt*" as specified here (l. 6). So the land here is likely not located adjacent to the Akip-tašenni Canal, i.e., in Zizza.

(A field of Akip-tašenni appears in the same text as a Zizza toponym [*JEN* 112:2, 4, 9] but the context does not permit the conclusion that the field itself was located in Zizza. Also, the text should be excluded from consideration here on chronological grounds. The reason given immediately below applies here as well.)

Urban real estate of "Akip-tašenni" is located in Turša (*JEN* 256:5-8; 272:5-6, 8-9). However, this designation applies to Akip-tašenni son of Teḫip-tilla and is probably exclusively post-Teḫip-tilla in date and thus irrelevant to this, a Teḫip-tilla, text.

Land of "Akip-tašenni" in Nuzi (*JEN* 779:5, 8-9) likewise probably refers to the son of Teḫip-tilla and should be excluded on chronological grounds.

Of the four most likely possibilities for locating this land, Artiḫi, Nuzi, Unap-še, and Zizza, one slight indication may favor Nuzi. The second seal impression is that of Zikaya (l. 33). If this Zikaya is the son of Elḫip-šarri (*NPN*, 175b *sub* ZIKAỊA 1)), then we may note that this person himself possessed real estate in Nuzi (*JEN* 279:10, 2, 5; cf. *JEN* 310:4, 8).

l. 20. After this line, the scribe has drawn a horizontal line. This line does not appear in the copy.

l. 25. Only the vaguest traces of probably four signs remain.

l. 27: [IGI DUMU] *Zi-ka*$_{4}$*-a-a*. *I-ru-ya* seems a likely candidate to bear this patronymic. See *NPN*, 175b *sub* ZIKAI̯A 8)-15).

l. 29: *Zi*!. The sign is a clear GI.

l. 30: [DINGIR-*ni-š*]*u*. For this restoration, cf. l. 35.

l. 31: [ÌR-DINGIR-š]*u*. This restoration is all but certain. See *NPN*, 160b, *sub* DÛR-ŠARRU.

JEN 692

OBVERSE

1 *ṭup-pí ma-ru-ti ša*

2 ^{m}*Ta-i-til-la* DUMU *Wa-an-ti-ya*

3 ^{m}*Te-ḫi-ip-til-la* DUMU *Pu-ḫi-še-en-ni*

4 *a-na ma-ru*!*-ti i-pu-us-sú-ma*

5 6 ^{GIŠ}APIN A.ŠÀ ⸢*ši*⸣*-qa i+na* AN.ZA.KÀR

6 *pí-ir-ša-an-ni i+na a-aḫ a-tap-pí*

7 *ša A-kip-ta-še-en-ni i+na*

8 *le-et* A.ŠÀ.ḪÁ *ša* ^{m}*Te-ḫi-ip-til-la*

9 *ki-ma* ḪA.LA-*šu a-na* ^{m}*Te-ḫi-ip-til-*[*la*]

10 *id-dì-in ù* ^{m}*Te-ḫi-*•*i*[*p*]*-*•*til-*•*la*

11 4 UDU.MEŠ 2 ANŠE ŠE.MEŠ *ki-ma*

12 NÍG.BA-*šu a-na* ^{m}*Ta-i-til-*[*la*]

13 ⸢*id*⸣*-dì-in-*<*na*>*-aš-šu šum-ma*

14 [A.ŠÀ *p*]*a-qí-ra-na i-*•*ra-*

15 [*a*]*š-ši* ^{m}*Ta-i-til-***la*

16 [*ú-za-ak-k*]*a*$_{4}$*-ma a-na* $^{m•}$*Te-*[*ḫi-ip-til-la*]

17 [*i-na-an-di*]*n šum-ma*

18 [^{m}*Ta-i-til-la*] KI.BAL-*a*[*t*]

LOWER EDGE

19 [2 MA.NA KÙ.BABBAR] ⸢*ù*⸣ 2 MA.NA KÙ.⸢SIG$_{17}$⸣

20 [*a-na* ^{m}*Te-ḫi*]*-ip-til-la*

21 [*ú-ma*]*-al-la*

REVERSE

22 [IGI *Ki-an-ni*]*-pu* DUMU IBILA-^{d}XXX

23 [IGI] DUMU IBILA-^{d}XXX

24 [IGI] DUMU *Ḫa-ma-an-na*

25 [IGI] ⸢*Pí-ru*⸣ +DUMU *[*N*]*a-***i*[*š*]*-ké-el-p*[*è*]

26 IGI *Ḫa-ma-an-**⸢*na*⸣ [DUMU *Ar*]*-*•*ša-an-*•*t*[*a*]

27 IGI *A-be-ya* +DU[MU *Na-iš-ké*]*-el-pè*

28 IGI *Ḫe-ša-al-*[*la* DUMU *Zu*]*-me*

29 IGI *Tu-ur-[še-en-ni* DUMU •*Ḫ]a-ma-*a[n-na]*
30 IGI *Ḫu-lu-•u[k-ka*$_4$ DUMU *Ku-š]u-ḫa-t[al]*
31 IGI *Ar-t[a?-* DUMU *]-ri-te*
32 ⸢IGI •*T*⸣*a-a-[a* DUMU IBILA-^{d}]XXX DUB.•SA[R]

.

.

.

UPPER EDGE

S.I.

33 ^{NA_4} KIŠIB ^{m} *Ki-an-ni-pu*

LEFT EDGE

S.I.

34 ^{NA_4} KIŠIB ^{m}•*Ta-*a-•a* DUB.SAR-*ru*??

TRANSLATION

(1-4) Tablet of adoption of Tai-tilla son of Wantiya. He adopted Teḫip-tilla son of Puḫi-šenni.

(5-10) He gave to Teḫip-tilla as his inheritance share a .6 homer irrigated field in the *piršanni dimtu*, on the bank of the Akip-tašenni Canal, adjacent to land of Teḫip-tilla.

(11-13) And Teḫip-tilla gave to Tai-tilla as his gift 4 sheep (and) 2 homers of barley.

(13-17) Should [the field] have claimants, Tai-tilla shall clear (it) and give (it) to Teḫip-tilla.

(17-21) Should [Tai-tilla] abrogate (this contract), he shall pay [to] Teḫip-tilla [2 minas of silver] and 2 minas of gold.

(22-32) [Before] Kiannipu son of Apil-sin; [before ...] son of Apil-sin; [before ...] son of Ḫamanna; [before] Piru son of Naiš-kelpe; before Ḫamanna [son of] Ar-šanta; before Abeya son of Naiš-kelpe; before Ḫešalla son of Zume; before Tur-šenni [son of] Ḫamanna; before Ḫulukka [son of] Kušuḫ-atal; before Ar-ta(?)-... [son of] ...-rite; before Taya [son of] Apil-sin, the scribe. ....

(33-34) (*seal impression*) seal impression of Kiannipu; (*seal impression*) seal impression of Taya, the scribe.

COMMENTS

This tablet is somewhat more damaged now than when copied. There is evidence to suggest that more seal impressions and PNs of sealers were preserved than are now visible. For one example, see below, note to l. 32.

NOTES

l. 4: *i-pu-us-sú-ma*. These signs are perfectly clear. The middle three signs of the *i-te-li-⸢x⸣-ma* of the copy are incorrect.

ll. 5-6: AN.ZA.KÀR // *pí-ir-ša-an-ni*. The real estate is, therefore, to be located in the town of Zizza. See, for example, *JEN* 244:5-6. On the use of *piršanni* as a virtual toponym and its geographical significance, see, for the moment, Maidman (1976, 180-83).

l. 10: *i*[*p*]. The trace is typical of IP, not the "MIN" of the copy.

l. 12: BA. The sign is more typical than the copy indicates.

l. 13: ⸢*id*⸣-*dì-in*-<*na*>-*aš-šu*. This reconstruction follows Lacheman. Cf. *JEN* 691:10. But note too another "defective" spelling of this word in *JEN* 688:5.

ll. 14-15: *i-ra-*//[*a*]*š-ši*. This form of word division is unusual if not unique. Lacheman reconstructs: *i-ra-*[*aš-ši*] // {[*i-ra-a*]*š-ši*}.

l. 22: [*Ki-an-ni*]-*pu*. This restoration is based on l. 33. Cf. *JEN* 271:20.

l. 27: [*Na-iš-ké*]-*el-pè*. This restoration seems probable. See *NPN*, 22b *sub* ABEI̯A 1)-7); and *AAN*, 24b *sub* ABEIA.

l. 29: *Tu-ur-*[*še-en-ni*]. The restoration is plausible on the basis of *NPN*, 51b, 42).

l. 30: [*Ku-š*]*u-ḫa-t*[*al*]. This restoration, following a suggestion of Lacheman, seems plausible. See *NPN*, 62b *sub* ḪULUKKA 1)-12); and *AAN*, 59b *sub* ḪULUKKA.

l. 31. [ ]-*ri-te*. In a note, Lacheman renders this patronymic: *Ar-te-*[ ].

l. 32. Below this line, Lacheman once read:

NA$_4$ [^{m}*Pí-r*]*u* DUMU *Na-*[*iš-ké-el-pè*]
S.I. Po 637

l. 34: *ru*??. These wedges comprise no sign with which I am familiar. They are certainly not the DUMU of the copy. To my eye, the sign appears as:

It is vaguely IL-like.

JEN 693

OBVERSE

1 [ṭup-p]í ma-ru-[ti ša]

2 [^{m}Wa-r]a-at-te-[ya DUMU -ya?/-e?]

3 [^{m}Te-ḫ]i-ip-til-l[a DUMU Pu-ḫi-še-en-ni]

4 [a-na m]a-ru-ti [i-te-pu-uš(-ma)]

5 [É.Ḫ]Á.MEŠ ku-up-pa-t[i]

6 ⸢60⸣?[+? i-n]a am-ma-ti [mu-ra-ak-šu-nu]

7 ⸢ù⸣ [? +]˙20 i+na am-[ma-ti ru]-pu-[us-sú-nu ù ^{GIŠ}A]PIN A.ŠÀ

8 <AŠ?> mi-<iṣ?>-ri-[š]u AŠ ^{GIŠ}⸢ta-a-a⸣-[ri]

9 É.⸢ḪÁ⸣.MEŠ ku-up-pa-t[i] ⸢ša? x⸣[ ] ⸢x x⸣

10 ù i-[n]a šu-pa-al [ ] ⸢x-šu⸣

11 ša ^{m}⸢Ḫi⸣-iš-mì-te-$^{+}$šu[p (ù) É.ḪÁ.M]EŠ ku-u[p-pa-ti]

12 ù i-˙na ⸢e⸣-le-en KA[SKAL ša UR]U Ú-lam-me

13 AŠ [U]RU [Nu]-zi AŠ ⸢x⸣ [ ]

14 ^{m}˙Wa-r[a]-at-te-ya D[UMU -y]a?/-⸢e⸣?

15 a-n[a ^{m}Te]-ḫi-ip-til-l[a DUMU Pu-ḫ]i-še-en-ni

16 ki-i-[ma Ḫ]A.LA.M[E]Š!-šú ⸢i⸣-[din] $^{+}$⸢ù⸣ ^{m}Te-ḫi-ip-[til-la]

17 4 AN[ŠE ŠE].MEŠ ⸢ù⸣ [ ] DIŠ [d]ú-uḫ-nu^{MEŠ}

18 a-na [^{m}Wa-ra-at-te-ya k]i-i-ma NÍG.BA.MEŠ-šu <i-din>

19 il-k[u$_8$ ša É.ḪÁ.MEŠ ku-up-pa-ti] ⸢ù⸣ ša A.ŠÀ

20 ^{m}Wa-ra-[at-te-ya na]-a-ši

21 šum-ma ⸢É⸣.[ḪÁ.MEŠ ku-up-pa-ti ù A.ŠÀ] pa-qí-ra-na

22 i-ra-aš-⸢šu ù ^{m}Wa-ra⸣-at-te-e

23 ú-za-ak-ka$_4$-ma a-na ^{m}Te-ḫi-ip-til-la i-na-an-din

24 šum-ma ^{m}Wa-ra-at-te-e KI.BAL-kat

25 1 MA.NA KÙ.BABBAR 1 MA.NA KÙ.SIG$_{17}$ ú-ma-al-la

26 ˙IGI It-ḫi-iš-ta DUMU A-ar-ta-<e>

LOWER EDGE

27 IGI Ur-ḫi-ya DUMU Še-ka$_4$-rù

28 IGI Ut-ḫáp-ta-e DUMU Zi-ké

29 IGI Ḫa-na-ak-ka$_4$ DUMU Še-ka$_4$-rù

REVERSE

30 an-nu-ti LÚ.MEŠ mu-še-el-mu-ú ša É.MEŠ ù A.ŠÀ

31 IGI Zi-ka$_4$-a-a DUMU ˙El-ḫi-ip-LUGAL

32 IGI Zi-ké DUMU Še-ka$_4$-rù

33 an-nu-ti IGI.MEŠ-ti ga$_5$-$^{+}$bá-šu-nu-ma

34 na-dì-⸢na⸣-nu ša ŠE.MEŠ ˙ù dú-uḫ-ni

35 ⸢IGI⸣ Ze-˙e-tu$_4$ DUMU I-ri-iš-a-bi

36 [IGI Ḫ]a-na-a-a DUMU Ta-e IGI Um-pí-ya
: <DUMU> Ar-ša-an-ta

37 [IGI T]a-i-na DUMU E-ra-ti

38 IGI *I*]*p-pa-a-a* DUMU KI.MIN
39 [IGI *T*]*a-a-a* DUMU IBILA-^{d}XXX DUB.SAR
40 [IG]I *Muš-te-ya* DUMU *Be-la-a-a*
41 ^{NA_4} KIŠIB ⸢^{m}⸣[ ]
S.I.
S.I. Po 634
42 ^{NA_4} KIŠIB ^{m}*Zi-ka*$_4$*-a-a* ^{NA_4} KIŠIB ^{m}*It-ḫi-iš-*⸢*ta*⸣
S.I. S.I.
43 ^{NA_4} KIŠIB ^{m}*Ta-a-a* DU[B.SA]R DUMU *Ar-ta-*⸢*e*⸣
S.I.
44 ^{NA_4} KIŠ[IB]
45 ^{m}*Ḫa-*[*na-ak-ka*$_4$]

LEFT EDGE

46 [*šu-un-d*]*u*$_4$ ^{m}*Ku*$_8$*-uš-ši-ḫar-pè*
47 [AŠ] ⸢URU⸣ *Nu-*⸢*zi*⸣ *ḫa-za-nu-ta* DÙ-*šú*
48 *ù* AŠ UD-⸢*šu*⸣ ^{m}*Te-ḫi-ip-til-la* $^{+}$É!.$^{+}$⸢ḪÁ!? $^{+}$ *ù*⸣ [A.ŠÀ *il*]-$^{+}$⸢*te-*$^{+}$*qè*⸣
S.I. Po 474
49 ^{NA_4} KIŠIB ^{m}*Muš-te-e*
S.I.
50 ^{NA_4} ⸢KIŠIB⸣ ^{m}*U*[*r-ḫi-y*]*a*

TRANSLATION

(1-4) Tablet of adoption [of] Waratteya [son of ...-ya?/-e?]. He adopted Teḫip-tilla [son of Puḫi-šenni].

(5-16) Waratteya son of ...-ya(?)/-e(?) gave to Teḫip-tilla [son of] Puḫi-šenni as his inheritance share ... *kuppu*-structures, (together measuring) 60 [+?] cubits [in length] and [?+] 20 cubits in width [and] a(n) (x).x homer field <on?> its border(?)—by the [...?] standard—(located) [to the ... of] the *kuppu*-structures [of] ..., and to the west [of] ... of Ḫišmi-tešup [and of?] the *kuppu*-structures, and to the east of the road [to] the town of Ulamme, in the town of Nuzi in(?) ... .

(16-18) And Teḫip-tilla <gave> to [Waratteya] as his gift 4 homers [of barley] and ... [of] millet.

(19-20) Waratteya shall bear the *ilku* [of the *kuppu*-structures] and of the field.

(21-23) Should the [*kuppu-*]structures [and the field] have claimants, then Waratteya shall clear (the real estate) and give (it) to Teḫip-tilla.

(24-25) Should Waratteya abrogate (this contract), he shall pay 1 mina of silver (and) 1 mina of gold.

(26-40) Before Itḫišta son of Ar-ta<e>; before Urḫiya son of Šekaru; before Utḫap-tae son of Zike; before Ḫanakka son of Šekaru. These are the measurers of the structures and field. Before Zikaya son of Elḫip-šarri;

before Zike son of Šekaru. These are the witnesses and all of them are the distributors of the barley and millet. Before Zetu son of Irîš-abi; before Ḫanaya son of Tae; before Umpiya <son of> Ar-šanta; before Taena son of Erati; before Ippaya son of the same; before Taya son of Apil-sin, the scribe; before Muš-teya son of Bêlaya.

(41-45) seal impression of ... (*seal impression*); (*seal impression*) seal impression of Zikaya; seal impression of Itḫišta (*seal impression*) son of Ar-tae; (*seal impression*) seal impression of Taya, the scribe; (*seal impression*) seal impression of Ḫanakka.

(46-48) At the time that Kušši-ḫarpe exercised the mayoralty [in] Nuzi; and on that day, Teḫip-tilla took the structures(?) and [the field].

(49-50) (*seal impression*) seal impression of Muš-teya; (*seal impression*) seal impression of Urḫiya.

COMMENTS

This tablet has suffered very little deterioration since the copy was made.

The relatively great length of the text has forced the scribe into some atypical practices. Narrative text appears on the left edge. The writing is very cramped; in places, especially parts of ll. 30, 34, it is almost microscopic. (In the latter case, *dú-uḫ-ni* is forced up by the overlapping end of l. 23 from the obverse.) A witness PN and patronymic have belatedly been appended to lines 36 and 37. Finally, one is tempted to consider that two, perhaps three, scribal omissions (ll. 18, 37, 8 [if AŠ has been correctly restored]) may represent purposeful saving of space. (One or two other omissions, ll. 26, 8 [if *iṣ* is correctly restored], are certainly accidental.) However, the unnecessary inclusion of patronymics perhaps argues against this last argument.

On the relationship of this text to *JEN* 715 and other texts, see below, note to *JEN* 715:9.

NOTES

l. 2: [DUMU -*ya*?/-*e*?]. The trace of the last sign survives in line 14.
The *CAD* Nuzi file rendering of line 14 includes the patronymic, *Pu-ḫi-ya*. A note of Lacheman's also reflects this reading. These transliterations may have been made prior to Lacheman's copy when more of the tablet was preserved. The hand copy and the tablet itself fail to preserve the patronymic. See below, notes to ll. 6, 13, 17 for further possible evidence of a fuller text.

l. 4: [*i-te-pu-uš(-ma)*]. Or the like.

l. 6: ⸢60⸣?. The *CAD* Nuzi file reads ⸢70⸣? at this point. See above, note to l. 2.

l. 7:]-*bu*-[. Though the sign fits the context admirably, it may belong to l. 8 rather than l. 7.

l. 8. The end of this line may indicate a northerly or southerly orientation of the ceded real estate relative to the structures noted in l. 9. Cf. the directions given in lines 10 and 12.

l. 8: <AŠ?> *mi-<iṣ?>-ri-*[*š*]*u*. The restorations, though yielding some sense, do so at the cost of awkward Akkadian, awkwardness reflected in the translation.

l. 9: ⸢x x⸣. These two signs may belong to line 8.

l. 13: ⸢x⸣. The *CAD* Nuzi file reads, at this point, *ṣé-ri-ti*, with no indication of a break. See above, note to line 2. The trace can certainly bear this reading.

l. 14: D[UMU -*y*]*a*?/-⸢*e*⸣?. See above, note to l. 2.

l. 17: DIŠ. The *CAD* Nuzi file reads, at this point: *ù* 1 [ANŠE] *dú-uḫ-nu*^{MEŠ}. See above, note to l. 2.

l. 18: <*i-din*>. This reading is also adopted in the *CAD* Nuzi file.

l. 26: <*e*>. The last sign on this line is TA, not E as copied. The tablet is well preserved at this point.

l. 30: LÚ.MEŠ. These signs represent a logographic unit, not a determinative. Cf. *JEN* 46:32, written by the same scribe, where these signs are followed by a phonetic complement. On the special relevance of *JEN* 46 for this text, see below, note to l.37.

l. 34: *ni*. This reading is probable. Owing to the extremely small size of the sign, however, a reading, NU, cannot entirely be ruled out.

ll. 36-37. The marginal "SIC!" and circle indicators in the copy are Lacheman's.

l. 37: <DUMU>. This reading is also adopted by the *CAD* Nuzi file. This restoration is logical. More important, it is supported by the all but certain reading of this individual's name in *JEN* 46:30. This is especially important since all the other witnesses appearing in *JEN* 46 reappear in *JEN* 693. (*JEN* 693 includes two or three additional witnesses as well.) Incidentally, it is peculiar that, given the identity of the witnesses, the order in which they appear is only generally similar.

l. 41: ⸢^{m}⸣[ ]. The *CAD* Nuzi file reads, at this point: "[ ] *ikkaru eqli*."

l. 43: DUMU *Ar-ta-*⸢*e*⸣. The patronymic belongs to Itḫišta (l. 42; cf. l. 26), not to Taya (l. 43, cf. l. 39).

l. 45: ^{m}*Ḫa-*[*na-ak-ka*$_4$]. This restoration (and not ^{m}*Ḫa-*[*na-a-a*] from l. 36) is based on two considerations: the presence of Ḫanakka as sealer in *JEN* 46:39 (for the relevance of that text to this one, see above, note to l.37); and Porada's identification of the seal impression below this line as that of Ḫanakka son of Šekaru.

ll. 46-48. *JEN* 46:23-25 offers a close parallel to this date formula.

l. 48: É!.⸢ḪÁ!? *ù*⸣ [A.ŠÀ *il*]-⸢*te-qè*⸣. The last copied sign is not precisely rendered. The tablet at this point is very damaged. The problematic traces appear as follows:

The interpretation of these traces, unsatisfactory as it is, is my own. One might even reverse the reading to yield: <A>.ŠÀ! ⸢*ù*! É⸣!.[ḪÁ(.MEŠ) *il*]-⸢*te-qè*⸣. The last two traces might represent ⸢*il-qè*⸣ (cf. *JEN* 46:25).

l. 50: *U*[*r-ḫi-y*]*a*. For this restoration, cf. l. 27 and *JEN* 46:27, 39.

JEN 694

OBVERSE

1 [*ṭup-p*]*í* ⸢*ma*⸣-*ru*-[*t*]*i* [*ša* ^{m}*Ḫu-ti*$_4$*-ya* DUMU]
2 [^{m}*T*]*e-ḫi-ip-til-la* +DUMU + *P*[*u-ḫi-še-en-ni*]
3 [*a-na*] *ma-ru-ti i-*+*pu*-[*uš(-ma)*]
4 [?]+ 1 +⸢ANŠE⸣ 2 ^{GIŠ}APIN A.ŠÀ
5 [AŠ] +⸢*e*⸣-+*le-en* AN.ZA.KÀR +*ša* +^{m}[ ]
6 +*i*++*na* KASKAL ⸢*ša*⸣ AN.ZA.KÀR *Ú*-[*lu-li-ya*]
7 ⸢*i-na*⸣ ^{IM}*še-ra-mu*-⸢*uḫ*⸣-[*ḫi*]
8 *i+na* [(x)] *⸢x⸣ A.GÀR URU *Ú-náp-š*[*e-w*]*a* [^{m}*Ḫu-ti*$_4$*-ya*]
9 •*a-na* *^{m}*Te-ḫi-ip-til-la* [*ki-ma* ḪA.LA-+*š*]*u* +*i*-+*din*
10 +⸢*ù*⸣ [ ] +1 [+1?] +⸢GUN⸣ 20 +MA.+NA [ ]
11 ^{m}⸢*Te*⸣-*ḫ*[*i*]-+*ip*-+*til*-+⸢*la*⸣ +*a*-+⸢*na*⸣ +^{m}[*Ḫu-ti*$_4$*-ya ki-ma* NÍG.BA-*šu i-din*]
12 ⸢*il-ku*⸣ *ša* A.ŠÀ $^{m+}$⸢*Ḫu*-+*ti*$_4$-+*ya*⸣ [*na-(a-)ši*]
13 *šum-ma* A.ŠÀ *pa*-+*qí-ra-na* [*i-ra-aš-ši*]
14 $^{m+}$*Ḫu*-+*t*[*i*$_4$]*-ya ú*-⸢*za*-+*ak*!-+*kà*⸣-[*ma*]
15 •*a*-•*na* ^{m}*Te-ḫi-ip-til*-⸢*la i*⸣-[*na-din*]
16 *šum-ma* ^{m}*Ḫu*-+*ti*$_4$*-ya i-ba*[*la*]-*k*[*a-at*]
17 2 MA.NA +KÙ.+SIG$_{17}$ *i-na*-+*din*

\+ ____

18 IGI *Ar-nu-zu* DUMU *Am-ma*-+*ak*-[*ka*$_4$]
19 •IGI *Ar-ti-ir-wi* DUMU *Ḫa*-+*na*-⸢*a-a*⸣
20 IGI *A*-+*ta-na-aḫ*-DINGIR DUMU *Na-a*[*n*]-*t*[*e-šup*]
21 +IGI +*Ḫa*-+*na-a-a* DUMU *Ar*-⸢*te*⸣-+*šup*
22 IGI *A*-+*ta-na-aḫ*-•DINGIR DUMU *Ip-ša*-**ḫa*-**lu*
23 +[I]GI +*Zi*-+⸢*zi*⸣-[*ya* DUMU *Pu*]*r*-+*na-pu*
24 [4+] 2 LÚ.M[EŠ (*an-nu-ti*) *mu-še*-+*e*]*l*-+*wu* + *ša* A.ŠÀ
+25 [IGI] ⸢*It*⸣-[*ḫi-iš-t*]*a* DUMU *A-ar-ta*-[*e*]
+26 [IGI *Ki*]-⸢*in*⸣-[*ki-ya* DU]M[U] *Ši-mi*-⸢*ka*$_4$⸣-*t*[*al*]

.

.

.

LOWER EDGE

27 [IGI DUMU] *Mu-*uš-[ ]

REVERSE

28 IGI *Um-pí-ya* DUMU *Ma-li-ya*

29 IGI MU-*lib*-<*ši*> DUMU *Ta-a-a* •DUB.*SA[R]

30 IGI *Šúk-ri-ya* <DUMU> *Ma-li-ya*

31 IGI ⌈*Ki*⌉-*pa-a-a* DUMU *I-la-ap*-•*ri*

32 IG[I] *Gi*$_5$-*mi-la-dá* DUMU *Zu-me*

33 [IG]I *Ḫa-na-ak-kà* DUMU *Še-kà-rù*

34 ⌈IGI⌉ *It-ḫa-pí-ḫe* DUB.S[A]R DUMU •⌈*Ta*⌉-**a*-**a*

35 IGI *Šúk-ra-pu* DUMU *Še*?-$^{+}$⌈*x-x*⌉-[ ]

36 *an-nu-tu*$_4$ IGI.MEŠ-*t*[*ù*]

S.I.

37 $^{\mathrm{NA_4}}$ KIŠIB ^{m}*It-ḫi-iš-ta* DUMU *A*-[*ar-ta-e*]

S.I.

38 $^{\mathrm{NA_4}}$ KIŠIB ^{m}*Ki-in*-$^{+}$*ki*-$^{+}$*ya*

S.I.

39 $^{\mathrm{[N]A_4}}$ KIŠIB ^{m}[ ]

LEFT EDGE

S.I. S.I.

40 •$^{\mathrm{NA_4}}$ KIŠIB MU-*lib*-<*ši*> DUMU *Ta-a-a* $^{\mathrm{NA_4}}$ •KIŠ[IB $^{\mathrm{(m)+}}$*I*]*t*-$^{+}$⌈*ḫa*-$^{+}$*pí*⌉-[*ḫe*]

TRANSLATION

(1-3) Tablet of adoption [of Ḫutiya son of ...]. He adopted Teḫip-tilla son of Puḫi-šenni.

(4-9) [Ḫutiya] gave to Teḫip-tilla [as] his [inheritance share] a(n) [x?+] 1.2 homer field [to] the east of the *dimtu* of ..., on the road to the *dimtu* of Ulūliya, to the north, in the ... *ugāru* of the town of Unap-še.

(10-11) And Teḫip-tilla [gave] to [Ḫutiya as his gift] ... [1?+] 1 talent (and) 20 minas (i.e., 1⅓ talents, altogether) of ... .

(12) Ḫutiya [shall bear] the *ilku* of the field.

(13-15) Should the field [have] claimants, Ḫutiya shall clear (it) [and] give (it) to Teḫip-tilla.

(16-17) Should Ḫutiya abrogate (this contract), he shall give 2 minas of gold.

(18-36) Before Ar-nuzu son of Ammakka; before Ar-tirwi son of Ḫanaya; before Âtanaḫ-ilu son of Nan-tešup; before Ḫanaya son of Ar-tešup; before Âtanaḫ-ilu son of Ipša-ḫalu; before Zizziya [son of] Purn-apu. [(These)] [4+] 2 men are the measurers of the field. [Before] Itḫišta son of

Ar-tae; [before] Kikkiya son of Šimika-atal; ... [before] ... [son of] Muš-...; before Umpiya son of Maliya; before Šumu-lib<šī> son of Taya, the scribe; before Šukriya <son of> Maliya; before Kipaya son of Ilapri; before Gimill-adad son of Zume; before Ḫanakka son of Šekaru; before Itḫ-apiḫe, the scribe, son of Taya; before Šukr-apu son of Še?-... . These are the witnesses ... .

(37-40) (*seal impression*) seal impression of Itḫišta son of Ar-tae; (*seal impression*) seal impression of Kikkiya; (*seal impression*) seal impression of ...; (*seal impression*) seal impression of Šumu-lib<šī> son of Taya; (*seal impression*) seal impression of Itḫ-apiḫe.

COMMENTS

This tablet was apparently far more legible in the period immediately before the copy was made. See the references to the *CAD* Nuzi file readings below, notes to ll. 18, 24, 26 (first note), 27, 35, 36. Furthermore, Porada's notes indicate that a further sealing and PN may once have been visible on the upper edge.

Since the copy was made, this tablet has suffered further, slight deterioration. However, it is in far better shape than the copy indicates. Collations yielded more partial signs, whole signs, even whole lines than are copied. For the most part, the lines are straight and continuous. They do not change direction (see lines 5 and 6).

NOTES

ll. 6-7. For the description of the real estate in these lines, cf. *JEN* 723:6 and the note to *JEN* 723:1.

l. 6: *Ú-[lu-li-ya]*. This restoration is based on the fact that "Ulūliya" (often written without the masculine determinative) is the most frequently mentioned *dimtu* name starting with Ú and connected to Teḫip-tilla real estate interests in the town of Unap-še (see, e.g., *JEN* 652:25-26; 770:8-9). The only other possibility is the *dimtu* of ^{m}*Ú-k[i?-*] in *JEN* 247:3 (cf. l.7 for the Unap-še connection of that GN). However, this latter *dimtu* name may also be interpreted as ^{m}*Ú-l[u-li-ya]*. At *JEN* 247:3, after *ša* ^{m}*Ú*, appears:

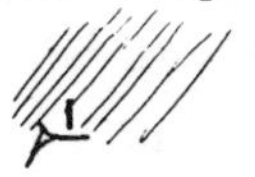

This is more like *l[u]* than Chiera's copy would indicate.

l. 8: *i+na* [(x)] ⌜x⌝ A.GÀR. Since the trace is not visible, it is possible that nothing intervenes between the two preserved words. If a word is effaced, then *[le-e]t* is a plausible reconstruction.

l. 10: MA.NA [ ]. URUDU.MEŠ may well fill the lacuna. See below, note to l. 36.

l. 13: *[i-ra-aš-ši]*. Or the like.

l. 14: *Ḫu*. The shape of this sign is normal and not as copied.

l. 17. After this line, the scribe has drawn a horizontal line. This line does not appear in the copy.

l. 18: *Am-ma-ak-*[*ka_4*]. The *CAD* Nuzi file has: *Am-ma-ak-* . On this basis, *NPN*, 20a *sub* AMMAKKA 2), reads, in effect: -⌜*ka_4*⌝. Cf. also *JEN* 709:26 and the note thereto. This restoration is slightly disquieting since the scribe in this text sometimes employs GA (= *kà*) where QA (= *ka_4*) might be expected (see ll. 14, 33; cf., though, ll. 16, 26).

Besides Ar-nuzu son of Ammakka, there is attested one Ar-nuzu son of Arim-matka (*JEN* 214:28, 34). These two individuals appear in similar contexts and it is tempting to identify them as the same person, i.e., to equate their patronymics, Ammakka and Arim-matka. The former name might evolve from the latter in three steps: the disappearance of the second, short, vowel (if short it is; cf. Arp-iššuḫre [<Arip-iššuḫre] and other examples discussed by Purves, *NPN*, 189) and the progressive assimilation of /r/ to /m/ and of /t/ to /k/. One element in this process, assimilation of /t/ to /k/, is reflected in the Nuzi PN, Arim-makka (see *NPN*, 27b *sub voce*; and *AAN*, 28a *sub voce*). That "Arim-makka" is a variant of "Arim-matka" is demonstrated by Fadhil (1972, 95, text no. 22 (= *IM* 73443):11, 15). Cf. Fadhil (1972, 96, note to l. 15). Thus, the process may be envisaged as follows: Arim-matka > Arim-makka > *Ar(m)-makka > Ammakka.

l. 19: *ti*. The shape of this sign is normal and not as copied.

l. 23: *Zi-*⌜*zi*⌝-[*ya* DUMU *Pu*]*r-na-pu*. The traces here preserved combined with those of *JEN* 723:21 lead to this plausible reconstruction, as it appears in *NPN*, p. 181a, *sub* ZIZZIJA.

l. 24: [4+] 2. The *CAD* Nuzi file reflects a fully preserved "6."

l. 26. After this line, the *CAD* Nuzi file places a line not now visible: [IGI]-*ip*-LUGAL DUMU *Ma-li-ya*. Apparently referring to this line, *NPN*, 95a *sub* MALIJA 13) (and only there), supplies *Ḫa* before *ip*.

l. 26: [*Ki*]-⌜*in*⌝-[*ki-ya*]. This restoration is based on l. 38 combined with the relatively well preserved patronymic of this line. The individual defined by these names appears elsewhere as a witness in the Teḫip-tilla corpus. Cf. *NPN*, 84b *sub* KIKKIJA 2), where the same reading is adopted.

l. 27: *Mu-uš-*[ ]. The *CAD* Nuzi file reads: *Mu-uš-te-ya*.

l. 29: MU-*lib-*<*ši*>. The apparently defective writing of the scribe's name here and in l. 40 would suggest that, of the two scribes mentioned in this text, Šumu-libšī and Itḫ-apiḫe (ll. 34, 40) sons of Taya, Itḫ-apiḫe actually wrote the document. However, the alternative proposition, that this writing of his name was Šumu-libšī's own, in the manner of an abbreviated autograph, may not, *a priori*, entirely be ruled out.

l. 30. This line is correct as copied. Restored <DUMU> results in a well attested individual. See *NPN*, 136b, 24).

l. 35: *Še*?-$^{+}$⌜x-x⌝-[ ]. The *CAD* Nuzi file reads: *Pu-i-ta-e*. The traces can bear this interpretation, i.e., *P*[*u*]-⌜*i*⌝-*t*[*a-e*]. (What is copied as a PA sign actually appears as:  .) However, this individual is nowhere else attested in the Nuzi texts.

l. 36. The *CAD* Nuzi file reads the latter part of this line as follows: IGI.MEŠ-*tù ga*$_{14}$-*ba-šu-nu-ma* URUDU.MEŠ [*i-di-nu*]. If this reading is correct, the writing must have been very cramped.

l. 40: MU-*lib*-<*ši*>. See above, note to l. 29.

JEN 695

OBVERSE

$^{+}$1 *ṭup-pí m*[*a-ru-ti ša* ^{m}*Aḫ-wa-qar* DUMU *A?-pil?-* *ù*]

2 *ša* $^{m+}$⌜X⌝-[-AḪ?-]

3 DUMU [^{m}*Te-ḫi-ip-til-la* DUMU *Pu-ḫi-še-e*]*n-ni*

4 •⌜*ù*⌝? [*a-na ma-ru-ti i-te-ep-šu-šu-ma*]

.

.

.

5 [-*m*]*a*?

.

.

.

6 $^{+m+}$*Aḫ-wa-qar ù* $^{m+}$⌜X⌝-[ ]-A[Ḫ?-]

7 [*ú*]-*za-ak-ku-ma a-na* ⌜^{m}⌝[*Te-ḫi*]-*i*[*p-til-la*]

8 [SU]M-*nu ma-an-nu* [*ša i-na bi*$_{4}$-*ri-šu-nu* KI.BAL] ⌜*ya*⌝

9 [2] MA.NA KÙ.SI[G$_{17}$ (?) *ú-ma-al*]-*la*!

LOWER EDGE

10 [I]GI *Ú-zi-ya* D[UMU *Pu-ḫi-ya*]

11 $^{+}$⌜IGI⌝ *Pí-ru* DUMU *N*[*a-iš-ké-el-*]
:[*pè*]

REVERSE

12 [IGI] *Še-ka*$_{4}$-*ru* DUMU *Ḫu*-⌜*ti*⌝-[*ya*]

13 [IGI] *It-ḫi-iš-ta* DUMU *Ar-t*[*a-e*]

14 [IGI *K*]*é-el-te-šup* DUMU *A-ri-ip-š*[*e-*]
:*el*-⌜*li*⌝

15 IGI ⌜ŠU-^{d}⌝IM DUMU *Zu-me*

16 IGI *Tar-mi-ya* [DU]MU *Eḫ-li-te-šup*

17 IGI DUMU-^{d}X DU[MU *Ku-uz-za*]-*ri-ya*

18 IGI *Ḫa-ma-a*[*n-na* DUMU] **A*-[ ]-⸢x⸣-RI
19 IGI *Ta*-[*a*]-*a* [DUMU *A-pil*]-XXX DUB.*S[A]R

S.I. Po 56

20 ^{NA_4} KIŠIB ⸢m⸣*Aḫ-wa-qar* DUMU *A-pil*-[ ]

S.I.

21 ^{NA_4} ⸢KIŠIB⸣ ^{m}⸢*Ú-zi-ya*⸣

S.I.

22 $^{[N]A_4}$ KIŠIB ^{m}*Ta-a-a*
23 DUB.SAR

LEFT EDGE

S.I. Po 114

24 ^{NA_4} KIŠIB ^{m}*Še-ka$_4$-ru* DUMU *Ḫu-ti-y*[*a*]

TRANSLATION

(1-4) Tablet of adoption [of Aḫu-waqar son of Apil?-... and] of X...AḪ(?) ... son of .... Now(?) [they adopted Teḫip-tilla son of] Puḫi-šenni.

(5) ....

(6-8) .... Aḫu-waqar and X...AḪ(?)... shall clear (it) and give (it) to Teḫip-tilla.

(8-9) Whichever [amongst them abrogates] (this contract) shall pay [2] minas of gold [(?)].

(10-19) Before Uziya son of [Puḫiya]; before Piru son of Naiš-kelpe; [before] Šekaru son of Ḫutiya; [before] Itḫišta son of Ar-tae; [before] Kel-tešup son of Arip-šelli; before Gimill-adad son of Zume; before Tarmiya son of Eḫli-tešup; before Mâr-ištar son of Kuzzariya; before Ḫamanna [son of] A...RI; before Taya [son of] Apil-sin, the scribe.

(20-24) (*seal impression*) seal impression of Aḫu-waqar son of Apil-...; (*seal impression*) seal impression of Uziya; (*seal impression*) seal impression of Taya, the scribe; (*seal impression*) seal impression of Šekaru son of Ḫutiya.

COMMENTS

This tablet has suffered minimal deterioration since the time it was copied.

Lacheman estimates some ten lines to be missing between lines 4 and 6.

The four signs near the ends of lines 6-9 are assigned to those lines with trepidation.

NOTES

l. 1: [*A?-pil?-*]. The partial restoration of the patronymic is based on line 20. It is possible, however, that the latter Aḫu-waqar is a mere witness and not the principal party mentioned in line 6 and restored here.

l. 2: ⸢X⸣. The trace appears as:  . See also below, note to l. 6.

l. 3: [^{m}*Te-ḫi-ip-til-la* DUMU *Pu-ḫi-še-e*]*n-ni*. This reconstruction is strong but not quite certain since evidence of the findspot of this tablet is lacking. The major strength of the reconstruction are the strong Teḫip-tilla connections of the scribe and most of the witnesses whose names are preserved. The surviving traces at the end of line 3 are consistent with this interpretation, not only in shape, but in their location on the tablet. They are on the reverse of what must have been, in any case, a very long line. It should be noted, though, that these traces might not belong to this line. See also below, note to line 7.

l. 4: ⸢*ù*⸣?. This reading follows a suggestion by Lacheman. The copy appears to record KI. The remaining trace is: . Ù is possible but not expected in the restored context.

l. 4: [*i-te-ep-šu-šu-ma*]. Or the like.

l. 6: ⸢X⸣. The sign is not as copied. It appears as:  . The traces should represent part of the same sign as is preserved in traces in l. 2. I cannot restore any single sign from these two sets of traces.

l. 7: [*Te-ḫi*]-*i*[*p-til-la*]. The restorations may indirectly be supported by a rendering of this line by Lacheman. He reads the end of this line as [*Te-ḫi-ip-t*]*il-la*.

l. 8: ⸢*ya*⸣. The assignment of this sign to this line as here restored yields no sense. Yet I can see no preferable alternative.

l. 9: [(?)]. The spacing of the preserved signs would definitely allow for more signs in the lacuna.

l. 9: *la*!. The sign appears, not as copied, but as: 

l. 10: [*Pu-ḫi-ya*]. The reconstruction is based on this Uziya's frequent appearance elsewhere as a witness for Teḫip-tilla. See *NPN*, 169a, *sub* UZIḚA 3). It is recognized that the force of this argument is diminished to the extent that Teḫip-tilla's presence in this text is not certain. See also below, note to l. 17.

l. 11: *N*[*a-iš-ké-el*] / / :-[*pè*]. Whether one or more signs were separated from l. 11 is uncertain.

l. 17: [*Ku-uz-za*]-*ri-ya*. The reconstruction is based on this Mâr-ištar's frequent appearance elsewhere as a witness for Teḫip-tilla. See *NPN*, 95b *sub* MÂR-IŠTAR 3). See also above, note to l. 10, regarding the implication of this argument in the present context.

l. 19: [*A-pil*]-XXX. The spelling of this PN may not be precisely as reconstructed but the name itself is certain.

l. 23. Before DUB, two wedges appear in the copy. This actually represents a partial recopying of the end of l. 3 from the obverse.

JEN 696

OBVERSE

1 *li-ša-an-šu*
2 *ša* ^{m}⸢*It-ḫi*⸣-*iš*!-*ta*
3 DUMU *A-ar-ta-e*
4 AŠ *pa-ni ši-bu-ti*
5 *an-nu-ti ki-na-*[*a*]*n-*⸢*na*⸣
6 *iq-ta-bi* [(?)]
7 NÍG.BA ⸢x⸣ [ ] ⸢x⸣ MEŠ
8 [^{m}*I*]*t-ḫ*[*i-iš-ta*]
9 [ ] ⸢x⸣
10 [ ] ⸢x⸣
11 [ ] ⸢x⸣
12 [ ] ⸢x⸣

LOWER EDGE

13 [ ] $^{+}$⸢x $^{+}$x⸣ MEŠ [ ]

REVERSE

14 [ ] ⸢x⸣
15 QA-*aš*-[ ]
16 [IGI -*t*]*i-ya* DUMU *A*-[ ]-*a*
17 [IGI *Ik-k*]*i-ya*•DUMU ^{d}IM-*še-m*[*i*]
18 [IGI DUMU] *Ka*$_{4}$-*a-a*
19 [IGI DUMU *Ar-š*]*a-tù-y*[*a*]
20 [IGI *Ta-a-a* DUMU *A-pil*-XXX DUB.SAR]-*rù*

.
.
.

21 •⸢^{NA_4} •KIŠIB •^{m}⸣•*Ta-a-a* •D[U]B.$^{+}$SAR

.
.
.

22 •⸢DUMU *Ar-ta*⸣-*e*

UPPER EDGE

S.I.

23 ^{NA_4} KIŠIB ^{m}*Ik-ki-ya* $^{+}$SIMUG

LEFT EDGE

24 [NA$_{4}$ ^{m}]-*ak-ka*$_{4}$

TRANSLATION

(1-6) Declaration of Itḫišta son of Ar-tae before these witnesses; he spoke as follows:

(7-15) "... gift ... Itḫišta .... ."

(16-20) [Before] ...-tiya son of A-...-a; [before] Ikkiya son of Adad-šēmī; [before ... son of] Kaya; [before ... son of] Ar-šatuya; [before Taya son of Apil-sin], the scribe .... .

(21-24) [....?] seal impression of Taya, the scribe; .... son of Ar-tae; (*seal impression*) seal impression of Ikkiya, the smith; .... [seal impression of] ...-akka.

COMMENTS

Except for line 21, this tablet has suffered virtually no deterioration since the copy was made.

The combination of a text beginning "*lišānšu*" (l. 1) and the statement itself being made before witnesses (l. 4; rather than before officials) is relatively rare. See, e.g., *JEN* 123, 186, 189. The form is not usually used for declarations involving real estate.

NOTES

l. 6. See below, note to l. 7: ⸢x⸣ MEŠ.

l. 7: NÍG.BA ⸢x⸣. The *CAD* Nuzi file (tentatively) and Lacheman (absolutely) read 4 *ma-t*[*i*].

l. 7: ⸢x⸣ MEŠ. Lacheman reads [x ANŠE Š]E.MEŠ and assigns these signs to the end of line 6.

l. 8: [^{m}*I*]*t-ḫ*[*i-iš-ta*]. The *CAD* Nuzi file and Lacheman read $^{[m]}$⸢*Te*⸣-*ḫi*-[*ip-til-la*]. The former sign more closely resembles IT than TE.

Nevertheless, it seems likely that this text does involve Teḫip-tilla son of Puḫi-šenni. The name of one of his witnesses appears here (l. 17) as well as that of one of his most frequently used scribes (l. 21). The principal himself, Itḫišta son of Ar-tae, is elsewhere a ubiquitous witness for Teḫip-tilla. He witnesses for Teḫip-tilla's son Enna-mati as well.

l. 12. Below the tail of the horizontal (i.e., all that remains of this line), the copy has a wedge. The tablet is clear at this point and the wedge is not there.

l. 13: ⸢x x⸣. These traces are not as copied. They appear as:

Lacheman reads, at this point, ANŠE ŠE and elsewhere, ANŠE ŠE.MEŠ.

l. 17: [*Ik-k*]*i-ya*. This restoration results from the almost entirely preserved patronymic. This PN as patronymic is attested for only three individuals. See *NPN*, 39b *sub* ADAD-ŠĒMĪ; and *AAN*, 37a *sub* ADAD-ŠĒMĪ. Ikkiya

is the likeliest candidate since the traces toward the start fit his name and, of the three, his name only. If the restoration is correct, cf. l. 23.

l. 18: *Ka$_{4}$-a-a*. [ ]-*ka$_{4}$-a-a* is equally possible.

l. 20. This line is restored essentially following a suggestion of Lacheman. The position of the scribe as last of the witnesses is common in declaration texts such as this. See, e.g., *JEN* 123:25; 186:20.

l. 23: SIMUG. This sign is typical and not as copied.

l. 24. Porada's notes indicate that, in recent times, a seal impression appeared above this line.

l. 24: [ ]-*ak-ka$_{4}$*. Lacheman renders this name as [*Ḫa-na-ak-ka$_{4}$*].

JEN 697

OBVERSE

1 [*i*]*t-*˹*ti*˺ [^{m}*It-ḫa-a-pu ù*]
2 •^{m}•*Ḫa-lu-še-en-n*[*i* DUMU.MEŠ]
3 A.ŠÀ.MEŠ *uš-te-pè-*[*i-lu*]
4 ^{m}*It-ḫa-a-pu* ˹*ù*˺ [^{m}*Ḫa-lu-še-en-ni* A.ŠÀ]
5 *i+na e-le-en* *AN.*ZA.[KÀR]
6 *a-na* ^{m}*Te-ḫi-ip-til-l*[*a it-ta-ad-nu*]
7 *ù* ^{m}*Te-ḫi-ip-til-*˹*la*˺ *i*[*p-le-ti-šu-nu*]
8 *ša* ^{m}*It-ḫa-a-pu ù š*[*a* ^{m}*Ḫa-lu-še-en-ni*]
9 *i+na* AN.ZA.KÀR *A-ni-i-ta u*[*n-te-el-l*]*i-*˹*ma it*˺*-ta-din*
10 *ša ma-an-ni-im-me-e* A.ŠÀ-**š*[*u*]
11 *pa-qí-ra-na i-ra-aš-ši* ⁺˹*ù ú*˺*-za-ak-*<*ka$_{4}$*>
12 *ù* ^{m}*Te-ḫi-ip-til-la* 4 ANŠE ŠE.MEŠ
13 *a-na* Ú-*ti a-na* ^{m}*It-ḫa-a-pu ù* ^{m}*Ḫa-lu-še-en-ni* SUM
14 *ma-an-nu ša* KI.BAL-*tu* 10 MA.NA KÙ.[SI]G$_{17}$ ˹*ú*˺*-ma-al-la*
15 IGI *Ḫ*[*a*]-⁺*ši-ú-ki* DUMU *Na-al-*[*t*]*ù-*[*ya*]
16 IGI *Še-er-pa-taš-ši* DUMU *Ku-ri-*˹*iš*˺*-*[*ni*]
17 IGI *Šur-*•*kip*-LUGAL ˹DUMU *A-ta*˺*-a-*˹*a*˺
18 [I]GI *Kip-ta-e* DUMU [*E*]*n-na-ma-*•*ti*
19 IGI *Te-ḫi-ip-a-pu* ˹DUMU˺ *Eḫ-li-t*[*e-šup*]

LOWER EDGE

20 IGI *Pí-ru* DUMU *Na-iš-ké-el-*⁺*pè*
21 IGI *Ḫa-ma-an-na* DUMU DUMU-*eš$_{15}$-ri*

REVERSE

22 IGI *Nu-i-*<*še*>*-ri* DUMU *Ka$_{4}$-lu-mi*
23 IGI ŠU-^{d}IM DUMU *Zu-me*
24 IGI *Ta-a-a* DUMU *A-pil*-XXX D[UB.SAR]
25 IGI ˹*Ḫa*˺*-ši-ip-a-pu* DUMU *A*[*r-te-ya*]

26 IGI Z[*i*?-⁺*l*]*i*?-*ip-til-*˺*la* ˹DUMU ˹*E*[*n*-]

S.I.

27 ^{NA_4} KIŠIB ^{m}*Ḫa-ši-ú-ki* DUMU *Na-al-tù-ya*

S.I.

28 ^{NA_4} KIŠIB ^{m}*Še-er-pa-taš-ši*

S.I.

29 ^{NA_4} KIŠIB ^{m}Š[U!?-$^{d?}$IM?]

.

.

.

LEFT EDGE

S.I.

30 ^{NA_4} KIŠIB ^{m}*Ta-a-a* DUB.SAR

TRANSLATION

....

(1-3) (together) with [Itḫ-apu and] Ḫalu-šenni [sons of ...] exchanged fields.

(4-6) Itḫ-apu and [Ḫalu-šenni gave] to Teḫip-tilla a ... [field] to the east of the *dimtu* [(of) ...].

(7-9) And Teḫip-tilla gave in full an equivalent (i.e., a field) for Itḫ-apu and for [Ḫalu-šenni] in the *dimtu* of Anita.

(10-11) Whose field has claimants shall clear (the field).

(12-13) And Teḫip-tilla gave to Itḫ-apu and Ḫalu-šenni as excess payment 4 homers of barley.

(14) Whoever abrogates (this contract) shall pay 10 minas of gold.

(15-26) Before Ḫašiuki son of Naltuya; before Šerpa-tašši son of Kurišni; before Šurkip-šarri son of Ataya; before Kip-tae son of Enna-mati; before Teḫip-apu son of Eḫli-tešup; before Piru son of Naiš-kelpe; before Ḫamanna son of Mâr-ešrī; before Nui-<še>ri son of Kalūmu; before Gimill-adad son of Zume; before Taya son of Apil-sin, the scribe; before Ḫašip-apu son of Ar-teya; before Zilip(?)-tilla son of En-... .

(27-30) (*seal impression*) seal impression of Ḫašiuki son of Naltuya; (*seal impression*) seal impression of Šerpa-tašši; (*seal impression*) seal impression of Gimill-adad(?); ....; (*seal impression*) seal impression of Taya, the scribe.

COMMENTS

This tablet has deteriorated only slightly since the copy was made.

The obverse is missing its first two lines:

ṭup-pí šu-pè-ul-ti ša

^{m}*Te-ḫi-ip-Til-la* DUMU *Pu-ḫi-še-en-ni*

NOTES

l. 1: *[i]t-⸢ti⸣* [ᵐ*It*]. The *CAD* Nuzi file records the first three signs as entirely preserved. Furthermore, Lacheman sees the fourth sign in part.

Beginning within the "wings" of the *Winkelhaken* representing the first part of TI, there appears the start of a horizontal wedge. This is not depicted in the copy of this tablet.

l. 5: AN.ZA.[KÀR]. The *dimtu* of Teḫip-tilla may be the missing toponym here. Cf. *JEN* 223:6; 238:6-7. For the relevance of *JEN* 223 and 238 to this text, see below, note to l. 25.

l. 6: *[it-ta-ad-nu]*. Or the like.

l. 7: *i[p-le-ti-šu-nu]*. Cf., e.g., *JEN* 223:8; 238:8; 254:12. This restoration is also adopted by Weeks (1972, 249).

The surviving trace, the foot of a vertical wedge, does not appear in the copy.

l. 8: *š[a]*. The beginning of this sign is represented by three stacked horizontal wedges, not two as depicted.

l. 9: AN.ZA.KÀR *A-ni-i-ta*. The *dimtu* of Anita is the same as the *dimtu* of Anitail. A comparison of the contexts and parties of *JEN* 60 (the *dimtu* of Anitail is mentioned in l. 7), 383, and 486 (the *dimtu* of Anita is mentioned in l. 6) demonstrates this equation.

Furthermore, *JEN* 486 links the *dimtu* of Anita with the *dimtu* of Teḫip-tilla (ll. 10-11). *JEN* 263 links the *dimtu* of Anitani (l. 8) with the Zizza *dimtu* of Teḫip-tilla (ll. 3, 5; one other *dimtu* [at least] of Teḫip-tilla is located in the town of Turša [Maidman 1976, 182-83]). In other words, the *dimtu* of Anitani = the *dimtu* of Anita = the *dimtu* of Anitail. See already Oppenheim (1938, 139-40). This *dimtu* is located in Zizza.

Regarding the linguistic composition of this toponym, Purves (*NPN*, 219b *sub* -il) assumes an underlying form "Anita." He considers the "-il" of Anitail the proto-Hattic gentilic ending. He further notes (*NPN*, 200b *sub* anita) the resemblance of this name to Anitta, Prince of Kuššara. A proto-Hattic suffix would, then, be appropriate to this name. As for the "-ni" of Anitani, Purves (*NPN*, 238b *sub* -ni) suggests identity with the Hurrian formative *-ni*.

Why a single toponym should assume three such distinct linguistic forms within a single corpus of material remains unexplained.

l. 9: *u[n-te-el-l]i-⸢ma⸣*. This reconstruction is based on the same formulation by the same scribe in *JEN* 238:10-11. For the particular relevance of that text to this one, see below, note to line 25. I am indebted to Professor Stephen Andrews for pointing out this and other parallels to the present passage and for this reconstruction.

l. 10: *ša*. The two horizontal "tails" preceding this sign in the copy are not present on the tablet.

l. 13: Ú-*ti*. This term signifies a price, in mobilia, paid by one of the exchanging parties, over and above the real estate ceded. See, for example, *JEN* 254:17. It is either a balance payment where the two properties are not of equal value (Gadd 1926, 118; Chiera 1938, 185) or an added inducement in the form of an excess payment for the receiving party to part with his property (so, essentially, H. Lewy 1942, 314). Most likely, the term includes both ideas (so Gordon 1936, 132, n. 1; Gordon 1938, 54; Steele 1943, 31, 51-53; Hayden 1962, 106; Young 1973, 229).

Despite relative clarity regarding the significance of the term, the word itself remains something of a mystery. The writing, Ú-*ti* (and variants, e.g., Ú-*ti*$_4$-*i* [*JEN* 239:16], Ú-*te-e* [*JEN* 810:39]), is most common. Less often, Ú-*ta* appears (see, e.g., *JEN* 247:8).

The signs have been rendered *šam-ti* (Gadd 1926, 118; Gordon 1936, 132 ["gratuity"]), *ú-ti* (Koschaker 1928, 54, n. 3; Koschaker 1936, col. 152 [a Hurrian word]; H. Lewy 1949, 3-4, n. 13 [*ú-ti* = *idu* as "side, remuneration for labor"]), and Ú (Young 1973, 229 [Ú as a Sumerogram, noting *CAD*, Z, 45b *sub zāninu*, lexical section; *-ti* is left unexplained]).

Now the term *utari* occasionally appears where Ú-*ti* is expected. See, for example, *JEN* 224:18. Oppenheim (1939-41, 76) already suggested that the two terms are synonymous. (Cassin's equation of *utena* with Ú-*ti* and *utaru* [1938, 266] is untenable: cf. Gordon [1938, 54], Goetze [1940, 169], and Oppenheim, [1939-41, 76].)

The attempts of Koschaker (1936, 152) and Steele (1943, 31) to see Hurrian *-ar*, "to give," in *utari*, are farfetched and, perhaps, unnecessary. Goetze's suggestion, *apud* Steele (1943, 31, n. 93), that *utari* derives from Akkadian *atāru* is far more attractive.

For it may be that Ú-*ti*, in light of the parallel *utari*, may represent Akkadian *atartu*, "excess, balance" (*CAD* A/2, 485b-486a). If *-ti/a* represents a phonetic complement (cf. Cross 1937, 30, n. 50), then may Ú be a local Nuzi graphic variant of, or development from, DIR (= *atartu*)? For DIR = *atartu*, see *CAD*, A/2, 485b-486a. The semantic ranges of *atartu* and Ú-*ti* are close. Cf. also *CAD*, A/2, 501b-502b *sub atru*.

l. 14: KÙ.[SI]G$_{17}$. For the restoration of this word, cf. *JEN* 223:16; 238:17. For the relevance of *JEN* 223 and 238 to this text, see below, note to l. 25. The *CAD* Nuzi file in effect reads, at this point, KÙ.SIG$_{17}$.

l. 16: ⸢*iš*⸣. The end of this sign is represented by the feet of the two vertical wedges. These traces are not depicted in the copy.

l. 19. This is the last line of the obverse, not the first line of the lower edge as copied.

l. 22. This line is correct as copied.

l. 25: *A*[*r-te-ya*]. The restoration of this patronymic is based on the appearance of the person so defined in *JEN* 238:18. *JEN* 223, 238, and 697 are relevant to each other since they share significant features. These include a common text genre, a common geographical horizon, and the involve-

ment of Teḫip-tilla son of Puḫi-šenni. Most striking, however, is the appearance of a largely common body of witnesses in roughly the same order. Of the twelve witnesses of *JEN* 697, six appear in both of the other texts while another four (not including the Ḫašip-apu here discussed) appear in one or another of them. (In fact, only two witnesses in all these three texts appear only once: See *JEN* 223:21 and 697:26.) Therefore, the restoration of the patronymic here from *JEN* 238:18 is reasonable. The same individual appears as a witness in another Teḫip-tilla text, *JEN* 447 (ll. 6, 17). Finally, Lacheman, in effect, also restores *A*[*r-te-ya*].

l. 26: *Z*[*i*?-*l*]*i*?. The restoration of the first sign is based on Lacheman's: *Z*[*i*]. The traces of the second sign are not as copied, but as:

l. 27. Lacheman's notes identify the seal in‚pression above this line as Po 37.

l. 28. Lacheman's notes identify the seal impression above this line as Po 587.

l. 28: *er*. The sign is typical, not as copied.

l. 29. Based on the analogous sections of *JEN* 223 and 238, there may well be below this line a gap consisting of a seal impression and identifying legend. Again, based on those texts (specifically, *JEN* 223:29; 238:28), the sealer may have been one of the two co-contractors with Teḫip-tilla. However, the upper edge is entirely destroyed; it cannot be determined if any additional sealing and legend were once present.

Lacheman's notes identify the seal impression above line 29 as Po 460.

l. 30. Lacheman's notes identify the seal impression above this line as Po 374.

JEN 698

OBVERSE

1 ⸢ṭup-pí⸣ ma-r[u-ti ša]
2 ^{m}Pu-un-*⸢ni⸣-[ya DUMU]
3 •⸢ù⸣ ^{m}Te-ḫi-⸢ip⸣-[til-la DUMU Pu-ḫi-še-eṇ-ni]
4 [a-n]a [m]a-⸢ru⸣-t[i i-pu-uš(-ma)]
5 [ ]⸢x⸣[ ]⸢x? i-na el-le⸣-et ⸢A⸣?.[ŠÀ?]
6 [ša AN.ZA.KÀR ša Ú-•k]i-•in-⸢za-aḫ⸣
7 [ ]⸢x x⸣ $^{+}$AN.$^{+}$ZA.$^{+}$KÀR ⸢ša Ú⸣-ki-in-za-⸢aḫ⸣-•ma
8 [ ]⸢x⸣ x šu? •x ⸢x⸣ [ ]u[š?]
9 [i-na] ⸢le-et⸣ a-ta-ap-[pí]•AN[ ]
10 ⸢^{m}Pu⸣-un-ni-ya ki-ma
11 ḪA.⸢LA⸣-šú ⸢a-•na⸣ ^{m}Te!-ḫi-ip-[til-la id-din]
12 [ù] ^{m}[Te-ḫi]-ip-•til-la 10 ⸢ANŠE⸣ [ŠE?].M[EŠ?]
13 [k]i-m[a N]ÍG.BA-šú a-na ^{m}Pu-[un]-⸢ni-$^{+}$ya⸣ [id-din]

14 [(?)]⸢il?-*ka$_4$?-ma⸣? ša A.ŠÀ a[n-ni]-⸢i⸣
15 [^{m}]Pu-[un]-⸢ni-ya⸣ [na-(a-)ši]
16 šum-ma A.ŠÀ ⸢pá-qí⸣-r[a-na i-r]a-aš-ši
17 ^{m}Pu-un-ni-ya ú-za-[ak-ka$_4$(-ma)]
18 a-na ^{m}Te-ḫi-•ip-til-la [i-na-an-din]

LOWER EDGE

19 ma-an-nu •ša BAL-tu$_4$
20 1 MA.NA KÙ.BABBAR 1 MA.NA KÙ.S[IG$_{17}$]
21 ú-ma-al-la-a

REVERSE

22 IGI ⸢A⸣-ri-ik-ké-e-a
23 DUMU Š[i]-il-wa-a-a
24 •IGI ⸢X⸣[ ]⸢X X⸣ DUMU E-$^{+}$ké!?-[ké?]
25 ⸢IGI Še-eḫ⸣-[l]i-ya DUMU IZI-⸢$^{d+}$x⸣
26 I[GI] ^{d}XXX-•⸢i-qí⸣-ša DUB.SAR
27 ⸢4⸣? ^{LÚ}IG[I.MEŠ]-tu$_4$ ù A.ŠÀ.M[EŠ?]
28 ú-še-el-w[u]-ú ù KÙ.BABBAR.MEŠ šu-nu-m[a S]UM-nu
29 IGI Ak-ku-te-[ ] DUMU Ḫa-ši-y[a]
30 IGI A-kip-LU[GAL? DU]MU Ak-ku-⸢te⸣-šu[p]
31 IGI Ar-ša-at-na DUMU Ša-am-⸢pí-ya⸣
32 IGI Ki-in-ni-ya DUMU Ta-ú-uḫ-[ḫe]
33 IGI Ú-kùr-L[U]GAL DUMU A-ri-ya
34 I[G]I ⸢Ni-x-x⸣ [DUM]U E-ké-ké

S.I.

35 NA$_4$ ^{m}[ ]

S.I.

36 [N]A$_4$ ^{m}A-ri-i[k-$^{+}$k]é-$^{+}$e-$^{+}$⸢a⸣

S.I.

37 NA$_4$ ^{m}Ḫu-pí-ta

.
.
.

38 [ ] AK [ ]

LEFT EDGE

39 [i-na $^{(GIŠ)}$]•⸢ta⸣-a-a-ri! ša ⸢É⸣.$^{+}$G[AL] •ša pí-<i?> ṭ[up?]-⸢pí⸣?[(?)]

TRANSLATION

(1-4) Tablet of adoption [of] Punniya [son of ...]. He adopted Teḫip-tilla [son of Puḫi-šenni].

(5-11) Punniya [gave] to Teḫip-tilla as his inheritance share ... to the east(??) of the field(?) [of ...? the *dimtu* of] Ukin-zaḫ, ... the *dimtu* of Ukin-zaḫ as well. ... adjacent to the ...-AN-...(?) Canal.

(12-13) And Teḫip-tilla [gave] to Punniya as his gift 10 homers of [barley?].

(14-15) And(?) Punniya [shall bear] the *ilku* of this field.

(16-18) Should the field have claimants, Punniya shall clear (it and) [give] (it) to Teḫip-tilla.

(19-21) He who abrogates (this contract) shall pay 1 mina of silver (and) 1 mina of gold.

(22-34) Before Arik-keya son of Šilwaya; before ... son of Ekeke(?); before Šeḫliya son of Nûr-^{d}...; before Sin-iqîša, the scribe. (Regarding these) 4(?) witnesses, they measured the field[s?] and, as well, they gave the silver. Before Akku-te-... son of Ḫašiya; before Akip-šarri(?) son of Akku-tešup; before Ar-šanta son of Šampiya; before Kinniya son of Tauḫḫe; before Ukur-šarri son of Ariya; before Ni-... son of Ekeke.

(35-38) (*seal impression*) seal impression of ...; (*seal impression*) seal impression of Arik-keya; (*seal impression*) seal impression of Ḫupita; ..... .

(39) [By] the palace standard, as per(?) (the) ... tablet(?).

COMMENT

This tablet has suffered some deterioration since the copy was made.

NOTES

l. 3: [*Pu-ḫi-še-en-ni*]. This restoration and, therefore, the identity of the adoptee, is assured by the archaeological context in which the tablet was found: room 15 or 16, the archive rooms of the family of Teḫip-tilla son of Puḫi-šenni.

l. 4: [*i-pu-uš(-ma)*]. Or the like.

l. 5: ⸢*el-le*⸣*-et*. This word also appears in *JEN* 420:6; 426:5; and *LG* 2:8. Its precise meaning is unknown although it should represent some sort of direction. It bears a resemblance to *elēnu*, "east" in the Nuzi texts. If the former is a variant of the latter, compare ^{IM}*su-ti-it* (*JEN* 467:11) with the standard *sūtānu*, "south" in the Nuzi texts. *AHw*, 203b *sub ellet, elliat*, links *ellet* with *lētu*, an interpretation apparently shared by Lacheman (1967, 8) who translates the term, "*à côté de.*"

l. 6: [AN.ZA.KÀR]. This reading (as opposed, say, to A.ŠÀ) is assured by the "*-ma*" following AN.ZA.KÀR ⸢*ša Ú*⸣*-ki-in-za-*⸢*aḫ*⸣ in the next line.

l. 7: AN.ZA.KÀR ⸢*ša Ú*⸣*-ki-in-za-*⸢*aḫ*⸣*-ma*. The signs directly below [*k*]*i-in* of line 6 are clearly AN.ZA.KÀR and not as copied.

The *dimtu* of Ukin-zaḫ is to be located in the vicinity of Malašu Stream (*JEN* 841:10, 5). This watercourse, in turn, is located within the boundaries of the town of Unap-še (*JEN* 63:5-7).

l. 8: *šu*? x ⸢x⸣. These signs might be rendered *Ma*!-*la*!-*š*[*u*]. (For the relevance of this toponym to this text, see above, note to line 7.) However, the signs immediately preceding these three signs would still remain obscure, not readily suggesting *a-aḫ*$_4$ (*JEN* 589:9) or *ḫar-ri* (e.g., *JEN* 98:6) or *le-et* (*JEN* 214:8) or *na-aḫ-li* (e.g., *JEN* 399:6) or *ša-pa-at* (e.g., *JEN* 63:6).

l. 11: *Te*!. The sign is a clear ŠE, as copied.

l. 12: [*ù*] ^{m}[*Te-ḫi*]. Lacheman once saw all four of these signs as preserved.

l. 13: ⸢*ya*⸣. The wedges after ⸢NI⸣ form a clearer ⸢YA⸣ than depicted.

l. 13: [*id-din*]. Or the like. Lacheman once saw, at this point, "⸢*iddin*⸣."

l. 14: ⸢*il*?-*ka*$_4$?-*ma*⸣?. The first trace may be nothing more than pitting in the tablet and the second trace is now totally effaced. The third unit has traces of three horizontal wedges. Yet Lacheman sees the start of this line as *ù* ⸢*il-ka*$_4$⸣. Ll. 14-15 certainly must contain the *ilku* clause.

l. 15: *Pu*. The sign is typical and not as copied.

l. 17: *ya*. The sign is typical and not as copied.

l. 18: [*i-na-an-din*]. Or the like.

l. 21: *al*. The sign is typical and not as copied.

l. 24: ⸢X⸣[ ]⸢X X⸣. But for the overly large gap between the first two signs, the traces could represent *Ḫ*[*u-pí*]-⸢*ta*⸣. Cf. line 37.

l. 24: *ké*!?-[*ké*?]. The sign appears as:  , i.e., as MUD.

If GI is to be read, then [*ké*] should be restored as the next, and last, sign. No other Nuzi PN known to me begins: *E-ké-*... .

l. 25: IZI-⸢^{d}x⸣. For this name type and writing at Nuzi, see *NPN*, p. 108b. The last sign is not as copied. Rather, it appears as:

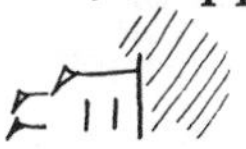

This name may also be *Pil-l*[*a*]-*r*[*a*]. See *P-S* 21:28. That text, like this one, was written by one Sin-iqîša.

l. 29: *Ak-ku-te-*[ ]. Lacheman reads *Ak-ku-Te-šup*.

l. 30: *Ak-ku-*⸢*Te*⸣-*šu*[*p*]. So too Lachemen. *Ak-ku-*⸢*le-en*⸣-[*ni*] is also possible although less likely.

l. 36: ^{m}. This sign is a clear DIŠ, not as copied.

l. 38. The AK is at the bottom of the reverse, on the same axis as ll. 1-34.

l. 39. The reading of this line is tentative. The traces are somewhat effaced and the sense not perfectly clear. At best, it represents the belated correction of an omission from line 5.

l. 39: G[AL]. The traces are not as depicted. Rather, they appear as: 

l. 39: ṭ[up?]. This trace is not as copied. Rather, it appears as: 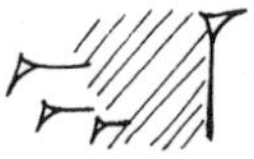

JEN 699

OBVERSE

1 [EME-šu ša ^{m}Še-eḫ-li]-⸢ya DUMU⸣ A!?-k[a?-a-a]
2 [EME-šu] *⸢ša⸣ [^{m}]*Ḫu-*ti-[ya ù EME]-•⸢šu •ša⸣ [^{m}Ar-te-ya]
3 [EME-šu] *ša *^{m}*Zi-*k[é ù EM]E-šu š[a ^{m}A-ta-a-a]
4 [(ù) EME-šu ša ^{m}Ki-pí]-•ya *DUMU.*MEŠ *^{m}*T[a-mar-t]a-⸢e⸣
5 [EME-šu] •ša ^{m}•Šúk-•ri-•ya *⸢ù⸣ [E]ME-šu
6 [ša ^{m}•Ḫ]a-ip-•LUGAL DUMU.•MEŠ *^{m}*Ma-[l]i-ya
7 [(ù) EME]-•šu •ša *^{m}•Eḫ-*l[i]-*⸢ya⸣ DU[MU] Ak-ku-[le-en-ni]
8 [um-ma] •⸢ŠEŠ⸣.MEŠ •an-nu-*tu$_{4}$-[m]a
9 [i-na pa]-na-nu-ma •a-bu-•ni-[m]i 5 ANŠE [A.ŠÀ.MEŠ]
10 [ša ^{m}•M]i-•na-aš-•šúk *[D]UMU *⸢Za⸣-[z]i-ya
11 [i-na *š]a-•pá-at a-•tap-*p[í N]i-ra-aš-[ši]
12 [i-na le]-et A.ŠÀ.MEŠ *š[a ^{m}]Ḫu-ti-ya
13 [DUMU Me-l]e-ya i-na •KASKAL.*MEŠ-•[n]i ša URU
14 [Ta-a]r-ku-ul-li *⸢i-*na x⸣-ú-ri-ni
15 [a-na ^{m}T]e-ḫi-ip-til-l[a] DU[MU P]u-ḫi-še-en-ni
16 ⸢it⸣-ta-ad-nu ⸢ù i⸣?-[na?-an?-na?] ⸢ni⸣?-[i?-nu?]
17 ni-⸢it⸣-ta-d[in šum-ma] ⸢i⸣+na EGIR
18 A.ŠÀ.MEŠ an-⸢ni⸣-[i ni-š]a-as-sí
19 ù 10 MA.NA K[Ù.SIG$_{17}$.MEŠ a-n]a ^{m}Te-ḫi-ip-til-la
20 •⸢ni-ma-•al⸣-[la-m]i um-ma ^{m}Ké-li-ya-m[a]
21 [DUMU] ⸢Un-te⸣-[šup] A.ŠÀ.MEŠ an-ni-i
22 [ ] ⸢ù⸣ a-na-ku i+na EGIR
23 [A].+ŠÀ.M[EŠ a]n-•ni-•⸢i⸣ ša ŠEŠ<.MEŠ>-⸢ya⸣
24 [a-na ^{m}T]e-ḫi-⸢ip⸣-til-la in-dì-nu
25 [i-na EG]IR ^{m}Te-ḫi-ip-til-la
26 [l]a [a]-•šá-as-sí šum-ma a-+ša-+as-+sí

LOWER EDGE

27 [10? MA.N]A +KÙ.+SIG$_{17}$.MEŠ a-na ^{m}Te-ḫi-ip-til-la
28 [ú]-ma-al-la-mi
29 [IGI] ⸢x x⸣ [D]UMU Pu-ḫi-ya
30 [IGI DUMU K]u-ri-iš-ni

REVERSE

31 [IGI DUMU En-n]a-ma-ti
32 [IGI] ⸢x x⸣ [DUMU]-⸢x⸣-a-ni
33 [IGI] •⸢Ḫa⸣-na-•ak-•kà DUMU [Še-ka$_{4}$-rù]

34 I[G]I •ŠU-•^{d}IM DUMU *Zu-[ú-me]
35 IGI Ma-*i-•it-•ta *DUMU [ ]
36 IGI •⸢Ḫu⸣-ti-ip-LUGAL DUMU •Te-[ ]
37 ⸢IGI⸣ Ḫé-šal-la DUMU Zu-ú-me
38 [IG]I •Ḫa-aš-ḫar-pá DUMU Mil-ku-ya
39 [IG]I •Ḫa-•⸢na⸣-a-a DUMU Ta-e
40 [IG]I Še-*⸢ka$_4$⸣-rù DUMU DINGIR-ŠEŠ
41 [IGI Ḫ]a-na-a-a DUMU Na-al-tùk-ka$_4$
42 [IGI U]r-ḫi-te-šup DUMU Kál-ma-aš-šu-•ra
43 [IGI U]r-ḫi-ya DUMU Še-ka$_4$-rù
44 [IG]I Ḫu-ti-ya DUMU Zi-li-ḫar-pè
45 [IGI] Ki-in-ki-ya DUMU Ši-mi-ka$_4$-tal
46 [i]l-ku ša A.ŠÀ.MEŠ an-ni-i šu-•nu-[ma]
47 [na]-šu-ú šum-ma A.ŠÀ.MEŠ pa-qí-•⸢ra⸣-*na
48 [i]-ra-aš-ši ⸢šu-•nu-ma⸣ ú-za-ak-ku-*ma

S.I.

49 $^{[N]A_4}$ KIŠIB ^{m}Ur-ḫi-ya

S.I.

50 [^{NA_4} KIŠI]B [^{m}]

S.I.

51 ^{NA_4} KIŠIB ^{m}Ḫa-na-ak-kà
52 ŠU ^{m}I-ni-ya
53 $^{+}$DUMU ⸢Ki⸣-[a]n-ni-pu

TRANSLATION

(1-7) [Declaration of] Šeḫliya son of Akaya; [declaration] of Ḫutiya [and declaration] of [Ar-teya], [declaration] of Zike [and] declaration of [Ataya] [(and) declaration of] Kipiya sons of Tamar-tae; [declaration] of Šukriya and declaration [of] Ḫaip-šarri sons of Maliya; [(and) declaration] of Eḫliya son of Akkul-enni.

(8-20) [Thus] (declared) these brothers: "Formerly, our fathers gave [to] Teḫip-tilla son of Puḫi-šenni a 5 homer [field of (i.e., which had previously belonged to)] Minaš-šuk son of Zaziya, (located) on the bank of the Nirašši Canal, adjacent to a field of Ḫutiya [son of] Meleya on the road to the town of Tarkulli, to the ... . And now(?), we have given (it again, i.e., have confirmed that cession). [If] we (hereafter) lodge a formal complaint regarding this field, then we shall pay to Teḫip-tilla 10 minas of gold."

(20-28) And thus (declared) Keliya [son of] Un-tešup: "... this field ... and I shall not (hereafter) lodge a formal complaint against Teḫip-tilla regarding ... this field which my brother<s> gave [to] Teḫip-tilla. If I lodge (such) a complaint, I shall pay to Teḫip-tilla [10?] minas of gold."

(29-45) [before] ... son of Puḫiya; [before] ... [son of] Kurišni; [before] ... [son of] Enna-mati; [before] ... [son of] ...-ani; [before] Ḫanakka son of [Šekaru]; before Gimill-adad son of Zume; before Maitta son of ...; before Ḫutip-šarri son of Te-...; before Ḫešalla son of Zume; before Ḫaš-ḫarpa son of Milkuya; before Ḫanaya son of Tae; before Šekaru son of Ili-aḫi; [before] Ḫanaya son of Naltukka; [before] Urḫi-tešup son of Kalmaš-šura; [before] Urḫiya son of Šekaru; [before] Ḫutiya son of Zili-ḫarpa; [before] Kikkiya son of Šimika-atal.

(46-47) [And] they (i.e., the declarers) shall bear the *ilku* of this field.

(47-48) And should the field have claimants, they (i.e., the declarers) shall clear (it).

(49-51) (*seal impression*) seal impression of Urḫiya; (*seal impression*) seal impression of ...; (*seal impression*) seal impression of Ḫanakka.

(52-53) Hand of Iniya son of Kiannipu.

COMMENTS

This tablet is somewhat unusual in its content. It is also unusual for the light it sheds on a long-standing crux in Nuzi studies. Together with *JEN* 467—a text describing the vicissitudes of the same plot of land as here described but at an anterior stage of its history—*JEN* 699 helps us to understand how the *ilku*-tax worked and how the ubiquitous *ilku* clause in real estate adoption texts is to be understood.

This tablet also relates directly to *JEN* 508, a list of names written after *JEN* 699. *JEN* 508:16-21 identify precisely the cocontractors of *JEN* 467:3-7. It is highly likely that *JEN* 508:1-10 identify precisely those parties identified here in *JEN* 699:1-7. On connections of *JEN* 467, 508, and 699, see already Maidman (1979, 180, n. 3) and Morrison (1987, 181-82 with n. 52).

The problem of the *ilku* as well as that of the complex interrelationship of *JEN* 467, 699, 508 cannot, of course, be explored here. I have devoted a lengthy study to these problems, a study which, with the publication and edition of *JEN* 699, can now be completed. I mention these issues here because *JEN* 699:1-7 are poorly preserved and restoration of the names once written in these lines is based on *JEN* 508:1-10 and, secondarily, *JEN* 467. Both *JEN* 467 and 508, as well as *JEN* 699, have been collated for the purpose of more precisely determining the meaning of these texts and their relationship to one another. In the case of *JEN* 508, collation was made from a pair of casts.

JEN 508:7-10 agree entirely with *JEN* 699:5-7 in identifying the last three of nine men who issue the initial declaration. The fragments of *JEN* 699:1-4 agree essentially with the list contained in *JEN* 508:1-6 and may be restored from that list. There seems to be some disagreement in the two texts regarding the identities of the first six parties. However, this is to be explained, in general terms, as follows. (Detailed argumentation appears in the study promised above.)

JEN 699 already suffered considerable deterioration in antiquity. By the time the scribe of *JEN* 508 wished to copy the names of *JEN* 699, he was faced with lacunae, partially preserved signs, and names appearing in no clear context. He interpreted the surviving text as best he could but with only partial success and with some hesitancy. See, for partial evidence of this, Chiera's marginal comments to *JEN* 508 and the nonsensical *JEN* 508:4-6.

The source of these errors can still be traced in the "modern" state of preservation of *JEN* 699. That is, the errors in the well preserved *JEN* 508 are explicable on the basis of the state of preservation of *JEN* 699 as and when recorded for the *CAD* Nuzi file. (Thus not only does *JEN* 508 aid in reconstructing *JEN* 699 but *JEN* 699 aids in understanding *JEN* 508.) This implies, of course, that little or no deterioration of *JEN* 699 took place between the writing of *JEN* 508 and the 1920s and 1930s.

By the time of Lacheman's copy, however, the tablet had further deteriorated. Some indication of this decay is reflected below in those notes where a lacuna is "filled in" by appeal to the *CAD* Nuzi file. Still, Lacheman's copy is a good indicator of the problems faced by the ancient scribe of *JEN* 508. Unfortunately, the tablet has deteriorated rather badly between the time of Lacheman's copy and my own initial collation. The many diacritical marks in the transliteration indicating partial and total obliteration of signs since the copy was made are symptoms of the great extent of the damage, especially in the crucial top half of the obverse.

NOTES

l. 1: [EME-*šu*]. This format is assured by the preserved last signs of line 5.

l. 1: [*ša* ᵐ*Še-eḫ-li*]-⸢*ya* DUMU⸣ *A*!?-*k*[*a*?-*a-a*]. Cf. *JEN* 508:1; 467:3 and its echo, 508:16-17. *JEN* 467:3 now lacks the last two signs and the "*A-kà*" of *JEN* 508:17 are now partially effaced (although recognizable).

The *CAD* Nuzi file reflects a reading: [ ] *ša* ᵐ*P*[*u*]-/*Še*-[ ]. These traces, no longer visible, are consistent with the ᵐ*Še-eḫ-li-ya* of *JEN* 508:1. The reading of this name is also supported by the visible ⸢*ya*⸣ in *JEN* 699:1.

The four partially preserved signs of line 1 are faint but clear. They are not part of Lacheman's original copy and they seem as well to have escaped the notice of the scribe of *JEN* 508.

The traces of the last two remaining signs are not easily rendered as *A-k*[*a*]. Nevertheless, the name of Šeḫliya's father is more or less clearly preserved in *JEN* 467:3 and its echo, 508:17.

Lacheman, at one point prior to the time he made his hand copy, apparently saw these traces as well. He seems to have interpreted the last three as DUMU *A-kà*-[ ] but assigned this patronymic to Ḫutiya (l. 2). This is incorrect. See below, note to line 2.

l. 2: [*ù* EME]-⸢*šu ša*⸣ [^{m}*Ar-te-ya*]. At this point in the text, the *CAD* Nuzi file reads: *ù* EME-*šu ša*. Though this writing favors the adopted reconstruction, in general, one should be aware that the Nuzi file is sometimes lax in the use of square brackets, and it may be, as suggested below, that the scribe of *JEN* 508 did not see these signs.

If the reading, [*ù* EME]-⸢*šu ša*⸣, is adopted, then a personal name must have appeared in the present lacuna and, consequently, the paternity of Ḫutiya (l. 2) is not established until line 4, with Tamar-tae. Yet *JEN* 508:2 assigns to Ḫutiya, as father, KU-GA-[ ]. *NPN*, 11b *sub* AKAI̯A 12), 64b *sub* ḪUTII̯A 1), interprets these signs as *A-kà-*[*a-a*], identifying this particular Ḫutiya with a well attested figure in the Teḫip-Tilla texts. The same KU-GA-[ ] may well have led Lacheman, in *JEN* 699, to assign his DUMU *A-kà-*[ ] to line 2 instead of l. 1 (see above, note to l. 1: [*ša* ^{m}*Še-eḫ-li*]-⸢*ya* DUMU⸣ *A*!?-*k*[*a*?-*a-a*]). However, even if the spacing permitted this shift of the patronymic to line 2 (it doesn't), Šeḫliya would then be deprived of *his* rightful father. Cf. *JEN* 467:3; 508:16-17. Aside from this, the initial interpretation of *NPN* is to be rejected. Collation of *JEN* 508 shows that the first sign of the patronymic is not A, but appears as:

and the second sign is a slightly damaged GA.

What, then, does the KU-GA-[ ] of *JEN* 508:2 represent? It is improbable that the scribe erred, as Lacheman did, and mistook the end of *JEN* 699:1 for the end of the following line, garbling the writing in the process. Rather, it appears somewhat more likely that he saw *JEN* 699:2 essentially as it appears in Lacheman's copy. He interpreted the last two signs (and others?) as a patronymic rather than as ⸢*šu ša*⸣, wrote what he thought these traces represented, and then supplied, by faulty deduction, "DUMU" in *JEN* 508:2. The scribe appears to have repeated this process in line 4. See below, note to l. 3: [^{m}*A-ta-a-a*].

If the name of Ḫutiya's father does not appear in this lacuna in *JEN* 699:2, what does? Most likely, ^{m}*Ar-te-ya*, as this PN appears in *JEN* 508:3, the line following the appearance of "Ḫutiya son of KU-GA-[ ]." P.M. Purves already deduced this in a comment in the *CAD* Nuzi file. Whence the scribe obtained this datum is unknown but he did not have it as he was initially writing this text. (It is less likely that he initially merely forgot to include precisely this datum.) As Chiera notes in a marginal note to *JEN* 508, the line was "added later" (Chiera 1934b, plate 476), an observation based on the fact that, though this is not indicated in the copy, the signs are written in miniature between lines 2 and 4. Line 2 was originally followed immediately by line 4, as if *JEN* 699:2 contained the name of one person, Ḫutiya, not two, and his name was to be followed by that of Zike (l. 3).

l. 3: [EME-*šu*]. The *CAD* Nuzi file records these signs as visible.

l. 3: [^{m}*A-ta-a-a*]. This restoration is based on *JEN* 508:4 (collation of that line shows that, after TA, only a single vertical now survives). There, this PN appears as Zike's patronymic. Yet *JEN* 467:4 assigns as father to Zike Tamar-tae. It is possible the scribe of *JEN* 508 mistook the wedges of *šu š*[*a*] in *JEN* 699:3 for DUMU and "copied" this sign in *JEN* 508:4 (*A-ta-a-a* will still have been preserved in *JEN* 699 at that time). The consequence of this error appears in *JEN* 508:5-6, where the "sons of PN" comprise but a single individual, Kipiya.

l. 4: [^{m}*Ki-pí*]-*ya*. The *CAD* Nuzi file reads: [ ]-*pí-ya*. The restoration is assured by *JEN* 508:5.

l. 4: *T*[*a-mar-t*]*a*-⌜*e*⌝. If the reconstruction of the text proposed to this point is correct, then Tamar-tae is the father of Ḫutiya (l. 2), Ar-teya (l. 2), Zike (l. 3), Ataya (l. 3), and Kipiya (l. 4). Since *JEN* 467:4 names Tamar-tae as the father of Zike (collation of that line reveals the first TA to be completely preserved and the MAR to be represented not only by two horizontals but by the first vertical as well), we venture the restoration of that patronymic here. The *CAD* Nuzi file renders: DUMU.MEŠ *Ta-e-*[ ]. This suggests that (a) *Ta-ma*[*r*] was visible and that (b) [*t*]*a*-⌜*e*⌝ at the end of the line was not noticed.

The scribe of *JEN* 508 gave up attempting to reproduce this name. The erased traces in *JEN* 508:6 do not appear as copied but as:

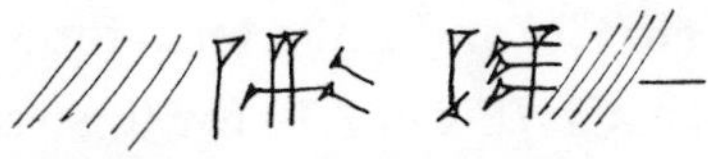

One might argue, though not strongly, that the scribe saw in *JEN* 699:4 *T*[*a*]-*ma*[*r*]-*t*[*a*], reconstructed the first two signs incorrectly, began the third, and abandoned the effort as yielding no sense when faced with the final traces of this line.

ll. 5-7. Cf. *JEN* 508:7-10. The text of *JEN* 508 becomes clearer where *JEN* 699 becomes less broken. This constitutes a further argument for (a) the dependence of *JEN* 508 on *JEN* 699; and (b) the damaged state of *JEN* 699 in antiquity.

l. 7: [(*ù*) EME]. The *CAD* Nuzi file reflects [ ] EME-*šu*.

l. 8: [*um-ma*] ⌜ŠEŠ⌝. The *CAD* Nuzi file reflects [ ]-*ma* ŠEŠ. Thus no number seems to have been lost in the lacuna.

l. 9: 5 ANŠE [A.ŠÀ.MEŠ]. Lacheman and the *CAD* Nuzi file read 5 ANŠE A.ŠÀ.MEŠ. The apparent lack of space for the last three signs thus seems illusory.

l. 11: [*N*]*i-ra-aš*-[*ši*]. Lacheman and the *CAD* Nuzi file read *Ni-ra-aš-ši*, i.e., with no missing wedges or signs.

Although the evidence is not conclusive, "Niraššì" is here capitalized as a probable toponym. Certainty is lacking since this term is associated

with more than one place. A Nirašši Canal is explicitly linked to the town of Artiḫi (*JEN* 4:4). However, the same canal is located in the town of Kipri (*EN*, 9/3, 58:6-7). And indirect evidence links this canal to probably two other towns as well. *JEN* 154:6 refers to land by an *atappi Nirašši ša āl Anzugal*<*li*?>. However, in the same context, the tablet mentions other land as being in Nuzi (*JEN* 154:7). In this connection, *JEN* 805:4 links this canal to the road to Atakkal and that route has but one known second terminus, Nuzi (*JEN* 137:8-9). Cf. also Morrison (1993, 41-42).

If only one watercourse is called Nirašši and it is indeed a toponym, then it passes through the four municipalities of Artiḫi, Kipri, Nuzi, and Anzugalli (so also K. Deller *apud CAD*, N/2, 260a). In any event, Nuzi is the likeliest location of the land mentioned in this text. Nirašši, of course, is mentioned (possibilities are: Artiḫi, Kipri, Nuzi, and Anzugalli).

A road to Tarkulli is mentioned (ll. 13-14). Roads bearing this name have two known second termini, Nuzi (Oppenheim 1938, 142, for circumstantial evidence) and Šinina (*JEN* 659:4-7). Finally *JEN* 699:12-13 links this land to that of Ḫutiya son of Meleya. This individual (though not his land) is elsewhere linked to Nuzi (*HSS*, V, 94:1-7).

Constraints of space preclude a discussion here of the etymology of this term and of the semantic contexts in which it appears. See, for the moment, Maidman (1976, 405-6, n. 699). In light of that discussion, and despite the multiplicity of towns linked with *Nirašši*, it seems that Nirašši is a discrete GN and not a term for a type of watercourse.

l. 13: [DUMU *Me-l*]*e-ya*. Cf. *JEN* 467:10 for this restoration.

l. 14: ⸢*x*⸣-*ú-ri-ni*. For ⸢*x*⸣, the *CAD* Nuzi file saw: 

In light of the parallel context, *JEN* 467:11, and if ^{IM}*su-ti-it* there is a variant of *sūtānu* (cf. above, note to *JEN* 698:5), perhaps these signs should be interpreted $^{\mathrm{[I]M}}$*sú*!-*ta*!-*ni*. Lacheman once hazarded PA$_{5/6}$ *sa-ra-e*.

l. 15: [*a-na* ^{m}*T*]*e*. The *CAD* Nuzi file records these signs as wholly preserved.

ll. 17-18. The *CAD* Nuzi file records these lines as wholly preserved.

l. 20: ⸢*ni-ma-al*⸣-[*la-m*]*i*. The *CAD* Nuzi file records these five signs as entirely preserved. However, at present all that remains of the disquieting NI is: 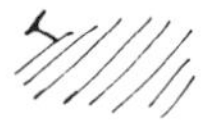

l. 21: [DUMU] ⸢*Un-te*⸣-[*šup*]. For this restoration, cf. *JEN* 467:6; 508:20.

l. 23: ⸢*i*⸣. Despite the MI of the copy, I is to be preferred: (a) both the *CAD* Nuzi file and Lacheman once did read I; (b) what remains is consistent with I: 

(c) it is what is expected. The MI of the copy is probably a copyist's lapse.

l. 26: *šá*. Only the last vertical remains of this sign. Note that ŠA, not ŠÁ, is used in the repetition of this word on the same line.

l. 28: [*ú*]. Given the ⸢*ni-ma-al*⸣-[*la-m*]*i* of l. 20, [*a*] is another possible restoration.

l. 29: ⸢x x⸣[ ]. Lacheman reads *Še-ka-ru* at this point in the text.

l. 31: [*En-n*]*a-ma-ti*. The *CAD* Nuzi file reads, at this point, [ ]-*na-ma-ti*.

l. 33: DUMU [*Še-*ka_4*-rù*]. The *CAD* Nuzi file and Lacheman both read, at this point, DUMU *Še-ka-rù*. Porada identifies the seal impression above l. 51 as that of Ḫanakka son of Šekaru. In light of the spelling of Šekaru in lines 40 and 43, we reconstruct here ka_4 rather than *ka*.

l. 36: ⸢*Ḫu*⸣. The *CAD* Nuzi file reflects an undamaged sign here.

l. 38: *Mil-ku-ya*. This PN is correct as copied. *NPN*, 56a *sub* ḪAŠ-ḪARPA 1), 78b *sub* KAKUịA 2) are to be corrected accordingly. This reference should be added to MILKUịA (*NPN*, 98a).

l. 42: [IGI *U*]*r*. The *CAD* Nuzi file records these signs as entirely preserved.

l. 43: [IGI *U*]*r*. The *CAD* Nuzi file records these signs as entirely preserved. Cf. also l. 49.

ll. 46-47. According to the *CAD* Nuzi file, these lines were entirely preserved. (Lacheman notes that the last sign of line 46 was preserved.)

l. 51. See above, note to l. 33.

l. 53. After this line, Lacheman once read:

54 DUB.SAR

LEFT EDGE

55 NA_4 ^{m}*Ḫu-*[*ti-ya*]

Neither of these lines appears in his copy, and neither is visible.

JEN 700

OBVERSE

1 [*ṭ*]*up-pí ma-r*[*u-ti ša* ^{m}*Ta-e*]

2 [DUM]U *Ta-i-š*[*u-uḫ*]

3 ^{m}*Te-ḫi-ip-til-*⸢*la*⸣ [DUMU *Pu-ḫi*]-⸢*še*⸣-[*en-ni*]

4 *a-na ma-ru-ti i-te-pu-*[*us-sú*]

5 1 ANŠE A.ŠÀ *i+na qí-na-at* [AN?.ZA?.KÀR? (*ša*) ^{m}*Š*]*ur-ku-ma-tal*

6 *i+na mi-in-dá-*ti_4 *ša* É.GAL GA[L *i-na* URU *A*]*r-*$^{+}ti_4$*-*$^{+}$*ḫi*

7 ^{m}⸢*Ta*⸣*-e a-na* ^{m}*Te-ḫi-ip-til-la*

8 *ki-*⸢*ma*⸣ [Ḫ]A.LA •*i-*•*din ù*

9 ^{m}*Te-ḫ*[*i-i*]*p-til-*•*la* 8 •ANŠE ŠE.[MEŠ]

10 *a-na* ^{m}⸢*Ta*⸣-[*e* •*k*]*i*!*-ma* NÍG.[BA] •*i-*⸢*din*⸣

11 *šum-ma* A.ŠÀ *pa-*[*qí*]-⸢*ra-na*⸣ *i-ra-*[*aš*]-$^{+}$⸢*ši*⸣

12 ^{m}*Ta-e-ma* [*ú*]-*za*-*ak-kà*
13 *il-kà ša* ⸢A⸣.ŠÀ ⸢*šu*⸣-*ma na*-⸢*ši*⸣
14 *šum-ma* ^{m}*Ta-e i*-[*bala*]-⸢*kat*⸣
15 1 MA.NA KÙ.[BABB]AR 1 MA.NA K[Ù.SIG$_{17}$ *i*]-*na-din*
16 IGI *A-ri-ḫar-pa* DUMU *E-en*-[*n*]*a-mil-ki*
17 IGI $^{+}$*It*-⸢*ḫi*⸣-*ip-til-la* DUMU *Tup-ki*-⸢*ya*⸣
18 IGI *Tar-mi-te-šup* DUMU *Ar-te*-⸢*ya*⸣
19 IGI *Ša-aš-ta-e* DUMU *E-eḫ*-[*li-ya*]
LOWER EDGE
20 IGI *Še-ḫi-rù* DUMU *Te-eš-šu-y*[*a*]
21 IGI *Te-ḫi-ip-til-la* DUMU *Ḫa-ši*-[*ya*]
22 IGI *Šu-ri-ša* DUMU *Mu-uš-te-šup*
REVERSE
23 IGI *A-kip-til-la* DUMU *Tù-ra-ri*
24 IGI *Wa-an-ti*$_4$-*ya* DUMU *Ḫa-ip*-LUGAL
25 5 ⸢LÚ⸣.MEŠ *mu-še-el-wu ša* A.ŠÀ
26 IGI *Mu-uš-te-šup* DUMU *Ḫa-š*[*i*!-*ya*]
27 IGI *It*-*ḫa*-*pí*-$^{+}$*ḫe* DUB.SAR[(-*rù*)]
28 IGI *I-li-ma-ḫi* DUMU *Ḫa-na*-[*an-ni-y*]*a*
S.I.
29 ^{NA_4} KIŠIB ^{m}*A*-[*ri-ḫ*]*ar-pa* DUMU *E*-[*en*-$^{+}$*n*]*a*-$^{+}$*mil*-$^{+}$*ki*
S.I.
30 $^{+[N]A_4}$ $^{+}$KIŠIB ^{m}*Mu-uš-te*-[*šup* DUMU *Ḫa-ši-ya*]
S.I.
31 ^{NA_4} KIŠIB ^{m}*A-kip-til-la* DUMU *Tù-ra-r*[*i*]
S.I.
32 [^{NA_4} KIŠIB ^{m}]$^{+}$*It*-$^{+}$*ḫi-ip-til-la* D[UMU **Tu*]*p*-[*ki-ya*]
UPPER EDGE
S.I.
33 ^{NA_4} KIŠIB ^{m}[*It-ḫa-pí-ḫe* DUB.SAR]

TRANSLATION

(1-4) Tablet of adoption [of Tae] son of Tāin-šuḫ. He adopted Teḫip-tilla [son of] Puḫi-šenni.

(5-8) Tae gave to Teḫip-tilla as an inheritance share a 1 homer field in the *qinnatu* (of) [the *dimtu*? of] Šurkum-atal—(measured) by the large palace standard—[in the town of] Artiḫi.

(8-10) And Teḫip-tilla gave to Tae as a gift 8 homers of barley.

(11-12) Should the field have claimants, Tae shall clear (it).

(13) And he (i.e., Tae) shall also bear the *ilku* of the field.

(14-15) Should Tae abrogate (this contract), he shall give (to Teḫip-tilla) 1 mina of silver (and) 1 mina of gold.

(16-28) Before Ariḫ-ḫarpa son of Enna-milki; before Itḫip-tilla son of Tupkiya; before Tarmi-tešup son of Arteya; before Šaš-tae son of Eḫliya; before Šeḫiru son of Teššuya; before Teḫip-tilla son of Ḫašiya; before Šuriša son of Muš-tešup; before Akip-tilla son of Turari; before Wantiya son of Ḫaip-šarri. (These) 5 men are the measurers of the field. Before Muš-tešup son of Ḫašiya; before Itḫ-apiḫe, the scribe; before Ili-ma-aḫi son of Ḫanannaya.

(29-33) (*seal impression*) seal impression of Ariḫ-ḫarpa son of Enna-milki; (*seal impression*) seal impression of Muš-tešup [son of Ḫašiya]; (*seal impression*) seal impression of Akip-tilla son of Turari; (*seal impression*) [seal impression of] Itḫip-tilla son of Tupkiya; (*seal impression*) seal impression of [Itḫ-apiḫe, the scribe].

COMMENT

This text has suffered slight damage since it was copied.

NOTES

ll. 5-6. The last signs of these lines, appearing on the reverse of the tablet, do indeed belong to lines 5 and 6. Contrary to the copy, they do not align with lines 4 and 5.

l. 5: *qí-na-at* [AN?.ZA?.KÀR?]. The tentative restoration is based on the fact that, as a topographical term in the Nuzi texts, *qinnatu* is most frequently linked to *dimtu*. The meaning of *qinnatu* in these contexts remains unclear. On the semantic environment and possible meanings of *qinnatu* in the Nuzi texts, see Maidman (1976, 385-86, n. 526).

l. 6. The *CAD* Nuzi file records this line as entirely preserved.

l. 6: *ti*$_4$-*ḫi*. These signs are clearly discernible; the "TUR" of the copy is inaccurate.

l. 9: [MEŠ]. The *CAD* Nuzi file records this sign as preserved.

l. 15: [*i*]-*na-din*. The second last sign is a clear NA, not TA as copied.

l. 19: *E-eḫ*-[*li-ya*]. This and other PN restorations in this text are based on a largely standard witness sequence common to *JEN* 4, 30, 34, 45, 54, 425, 700, *JENu* 973a+1077f(+)973b, 1163, 1183. See already Weeks (1972, 204-5; *JEN* 30 and the three *JENu* items should be added to his list) and Fadhil (1983, 53b; the last *JENu* item should be added to his list).

l. 20. This line begins the lower edge.

l. 28: *Ḫa-na*-[*an-ni-y*]*a*. The second sign is a clear NA, not as copied. The *CAD* Nuzi file sees this PN as completely preserved, ending with *-e*. However, such an ending for this PN is nowhere else attested whereas *-ya* is. *-ya* is asserted at this point in *NPN* (whose entire reading of this PN is adopted here), 53a *sub* ḪANANNAJA 1), 69a *sub* ILI-MA-AḪI 1).

JEN 701

OBVERSE

1 *ṭup-pí m[a]-ru-t[i ša]*
2 ^{m}*Ka-pá-*⸢*at*⸣*-t[a]* •DUMU ⸢X⸣-[ ]
3 *ù* ^{m}*Te-ḫi-*•⸢*ip*⸣*-til-l[a]*
4 DUMU *Pu-ḫi-še-[e]n-ni a-[na]*
5 *ma-ru-ti i-pu-us-s[ú(-ma)]*
6 1 •ANŠE A.ŠÀ *ša-qú-ú i+na*
7 *ú-ga-ri a-na* ^{m}*Te-ḫi-ip-[til-la* SUM*-din]*
8 *ù* ^{m}*Te-ḫi-ip-til-la*
9 1 GUD *it-ti bu!-*⸢*ri*⸣*-šu-ma*
10 *ù* 2 ANŠE ŠE.MEŠ ⸢*ki*⸣*-ma* 20 GÍN KÙ.BABBAR.MEŠ *k[i?-m]a?* •NÍG!.•BA
11 *a-na* ^{m}*Ka-pá-at-t[a]* SUM-⸢*din*⸣
12 *šum-ma* A.ŠÀ *pí-*•⸢*ir*⸣*-*•*[q]à i[r-*t]a-*ši*
13 ^{m}*Ka-pá-at-ta ú-*⸢*za-ak*⸣*-[ka$_{4}$-ma?]*
14 *ù a-na* ^{m}*Te-ḫi-ip-Til-la i-[na-an-din]*
15 *ma-an-nu ša* BAL*-tu*

LOWER EDGE

16 1 MA.NA KÙ.BABBAR 1 MA.N[A KÙ.SIG$_{17}$]
17 *ú-ma-al-la*

REVERSE

18 IGI *Pí-im-pí-li* *DUMU *K[u?-pa?-ti?-ya?]
19 IGI *Ḫu-ti-ya* *DU[MU] ⸢X⸣*-at-*tù-*[ ]
20 IGI *A-[r]i-ip-šar-*⸢*ri*⸣ [DUMU]
21 IGI *W[a]-an-*⸢*ti*⸣*-*ya* [DUMU]
22 IGI ⸢*Eḫ-li*⸣*-[y]a* DUMU ⸢*E*⸣*-[ké?]-*⸢*ké*⸣?
23 IGI ⸢*Al*⸣*-ki-t[il?-la?* DUMU] *A-r[i?]-*⸢*x-x*⸣*-la-*⸢*x*⸣
24 IGI *Zi-il-*•*te-[y]a*
25 DUMU *Ta-ú-*[k]a$_{4}$?*
26 IGI *Ḫu-ti-[ya* DUMU] •^{d}UTU-ma.[an.s]ì DUB.SAR

[S.I.]

27 ^{NA_4} KI[ŠIB ^{m}]*Ḫu-*⸢*ti*⸣*-[ya]*
28 *ša* U[RU?]

[S.I.]

29 ^{NA_4} KIŠIB ^{m}*Tar-m[i?-*]

UPPER EDGE

[S.I.?]

30 $^{[NA_4?]}$ +KI[ŠIB?]

LEFT EDGE

[S.I.]

31 ^{NA_4} KIŠIB ^{m}*Pí-im-pí-li*

TRANSLATION

(1-5) Tablet of adoption [of] Kapatta son of .... He adopted Teḫip-tilla son of Puḫi-šenni.

(6-7) [He gave] to Teḫip-tilla a 1 homer irrigated field in the *ugāru*.

(8-11) And Teḫip-tilla gave to Kapatta as(?) a gift 1 ox (*sic*) with its calf and 2 homers of barley, (these items being) the equivalent of 20 sheqels of silver.

(12-14) Should the field have a claim, Kapatta shall clear (the field) and give (it) to Teḫip-tilla.

(15-17) Whoever abrogates (this contract) shall pay 1 mina of silver (and) 1 mina [of gold].

(18-26) Before Pimpili son of Kuppatiya(?); before Ḫutiya son of X-attu-...; before Arip-šarri [son of ...]; before Wantiya [son of ...]; before Eḫliya son of Ekeke(?); before Alki-[tilla? son of] A-ri(?)-...-la-...; before Zil-teya son of Tauka; before Ḫutiya [son of] ^{d}UTU-ma.an.sì.

(27-30) [(*seal impression*)] seal impression of Ḫutiya of the town(?) of ...; [(*seal impression*)] seal impression of Tarmi(?)-...; [(*seal impression*)?] seal(?) impression(?) of(?) ...; [(*seal impression*)] seal impression of Pimpili.

COMMENTS

This tablet has suffered some deterioration, especially on the reverse, since the copy was made. Line 1 begins *ṭup-pí*. The remnant of a sign appearing above line 1 is on the upper edge (i.e., near the end of the text).

NOTES

l. 2: In his notes, Lacheman records this trace as: 

l. 6: *ša-qú-ú*. The term most likely describes irrigation (a variation on the more common *ši-qú*) rather than height. That is, it derives from von Soden's *šaqû(m)* III (see *AHw*, 1181b, par. 5) rather than from his *šaqû(m)* I (see *AHw*, 1180a, par. 2).

l. 9: *bu*!. The scribe wrote MU and then attempted to correct himself.

l. 10: KÙ.BABBAR.MEŠ *k*[*i*?-*m*]*a*? NÍG!.BA. The last three signs appear on the reverse. They have actually been copied, upside down, at the end of line 25. The *CAD* Nuzi file reads, after MEŠ, *a-na* [ ] MEŠ.

l. 13: [ka_4-*ma*?]. The *CAD* Nuzi file records the line as completely preserved, including these two signs.

l. 15. This line is the last line of the obverse. The line starts with *ma*. The DIŠ of the copy does not appear on the tablet.

l. 18: *K*[*u?-pa?-ti?-ya?*]. The suggested restoration of the patronymic is based on the extreme rarity of the PN, Pimpili. It appears only once elsewhere, *JEN* 519:13. There, the patronymic is *Ku-pa-ti-ya*.

l. 19: ⸢*X*⸣*-at-tù-*[ ]. In his notes, Lacheman restores, in effect, [*Š*]*a-at-tù-*[ ]. Elsewhere he interprets the first sign as: 

l. 23: ⸢*x-x*⸣. Lacheman interprets these traces as IL.

l. 25. See above, second note to line 10.

l. 28. Instead of constituting an independent line following line 27, these signs could be the latter part of line 29.

l. 30. The trace appears, not as copied, but, rather, as:

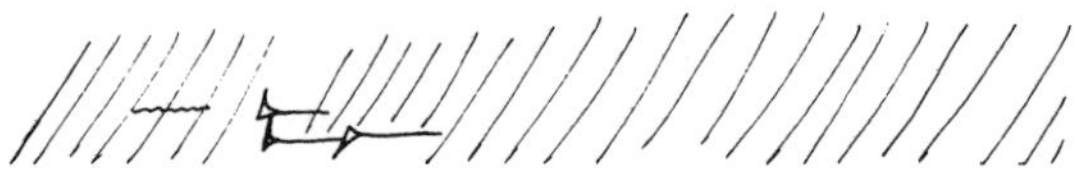

JEN 702

OBVERSE

1 *ṭup-•pí* [*ma-ru*]*-•ti* **š*[*a*]
2 •^{m}*Še-•e*[*l*]*-w*[*i-*n*]*a-tal* *DUMU *⸢*A*⸣-[*a*]*r-ša-li-ip*
3 ^{m}*Te-ḫi-ip-•til-**[*l*]*a* DUMU **Pu-*ḫi-*še-en-ni*
4 *a-na ma-ru-*[*ti*] *i-•pu-uš*
5 1 ANŠE 5 ^{GIŠ}[APIN] A.ŠÀ.MEŠ *ša* URU *Ar-ti-ḫi*
6 [ ] ⸢x⸣ TA *a* ⸢x⸣ [ ] ⸢x⸣
7 [*i?-na? mi*]-⸢*in*⸣*-dá-ti* •*ša* *⸢É.*GAL-*li*⸣
8 [*i-na le*]*-et* A.ŠÀ *ša* *^{m}*Ki-ip-*⸢*ta*⸣*-li-li*
9 [^{m}*Še*]-⸢*el*⸣*-wi-na-tal* •*a-na*
10 [^{m}*Te*]*-ḫi-ip-til-la ki-ma* ḪA.LA-*šú* SUM-*nu*
11 [*ù*] ^{m}*Te-ḫi-ip-til-la a-na*
12 [^{m}*Š*]*e-el-wi-na-tal* 3 ANŠE ŠE
13 [*ki-m*]*a* NÍG.BA-*šú i-dì-na-aš-šu*
14 [*šu*]*m-ma* A.ŠÀ *pa-qí-ra-na ir-ta-ši*
15 ^{m}*Še-el-wi-na-tal ú-za-ak-*ka_4
16 *a-na* ^{m}*Te-ḫi-ip-til-la i-na-an-din*
17 *ù il-ki ša* A.ŠÀ.MEŠ
18 ^{m}*Še-el-wi-na-*⸢*tal*⸣*-ma na-ši*
19 ^{m}*Te-ḫi-ip-til-la* [*u*]*l-la-ši*
20 *šum-ma* ^{m}*Še-el-*w*[*i*]*-na-tal* KI.BAL
21 1 MA.NA KÙ.BABBAR [1 MA].NA KÙ.SIG_{17}
22 *a-na* ^{m}*Te-ḫi-ip-*[*ti*]*l-la ú-ma-al-la*

---

23 •⸢IGI⸣ •*Ša-t*[*u-ša*] DUMU *Tu-ra-ri*
24 •IGI •*Ut-ḫi-ip-*[*til-*•*l*]*a* DUMU *Tu-up-*⁺*ki-*⁺⸢*ya*⸣
25 ⁺IGI •⸢*El*⸣*-ḫi-i*[*p*-LUGA]L DUMU *Gi*$_5$*-mi-*⁺*li-*⁺*ya*
26 [IGI *A-ki-ip*]*-til-la*

LOWER EDGE

27 [DUM]U *Tu-ra-ri*

REVERSE

28 •⸢IGI⸣ •*Ú-na-ap-še*
29 DUMU *A-ḫi-ya*
30 5 $^{\text{LÚ.MEŠ}}$IGI.MEŠ A.ŠÀ.MEŠ
31 *ú-*[*uš*]*-*⸢*te*⸣*-el-*⸢*wu*⸣
32 IG[I] •*Wi-ir-ra-aḫ-ḫe* DUMU *Ḫa-*[ ]
33 IGI *Še-en-na-ya* DUMU *Ḫa-š*[*i*]*-in-na*
34 IGI *A-bi-*DINGIR DUMU *Ša-ri-iš-še*
35 IGI *A-ri-ḫar-pá* DUMU *En-na-mi-*•*il-ki*
36 ŠU ^{md}*Iškur-an-dùl*! DUB.SAR
37 DUMU ⸢*Zi*⸣*-ni-*⸢*ya*⸣

S.I. Po 980

38 [NA$_4$] ^{m}*Wi-ir-ra-aḫ-ḫe*

S.I.

39 NA$_4$ ^{m}*A-*⸢*ri*⸣*-ḫar-pa*

S.I. Po 161

40 $^{\text{NA}_4}$ KIŠIB ^{m}*El-ḫip-*LUGAL

S.I.

UPPER EDGE

41 NA$_4$ $^{\{\text{m}\}\text{md}}$•*Iškur-*•*an-dùl*! DUB.SAR

LEFT EDGE

S.I.

42 $^{\text{NA}_4}$ KIŠIB ^{m}•*Ša-*[*tu-ša*]

TRANSLATION

(1-4) Tablet of adoption of Šelwin-atal son of Ar-šalipe. He adopted Teḫip-tilla son of Puḫi-šenni.

(5-10) Šelwin-atal gave to Teḫip-tilla as his inheritance share a 1.5 homer field of the town of Artiḫi .... [by?] the palace standard, adjacent to the field of Kip-talili.

(11-13) [And] Teḫip-tilla gave to Šelwin-atal as his gift 3 homers of barley.

(14-16) Should the field have claimants, Šelwin-atal shall clear (it and) give (it) to Teḫip-tilla.

(17-19) And Šelwin-atal shall also bear the *ilku* of the field. Teḫip-tilla shall not bear (it).

(20-22) Should Šelwin-atal abrogate (this contract), he shall pay to Teḫip-tilla 1 mina of silver (and) [1] mina of gold.

(23-37) Before Šatuša son of Turari; before Itḫip-tilla son of Tupkiya; before Elḫip-šarri son of Gimilliya; before Akip-tilla son of Turari; before Unap-še son of Aḫiya. (These) 5 witnesses have measured the field. Before Wirraḫḫe son of Ḫa-...; before Šennaya son of Ḫašin-na; before Abi-ilu son of Šariške; before Ariḫ-ḫarpa son of Enna-milki. Hand of Iškur-andul, the scribe, son of Ziniya.

(38-42) (*seal impression*) seal impression of Wirraḫḫe; (*seal impression*) seal impression of Ariḫ-ḫarpa; (*seal impression*) seal impression of Elḫip-šarri; (*seal impression*) seal impression of Iškur-andul, the scribe; (*seal impression*) seal impression of Šatuša.

COMMENT

This tablet has suffered deterioration since the copy was made, especially in the first lines of the obverse.

NOTES

l. 2: ⸢*A*⸣-[*a*]*r*. Lacheman records these signs as entirely preserved.

l. 5: *ša*. *i-na* is expected. Yet the same scribe uses *ša* in a similar context, *JEN* 214:7.

l. 6. Lacheman reads this line, in effect, as: *i-na* ^{GIŠ}*ta-a-*[*ri* GAL *i-n*]*a*, while the *CAD* Nuzi file has: [*i-na*] ⸢^{GIŠ}⸣*ta-a-*[*a-ri* GAL *ša* É.GAL]. Following these leads, we might render this line as: [*i-na* $^{\text{GI}]\text{Š}}$*ta-a-r*[*i ša* É.GAL(*-li*) *i-n*]*a* (a reading found, in fact, elsewhere among Lacheman's papers) so that line 7 would represent a gloss of line 6. (The same scribe elsewhere writes *ta-a-ri* instead of the more usual *ta-a-a-ri*; see *JEN* 38:8—*ta-*⸢*a-ri*⸣—and perhaps 743:4—*ta-a-*[*ri*]—and 792:8—*ta-a-ri*—all three collated.) However, the reason for this gloss is not apparent. Both formulae are ubiquitous in the Nuzi texts.

l. 13: *šú*. This sign is normal, not as copied.

l. 13: *dì*. The sign might also represent *din*.

l. 23. The *CAD* Nuzi file records this line as completely preserved.

l. 24: *Tu-up-ki-*⸢*ya*⸣. The second sign is a typical UB, not GUD as copied. After this sign, KI ⸢YA⸣ is clear.

l. 26. The *CAD* Nuzi file renders this line, in effect, as: IGI [*A*]-*ki-*[*ip*]*-til-la*. The identity of the witness thus established is probably to be accepted. He is elsewhere a common witness in Artiḫi texts. See the references in *NPN*, 16b *sub* AKIP-TILLA 24).

l. 31: ⸢*te*⸣. The *CAD* Nuzi file records this sign as completely preserved.

l. 32: *aḫ*. This sign is typical, not as copied.

l. 32: *Ḫa*-[ ]. *NPN*, 54b *sub* ḪANIU 19), 173b *sub* WIRRAḪḪE 1), reads *Ḫa-ni-ù*. Lacheman reads *Ḫa*-⸢*ni-ú*⸣. The *CAD* Nuzi file reads *Ḫa*-[ ]-*ya*.

l. 36: ŠU. This sign is typical, not as copied.

l. 36: *Iškur*. Spellings of this name such as *Iš-kùr-a-an-dì-il* (*JEN*265:40) demonstrate the phonetic value, *iškur*, for IM.

JEN 703

OBVERSE

1 *ṭup*-•*pí* [*ma-ru-ti ša*]

2 [^{m}]*Šúk-r*[*a-pu* DUMU *E-te-ya*]

3 *ša* ^{m}*Ni-i*[*ḫ-ri-ya* DUMU *En-na-a-a*]

4 *ša* ^{m}*Túr*-[*še-en-ni*] DU[MU! Z]*i*-⸢*li*-•*ip*⸣-[*ka*$_{4}$-*na-ri*]

5 *ša* ^{m}⸢*Na-ni*!-*ya*⸣ DUMU *Šu-ru-ka*$_{4}$-*a-a*

(erasure)

6 5 LÚ.ME[Š] *an-nu-tù ša* URU *Ú-nap-še-wa*

7 ^{m}*Te-ḫi-ip-til-la* DUMU *Pu-ḫi-še-en-ni*

8 ⸢*a-na*⸣ *ma*-⸢*ru*⸣-*ti i-te-ep-šu-uš*

9 [6] ANŠE A.ŠÀ AŠ *ta-a-a-ri* GAL *ša* É.GAL[(-*lì*)]

10 [*i-n*]*a* [*š*]*u-pa-al* AN.ZA.KÀR *ša A-ka*$_{4}$-*wa-til*

11 *⸢*i*!-•*na*⸣ *e-le-en* AN.ZA.KÀR *ša*

12 [$^{m?}$]*⸢*Um*⸣-*pí-na-pí* ^{m}*Šúk-ra-p*[*u*] ^{m}*Ni*-[*iḫ-r*]*i-ya*

13 *^{m}•*Túr-še-en-ni* ^{m}*Na-ni-ya*

14 ([attempted] erasure) *ki*-[*m*]*a* ḪA.⸢LA⸣-[*šu*]

15 [*a-na* ^{m}]*Te-ḫi-ip-til-la it-ta-ad-nu*

16 [*ù*] ^{m}*Te-ḫi-ip-til-la* •39 ANŠE ŠE.MEŠ

17 [*ki-ma*] NÍG.BA-*šu-nu it-ta-din*

18 [*šum-ma*] A.ŠÀ *pa-qí-ra*-⸢*na*⸣ TUK-*ši*

19 [^{m}*Šúk-r*]*a*-⸢*pu*⸣ ^{m}*Ni-iḫ-ri-ya*

20 [^{m}*Túr-še-en-ni*] ^{m}*Na-ni-ya*

21 (erasure) *ú-za-ku-ma*

22 [*a-na* ^{m}]$^{+}$*Te-ḫi-ip-til-la i+na-an-dì-nu*

23 •⸢*il*⸣-*ka*$_{4}$ *ša* A.ŠÀ *šu-nu-ma na-šu-ú*

24 $^{+}$⸢*šum*⸣-*ma* LÚ.MEŠ *an-nu-ti* KI.BAL-$^{+}$*tù*!

LOWER EDGE

25 10 MA.NA KÙ.SIG$_{17}$ *a+na* ^{m}*Te-ḫi-ip-til*-[*la*]

26 *i+na-an-dì-nu*

\+ ____

REVERSE

27 $^{+}$IGI $^{+}$Ze-$^{+}$en-$^{+}$ni $^{+}$DUMU Ḫa-ma-⸢an-na⸣

28 $^{+}$IGI $^{+}$Zi-ka$_4$-a-a DUMU Ku-tùk-ka$_4$

29 $^{+}$IGI $^{+}$DUMU-$^{+d}$X DUMU Ku-za-ri-ya

30 $^{+}$[IG]I $^{+}$Ur-$^{+}$ḫi-$^{+}$ya DUMU Še-ka$_4$-rù

31 [IG]I $^{+}$⸢E-$^{+}$ni⸣-[i]š-ta-e DUMU Ak-ka$_4$-pa

32 IGI [A-ri]-*ma-*⸢at⸣-•ka$_4$ DUMU DINGIR-a-ḫi

33 IGI *⸢Ḫu-*ti⸣-*ya •DUMU A-ri-ma-at-ka$_4$

34 IGI It-•ḫa-*pí-•⸢ḫe⸣ DUMU Ta-a-a

35 IGI Ip-ša-ḫa-lu DUMU Ar-te-ya

36 IGI Ta-a-a DUMU A-pil-XXX DUB.SAR

37 IGI ^{d}IM-te-ya DUMU Im-bi-^{d}UTU

38 11 $^{LÚ.MEŠ}$IGI.•⸢MEŠ⸣ an-nu-tù A.ŠÀ.MEŠ

39 šu-nu-ma il-⸢mu⸣-ú ù ŠE.MEŠ AŠ pa-•ni-•šu-nu

40 ma-dì-id IGI Um-pí-⸢y⸣a DUMU Ki-pè-er-•ḫa

S.I. Po 228

41 ^{NA_4}KIŠIB ^{m}Ur-•ḫi-•ya

S.I. Po 340

42 ^{NA_4}KIŠIB ^{m}DUMU-⸢^{d}⸣[X DUMU] ⸢Ku⸣-[za-ri-ya]

S.I.

43 $^{+NA_4}$ $^{+}$KIŠIB ^{m}⸢X⸣-[ ]

UPPER EDGE

[S.I.]

$^{+}$44 ^{NA_4}KIŠ[IB ^{m}]

LEFT EDGE

S.I. S.I.

45 ^{NA_4}KIŠIB ^{m}Ta-a-a DUB.SAR NA$_4$ ^{m}I[t]-ḫa-pí-[ḫe (DUMU Ta-a-a)]

TRANSLATION

(1-8) Tablet of [adoption of] Šukr-apu [son of Eteya], of Niḫriya [son of Ennaya], of Tur-šenni son of Zilip-kanari, (and) of Naniya son of Šurukkaya. These 5 (*sic*) men of the town of Unap-še adopted Teḫip-tilla son of Puḫi-šenni.

(9-15) Šukr-apu, Niḫriya, Tur-šenni, (and) Naniya gave [to] Teḫip-tilla as [his] inheritance share a field, [6] homers by the large standard of the palace, to the west of the *dimtu* of Akawatil (and) to the east of the *dimtu* of Umpin-api.

(16-17) [And] Teḫip-tilla gave (to them) [as] their gift 39 homers of barley.

(18-22) [Should] the field have claimants, Šukr-apu, Niḫriya, [Tur-šenni], (and) Naniya shall clear (it) and give (it) [to] Teḫip-tilla.

(23) They shall also bear the *ilku* of the field.

(24-26) Should these men abrogate (this contract), they shall give to Teḫip-tilla 10 minas of gold.

(27-40) Before Zenni son of Ḫamanna; before Zikaya son of Kutukka; before Mâr-ištar son of Kuzzariya; before Urḫiya son of Šekaru; before Eniš-tae son of Akkapa; before Arim-matka son of Ili-aḫi; before Ḫutiya son of Arim-matka; before Itḫ-apiḫe son of Taya; before Ipša-ḫalu son of Ar-teya; before Taya son of Apil-sin, the scribe; before Adatteya son of Inbi-šamaš. It was these 11 witnesses who encircled the field. Also, the barley was measured in their presence. Before Umpiya son of Kip-erḫan.

(41-45) (*seal impression*) seal impression of Urḫiya; (*seal impression*) seal impression of Mâr-ištar [son of] Kuzzariya; (*seal impression*) seal impression of ...; [(*seal impression*)] seal impression of ...; (*seal impression*) seal impression of Taya, the scribe; (*seal impression*) seal impression of Itḫ-apiḫe [son? of? Taya?].

COMMENTS

This tablet has suffered some deterioration since the copy was made. On the other hand, a small, squarish fragment, attached when the tablet came to Chicago but absent when Lacheman made his copy, has since been restored to its place at the top left of the reverse. The fragment contributes practically all the initial signs of ll. 28-31 (line 27 is part of the main tablet; additions to this line are unrelated to the presence of the fragment).

The transaction recorded on this tablet is the basis of the litigation described in *JEN* 651. Certain broken passages in *JEN* 703 may be restored on the basis of *JEN* 651. See below, notes to ll. 2-4, 9.

NOTES

l. 2-4. These lines are restored on the basis of ll. 12-13 and *JEN* 651:8-10.

l. 4: *Túr*-[*še-en-ni*]. This spelling is restored here and in line 20 on the basis of line 13. Therefore, the spelling in *NPN*, 160b *sub* TUR-ŠENNI 8), 178b *sub* ZILIP-KANARI 2) should be corrected accordingly.

l. 6: 5 LÚ.ME[Š]. Lines 2-5 list but four adopters. A fifth was once listed but his name has systematically been erased. Thus, an erasure appears between the present lines 5 and 6 and at the beginning of line 21. A third attempted erasure at the start of line 14 was unsuccessful, leaving clear traces of the name of this erstwhile adopter: Zilip-apu.

In fact, Lacheman interprets the traces remaining from the erasure between lines 5 and 6 as: *ù ša* ^{m}*Zi-li-ip-a-pu* DUMU *Ip-ša-*[*ḫa-lu*]. His restoration of the damaged patronymic would almost certainly be correct. The individual so identified has close links elsewhere both to Teḫip-tilla

real estate interests in the area described in this text and to one of the adopters in this text, Niḫriya son of Ennaya (l. 3). See *JEN* 38, 52.

The start of line 6 suggests that, while the fifth name and patronymic were erased, the number "5" was left undisturbed because it was an unimportant contractual element of the text. Cf. above, note to *JEN* 676:7. (A certain carelessness in scribal practice may also be discerned in this text in line 40. There, a last witness is named after what is presumably a summary statement following the list of witnesses.)

As is to be expected, *JEN* 651:8-11 identify only the four adopters appearing in *JEN* 703:2-5.

ll. 9-10. The beginnings of these lines appear in the copy to be elevated with respect to the rest of the same lines. This is a correct impression. It is due to physical distortion resulting from damage to the tablet.

l. 9: [6]. This restoration is based on *JEN* 651:5.

l. 10: AN.ZA.KÀR *ša A-ka*$_4$*-wa-til*. The land is thus to be located in the town of Unap-še. See, for example, *JEN* 709:7-8.

l. 11. According to the *CAD* Nuzi file and Lacheman, this line begins: *ù i-na*.

l. 14. As stated above, note to line 6, an unsuccessful attempt has been made to erase all the signs preceding KI, i.e., what now appears as: ⸢*ù*⸣ [m]*Zi-li-ip-a-pu*.

Since the intent of the scribe was to delete this datum, the transliteration is relegated to this note, and not included in the main transliteration of *JEN* 703. Nor is this name included in the translation.

l. 20: [m*Túr-še-en-ni*]. See above, note to l. 4.

l. 21. The *CAD* Nuzi file and Lacheman record, for the first part of this line: *ù* m. These signs presumably will have survived a scribal attempt at erasure. No doubt, *Zi-li-ip-a-pu* was also erased. Parts of LI or IP and PU are still visible.

l. 24: *tù*!. The sign appears, not as copied, but as: 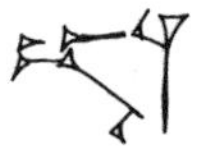

l. 26. Below this line appears a horizontal line. This is not indicated in the copy.

l. 27. But for the last two signs, the line is perfectly preserved, not as copied.

ll. 28-31. See above, comments.

l. 31: ⸢*E-ni*⸣. The traces appear as: 

l. 40. See above, note to l. 6.

l. 41. Lacheman, in effect, reads after *-ya*: DU[MU *Še-ka*$_4$*-rù*].

l. 42: ⸢*Ku*⸣-[*za-ri-ya*]. The *CAD* Nuzi file reads, at this point: [*K*]*u-za-*⸢*ri*⸣-[*ya*].

JEN 704

OBVERSE

1 ṭup-pí •ma-*⸢ru⸣-[t]i •ša

2 ^{m}Im-bi-l[i-*š]u •DUMU ŠU-•ma-^{d}IM

3 ^{m}Te-ḫi-ip-•til-*⸢la⸣ *DUMU Pu-ḫi-še-ni

4 •a-na ma-ru-t[i DÙ]-ma

5 1 ANŠE A.ŠÀ AŠ? [šu-pa]-al

6 •URU •Ḫu-•lu-me-n[i]-wa ki-ma ḪA.LA-šú

7 a-na $^{m•}$⸢Te⸣-ḫi-i[p-t]il-la

8 $^{+}$⸢it⸣-ta-din •⸢ù⸣ ^{m}Te-ḫi-ip-til-la

9 •5 ANŠE •ŠE.MEŠ ki-ma NÍG.BA-šu

10 a-na ^{m}I[m]-•⸢bi-li⸣-šu!

11 [i]t-•t[a-ad-na]-•aš-šu

12 [š]um-ma A.ŠÀ [d]i-n[a] TUK-ši

13 ^{m}Im-bi-[l]i-⸢šu⸣ ú-za-ka$_{4}$-ma

14 a-na $^{m•}$Te-⸢ḫi⸣-ip-[til-l]a

15 i+na-an-din i[l]-ka$_{4}$ ša A.[Š]À

16 ^{m}I[m]-bi-li-š[u-m]a •na-ši

LOWER EDGE

17 š[um-ma ^{m}I]m-bi-l[i-šu] KI.[BAL-at]

18 ⸢x⸣[ ] 5 MA.$^{+}$NA [KÙ.SIG$_{17}$ a-na]

REVERSE

19 ^{m}Te-ḫ[i-ip-til-•l]a SI.A

20 IGI •Ḫu-ti-⸢ya⸣ •[D]UMU •⸢A⸣-ka$_{4}$-a-a

21 IGI E-mu-⸢ya⸣ DUMU Ip-ša-ḫa-[lu]

22 •IGI ÌR-DINGIR-šu [DUMU B]ÀD-⸢LUGAL⸣

23 IGI Ké-li-•ya [DUMU A]-ar-•ta-e

24 IGI [Š]ur-kip-LUGAL $^{+}$⸢DUMU⸣ Ka$_{4}$-lu-li

25 •IGI •[Ḫ]a-•ši-pa-pu [DUM]U A-•⸢kip⸣-a-pu

26 •IGI Pí-⸢ru⸣ DUMU N[a]-iš-ké-el-pè

27 IGI It-ḫa-p[í-ḫ]e DUMU Ta-a-a

28 IGI Ta-a-a DU[MU A-•p]il-XX[X] DUB.SAR

S.I. Po 637

29 ^{NA_4} KIŠIB ^{m}Pí-⸢ru⸣

S.I. Po 968

30 *^{NA_4} *K[IŠIB $^{m•}$Ì]R-[•DIN]GIR-šu

UPPER EDGE

[S.I.]

31 NA$_{4}$ ^{m*}⸢X⸣-[ ]-•⸢ya⸣

LEFT EDGE

S.I.

32 NA$_{4}$ ^{m}Ké-[l]i-ya

TRANSLATION

(1-4) Tablet of adoption of Inb-ilišu son of ŠU-ma-^{d}IM. He adopted Teḫip-tilla son of Puḫi-šenni.

(5-8) He gave to Teḫip-tilla as his inheritance share a 1 homer field to the west of the town of Ḫulumeni.

(8-11) And Teḫip-tilla gave to Inb-ilišu as his gift 5 homers of barley.

(12-15) Should the field have a case (against it), Inb-ilišu shall clear (the field) and give (it) to Teḫip-tilla.

(15-16) Inb-ilišu shall also bear the *ilku* of the field.

(17-19) Should Inb-ilišu abrogate (this contract), he shall pay [to] Teḫip-tilla ... (and?) 5 minas [of gold].

(20-28) Before Ḫutiya son of Akaya; before Emuya son of Ipša-ḫalu; before Ward-ilišu [son of] Dûr-šarru; before Keliya [son of] Ar-tae; before Šurkip-šarri son of Kaluli; before Ḫašip-apu son of Akip-apu; before Piru son of Naiš-kelpe; before Itḫ-apiḫe son of Taya; before Taya son of Apil-sin, the scribe.

(29-32) (*seal impression*) seal impression of Piru; (*seal impression*) seal impression of Ward-ilišu; [(*seal impression*)] seal impression of ...-ya; (*seal impression*) seal impression of Keliya.

COMMENTS

This tablet has suffered considerable deterioration since the copy was made.

In the copy, the lines on the obverse appear to slant upwards to the right; those on the reverse downwards. On the tablet itself, the lines appear straight. This slant in the copy results in a certain ambiguity where lines are broken in the middle, i.e., it is difficult, at times, to see which second half of a line belongs to which first half. To forestall such confusion, Lacheman "connected" isolated halves of lines by means of horizontal lines for lines 6-8 and 21-25. These connections are correct (again, the lines are quite straight on the tablet itself) but the lines themselves do not appear on the tablet.

NOTES

l. 2: ŠU-*ma*-^{d}IM. The first sign is a normal ŠU, not as copied. The second sign, though now partially effaced, seems a clear MA.

The rendering of the first two signs is problematic. "*Šu-ma-*" as an element preceding a DN is, to my knowledge, otherwise unattested at Nuzi. Perhaps the scribe omitted a sign and we should read *Šu-<um>-ma-*^{d}IM. Cf. *NPN*, 138a *sub* ŠUMMA-ILU. Or perhaps one should consider the second sign to be an incomplete dittograph (left unfinished when the scribe realized his error?) and render the name ŠU-{ŠU!}-^{d}IM, i.e., Gimill-adad. See, for this PN, *NPN*, 85b.

l. 4: [DÙ]. Cf. *JEN* 43:4, written by the same scribe. On other connections between *JEN* 43 and 704, see below, next note.

l. 5: 1 ANŠE. The space to the left of the number is broken. In theory, therefore, more than one homer of land could be involved. However, it is likely that no sign is lost. The reason is as follows.

JEN 41, 43, and 704 share many features. These include a largely common witness list and the location of real estate in Ḫulumeni (the only times, it seems, this GN appears in the Nuzi texts). This cluster of texts was already noted by Lacheman and by Weeks (1972, 209-10). Also common to the first two of these real estate adoption texts is the price ratio, 1 homer of land : 5 homers of barley (*JEN* 41:5, 8; 43:5, 9). The price paid for the Ḫulumeni land in this text appears in line 9. Parallel to the case of the number of homers in line 5, in line 9 two vertical wedges (but not a *Winkelhaken*) may, in theory, have been lost. However, the "surviving" pair of numbers yields the expected 1:5 ratio. It is therefore assumed that no wedges have been lost at the start of either line.

l. 5: AŠ?. ⸢*i*⸣-[*na*] is also possible.

l. 8: ⸢*it*⸣. The wedges before TA constitute a clear, almost completely preserved IT, not as copied.

l. 9: 5 ANŠE. See above, note to l. 5: 1 ANŠE.

l. 10: *šu*!. This sign appears as copied. The two small circles on either side of the sign do not appear on the tablet.

l. 15: [Š]À. The configuration of the remaining wedges more clearly represents ŠÀ than the copy indicates.

l. 18: 5 MA.NA [KÙ.SIG$_{17}$]. The NA is complete and normal, not as copied.

The penalty of five minas of gold is found in the other Ḫulumeni texts, *JEN* 41:15; 43:15, and so may well be restored here. (The partially preserved sign at the start of this line remains problematical.)

l. 22: [B]ÀD. The traces clearly reflect this sign, more so than the copy.

l. 31: ^{m}⸢X⸣-[ ]-•⸢*ya*⸣. This PN could be *Ḫu-ti-ya* (cf. l. 20) or *E-mu-ya* (cf. l. 21).

l. 32. Lacheman reads, below this line on the left edge: NA$_4$ ^{m}*Ta-a-a* DUB.[SAR]. It is difficult to envision there the space required for this line and for the seal impression which should have accompanied it.

JEN 705

OBVERSE

1 *ṭup-pí ma-ru-ti ša*

2 ^{m}*Še-ḫa-la* DUMU *Ar-te-šup*

3 ^{m}*Te-ḫi-ip-til-la* DUMU *Pu-ḫi-še-en-ni*

4 *a-na ma-ru-ti i-pu-sú*

5 8 ^{GIŠ}APIN A.ŠÀ *i+na ša-pa-at*

6 KASKAL *ša* URU *Du-ru-ub-la*

7 *a-na* ^{m}*Te-ḫi-ip-til-la ki-ma* ḪA.LA *i+din*

8 *ù* ^{m}*Te-ḫi-ip-til-la* 6 ANŠE 4 BÁN ŠE *ki-ma* NÍG.BA

9 *a-na* ^{m}*Še-ḫa-la i+din*

10 *il-ka*$_4$ *ša* A.ŠÀ *šu-ma na-a-ši*

11 *šum-ma* A.ŠÀ *pa-qí-ra-na i-ra-aš-ši*

12 •*šu-ú-ma na-a-ši*

13 •*šum*!-•⸢*ma*⸣ [^{m}*Še-ḫ*]*a-la i-bala-k*[*a*$_4$*-at*]

14 2 MA.N[A KÙ.SIG$_{17}$ *i-n*]*a-din*

15 IGI *A-ki*[*p-til-la* DUMU *Tù-ra-ri*]

16 IGI *Pí-*[*ri-ku* DUMU *I-ip-pa-ri*]

17 IGI *It-*[*ḫi-ip-til-la* DUMU *Tup-ki-ya*]

LOWER EDGE

18 3! L[Ú(.MEŠ) *mu*]-⸢*še-el*⸣-*wu* $^{+}$*ša* $^{+}$⸢A⸣.$^{+}$ŠÀ ⸢*ù*⸣

19 •*na-*[*di-na-nu*] *ša* ŠE.MEŠ

REVERSE

20 IGI [*Mu-ḫu-ur*]-*sú* DUMU *Mil-ku-*⸢*ya*⸣

21 $^{+}$IGI [*Ar-zi-iz*]-⸢*za* DUMU *Mil-ku*⸣-[*ya*]

22 IGI [DUMU]

23 •IGI [DUMU]

24 •IGI [DUMU]

25 ⸢IGI⸣ [DUMU]

26 [IGI DUMU]-*a*

S.I. Po 21A

27 ^{NA_4} KIŠIB ^{m}*Še-el-wi-na-tal* DUMU *A-kap-tùk-ke*

S.I. Po 306

28 ^{NA_4} KIŠIB ^{m}MI.NI-*ya* DUMU *Te-ḫi-ip-*LUGAL

UPPER EDGE

S.I. Po 104

29 $^{⸢NA_4⸣}$ KIŠIB ^{m}*Ar-zi-iz-za*

30 DUMU *Mil-ku-ya*

LEFT EDGE

S.I.

31 $^{[N]A_4}$ KIŠIB ^{m}*It-ḫa-pí-ḫe* DUB.SA[R]

TRANSLATION

(1-4) Tablet of adoption of Šeḫala son of Ar-tešup. He adopted Teḫip-tilla son of Puḫi-šenni.

(5-7) He gave to Teḫip-tilla as an inheritance share a .8 homer field abutting the road to the town of Dūr-ubla.

(8-9) And Teḫip-tilla gave to Šeḫala as a gift 6.4 homers of barley.

(10) And he (i.e., Šeḫala) shall bear the *ilku* of the field.

(11-12) Should the field have claimants, he shall bear (it) (*sic*).

(13-14) Should Šeḫala abrogate (this contract), he shall give 2 minas [of gold].

(15-26) Before Akip-tilla [son of Turari]; before Piriku [son of Ippari]; before Itḫip-tilla [son of Tupkiya]. (These) 3 men are the measurers of the field and the distributors of the barley. Before Muḫur-sin son of Milkuya; before Ar-zizza son of Milkuya; before [... son of ...]; before [... son of ...]; before [... son of ...]; before [... son of ...]; before [... son of] ...-a.

(27-31) (*seal impression*) seal impression of Šelwin-atal son of Akap-tukke; (*seal impression*) seal impression of Ziliya son of Teḫip-šarri; (*seal impression*) seal impression of Ar-zizza son of Milkuya; (*seal impression*) seal impression of Itḫ-apiḫe, the scribe.

COMMENTS

The condition of this tablet is virtually unchanged from when the copy was made.

Note that, in the copy, the seal impression and text of the left edge appear immediately below the obverse. They represent, of course, the very end of this document.

According to the *CAD* Nuzi file, a separate fragment associated with this text reads: [ ]-*šú* DUMU *Mil-ku-ya*. The fragment is no longer present. Since it repeats *JEN* 705:20, that fragment appears to have been joined to the main tablet. (Only a cast was available for collation; it is not clear whether or not such a join has been made.)

NOTES

l. 6. For the location of this road, see below, note to l. 15.

l. 8: 4 BÁN. This manner of writing 4 BÁN is most unusual, as already noted by Fadhil (1983, 37a). For the typical writings of 1-5 BÁN, see Goetze (1956, 186). This writing can hardly represent "4 (PI) 1 BÁN" since 1 PI = .6 ANŠE and, typically, only the number "1" appears with this measure. For the dry measures in the Nuzi texts, see the reference above, second note to *JEN* 687:8.

l. 8: BA. This sign is clear and complete, not as copied. It is the last sign on the line.

l. 12. The scribe has repeated the end of the *ilku* clause (cf. l. 10) instead of the end of the clear title clause. Cf., for the same phenomenon, *JEN* 37:17. For further on this latter text, see below, note to line 15.

l. 13: *-k*[*a*$_4$*-at*]. Cf. *JEN* 15:15; 37:20; 687:16. For further on these texts, see below, note to line 15. The *CAD* Nuzi file reflects "*-kat*."

l. 14: [KÙ.SIG$_{17}$]. For this restoration, cf. *JEN* 37:20; 687:16. For the relevance of *JEN* 37 and 687 to this text, see below, next note.

l. 15. The restoration of the PN and patronymic in this line and the restorations of lines 14, 16, 17, and 20 are based on a largely shared list of witnesses in this document, *JEN* 15, 37, and 687. The last two texts resemble each other most closely in this respect. Weeks (1972, 206) already pointed out certain similarities between *JEN* 37, 687, and 705. Fadhil (1983, 39a) notes similarities between *JEN* 37 and 705.

Since the other texts all deal with real estate in Artiḫi (*JEN* 15:7; 37:7; 687:6), it is very likely that the land described in this text is to be located in this town as well.

l. 17: *It-*[*ḫi-ip-til-la*]. Although *JEN* 15:18; 37:23; and 687:20 spell this PN with initial UD, the same name is often written with initial ID. See *NPN*, 76a *sub* ITḪIP-TILLA. The restoration is thus plausible.

l. 18: 3!. The number of wedges is slightly ambiguous. The intent is not.

l. 21. Cf. lines 29-30 for this restoration.

ll. 22-25. Two of these four witnesses are most likely identified as sealers in lines 27-28.

l. 26. Based on the analogous *JEN* 15:28; 37:32; 687:30, as well as on *JEN* 705:31, this line might be restored: [IGI *It-ḫa-pí-ḫe* (DUB.SAR) DUMU *Ta-a*]*-a*.

JEN 706

OBVERSE

1 [*l*]*i-š*[*a-an-šu ša*]

2 ^{m}*Te-ḫ*[*i?*]-⸢*ip?-x*⸣[*-x?* DUMU]

3 AŠ *pa-ni ḫal-ṣ*[*ú-uḫ-le-e*]

4 •⸢*ù*⸣ AŠ *pa-ni* D[I.KU$_5$.MEŠ]

5 *k*[*i-na*]*-an-na iq-ta-bi*

6 *i*[*t-t*]*i* ^{m}*Te-ḫi-ip-til-l*[*a*]

7 ⸢A⸣.ŠÀ [*uš*]*-te-pè-é*[*l-m*]*i*

8 [x?+1]+⸢1⸣ANŠE 5 ^{GIŠ}APIN A.ŠÀ [*i-na*]

9 [A]N.ZA.•[K]ÀR *ša Kip-te-*[*š*]*up a-*[*na*]

10 [^{m}*Te*]-*ḫi-ip-til*-[*la a*]*t-t*[*a-din*]
11 ⸢*ù*⸣ ^{m}⸢*Te*⸣-*ḫi-i*[*p-ti*]*l-la*
12 [x?+] 2 A[NŠE 5 ^{GIŠ}APIN] •A!.ŠÀ! ⸢x⸣ [ ]
13 *ša* $^{m?}$[ ]-⸢*x*⸣-*iš-ti a-n*[*a ya-ši*]
14 *it-t*[*a-ad-n*]*a ša* ⸢*ma*⸣-*a*[*n-ni-im-me-e*]
15 A.ŠÀ-*š*[*u pí-ir-qa* TU]K-⸢*ši*⸣
16 ⸢*ù*⸣ [*ú-za-ak-ka*$_{4}$]
17 *u*[*š-tu u*$_{4}$*-mi an-ni-im an-nu-um*]
18 AŠ [EGIR *an-ni-im*]

LOWER EDGE

19 *l*[*a i-ša-(as-)sí*]

.

.

.

REVERSE

S.I. Po 924

20 ^{NA_4} KIŠIB [^{m}**T*]*ar-mi-ya*
21 DUMU •*Ú*-[*n*]*a*-$^{+}$⸢*ap*⸣-*ta*-⸢*e*⸣

S.I. Po 663

22 ^{NA_4} KIŠIB ^{m}*Te-ḫi-i*[*p-til-la* (DUMU *Pu-ḫi-še-en-ni*)]

S.I. Po 492

.

.

.

TRANSLATION

(1-5) Declaration [of] Teḫip(?)-... [son of ...] before lands officer(s) and before judge[s]; thus he spoke:

(6-14) "I have exchanged land with Teḫip-tilla. I have given to Teḫip-tilla a(n) [x?+1+]1.5 homer field [in] the *dimtu* of Kip-tešup and Teḫip-tilla has given to [me] a(n) [x?+]2[.5] homer field(!) ... of ... ."

(14-16) Whose field has a [claim] (against it), [he shall clear] (the field).

(17-19) From [this day forward], n[either shall hai]l [the other (into court)].

(20-22) .... *seal impression*) seal impression of Tarmiya son of Unap-tae; (*seal impression*) seal impression of Teḫip-tilla [(son of Puḫi-šenni)] (*seal impression*) .... .

COMMENTS

Lacheman copied this tablet twice. The other copy (unaltered) is published as *JEN* 793. *JEN* 706 is generally the better copy. However, the

appearance of the tablet's reverse is better represented by *JEN* 793. In *JEN* 706, as in many of his copies, Lacheman has truncated those parts of the surface containing seal impressions, presumably to save space.

The tablet has suffered little deterioration since it was copied.

NOTES

l. 1. The restoration of this line and of other formulaic sections of this text are based on the standard form of Teḫip-tilla declarations of real estate exchange. See, for example, *JEN* 104.

l. 8: [x?+1]+⌜1⌝ANŠE 5 GIŠAPIN. Lines 8 and 12 should complement each other: in real estate exchange transactions, especially where (as in this text) no additional payment of mobilia is made, the amounts of land are most often equal. If this be the case here, then line 12 shows that at least one vertical wedge is missing at the start of line 8. Conversely, the "5 GIŠAPIN" of line 8 is to be restored in the major lacuna of line 12.

The "5" of this copy is correct. The "4" of *JEN* 793:"8" is not.

l. 9: [A]N.ZA.[K]ÀR *ša Kip-te-*[*š*]*up*. This *dimtu* is located in Nuzi. See, for example, *JEN* 310:4, 8. If this transaction follows the pattern of practically all other Nuzi real estate exchanges, then the *quid pro quo*, described in lines 12-13, is also to be located in the vicinity of Nuzi.

l. 12: [x?+] 2 A[NŠE 5 GIŠAPIN]. See above, note to line 8.

l. 12: A!.ŠÀ!. The last two verticals of "ZA" and all of "AḪ" appear clearly on the tablet. "A.ŠÀ" is the preferred interpretation for reasons of space. There appears to be too little room for A.ŠÀ in the lacuna after the statement of the *amount* of land involved. See above, note to line 8. And although "*-zaḫ*" is a well attested final element in Nuzi PNs (see, for example, *NPN*, 276), there would certainly be too little space in the lacuna for A.ŠÀ *and* the start of a PN *and* signs between A.ŠÀ and the PN. (Not even a "klein *-zaḫ*" would help!)

ll. 12-13: ⌜x⌝ [ ] // *ša* m?[ ]-⌜*x*⌝*-iš-ti*. This section should describe the location of the real estate, perhaps along the lines of "adjacent to the field/*dimtu* of PN" (PN=...-išti?; for "*-išti*" names, see *NPN*, 258a). However, a reasonable interpretation of these signs eludes me.

ll. 17-18. The restoration of these lines is based on *JEN* 104:15-16. For variations on this construction, cf., for example, *JEN* 114:17-18; 137:15-16.

l. 18. This line appears on the obverse, not as copied.

l. 19. After this line, there must once have appeared: ŠU mPN DUB.SAR. Cf., for example, *JEN* 144:20.

l. 21: ⌜*ap*⌝. The sign is perfectly clear (only the lower left horizontal wedge is wanting), not as copied. For a similar error, see *JEN* 793:"18."

l. 22. Below the seal impression below this line, there must once have appeared ^{NA_4} KIŠIB ^{m}*Tar-mi-te-šup* DUMU *Eḫ-li-te-šup*. Cf., for example, *JEN* 137:21. Lacheman's identification of the seal impression as "Po 492" also points to this individual. See Porada (1947, 132b). See also, on this individual and his role in declaration documents, Maidman (1981, 237-38, n. 17).

JEN 707

OBVERSE

1 [ṭ]*up-pí ma-r*[*u-ti ša* ^{m}*Te-eš-šu-a-a* DUMU]
2 ^{m}*Al-ki-y*[*a* DUMU *Mi*]*l-*[*ki-te-šup*]
3 *a-na ma-ru-*[*t*]*i i-te-p*[*u-uš*]
4 É.ḪÁ.MEŠ GI[Š].ŠAR.MEŠ *ù ḫ*[*a-la-aḫ-wa*]
5 *i+na šu-pa-al ku-pa-ti* [*ša*]
6 *i+na* ˹*ša-pa-at*˺ *a-ta-*$^{+}$*pi* [*ša* ^{m}*Ki-il-li*]
7 ^{m}˹*Te*˺-[*eš-šu-a*]-˹*a*˺ *a+na* <m>*A*[*l-ki-ya*]
8 ˹x˺[ ]-*šu* $^{+}$TUR? ˹x˺[ ]
9 [ ]˹x x˺[ ]˹x˺[(?)]
10 [ ]˹x x x x˺[(?)]
11 *šum-*[*ma* É.ḪÁ.MEŠ-*t*]*u*$_{4}$ GIŠ.ŠAR.MEŠ [*ù ḫa-la-aḫ-wu*]
12 *di-*[*na ir-t*]*a-šu-ú* ^{m}*T*[*e-eš-šu-a-a*]
13 *ú-z*[*a-ak-ka*$_{4}$] ˹*ù*˺ *a-na* ^{m}*Al-*[*ki-ya i-na-di-in*]
14 *i*[*l-ka*$_{4}$ *ša* É].ḪÁ.MEŠ GIŠ.Š[AR.MEŠ *ù ḫa-la-aḫ-wi*]
15 ^{m}*T*[*e-eš-šu-a*]-˹*a-ma*˺ *na-ši*
16 *šum-m*[*a* ^{m}*Te-e*]*š-šu-a-a* KI.[BAL(-*at*)]
17 2 MA.•NA K[Ù.BAB]BAR 2 MA.NA KÙ.SIG$_{17}$ [*a-na*]
18 ^{m}*Al-ki-ya i-na-di-*[*in*]

LOWER EDGE

19 ^{NA_4} KIŠIB ^{m}*A-ri-ḫ*[*ar-pa*$_{12}$]
S.I.

REVERSE

20 ^{NA_4} KIŠIB ^{m}*Ur-ḫi-ya* DUMU *A-*˹*ru*˺-[*um-pa*$_{12}$]
S.I.
21 IGI *Ar-zi-iz-za* DUMU *Mil-*˹*ku*˺!-[*y*]*a*!
22 IGI ˹*Ki-li*˺*-li-ya* DUMU •*Šur*!-*ri-*[ ]
23 IGI *Ur-ḫi-ya* DUMU *A-ru-um-pa*$_{12}$
24 •IGI *A-*•*ri-*•*ḫar-pa*$_{12}$ DUMU *E-na-mil-ki*
25 [IGI] •*Ḫa-ni-a-aš-ḫa-ri* DUMU *A-ri-ya*
26 [IGI •*I*]*t-ḫi-zi-iz-za* DUMU *E-na-mil-k*[*i*]
27 [IGI *A-k*]*ip-til-la* DUMU *Tu-ra-ri*

28 [IGI *W*]*u-ur-tù-ru-*⌜*uk* DUMU *Ma*⌝-[*li-ya*]
29 [IGI]-*in*-[DUMU]

.
.
.

S.I.

.
.
.

LEFT EDGE

S.I.

30 ^{NA_4} KIŠIB A?-[ ]

TRANSLATION

(1-3) Tablet of adoption [of Teššuya son of ...]. He adopted Alkiya [son of] Milki-tešup.

(4-8) Teššuya [gave] to Alkiya .... buildings, orchards, and *ḫalaḫwu* (-land) to the west of the *kuppu*-structures [of ...], on the bank of the [Killi] Canal.

(8-10) ....

(11-13) Should the buildings, orchards, [and *ḫalaḫwu*(-land)] have a case (against them), Teššuya shall clear (the real estate) and [give] (it) to Alkiya.

(14-15) Teššuya shall also bear the *ilku* [of] the buildings, orchards, [and *ḫalaḫwu*(-land)].

(16-18) Should Teššuya abrogate (this contract), he shall give [to] Alkiya 2 minas of silver (and) 2 minas of gold.

(19-20) Seal impression of Ariḫ-ḫarpa (*seal impression*); seal impression of Urḫiya son of Arrumpa (*seal impression*).

(21-29) Before Ar-zizza son of Milkuya; before Kilīliya son of Šurri-...; before Urḫiya son of Arrumpa; before Ariḫ-ḫarpa son of Enna-milki; [before] Ḫaniašḫari son of Ariya; [before] Itḫi-zizza son of Enna-milki; [before] Akip-tilla son of Turari; [before] Wur-turuk son of Maliya; [before] ...-in-... [son of ...] ....

(30) .... (*seal impression*); (*seal impression*) seal impression of A(?)-.... .

COMMENT

This tablet has suffered very little deterioration since it was copied.

NOTES

l. 2: [*Mi*]*l*-[*ki-te-šup*]. It must be noted that explicit evidence for this restoration is wanting. At most, one may say that the trace of two verticals toward the end of line 2 is not inconsistent with the reading, [*Mi*]*l*, and that Lacheman reads at this point: [ ]-*te-šup*.

Nevertheless, this restoration rests on firm foundations. The adoptee here is to be identified with Alkiya son of Milki-t[ešup], an adopter in *JEN* 206. (The restoration of the last part of the patronymic in *JEN* 206:2 is itself no problem. See *NPN*, 19a *sub* ALKIḪA 6).) This identification is secured by a number of significant parallels between *JEN* 206 and 707. First, the witnesses of the two texts overlap somewhat. Compare *JEN* 707:24, 25, 26 with, respectively, *JEN* 206:34, 37, 36. Second, the location of the real estate involved in both these texts is almost certainly the town of Artiḫi. In the case of the land mentioned in *JEN* 206, that text is most likely related to *JEN* 400 which probably involves nearby real estate. (Zaccagnini [1984, 88] considers this a certainty.) *JEN* 400:7 locates that land in Artiḫi. As for *JEN* 707, the witnesses of this text are largely part of a standard witness sequence from texts dealing with Artiḫi real estate. Cf., for example, *JEN* 707:23, 24, 25, 27, 28 with, respectively, *JEN* 419:31, 27, 26, 16, 17. For the Artiḫi witness sequence of which *JEN* 419:16-31 in an example, see above, first note to *JEN* 686:5. The third significant parallel between *JEN* 707 and *JEN* 206 centers on the description of the real estate itself. The description in *JEN* 206 is unusual and lengthy. It is echoed, where the text is sufficiently preserved, in *JEN* 707. Cf. *JEN* 206:6-7 with *JEN* 707:4a, 4c (probably); and *JEN* 206:10-12 with *JEN* 707:4b, 5, 6 (probably).

For these three reasons (i.e., common witnesses, location of real estate, and description of real estate) and because the surviving traces of the patronymic do not contradict this proposition, the restoration "Milki-tešup" is considered all but assured. It is most likely because of the echoes of *JEN* 206 in *JEN* 707 that the *CAD* Nuzi file restores, in this part of line 2: "[Milki-tešup]."

Employing the rationale just delineated, it is difficult to avoid the conclusion that *JEN* 206 describes another stage in the same course of events described in *JEN* 707.

If we accept this perspective, then another problem is solved. *JEN* 707 is said to come from room 16, a Teḫip-tilla Family context. Yet nowhere in the text is a member of this family mentioned. The question arises: what is this text doing in room 16? *JEN* 206 (from the adjoining room 15) describes the cession of real estate from Alkiya son of Milki-tešup and others to Teḫip-tilla son of Puḫi-šenni. *JEN* 707 describes how the same Alkiya (representing himself and others?) obtained the same real estate at an earlier moment. When Teḫip-tilla obtained these properties,

he had *JEN* 206 drawn up and also acquired *JEN* 707, the old title, from Alkiya as part of the transaction.

JEN 707 is, therefore, a "background" text, a category of text already known elsewhere in the Teḫip-tilla Family archives. For further details on this type of text and its archival function, see Maidman (1979, 182-83 with n. 14). To the list of "background" texts there given, *JEN* 707 (vis-à-vis *JEN* 206) may be added. Thus, the presence of *JEN* 707 in room 16 poses no difficulty if the Alkiyas of these texts are, in fact, a single individual.

Another benefit of linking *JEN* 707 to *JEN* 206 is the restoration of gaps in the former text in light of the latter. For specific instances, see below, notes to lines 4, 5, 6. Cf. also below, note to line 8.

l. 4: *ḫ*[*a-la-aḫ-wa*]. This restoration is based on *JEN* 206:7, alluding, probably, to part of the real estate described here. See above, note to line 2, on the relation of this text to *JEN* 206. The *CAD* Nuzi file already proposed this restoration.

l. 5: *ku-pa-ti* [*ša*]. In light of *JEN* 206:10-11, the area of the lacuna might well have contained *ša* ᵐ*Te-ḫi-ip-til-la* or the like.

l. 6: ⸢*ša-pa-at*⸣ *a-ta-pi* [*ša* ᵐ*Ki-il-li*]. The restoration of the first word is suggested by *JEN* 206:12. The *CAD* Nuzi file reads, at this point, *ša-pa-at*. *JEN* 206:12 further identifies the canal as *ša* ᵐ*Ki-il-*[*l*]*i*. That identification should apply here as well and is thus restored. Cf. already Fadhil (1983, 40b).

The last preserved sign is a clear PI (a good UD+AŠ), not as copied. It should, therefore, be rendered: *pi*. Thus, Gelb's comment, *NPN*, 4, that "the sign PI has at Nuzi the values *wa, we, wi, wu, wo*, never the value *pi*," appears not to be true. In light of this value, note also the likely pa_{12} value of PI elsewhere in this tablet in lines 23 (*A-ru-um-*pa_{12}) and 24 (*A-ri-ḫar-*pa_{12}). In the case of the PN of line 23, cf. *A-ru-*pa_{12} in *JEN* 686:33 and 710:35. See also above, note to *JEN* 686:33-34. On the latter PN (l. 24), cf. below, note to *JEN* 728:27. Note that Gelb adopts the value *wa* for PI in the case of these two names. See *NPN*, 25b *sub* ARIḪ-ḪARPA, 36a *sub* ARRUMPA.

l. 8: ⸢x⸣ (first). This trace must begin some form of *nadānu*.

l. 8: TUR?. The sign is not PA, as copied. It shows as a faint TUR. However, the vertical wedge is not at all clear; the sign may represent I. The *CAD* Nuzi file in fact interprets this line as: [*i-din ù* GÌR]-*šu i-*[*il-li*], based on the similar phraseology of *JEN* 206:15.

ll. 9-10. If line 8 is parallel to *JEN* 206:15 (see note immediately above), then these lines may well be the analogues of *JEN* 206:16.

l. 13: *ú-z*[*a-ak-*ka_4]. Or the like.

l. 13: ⸢*ù*⸣. The *CAD* Nuzi file reads, at this point, *ù*.

l. 14: *i*[*l-*ka_4]. Or the like.

l. 20: ⸢*ru*⸣. The sign, as copied, looks like RI. However, it is faint and ⸢RU⸣ is certainly possible. In light of line 23, it is certain. Also, Porada links the seal impression below this line with Urḫiya son of Arrumpa. The *CAD* Nuzi file at this point reads: *ru*.

l. 22: *Šur*!-*ri*-[ ]. Cf. *NPN*, pp. 85a *sub* KILĪLIḪA 1), 139a, *sub* ŠURRI...: "*Šur*$_{x}$(PAD)-*ri*-[...]."

l. 23: *A-ru-um-pa*$_{12}$. See above, note to line 6.

l. 24: *A-ri-ḫar-pa*$_{12}$. See above, note to line 6.

l. 28: ⸢*Ma*⸣-[*li-ya*]. The restoration is all but certain. See *NPN*, 174b *sub* WURTURUK.

l. 30: A?-[ ]. Although *A*-[*kip-til-la*] would seem to be the most likely restoration (cf. l. 27), the *CAD* Nuzi file here reads *Ḫa*-[ ], indicating a restoration, *Ḫ*[*a*!-*ni-a-aš-ḫa-ri* (DUMU *A-ri-ya*)] (cf. l. 25). Porada links the seal impression above this line with Ḫaniašḫari son of Ariya.

JEN 708

OBVERSE

.
.
.

1 [ ] ⸢^{f}?[*Ḫa?-ši?*]-•⸢*il!?-lu*⸣?-[*um?*]-•*ti*
2 [*a-na* **k*]*a*-•*al-lu-ti* SUM-*in* ⸢x⸣ [(?)]
3 [*ù*] ^{m}*Te-ḫi-ip-til-la a+na* Ì[R.MEŠ-*šu*]
4 [*ga*$_{14}$-*a*]*b*!-*bi-im-ma* SUM-*in šum*-•*m*[*a*]
5 [1-*e*]*n mu-us-sú im-tu*-•*ut ù* [*a-na ša-ni-i*] SUM-[*in*]
6 [**šu*]*m*-•*ma ša-nu-ú im-t*[*u*]-•*ut* •*ù* [*a-na ša-aš-ši*] SU[M-*in*]
7 [*šum-m*]*a re-bu-ú im*-**t*[*u-ut*] *⸢*ù*⸣ [*a-na ḫa-am-ši* SUM-*in*]
8 [*a-d*]*i ṣú-ḫa*-•*ar*-**tu*
9 [^{f}]•*Ḫa*-•*ši-il*-[*lu-u*]*m*-[*ti bal-ṭù i-na* É ^{m}*Te-ḫi-ip-til-la*]
10 [*l*]*a ú-uṣ-ṣ*[*í šum-ma ṣú-ḫa-ar-tu*]
11 [*pa-r*]*i*!-*qa-na ir*-[*ta-ši ù* ^{f}*Ša*]-*áš-k*[*u-li*] ⸢*ú-za-ak*⸣-*ka*$_{4}$
12 [*ù* ^{m}]•⸢*Te*⸣-*ḫi*-⸢*ip*⸣-[*til-la a-n*]*a* ^{f}*Ša-áš-k*[*u-li*]
13 [*ša*? K]I?.BAL!?-*tu* 2 MA.[NA] ⸢KÙ⸣.[BABBAR? SUM?]
14 [IGI]-⸢*x*⸣-*ya* DUMU *Ik-ku-ya*
15 [IGI *Mu-uš-te-šup*] DUMU *Ar-na-pu*
16 [IGI DUMU] ⸢X X⸣ [ ]

.
.
.

REVERSE

.
.
.

17 [IG]I ⸢X⸣-[DUMU]
18 IGI *Še-el-la-*[*pa-i* DUMU]
19 IGI ⸢*Ip-ša*⸣-*ḫa-lu* DUMU *It-ḫi-iš-t*[*a*]
20 IGI [DUMU]-•^{d}INNIN! DUMU *Ku-uz-za-ri-ya*
21 [I]GI ⸢*It*⸣-*ḫi-iš-ta* DUMU *Ar-ta-e*
22 IGI *El-ḫi-ip*-LUGAL DUMU SILIM-^{d}IM
23 IGI *Ta-a-a* DUB.SAR
S.I. Po 47
24 ^{NA_4} KIŠIB ^{m}*Ša-áš-ku-li* DUMU.MÍ ^{m}*Pí-si*?-[(?)]
S.I.
25 [^{NA_4} KIŠIB ^{m}*Mu-uš-te-š*]*up* DUMU •*Ar-**⸢*na-***pu*⸣

TRANSLATION

....

(1-2) ... gave Ḫašil-lumti(?) [into] "daughter-in-lawship" [...?].

(3-7) [And] Teḫip-tilla may give (her) to any of [his] slave[s]. If her (lit. "his") first husband shall have died, then he may give (her) [to a second]. If the second shall have died, then he may give (her) [to a third]. If the fourth shall have died, then [he may give (her) to a fifth].

(8-10) As long as the slave girl, Ḫašil-lumti, [lives], she shall not depart [Teḫip-tilla's household].

(10-11) [Should the slave girl] have claimants, [then] Šaš-kuli shall clear (her).

(12-13) [And] Teḫip-tilla ... to Šaš-kuli ... .

(13) [Whoever?] abrogates(?) (this contract) [shall give(?) 2 minas of [silver?].

(14-23) [Before] ...-ya son of Ikkuya; [before Muš-Tešup] son of Arn-apu; [before ... son of] ...; ....; before ... [son of ...]; before Šellapai [son of ...]; before Ipša-ḫalu son of Itḫišta; before Mâr-ištar son of Kuzzariya; before Itḫišta son of Ar-tae; before Elḫip-šarri son of Šulm-adad; before Taya, the scribe.

(24-25) (*seal impression*) seal impression of Šaš-kuli daughter of Pi-si(?)-...; (*seal impression*) [seal impression of] Muš-tešup son of Arn-apu.

COMMENTS

This tablet has suffered considerable additional deterioration since the copy was made. This is especially the case around the edges of the preserved parts of the upper obverse of the tablet.

The text, even in its partially preserved state, is not difficult to fathom. It is a contract describing the sale of a young female into "daughter-in-lawship." Such contracts are occasionally attested elsewhere in the Nuzi corpus. The contracts assume a variety of textual formats. One text in particular, *JEN* 437, has a formulary extremely close to the preserved portions of *JEN* 708. So marked is the resemblance between these two texts (*JEN* 437:4-19 is substantially parallel to *JEN* 708:2-13) that significant lacunae in *JEN* 708 are filled in based on the preserved text of *JEN* 437. (Note further that the purchaser is the same in both texts [cf. *JEN* 437:4-6 with *JEN* 708:3]; the two texts share a scribe and even a witness [cf. *JEN* 437:27, 26 with *JEN* 708:23, 21].) A discussion and partial translation of *JEN* 437 appear in J. Lewy (1940, 54-55).

On the basis of *JEN* 437, one surmises that perhaps two lines are missing at the start of *JEN* 708. These, together with the badly damaged line 1, would have identified the vendor (Šaš-kuli [l. 24]; see below, second note to line 11), possibly the purchaser (Teḫip-tilla [l. 3]), and the female being sold (Ḫašil-lumti [l. 9]).

NOTES

l. 2: ⸢x⸣ [(?)]. *JEN* 437 offers no clue as to how the end of this line might be restored.

l. 3: [*ù*]. Lacheman records this sign as entirely preserved.

l. 3: Ì[R.MEŠ-*šu*]. The remaining trace resembles MU and, in fact, Lacheman reads *mu-ti*. However, the analogue in *JEN* 437:6, ÌR.MEŠ-*šu*, is to be preferred.

l. 4: [*ga*$_{14}$-*a*]*b*!-*bi-im-ma*. The initial surviving trace does not appear to point to the usual AB sign. Lacheman reads here, *ra*. However, the *ga*$_{14}$-*ab-bi-im-ma* of *JEN* 437:7 indicates the reading here. Note that, after this word, *JEN* 437:7 has *a-na aš-šu-ti*.

l. 5: *mu-us-sú*. The same error (i.e., *mussu* for *mussa*) is committed by this scribe in *JEN* 437:8.

l. 5: [*a-na*]. The *CAD* Nuzi file records these two signs as wholly preserved.

ll. 6-7. It would appear that the scribe inadvertently omitted a sentence between these two lines: *šum-ma ša-aš-šu im-tu-ut ù a-na re-bi-i* SUM-*in*. Cf. *JEN* 437:11-12. The reason behind this mental lapse might the scribe's mechanical "counting" from "3" at the end of line 6 to "4" at the start of line 7.

For further examples of this formula in the Nuzi texts, see Maidman (1990, 80).

l. 6: [*a-na*]. The *CAD* Nuzi file records these two signs as wholly preserved.

l. 8. This line appears anomalously (and disturbingly) short. However, no restoration presents itself or appears necessary.

l. 9: [f]*Ḫa-ši-il-[lu-u]m-[ti]*. According to Lacheman, the female determinative is entirely preserved.

The restoration of the name is likely, but not entirely certain. The ending, *-um-ti*, is based on the last trace of line 9 and especially on the *-ti* of line 1, *if* the traces of this line represent the PN of the female being sold. For the fPN, "Ḫašil-lumti," cf., e.g., *JEN* 516:15 (the same female might even be meant; cf. *HSS*, XVI, 333:11, 16). The other possibility for this PN is [f]*Ḫa-ši-il-[lu]* (followed by the traces of a following sign). For the fPN, "Ḫašil-lu," cf., e.g., *P-S* 52:3. *NPN*, 57a, recognizes neither of these possibilities for the slave girl of *JEN* 708.

l. 9: [*bal-ṭù*]. This grammatically incorrect form (cf. *bal-ṭá-at* [*JEN* 26:12]) is taken from *JEN* 437:13, written by the same scribe.

l. 9: [*i-na*]. Cf. *JEN* 26:13 and the trace in *JEN* 437:14.

l. 11: [*pa-r*]*i!-qa-na*. The trace of RI is not as copied. It appears more as DIŠ+A. For other examples of this form of the word instead of the usual *pa-qí-ra-na*, see *AHw*, 105a *sub* bāqirānum.

l. 11: [f*Ša*]*-áš-k*[*u-li*]. The spelling in *NPN*, 126a *sub* ŠAŠ-KULI, is to be corrected accordingly. This PN is better preserved in line 12. The restoration here and in the next line is based on the following reasoning. *JEN* 437 is sealed by three individuals: the vendor (l. 28; cf. ll. 1-2), a witness (l. 29; cf. l. 26), and the scribe (l. 30; cf. l. 27). *JEN* 708 has two surviving seal impressions with accompanying legends identifying the sealers. The second sealer is a witness (l. 25; cf. l. 15). The first (l. 24) is not the scribe (cf. l. 23). Nor does she appear in the surviving list of witnesses. On the analogy of *JEN* 437, it is suggested that she is the vendor in this contract. The surviving traces in lines 11 and 12 fit her PN admirably. And the vendors's name is expected in lines 11 and 12. Cf. *JEN* 437:16, 17. (Lacheman's papers suggest that he may have reached this conclusion as well.)

l. 12: f*Ša-áš-k*[*u-li*]. On the identity of this person, see the note immediately above.

Following this fPN should appear the price paid by Teḫip-tilla for Ḫašil-lumti. Cf. *JEN* 437:17-18. The relevant words would have appeared at the end of line 12 and possibly at the start of line 13. For another possibility, see the following note.

l. 13: [*ša?* K]I?.BAL!?*-tu*. This reconstruction assumes that the remaining signs and traces of line 13 represent the fine of a penalty clause. Cf. the *CAD* Nuzi file: [*ma-an-nu ša* K]I.BAL*-tu*, and *JEN* 437:19, itself only partially preserved. However, even if this clause started with an abbreviated "[*ša* K]I," the preceding space on line 13 and the end of line 12 appear to allow scant room for describing the price paid to the vendor. As an alternative, one might consider that lines 12-13 contain only the price clause and that there is no penalty clause at all. (Note that

the BAL of this line actually resembles IG quite closely. Cf. the sign form immediately below, on the next line. Might [(?)]-⸢x⸣-IG-*tu* describe [part of?] the price?)

l. 13: ⸢KÙ⸣.[BABBAR?]. Thus a metal is involved in any case.

l. 14: [IGI]-⸢*x*⸣-*ya*. Lacheman makes the plausible restoration: IGI *Ni-iḫ-ri-ya*. See *NPN*, 67b *sub* IKKUI̯A; and *AAN*, 66a *sub* IKKUIA.

l. 15: [IGI *Mu-uš-te-šup*]. The last sign of this PN is mostly preserved in line 25. "[Muš-teš]up DUMU Arn-apu" is the only reasonable restoration for "[-R]U DUMU Arn-apu." See *NPN*, 30b *sub* ARN-APU; and *AAN* 30b *sub* ARN-APU. Lacheman restores [*Mu-uš-te-šup*].

l. 17: [IG]I ⸢X⸣. Rather than the traces as copied, this part of the tablet preserves:

l. 18. The patronymic should likely be restored, [*Ar-ta-e*]. See *NPN*, 129b *sub* ŠELLAPAI 3).

l. 20: [DUMU]-^{d}INNIN!. The last sign appears clearly as ŠUR. The *CAD* Nuzi file also reads ŠUR. Cf. the identical sign form in the name of the same individual in *JEN* 302:18. The interpretation, INNIN!, is assured by the ubiquity of the resulting PN and patronymic. See *NPN*, 95b *sub* MÂR-IŠTAR 3). The ^{d}X asserted for this line in *NPN*, 95b and 93b *sub* KUZZARII̯A 6) is incorrect.

l. 24: ^{m}*Ša*. The male determinative is clear. The tablet is well preserved at this point.

l. 24: ^{m}*Pí-si*?-[(?)]. The male determinative is unexpected in a patronymic but clearly present.

As reflected in the copy, the last preserved sign is indistinct. The reading adopted here tentatively follows Lacheman and the "*Bi*-si-[....]" of *NPN*, 115b *sub* PISI....?, 126a *sub* ŠAŠ-KULI. This last sign might also be RA. The *CAD* Nuzi file opts for RU. If the last alternative is correct, then the vendor might well be the daughter of that most ubiquitous of Teḫip-Tilla witnesses, Piru son of Naiš-kelpe. See *NPN*, 115 *sub* PIRU 1).

l. 25. See above, note to line 15.

Lacheman identifies the seal impression above this line as "Po 917."

If the parallels between this tablet and *JEN* 437 persist to the end, then, below line 25, there once should have appeared another seal impression followed by a last line of text: ^{NA_4} KIŠIB DUB.SAR-*ri*.

JEN 709

OBVERSE

1 *ṭup-pí m[a-r]u-ti ša*

2 ^{m}*Ta-a-[a]* DUMU *Ip-ša-ḫa-•lu*

3 ^{m}*Te-ḫi-i[p-ti]l-la* ⸢DUMU⸣ *P[u]-ḫi-še-en-n[i]*

4 *a-na ma-r[u]-ti i-*⸢*te-pu*⸣*-uš-ma*

5 1 ANŠE 2 $^{⸢GIŠ⸣}$APIN A.ŠÀ ⸢*i-na*⸣ ^{GIŠ}*ta-a-a-r[i]* GAL

6 [AŠ] *šu-pa-al* AN.ZA.KÀR ⸢*ša*⸣ $^{m?}$*Ap-li-a*

7 [*ù* AŠ] ⸢*e-le*⸣*-nu* AN.ZA.KÀR ⸢*ša*⸣ ^{m}*A-ka*$_{4}$*-wa-til*

8 [AŠ] ⸢A⸣.GÀR [UR]U *Ú-nap-še-wa*

9 [*ki-m*]*a* Ḫ[A].LA-*šu* ^{m}*Ta-a-a*

10 [*a-na*] ^{m}*Te-ḫi-ip-til-la* ⸢*it*⸣*-ta-din*

11 [*ù*] ^{m}*Te-[ḫ]i-ip-til-la*

12 [A]NŠE ŠE.MEŠ *ki-ma* NÍ[G].BA-*šu*

13 ⸢*a*⸣-[*na*] ^{m}*T[a]-a-a it-ta-ad-na-aš-šu*

14 *šum-*⸢*ma*⸣ [A.ŠÀ] *an-nu-um di-na* TUK-*ši*

15 ^{m}*Ta-a-*⸢*a ú*⸣*-za-ak-ka*$_{4}$*-ma*

16 *a-na* ^{m}*Te-ḫi-ip-til-la i+na-an-*⸢*din*⸣

17 *il-ka*$_{4}$ *ša* A.ŠÀ ^{m}*Ta-a-a-ma* ⸢*na*⸣-[*š*]*i*

18 *šum-ma* ^{m}*Ta-a-a* KI.BAL-*at*

19 10 MA.N[A] KÙ.SIG$_{17}$ *a-na* $^{m⸢}$*Te*⸣*-ḫi-ip-til-la*

20 *ú-ma-al-la*

---

21 IGI *Ḫu-[lu]-*⸢*uk*⸣*-ka*$_{4}$ •DUMU *Ku-ra-sú*

22 IGI *Ur-ḫ[i]-ya* DUMU *Š[e]-ka*$_{4}$*-rù*

23 IGI ⸢*Tar*⸣*-mi-ya* DUMU *Ma-ša-an-ta*

LOWER EDGE

24 IG[I] *Wu-un-nu-ki-ya* DUMU *Tar-•mi-•ya*

25 ⸢IGI⸣ *Ma-li-ya* DUMU *Ḫu-pí-t[a]*

26 ⸢IGI⸣ *Ar-nu-zu* DUMU *Am-ma-ak-k[a*$_{4}$*]*

REVERSE

27 IGI ⸢*It-ḫa*⸣*-pí-*⸢*ḫe*⸣ DUMU *Ta-a-a*

28 IGI *Na-ḫi-še-ya* DUMU *Ki-pè-er-ḫa*

29 IGI DINGIR-KI-*ya* DUMU *Ki-pè-er-ḫa*

30 IGI ⸢*Ta*⸣*-a-a* DUB.SAR-*rù*

31 *ši-bu-tù-ma* A.ŠÀ *il-*⸢*mu*⸣*-ú*

32 ⸢*ù*⸣ ŠE.MEŠ *id-dì-nu*

S.I. Po 141

33 ^{NA_4} KIŠIB ^{m}*Tar-mi-ya* DUMU *Ma-ša-an-te*

S.I. Po 498

34 ^{NA_4} [KI]ŠIB ^{m}*It-ḫa-pí-ḫe* DUMU *Ta-[a-a]*

S.I. Po 508

35 [^{NA_4} KIŠIB ^{m}]⌜x x⌝

LEFT EDGE

S.I. Po 199

36 [^{NA_4} KI]ŠIB ^{m}*Ur-*$^{+}$*ḫi-ya* ⌜DUMU *Še*⌝-*ka*$_4$-*rù*

TRANSLATION

(1-4) Tablet of adoption of Taya son of Ipša-ḫalu. He adopted Teḫip-tilla son of Puḫi-šenni.

(5-10) Taya gave [to] Teḫip-tilla as his inheritance share a field, 1.2 homers by the large standard, [to] the west of the *dimtu* of Apliya [and to] the east of the *dimtu* of Akawatil, [in] the *ugāru* of the town of Unap-še.

(11-13) [And] Teḫip-tilla gave to Taya as his gift x homer(s) of barley.

(14-16) Should this [field] have a case (against it), Taya shall clear (the field) and give (it) to Teḫip-tilla.

(17) Taya shall also bear the *ilku* of the field.

(18-20) Should Taya abrogate (this contract), he shall pay to Teḫip-tilla 10 minas of gold.

(21-32) Before Ḫulukka son of Kurasu; before Urḫiya son of Šekaru; before Tarmiya son of Mašante; before Wunnukiya son of Tarmiya; before Maliya son of Ḫupita; before Ar-nuzu son of Ammakka; before Itḫ-apiḫe son of Taya; before Naḫiššeya son of Kip-erḫan; before Ili-ittiya son of Kip-erḫan; before Taya, the scribe. And (these) witnesses encircled the field and distributed the barley.

(33-36) (*seal impression*) seal impression of Tarmiya son of Mašante; (*seal impression*) seal impression of Itḫ-apiḫe son of Taya; (*seal impression*) [seal impression of] ...; (*seal impression*) seal impression of Urḫiya son of Šekaru.

COMMENT

Only four signs (see lines 2, 21, 24) have suffered partial damage since the tablet was copied.

NOTES

l. 6: [AŠ]. The *CAD* Nuzi file reads: *i-na*. Lacheman reads: AŠ. The spacing favors the latter.

l. 6: *Ap-li-a*. The end of this line is correct as copied.

l. 7: [*ù* AŠ] ⌜*e-le*⌝-*nu*. The *CAD* Nuzi file records the first four signs as completely preserved.

ll. 8-13. Note that the left hand parts of these lines appear higher than their continuations on the right. The difference in height is not as exaggerated

as the copy suggests. Line 13 especially might cause confusion. It starts at the left edge, continues on a higher level, and resumes (for the rest of the line) at a lower "latitude."

l. 8: ⌜A⌝.GÀR [UR]U. The *CAD* Nuzi file records these signs as completely preserved. Lacheman records A.GÀR *ša* URU as completely preserved.

l. 12: [A]NŠE. The *CAD* Nuzi file records "5 ANŠE" as entirely preserved.

l. 13. See above, note to ll. 8-13.

l. 19: 10. The *Winkelhaken* is clearly preserved. Contrary to the copy, there is no DIŠ sign.

l. 24. Despite the appearance of the copy, there is no open space above line 24 on the lower edge.

l. 26: *Am-ma-ak-k*[*a*$_4$]. See also above, note to *JEN* 694:18. The last sign was once entirely preserved according to Lacheman, the *CAD* Nuzi file, and *NPN*, 20a *sub* AMMAKKA 2), 31a *sub* AR-NUZU 1). In the only other attestation of this person, *JEN* 694:18, the last sign is wholly effaced.

l. 35. It is possible that, below this line, additional text has been lost.

l. 35: ⌜x x⌝. Porada suggests that S.I. Po 508 might be the seal impression of Taya the scribe. If so, these traces might well reflect: [DU]B.⌜SAR⌝.

l. 36: *ḫi*. This sign is clear and wholly preserved.

JEN 710

OBVERSE

1 [*ṭup-p*]*í ma-ru-t*[*i ša* ^{m}*Ki-it-ta-a-a*]

2 [DUMU M]I.NI-*a-bi* ^{m}·⌜*Te*⌝-[*ḫi-ip-til-la*]

3 [DUMU] *Pu-ḫi-še-en-ni a-na*

4 [*m*]*a-ru-ti i-pu-us-s*[*ú*]

5 [x?+] 1 ANŠE 2 ^{GIŠ}APIN A.ŠÀ AŠ? [ ]⌜x⌝ *mi a aḫ ḫi*

6 [x?+] 1 ANŠE 2 ^{GIŠ}APIN A.ŠÀ AŠ? [*t*]*i?-li-i*

7 *ša zi-li*-UR-*ki+i* AŠ *ú-gà*[*r* (*ša*) URU *A*]*r-ti*$_4$-*ḫi* AŠ *ta-a-a-*[*r*]*i* GAL *ša* É.GAL

8 *a-na* ^{m}*Te-ḫi-ip-til-la* [*k*]*i-*·*ma* *⌜ḪA⌝.[L]A *i-din*

9 *ù* ^{m}*Te-ḫi-ip-til-l*[*a* x?+]·13 ANŠE ŠE

10 30 MA.NA URUDU!.MEŠ *a-na* ^{m}[*K*]*i-it-ta-a-a i+din*

11 *il-ka*$_4$ *ša* A.ŠÀ *šu-m*[*a n*]*a-ši*

12 *šum-ma* A.ŠÀ *pa-*⌜*qí*⌝*-ra-*·*n*[*a*]

13 *i-ra-aš-ši šu-ú-ma* ⌜*ú*⌝*-za-ak-kà*

14 *šum-ma* ^{m}*Ki-*⌜*it*⌝*-ta-a-*·*a*

15 *i-bala-kat* 10 MA.NA KÙ.SIG$_{17}$!

16 *ú-ma-al-la*

---

17 IGI *A-kip-til-la* DUMU *Tù-ra-ri*
18 IGI *Wu-ur-tù!-ru-uk!* DUMU *Ma-li-•ya*
19 IGI *Ša-tù-ša* DUMU *Tù-⸢ra⸣-ri*
20 IGI *Ut-ḫi-ip-til-la* DUMU *Tu[p-ki]-ya*

LOWER EDGE

21 •4 LÚ.MEŠ *an-nu-•tu*$_4$
22 [*m*]*u-še-el-•wu •š*[*a* A.ŠÀ *ù*]
23 *na-di-•na-*[*nu*] *⸢*ša*⸣ [ŠE.MEŠ *ù*? URUDU?.MEŠ?]
24 [IG]I ⸢x x x⸣ [DUMU]

REVERSE

25 ⸢IGI⸣ *Ar-*[*t*]*e-*[*šup* DUMU *It-ḫi-iš-ta*]
26 IGI *Pu-*[*ḫi-še-en*]*-⸢ni⸣* [DUMU] *A-ta-a-⸢te⸣*
27 IGI *Tar-*[*mi*]*-•te-šup* DUMU *Ar-te-ya*
28 IGI •*Te-šu-up-er-•wi* •DUMU •*Šúk-•ri-ya*
29 •IGI *Ḫa-ni-a-aš-ḫa-•ri* [DUMU *A-ri*]*-ya*
30 IGI *A-ri-ḫa-ar-*[*me* DUMU *E-en*]*-na-mil-ki*
31 IGI *Šúk!-ri-ya* D[UMU *X-li-ya*]
32 •IGI *It-ḫa-*p*[*í-ḫe* DUMU *Ta-a-a* •D]UB.•SAR
33 IGI •*Ki-•ip-ta-*[*li-li* DUMU] *⸢E⸣-•en-•na-mil-•ki*
34 IGI *Tar-mi-ya* DUMU *Ma-*[*ša*]*-an-te*
35 IGI *Ur-ḫi-ya* DUMU *A-ru-pa*$_{12}$

S.I. Po 636

36 ^{NA_4} KIŠIB ^{m}*Ur-ḫi-ya*

S.I. Po 720

37 ^{NA_4} KIŠIB ^{m}*Tar-mi-te-šup*

S.I.

38 [^{NA_4} KIŠIB ^{m}]⸢X X⸣

UPPER EDGE

[S.I.]

39 [^{NA_4} KIŠIB ^{m}]⸢X⸣[ ]

LEFT EDGE

S.I.

40 •^{NA_4} •KIŠIB ⸢DUB⸣.SAR

TRANSLATION

(1-4) Tablet of adoption [of Kittaya son of] Ṣill-abi. He adopted Teḫip-tilla [son of] Puḫi-šenni.

(5-8) He gave to Teḫip-tilla as an inheritance share a(n) [x?+]1.2 homer field in(?) ..., a(n) [x?+]1.2 homer field in(?) ... Tel(?) ZiliURki in the *ugāru* [of the town of] Artiḫi, (the land being measured) by the large standard of the palace.

(9-10) And Teḫip-tilla gave to Kittaya [x?+]13 homers of barley (and) 30 minas of copper.

(11) And he shall bear the *ilku* of the field.

(12-13) Should the field have claimants, he shall clear (the field) as well.

(14-16) Should Kittaya abrogate (this contract), he shall pay 10 minas of gold.

(17-35) Before Akip-tilla son of Turari; before Wur-turuk son of Maliya; before Šatuša son of Turari; before Itḫip-tilla son of Tupkiya. These 4 men are the measurers of [the field and] the distributors of [the barley and? copper?]. Before ... [son of ...]; before Ar-tešup [son of Itḫišta]; before Puḫi-šenni [son of] Adatteya; before Tarmi-tešup son of Ar-teya; before Tešup-erwi son of Šukriya; before Ḫaniašḫari [son of] Ariya; before Ariḫ-ḫarpa [son of] Enna-milki; before Šukriya son of [...-liya]; before Itḫ-apiḫe [son of Taya], the scribe; before Kip-talili [son of] Enna-milki; before Tarmiya son of Mašante; before Urḫiya son of Arrumpa.

(36-40) *(seal impression)* seal impression of Urḫiya; *(seal impression)* seal impression of Tarmi-tešup; *(seal impression)* [seal impression of] ...; [*(seal impression)* seal impression of] ...; *(seal impression)* seal impression of the scribe.

COMMENT

This tablet has suffered some damage, especially on the reverse, since the copy was made.

NOTES

l. 1. The four upside down wedges at the end of this line are from the end of the reverse, and are represented in the transliteration as line 38.

ll. 5-7. The interpretation of parts of these lines is problematical. However, the signs are correct as copied.

l. 5: [x?+] 1. Lacheman and the *CAD* Nuzi file see no gap at the start of this line. The number "1" is written over an erasure.

l. 5: [ ]⸢x⸣ *mi a aḫ ḫi*. I can suggest no interpretation for these signs. Lacheman reads, in effect: [*ti-l*]*i Mi-a-aḫ-ḫi*. Cf. Weeks (1972, 191): "[...] Mi-a-aḫ-ḫi." However, as a PN or GN, Miaḫḫi is elsewhere unattested in the Nuzi texts. (Fadhil [1983, 43a] reads: [AN.ZA.KÀR *M*]*a-mi-a-aḫ-ḫi*. It is unlikely that the initial trace represents [M]A.) The latter element (if it is an element), *-aḫḫi, is* attested elsewhere at Nuzi (e.g., *piršaḫḫi, kinaḫḫi*). See Maidman (1976, 180, note to line 31) and compare Astour (1981, 14, nos. 16, 17).

The *CAD* Nuzi file rendering: [ ]-*mi a-ḫi-ri-ḫi*, is hardly more enlightening.

Perhaps militating against interpreting this series of signs as a toponym is the following observation. It appears that the same land is described in lines 5 and 6, especially since the number of homers in each

line is written over an erasure (see note immediately above and note immediately below). If this is so and if lines 6-7 describe the topographical environment of the land (see below, notes to line 6 [second note] and 7 [second note]), then this line should define the land in other than topographical terms (e.g., in terms of crop[s] grown or legal status).

l. 6: [x?+] 1. As with line 5, Lacheman and the *CAD* Nuzi file see no gap at the start of this line. As with line 5, the number "1" is written over an erasure.

l. 6: [*t*]*i*?-*li*-*i*. [*t*]*i*-*li*-*i* is restored both by Lacheman and by the *CAD* Nuzi file.

l. 7: *zi*-*li*-UR-*ki*+*i*. This group of signs with something like these values may well represent a toponym. On this issue and a possible second occurrence of this very name, see already above, note to *JEN* 687:6.

This configuration, however, permits more than that interpretation alone. A personal name could be represented by these signs. However, no known Nuzi PN is suggested by the signs as here rendered. An ingenious solution to this dilemma is suggested by Lacheman: "*Zi*-*li*-*ip*-*ki*-*mâr*" (cf. the *CAD* Nuzi file's: *Zi*-*li*-*lik*-*ki*+TUR), i.e., *Zi*-*li*-*ip*!-*ke*+*már*!. Although this PN is not attested at Nuzi, the initial element, "Zilip-," and the final element, "-kewar," are both well represented in the onomasticon. (The meaning of neither element is known.) See *NPN*, 277b, 226, respectively, for these two elements.

That two signs out of five are irregularly rendered weakens Lacheman's interpretation, but not badly. For some reason, the scribe displays an unsure hand elsewhere in this text. Note the number "1" in lines 5 and 6, impressed over erasures; the somewhat unusual URUDU of line 10; the incomplete SIG_{17} of line 15 (see below, note to line 15); the defective DU of line 18; the imprecise UG (=AS) also of line 18 (this particular peculiarity is repeated in the same PN in *JEN* 419:17; 716:21; 728:16); and the overly complete MUG of line 31. Note further the scribe's peculiar omission of NÍG.BA in the gift clause (ll. 9-10); of the second half of the clear title clause (ll. 12-13); and of *ana Teḫip-tilla* in the penalty clause (ll. 14-16).

For the PN, Zilip-kewar, more peculiar than the sign forms is the use of TUR for *már*. To my knowledge, this is the only time at Nuzi that the sign would assume this phonetic value. This tells more seriously against Lacheman's interpretation. Yet the suggestion remains attractive.

l. 7: É.GAL. There is no break (and therefore no missing signs) after this sign.

l. 9: [x?+]13. Lacheman considers the number complete as is.

l. 9: ŠE. There is no break after this sign.

l. 15: 10 MA. No sign intervenes between these two signs.

l. 15: SIG_{17}!. The first half of this sign does not appear on the tablet. The surface is well preserved at this point.

l. 23: [*ù*? URUDU?.MEŠ?]. This reconstruction is possible but not necessary. See below, note to *JEN* 728:21.

l. 24. Lacheman and the *CAD* Nuzi file judge this line to have been erased. Of the four other texts in this series (see below, note to line 25), three identify Ar-tešup son of Itḫišta as the fifth witness (*JEN* 419:22; 716:26; 728:22) while one (like the present text) has an effaced line before the appearance of Ar-Tešup son of Itḫišta as the fifth witness (*JEN* 686:22). The possibility of erasure here, then, cannot be excluded. (Collation from a cast suggests that the line may indeed have been erased; certainty is lacking.)

l. 25. The restoration of this line is based, as are all witness PN restorations in this text, on the largely common Artiḫi witness sequence in *JEN* 419, 686, 710, 716, 728. See above, first note to *JEN* 686:5.

l. 30: *ki*. This last sign is a clear KI, not as copied.

l. 31: [X-*li-ya*]. This restoration is based on *JEN* 728:28. This person is not part of the witness sequence. See above, note to *JEN* 686:32.

l. 35: *A-ru-pa*$_{12}$. On this spelling, see above, note to *JEN* 686:33-34.

l. 38: ⸢X X⸣. In the copy, these traces appear upside down at the end of line 1.

l. 39: ⸢X⸣. In the copy, this trace appears above line 1. In apparent reference to this trace, Lacheman reads: [NA$_4$ ^{m}*A*]-*ri*-[*ḫar-pa*]. Cf. *JEN* 419:36 and 716:39, from the same cluster of texts.

JEN 711

OBVERSE

1 AŠ *Šu-ma-•š*[*a-wa-al-li*]
2 *i+na ša-pa-*[*a*]*t* ⸢X⸣ [ ]
3 ⸢*a*⸣-*na* ^{m}*Te-ḫi-•ip-til-la i*[*t*!-*ta-din*]
4 ⸢*ù*⸣ ^{m}*Te-ḫi-ip-til-la* 2 AN[ŠE A.ŠÀ]
5 *i+na Šu-ma-ša-wa-al-l*[*i*]
6 ⸢*a*⸣-*na ya-ši i-di-na*
7 [*š*]*a ma-an-ni-me-e* A.ŠÀ *pa-qí-r*[*a-na*]
8 *i-ra-aš-ši ù ú-za-ak-kà*
9 *ma-am-ma i+na* EGIR-*ki ma-am-ma la i-*[*sà-as-sí*]

S.I. Po 924

10 ^{NA_4} KIŠIB ^{m}*Tar-mi-ya* DUMU *Ú-náp-t*[*a*]-⸢*e*⸣

S.I. Po 793

11 ^{NA_4} KIŠIB ^{m}*Tar-mi-te-*⸢*šup*⸣
12 DUMU *E-ḫe-e*[*l-te-šup*]

REVERSE

S.I. Po 632

13 ^{NA_4} KIŠIB ^{m}*Te-eš-šu-ya* DUMU LUGAL

14 [Š]U! ^{m}⸢*It*⸣-[*ḫa-pí-ḫe* DUB.SAR]

TRANSLATION

....

(1-6) "I (lit. "he") have given to Teḫip-tilla .... in (the *dimtu* of) Šumaššawalli, on the bank/edge of ...; and Teḫip-tilla has given (lit. "gave") to me a 2 homer [field] in (the *dimtu*) of Šumaššawalli."

(7-8) Whose field has claimants, he shall clear (the field).

(9) Neither shall hail the other (into court).

(10-13) (*seal impression*) seal impression of Tarmiya son of Unap-tae; (*seal impression*) seal impression of Tarmi-tešup son of Eḫli-tešup; (*seal impression*) seal impression of Teššuya son of the king.

(14) Hand of Itḫ-apiḫe, [the scribe].

COMMENTS

This tablet has suffered only slight damage since the copy was made. Five or six lines at the start of the text are missing. The remaining context makes it clear that the tablet records a declaration of real estate exchange. Cf. *JEN* 199 for a better preserved example of this genre, written by the same scribe and also involving Teḫip-Tilla. The missing portion of the obverse should be roughly parallel to the contents of *JEN* 199:1-6:

li-ša-an-šu ša ^{m}PN
DUMU PN$_2$ *a-na pa-ni* (*ḫal-ṣú-uḫ-le-e*
ù a-na pa-ni) DI.KU$_5$.MEŠ
ki-a-am iq-ta-bi
it-ti ^{m}*Te-ḫi-ip-til-la*
nu-uš-te-pè-i-il 2 ANŠE A.ŠÀ

Cf. also above, *JEN* 706.

NOTES

l. 1: *Šu-ma-š*[*a-wa-al-li*]. This restoration is based on line 5 and on the assumption that this real estate exchange involves two plots of land in proximity to each other.

The term is to be considered a toponym. It is preceded by AN.ZA.KÀR in *JEN* 140:6; 180:8; 746:9 (probably—see below, note to *JEN* 746:9; and note the anomalous writing there, *Šu-ma-ša-wa-al-*⸢*ḫi*⸣, as opposed to the usual *Šu-ma(-aš)-ša-wa-al-li*). It should be noted that *JEN* 153:8 and 172:8 (partially broken), in addition to the present text, fail to define Šumaš-

šawalli as a *dimtu*. Land designated by this term is located in Nuzi. See *JEN* 746:8-9. *JEN* 140:6-7 links this *dimtu* with the *dimtu* of Awīlu, itself located in Nuzi, according to *JEN* 662:9, 13.

l. 2: ⌜X⌝. Lacheman reads, at this point: ⌜KASKAL *ša*⌝ [URU x x x].

l. 3: *i*[*t*!]. The sign does not appear as copied but, rather, as:  The sign, *at*, is expected. Cf., e.g., *JEN* 199:8.

l. 5: *l*[*i*]. Lacheman implies that this is the last sign on this line.

ll. 8-9. Between these two lines, one expects: *iš-tu*$_4$ *u*$_4$*-mi an-ni-i* (*JEN* 199:13-14) or the like.

l. 9: *i*-[*sà-as-sí*]. For this restoration, see *JEN* 122:24; 199:16, written by the same scribe.

l. 12: *E-ḫe-e*[*l-te-šup*]. This restoration is based on the ubiquitous presence of this particular Tarmi-tešup (together with the Tarmiya son of Unaptae of line 10) in declaration texts. See, e.g., *JEN* 122:27; 153:20; 172:19.

l. 14. One expects the identity of the scribe to be noted in the last section of declaration texts of this type. (This would not be accompanied by a seal impression and, on the copy, Lacheman correctly notes this absence.) The identification, however, usually precedes that of the sealers. See, e.g., *JEN* 172, 179. Cf., however, *JEN* 176.

l. 14: ⌜*It*⌝. These traces lead to the restoration of the name and title of Itḫapiḫe, the only Teḫip-tilla scribe whose name starts with this element.

JEN 712

(see *JEN* 753)

JEN 713

OBVERSE

1 ^{m}*Te-ḫi-ip-*[*til-la*]
2 *it-ti* ^{m}*Ḫu*!-[*i-iš-ša*]
3 DUMU *Ḫur-pí-š*[*e-en-ni*]
4 AŠ *di-ni* AŠ ⌜*pa*⌝-[*n*]*i* DI.KU$_5$.MEŠ
5 *i-te-lu-ú-ma* ^{m}*Te-ḫi-ip-til-*⌜*la*⌝
6 *i+na di-ni il-te-i-ma*
7 *ù* ^{m}*Ḫu-i-iš-ša*
8 *a-na* 24 UDU.MEŠ *a-na*
9 ^{m}*Te-ḫi-ip-til-la it-ta-du-u*[*š*]

S.I. Po 647

LOWER EDGE

10 [$^{\text{NA}_4}$ KIŠIB ^{m} *-t*]*e?-šup*

REVERSE

S.I.

11 $^{\text{NA}_4}$ KIŠIB ^{m}[ ]-⸢*ir*⸣ *⸢X X *X⸣

S.I.

12 $^{\text{NA}_4}$ KIŠIB ^{m}*Ḫa-ši-*⸢*x*⸣ [(?)]

S.I. Po 632

13 $^{\text{NA}_4}$ KIŠIB ^{m}*T*[*e-eš-šu-ya* DUMU LUGAL]

TRANSLATION

(1-9) Teḫip-tilla took to court, before judges, Ḫuišša son of Ḫurpi-šenni. Teḫip-tilla won the case and they (i.e., the judges) sentenced Ḫuišša (to pay) 24 sheep to Teḫip-tilla.

(10-13) (*seal impression*) [seal impression of] ...-tešup(?); (*seal impression*) seal impression of ...; (*seal impression*) seal impression of Ḫaši-...; (*seal impression*) seal impression of Teššuya [son of the king].

COMMENTS

Only line 11 has suffered some damage since the copy was made.

This record of litigation is unusual: standard introduction, verdict, and sealer formulas are present but no description of the court proceedings is given. For very similar texts, see *HSS*, V, 45, 50; *G* 37. The function of texts such as these—and a primary function even of the lengthier, more descriptive trial texts (far more numerous than the short texts)—is very probably the notation of the disposition of the case. In this text, it is a penalty (ll. 7-9). Litigation texts record goods owed to (or recovered by) the winner; and protection of the winner's property is, ultimately, the *raison d'être* of such documents. Description of the trial itself—often truncated and, therefore, yielding little connected sense—is, at best, of secondary importance to those who commissioned these tablets. The recording of court proceedings is not, *per se*, a function of this genre of text. These ideas are more fully developed in Maidman (1993, 47-51).

NOTES

l. 1: [*til-la*]. Lacheman implies that the patronymic was never written. This is plausible, given the spacing of the signs. Very likely, the son of Puḫi-šenni is meant. The other principal party appears as a witness in three other Teḫip-tilla texts, and there only. See *NPN*, p. 62a *sub* ḪUIŠŠA 1).

l. 2: *Ḫu*!. The "AK"-like appearance of this sign is clear on the tablet.

l. 3: *Ḫur-pí-š[e-en-ni]*. This restoration is based on a perusal of all attested persons bearing the name, Ḫuišša. See *NPN*, 62a *sub* ḪUIŠŠA; and *AAN*, 59a *sub* ḪUIŠŠA. The evidence suggests no other possible reconstruction.

l. 11: ⸢X X X⸣. Only the single horizontal line remains visible.

l. 13: *T[e-eš-šu-ya* DUMU LUGAL]. Porada (1947, 134) identifies S.I. 632 with this person in *JEN* 178. The trace of the PN in this line suggests that the same PN and title belong here.

JEN 714

OBVERSE

1 •*ṭup-pí ma-r[u-ti ša]* ^{m}*Te-ḫ]i-i[p-til-la]*

2 •DUMU *Pu-ḫi-še-e[n-n]i* ^{m}*Šu-um-ma-*•⸢*i*⸣-[*il*]

3 DUMU *Ik-ki-in* ⸢*a*⸣*-na ma-ru-ti*$_4$ *i-p[u-us-sú* GIŠ.ŠAR]

4 42 *i+na am-ma-ti*$_4$ *mu-ra-*⸢*ak*⸣-[*šu ù*]

5 38 *i+na am-ma-ti*$_4$ *ru-up-šu ša* GIŠ.Š[AR]

6 *i+na* URU *Ú-lam-me* ^{m}*Šu-um-ma-i-i[l]*

7 *a-na* ^{m}*Te-ḫi-*⸢*ip*⸣*-til-la ki-mu* ḪA.LA-*š[u] i+din*

8 *ù* ^{m}*Te-ḫi-ip-til-la a-na*

9 ^{m}*Šu-um-ma-i-[i]l* 30 MA.⸢NA⸣ URUDU.ME[Š]

10 5 UDU.MEŠ 7 ⸢ANŠE⸣ 3? BÁN ŠE.[ME]Š [*ki*]-*m*[*u*]

11 NÍG.BA *i+din š[um!-ma* ^{m}*Šu]-*⸢*um*⸣-[*ma-i-i*]*l*

12 *i-bala-ka*$_4$-⸢*at*⸣ [1?] ⸢MA.NA⸣ [KÙ?.BABBAR?] ⸢*ù*⸣?

13 1 MA.NA ⸢KÙ⸣.[SIG$_{17}$?] *ú-ma-[al-la]*

14 ⸢IGI⸣ *Pí-*⸢*i-ru*⸣ DUMU *Na-i-iš-*⸢*ké*⸣*-e[l-pé]*

15 I[GI *E-mu-y*]*a* DUMU *Ip-ša-ḫa-lu*

16 IGI *M[u-uš-t]e-šup* DUMU *Ar-na-pu*

17 IGI *Še-*⸢*la*⸣-[*pa*]-⸢*i*⸣ DUMU *A-ri-ya*

18 •IGI *Pa-li-*⸢*ya*⸣ DUMU *Ḫu-ti*$_4$*-ya*

19 [I]GI +*It-ḫi-iš-ta* ⸢DUMU⸣ *A-ar-t[a-e]*

20 IGI [ ]-⸢*x*⸣*-ni-ya* [DUMU]

LOWER EDGE

21 [IGI] **Ḫu-*⸢*x-x*⸣ [DUMU]

22 [IGI]⸢X X⸣ [DUMU]

23 I[GI DUMU]

REVERSE

24 [IGI] *It-ḫa-p[í-ḫe* DU]B.⸢SAR⸣-*rù*

S.I. Po 291

25 ^{NA_4} KIŠIB ^{m}*Ta-an-te-ya* D[UMU *A-ka*$_4$*-a-a*]

S.I. Po 301

26 ^{NA_4} KIŠIB ^{m}*E-[mu-ya* DUMU ⸢*Ip*⸣?-[*ša?-ḫa?-lu?*]

S.I. Po 637

27 •^{NA_4} KIŠIB ^{m}*Pí-i-*⸢*ru*⸣ DUMU •*Na-i-iš-*⸢*ké*⸣-

•: •*e*[*l-p*]*é*

S.I. Po 309

28 ^{NA_4} KIŠIB ^{m}⸢x⸣[ ]

S.I.

UPPER EDGE

29 ^{NA_4} KIŠIB ^{m}[ ]-⸢x-*te*?-x⸣

TRANSLATION

(1-3) Tablet of adoption [of] Teḫip-tilla son of Puḫi-šenni. Šumma-ilu son of Ikkin adopted him.

(3-7) Šumma-ilu gave to Teḫip-tilla as his inheritance share [an orchard], 42 cubits in length [and] 38 cubits in width (lit. "the width of the orchard"), in the town of Ulamme.

(8-11) And Teḫip-tilla gave to Šumma-ilu as a gift 30 minas of copper, 5 sheep, (and) 7.3(?) homers of barley.

(11-13) Should Šumma-ilu abrogate (this contract), he shall pay [1?] mina of ...(?) [silver?] and(?) 1 mina of gold(?).

(14-24) Before Piru son of Naiš-kelpe; before Emuya son of Ipša-ḫalu; before Muš-tešup son of Arn-apu; before Šellapai son of Ariya; before Paliya son of Ḫutiya; before Itḫišta son of Ar-tae; before ...-niya [son of ...]; [before] Ḫu-... [son of ...]; [before] ... [son of ...]; before [... son of ...]; [before] Itḫ-apiḫe, the scribe.

(25-29) *(seal impression)* seal impression of Tanteya son of [Akaya]; *(seal impression)* seal impression of Emuya [son of] Ipša-ḫalu; *(seal impression)* seal impression of Piru son of Naiš-kelpe; *(seal impression)* seal impression of ...; *(seal impression)* seal impression of ... .

COMMENT

This tablet has suffered slight damage since it was copied.

NOTES

l. 2: *Šu-um-ma-*⸢*i*⸣-[*il*]. The entry, ŠUMMAI̯A, in *NPN*, 138a, is to be deleted. That interpretation, as the succeeding entry, ŠUMMA-ILU, shows, was made before *JENu* 300 and *JENu* 1142 were joined. Apropos the latter entry, the interpretation of the last sign as *il* is not to be doubted, as its appearance in line 9 demonstrates. See also next note.

l. 3: *Ik-ki-in* ⸢*a*⸣-. There appears to be no room after *in* for another sign before ⸢*a*⸣. Therefore, there seems to be no good reason for the *NPN*'s interpretation of this name as "IKKIN...." (67b). (In this entry, correct

"*Šu-um-ma-ia*"; see above immediately preceding note). *AAN*, 65b, correctly notes the PN, Ikkinna, spelled *Ik-ki-in-na* (see now, as well, *EN*, 9/1, 140:1 [reference from Lacheman's notes]). If that name is meant to be represented here, then a defective spelling, *Ik-ki-in-*<*na*>, may have to be posited.

l. 5: GIŠ.Š[AR]. Lacheman and the *CAD* Nuzi file record both signs as completely preserved.

l. 10: 3? BÁN. The bottom half of the number is completely effaced. Lacheman records, not "3," but "6."

For this way of writing "3 (or "6") BÁN," see above, first note to *JEN* 705:8.

l. 11. Between the "gift" clause (ending in this line) and the penalty clause (beginning with this line), one expects the clear title clause.

l. 11: *š*[*um*!-*ma* ᵐ*Šu*]-⸢*um*⸣-[*ma-i-i*]*l*. Lacheman interprets these traces as: *m*[*a-an-nu*]-*um*-[*me-e š*]*a*. Although the first trace would appear to bear this out, this scribe's practice elsewhere favors the adopted restoration. See, for example, *JEN* 4:12; 12:15.

l. 12: ⸢*at*⸣. Lacheman reads *tu*.

l. 13: KÙ.[SIG$_{17}$?]. The *CAD* Nuzi file reads, at this point: KÙ.SIG$_{17}$.

l. 15: [*E-mu-y*]*a*. For the restoration of this name, see below, note to line 26.

l. 20. For this line, Lacheman reads: IGI *Na-ni-ya* DUMU [ ].

l. 21. At one time, Lacheman saw and restored: IGI *Ḫu-lu-uk-ka*$_4$ [DUMU *Ku-šu-ḫa-tal*].

l. 22: ⸢X X⸣. The first of these traces is not as copied. Rather, it appears as:

l. 25: [*A-ka*$_4$*-a-a*]. This is the only plausible restoration of Tanteya's patronymic. See *NPN*, 147 *sub* TANTEI̯A.

l. 26. The restoration of this line is based on Porada's identification (1947, 130) of S.I.. Po 301 with Emuya son of Ipša-ḫalu in *JEN* 2. The [-*y*]*a* DUMU *Ip-ša-ḫa-lu*, preserved in line 15 of our text, is most likely the same person.

The question marks accompanying the patronymic in this line indicate uncertainty regarding the interpretation of the trace, not regarding the patronymic itself.

l. 27: *Pí*. The sign is typical, not as copied.

l. 28: ⸢X⸣[ ]. Lacheman restores: *I*[*t-ḫi-iš-ta*]. Cf. line 19.

l. 29: [ ]-⸢x-*te*?-x⸣. Lacheman reads and restores: [*Mu-uš*]-*te*-[*šup*]. Cf. line 16.

JEN 715

OBVERSE

1 ṭup-pí ma-[ru-ti ša]
2 ^{m}Šúk-ri-[DUMU]
3 ^{m}Te-ḫi-i[p-til-la DUMU Pu-ḫi-še-en-ni]
4 a-na ma-•ru-[ti i-te-pu-uš(-ma)]
5 +ki-ma ḪA.[L]A-[šu GIŠ?.ŠAR?]
6 40+⁺⸢10⸣? i+na a[m-m]a-[ti mu-ra-ak-šu]
7 30 i+na [am-m]a-[ti ru-pu-us-sú]
8 i+na šu-p[a]-⸢al⸣ [É?.ḪÁ?.MEŠ? (ku-up-pá-ti)]
9 ša ^{m}Ḫi-iš-mi-t[e-šup i-na]
10 le-et ku-up-p[á-ti ša]
11 ^{m}Wa-[an?-t]i-i[p- (^{m}Šúk-ri-)]
12 a-na ^{m}[Te-ḫi-ip-til-la]
13 it-[ta-din ù]
14 ^{m}Te-[ḫi-ip-til-la a-na]
15 ^{m}Šúk-[ri-]
16 ki-ma NÍ[G.BA-šu it-ta-din]
17 ⸢šum⸣-ma [^{m}Šúk-ri-]

LOWER EDGE

18 +KI.+BAL-⸢tu 2⸣ [MA.NA]
19 +KÙ.SIG$_{17}$ ú-ma-a[l-la]

REVERSE

20 IGI [Ut]-ḫap-ta-e DUMU Z[i-ke]
21 [IGI] •⸢Ḫa⸣-na-ak-ka$_4$ DUMU ⸢Še-ka$_4$⸣-rù
22 [IGI] Ḫé-ša-al-la DUMU Zu-•me
23 [IG]I It-ḫi-iš-ta DUMU Ar-ta-e
24 [I]GI Zi-ke DUMU Še-ka$_4$-rù
25 [3]+2 LÚ.MEŠ an-nu-tu$_4$ A.ŠÀ
26 šu-nu-ma ⸢il⸣-mu-ú ù šu-[nu-ma]
27 KÙ.BABBAR it-⸢ta⸣-ad-nu
28 IGI Ḫu-un-ni-ya DUMU Ḫa-ma-an-[na]
29 IGI Mu-uš-te-ya DUMU Te-ḫi-ya
30 IGI Ki-pá-a-a DUMU I-⸢la⸣-ap-*r[i]
31 IGI Ḫa-i-⸢x⸣-[ ] DUMU Su-um-mi-[ ]
32 IGI $^{d\bullet}$⸢ŠEŠ.KI⸣-•ma.an.sì
33 DUMU •Ta-a-a DUB.SAR

S.I.

34 ^{NA_4} KIŠIB ^{m}It-ḫi-iš-ta

S.I.

35 ^{NA_4} KIŠIB ^{m}Mu-uš-+te-+ya

S.I.

36 NA_4 $^{m⌜}$*Ḫa*⌝*-na-ak-ka*$_4$

UPPER EDGE

S.I.

37 $^{[N]A_4}$ KIŠIB ^{d}Š[EŠ?.KI?-ma?.an?.sì? (DUB.SAR)]

LEFT EDGE

[S.I.] S.I.

38 ^{N}[^{A_4} KIŠIB]-⌜X⌝ ^{NA_4} KIŠIB *Ḫu-un-ni-ya*

TRANSLATION

(1-4) Tablet of adoption [of] Šukri-... [son of ...]. He adopted Teḫip-tilla [son of Puḫi-šenni].

(5-13) As his inheritance share, [Šukri-.../he] gave to [Teḫip-tilla an orchard?], 40+10(?) cubits [in length] (and) 30 cubits [in width], to the west of the [(*kuppu*)-structures?] of Ḫišmi-tešup, adjacent to the *kuppu*(-structures) [of] Wa[n?]tip-... .

(13-16) [And] Teḫip-tilla [gave to] Šukri-... as [his] gift ... .

(17-19) Should [Šukri-...] abrogate (this contract), he shall pay 2 [minas] of gold.

(20-33) Before Utḫap-tae son of Zike; [before] Ḫanakka son of Šekaru; [before] Ḫešalla son of Zume; before Itḫišta son of Ar-tae; before Zike son of Šekaru. (As to) these [3]+2 men, they encircled the field and have distributed the silver. Before Ḫunniya son of Ḫamanna; before Muš-teya son of Teḫiya; before Kipaya son of Ilapri; before Ḫai-... son of Summi-...; before Nanna-mansi son of Taya, the scribe.

(34-38) (*seal impression*) seal impression of Itḫišta; (*seal impression*) seal impression of Muš-teya; (*seal impression*) seal impression of Ḫanakka; (*seal impression*) seal impression of Nanna-mansi(?) [(the scribe)]; (*seal impression*) seal impression of ...; (*seal impression*) seal impression of Ḫunniya.

COMMENT

This tablet has deteriorated slightly since it was copied.

NOTES

l. 3: ^{m}*Te-ḫi-i*[*p-til-la*]. The *CAD* Nuzi file records this PN as completely preserved.

l. 4: [*i-te-pu-uš(-ma)*]. Or the like.

l. 5: [GIŠ?.ŠAR?]. This restoration or that of some other specialized land (e.g., *paiḫu*) seems reasonable since (a) measurement in cubits is given (ll. 6-7) as is usual when orchards are described (e.g., *JEN* 42:5, 7-8; 714:4-5); and (b) the real estate is land, that is, A.ŠÀ, of one sort or another according to line 25. That A.ŠÀ is, on occasion, a general designation for

particular types of land has already been pointed out by Cassin (1938, 9, n. 1). See *JEN* 64:4, 25 (A.ŠÀ = GIŠ.ŠAR; as here but in reverse order); and *L-O* 15:5, 10 (*qaqqara paiḫa* = A.ŠÀ). A.ŠÀ may also mean "real estate" in general, not just land. See below, note to *JEN* 757:13.

l. 6: 40+⸢10⸣?. Both Lacheman and the *CAD* Nuzi file read "40." However, an impression to the upper right of the number, if not a gouge, could be the remnant of a fifth *Winkelhaken*.

l. 7: [*ru-pu-us-sú*]. Or [*ru-up-šu*]. See, for example, *JEN* 714:5.

l. 8: [É?.ḪÁ?.MEŠ? (*ku-up-pá-ti*)]. This restoration is based on *JEN* 213:14-16. On the relationship between that text and *JEN* 715, see below, next note.
In light of *JEN* 715:10, the lacuna here might even be filled by *ku-up-pá-ti* alone.

l. 9: ^{m}*Ḫi-iš-mi-t*[*e-šup*]. The restoration of this PN as toponym seems very likely in light of similar instances in other Teḫip-tilla texts: *JEN* 145:9-10; 259:6-7; 693:10-11; and probably 213:14-16. Indeed, the similarity of description shared by those texts and *JEN* 715 suggests that the same general vicinity in Nuzi itself (for this locus, see, e.g., *JEN* 145:8; 693:13) is indicated in all these cases. The overlap of witnesses in *JEN* 213, 259, 693, and 715 is also marked, if not thoroughgoing. Restorations of partially effaced witness PNs may be hazarded in light of the other three texts.

l. 11. What appears to be a horizontal trace at the start of this line is in fact a vertical trace from line 38, on the left edge.

l. 11: ^{m}*Wa-*[*an?-t*]*i-i*[*p*]. The suggested restoration of AN results in an initial PN element, "Wantip-," well attested in the Nuzi texts. See *NPN*, 274b. Lacheman suggests that the last sign fragment represents *i*[*k*].

l. 13: *it-*[*ta-din*]. The *CAD* Nuzi file reads: *it-ta-ad-nu*. No break is indicated.

l. 15. See below, note to line 27.

ll. 16-17. Between the "gift" clause (ending with line 16) and the penalty clause (starting with line 17), a clear title clause is expected.

l. 20: *Z*[*i-ke*]. The surviving trace does not appear as copied but, rather, as:

For the restoration of this PN, cf., *JEN* 213:29; 259:31; 693:28. On the relevance of those texts for *JEN* 715, see above, note to line 9.

l. 22: *me*. The sign appears normal, not as copied (i.e., as LÁ).

l. 25: [3]+2. Lacheman sees: [ ] 3. The *CAD* Nuzi file records "5."

l. 25: *an-nu-*tu_4. All these signs are quite clear. The ŠI BU of the copy (for AN NU) is not there.

l. 26: *ú*. This sign is typical, not as copied.

l. 26: *šu-*[*nu-ma*]. The surviving sign is typical, not as copied.

l. 27: KÙ.BABBAR. This designation of the mobilia does not necessarily define precisely the *quid pro quo* for the real estate, just as A.ŠÀ does not here precisely define the real estate (see above, note to line 5). The missing commodity of line 15 might be silver or some other movable (cf., e.g., *JEN* 687:8-9, 22-23; 761:10-12, 34, 35; 772:11, 24, 33). *kaspu* thus represents "money" in the sense that money is a standard of value by which different commodities can be compared. See, most recently, Zaccagnini (1989, 425a).

Note, on the other hand, that where the gift is said to consist of barley and is later designated as silver, the amount of barley could represent the value of a certain amount of silver.

l. 28: *-an-*[*na*]. The surviving sign is typical, not as copied. The *CAD* Nuzi file records "*-an-na*," with no indication of a break.

l. 31. Based on the interpretation of *NPN*, 55a *sub* ḪAPIRA 3), 138a *sub* ŠUMMIḪA 14), this line should likely be rendered: IGI *Ḫa-pí*!-⸢*ra*⸣ DUMU *Su-um-mi-*[*ya*]. It should be noted that, between the second and third signs, there appears:  This trace might be the remainder from an erasure.

l. 32: ^{d}⸢ŠEŠ.KI⸣. Despite the apparent "^{d}XXX," a reading also implied in the *CAD* Nuzi file, "^{d}⸢ŠEŠ.KI⸣" is the preferred reading for several reasons. A scribe, "^{d}XXX-ma.an.sì," is nowhere else attested at Nuzi, while "^{d}ŠEŠ.KI-ma.an.sì" is attested eight times. See *NPN*, 103a *sub* NANNA-MANSI; *AAN*, 98a *sub* NANNA-MA.AN.SÌ; and Lacheman, Owen, Morrison, *et al.* (1987, 384 *sub* ^{d}NANNA.MA.AN.SÌ). Of course, this is not evidence. However, it does, at least, mark "^{d}XXX-ma.an.sì" as a peculiar reading.

In its present state, the tablet preserves only the first *Winkelhaken*, not all three. The original sign could, therefore, conceivably have been "ŠEŠ." (Perhaps Lacheman saw "ŠEŠ," then thought "EŠ" [a mental *Hörfehler*], then "copied" "EŠ." Since "^{d}XXX" would yield sense, he would not have caught his error. Note that, already in line 25 of this text, he "copied" something he thought rather than saw. See above, note to line 25. *JEN* 715 is not, in other respects, one of Lacheman's better copies. See above, notes to lines 20, 22, 26 [both notes], and 28.)

Furthermore, the space between "XXX" and "MA" almost demands the presence of a sign. The horizontal wedge (not noted by Lacheman) could well represent ⸢KI⸣. Also, line 37 might preserve "^{d}Š[EŠ]."

Finally, *NPN*, 103a, seems in fact to reflect a preserved "ŠEŠ.KI."

l. 32: *sì*. After this sign, NA was once written, but then erased. Apparently, the scribe momentarily thought "SUM" (=*iddin*) to which he mechanically appended *na*. He then realized that "*sì*" was called for and erased the NA.

JEN 716

OBVERSE

1 [ṭup-p]í ma-ru-ti ša ^{m}Túl-pí-še-en-ni
2 [DUMU •T]ù-ra-ri ^{m}⸢Teḫ-ḫi-ip-til-la
3 [DUMU Te]-⸢ḫi-ip⸣-til-la a-na ma-ru-•ti
4 [i-pu-us-•s]ú! 2 ANŠE A.ŠÀ AŠ ^{GIŠ}ta-a-a-ri GAL $^{+}$ša $^{+}$É.$^{+}$GAL
5 [ ]⸢x⸣-RI i-⸢na⸣? É.GAL
6 [ša?/i?-na? URU Lu]-up-ti$_4$
7 [a-na ^{m}Te-ḫi-i]p-til-la ^{m}Túl-pí-še-en-ni
8 [ki-ma ḪA.LA i]-din ù
9 [^{m}Te-ḫi-ip-til]-la 30 ANŠE ŠE
10 10 [+? MA.NA URUDU.MEŠ a-n]a ^{m}Túl-pí-še-en-ni
11 k[i-ma NÍG.BA i-din il]-⸢ka$_4$ ša A⸣.ŠÀ
12 [^{m}Túl-pí-še-en]-⸢ni-ma⸣ na-ši
13 [šum-ma A.ŠÀ pa-q]í-ra-na
14 •⸢i⸣-[ra-aš-ši] ^{m}Tù-ul-pí-še-ni
15 ú-[za-ak-kà] ⸢a⸣-na ^{m}Te-ḫi-ip-til-⸢la⸣
16 ⸢i⸣-[na-di]-in
17 š[um]-•⸢ma⸣ ^{m}•Túl-*p[í]-še-en-ni
18 i-[ba]la-kat •10 MA.[N]A KÙ.SIG$_{17}$
19 ú-[m]a-al-[l]a

---

20 [IG]I A-kip-til-la DUMU Tù-ra-ri

LOWER EDGE

21 [IG]I Wu-ur-tù-ru-uk! DUMU Ma-li-ya
22 [IG]I Ša-tù-ša DUMU Tù-ra-ri
23 [IG]I Ut-ḫi-ip-til-la DUMU Tup-ki-ya

REVERSE

24 4 LÚ.MEŠ! mu-še-el-wu ša <A.ŠÀ ù>
25 na-di-na-nu ša ⸢ŠE⸣.MEŠ
26 IGI Ar-te-šup DUMU I[t]-ḫi-iš-ta
27 IGI Pu-ḫi-še-en-ni DUMU A-ta-a-te
(erasure)
28 IGI Te-šu-up-er-wi DUMU A-ri-ya
29 •IGI Ḫa-ni-a-aš-ḫa-ri DUMU A-ri-ya
30 [IGI] ⸢A⸣-ri-ḫa-ar-me DUMU E-en-na-mil-ki
31 IGI Ki-ip-ta-li-li ŠEŠ-šú
32 IGI Tar-mi-ya DUMU Ma-[š]a-an-te
33 IGI Ur-ḫ[i-y]a DUMU Ar-•ru-um-pa
34 IGI It-ḫa-pí-ḫe DUMU Ta-a-a DUB.SAR
+ ---

S.I. Po 636

35 $^{⸢\text{NA}_4⸣}$ KIŠIB ^{m}*Ur-ḫi-ya*

36 +DUMU *Ar-ru-pa*

37 $^{\text{NA}_4}$ KIŠIB

S.I. Po 265

38 ^{m}*⸢T⸣e-•⸢šu-up⸣-er-[w]i*

S.I.

UPPER EDGE

+39 $^{[\text{NA}_4]}$ ⸢KIŠIB⸣ ^{m}*A-ri-⸢ḫa⸣-ar-pa*

LEFT EDGE

40 [$^{\text{NA}_4}$ KIŠIB?] •DUB.SAR

S.I.

TRANSLATION

(1-4) Tablet of adoption of Tulpi-šenni [son of] Turari. He adopted Teḫip-tilla son of Teḫip-tilla (*sic*).

(4-8) Tulpi-šenni gave [to] Teḫip-tilla [as an inheritance share] a field, 2 homers by the large standard of the palace, ... in(?) the palace (precinct?) [of?/in? the town of] Lupti.

(8-11) And Teḫip-tilla [gave] to Tulpi-šenni as [a gift] 30 homers of barley (and) 10 [+? minas of copper].

(11-12) And Tulpi-šenni shall bear the *ilku* of the field.

(13-16) [Should the field] have claimants, Tulpi-šenni shall clear (it); he shall give (it) to Teḫip-tilla.

(17-19) Should Tulpi-šenni abrogate (this contract), he shall pay 10 minas of gold.

(20-34) Before Akip-tilla son of Turari; before Wur-turuk son of Maliya; before Šatuša son of Turari; before Itḫip-tilla son of Tupkiya. (These) 4 men are the measurers of <the field and> the distributors of the barley. Before Ar-tešup son of Itḫišta; before Puḫi-šenni son of Adatteya; before Tešup-erwi son of Ariya; before Ḫaniašḫari son of Ariya; [before] Ariḫ-ḫarpa son of Enna-milki; before Kip-talili, his brother; before Tarmiya son of Mašante; before Urḫiya son of Arrumpa; before Itḫ-apiḫe son of Taya, the scribe.

(35-40) (*seal impression*) seal impression of Urḫiya son of Arrumpa; seal impression of (*seal impression*) Tešup-erwi; (*seal impression*) seal impression of Ariḫ-ḫarpa; [seal impression of] the scribe (*seal impression*).

COMMENT

This tablet has suffered some additional damage since the copy was made.

NOTES

l. 3: [DUMU *Te*]-⌜*ḫi-ip*⌝-*til-la*. This is an obvious scribal error for DUMU *Pu-ḫi-še-en-ni*. The scribe has simply repeated the personal name of the adoptee. (*NPN*, 153a, entry 15) is to be corrected.)

He committed a similar error later in the same text. *JEN* 716 contains a standard Artiḫi witness sequence common to this and four other texts (see above, first note to *JEN* 686:5). According to the sequence, the witness expected to appear at *JEN* 716:28 is Tešup-erwi son of Šukriya. Cf. *JEN* 686:26; 710:28; 728:25. Instead, line 28 has "*Tešup-erwi mār Ariya*." Whereas in line 3 the scribe has repeated a PN appearing previously, in line 28 he anticipates the (correct) patronymic of the succeeding witness of line 29, Ḫaniašḫari son of Ariya. (*NPN*, 155a *sub* TEŠUP-ERWI 3), already points out the error here and a parallel confusion of "Ariya" for "Šukriya" in *JEN* 419:33 [cf. *JEN* 419:25], written by the same scribe. There, however, the basis for the confusion is not clear.) For another example of this kind of confusion, see below, *JEN* 722:33 and the note thereto.

A third instance of scribal difficulties with PNs in the present text occurs between lines 27 and 28. In line with the witness sequence, one expects, in that space: IGI *Tar-mi-te-šup* DUMU *Ar-te-ya*. Cf. *JEN* 419:24; 686:25; 710:27; 728:24. And, in fact, that name apparently was written here as well, only to be erased subsequently. We do not know why. The supposition of the name's appearance and subsequent erasure—if correct—supports the idea that we are dealing with a witness sequence, fixed and standardized, not only in fact, but either in the scribe's "notes" or even in his mind. The scribe inserted the name mechanically, as he did in other texts. The same mechanical procedure may well have led to the errors of lines 28 and 3. Perhaps *JEN* 716 was the last (and *JEN* 419 next to last?) of a mind-numbing series of practically identical texts written up on a single occasion. For this phenomenon elsewhere, cf. above, Introduction, n. 26.

l. 4: [*i-pu-us-s*]*ú*!. What appears to be a *Winkelhaken* on the copy is now effaced. Although [*i-te-pu-u*]*š* would fit the copied traces better, the scribe of the series of texts of which *JEN* 716 is one (see above, immediately preceding note) writes *i-pu-us-sú* consistently. Cf. *JEN* 419:4; 686:3; 710:4; 728:4.

ll. 5-6. In these two lines, only É.GAL (l. 5) appears certain. [URU *Lu*]-*up-ti*$_4$ (l. 6) is very likely. As for the rest, the *CAD* Nuzi file has "*i-na*" where *i*-

⸢*na*⸣? now appears (l. 5), and restores "[*ša* URU *Lu*?]-*up-ti*$_4$" in the next line. Karlheinz Deller, personal communication, 18 June 1977, proposes: "[*ina miṣ*]*ri ša ekalli* [*ša* URU *L*]*upti*." The trace before RI (l. 5) does not support an interpretation [I]S; nor do the wedges and spacing between RI and É (l. 5) allow for ŠA alone to be partially restored. Nevertheless, Deller's proposal has the virtue of supplying a complete reading of these two lines.

The presence of [URU *Lu*]-*up-ti*$_4$ is disturbing because the rest of the texts in this series are Artiḫi texts (only *JEN* 728 is not explicit on this point), as is *JEN* 521 to which *JEN* 716 may be related. (See further, Catalogue of Interrelated Texts, p. 429 n. 5.) In light of this, and if the real estate described in *JEN* 716 is Artiḫi real estate, then perhaps line 6 ought to be restored: [*i-na* KASKAL *ša* URU *Lu*]-*up-ti*$_4$. Two obstacles, however, stand in the way of this restoration. First, no explicit Artiḫi-Lupti connection, to my knowledge, is attested in the Nuzi texts. Second, the available space is, perhaps, too little to allow for the reconstruction of six such signs.

Line 5 remains a conundrum.

l. 10: 10 [+? MA.NA URUDU.MEŠ]. The pattern of clauses appearing in the other texts of this series suggests that (a) *k*[*i-ma* NÍG.BA] is probably not to be restored at this point; and (b) copper would be the second commodity given as a "gift." Cf. *JEN* 419:8; 710:10; 728:8. The fact that line 25 mentions barley only does not tell against this restoration, as *JEN* 728:7-8, 21, a parallel context, may demonstrate. However, see below, second note to *JEN* 728:21.

l. 14: *pí*. This sign is normal, not as copied.

l. 23: *ḫi*. This sign does not appear as copied. Rather, it consists of three wedges, as in the ḪI of line 34.

l. 24. This line begins the reverse.

l. 24: 4. Despite the "6" of the copy, "4" is (a) recorded as preserved in the *CAD* Nuzi file; (b) recorded as partially preserved by Lacheman; and (c) called for by the context. The wedges themselves are, in any case, very indistinct.

l. 24: MEŠ!. Two, not three, *Winkelhakens* are used for this sign.

l. 24: <A.ŠÀ *ù*>. This omission is noted by Lacheman on the copy.

ll. 27-28. On the erasure between these lines, see above, note to line 3.

l. 28: *A-ri-ya*. See above, note to line 3.

l. 34. Below this line appears a horizontal line. This is not indicated in the copy.

l. 38: ⸢*up*⸣. The upper left wedge of the copy does not appear on the tablet. The tablet is clear at that spot.

l. 39. The seal impression above this line extends the entire width of the tablet, not as indicated in the copy.

l. 40: [^{NA_4} KIŠIB?]. Cf. *JEN* 710:40. The *CAD* Nuzi file reads: NA_4 DUB.SAR (cf. *JEN* 419:35).

JEN 717

OBVERSE

1 [*ṭup-pí ma-ru-ti* $^{+}$*š*]*a* $^{\langle m\rangle}$*El-ḫi-*⸢*ip*⸣-[DUMU]
2 [^{m}*T*]*e-*•*ḫi-*[*i*]*p-til-la* DUMU *Pu-ḫi-še-e*[*n-ni*]
3 [*a-n*]*a ma-ru-ti i-pu-sú*
4 [ ] •*a-wi-ḫa-ri* A.ŠÀ *i+na qí-na-at* •AN.ZA.⸢KÀR⸣
5 [*ša*] ^{m}*Te-ḫi-ip-til-a* $^{\langle m\rangle}$*El-*[*ḫ*]*i-i*[*p-*]⸢x⸣[ ]
6 [*a-n*]*a* ^{m}*Te-ḫi-ip-til-la ki-*[*mu* Ḫ]A.LA *i-*[*dì*]*-nu*
7 •⸢*ù*⸣ ^{m}*Te-ḫi-ip-til-la* 1 A[N]ŠE ŠE
8 *[*k*]*i-*•*mu* NÍG.BA-*šu i-dì-in*
9 [*ma*]*-an-nu-me i+bala-kà-*tu_4 1 MA.NA KÙ.BABBAR *i+na-din*
10 [IGI] ÌR-DINGIR-*šu* DUMU BÀD-LUGAL
11 [IGI] *Pí-i-*•⸢*ru*⸣ DUMU *Na-i-iš-*⸢*ké-él*⸣*-pè*
12 [IGI] ⸢*El*⸣*-ḫi-*⸢*ip*⸣-LUGAL DUMU *Šu-ul-ma-*⸢*dá*⸣?
13 [IGI •*T*]*a-i-še-en-ni* DUMU *Ti-*•*x-*[ ]
14 [IGI *I*]*t-ḫi-iš-ta* DUMU *Ta-an-*[ ]
15 [IGI *Ni-n*]*u-a-tal* DUMU *Ar-ša-a*[*n-ta*]
16 [IGI *Ki*]*-pá-an-ti-il* DUMU ⸢X⸣-[ ]
17 [IGI *Ḫa*]*-ma-an-na* DUMU *Šu-ru-u*[*k-*ka_4]
18 [IGI]-^{d}$iš_8$*-tár* DUMU [ ]

REVERSE

19 [IGI] •⸢*It-ḫa*⸣*-pí-ḫé* DUB.SAR

S.I. Po 637

20 ^{NA_4} KIŠIB ^{m}*Pi-i-ru-*$^{+}$*ú*

S.I.

21 ^{NA_4} KIŠIB DUB.SAR

S.I.

22 $^{[NA_4]}$ •⸢KIŠIB⸣ *^{m}[ ]

TRANSLATION

(1-3) [Tablet of adoption] of Elḫip-... [son of ...]. He adopted Teḫip-tilla son of Puḫi-šenni.

(4-6) Elḫip-... gave to Teḫip-tilla as an inheritance share a .x homer field in the *qinnatu* of the *dimtu* of Teḫip-tilla.

(7-8) And Teḫip-tilla gave as his gift 1 homer of barley.

(9) Who abrogates (this contract) shall give 1 mina of silver.

(10-19) [Before] Ward-ilišu son of Dûr-šarru; [before] Piru son of Naiš-kelpe; [before] Elḫip-šarri son of Šulm-adad; [before] Tai-šenni son of Ti-...; [before] Itḫišta son of Tan-...; [before] Ninu-atal son of Ar-šanta; [before] Kipantil son of ...; [before] Ḫamanna son of Šurukka; [before] ...-ištar son of ...; [before] Itḫ-apiḫe, the scribe.

(20-22) (*seal impression*) seal impression of Piru; (*seal impression*) seal impression of the scribe; (*seal impression*) seal impression of ... .

COMMENTS

This tablet has deteriorated somewhat since the copy was made.

The reverse is somewhat longer than it appears in the copy. Lacheman here, as elsewhere, indicates this shortening by means of the broken outline of the reverse.

Lacheman links this text to *JEN* 778. For further on this alleged linkage, see in part two of this volume, note to *JEN* 778:4.

NOTES

l. 1: *[š]a* $^{<m>}$*El-ḫi-*⸢*ip*⸣-[DUMU]. The adopter in this text may well be Elḫip-šarri son of Turru. The latter appears in *JEN* 641:4 in what may be a reference to the very transaction here described. For further details on the connection of these two texts and other possible text connections involving *JEN* 717, see Catalogue of Interrelated Texts, pp. 429-30 with nn. 6-10. See also below, note to line 18.

The first two surviving signs of this line appear as:

The omission of the male determinative here and in line 5 may be due to haplography in the environment preceding the first vertical of the following EL.

l. 2: *til*. This sign is typical, not as copied.

l. 4: [ ] *a-wi-ḫa-ri*. The *CAD* Nuzi file reflects "1 *a-wi-ḫa-ri*" and implies that the start of the line is unbroken.

ll. 4-5: AN.ZA.⸢KÀR⸣ // *[ša]* ^{m}*Te-ḫi-ip-til-a*. Although there are two geographical entities called "*dimtu* of Teḫip-tilla," the *dimtu* as described here (i.e., containing a *qinnatu*) refers to the Zizza *dimtu* of that name, not to the Turša *dimtu* (cf., e.g., *JEN* 72:4-5). See, further, the discussion in Maidman (1976, 181-82).

The curious spelling, *Te-ḫi-ip-til-a*, is correct as copied. In this text, the scribe employs several unusual spellings for PNs and other words. See,

for example, ll. 16, 20. Note also the inappropriately plural form of *nadānu* in line 6.

l. 5: $^{<m>}$*El*. See above, note to line 1.

l. 6: *i-[dì]-nu*. See above, note to lines 4-5.

ll. 8-9. Between the "gift" clause (ending with line 8) and the penalty clause (starting with line 9), the clear title clause is expected.

l. 11: *pè*. *NPN*, 102a *sub* NAIŠ-KELPE 4), adopts the interpretation, ⌜*pé*⌝. This is quite possible. Note that this interpretation does not appear in *NPN*, 115a *sub* PIRU 1).

l. 12: ⌜*dá*⌝?. This interpretation is a tentative acceptance of the reading of *NPN*, 43b *sub* ELḪIP-ŠARRI 7), 137b *sub* ŠULM-ADAD.

l. 13: *Ti-x-*[ ]. Lacheman, the *CAD* Nuzi file, and *NPN*, 144b *sub* TAI-ŠENNI 12), 156a *sub* TIWIRA.... read: *Ti-wi-ra-*[ ].

l. 14: *Ta-an-*[ ]. The *CAD* Nuzi file reads: *Ta-an-ti-*[*ya*]. Lacheman, at one point, and *NPN*, 76b *sub* ITḪIŠTA 9), 147b *sub* TANTEJA 4), identify this witness with the Itḫišta son of *Ta-an-te-ya* of *JEN* 11:22.

l. 18. *NPN*, 96a *sub* MÂR-IŠTAR 18), proposes the restoration: [DUMU]-*iš*$_8$-*tár*. If correct, this witness might be the son of Ataya, who elsewhere appears in a Teḫip-tilla Zizza real estate adoption text, *JEN* 201:19, 35, as a witness. Cf. his appearance as a witness in a Teḫip-tilla Zizza real estate exchange text, *JEN* 277:27. In that text, Teḫip-tilla cedes land in the *dimtu* of Elḫip-šarri (ll. 13-14)!

l. 20: *ú*. This last sign is perfectly preserved.

l. 21. Porada states that the seal impression above this line was made, not from the scribe's seal, but from a seal of Ward-ilišu son of Dûr-šarru (cf. l. 10) and that this impression was subsequently erased.

l. 22. The line is all but obliterated. Only  appears, directly below the "L" of the word, "SEAL," in the copy.

JEN 718

OBVERSE

1 *ṭup-pí ma-ru-ti*
2 *ša* ^{m}*Te*!(=UD)-*ḫi-ip-til-la* DUMU *Pu-ḫi-še-ni*
3 ^{m}•*Ta-i-še-en-ni* DUMU *A-kap-tùk-ke*
4 *a-na ma-ru-ti i-pu-sú-ma*

---

5 9 ^{GIŠ}APIN A.ŠÀ *i+na* KASKAL *Na-aš-mur*
6 *ù* ^{m}*Ta-i-še-ni a-*$^{+}$*na* $^{<m>}$*Te-ḫi-ip-til-la* SUM

7 *ki-ma* ḪA.LA-*šú*
8 *ù* ^{m}*Te-ḫi-ip-til-la* 9 ANŠE ŠE
9 45 MA.NA URUDU.MEŠ *a-na* ^{m}*Ta-i-še-en-ni ki-ma* •⸢NÍG⸣.•BA •SUM
10 *šum-ma* A.ŠÀ *pa-qí-ra-na ir-ta-ši*
11 *ù* ^{m}*Ta-i-še-en-ni ú-za-ka$_{4}$-ma*
12 ⸢*a-na*⸣ ^{m}*Te-ḫi-ip-til-la ina-*⸢*di*⸣*-in*

---

13 [*šum*]-•*ma* ^{m}*Ta-i-še-ni* K[I!?.BAL?-*a*]*t*?
14 [1 MA.NA K]Ù.[BAB]BAR 1 MA.[N]A *KÙ.*SIG$_{17}$
15 [*a-na* ^{m}]*Te-*⸢*ḫi*⸣*-ip-til-***la* [*ú-ma-al-la*]

---

16 [IGI ^{m}*Tu*]*p-*⁺*ki-til-la* DUMU ⸢*It-ḫi*⸣*-til-l*[*a*]

\+ ---

17 [IGI ^{m}X?]-⸢*x*⸣*-pá-ya* DUMU ⸢*Ki*/⸢*Di-*•x⸣-[ ]
18 [IGI ^{m}]-LI-⸢*x*⸣*-ni* DUMU BE?-[ ]⸢X⸣
19 [IGI ^{m} DUMU]⸢X⸣

LOWER EDGE

20 [4? LÚ.MEŠ *an*]*-nu-*⸢*tu$_{4}$*⸣ *ša* ⸢X⸣[ ]
21 [ ] ⸢X⸣ *ša* A.ŠÀ

\+ ---

22 [IGI ^{m}*Zi-i*]*l$_{5}$-te-ya sà-sú-ku*

REVERSE

23 [IGI ^{m}*I?-ri?-r*]*i?-til-la* DUMU *Še-ka$_{4}$-*[*ru*?/*-rù*?]

---

24 [IGI ^{m} DUMU]-•*a*
25 [IGI ^{m} DUMU]-**til-*•⸢*la*⸣
26 [IGI ^{m}]⸢X⸣ [DUMU?] •⸢TU⸣ [ ]-*ni*?/-RU?

---

27 [IGI ^{m} DUMU]*-til-la*
28 [IGI? $^{m?}$ DUMU?] ⸢*x-x*⸣*-ni-te-š*[*u-up*?]

---

29 3 LÚ.M[EŠ] *la-*•*mu-*⸢*ú*⸣ [*š*]*a* [A.ŠÀ (?)]
30 *ša* ⸢URUDU⸣ *ú-*⸢*x-x*⸣ [(?)]

---

31 IGI ^{md}UTU-DINGIR-[AŠ-KUR DUB?.SA]R?
32 *an-nu-tu$_{4}$* LÚ.MEŠ *š*[*a*]

S.I.

33 ^{NA_4} KIŠIB *ša* ^{m}*Ta-i-še-e*[*n*]*-ni ša* EN A.ŠÀ

S.I. Po 354

UPPER EDGE

34 ^{NA_4} KIŠIB *ša* ^{m}*Zi-il$_{5}$-te-ya ši-bi*

S.I.

35 NA$_{4}$ *ša* ^{m}*Ki-pa-še-ni ši-bi*

LEFT EDGE

36 ^{NA_4} KIŠIB *ša* ^{md}UTU-DINGIR-AŠ-KUR

S.I.

TRANSLATION

(1-4) Tablet of adoption of Teḫip-tilla son of Puḫi-šenni. Tai-šenni son of Akap-tukke adopted him.

(5-7) A .9 homer field on the road to (the town of) Našmur is what Tai-šenni gave to Teḫip-tilla as his inheritance share.

(8-9) And Teḫip-tilla gave to Tai-šenni as a gift 9 homers of barley (and) 45 minas of copper.

(10-12) Should the field have claimants, Tai-šenni shall clear (it) and give (it) to Teḫip-tilla.

(13-15) Should Tai-šenni abrogate (this contract), [he shall pay to] Teḫip-tilla [1 mina of] silver (and) 1 mina of gold.

(16-32) [Before] Tupki-tilla son of Itḫip-tilla;

[before] ...-paya son of ...; [before] ... son of ...; [before ... son of] ... . These [4? men] are the ones who .... of the field.

[Before] Zilteya, the bookkeeper; [before] Iriri(?)-tilla son of Šeka[ru?];

[before ... son of] ...; [before ... son of] ...-tilla; [before] ... [son of] ...;

[before ... son(?) of(?)] ...-tilla; [before? ... son? of? ... .

(These) 3 men are the one who encircled [the ...? field] (and) who ...-ed the copper.

Before ^{d}UTU-DINGIR-AŠ-KUR, the scribe(?). These are the men who ... .

(33-36) (*seal impression*) seal impression of Tai-šenni, (i.e.,) of the (erstwhile) owner of the field; (*seal impression*) seal impression of Zilteya, witness; (*seal impression*) seal impression of Kipa-šenni, witness; seal impression of ^{d}UTU-DINGIR-AŠ-KUR (*seal impression*).

COMMENTS

This tablet has suffered considerable additional damage since the copy was made. In addition to the effacement of whole signs and parts of signs, gradual deterioration has resulted in the survival of vague shapes and

outlines of signs in places where, in the copy, the signs are clear. Where these remnants appear consistent with the copy, their poor condition is not noted.

The text itself is unusual in several respects. The presence of horizontal lines at various places in the text, atypically phrased clauses, some relatively archaic sign shapes (e.g., note the similarity of ANŠE in line 8 to that in *JEN* 552:7 [*JEN* 552 was written for Teḫip-tilla's father]), and perhaps prosopographical considerations (see below, note to line 22, on the possible identity of ᵈUTU-DINGIR-AŠ-KUR [ll. 31, 36]) all suggest that *JEN* 718 is one of Teḫip-tilla's earlier texts.

NOTES

l. 2: *Te*!. The sign is correct as copied.

l. 5: *Na-aš-mur*. This is the name of a town. This fact and the interpretation of the last sign as *mur* are confirmed by other attestations of this GN in the Nuzi texts. See *HSS*, XIII, 441:24, 29, 33, 37; XV, 256:12. These references are collected by Fisher (1959, 66, no. 465). Also, cf. below, *JEN* 731:6 and the note thereto.

l. 6: *a-na* <m>. After A, NA is clearly preserved. No DIŠ sign follows NA.

l. 12: *ina-*⸢*di*⸣*-in*. To my knowledge, this is the first attestation in the Nuzi texts of the phonetic value, *ina*, for AŠ.

I fail to understand the need for Lacheman's "sic!" (referring to "⸢*di*⸣*-in*"). Perhaps he mistakenly considered these signs to represent an incorrectly used preterite form, i.e., ⸢*i-di*⸣*-in*.

l. 15: [*ú-ma-al-la*]. [*ina-di-in*] is also plausible, if less likely.

l. 16. On the possible further identity of this witness, see below, note to line 22. Below this line appears a horizontal line. This is not indicated in the copy.

l. 17. In his papers, Lacheman renders these names: [ ]*e*- (in another paper: *a*-) -⸢*pá-ya*⸣ DUMU *Ki-*⸢*in*⸣-[ ]. After ⸢KI⸣/⸢DI⸣, the tablet now has:

"Apaya" is attested as a PN. See *NPN*, 22a *sub* APAỊA; *AAN*, 24a *sub* APAIA. "Epaya" is not. On the other hand, the traces are more easily explained by E than by A. It is unclear if this sign begins the PN.

ll. 18-19. The second last (partially preserved) sign on line 18 is indeed on the right side of the tablet but is too high up in the copy. That is, the "longitude" is correct but the "latitude" is not. This trace is on line 19. In fact, this trace constitutes line 19.

l. 18. Lacheman reads: [IGI *Ak*]*-ku-le-en-ni* DUMU *A*[*r*]*-ḫa-m*[*a-an-na*]. Thus, the text appears to have been better preserved at the time of that note. However, his reading of the patronymic is difficult, given the surviving

traces. Furthermore, the only clear attestation of this individual (*JEN* 386:46-47) comes from at least two generations later.

l. 18: ⌜X⌝. This last trace does not appear as copied but, rather, as: 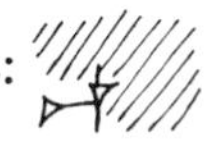

l. 20: [4?]. Lacheman restores [3].

l. 21. Lacheman restores the first part of the line, [*la-mu*]-*ú*. This is obviously based on line 29. However, for this very reason, a second appearance of this formula here is unexpected. Cf. also line 32 for yet another possible appearance of this clause. On the other hand, what appears on the copy as "DIŠ MEŠ" is a clearly preserved "*ša* A.ŠÀ."

Below this line appears a horizontal line. This is not indicated in the copy.

l. 22: [IGI ᵐ*Zi-i*]*l*$_5$-*te-ya*. The restoration of this name and the establishment of this witness's identity and function are related issues involving, among other texts, *JEN* 718, 731, 739, 759—all edited in this volume. For the sake of convenience and coherence, discussion of pertinent data and problems in all these texts are gathered here in this note. Establishment of the reading adopted here for this PN is the formal justification of this note.

Who is the individual upon whom this discussion focuses? His identity is most clearly established in *JEN* 739, where he appears as a sealer:

24 ... ᵐ*Zi-il*$_5$-[*te-y*]*a*
25 [DUMU *Ta*]-*ú-ka*$_4$ *sà-s*[*ú-u*]*k*-⌜*ki*⌝

The restoration of the name and patronymic are assured by his initial appearance in that text as a witness:

21 ... ᵐ*Zi-il*$_5$-*te-ya*
22 DUMU *Ta-ú-ka*$_4$

The name thus established, the following discussion assumes that, where Zil-teya the *sassukku* is mentioned, this Zil-teya is, by definition, the son of Tauka. This is a reasonable assumption in itself since both the PN, Zil-teya, and the profession, *sassukku*, are each relatively rarely attested. (The situation might not be the same were we dealing with a hypothetical, "Ḫašiya the scribe" or some other combination of common PN and commonly attested profession.) This assumption becomes even stronger when "Zil-teya the *sassukku*" and "Zil-teya" (with or without patronymic) appear in directly related contexts.

Where else, then, apart from *JEN* 739, does this individual appear? Given the assumptions posited above, he appears clearly in *JEN* 759 as a sealer:

23 ... ᵐ*Zi-il-te-ya*
24 ᴸ[ᵁ *s*]*à-sú-uk-ki*

As a sealer, he is drawn, as is customary in these texts, from the ranks of the witnesses. Thus he first appears in this text among those witnesses:

20 ... ^{m}*Zi-il-te-ya* DUMU *T[a-ú-ka$_4$]*

where his patronymic can be restored with confidence.

He appears again as a sealer in *JEN* 731:

23 ... ^{m}*Zi-il-te-ya* ^{LÚ}*sà-sú-⌜uk⌝-ki*

(This reference should be added to *NPN*, 179b, *sub* ZIL-TEJA 4). *NB*: Such additions to *NPN* are not routinely noted in this volume.) His name does not appear in this text among the witnesses, most likely because that part of the witness list in which it would have been preserved is now destroyed.

And finally, his name may be restored as [^{m}*Zi-i*]*l$_5$-te-ya* in *JEN* 718:22, the present text, although only [ ]-⌜*x*⌝-*te-ya* remains of this PN. This not very daring restoration is confirmed by the witness's reappearance as a sealer in line 34, with the PN there perfectly preserved. Should lingering doubts remain regarding this identification (in theory, the Zil-teya of line 34 could be a witness whose name is now lost in one of the text's lacunae), two other bits of circumstantial evidence can be mustered to fortify the case. First, no other known *sassukku* bears a name ending in "-teya." See Mayer (1978, 138). (To be sure, Mayer musters only five PNs holding this position.) Second, the connection of "[ ]-teya, the *sassukku*" of *JEN* 718 with "Zil-teya son of Tauka, the *sassukku*" of *JEN* 739 is strengthened by other features linking these two texts. A principal party of *JEN* 739, Iriri-tilla son of Šekaru (ll. 3-4, 11) seems to appear in *JEN* 718 as the witness, [ ]-⌜*x*⌝-*til-la* DUMU *Še-ka$_4$*-[ ] (l. 23). A witness in *JEN* 739, Ḫanaya son of Itḫip-tilla (l. 18) may be a brother of a witness in *JEN* 718, Tupki-tilla son of Itḫip-tilla (l. 16). (Cf. also, *JEN* 730:1, 8-9; and see below, notes to *JEN* 730:1 and 8.) In both texts, payment for land is made by Teḫip-tilla in barley and copper, probably employing the same scale of value: .1 homer of land = 1 homer of barley + 5 minas of copper. Cf. *JEN* 718:5, 8-9 with *JEN* 739:7, 13-14. See also below, note to *JEN* 739:13. These several connections between *JEN* 718 and 739 all but assure the conclusion that Zil-teya son of Tauka, the *sassukku*, appears in both.

Summarizing thus far, Zil-teya son of Tauka, the *sassukku*, appears in *JEN* 718, 731, 739, and 759. In each instance he is both a witness (assumed for *JEN* 731, a broken text) and a sealer, and is identified as a *sassukku*.

Zil-teya son of Tauka reappears in *JEN* 10:21; 40:23; 49:27; 86:24; 401:18; 411:27; 701:24-25; 763:21. The Zil-teya of *JEN* 614:19 is likely the same person as well. (Other "Zil-teyas" lacking patronymic are attested in the Nuzi texts; see *AAN*, 174b *sub* ZIL-TEIA. To that list may be added *EN*, 9/1, 122:41 and *SMN* 1696:7; 2384:25 [both unpublished; references from Lacheman]. But for the last two [unavailable to me], none of those attestations seems relevant here.) In all those instances, he appears as a witness, but not as a sealer, and he is never given his professional title.

Can *JEN* 718, 731, 739, and 759 tell us anything about the function of the *sassukku*? There is a possibility, albeit not a strong one, that in these

four texts, Zil-teya, in his capacity as *sassukku*, acts as scribe, i.e., he may have written these texts.

Before reviewing the evidence for this possibility, it should be recognized that these four texts pattern out in different ways. It has already been argued above that *JEN* 718 and 739 have several common features. *JEN* 731 and 759, are far more strongly linked to each other. They bear striking similarities. First, where the two texts may be compared, they share an identical witness sequence and a nearly identical sealing sequence. Indeed, witness PN restorations in this edition of *JEN* 731 are based on readings from *JEN* 759. Collation reveals, incidentally, that Zil-teya used the same seal in both of these texts, a seal marked by a lattice pattern similar to that of Po 72, 74, and 86 (Porada 1947, plate V). He did *not* use Po 354, his seal in *JEN* 718 (Porada 1947, 130b; now collated, and contra Lacheman and Maidman 1989, 108). (His seal impression in *JEN* 739 is indistinct.) Both *JEN* 731 and 759 are sealed lengthwise rather than widthwise, a somewhat unusual phenomenon in this corpus. The similarities between these texts is so stark that the conclusion is inevitable; whoever wrote one of these texts also wrote the other.

Now we return to the evidence for Tauka's having written these texts. This evidence is ambiguous, yet tantalizing.

In *JEN* 739, no scribe is mentioned either in the witness list or among the sealers. Neither section is entirely preserved, to be sure, yet the appearance of a *sassukku* may have obviated the mention of a scribe.

The same may hold true of *JEN* 718. Here, however, another difficulty arises. ^{d}UTU-DINGIR-AŠ-KUR appears in lines 31 and 36. Elsewhere, this name is always associated with the father of a scribe, Enna-mati. See *NPN*, 124a *sub* ŠAMAŠ-ILU-INA-MÂTI. (Note that this PN is nowhere in the Nuzi texts rendered phonetically; its interpretation must, therefore, for the moment remain uncertain.) The suspicion arises that we are dealing with the same person here and that he too may be, like his son (if it is his son), a scribe. Note that this person may, in line 31, actually be called scribe. (Is it a coincidence that Zil-teya son of Tauka appears in perhaps five texts where Enna-mati [only once with patronymic] is the scribe: *JEN* 40:28; 49:35; 401:30; 614:30 [with patronymic], 36 [note that both *JEN* 614 and 718 are written in a relatively archaic style]; and possibly 763:39?) It may turn out, in other words, that a scribe *is* mentioned in *JEN* 718. Yet even were this so, it would not, as we shall see, automatically preclude the possibility that the *sassukku* wrote the text.

Turning to *JEN* 759, there the evidence is clear. A scribe, Erwi-šarri, is present (l. 25). Since, as noted above, the scribe of *JEN* 759 is the scribe of *JEN* 731, it comes as no surprise that an "Erwi-šarri" appears there as well, in line 20. Although *JEN* 731:21 appears to preserve Erwi-šarri's patronymic, "[ ]-*ma*-RI," and the MA is clear, perhaps the line ought to be restored [DUB.S]AR!-*ri*. This emendation would be convenient

because, as regards the seal impression associated with this person here, it is the same one identified by Porada (1947, 130a) as no. 302, and that impression is linked elsewhere with Erwi-šarri son of *Teššuya*. It appears clear, in any case, that the Erwi-šarri of *JEN* 759 reappears in *JEN* 731 and that this person is a scribe.

And yet this does not entirely preclude Zil-teya's having functioned as a scribe. He too, as *sassukku*, appears in both texts. It is possible that, in *JEN* 759 (and perhaps *JEN* 731; also possibly in *JEN* 718), we have a case parallel to that, for example, of *JEN* 694:29, 34 (cf. l. 40), where two scribes (so defined) appear in a single text.

Summing up, in one text at least (*JEN* 739), the *sassukku* would seem to appear instead of the DUB.SAR and in two texts (*JEN* 759 and, by extension, 731) the *sassukku* would seem to appear beside the DUB.SAR. A fourth text (*JEN* 718) is unclear on this point.

Zil-teya the *sassukku*, then, could, in these four real estate texts (with *JEN* 739 providing the strongest evidence) have been the *functional* (not linguistic) equivalent of the *ṭupšarru*, a supposition supported by the attestations elsewhere of *šassukku*, cited in *AHw*, 1194b. Cf. the discussions of *sassukku* of Mayer (1978, 137-38 ["Zil-teya son of Tauka" should be added to Mayer's list of those holding this office] and Fadhil (1983, 231-32).

(*JEN* 603:32 also mentions another *sassukku* as witness but the text is broken at a crucial point and thus is inconclusive for our problem. Zil-teya son of Tauka appears in another text apparently lacking a named scribe, *JEN* 763 [however, cf. l. 39; Zil-teya appears in l. 21]. However, there he is not called by his professional title.)

l. 23. On the restoration of this line, see above, immediately preceding note.

l. 26. Lacheman at one point read: [IGI]-*ta* DUMU *Tu*-[ ]-*ni*.

ll. 27-28. Lacheman believes a single PN to have been contained in line 27 with the patronymic appearing in line 28.

l. 28. If the surviving signs actually represent a PN, then [*Ḫu-t*]*a*-[*a*]*n-ni-te-š*[*u-up*] is the only possibility that comes to mind. See *NPN*, 64a *sub* ḪUTANNI-TEŠUP; and *AAN*, 61a *sub* ḪUTANNI-TEŠUP for the evidence for this name.

l. 30. Lacheman reads: *ša* URU *Ú-lam-me*, an attractive solution (the last horizontal is part of a sign, not a surface scratch). However, the second sign appears far closer to URUDU than to URU. Furthermore, this text has no distinguishing features in common with other known Teḫip-Tilla Ulamme texts.

Perhaps one ought to read: *ša* URUDU *i*!-⌜*di*⌝-[*n*]*u*.

l. 31: ᵈUTU-DINGIR-[AŠ-KUR]. This name has not been normalized as Akkadian since, as noted above, note to l. 22, no other spelling which might reflect pronunciation is attested in the Nuzi texts.

l. 31: [DUB?.SA]R?. For this possible restoration, see above, note to line 22.

l. 32: š[a]. Lacheman restores: š[a URU A-pè-na-aš].

l. 33. For the more common form of this type of legend, see, for example, *JEN* 721:25; 724:33.

l. 34. The seal impression above this line is Po 354 (collated), not Po 314 (as in Lacheman and Maidman 1989, 108).

JEN 719

OBVERSE

1 ṭup-pí *ma-*⸢ru⸣-ti ša ^{m}Te-ḫ[i-ip-til-la]
2 DUMU Pu-*ḫi-*še-en-ni ^{m}[N]a-⸢x⸣-[(?)]-•⸢ya⸣?
3 DUMU Ki-•in-tar ^{m}Šu-•un-ta-ri
4 DUMU •Ḫa-ni-•ku-•uz-zi
5 ^{m}•Na-•i-še-*ri DUMU A-pu-zi
6 ^{m}A-•mi-*ni-pè DUMU Wa-an-ti$_4$-•ya
7 ^{m}•⸢Mil⸣-*ki-•ya DUMU A-pu-zi
8 *^{m}•Ni-*nu-•a-tal DUMU A-pu-zi
9 6 LÚ.•MEŠ an-nu-tu$_4$ ^{m}Te-ḫi-ip-til-la
10 a-na ma-ru-ti i-pu-šu
11 •6 ^{GIŠ}APIN A.ŠÀ i+na URU E-ri-iš-pa
12 a-na ^{m}Te-ḫi-ip-til-la i-di-*nu
13 ù ^{m}Te-ḫi-ip-til-la a-na ^{m}⸢Na⸣-[x-x?-ya?]
14 ^{m}Šu-un-•ta-ri ^{m}Na-i-še-ri
15 ^{m}A-mi-ni-pè ^{m}Mil-ki-ya [(ù) ^{m}Ni-nu-a-tal]
16 •6 •LÚ.•MEŠ [an-n]u-ti 10 UDU.MEŠ ⸢i⸣?-[din?]
17 šum-•ma [A.ŠÀ p]a-qí-ra-na
18 ⸢i⸣-[r]a-[aš-š]i!? L[Ú.MEŠ an-nu-ti]
19 [ú]-za-[ak-k]u-ú
20 [š]um-m[a i-bal]a-ka$_4$-tu$_4$ L[Ú.MEŠ an-nu-ti]
21 ⸢X⸣[M]A? MA.•NA [ ]
22 [a-na] ^{m}?[Te-ḫ]i?-[ip-til]-l[a? ú-ma-al-lu(-ú)]

LOWER EDGE

23 *IGI •A-•ki-•ya DUMU ⸢Mu⸣-uš-⸢te⸣-[šup]
24 IGI ⸢Ta⸣?-*a-[a? DUMU] •Pu-•i-ta-•e
25 IGI •Še-*e[r]-•ši-•ya •DUMU Šúk-ri-y[a]

REVERSE

26 [IGI Al-p]u-ya DUMU A-ri-•ya
27 [IGI]-⸢x⸣-im-pa DUMU Pil-maš-še
28 [IGI] DUMU Ka$_4$-a-a
29 [IGI]-⸢x⸣-ú-ša DUMU Tù-ra-ri

30 [IGI]-⸢*a*⸣?-*a* [DUM]U *Ru-ú-sa*
31 [IGI -*u*]*š*?-⸢*x*⸣-*e* DUM[U *T*]*a*?-*mar*-•*t*[*a*?-*e*?]
32 [IGI]-*til-la* DUMU *Ak*-[(?)]-*kà-e-ni-a*
33 [IGI] •*Zi-li-pa-a-pu* DUMU [*Na*]-*al-tù-ya*
34 $^{+}$IGI •*Pá*-•*i-še-en-ni* DUMU ⸢*Še*⸣?-*el-la*
35 $^{+}$IGI [*I*]*t-ḫa-pí-ḫe* DUB.SAR

S.I.

36 $^{[NA_4]}$ KIŠIB ^{m}*Al-pu-ya* DUMU *A-ri*-•*ya*

S.I. Po 647

37 $^{+⸢NA_4⸣}$ [KIŠIB ^{m}]*A-ki-ya* DUMU *Mu-uš-te-šup*

S.I.

38 $^{+NA_4}$ [KIŠIB ^{m}*Zi-li-pa*]-*⸢*a*⸣-*pu* DUM[U] •*Na-al-tù-ya*

LEFT EDGE

S.I.

39 ^{NA_4} KIŠIB DUB.•SAR-$^{+}$[*r*]*u*/[*r*]*i*

TRANSLATION

(1-10) Tablet of adoption of Teḫip-tilla son of Puḫi-šenni. Na-...-ya(?) son of Kintar, Šun-tari son of Ḫanikuzzi, Nai-šeri son of Apuzi, Aminipe son of Wantiya, Milkiya son of Apuzi, (and) Ninu-atal son of Apuzi, these 6 men adopted Teḫip-tilla.

(11-12) They gave to Teḫip-tilla a .6 homer field in the town of Erišpa.

(13-16) And Teḫip-tilla gave to Na-...-ya(?), Šun-tari, Nai-šeri, Aminipe, Milkiya, [(and) Ninu-atal], (to) these 6 men, 10 sheep.

(17-19) Should [the field] have claimants, [these] men shall clear (it).

(20-22) Should [these] men abrogate (this contract), [they shall pay to] Teḫip-tilla ... mina(s) ... .

(23-35) Before Akiya son of Muš-tešup; before Taya(?) son of Pui-tae; before Šeršiya son of Šukriya; [before] Alpuya son of Ariya; [before] ...-impa son of Pilmašše; [before ...] son of Kaya; [before] ...-uša son of Turari; [before] ...-aya(?) son of Rusa; [before] ... son of Tamar-tae(?); [before] ...-tilla son of Ak-x(?)-kaenia; [before] Zilip-apu son of Naltuya; before Pai-šenni son of Šella(?); before Itḫ-apiḫe, the scribe.

(36-39) (*seal impression*) seal impression of Alpuya son of Ariya; (*seal impression*) seal impression of Akiya son of Muš-tešup; (*seal impression*) seal impression of Zilip-apu son of Naltuya; (*seal impression*) seal impression of the scribe.

COMMENTS

This tablet has suffered serious deterioration since the copy was made, especially on the obverse and lower edge. Recent joins of three small

fragments to the tablet add text (over and above what is represented in the copy) to lines 37-39, as indicated in the transliteration.

The text is noteworthy for its abundance of unique and rare PNs (e.g., Aminipe [ll. 6, 15], Pai-šenni [l. 34]), for a rare (if not unique) GN (i.e., URU Erišpa [l. 11]), and for the paltry amount of land involved (l. 11), especially given the large number of vendors.

NOTES

l. 2: ⸢*ya*⸣?. Lacheman reads: *-e-a*.

l. 3: *Šu-un-ta-ri*. The spelling of this PN here and in line 14 seem quite clear. The hesitancy of *NPN*, 54a *sub* ḪANIKUZZI 4), 139a *sub* ŠUN-TARI?, in accepting this PN appears unwarranted.

l. 11: 6. The lower left and lower center wedges are no longer preserved.

l. 13: ⸢*Na*⸣. The KI sign of the copy does not appear on the tablet. Rather, the sign appears as:

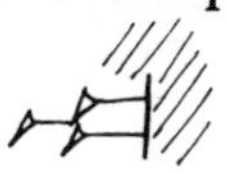

l. 14: *Šu-un-ta-ri*. See above, note to line 3.

l. 16: 6. Only the two left wedges are clearly discernible.

l. 21. This line specifies the penalty. "MA.NA" confirms this. Yet the preceding [M]A? seems out of place. Perhaps [M]A MA represents a dittograph. [*ma-a*]*t* would lead to an unacceptably onerous penalty, even as a literary device, while ⸢X⸣ 1 MA.NA is not supported by the surviving trace.

The first sign of this line is also peculiar. Lacheman reads: *i*-[ ]. The sign does not appear as copied, but, rather, as:

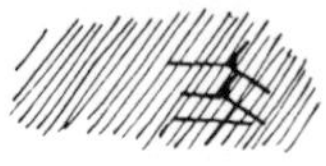

l. 22: [*ú-ma-al-lu(-ú)*]. Or the like.

l. 29: [IGI]-⸢*x*⸣-*ú-ša*. The *CAD* Nuzi file and *NPN*, 159b *sub* TURARI 65), 127a *sub* ŠATUŠA, restore [IGI *Ša-t*]*ù-ú-ša*. This would be a unique spelling for this PN. Furthermore, it would appear that perhaps more than two signs were lost in this lacuna. (However, cf. the restoration of line 26.)

l. 30: [DUM]U *Ru-ú-sa*. This is a unique PN among the Nuzi texts. Lacheman reads [DUMU] *Pu-ru-ú-sa*. However, one cannot here posit further deterioration of the tablet since Lacheman wrote this note on this PN. The round lacuna is in fact a hole extending from this surface through to line 17. This gap is too small to accommodate "[DUMU *P*]*u*!." <*Pu*>*-ru-ú-sa* is possible, yet, given the rarity of so many PNs in this text (see above, comments), perhaps one should allow this unique name to remain unique.

l. 31. The proposed restoration [*T*]*a*?-*mar*-•*t*[*a*?-*e*?] is accepted by *NPN*, 146a *sub* TAMAR-TAE 13). If this is correct, then the first part of the line might

be restored: [IGI *Mu-u*]*š-t*[*e*]*-e*. The individual thus identified engaged in a real estate exchange transaction with Teḫip-tilla according to *JEN* 268:1-4.

l. 32: *Ak-*[(?)]*-kà-e-ni-a*. I can make no prosopographical sense of these signs.

l. 33: *al*. This sign appears typical, not as copied.

l. 34: ⸢*Še*⸣?*-el-la*. Lacheman reads *Še-el-la*. The name appears neither in *NPN* nor in *AAN*.

l. 37: ⸢NA_4⸣. This sign appears as: 

l. 39: [*r*]*u*/[*r*]*i*. The trace appears as: 

JEN 720

OBVERSE

1 *ṭup-pí ma-ru-ti ša*

2 ^{m}*Te-ḫi-ip-til-la* DUMU *Pu-ḫi-še-en-ni*

3 ^{m}*Ḫu-i-te-šup* DUMU *Na-ni-ya*

4 *a-na ma-ru-ti i-pu-us-sú*

5 3 ^{GIŠ}APIN A.ŠÀ *i+na le-et Ya-ar-ru*

6 *i+na mi-in-dá-*ti_4 GAL [*ša* É].GAL

7 ^{m}*Ḫu-i-te-šup a-na* ^{m}[*Te-ḫi-ip-til-l*]*a*

8 *ki-ma* ḪA.LA*-šú i-d*[*in*]

9 *ù* ^{m}*Te-ḫi-*⸢*ip*⸣*-*[*til-la*]

10 1 ANŠE *ki-ba-t*[*ù*? *a-na* ^{m}*Ḫu-i-te-šup*]

11 *ki-ma* NÍG.BA-[*šú i-din* $^{+}$*šu*]*m-*$^{+}$*m*[*a* A.ŠÀ]

12 *pa-qí-r*[*a-na i-*$^{+}$*r*]*a-*$^{+}$*aš-*$^{+}$*š*[*i*]

13 ^{m}*Ḫu-*⸢*i*⸣*-*[*te-*$^{+}$*šu*]*p* $^{+}$*ú-*$^{+}$*za-*$^{+}$*a*[*k-kà-ma*]

14 *a-na* ^{m}[*Te-ḫi-ip-til*]*-*$^{+}$⸢*la*⸣ $^{+}$*i-*$^{+}$*na-*$^{+}$*din*

15 *i*[*l-*ka_4 *ša* A.$^{+}$Š]À $^{+m}$*Ḫu-*$^{+}$*i-*$^{+}$*te-*$^{+}$*šup*

$^{+}$16 [*na-(a-)š*]*i* ⸢*šum-ma*⸣ ^{m}*Ḫu-i-te-šup*

$^{+}$17 [*i-bal*]*a-kat* 2 MA.NA $KÙ.SIG_{17}$ *i-na-d*[*in*]

$^{+}$18 [*a-na* ^{m}*Te-ḫi-ip-t*]*il-la* IGI *Ša-*⸢*tù-ša*⸣

$^{+}$19 [DUMU *Tù-r*]*a-ri*

LOWER EDGE?

$^{+}$20 [IGI *Ut*?*-ḫi*?*-i*]*p*!?*-til-la* D[UMU *Tup*?*-ki*?*-ya*?]

$^{+}$21 [IGI]-⸢*x-x*⸣-[DUMU]

REVERSE

.

.

.

22 IGI ⌈X⌉[DUMU]
23 IGI *I*[*t-ḫa-pí-ḫe* DUMU *Ta-a-a* DUB].⌈SAR⌉-*rù*?
S.I. Po 937
24 ^{NA_4} KIŠIB ^{m}*Pa-a-a* DUMU *Pu-i-ta-e*
S.I. Po 4
25 ^{NA_4} KIŠIB ^{m}*Al-ki-te-šup* DUMU *Tù-uḫ-mì-y*[*a*]
S.I. Po 945

UPPER EDGE
26 ^{NA_4} KIŠIB ^{m}*Pár-ta-su-a* DUMU LUG[AL]

LEFT EDGE
27 [IGI *Pè-ti*$_4$*-ya* DUMU *Ku*]*-ri-iš-ni* S.I. Po 349
28 [IGI *Ḫu-un-ni-y*]*a* DUMU *Ḫa-ma-*<*an*>*-na* NA$_4$ DUB.SAR

TRANSLATION

(1-4) Tablet of adoption of Teḫip-tilla son of Puḫi-šenni. Ḫui-tešup son of Naniya adopted him.

(5-8) Ḫui-tešup gave to Teḫip-tilla as his inheritance share a .3 homer field adjacent to Yarru, (the field measured) by the large standard [of] the palace.

(9-11) And Teḫip-tilla [gave to Ḫui-tešup] as [his] gift 1 homer of wheat.

(11-14) Should [the field] have claimants, Ḫui-tešup shall clear (it) [and] give (it) to Teḫip-tilla.

(15-16) Ḫui-tešup shall bear the *ilku* [of] the field.

(16-18) Should Ḫui-tešup abrogate (this contract), he shall give 2 minas of gold—to Teḫip-tilla.

(18-23) Before Šatuša [son] of Turari; [before] Itḫip(?)-tilla son of [Tupkiya?]; [before] ... [son of ...]; ....; before ... [son of ...]; before Itḫ-apiḫe [son of Taya], the scribe.

(24-26) (*seal impression*) seal impression of Paya son of Pui-tae; (*seal impression*) seal impression of Alki-tešup son of Tuḫmiya; (*seal impression*) seal impression of Partasua, son of the king.

(27-28) [Before Petiya son of] Kurišni; [before] Ḫunniya son of Ḫama<n>na. (*seal impression*) seal impression of the scribe.

COMMENTS

Published as *JEN* 720, *JENu* 555 can be restored virtually in its entirety since it shares peculiar features with *JEN* 22 and 409. The three texts share the same scribe. The orthography of these texts is similar, as is the formulation of clauses. As well, the identity of the sealers corresponds almost precisely. Especially significant, the three texts share the unusual feature that witnesses are identified on the left edge. (As well, the better preserved

JEN 22 and 409 share a largely common witness sequence throughout.) It is reasonable to suggest that the scribe wrote these texts on a single occasion. He may initially have forgotten to include these witnesses in the appropriate section and then corrected himself by inserting these names in what room was left to him. *JEN* 22 and 720 identify the same two individuals (enough of *JEN* 720 is preserved at this point to consider this all but certain) while *JEN* 409 identifies just one of these. On a parallel type of displacement, see below, note to *JEN* 721:28-29.

Having established that *JEN* 720 together with *JEN* 22 and 409 constitute a homogeneous cluster of texts, it may now be asserted that *JENu* 1076a belongs to *JEN* 720 although it does not now physically join this tablet. This recently discovered item visibly resembles closely the main piece, it supplements the main piece where the latter is missing, and its text mirrors faithfully the pattern of *JEN* 22 and 409. (The fragment may even show that *JEN* 720 shares the same witness sequence as the other two texts.) Most telling, the vendor in the fragment is one Ḫui-tešup, the very name of the vendor in *JENu* 555.

The new fragment contributes to the second halves of lines 11-15 and adds lines 16-21. All these additions are indicated in the transliteration. The line numbering of this text in Lacheman and Maidman (1989, 111) should be adjusted accordingly. Sign fragments from the new piece are not shown in the notes below except in the case of PNs, where the reading is not transparent.

With the new piece now incorporated into the text, one can estimate the gap at the start of the reverse as amounting to about seven lines, corresponding to the latter part of the witness lists in *JEN* 22 and 409.

Various restorations in this text, substantive and otherwise, are based on *JEN* 22 and 409.

NOTES

l. 5: *Ya-ar-ru*. On this toponym and its Artiḫi connection, see above, first note to *JEN* 686:5.

ll. 17-19. The scribe evidently forgot to include "*ana Teḫip-tilla*" in its normal position, immediately before the verb (cf. *JEN* 22:16; 409:15-16), and so he placed it just after the verb (l. 18). He consequently began the witness list anomalously, in the middle of this line, continuing with the witness' patronymic at start of the next line (l. 19). He appears to have arrested this pattern by leaving line 19 with the patronymic only, beginning the name of the next witness on the line after that. Note that, after the patronymic on line 19, the fragment is preserved and the space (room enough for one or two signs) is blank.

On the restoration of the name of the first witness, cf. *JEN* 409:17 (no parallel in *JEN* 22). The traces of the last two signs of line 18 appear as:

l. 20. For the identity of this witness, cf. *JEN* 22:19; 409:19 (there, read "IGI *Ut*..."; cf. *NPN*, 153a 12)). His identity here depends on the reading of the first trace. It appears as: 

l. 21. The traces are directly below "*-til-la*" (l. 20) and appear as:

They are too ambiguous for the line to be restored.

l. 22. Cf., perhaps, *JEN* 409:30. Cf. *JEN* 720:27.

l. 25: *-mì-y*[*a*]. What appears in the copy as MI is actually a complete ME (where the non-existent *Winkelhaken* appears) plus the start of YA (i.e., the four horizontals which are correctly rendered).

ll. 27-28. The witness names on these lines are restored following *JEN* 22:36-37, also on a left edge. Cf. also *JEN* 409:35 (again on a left edge) for the restoration of the second of these two witnesses.

On the interconnections of *JEN* 22, 409, 720, see already above, comments.

l. 28: *Ḫa-ma-*<*an*>*-na*. For this spelling, cf. *JEN* 22:37; 409:35.

JEN 721

OBVERSE

1 [*ṭup-p*]*í ma-ru-ti*! *š*[*a* ^{m}*Ar-ša-lim*] $^{+}$DUMU $^{+}$*Šúk-*$^{+}$⸢*ri*⸣*-*$^{+}$*ya*
2 [^{m}*T*]*e-ḫi-ip-til-la* DU[MU *Pu-ḫi-še*]*-en-ni*
3 *a-na ma-ru-ti i-pu-*⸢*uš*⸣
4 2 ANŠE A.ŠÀ *i+na le-et* A.ŠÀ *ša* $^{m+}$*Mu-šu-ya*
5 ^{m}*Ar-ša-lim a-na* ^{m}*Te-ḫi-ip-til-la*
6 *ki-ma* ḪA.LA *i-din* ⸢*ù*⸣
7 ^{m}*Te-ḫi-ip-til-la* 10 ⸢ANŠE⸣ ŠE.ME[Š]
8 *a-na* $^{m!}$*Ar-ša-lim* [*ki-ma* NÍ]G.BA *i-•d*[*in*]
9 [*šum-m*]*a* ^{m}*Ar-ša-li*[*m i*]*-bala-•kat*
10 ⸢1 MA⸣.NA KÙ.BABBAR 1 MA.[N]A KÙ.SIG$_{17}$ [*ú-ma-al-la*]

---

11 ⸢IGI *Ap*⸣-[*x-u*]*š*/[*t*]*a* DUMU ^{d}IM-LUGA[L]
12 IGI *Wa-*[*at-wa* DU]MU ^{d}XXX*-na-*⸢*x*⸣-[(*x-*)*a-nu*?]
13 IGI *Zi-*[*li-ya* DUMU *Ḫé-el*?*-l*]*a-*⸢*kál*⸣!?
14 IGI *Wi-r*[*a-a*]*ḫ-ḫe* DUMU *A*[*t*!?*-ti*$_4$*-la-am-mu*]

15 4 LÚ.MEŠ *ša* A.ŠÀ.MEŠ *ú-*⸢*še*⸣*-*$^{+}$*e*[*l-wu-ú*]

$^{+}$ ---

16 IGI *A-ri-ḫa-ma-an-na* DUMU *Ḫa-*[*tar-te*]

17 IGI *Pa-i-til-la* DUMU *Ké-li-*[*ya*]

18 IGI *A-ta-a-a* DUM[U] *Tù-ra-r*[*i*]

19 IGI *Na-aḫ-ši-*[*y*]*a* DUMU *Še-*[*ḫu-ur-x*?]

LOWER EDGE

20 IGI *Pal-te-šup* DUMU *Ḫe-er-p*[*u*?*-ya*?]

REVERSE

21 IGI *It-ḫi-til-la* DUMU *Ip-ša-•ḫa-*[*lu*]

22 ⸢IGI⸣ *It-ḫa-pí-ḫe* DUB.SAR

23 DUMU *Ta-a-a*

$^{+}$ ---

S.I. Po 507

24 ^{NA_4} •KIŠIB ^{m}*A-ta-a-a* DUMU *Tù-r*[*a-ri*]

S.I. Po 347

25 $^{[N]A_4}$ KIŠIB ^{m}*Ar-ša-lim* EN A.Š[À]

S.I. Po 508A

26 $^{+NA_4}$ $^{+}$KIŠIB $^{+m+}$*Pa-*$^{+}$*i-til-la* $^{+}$DUMU $^{+}$*K*[*é-*$^{+}$*l*]*i-*[*ya*]

$^{+}$S.I.

$^{+}$27 [^{NA_4} KIŠIB] ⸢^{m}⸣*It-ḫa-pí-ḫe* DUB.SAR

LEFT EDGE

28 [*šu*]*m-ma* A.ŠÀ.M[EŠ *pí-i*]*r-*[*qa*] *i-ra-šu*

29 $^{[m]}$*Ar-š*[*a-lim*] *ú-za-ka*$_4$*-šu-nu-*<*ti*?>

TRANSLATION

(1-3) Tablet of adoption of [Ar-šalim] son of Šukriya. He adopted Teḫip-tilla son of Puḫi-šenni.

(4-6) Ar-šalim gave to Teḫip-tilla as an inheritance share a 2 homer field adjacent to the field of Mušuya.

(6-8) And Teḫip-tilla gave to Ar-šalim [as] a gift 10 homers of barley.

(9-10) Should Ar-šalim abrogate (this contract), [he shall pay] 1 mina of silver (and) 1 mina of gold.

(11-23) Before Ap…uš/ta son of Adad-šarri; before Watwa son of Sinna…a-nu(?); before Ziliya [son of] Ḫellakal(?); before Wiraḫḫe son of Attilammu. (These are) the 4 men who measured the field.

Before Ariḫ-ḫamanna son of Ḫatarte; before Pai-tilla son of Keliya; before Ataya son of Turari; before Naḫšiya son of Šeḫur-x(?); before Pal-tešup son of Ḫerpuya; before Itḫip-tilla son of Ipša-ḫalu; before Itḫ-apiḫe, the scribe, son of Taya.

(24-27) (*seal impression*) seal impression of Ataya son of Turari; (*seal impression*) seal impression of Ar-šalim, (erstwhile) owner of the field; (*seal impression*) seal impression of Pai-tilla son of Keliya; (*seal impression*) [seal impression of] Itḫ-apiḫe, the scribe.

(28-29) Should the field have a claim (against it), Ar-šalim shall clear (the field).

COMMENTS

This tablet has suffered only slight damage since it was copied.

The reverse of the tablet has been shortened in the copy.

Both Lacheman and the *CAD* Nuzi file record fuller texts at various points than what appears in the copy. Although there are many cases in the corpus where the *CAD* Nuzi file seems to have been authored by Lacheman, this is an absolute certainty in the case of *JEN* 721. Therefore, in citing the *CAD* Nuzi file below in the notes, these citations are to be understood as Lacheman's contributions.

NOTES

l. 1: [*ṭup-p*]*í*. The *CAD* Nuzi file records the initial word as entirely preserved.

l. 1: ⸢*ri*⸣. The sign appears as:

l. 2. The *CAD* Nuzi file records this line as entirely preserved.

l. 3. The last sign on this line is ⸢UŠ⸣. The MA of the copy does not appear on the tablet. The surface is well preserved at this point.

l. 4. The land here described may be located in Arrapḫa. See *JEN* 726:5. On the relevance of *JEN* 726 for the present text, see below, note to line 11.

l. 4: *Mu*. The sign is entirely preserved and is located where "AŠ" appears in the copy.

ll. 7-8. The *CAD* Nuzi file records these lines as entirely preserved.

l. 7: ⸢ANŠE⸣. Only one horizontal wedge appears at the start of this sign, the "top" one, not two, as copied.

l. 8: m!. In the copy, the abnormal male determinative appears incorrectly in line 9 rather than here. The male determinative in line 9 is typical.

l. 9: [*šum-m*]*a*. The *CAD* Nuzi file records this word as completely preserved.

l. 9: m. See above, note to line 8.

l. 10: [*ú-ma-al-la*]. Or the like.

l. 11: ⸢*Ap*⸣-[*x-u*]*š*/[*t*]*a*. For this restoration, cf. *JEN* 726:12. The reconstruction of this PN and that of all witness PNs in this text are based on the witness sequence of *JEN* 726, virtually identical to that of *JEN* 721 where the texts

can be compared. The linkage of these two texts is noted by Lacheman and by Weeks (1972, 210). On a further connection between these two texts, see also below, note to lines 28-29.

The *CAD* Nuzi file reads, in effect: *Tup*-[ ]. On this suggestion and the rendering of the name of this witness in *JEN* 726, see below, note to *JEN* 726:12.

l. 13: [*Ḫé-el?-l*]*a*-⌜*kál*⌝!?. See below, note to *JEN* 726:15.

l. 14: *r*[*a*]. The *CAD* Nuzi file records this sign as completely preserved.

l. 14: *A*[*t*!?]. The trace appears, not as copied, but as:

l. 15. Below this line appears a horizontal line. This is not indicated in the copy.

l. 15: *e*[*l*]. This trace does not appear as copied but, rather, as:

l. 20. This is the only line on the lower edge. Contrary to what is indicated on the copy, no erasure has been made between lines 20 and 21.

l. 20: *Ḫe-er-p*[*u?-ya?*]. This restoration assumes the identity of this witness with the witness identified in *JEN* 726:22. However, the combination of signs from these two texts resulting in this proposed patronymic is difficult—no such PN is elsewhere attested at Nuzi.

l. 21. This line begins the reverse.

l. 23. Below this line appears a horizontal line. This is not indicated in the copy.

l. 26: *K*[*é-l*]*i*-[*ya*]. The traces appear as:

l. 27. Lacheman identifies the seal impression above this line as "Po 353." This agrees with Porada (1947, 130b). See also below, third note to *JEN* 726:29.

l. 27: ⌜m⌝. The head of this wedge is no longer preserved.

ll. 28-29. The *CAD* Nuzi file records these lines as entirely preserved.

The text of these lines faces away from the obverse.

Both here and in *JEN* 726:30-32 the clear title clause has been displaced from its usual position following the gift clause. Is the scribe correcting an omission by placing the clauses here or is he being whimsical? Cf. a similar phenomenon, described above, *JEN* 720, comments.

JEN 722

OBVERSE

1 ⌜ṭup⌝-p[í ma-ru]-ti ša ^{m}Te-ḫi-ip-til-la DUMU Pu-ḫi-š[e-e]n-[ni]

2 ^{f}Pu-ḫ[u]-m[é-n]i DUMU.MÍ Ḫa-•na-[ ]

3 ^{m}Še-eš-wi-•ka$_4$ [ù] ^{m}Wa-an-ti$_4$-pu-$^{+}$ku-⌜ur⌝

4 DUMU.MEŠ Tù-r[a-r]i ^{m}Te-ḫi-ip-til-la

5 •⌜a⌝-na ma-ru-[ti] ⌜i-pu-šu?-ma⌝?

6 [x?+]⌜1⌝ ^{GIŠ}APIN A.Š[À] ⌜X X i+na⌝ ^{GIŠ}⌜ta-a-a⌝-ri ⌜GAL⌝ [š]a É.GAL
ki-ma ḪA.LA

7 [i]-$^{+}$na le-e[t ku(-up)]-⌜pa-ti⌝ ša ^{m}Te-ḫi-ip-til-la AŠ ša-pa-at [KASKAL š]a!
URU An-zu-gal-li

8 [i?-n]a? mi-i[ṣ?-ri?-š]ú? ša A.ŠÀ ša ^{m}A-ri-ya NAGAR

9 ⌜a-na ^{m}Te⌝-[ḫi-i]p-til-la ki-ma ḪA.LA SUM-nu

10 ⌜ù⌝ ^{m}⌜Te⌝-ḫ[i-i]p-til-la 6 ANŠE ŠE

11 2 UDU 2 en-[z]i a-na ^{f}Pu-ḫu-mé-ni

12 a-na ^{m}Še-eš-[wi-k]a$_4$ ù ^{m}Wa-an-ti$_4$-pu-ku-ur ki-⌜ma NÍG.BA⌝-šu-nu

13 i-di-in šum-m[a] A.ŠÀ pa-qí-ra-na

14 i-ra-aš-ši šu-nu-ma ú-za-ku

15 a-na ^{m}Te-ḫi-ip-til-la i-na-di-nu

16 il-ka$_4$ ša A.ŠÀ ⌜šu⌝-nu-ma na-šu-ú

17 šum-ma ^{f}Pu-ḫu-[mé]-ni

18 ^{m}Še-eš-wi-ka$_4$ ⌜ù⌝ ^{m}Wa-an-ti$_4$!-pu-kùr!

19 i-bala-ka$_4$-⌜tu$_4$ 2⌝[+x? M]A.NA KÙ.SIG$_{17}$

20 i-na-di-n[u]

---

21 IGI Ḫu-⌜un⌝-ni-ya DUMU Ḫa-ma-an-[na]

22 IGI Ḫa-na-ak-ka$_4$ DUMU Š[e]-k[à-rù]

23 IGI Ḫu-ti$_4$-ya DUMU ⌜A⌝-[ka$_4$-a-a]

LOWER EDGE

24 IGI Ḫu-ti$_4$-ya D[UMU]

25 IGI It-ḫi-ip-⌜X⌝[DUMU]

REVERSE

26 IGI Ar-te-ya DU[MU A-ka$_4$-a-a]

27 IGI Ḫe-šal-⌜la⌝ DUMU Zu-me

28 IGI Šúk-⌜ri⌝-ya •DUMU •Ma-li-y[a]

29 IGI Ḫu-i-t[e DU]MU KI.MIN

30 IGI It-ḫa-•pí-[ḫe] •DUB.SAR DUMU!? [Ta?-a?-a?]

\+ ---

31 an-nu-tu$_4$ LÚ.MEŠ [mu-še-e]l-wu ⌜ša⌝ A.ŠÀ

32 [ù] na-di-n[a]-•nu [š]a ŠE.MEŠ UDU.MEŠ ù en-zi

S.I. Po 699

33 ^{NA_4} KIŠIB ^{m}Ḫu-•un-[ni-y]a DUMU Še-kà-rù

S.I. Po 684

34 ^{NA_4} KIŠIB $^{m\bullet}$*Ḫa-na-ak-ka*$_4$ DUMU *Še-kà-rù*

S.I. Po 589

35 ^{NA_4} KIŠIB ^{m}⌈*Ḫu*⌉!-*ti*$_4$-*ya* DUMU *A-ka*$_4$-*a-a*

UPPER EDGE

S.I.

36 $^{N[A_4}$ KIŠIB] ^{m}*Ar-te-ya* DUMU *A-ka*$_4$-*a-a*

LEFT EDGE

37 ^{NA_4} KIŠIB ^{m}*It-ḫa-pí-ḫe* DUB.SAR

S.I. Po 691

TRANSLATION

(1-5) Tablet of adoption of Teḫip-tilla son of Puḫi-šenni. Puḫu-menni daughter of Ḫana... (and) Šešwikka [and] Wantip-ukur sons of Turari adopted Teḫip-tilla.

(6-9) They gave to Teḫip-tilla as an inheritance share a ... field, .1[+x?] homer by the large standard of the palace, as an inheritance share (*sic*), adjacent to the *kuppu*(-structures) of Teḫip-tilla, abutting [the road] to the town of Anzugalli, on(?) the border(?) of the field of Ariya, the carpenter.

(10-13) And Teḫip-tilla gave to Puḫu-menni (and) to Šešwikka and Wantip-ukur as their gift 6 homers of barley, 2 sheep, (and) 2 goats.

(13-15) Should the field have claimants, they shall clear (it and) give (it) to Teḫip-tilla.

(16) And they shall bear the *ilku* of the field.

(17-20) Should Puḫu-menni, Šešwikka, and Wantip-ukur abrogate (this contract), they shall give 2[+x?] minas of gold.

(21-32) Before Ḫunniya son of Ḫamanna; before Ḫanakka son of Šekaru; before Ḫutiya son of Akaya; before Ḫutiya son of ...; before Itḫip-... [son of ...]; before Ar-teya son of [Akaya]; before Ḫešalla son of Zume; before Šukriya son of Maliya; before Ḫui-te son of the same; before Itḫ-apiḫe, the scribe, son(?) of(?) [Taya?].

These are the measurers of the field [and] distributors of the barley, sheep, and goats.

(33-37) (*seal impression*) seal impression of Ḫunniya son of Šekaru (*sic*); (*seal impression*) seal impression of Ḫanakka son of Šekaru; (*seal impression*) seal impression of Ḫutiya son of Akaya; (*seal impression*) seal impression of Ar-teya son of Akaya; seal impression of Itḫ-apiḫe, the scribe (*seal impression*).

COMMENTS

This tablet has suffered slight damage since the copy was made. The unevenness of the lines at the start of the tablet is due to a misaligned join of a fragment in the upper left of the obverse.

As in the case of *JEN* 721, for *JEN* 722, the *CAD* Nuzi file was authored by Lacheman. All references below to readings of *JEN* 722 from the *CAD* Nuzi file are to be considered as contributions of Lacheman.

The writing of this tablet is punctuated by several scribal errors and lapses. These are both mechanical and ideational. See below, notes to lines 6-7, 18 (both), 30 (second note), 33 (second note).

NOTES

l. 1. The *CAD* Nuzi file records this line as entirely preserved.

l. 4: *r*[*a*]. The traces are more characteristic of RA than the copy indicates. They appear on the tablet as: 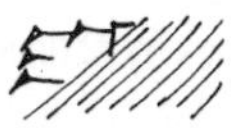

ll. 6-7. These lines are extraordinarily long. They cover the obverse, continue over the entire reverse, and extend back again to the left edge of the obverse. Perhaps scribal inattention or daydreaming is responsible for this aberration.

In this connection, note that the last words of line 6, *kīma zitti*, are inappropriate at that point. Realizing this, the scribe never finished the phrase. The full phrase appears (correctly) in line 9.

It should further be noted that the second part of line 7, beginning with "AŠ *ša-pa-at*," actually appears between lines 7 and 8. This phenomenon might suggest, not inattention, but a return to the text by the scribe after he had once finished this part of the tablet. However, if the ends of lines 6 and 7 (starting with ^{GIŠ} [l. 6] and AŠ [l. 7]) represent a later addition to the text, I fail to understand how the scribe could have written "*ki-ma* ḪA.LA" in line 6. The lowering of the end of line 7 might, after all, be simply another example of scribal carelessness in this text.

Regarding the reading of this lower segment, it is indeed to be read with line 7 because of the context (cf. comparable descriptions in texts cited below, note to line 7) and because it would then be immediately adjacent to the similarly long line 6. By contrast, the *CAD* Nuzi file reads, in effect, ... NAGAR AŠ *ša-pa-at*..., reading the segment with line 8.

l. 6: ⸢X X⸣. The *CAD* Nuzi file reads, at this point: *aš*?-*ta*. These signs make no sense to me.

l. 6: *ki-ma* ḪA.LA. See above, note to lines 6-7.

l. 7: *ša-pa-at* [KASKAL]. The lacuna might, in theory, have contained either "KASKAL" (cf., e.g., *JEN* 152:8) or "*atappi*" (cf., e.g., *JEN* 228:7-8). The former alternative is far more likely for two reasons. First, there is proba-

bly not enough room for a phonetic spelling of "*atappi*" (the phonetic being, by far, the preferred way of spelling this word in the Nuzi texts). More important, the real estate is also described as "*ina lēt kuppāti ša* ^{m}*Teḫip-tilla*" (l. 6). Teḫip-tilla elsewhere obtains real estate which is so described and which is further localized as being "*ina ḫarrāni* (*ša*) (*āl*) *Anzugalli*" (and never "*ina šapat atappi* (*ša*) (*āl*) *Anzugalli*"). See *JEN* 146:10-11; 194:6-8; 242:5-7. (Although a location on the "road to Anzugalli" describes land in both Nuzi [e.g., *JEN* 740:8] and Zizza [e.g., *JEN* 250:9-10], *JEN* 194:6-8 demonstrates that Nuzi is definitely the location of the land described here. Zizza land lacks comparable description.)

Although the term, *šapat*, is more common with *atappi* than with *ḫarrāni*—and, except for here, it never appears with *ḫarrāni* (*ša*) (*āl*) *Anzugalli*—this usage poses no difficulty to the restoration proposed here. On "*šapat ḫarrāni*," see already above, first note to *JEN* 686:5.

l. 8. This line ends with "NAGAR." See above, note to lines 6-7.

l. 12. In the copy, the last four signs of this line appear below *-ku-ur ki-*⌜*ma*⌝. In fact, these last signs are on the same line, on the reverse of the tablet.

l. 18: *ti*$_4$!. The sign appears, not as copied, but as: 

l. 18: *kùr*!. The sign appears, not as copied, but as:  , i.e., SI.

l. 19: ⌜2⌝[+x? M]A.NA. The *CAD* Nuzi file reads, at this point: 3 MA.NA.

l. 30. Below this line appears a horizontal line. This is not indicated in the copy.

l. 30: DUMU!? [*Ta?-a?-a?*]. This restoration is difficult because of apparent lack of space. "DUB.SAR-*i*" would solve this problem but is less likely since "*i*" would constitute a very peculiar phonetic complement here.

l. 33: *Še-kà-rù*. The patronymic should be: *Ḫa-ma-an-na*. See above, line 21. Also, the associated sealing is identified as "Po 699." Porada (1947, 135a) identifies sealing no. 699 with Ḫunniya son of Ḫamanna in *JEN* 91. The scribe has here inadvertently anticipated the patronymic of the next sealer (l. 34; cf. l. 22). For other examples of this type of error, committed by the same scribe, see above, note to *JEN* 716:3.

The second sign of this name, GA, has two verticals, not three as depicted.

JEN 723

OBVERSE

1 [ṭu]p-p[í ma-ru-ti ša ^{m}Ar-te-šup DUMU Ip?-ša?-ḫa?-lu?]

2 [^{m}Te-ḫi]-ip-[til-la DUMU Pu-ḫi-še-en-ni]

3 a-na •ma-*[r]u-[ti i-te-pu-uš]

4 1 A[NŠE? A.ŠÀ] AŠ? [ ]⸢X X⸣ [ ]

5 [ ]•⸢X⸣ •šu •ù [ ]⸢X⸣ ú ⸢X⸣

6 AŠ še-•ra-mu-ḫi ša AN.ZA.KÀR š[a]

7 AŠ •e-•le-nu š[a] ku-ut-•li [ša? (?)]

8 ^{m}•A[r]-•te-⸢šup⸣ [a-n]a ^{m}⸢Te⸣-[ḫi-ip]-til-[la]

9 ki-•ma ḪA.LA-š[ú?]⸢X⸣[ ]

10 ù ^{m}Te-ḫi-ip-*ti[l-la]⸢1? GUD? X⸣[ ]1 BÁN ŠE ki-ma NÍG.BA.MEŠ-šu

11 a-na ^{m}Ar-te-•⸢šup i⸣-di-in

12 il-ka$_4$ ša A.Š[À š]u-ma na-a-š[i]

13 šum-ma A.ŠÀ pa-[qí-r]a-na

14 i-ra-aš-[š]i ^{m}[A]r-te-šup

15 ú-za-ka$_4$-ma •⸢a⸣-[na ^{m}]Te-ḫi-ip-⁺til-⁺la

16 i-na-din šu[m-ma ^{m}]⸢Ar⸣-Te-šup

17 i-bala-kat 2 •MA.[NA] KÙ.SIG$_{17}$ a-na

18 ^{m}Te-ḫi-ip-til-la i-na-din

---

19 •IGI A-pa-*a-*a DUMU Ḫa-na-a-a

20 •IGI I-[lu-•n]a-mé-er DUMU •Pu-re-ya

21 •IGI •Zi-zi-•ya DUMU ⸢Pur-na-pu⸣

22 •IGI •Ar-nu-z[u DUMU]

23 •[I]GI •Ú-[(?)]-kùr!-⸢X⸣[DUMU]-⸢a⸣?

LOWER EDGE

24 [IGI] ⸢A⸣?-[ ]-⸢X-•X⸣-[DUMU N]a-an-te-•šup

25 [(6? LÚ.MEŠ) an-nu-tu$_4$ mu?-ša?]-a[l?-mu?]

26 [š]a? A.ŠÀ [ù na-di-na-nu] ša 1 GUD

REVERSE

27 [I]GI Zi-ka$_4$-⸢a⸣-[a DUMU E]l-ḫi-ip-LUGAL

28 IGI Te-ḫu-up-še-ni DUMU *Pí-i-rù

29 IGI Ta-i-šu-uḫ DUMU Še-•kà-rù

30 IGI Ḫu-i-te DUMU Ma-li-ya

31 IGI It-ḫa-pí-ḫe DUB.SAR DUMU Ta-a-a

\+ ---

32 IGI Ḫu-un-ni-ya DUMU Ḫa-ma-an-na

33 IGI Um-pí-ya DUMU Al-pu-ya

S.I. Po 198

34 ^{NA_4} KIŠIB ^{m}Te-ḫu-up-še-•ni •DUMU Pí-i-rù

S.I. Po 498

35 NA_4 DUB.SAR

S.I.

36 •^{NA_4} KIŠIB ^{m}⌜X⌝-[ ]

LEFT EDGE

37 [IGI]-⌜*x*⌝-*i* DUMU *A-ri-ya*

38 [IGI *Ḫe/Ḫé-šal-l*]*a* DUMU *Zu-me* •IGI •⌜*Ta*⌝-•*a-a* DUMU *A-pil*-XXX

39 [IGI]-⌜X⌝ DUMU *Še-ka₄-rù*

TRANSLATION

(1-3) Tablet of [adoption of Ar-tešup son of Ipša-ḫalu?]. He adopted Teḫip-tilla [son of Puḫi-šenni].

(4-9) Ar-tešup gave to Teḫip-tilla as his(?) inheritance share a 1 homer(?) [field] in(?) .... and ...., to the north of the *dimtu* of ..., to the east of the wall [of? ...?].

(10-11) And Teḫip-tilla gave to Ar-tešup as his gift [...?,] 1(?) ox(?), [(and) x?+] .1 homer(s) of barley.

(12) And he shall bear the *ilku* of the field.

(13-16) Should the field have claimants, Ar-tešup shall clear (it) and give (it) to Teḫip-tilla.

(16-18) Should Ar-tešup abrogate (this contract), he shall give to Teḫip-tilla 2 minas of gold.

(19-33) Before Apaya son of Ḫanaya; before Ilu-namer son of Pureya; before Zizziya son of Purn-apu; before Ar-nuzu [son of ...]; before Ukur(?)-... [son of] ...; [before] ... [son of] Nan-tešup. [These (6? men) are the] measurers(?) of(?) the field [and the givers] of the single ox. Before Zikaya son of Elḫip-šarri; before Teḫup-šenni son of Piru; before Tain-šuḫ son of Šekaru; before Ḫui-te son of Maliya; before Itḫ-apiḫe, the scribe, son of Taya;

---

before Ḫunniya son of Ḫamanna; before Umpiya son of Alpuya.

(34-36) (*seal impression*) seal impression of Teḫup-šenni son of Piru; (*seal impression*) seal impression of the scribe; (*seal impression*) seal impression of ... .

(37-39) [Before] ...-i son of Ariya; [before] Ḫešalla son of Zume; before Taya son of Apil-sin; [before] ... son of Šekaru.

COMMENTS

This tablet is in wretched condition. In addition, it has been coated with a glaze which further impedes decipherment. Indeed, in places, the glaze has rendered some signs all but invisible. The tablet has also suffered considerable additional surface damage since it was copied.

NOTES

l. 1: [*Ip?-ša?-ḫa?-lu?*]. *A propos* this restoration, Lacheman reads the first lines of this text, in effect, as follows:

1 *ṭup-pí* [*ma-ru-ti ša* ᵐ*Ar-te-šup*]
2 DUMU *Ip-ša-ḫa-lu*
3 ᵐ*Te-ḫi-ip-til-la* [ ]
4 [*a-na ma-ru-ti*]
5 *i-pu-šu ù ú-ta* [ ]

Despite the implication that line 2 was undamaged when this note was made, it is difficult to accept this rendering. Not only do the contents of lines 2 and 4 appear to be too short, the traces of line 3 are quite unambiguous and preclude Lacheman's interpretation.

For these lines, the *CAD* Nuzi file reads, in effect:

1 *ṭup-pí* [*ma-ru-ti ša* ᵐ*Ar-te-šup*]
2 DUMU *I*-[ ]
3 *a-na* [ ]
4 [ ]
5 *i-pu-šu ù ú-ta* [ ]

Now line two as there rendered is apparently a misinterpretation of the *ip* of what was once "ᵐ*Te-ḫi-ip-til-la*" and the "*i-pu-šu*" of line 5 is a (misplaced) attempt to conclude the first clause of the contract. These misinterpretations gave rise to Lacheman's rendition of these lines.

Yet Lacheman's identification of this Ar-tešup (this PN is almost entirely preserved in line 16) with the like-named son of Ipša-ḫalu is attractive and not to be dismissed summarily.

According to *JEN* 742, Ar-tešup son of Ipša-ḫalu and his brother adopt Teḫip-tilla and cede land to him. That land is in Unap-še: the *dimtu* of Eniya is mentioned there (l. 7), a toponym elsewhere linked to Malašu Stream (*JEN* 185:11-13). This stream, in turn, is located in Unap-še (e.g., *JEN* 214:7-8). *JEN* 808 describes a real estate exchange involving this Ar-tešup together with another individual and Teḫip-tilla. The land Ar-tešup cedes may have been located by the *dimtu* of Zaziya (l. 6). If so, this land too is in Unap-še. See *JEN* 70:6-7. Finally, *JEN* 747 explicitly describes land of this same Ar-Tešup as located in Unap-še (ll. 4-6).

Although *JEN* 723 is badly broken at crucial points, slight evidence does survive to indicate that the land ceded here by this Ar-tešup is also Unap-še real estate. Several witnesses have Unap-še connections. Especially impressive are two witnesses in this text who appear rarely elsewhere. Zizziya son of Purn-apu (l. 21) reappears in only one other place, as a witness in *JEN* 694:23. That text involves Unap-še real estate (l. 8). Ar-nuzu (*JEN* 723:22) is a witness whose patronymic does not survive. Yet the name is unusual and in only four other instances does an Ar-nuzu witness for Teḫip-tilla (*JEN* 214:28, 34; 586:24; 694:18; 709:26). One, two, or three individuals named Ar-nuzu may be involved

in these four texts, but all four texts deal with Unap-še real estate. See *JEN* 214:7; the adopters in *JEN* 586 belong to a family commonly linked to Teḫip-tilla real estate interests in Unap-še, as in, for example, *JEN* 652:23-28; 651:5-8, 12-13; see *JEN* 694:8 (there may even be a connection between the real estate description of *JEN* 694:6-7 and that of *JEN* 723:6); see *JEN* 709:8.

If the Unap-še real estate connections of these witnesses are significant, and *if* we legitimately may deduce that, in consequence of the presence of these witnesses, Unap-še real estate is involved in this text as well, then the adopter in this text, Ar-tešup, *may* indeed be the son of Ipša-ḫalu.

l. 3: [*i-te-pu-uš*]. Or the like.

l. 4: A[NŠE?]. ^{GIŠ}[APIN] is also possible.

l. 5: *ù*. The sign is very indistinct.

l. 5: *ú* ⸢X⸣. The former sign is clear, not as copied. Regarding the latter sign, Lacheman and the *CAD* Nuzi file read TA.

l. 9: ⸢X⸣. Most likely, this trace was part of the writing of *i-di-in* or the like.

l. 10: *ḫi*. This sign consists of three wedges, not four as copied. The top wedge of the copy is not present on the tablet. The tablet is clear at this point.

ll. 13-17. The *CAD* Nuzi file records these lines as completely preserved.

l. 20: *I-*[*lu-n*]*a-mé-er*. The *CAD* Nuzi file reflects: *I-lu-na?-mé-er*.

l. 21: ⸢*Pur-na-pu*⸣. It is now most difficult to discern these traces.

l. 23: *Ú-*[(?)]*-kùr*!-⸢X⸣. *NPN*, 162b *sub* UKUR-ŠARRI 4), reads, in effect: *Ú-kùr-*LU[GAL]. The last trace does not appear as copied but, rather, as:

ll. 24-25. The copy of these lines does not adequately portray the spatial relationship of the signs. Directly above the ŠA of line 26 appears the trace of a sign, perhaps A[L]. This trace lies below the other signs, from ⸢A⸣? on the left to RU on the right. The trace, in fact, is all that remains of line 25. The rest constitutes line 24.

l. 24: [*N*]*a*. The *CAD* Nuzi file records this sign as completely preserved.

l. 25. If *a*[*l*] is correctly restored (cf. above, note to ll. 24-25), then the remainder of the restoration (or its like) is plausible. In any case, something like the present restoration is called for.

l. 26: [*š*]*a*?. The *CAD* Nuzi file records a completely preserved ŠA.

l. 27. This line begins the reverse.

l. 31. Below this line appears a horizontal line. This is not indicated in the copy.

l. 36. Porada identifies this sealer as Zikaya son of Elḫip-šarri. Cf. line 27.

ll. 37-39. The text of the left edge faces toward the obverse.

l. 37: [IGI]-⸢*x*⸣-*i*. The only attested PN ending in "*-i*" and with Ariya as a patronymic is Šellapai. See *NPN*, 25a *sub* ARIḪA 22). Therefore, one should, perhaps, restore: [IGI *Še-(el-)la-p*]*a-i*.

l. 38: [*Ḫe*/*Ḫé-šal-l*]*a*. The *CAD* Nuzi file records *la* as entirely preserved. This is also implied by *NPN*, 60b *sub* ḪEŠALLA 4); 181b *sub* ZUME 1). It is possible that the trace could represent a spelling of "Gimill-adad." See *NPN*, 181b *sub* ZUME 2).

JEN 724

OBVERSE

1 *ṭup-pí ma-r*[*u-ti š*]*a* ^{m}⸢*Še-e*⸣-[*mi* DUMU] *E-*•*eḫ-li-pa-pu*

2 ^{m}*Te-*⸢*ḫi*⸣*-ip-***til-*[*l*]*a* DUMU *Pu-ḫi-š*[*e-en-ni*]

3 *a-na ma-ru-*•⸢*ti*⸣ *i-pu-sú*

4 2 ANŠE •A.[ŠÀ *š*]*a*? ^{m}*Ḫu-i-ip-**⸢X⸣[*i-na*]

5 *e-le-e*[*n* KASKAL? *š*]*a* URU *Nu-uḫ-*[ ]

6 ⸢*a*⸣?-*š*[*ar*?] *i+na le-et* •A.*Š[À **š*]*a*? É.GAL

7 [•*š*]*a*? GIŠ.ŠAR *ša* ^{m*}⸢*A*⸣?-[*kip*?]-*ta-še-e*[*n*?-*ni*?]

8 [*ki-ma* ḪA.LA]-⸢*šu*⸣ *a-na* ^{m}*Te-ḫi-*•⸢*ip*⸣-[*til*]-*la i-din*

9 [*ù* ^{m}*Te*]-*ḫi-ip-til-la*

10 [1? ANŠE.KU]R.RA [*k*]*i-ma* NÍG.⸢BA⸣-[*š*]*u*

11 [*a-na* ^{m}*Še*]-*e-mi i-*⸢*din*⸣

12 [*il-ka*$_4$] *ša* A.ŠÀ ⸢^{m}*Še*⸣-[*e-mi-m*]*a*

13 [*na-(a-)ši*] *šum-ma* A.ŠÀ *p*[*a-qí-r*]*a-na*

14 [*i-ra*]-*aš-ši* ^{m}*Še-e-*$^{+}$*m*[*i*]

15 [*ú-za*]-•*ak-kà-ma a-*$^{+}$⸢*na*⸣

16 [^{m}*Te*]-*ḫi-*⸢*ip*⸣-*til-la* [*i*]-•*na-*[*din*]

17 ⸢*šum*⸣-*ma* ^{m}*Še-e-mi* [KI?].BAL-[*at*?]

18 10 MA.NA ⸢KÙ⸣.SIG$_{17}$ *i-na-*$^{+}$⸢*din*⸣

---

19 IGI *Ḫe-šal-la* DUMU ⸢*Zu-me*⸣

20 IGI *Ḫa-na-a*[*k-k*]*à* ⸢DUMU⸣ [*Še*]-⸢*kà*⸣-[*rù*]

21 IGI *It-ḫi-*⸢*x*⸣-[(?)]-X DUMU ⸢X⸣-[ ]-IT-[(?)]

22 IGI *Tù-*⸢*x*⸣-[ ]-⸢*x-x*⸣ DUMU ⸢X-X⸣[ ]

LOWER EDGE

23 IGI *Ki-pí-y*[*a* DUMU *Ta*]-⸢*mar*⸣-*ta*!-⸢*e*⸣

24 IGI *Zi-ké* D[UMU *Iš*]-$^{+}$*ka*$_4$-$^{+}$*ar-*$^{+}$*pa*

25 IGI *It-ḫa-pí-ḫ*[*e*] DUB.SAR

REVERSE

26 7 LÚ.MEŠ *mu-***š*[*e*]-*el-wu ša* A.ŠÀ

27 IGI *Túl-pí-*•*še-*[*en-ni* DU]MU •*Iš-ka*$_4$-⸢*ar*⸣-**p*[*a*]

28 IGI *Tar-mi-ya* ⸢DUMU⸣ $^{+}$*Ta-a-a*

29 IGI *Zi-ké* DUMU *Ḫu-pa-pè-*$^{\bullet}$*e*

30 10 LÚ.MEŠ *an-nu-tu*$_4$ *na-di-na-*$^{\bullet}$*nu* **š*[*a* ANŠE.KU]R.RA

S.I. Po 179

31 $^{\mathrm{NA}_4}$ KIŠIB ^{m}*Ki-pí-ya* DUMU *Ta-mar-*⸢*ta*⸣-[*e*]

S.I.

32 $^{\mathrm{NA}_4}$ KIŠIB ^{m}*Zi-ké* ⸢DUMU *Iš-ka*$_4$⸣-$^{\bullet}$*ar-p*[*a*]

S.I.

33 $^{\mathrm{NA}_4}$ KIŠIB ^{m}*Še-e-mì* EN A.ŠÀ

UPPER EDGE

S.I.

34 $^{\mathrm{NA}_4}$ KIŠIB [^{m}] ⸢X⸣ [ ]

LEFT EDGE

S.I.

35 ⸢$^{\mathrm{NA}_4}$⸣ KIŠIB ^{m}*It-ḫa-pí-ḫe* DUB.SAR

TRANSLATION

(1-3) Tablet of adoption of Šemi [son of] Eḫlip-apu. He adopted Teḫip-tilla son of Puḫi-šenni.

(4-8) He gave to Teḫip-tilla [as] his [inheritance share] a 2 homer field of(?) Ḫuip-..., [to] the east of [the road?] to the town of Nuḫ-..., at(?) ..., adjacent to the land of(?) the palace, ... of(?) the orchard of Akip-tašenni(?).

(9-11) [And] Teḫip-tilla gave [to] Šemi as his gift [1?] horse.

(12-13) And Šemi [shall bear the *ilku*] of the field.

(13-16) Should the field have claimants, Šemi shall clear (it) and give (it) to Teḫip-tilla.

(17-18) Should Šemi abrogate (this contract), he shall give 10 minas of gold.

(19-30) Before Ḫešalla son of Zume; before Ḫanakka son of Šekaru; before Itḫi-... son of ...; before Tu-... son of ...; before Kipiya [son of] Tamar-tae; before Zike son of Iškarpa; before Itḫ-apiḫe, the scribe. (These) 7 men are the measurers of the field. Before Tulpi-šenni son of Iškarpa; before Tarmiya son of Taya; before Zike son of Ḫumpape. These 10 men are the givers of the horse.

(31-35) (*seal impression*) seal impression of Kipiya son of Tamar-tae; (*seal impression*) seal impression of Zike son of Iškarpa; (*seal impression*) seal impression of Šemi, (erstwhile) owner of the field; (*seal impression*) seal impression of ...; (*seal impression*) seal impression of Itḫ-apiḫe, the scribe.

COMMENTS

This tablet has suffered some deterioration since the copy was made. Also, I have joined three small chips (unnumbered) to the tablet. These have added to lines 14, 15, 18, and 34 and (except in the last case where the partial sign was already added to the copy) are noted at those spots in the transliteration.

The *CAD* Nuzi file on this text was authored by Lacheman. Notes below alluding to this file, therefore, also signify contributions by Lacheman.

This text contains several peculiar features: the gift is a horse (ll. 10, 30); the penalty is extraordinarily high (l. 18); seven persons measure the field (l. 26) while ten (including the first seven) transfer the horse (l. 30).

NOTES

ll. 2-3. The *CAD* Nuzi file records these lines as completely preserved.

l. 2: ⸢*ḫi*⸣. The sign does not appear as copied, but, rather, as: 

l. 4: [*š*]*a*?. If this trace is correctly interpreted, then the very unusual situation results whereby a field to be ceded is designated by a PN. Furthermore, the PN is not that of the ceder. It may represent the name of the owner of the land prior to Šemi. Note that Šemi is himself designated owner of the field later in this text (l. 33) although title has, by this time, passed to Teḫip-tilla.

l. 5: *Nu-uḫ*-[ ]. The town name starting "Nuḫ-..." is otherwise unknown to me. One is tempted to consider UḪ to be an error for ZI by a kind of graphic metathesis. The resulting "*Nu-zi*" would, of course, eliminate the need to posit a new town name.

l. 6: [*š*]*a*? É.GAL. The *CAD* Nuzi file records, at this point: *ša* É.GAL [(?)]

l. 8: ⸢*šu*⸣. The *CAD* Nuzi file suggests [L]A. This is quite possible.

l. 10: [1?]. This tentative restoration is based on the fact that, in line 30, there seems to be no room in the lacuna for any number at all. This may mean that but a single horse is given in payment.

l. 15. In the copy, two peculiarly directed wedges appear at the far right of this line. I could not clearly make out these wedges. If they are indeed present, they would appear to be the upside down end of a line from the reverse. See the end of line 19 and the note thereto for a clearer example of the copying on the obverse of the end of a line from the reverse.

l. 17: [KI?].BAL-[*at*?]. [*i*]-*bala*-[*kat*] is also possible.

l. 18: ⸢*din*⸣. The sign does not appear as copied but, rather as: 

This depiction includes a "contribution" from a newly joined chip.

l. 19. At the end of this line appear parts of two signs, upside down. The signs in fact end line 30 on the reverse and have been recopied at that point; the signs do not appear as "10 ANŠE" (l. 19) but as "[KU]R.RA" (l. 30).

l. 20: *a*[*k*]. The trace does not appear as copied, but, rather, as:

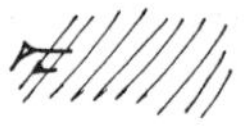

l. 20: [*Še*]-⸢*kà*⸣-[*rù*]. This is the only plausible restoration of the patronymic given the remaining sign. See *NPN*, 53a *sub* ḪANAKKA 1)-6); *AAN*, 50b *sub* ḪANAKKA.

l. 25: DUB.SAR. These signs appear directly after the scribe's name. By mistake, they have been copied at the top of the reverse.

l. 27: [DU]MU. The sign does not appear as copied but, rather, as: 

l. 30. See above, notes to lines 10 and 19.

JEN 725

OBVERSE

1 *ṭup-pí ma-ru-ti ša* ^{m}⸢*Te*⸣-[*ḫi-ip-til-la*]
2 DUMU *Pu-ḫi-še-en-ni* ^{m}*E-en-na-m*[*a-ti*$_4$]
3 DUMU *Ka*$_4$*-am-pu-tu*$_4$ *a-na ma-ru-*[*ti i?-pu?-sú?*]
4 11 ANŠE A.ŠÀ *i+na ú-ga*$_5$*-a*[*r*]
5 *i+na* ^{GIŠ}*ta-a-a-ri* GAL *š*[*a* É.GAL(-*li*)]
6 *i+na ša-pa-at* KASKAL *ša* URU ⸢X⸣-[ ]
7 ^{m}*E-en-na-ma-ti*$_4$ *a-na* ^{m*}*T*[*e-ḫi-ip-til-la*]
8 *ki-ma* ḪA.LA *i-din ù*
9 ^{m}*Te-ḫi-ip-til-*[*l*]*a* 5 GU[N URUDU.MEŠ (*ù*)]
10 7 ANŠE ŠE ⸢*a-na* ^{m}⸣*E-*en-*⸢*na*⸣*-m*[*a-ti*$_4$]
11 *ki-ma* NÍG.BA-*šú i-din*
12 *šum-ma* A.ŠÀ *pa-qí!-ra-na*
13 *i-ra-aš-ši* ^{m}*E-en-na-ma-ti*$_4$
14 *ú-*⸢*za*⸣*-ak-kà a-na* ^{m}*Te-ḫi-ip-til-la i+na-din*
15 *il-ka*$_4$ *ša* A.ŠÀ ^{m}*E-en-na-ma-ti*$_4$*-ma*
16 *na-a-ši šum-ma* ^{m}*E-en-na-ma-ti*$_4$
17 *i-bala-kat* 10 MA.NA KÙ.SIG$_{17}$ *i+na-din*
18 IGI *Šum-mi-ya* DUMU *A-ri-ka*$_4$*-na-ri*
19 IGI *Mu-uš-te-ya* DUMU *Ar-še-en-ni*
20 IGI *Ib-na-*ša-ru* DUMU *I-lu-ma-*lik*
21 3 LÚ.MEŠ *an-nu-*⸢*tù mu-še-el*⸣*-*wu*

22 ⸢*ša*⸣ A.ŠÀ *n*[*a-di-na-nu ša* ŠE]

LOWER EDGE

23 *ù* URUDU.M[EŠ]

24 IGI *Ta-a-a* [DUMU *A-pi*]*l*-XXX

REVERSE

25 IGI *Ḫa-ta-pí-a-šu* DUMU *Te-ḫi-ip-til-*⸢*la*⸣

26 IGI *Še-eḫ-li-ya* DUMU *Zi-li-ya*

27 IGI *E-ḫe-•el-te-*⸢*šup*⸣ DUMU *La-al-lu-ta-ri*

28 IGI *A-ri-ḫa-ma-an-na* DUMU *Tù-ri-ki-in-tar*

29 IGI *Šur-ki-til-la* DUMU *Ḫi-in-ti*$_4$*-ya*

30 IGI *Ki-iz-zi-ri* DUMU *Še-en-na-a-a*

31 IGI *Ni-ki-ya* DUMU *Tar-mi-te-šup*

32 IGI *It-ḫa-pí-ḫe* DUB.⸢SAR⸣ DUMU *Ta-a-a*

S.I. Po 629A

33 $^{\mathrm{NA}_4}$ KIŠIB ^{m}*E-ḫe-el-te-šup* DUMU [*La-al-lu-ta-ri*]

S.I. Po 329

34 $^{\mathrm{[N]A}_4}$ KIŠIB ^{m}*Ḫa-ta-pí-a-šu* [DUMU *Te-ḫi-ip-til-la*]

S.I. Po 609

35 $^{\mathrm{NA}_4}$ KIŠIB! ^{m}*Šur-ki-til-la* DUMU [*Ḫi-in-ti*$_4$*-ya*]

UPPER EDGE

S.I.

36 $^{\mathrm{NA}_4}$ KIŠIB ^{m}*It-ḫa-*[*pí-ḫe* DUB.SAR]

TRANSLATION

(1-3) Tablet of adoption of Teḫip-tilla son of Puḫi-šenni. Enna-mati son of Kamputtu adopted him.

(4-8) Enna-mati gave to Teḫip-tilla as an inheritance share an 11 homer field in the *ugāru* of ..., (measured) by the large standard of [the palace], abutting the road to the town of ... .

(8-11) And Teḫip-tilla gave to Enna-mati as his gift 5 talents [of copper (and)] 7 homers of barley.

(12-14) Should the field have claimants, Enna-mati shall clear (it and) give (it) to Teḫip-tilla.

(15-16) Enna-mati shall also bear the *ilku* of the field.

(16-17) Should Enna-mati abrogate (this contract), he shall give 10 minas of gold.

(18-32) Before Šummiya son of Arik-kanari; before Muš-teya son of Ar-šenni; before Ibnā-šarru son of Ilu-mālik. These 3 men are the measurers of the field (and) distributors [of the barley] and copper. Before Taya [son of] Apil-sin; before Ḫatapi-ašu son of Teḫip-tilla; before Šeḫliya son of Ziliya; before Eḫli-tešup son of Lallu-tari; before Ariḫ-ḫamanna son of Turi-kintar; before Šurki-tilla son of Ḫintiya; before Kizziri son of Šennaya; before Nikiya son of Tarmi-tešup; before Itḫ-apiḫe, the scribe, son of Taya.

(33-36) (*seal impression*) seal impression of Eḫli-tešup son of [Lallu-tari]; (*seal impression*) seal impression of Ḫatapi-ašu [son of Teḫip-tilla]; (*seal impression*) seal impression of Šurki-tilla son of [Ḫintiya]; (*seal impression*) seal impression of Itḫ-apiḫe, [the scribe].

COMMENT

The tablet has deteriorated but slightly since the copy was made.

NOTES

ll. 1-2. The *CAD* Nuzi file records these lines as being completely preserved.

l. 3: [*i?-pu?-sú?*]. Or the like. The *CAD* Nuzi file at this point reads, in effect: [ ]-*sú*.

l. 4: 11. The number is correct as copied.

l. 4: *ú-ga*$_5$*-a*[*r*]. The *CAD* Nuzi file reads the end of this line as: *ú-ga*$_5$*-ar* [ ] SAR. If this last sign was indeed once visible, then the only toponym that comes to mind as having both this sign and an *ugāru* is the town of Ṭupšarri. See *HSS*, XIX, 97:3 (A.GÀR ⌜*ša*⌝ URU DUB.SAR-*ri*-WA); IM 70882 (=TF$_1$ 258):3 (A.GÀR URU DUB.SAR-*ri-ni*-WA). The latter text was published by al-Rawi (1980, 134-35, 137). Cf. a preliminary edition by Fadhil (1972, 90-91 [text #18]).

l. 14: ⌜*za*⌝. It appears that the space between Ú and AK has been erased.

l. 14: *i+na-din*. The AN of the copy (between NA and DIN) does not appear on the tablet. The tablet is well preserved at this point.

l. 25: *ḫi*. This sign consists of three wedges only, not four as copied. The top wedge of the four does not appear on the tablet. The tablet is well preserved at this point.

l. 28: *in-tar*. These signs are rather clearer on the tablet than in the copy.

ll. 29-32. On the tablet, the IGI signs are somewhat higher than the rest of their respective lines. The copy renders well this peculiarity.

ll. 32-36. The *CAD* Nuzi file records these lines as wholly preserved.

JEN 726

OBVERSE

1 ṭup-pí ma-ru-t[i ša] ^{m}Za-zi-ya [DUMU Ḫa?-ši?-pa?-a?-pu?]
2 ^{m}Te-ḫi-ip-til-*la *DUMU Pu-ḫi-še-en-*⌜ni⌝
3 a-na ma-[r]u-ti i-pu-uš
4 1 *ANŠE *1 ^{GIŠ}APIN A.ŠÀ.MEŠ i+na ⌜le⌝-*e[t]
5 [i?-n]a? *⌜KASKAL? ša⌝ URU Ar-ra-ap-ḫe *⌜X⌝[ ]
6 *ù i+na le-et A.ŠÀ ša ^{m}Ḫa-ši-pa-a-pu
7 ^{m}Za-zi-ya a-na ^{m}Te-ḫi-⌜ip⌝-[ti]l-la ki-ma ḪA.LA-⁺⌜šu⌝ [i-din]
8 ù ^{m}Te-ḫi-ip-til-la •4 [ ]
9 [k]i-ma NÍG.BA a-na ^{m}Za-zi-[ya i-din]
10 šum-ma ^{m}Za-zi-⌜ya KI⌝.[BAL-at]
11 1 MA.NA KÙ.BABBAR [1 MA.NA KÙ.SIG$_{17}$ ú-ma-al-la]

---

12 [IG]I Ap-⌜x-uš/ta⌝ DUMU ⌜^{d}⌝[IM-LUGAL]
13 [IGI] Wa-⌜at⌝-wa DUMU ⌜Sí⌝?-[in?-n]a?-a-nu?
14 [IGI] Ar-⌜ša⌝-[l]im ⌜DUMU⌝ Šúk-ri-ya
15 IGI Zi-li-ya DUMU Ḫé-[e]l?-la-kál
16 [IGI] Wi-ir-[ra-a]ḫ!-[ḫe DUMU A]t-ti$_{4}$-la-a[m-mu]
17 [5 LÚ].*MEŠ [ša A.ŠÀ.MEŠ ú-še]-el-wu-ú
18 IGI Pa-i-til-la [DUMU] ⌜Ké⌝-l[i]-ya
19 IGI A-ri-ḫa-m[a]-an-na DUM[U] ⌜Ḫa⌝-tar-te
20 IGI A-•ta-*a-a *DUMU Tù-⌜ra⌝-ri
21 IGI Na-a[ḫ-ši-y]a DUMU Še-ḫu-ur[-x?]
22 [I]GI ⌜Pal?-te⌝?-[šup? DUMU] ⌜Ḫe?-er⌝?-pu-ya

REVERSE

23 IGI It-ḫi-til-l[a] DUMU Ip-ša-ḫa-lu
24 IGI It-ḫa-pí-ḫe DUB.SAR
25 •DUMU Ta-a-a

S.I.

26 ^{NA_4} KIŠIB Pa-⌜i⌝!-til-l[a DUMU] Ké-l[i-ya]

S.I. Po 507

27 $^{[N]A_4}$ KIŠIB A-ta-a-[a] ⌜DUMU⌝? [Tù-ra-ri]

S.I. Po 42

28 ^{NA_4} KIŠIB X EN A.ŠÀ

S.I. Po 353

⁺29 ^{NA_4} ⌜KIŠIB⌝! [D]UB.[SAR]

LEFT EDGE

30 šum-ma [A].Š[À pa-qí-*r]a!-*na *i-ra-aš-ši
31 ^{m}Za-•zi-[ya ú-za]-ak-⌜kà⌝-ma a-na
32 ^{m}T[e-ḫi-ip-til]-la i+⌜na⌝-an-[din]

TRANSLATION

(1-3) Tablet of adoption [of] Zaziya [son of Ḫašip-apu?]. He adopted Teḫip-tilla son of Puḫi-šenni.

(4-7) Zaziya [gave] to Teḫip-tilla as his inheritance share a 1.1 homer field adjacent to—in(?)—the road(?) to the town of Arrapḫa ...(?), and adjacent to the field of Ḫašip-apu.

(8-9) And Teḫip-tilla [gave] to Zaziya as a gift 4 ... .

(10-11) Should Zaziya abrogate (this contract), [he shall pay] 1 mina of silver [(and) 1 mina of gold].

(12-25) Before Ap...uš\ta son of Adad-šarri; [before] Watwa son of Sinnanu(?); [before] Ar-šalim son of Šukriya; before Ziliya son of Ḫellakal(?); [before] Wiraḫḫe [son of] Attilammu. [(These are) the 5] men [who] measured [the field.] Before Pai-tilla [son of] Keliya; before Ariḫ-ḫamanna son of Ḫatarte; before Ataya son of Turari; before Naḫšiya son of Šeḫur-x(?); before Pal-tešup(?) [son of] Ḫerpuya(?); before Itḫip-tilla son of Ipša-ḫalu; before Itḫ-apiḫe, the scribe, son of Taya.

(26-29) (*seal impression*) seal impression of Pai-tilla [son of] Keliya; (*seal impression*) seal impression of Ataya son of [Turari]; (*seal impression*) seal impression of ...(?), (erstwhile) owner of the field; (*seal impression*) seal impression of the scribe.

(30-32) Should the field have claimants, Zaziya shall clear (it) and give (it) to Teḫip-tilla.

COMMENTS

Lacheman's copy has not been checked against the original, since the tablet was returned to Baghdad before collation could be undertaken. Prior to the tablet's return, a pair of casts was made but with only partial success. Much of the surface is difficult to interpret and there is much I cannot read. Where I can read the casts with the help of the copy, I assume the copy to be accurate. Notation of signs indicating they are now partially or totally destroyed means that these signs are not entirely visible on the casts. In sum, collation of this text must be considered unsatisfactory. It has only approximate, not precise, value.

It appears that the tablet has suffered some additional damage since the copy was made, especially toward the top of the obverse.

NOTES

l. 1: [DUMU *Ḫa?-ši?-pa?-a?-pu?*]. These signs, clear on the copy, are not visible on the casts. Collation with the original would be enlightening. We may not assume, *a priori* that failure to see these signs is due to the

quality of the casts or to the deterioration of the original since the copy was made. Lacheman's original copy of the tablet did not contain these signs. They were added later. To be sure, further collation may have taken place. Yet Lacheman's papers are ambiguous on this point as well: this patronymic appears in transliteration but there is also a notation that the first line must be rechecked against the original. Whether the transliteration came before the notation or afterward is difficult to tell.

To my knowledge, Zaziya son of Ḫašip-apu is nowhere else attested in the Nuzi texts.

Somehow, this issue is likely related to the appearance of the PN, Ḫašip-apu, in line 6.

l. 4: 1 ANŠE. The initial wedges of this line are unclear. The number, "1," is possible according to what is visible.

l. 5: [*i*?-*n*]*a*? ⌜KASKAL⌝?. Lacheman reads, at this point: *i-na lìb-bi*. Following *ina lēt*, the sense of this part of the line is difficult in any case.

l. 6: *pu*. This sign is clearly preserved and typical. It does not appear as the NU of the copy.

l. 7: ⌜*šu*⌝. This sign is almost completely preserved. Only the lowest horizontal seems effaced.

l. 7: [*i-din*]. Lacheman records these signs as completely preserved.

l. 8: 4 [ ]. The upper right wedge seems effaced. Lacheman at one time read, in effect: 4 [+x ANŠE] ŠE. On another occasion, he read: 2 [+x ANŠE x+]1 BÁN ŠE.

l. 10: ⌜KI⌝.[BAL-*at*]. The copy supports this rendering. However, Lacheman reads, *i*-[*bala-kat*], a restoration supported by *JEN* 721:9. On the connections between *JEN* 721 and 726, see below, note to line 12.

l. 11. This line is restored on the basis of *JEN* 721:10. On the connections between *JEN* 721 and 726, see below, note to line 12.

As for the initial number, Lacheman once read "1" (as indicated in this edition) and once "2." If the latter is correct, then the restoration should be: [2 MA.NA KÙ.SIG$_{17}$ *ú-ma-al-la*].

l. 12. The restoration of this line is based on *JEN* 721:11. All witness PN restorations in this text are based on the combined evidence of this text and *JEN* 721. On the parallels connecting these two texts, see above, notes to *JEN* 721:11, 28-29.

The *CAD* Nuzi file for *JEN* 721:11 has "*Tup*-[ ]." In light of this, one is tempted to restore ⌜*Tup-ki-ya*⌝! DUMU ^{d}IM-LUGAL here (and there as well). This individual is attested in *HSS*, XIV, 619:24. The traces of the personal name, however, do not appear to favor this restoration.

l. 13: ⌜*at*⌝. Lacheman records this sign as wholly preserved.

l. 13: ⌜*Si*⌝?-[*in*?-*n*]*a*?-*a-nu*?. Lacheman reads, in effect: *Zi-ka*$_4$*-a-rù*. However, cf. the parallel traces in *JEN* 721:12.

l. 15: *Ḫé-[e]l?-la-kál*. This PN is difficult: (a) it is not clearly attested elsewhere at Nuzi; (b) it does not seem to accord with *JEN* 721:13 with which it is likely linked; and (c) Lacheman reads *At-ti$_4$-la-am-mu*. Regarding (c), the traces here appear not to favor that reading.

l. 16: *[a]ḫ!*. At this point, Lacheman reads RI. In light of *JEN* 721:14, a restoration of [A]Ḫ seems to reflect what Lacheman saw.

l. 16: *[A]t-ti$_4$-la-a[m-mu]*. Lacheman records these signs as completely preserved.

l. 17: [LÚ]. Lacheman records this sign as completely preserved.

l. 19: *na*. This sign appears normal, not as copied (i.e., "LA").

l. 21: IGI. This sign appears as copied, i.e., higher than the rest of the line.

l. 21: *a[ḫ]*. After the ḪI element, a horizontal may be preserved. The state of the cast makes it difficult to be sure. Lacheman reads: *Na-ḫi-šal-[mu]*.

l. 21: *Še-ḫu-ur[-x?]*. Lacheman reads: *Še-ḫu-ur-r[a]*.

l. 22. The first name is based on *JEN* 721:20. It is questionable only because the patronymic is not sure. See above, second note to *JEN* 721:20.

By combining several references from Lacheman's papers, it seems he once read this line as: IGI *Tar-mi-ya* DUMU *Al-pu-ya*.

Lacheman at one point suggested that, below this line on the lower edge, two lines are now missing. Elsewhere in his papers, he fails to note this. To judge from the parallel witness list of *JEN* 721, no lines seem to be missing.

l. 26. Lacheman records the seal impression above this line as Po 508A. This would accord with *JEN* 721:26 and its associated seal impression.

l. 27: ⸢DUMU⸣. The meaning of the trace is in doubt, but not the filiation thereby established.

l. 28: X. These two wedges are not distinct on the cast. Perhaps it is a partial recopying of the end of KIŠIB. Weeks suggests *ša* (1972, 196). Or it may simply be an idiosyncratic shorthand (suggested by "(KI.)MIN"?), referring, of course, to the vendor.

l. 29. Below this line, on the upper edge, Lacheman records, in effect:

[^{NA_4} KIŠIB]-*na*-[ ]. *JEN* 721 offers no support for this restoration.

l. 29: ⸢KIŠIB⸣!. The wedges appear as ⸢KIŠIB⸣ DIŠ. Cf. above, note to l. 28.

l. 29: [D]UB.[SAR]. The trace appears as: 

In this connection, seal impression Po 353, with which this line is associated, reappears above, *JEN* 721:27, in connection with Itḫ-apiḫe, the scribe. See above, note to *JEN* 721:27.

ll. 30-32. On the position of the clear title clause in this text, see above, note to *JEN* 721:28-29.

l. 30: [*pa-qí-r*]*a*!-*na*. In light of *JEN* 721:28, perhaps one ought to restores [*pí-i*]*r*!-*qa*! here.

JEN 727

OBVERSE

1 •*ṭup*-•*pí* •*ma*-*[*r*]*u-ti ša* ^{m}[*Ši*]-⸢*il*⸣-*wa*-[*te-šup*]

2 DUMU *A*-•⸢*x*-**x*⸣-**a*-•*a* ⸢*ù*⸣ ^{m}[*Te-ḫi-ip-til-l*]*a* DUMU •*Pu*-**ḫi*-**še*-[*en-ni*]

3 *a-na ma-r*[*u-ti*] *i-te*-[*pu-u*]*š-ma*

4 2 ANŠE *A.[ŠÀ] *⸢*i-na*⸣ AN.*Z[A.KÀR] *ša* ⸢*Ki*⸣-*pá-an-til i+na il-ta-ni-šu*

5 *a-na* ^{m}*T*[*e-ḫi-ip*]-*til-la* [*ki*]-*ma* ḪA.LA-*šu*

6 ⸢*it*?-*ta*?-*din*⸣? *šum-ma* $^{[m]}$*Ši-il-wa-te-šup*

7 [*i*]-*ba-la-ka*$_4$-*at* 1 MA.NA KÙ.BABBAR 1 MA.⸢NA KÙ.SIG$_{17}$⸣

8 [*a-n*]*a* ⸢^{m}⸣[*T*]*e-ḫi-ip-til-l*[*a*] *i+na-an-dì*-⸢*in*⸣

9 IGI ^{m}*Pí*-⸢*ru*⸣ DUMU *Na*-[*i*]*š-ké-el-pé*

10 IGI ^{m}Ì[R-D]INGIR-*šu* DUMU [*D*]*u-ur-šar-ru*

11 IGI ^{m}*Ni-nu-a-tal* DUMU *Ar-ša-wu-uš-ka*$_4$

12 IGI ^{m}•*Ta*-⸢*a*⸣-•*ú*-⸢*ki*⸣? DUMU *Ka*$_4$-*am-pá-tu*$_4$

13 IGI ^{m}*Ki-iz*-[*zi-ḫar*]-*pá* DUMU *A-ki-ya*

14 IGI ^{m}*Ḫa-ma-a*[*n*]-*n*[*a*] DUMU *Šu*-⸢*ru-uk*⸣-*ka*

15 IGI ^{m}*Ḫa-n*[*a*?-]DUMU *Ar*-[*š*]*a-tù-ya*

16 IGI ^{m}⸢X⸣-[DUMU] ⸢X⸣-[ ]-⸢X⸣-[ ]

17 IGI ^{m}[DUMU]

.

.

.

REVERSE

.

.

.

S.I.

18 ^{NA_4} [KIŠIB ^{m}] DUMU *Ta-a*-[ ]

S.I. Po 637

19 [^{NA_4} KIŠI]B ^{m}⸢*Pí*-•*ru*⸣ DUMU *Na-iš-ké-el-pé*

S.I.

20 ^{NA_4} KIŠIB ÌR-DINGIR-⸢*šu*⸣ DUMU *Du-ur-šar-ru*

S.I.

21 *^{NA_4} KIŠIB ^{m}*Ki-iz-z*[*i*-•*ḫ*]*ar-pá*

TRANSLATION

(1-3) Tablet of adoption of Šilwa-tešup son of A[ta?]ya. And he adopted Teḫip-tilla son of Puḫi-šenni.

(4-6) He gave to Teḫip-tilla as his inheritance share a 2 homer field in the *dimtu* of Kipantil, in its north(ern part).

(6-8) Should Šilwa-tešup abrogate (this contract), he shall give to Teḫip-tilla 1 mina of silver (and) 1 mina of gold.

(9-17) Before Piru son of Naiš-kelpe; before Ward-ilišu son of Dûr-šarru; before Ninu-atal son of Ar-šawuška; before Tayuki son of Kampatu; before Kizzi-ḫarpa son of Akiya; before Ḫamanna son of Šurukka; before Ḫan[a?-...] son of Ar-šatuya; before ... [son of] ...; before ... [son of ...].

(18-21) (*seal impression*) seal impression of ... son of Ta-...; (*seal impression*) seal impression of Piru son of Naiš-kelpe; (*seal impression*) seal impression of Ward-ilišu son of Dûr-šarru; (*seal impression*) seal impression of Kizzi-ḫarpa.

COMMENT

This tablet has deteriorated badly since it was copied. Many signs, clear to Lacheman, are now difficult to make out. Much else is simply no longer visible.

NOTES

l. 2: *A-⌈x-x⌉-a-a*. Lacheman reads, variously, *A-ta-*[*a-a*] and *A-ta-a-a*. According to *NPN*, 134a *sub* ŠILWA-TEŠUP 3), 29a *sub* ARIP-ḪURRA 4), the patronymic is *A-ri-ip-ḫur-ra*.

l. 2: [*Te-ḫi-ip-til-l*]*a* DUMU *Pu-ḫi-še-*[*en-ni*]. At one point, Lacheman read *Te-ḫi-ip-*[*til-l*]*a* DUMU *Pu-ḫi-še-en-ni*. Elsewhere, he saw the patronymic as *Pu-ḫi-še-ni*.

l. 3: *i-te-*[*pu-u*]*š-ma*. Lacheman and the *CAD* Nuzi file record this word as completely preserved.

l. 4: AN.Z[A.KÀR] *ša* ⌈*Ki*⌉*-pá-an-til*. The land is thus located in Nuzi. The *dimtu* of Kipantil lies adjacent to the *dimtu* of Kip-tešup (see, e.g., *JEN* 493:2-3) which itself is located in Nuzi (see, e.g., *JEN* 310:4, 8).

l. 4: *il*. The sign appears, not as copied, but as:

l. 5. Lacheman records this line as completely preserved.

l. 6: ⌈*it?-ta?-din*⌉?. Some form of the verb, *nadānu*, is called for. Lacheman interprets these traces as [*i*]-⌈*di*⌉*-n*[*a*]*-aš-šu*. The *CAD* Nuzi file reads *id-*[*din*].

l. 7: [*i*]*-ba-*. Lacheman and the *CAD* Nuzi file read, at this point: *i-ib-ba-*.

l. 12: *ki*?. The copy reflects KA. However, the sign itself is no longer clear. The *CAD* Nuzi file reflects KI. This is to be preferred since Tayuki son of Kampatu is a frequent witness for Teḫip-tilla. See *NPN*, 145a *sub* TAI̯UKI 8).

l. 15: *Ḫa-n*[*a*?-]. At various times, Lacheman read *Ḫa-ni-*[*ku-y*]*a* and *Ḫa-am-ni-*[*pi-zi*] (*sic*). For Ḫampizi son of Ar-šatuya, see *NPN*, 52a *sub* ḪAMPIZI 1), 32a *sub* AR-ŠATUI̯A 5).

l. 18. Lacheman notes the possible restoration: ^{NA_4} [KIŠIB ^{m}*It-ḫa-pí-ḫé*] DUMU *Ta-a-*[*a*]. The tablet, he observes, is in the "writing of Ithapihe." However, he also notes, regarding the seal impression above line 18: "the fragmentary seal is unlike those in Po," i.e., Itḫ-apiḫe seal impressions attested in Porada (1947).

l. 20. The seal impression above this line is identified by Lacheman, unpublished papers, as "Po 996," not the "Po 998" of the copy. Porada (1947, 138 *ad* no. 996) identifies Po 996 elsewhere with Ward-ilišu son of Dûr-šarru, the same individual identified here in line 20. Collation reveals, however, that the seal impression here, although it resembles both Po 996 and Po 998, is identical to neither.

JEN 728

OBVERSE

1 *ṭup-pí ma-ru-ti ša* ^{m}*Ip-*⸢*ša*⸣-[*a-a*]
2 DUMU *Ké*!-*li-ya* ^{m}*Te-ḫi-ip-til-*[*la*]
3 DUMU *Pu-ḫi-še-en-ni a-na ma-ru-t*[*i*]
4 *i-pu-us-sú* 2 ANŠE 2 ^{GIŠ}A[PIN] ⸢A⸣.ŠÀ *a-šar* A.ŠÀ.MEŠ *si-ip-si-*[*wa-na*]
•:*a-šar ku-ur-ki-iz-zi*(-)[ ]
5 AŠ ^{GIŠ}*ta-a-a-ri* GAL *ša* É.GAL [ ]-**še-*•*ni*
6 [*a*]-*n*[*a*] ^{m}*Te-ḫi-ip-til-la ki-ma* ḪA.•LA [*i-di-in*]
7 [*ù* ^{m}]•*Te-ḫi-ip-til-la* 20 ANŠE 5 [BÁN ŠE]
8 [MA.NA] URUDU.MEŠ *a-na* ^{m}*Ip-ša-a-*⸢*a*⸣
9 [*ki-ma* NÍG].⸢BA⸣ •*i-di-in*
10 [*šum-ma* A.*Š]À *p*[*a-q*]*í-ra-na i+ra-*[*aš-ši*]
11 [^{m}*Ip-ša*]-⸢*a*⸣-*a-ma ú-za-ak-k*[*à*]
12 [*il-ka*$_4$ *š*]*a* A.ŠÀ *šu-ma* [*na*(-*a*)]-⸢*ši*⸣
13 [*šum-ma* ^{m}*I*]*p-ša-a-a* [*i-bala-kat*]
14 10 [M]A.⸢NA⸣ [KÙ.SIG$_{17}$ *ú-ma-al-la*]
15 IGI [*A-ki*]*p-til-*•*la* DUMU *Tù-*•*ra-ri*
16 [I]GI [*W*]*u-ur-tù-ru-uk*! DUMU •⸢*Ma*⸣-*li-ya*
17 IGI *Ša-tù-ša* DUMU *Tù-*•*ra-*•*ri*
18 IGI *Ut-***ḫ*[*i*]-•*ip-til-la* DUMU *Tup-*⸢*ki*⸣-[*ya*]
19 [4] LÚ.MEŠ *an-*[*n*]*u-tu*$_4$ ⸢A⸣.[ŠÀ]

LOWER EDGE

20 ⸢X⸣ [X] +*ú-še-el-w[u] ù*

21 *na-di-na-nu ša* ŠE.MEŠ <*ù*? URUDU?.MEŠ?>

REVERSE

+ ____

22 [I]GI *A[r]-te-šup* DUMU *It-ḫi-iš-ta*

23 IGI *P[u-ḫi-še]-en-ni* DUMU *A-ta-a-te*

24 IGI *Tar-[mi]-•te-šup* *DUMU *Ar-te-ya*

25 IGI *Te-š[u]-up-er-wi* •DUMU *Šúk-ri-ya*

26 IGI *Ḫa-n[i-a]-•aš-ḫa-ri* DUMU *A-ri-ya*

27 IGI *A-r[i-ḫa]-⸢ar-+pa⸣*? *DUMU *E-en-na-mil-ki*

28 IGI *Šúk-[ri-ya* DUMU] ⸢*X*⸣*-li-ya*

29 IGI *Ki-*i[p-ta-li-l]i* DUMU *E-en-na-mil-ki*

30 IGI *Tar-[mi-ya* DUMU *Ma-ša-an-t]e*

.

.

.

S.I.

31 [^{NA_4} KIŠIB ^{m}*U]r-ḫi-ya*

32 [DUMU *Ar-•r]u-pa*

S.I.

33 ^{NA_4} KIŠ[IB ^{m}]

34 ^{NA_4} KIŠIB [^{m}*Tar-mi]-te-šup*

S.I.

35 [DUMU] *Ar-te-ya*

RIGHT EDGE

S.I.

36 ^{NA_4} KIŠIB ^{m}*Te-šu-up-er-w[i]*

TRANSLATION

(1-4) Tablet of adoption of Ipšaya son of Keliya. He adopted Teḫip-tilla son of Puḫi-šenni.

(4-6) [He gave] to Teḫip-tilla as an inheritance share a 2.2 homer field, among the *sipsiwana* fields, among the *kurkizzi*...(?), (measured) by the large standard of the palace ... .

(7-9) [And] Teḫip-tilla gave to Ipšaya [as] a gift 20.5 homers [of barley (and) x minas of] copper.

(10-11) [Should] the field have claimants, it is Ipšaya who shall clear (it).

(12) And he shall bear [the *ilku*] of the field.

(13-14) [Should] Ipšaya [abrogate (this contract), he shall pay] 10 minas of [gold].

(15-30) Before Akip-tilla son of Turari; before Wur-turuk son of Maliya; before Šatuša son of Turari; before Itḫip-Tilla son of Tupkiya. These

[4] men measured the ... field and are the distributors of the barley <and? the? copper?>.

Before Ar-tešup son of Itḫišta; before Puḫi-šenni son of Adatteya; before Tarmi-tešup son of Ar-teya; before Tešup-erwi son of Šukriya; before Ḫaniašḫari son of Ariya; before Ariḫ-ḫarpa son of Enna-milki; before Šukriya [son of] ...-liya; before Kip-talili son of Enna-milki; before Tarmiya [son of] Mašante; .... .

(31-36) (*seal impression*) [seal impression of] Urḫiya [son of] Arrumpa; (*seal impression*) seal impression of ...; seal impression of Tarmi-tešup (*seal impression*) [son of] Ar-teya; (*seal impression*) seal impression of Tešup-erwi.

COMMENTS

This tablet has suffered additional deterioration since the copy was made.

Restorations in this text, including that of witness PNs, are based on the fact that *JEN* 728 together with *JEN* 419, 686, 710, and 716 constitute a homogeneous group of Artiḫi texts. See above, first note to *JEN* 686:5.

NOTES

ll. 4-5. The text of these two lines extends from the obverse across the entire reverse.

l. 4: *si-ip-si-[wa-na]*. This restoration is based on *JEN* 12:5 and 55:5. The meaning of the word is unknown. The three contexts in which the term appears are insufficient to establish a definition. However, *JEN* 12, 55, 728 are all Artiḫi texts: *JEN* 728 is linked to other Artiḫi texts by a standard witness sequence (see above, comments) and *JEN* 12 and 55 have witness sequences which significantly overlap that of *JEN* 728. Therefore, *sipsiwana* may be a term identifying a feature of the Artiḫi landscape—in effect, a toponym.

One may here note that several peculiar terms in the Teḫip-tilla corpus are confined to the Artiḫi environment: *yarru* (see above, first note to *JEN* 686:5), *alupatḫi* (see above, first note to *JEN* 687:6), *Nirašši* (see above, note to *JEN* 699:11; unusual, but not as mysterious as the others or as exclusively Artiḫian), *kurkizzi* (see below, third note to line 5), and, of course, *sipsiwana*.

l. 5: AŠ GIŠ. These wedges might, with less probability, be interpreted as: [*i*]-*na*.

l. 5: [ ]-*še-ni*. Less likely, IN. I cannot make any sense of these signs (or sign) in this context. The first element (or sign) is now entirely effaced, the second nearly so.

l. 5: *ku-ur-ki-iz-zi*(-)[ ]. Unless the reference is to some locale known for its piglet (i.e., *kurkizannu*) population, I am at a loss to understand this term.

l. 7: *ḫi*. This sign consists of three wedges, not four as depicted in the copy. The top wedge of the copy is not present on the tablet. The tablet is well preserved at this point.

l. 7: 20. Although three wedges appear in the copy, the first of these is a depression made in the clay, not a typical impression of the stylus. Joachim Oelsner, observing this phenomenon, notes similar scribal quirks in the Middle Babylonian texts from Nippur (personal communication, 3 August 1983).

l. 7: [BÁN]. For this restoration, see above, note to *JEN* 705:8.

l. 10: *p*[*a*]. Although the sign appears to be BA, what is preserved is:  In light of the spelling of the same word in *JEN* 419:11; 686:10; etc., with PA, not BA, it is likely that the former sign was written here as well.

ll. 13-14. These lines are restored on the basis of *JEN* 686: 14-15; 710:14-16; 716:17-19. On the relevance of these texts, see above, comments. It is possible that *i-bala-kat* appeared at the start of line 14 rather than at the end of line 13.

A line may well be missing after line 14. If so, one might replace *ú-ma-al-la* on line 14 with *a-na* ᵐ*Te-ḫi-ip-Til-la i-na-din* on the missing next line. Cf. *JEN* 419:15.

l. 21: <*ù*? URUDU?.MEŠ?>. Although copper, as well as barley, was given as the "gift," it need not be so noted at this point. Cf. *JEN* 716:25 (this assumes a restoration in *JEN* 716:10; see above, note to that line). Since, however, "*ù* URUDU.MEŠ" does appear in a comparable context, *JEN* 419:21, the scribe may inadvertently have omitted it here. Another possibility is that noted by Lacheman and the *CAD* Nuzi file: a third line on the lower edge is now effaced. It contained: *ù* URUDU.MEŠ.

l. 22. Immediately above this line, on the reverse, appears a horizontal line. This is not indicated in the copy.

l. 27: ⸢*pa*⸣?. After ⸢AR⸣ and before DUMU (itself now effaced) appears the following (absent from the copy): 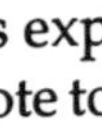 . Although ME is expected here (cf. *JEN* 419:27; 716:30), PA (or BA or even WA; see above, note to *JEN* 707:6) seems to be represented by these traces.

l. 28: *Šúk*-[*ri-ya*]. Cf. *JEN* 710:31. See also above, note to *JEN* 686:32.

l. 30. Two lines appear to be missing after line 30. They would have contained the names of two additional witnesses: Itḫ-apiḫe, the scribe, son of Taya and Urḫiya son of Arrumpa. Cf., e.g., *JEN* 419:30-31. For the latter witness, see in fact, below, lines 31-32.

l. 33. The identity of the sealer may well be Ariḫ-ḫarpa (son of Enna-milki). Cf., e.g., *JEN* 716:39. The sealing itself actually appears on the right edge of the reverse.

l. 36. Porada indicates that, following line 36, a seal impression was once visible on the left edge. If so, it was probably that of Itḫ-apiḫe the scribe. Cf., e.g., *JEN* 710:40; 716:40.

JEN 729

OBVERSE

1 [ṭup-pí ma-ru]-˹ti ša˺ [^{m}Ip-š]a-+ḫa-+lu DUMU Šu-ur-ku-ma-tal
2 [^{m}Te-ḫi-ip-ti]l-la DUMU Pu-˹ḫi-še-en˺-ni
3 [a-na ma]-˹ru-ti˺ i-pu-uš-ma
4 •2 •AN[ŠE] *˹A.*ŠÀ˺ [i?-na?] ˹URU? X •X i?-na? ṣe?-ri?-ti˺?
5 ^{m}Ip-[ša-ḫa-lu a-na ^{m}Te-ḫi-ip-til-la]
6 ki-˹ma ḪA˺.*L[A-šu SUM-in]
7 [x?+]40 GÍN KÙ.*B[ABBAR ^{m}Te-ḫi]-•ip-•til-•la
8 a+˹na˺ ^{m}Ip-ša-˹ḫa˺-lu •ki-ma NÍG.BA-šu ˹SUM˺-in
9 šum-ma A.ŠÀ pa-qí-•ra-•an-na i-ra-aš-še
10 ^{m}Ip-ša-ḫa-lu ú-za-ak-•kà-•ma
11 a+na <m>Te-ḫi-ip-til-la SUM-*in
12 [š]um-ma ^{m}Ip-ša-ḫa-lu ib-˹ba˺-la-ak-[ka$_4$-at x?+1 MA.N]A KÙ.BABBAR
13 [x?+]˹1˺ MA.NA KÙ.˹SIG$_{17}$˺ ú-•ma-˹al˺-la

---

14 IGI Mu-uš-te-eš-šup DUMU Ḫa-ši-•ya
15 IGI ˹A˺-kip-še-•en-ni DUMU •˹Ni˺-•iḫ-[ri-y]a
16 IGI [P]í-i-˹ru˺ [DUMU Na]-iš-[k]é-[el-p]è
17 I[GI M]u•u[š-še]-˹en-•ni˺ [DUM]U Ni-nu-[a]-tal
18 [IGI] •E-wi-in$_4$-na-an-ni [DUMU] Še-en-na-a-a
19 [IGI] Gi$_5$-mil-l[i-^{d}I]M [DUMU •Z]u-ú-me
20 [IGI] •It-ḫi-•iš-•˹ta˺ D[UMU] A-ar-ta-e
21 [IGI] Zi-kà-*a-*˹a˺ [DUMU] ˹Éḫ˺-li-ip-LUGAL

LOWER EDGE

22 [IGI] ˹Tu˺-ra-r[i ^{L}]$^{Ú?}$ ŠITIM
23 •IGI I-ri-•ya *˹DUMU? *A˺?-ḫi-i-ú?
24 IGI Ar-ta-še-•en-•ni DUB.SAR-rù

REVERSE

25 DUMU IBILA-^{d}XXX

\+ ---

\+ ---

S.I. Po 17

26 $^{\text{[N]A}_4}$ KIŠIB ^{m}*Ar-ta-še-en-ni* ⸢DUB⸣.SAR-*ri*

S.I.

27 $^{\text{NA}_4}$ KIŠIB ^{m}*Ip-ša-⸢ḫa⸣-lu*

28 DUMU *Šu-ur-ku-⸢ma⸣-tal*

S.I. Po 917

29 $^{\text{NA}_4}$ KIŠIB ^{m}⸢*Mu-uš-te-eš-šup*⸣ DUMU ⸢*Ḫa-ši-ya*⸣

S.I. Po 637

UPPER EDGE

30 $^{\text{NA}_4}$ KIŠIB ^{m}*Pí-i-ru* DUMU *Na-iš-ké-⁺el-⁺pè*

TRANSLATION

(1-3) [Tablet of] adoption of Ipša-ḫalu son of Šurkum-atal. He adopted Teḫip-tilla son of Puḫi-šenni.

(4-6) Ipša-ḫalu [gave to Teḫip-tilla] as [his] inheritance share a 2 homer field, [in?] the town(?) of …, in(?) the suburbs(?).

(7-8) Teḫip-tilla gave to Ipša-ḫalu as his gift [x?+]40 sheqels of silver.

(9-11) Should the field have claimants, Ipša-ḫalu shall clear (it) and give (it) to Teḫip-tilla.

(12-13) Should Ipša-ḫalu abrogate (this contract), he shall pay [x?+1] mina(s) of silver (and) [x?+]1 minas of gold.

(14-25) Before Muš-tešup son of Ḫašiya; before Akip-šenni son of Niḫriya; before Piru [son of] Naiš-kelpe; before Muš-šenni son of Ninu-atal; [before] Ewinnanni [son of] Šennaya; [before] Gimill-adad [son of] Zume; [before] Itḫišta son of Ar-tae; [before] Zikaya [son of] Elḫip-šarri; [before] Turari, the house builder; before Iriya son(?) of(?) Aḫiu(?); before Artašenni, the scribe, son of Apil-sin.

(26-30) (*seal impression*) seal impression of Artašenni, the scribe; (*seal impression*) seal impression of Ipša-ḫalu son of Šurkum-atal; (*seal impression*) seal impression of Muš-tešup son of Ḫašiya; (*seal impression*) seal impression of Piru son of Naiš-kelpe.

COMMENT

This tablet has suffered considerable damage since it was copied.

NOTES

l. 4: ⸢URU? X X⸣. A town name would be expected at this point in the text. One would like to restore here: URU *Zi-iz-za*. The reason for this is a

largely overlapping witness sequence (including a rarely attested scribe) shared by this text and *JEN* 77. The real estate described in that text is located in Zizza (l. 5). However, I find no text where a *ṣēru* or *ṣērītu* is connected with Zizza. This may be relevant if *ṣērīti* is correctly restored on this line (see below, next note).

l. 4: ⸢*ṣe?-ri?-ti*⸣?. On the meaning of *ṣēru*, *ṣērītu* as "suburbs" or the like in the Nuzi texts, see Maidman (1976, 145 with notes) and compare the remarks of Oppenheim (1964, 112, 115). To the references cited in Maidman may be added H. Lewy (1964, 187, n.1); Zaccagnini (1979c, 20 [arguing against my position]); Cassin (1982, 102, n. 14); and Wilhelm (1983, 312-13).

l. 7: [x?+]40. Lacheman sees no lacuna at the start of this line and reads "40." The *CAD* Nuzi file reads "5." Might this have been an error for "50?"

l. 9: *an*. This sign is partially effaced (it now looks like MAŠ) but is, most likely, AN, as copied.

l. 9: *še*. The sign is correct as copied.

l. 12: [x?+1 MA.N]A. See below, next note.

l. 13: [x?+]⸢1⸣. Lacheman and the *CAD* Nuzi file see no lacuna at the start of this line and read "1." If this is so, then "[1 MA.N]A" is to be restored in line 12.

l. 16. The *CAD* Nuzi file records this line as completely preserved.

l. 17. The *CAD* Nuzi file records this line as completely preserved. Lacheman, at one point, saw parts (at least) of every sign.

l. 22: ŠITIM. The sign appears, not as copied, but, rather, as:

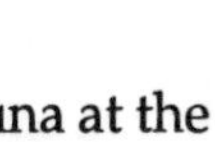

l. 23. Lacheman and the *CAD* Nuzi file record this line as completely preserved. The patronymic (if it is a patronymic) is, to my knowledge, otherwise unattested at Nuzi.

l. 25. Below this line appears a double line. This is not shown on the copy.

l. 29. The *CAD* Nuzi file records this line as completely preserved.

l. 30. This line appears on the upper edge, not on the reverse as depicted. After line 30, the rest of the upper edge is blank.

JEN 730

OBVERSE

1 $^{[m]}$⸢*Tup*⸣$^{-u}$[^{p}*-ki-til-la* DUMU? PN?]
2 ^{m}*Te-ḫi-•ip-til-la*
3 DUMU *Pu-ḫi-še-en-*⸢*ni*⸣
4 *a-na ma-ru-ti i-p*[*u-uš-ma*]
5 GIS.ŠAR *i+na* URU *Nu-z*[*i*]
6 *i+na le-et* GIS.ŠAR *š*[*a*]
7 ḪA.LA-*šu* <*ša*?> ^{m}*Tup*$^{-up}$*-ki-*[*til-la*]
8 *ù* GIS.ŠAR *ša* ^{m}*Ḫa-*⸢*x*⸣-[ ]
9 DUMU *It-ḫi-til-la* [(?)]
10 ⸢*ù*⸣ <m>*Tup*$^{-up}$*-ki-*[*til-l*]*a*
11 *a-*[*n*]*a* <m>*Te-ḫi-i*[*p-til*]*-la ki-mu*

(erasure)

---

12 ⸢ḪA⸣.LA-*šu* (erasure) *in-*[*d*]*ì-*⸢*in*⸣
13 [GÍN •K]Ù.BABBAR ⸢*ù*⸣? [(?)]
14 [*ù* ^{m}*Te-ḫ*]*i-ip-til-l*[*a*]
15 [*a-na* ^{m}*Tup*$^{-u}$]^{p}*-ki-til-l*[*a*]

LOWER EDGE

16 [*ki-mu* NÍG].⸢BA⸣-*šu i*[*n-dì-in*]

\+ ---

17 [*ma-an-nu š*]*a* KI.BAL-*t*[*u*]

REVERSE

18 [MA.N]A KÙ.SIG$_{17}$ Ì.L[Á.E]
19 [I]G[I *M*]*u-uš!-še-en-ni* DUMU *Ni-*[*nu-a-tal*]
20 I[GI *P*]*í-e-ru* [D]UMU •*Na-•iš-•k*[*e-el-pè*]
21 IG[I] *Ar-ša-lim* DUMU ⸢*Tam*⸣*-pu-uš-til*
22 [IGI] ⸢*Ú*⸣*-na-ap-ta-*<*e*> DUMU *Še-er-wi*
23 •IG[I *I*]*k-ka-ri-ya* DUMU *Ḫa-ni-ku-ú-•a*
24 •IGI•⸢*Še*⸣*-él-la-pá-e* DUMU *A-ar-ta-e*
25 IGI ⸢*Ar*⸣*-ta-še-en-ni* DUB.SAR

S.I. Po 792

26 ^{NA_4} KIŠIB *Ar-ta-še-en-*[*ni*]

S.I. Po 637

TRANSLATION

....

(1-4) Tupki-Tilla [son? of? ...?]. He adopted Teḫip-tilla son of Puḫi-šenni.

(5-12) Now Tupki-tilla gave to Teḫip-tilla as his inheritance share an orchard in the town of Nuzi, adjacent to the orchard of ..., the inheritance share <of?> Tupki-tilla, and an orchard of Ḫa-... son of Itḫip-tilla [...?].

(13-16) [And] Teḫip-tilla gave [to] Tupki-tilla [as] his gift [... sheqels] of silver and(?) [...?].

(17-18) [He] who abrogates (this contract) shall weigh out X mina(s) of gold.

(19-25) Before Muš-šenni son of Ninu-atal; before Piru son of Naiš-kelpe; before Ar-šalim son of Tampuštil; [before] Unap-ta<e> son of Šerwi; before Ikkariya son of Ḫanikuya; before Šellapai son of Ar-tae; before Artašenni, the scribe.

(26) (*seal impression*) seal impression of Artašenni; (*seal impression*) ....

COMMENTS

This tablet has suffered slight damage since it was copied.

The first line of the obverse and at least one line after line 26 are missing. The first line read: *ṭup-pí ma-ru-ti ša*. For another possibility, see below, note to line 1.

The line after line 26 (if line *27 was the last line, it likely appeared on the upper edge) would have identified the one who rolled the seal whose impression Lacheman identifies on the copy as Po 637. Collation confirms that identification. Porada (1947, 134 *ad* no. 637) identifies the sealing bearing this number as that made elsewhere by Piru son of Naiš-kelpe. That person appears here, line 20. It is, therefore, likely that line *27 read: $^{\text{NA}_4}$KIŠIB *Pí-e-ru* (DUMU *Na-iš-ke-el-pè*) or the like.

NOTES

l. 1. In light of the spacing of lines 2-3, it appears at first glance that only one PN would be written on line 1. (Cf. the short lines of *JEN* 762, almost certainly written by the same scribe.) However, it would be almost inconceivable that, in a contract document of this sort, the scribe would omit the patronymic. Any temptation to do so would be discouraged by the knowledge that "Tupki-tilla" is not a particularly rare name at Nuzi. See *NPN*, 158b *sub* TUPKI-TILLA; *AAN*, 150b-151a *sub* TUPKI-TILLA. It should be noted further that, the length of lines 2 and 3 notwithstanding, almost half of line 1 would remain for the inclusion of the patronymic.

If the patronymic was indeed omitted, one is tempted to see in Itḫip-tilla (l. 9) a possible candidate for Tupki-tilla's father. Lines 5-9 could imply that Tupki-tilla and Ḫa-... were brothers. A Tupki-tilla son of Itḫip-tilla is attested. See *JEN* 718:16.

Another possibility, still less likely, is that line 1 contained the patronymic (e.g., *Um-p*[*í-ya*] or the like) and that *two* lines are missing at the start. The first would have contained the opening formula (as reconstructed above, see comments) and the second would have contained: ^{m}*Tup-up-ki-til-la* DUMU.

l. 4: *i-p*[*u-uš-ma*]. Or the like. The *CAD* Nuzi file records the second sign as completely preserved.

ll. 5-12. The sense of these lines is not entirely transparent. Two possible interpretations present themselves. In describing the inheritance share due to Teḫip-tilla, the scribe may have made a false start with incorrect information. This false start would be represented by lines 5-7, which appear to end with the partially preserved, partially completed statement that orchard land is what Tupki-tilla was ceding to Teḫip-tilla as an inheritance share. The correct version of the clause then continues the text in lines 8-12. Were this the case, however, one would expect the scribe to have erased the faulty lines (he does erase such a line, in fact, after line 11) or simply to have started afresh with a new tablet.

More likely, we have but a single clause wherein the scribe notes that two plots of orchard land were ceded to Teḫip-tilla, the first having been Tupki-tilla's own inheritance share (ll. 5-7), the second the erstwhile property of another individual, perhaps Tupki-tilla's brother (ll. 8-9). (For this possible relationship, cf. above, note to line 1.) The clause ends typically (ll. 10-12). The difficulty with this interpretation is the syntax of line 7. One might assume that the referent of the pronominal suffix in "*zittišu*" is implicit (i.e., Tupki-tilla [l. 1]) in which case the following "Tupki-tilla" would represent a preliminary statement of the subject of the verb (l. 12). A less difficult way out of this dilemma involves the assumption that the scribe accidentally omitted *ša* after ḪA.LA-*šu*. The referent of the suffix would then be the following personal name. The difficulty with this solution is that it assumes a scribal omission. Yet this is no great impediment since the text contains other, unambiguous, scribal omissions. See lines 10, 11, 22.

(The omission of the male determinative in lines 10 and 11, however, may be characteristic of a peculiar [early?] scribal tradition. Cf., for example, the similar omissions in *JEN* 566:1, 4, 8, 10; 733:6, 9; 734:1, 5; 739:12, 14; 742:2, 14, 15, 18; possibly 748:3, 8; 760:12; 774:7. In some of these cases, haplography may come into play. See below, comments on *JEN* 739 and 742.)

Furthermore, he may accidentally have omitted the clear title clause which should have appeared after line 16. In addition, as noted above, the scribe must have erred (albeit not by omission) in the line following line 11. He then erased that line to correct the error. On this error, see also below, note to lines 11-12. Finally, he erased a further error in line

12. For this last item, see below, note to line 12. In sum, asserting that the scribe accidentally omitted *ša* in line 7 does not strain one's credulity.

l. 6: *š*[*a*]. The sign appears, not as copied, but, rather, as:

l. 7: <*ša*?>. See above, note to lines 5-12.

l. 8: ^{m}*Ḫa*-⌜*x*⌝-[ ]. *NPN*, 52b *sub* ḪANAIA 15), 76a *sub* ITḪIP-TILLA 14), reads, it seems: *Ḫa-n*[*a-a-a*]. The trace does not support the reading, NA. Note, however, that one Ḫanaya son of Itḫip-tilla appears as a witness in *JEN* 739 (l. 18). That text is closely connected to *JEN* 718 (see above, note to *JEN* 718:22), the very text in which Tupki-tilla son of Itḫip-tilla appears (l. 16)! See already above, note to line 1.

To the references in *NPN* for Ḫanaya son of Itḫip-tilla may now be added *L-O* 16:1-2, 4, 10.

ll. 11-12. Between these lines, the scribe wrote a line of text he subsequently erased. This erasure is not noted in the copy. He then marked that erasure by enclosing it in a double horizontal line all the way across the obverse.

(These horizontal lines are not represented in the translation since the scribe did not mean them to set off one section from another.)

l. 12: *šu*. Following this sign appears GI in a form typical of the sign in the environment before KÙ. The scribe (unsuccessfully) erased this GI although this erasure is not noted in the copy.

The error stemmed from an automatic motor reflex. In writing ŠU, the scribe approximated KÙ and "naturally" his hand completed the complex with "GI." (However, cf., by contrast, the sign form of GI in line 18.) Recognizing his error, he of course erased the GI element.

l. 16. Immediately below this line appears a horizontal line. This is not indicated in the copy.

l. 17. Lacheman once saw this line as wholly preserved.

l. 19. This line is restored following Lacheman and *NPN*, 99b *sub* MUŠ-ŠENNI 1), 106b *sub* NINU-ATAL 27). This witness also appears in *JEN* 729:17. That text was likely written by the same scribe as this text. See below, note to line 25.

l. 20: [*pè*]. Or the like.

l. 25. Porada associates this scribe with the like named son of Apil-sin. Regarding the seal impression associated with this line, cf. Porada, (1947, 136a *ad* no. 792), where she again expresses the same conclusion regarding the scribe's paternity. Collation confirms that this seal impression is indeed Po 792.

JEN 731

OBVERSE

1 ṭup-[pí] ma-ru-ti ša
2 ^{m}Mu-[u]š-te-•ya DUMU •E-en-ša-ku
3 •ù [^{m}T]e-⸢ḫi⸣-ip-til-la DUMU Pu-ḫi-še-en-ni
4 a-na [ma-ru-*t]i •i-te-pu-us-sú
5 4? ^{GI}[$^{Š?}$APIN? A.Š]À i+na le-et bu-ur-ti ša ^{m}Te-ḫi-ip-*til-•la
6 i-na [ ]-ur ki-ma
7 ḪA.•LA-[šu ^{m}Mu-u]š-te-ya a-na
8 ^{m}Te-ḫi-[ip-til-la] •SUM ù ^{m}[Te-ḫi]-⸢ip⸣-til-la [ki]-ma NÍG.BA-šu
9 4? ANŠE *⸢ŠE⸣[(.MEŠ) a-na ^{m}]Mu-uš-t[e-ya SUM]
10 šum-ma A.[ŠÀ pa-i-i]q-ra-n[a ir-ta-ši]
11 ^{m}Mu-uš-[te-ya ú-za]-ak-[ka$_4$-ma ù]
12 a-na ^{m}Te-ḫ[i-ip-til-la] ⸢i⸣-n[a-din]
13 šum-ma ^{m}Mu-uš-te-ya KI.B[AL-kat?]
14 1 MA.NA KÙ.BABBAR 1 MA.NA KÙ.S[IG$_{17}$]
15 ú-ma-al-⸢la⸣

---

16 IGI ^{m}Ma-ti-⸢ya⸣ DUMU Ma-•r[a?-]
17 IGI ^{m}Zi-il-te-eš-šup •DUMU [Te-eš-šu-ya]
18 IGI $^{m⸢}$Eḫ⸣-li-⸢ya DUMU Pur⸣-[ni-tù-ru/rù]
19 [IGI ^{m}A-ka$_4$-we DUMU I-l]u-[ša]

.
.
.

REVERSE

.
.
.

[S.I.] S.I.
20 [^{NA_4} KIŠI]B! ^{m}M[u!?-uš?-te?-ya?] $^{[N]A_4}$ KIŠIB ^{m}Er-wi-LUGAL
21 S.I. [DUMU?]-ma-RI
22 [^{NA_4} KIŠIB ^{m}]Eḫ-li-ya DU[MU Pur-ni-tù-ru/rù]
S.I.

LEFT EDGE

23 [N]A$_4$ ^{m}Zi-il-te-ya ^{LÚ}sà-sú-⸢uk⸣-ki

TRANSLATION

(1-4) Tablet of adoption of Muš-teya son of En-šaku. He adopted Teḫip-tilla son of Puḫi-šenni.

(5-8) Muš-teya gave to Teḫip-tilla as [his] inheritance share a .(?)4(?) homer field adjacent to the well of Teḫip-tilla in … .

(8-9) And Teḫip-tilla [gave to] Muš-teya as his gift 4(?) homers of barley.

(10-12) Should the field [have] claimants, Muš-teya shall clear (it) [and] then give (it) to Teḫip-tilla.

(13-15) Should Muš-teya abrogate (this contract), he shall pay 1 mina of silver (and) 1 mina of gold.

(16-19) Before Matiya son of Ma-ra(?)-…; before Zil-tešup son of [Teššuya]; before Eḫliya son of Purni-turu; [before Akawe son of] Iluša; …. .

(20-23) [(*seal impression*)] seal impression of Muš-teya(?); (*seal impression*) seal impression of Erwi-šarri [son? of?] …; (*seal impression*) [seal impression of] Eḫliya son of [Purni-turu]; (*seal impression*) seal impression of Zil-teya, the bookkeeper.

COMMENTS

The surface of this tablet is badly worn, especially the upper obverse, lines 1-5. The tablet also appears to have suffered additional deterioration since the copy was made.

JEN 731 and 759 share an identical witness sequence and nearly identical sealing sequence as well as other significant features. For further details, see above, note to *JEN* 718:22. Witness PN restorations and other, formulaic, restorations in *JEN* 731 are based on readings from *JEN* 759.

NOTES

ll. 1, 3, 4. Lacheman and the *CAD* Nuzi file record these lines as entirely preserved.

l. 5: 4?. The number may well be "4," as copied. However, the stylus impressions are very faint and the number could be "3." Cf. below, first note to line 9.

l. 5: ^{GI}[$^{\text{Š?}}$APIN?]. These traces could represent A[NŠE] as well as ^{GI}[Š]. ^{GI}[^{Š}APIN], however, is to be preferred for the following reasons. First, the size of the gift is small (l. 9) and seems to correspond to a relatively small amount of land. Second, by interpreting this part of the text as ^{GI}[^{Š}APIN], the scale of value of land to barley is about the same as in *JEN* 759, a text closely related to this one (see above, comments).

l. 5: [A.Š]À. The *CAD* Nuzi file records these signs as completely preserved.

l. 6: *i-na* [ ]-*ur*. This lacuna might be filled by appeal to *JEN* 718 since there exists a slight connection between that text and this: the witness, Zil-teya, the bookkeeper, of *JEN* 731:23 also appears as a witness in *JEN*

718:22, 34. See already above, note to *JEN* 718:22. Now the land which Teḫip-tilla obtains, according to *JEN* 718, is *i+na* KASKAL *Na-aš-mu-ur* (l. 5). So, if the connection between these two texts has any meaning, perhaps this passage ought to be restored: *i-na* [KASKAL (URU) *Na-aš-mu*]*-ur*. In any case, no other restoration comes to mind.

l. 9: 4?. "3" is possible for the same reason that "3" is possible in line 5. See above, first note to line 5.

l. 9: *t*[*e-ya* SUM]. The *CAD* Nuzi file records these signs as completely preserved.

l. 10: [*pa-i-i*]*q-ra-n*[*a*]. For this restoration, cf. *JEN* 759:10. This interpretation seems preferable to [*pa-q*]*i*!*-ra-n*[*a*]. For this peculiar form of *pāqirāna*, see below, note to *JEN* 759:10.

l. 10: *n*[*a ir-ta-ši*]. The *CAD* Nuzi file records these signs as completely preserved.

l. 11: [*ka*$_4$*-ma ù*]. The *CAD* Nuzi file records these signs as completely preserved.

l. 13: B[AL-*kat*?]. The *CAD* Nuzi file records BAL as preserved and as the last sign of this line. Cf., however, the form of the parallel word in *JEN* 759:13: KI.⌜BAL⌝*-kat*.

l. 14: S[IG$_{17}$]. The *CAD* Nuzi file records this sign as completely preserved and as ending this line.

l. 16: *Ma-r*[*a*?-]. If the patronymic truly starts: *Ma-ra-*[ ], then perhaps these signs represent "Mâr-adad." For this PN, see *NPN*, 95b *sub* MÂR-ADAD; and *AAN*, 91b *sub* MĀRAT-ADAD (the name should be interpreted [as Lacheman already understood] as MĀR-ADAD, i.e., *Ma-ra-dá*^{d}IM, not *Ma-ra-ta-*^{d}IM). No other appropriate, attested PN from the Nuzi texts is known to me.

l. 18: ⌜*Pur*⌝. This sign does not appear as depicted, but, rather, as: . Compare *JEN* 759:18, 26.

l. 19. For this restoration, cf. *JEN* 759:19.

Below this line, three lines are missing, to judge from the equivalent section of *JEN* 759. The first of these probably contained: IGI ^{m}*Zi-il-te-ya* DUMU *Ta-ú-ka*$_4$. Cf., in fact, *JEN* 731:23 and see the note thereto. The next two lines identified the witnesses as measurers of the field and, possibly, distributors of the barley. These lines probably occupied the rest of the obverse and the lower edge, but not the start of the reverse.

l. 20: [^{NA_4} KIŠI]B! ^{m}*M*[*u*!?*-uš*?*-te*?*-ya*?]. *JEN* 759:22, the equivalent line, contains the name of the adopter. Therefore, the initial sealing here may have been that of the adopter as well. The surviving trace of the PN does not, in any case, fit the initial sign of any of the surviving witness PNs in *JEN* 731. One might interpret these traces as [^{NA_4} KIŠIB ^{m}*Mu-u*]*š*!*-t*[*e-ya*]. But

the traces could easily accommodate parts of the names of the witnesses on lines 17 and 18 as well.

l. 20: $^{[N]A_4}$ KIŠIB ^{m}*Er-wi*-LUGAL. Lacheman notes that the seal impression above this part of the line is broken. On the identification of this seal impression, see above, note to *JEN* 718:22.

l. 21. On the interpretation of this line, see above, note to *JEN* 718:22.

ll. 22-23. According to Lacheman, the seal impressions above these lines are not to be found in Porada (1947). Furthermore, he notes that a seal impression was once visible below line 23 and that that impression too is absent from Porada's work.

l. 23. The individual identified in this line is Zil-teya son of Tauka. See above, notes to *JEN* 718:22 and *JEN* 731:19. He may be the scribe of this text.

JEN 732

OBVERSE

1 [*ṭup-pí*] *ma-ru-ti ša* ^{m}*Šúk-*$^{+}$*r*]*a-a-pu* DUMU! $^{+}$⸢X⸣-[ ]

2 [^{m}*Te-ḫi-ip-til-la* DUMU *Pu-ḫi*]*-še-en-ni*

3 [*a-na ma-ru-ti i-*(*te-*)*pu-u*]*s-sú*

4 [A.ŠÀ] *i-na l*]*e-et* A.ŠÀ

5 [*ša?*]⸢^{m}⸣*Šúk-ra-a-pu*

6 [*a-na* ^{m}*Te-ḫi-ip*]*-til-la ki-ma* ḪA.LA-*šú i+din*

7 [*ù* ^{m}*Te-ḫi-i*]*p-til-la* 7 ANŠE 5 BÁN ŠE.MEŠ

8 [*a-na* ^{m}*Šúk-r*]*a-a-pu ki-*[*ma* NÍG].⸢BA⸣-*šú i+din*

9 [*šum-ma* A.$^{+}$Š]À *pa-qí-ra-n*[*a i-ra-a*]*š-*$^{+}$*ši*

10 [^{m}*Šúk-ra*]*-a-pu ú-za-*[*ak-ka*$_{4}$*-ma*]

11 [*a-na* ^{m}*T*]*e-ḫi-ip-til-*[*la i-na-din*]

12 ⸢*ù*⸣? [*i*]*l*!*-ka*$_{4}$ *ša* [A.ŠÀ ^{m}*Šúk-ra-a-pu*]

13 ⸢*na*⸣*-ši-i šum-m*[*a* ^{m}*Šúk-ra-a-pu*]

14 *i-bala-kat* 1[+1? MA.NA KÙ.SIG$_{17}$ (*a-na* ^{m}*Te-ḫi-ip-til-la*)]

15 *i-na-din*

16 IGI ⸢X⸣-[ ]-⸢X⸣ DUMU! [ ]

17 IGI *Mu-uš-t*[*e-ya* DUMU *Ar-še-en-ni*]

18 IGI *Ḫu-ti*$_{4}$*-p*[*u-kùr* DUMU *Ni-iš-ḫu-ḫa*]

19 3 LÚ.MEŠ A.[ŠÀ *il-mu-ú*]

REVERSE

S.I.

20 ^{NA_4} KIŠIB ^{m}*Ki-pé-er-ḫa* DUMU ⸢*Ar*⸣-[*tù-*(*un-*)*ni*]

S.I. Po 637

21 ^{NA_4} KIŠIB ^{m}*Pí-i-rù* DUMU *Na-iš-ké-*[*e*]*l-pè*

S.I. Po 152

22 [^{NA_4} KIŠIB ^{m}*Mu-u*]*š-te-ya* DUMU

23 [*Ar-še*]-*en-ni*

S.I.

UPPER EDGE

+24 [^{NA_4} KIŠIB ^{m}](-)⌈*x*⌉-*ya*

TRANSLATION

(1-3) [Tablet of] adoption of Šukr-apu son of .... He adopted [Teḫip-tilla son of] Puḫi-šenni.

(4-6) Šukr-apu gave [to] Teḫip-tilla as his inheritance share [a ... field] adjacent to the field [of? ...].

(7-8) [And] Teḫip-tilla gave [to] Šukr-apu as his gift 7.5 homers of barley.

(9-11) [Should] the field have claimants, Šukr-apu shall clear (it) [and give (it) to] Teḫip-tilla.

(12-13) And(?) [Šukr-apu] shall bear the *ilku* of [the field].

(13-15) Should [Šukr-apu] abrogate (this contract), he shall give [(to Teḫip-tilla)] 1[+1? mina(s) of gold].

(16-19) Before ... son of ...; before Muš-teya [son of Ar-šenni]; before Ḫutip-ukur [son of Niš-ḫuḫa]. (These) 3 men [encircled] the field.

(20-24) (*seal impression*) seal impression of Kip-erḫan son of Ar-tunni; (*seal impression*) seal impression of Piru son of Naiš-kelpe; (*seal impression*) [seal impression of] Muš-teya son of Ar-šenni; (*seal impression*) [seal impression of] ... .

COMMENTS

This tablet preserves part of every line written on the obverse, from the last part of the first line to the first part of the last line; and every part of the reverse, from the first part of the first seal impression to the last part of the last seal impression. It also preserves the last part of the line on the upper edge.

The following illustration (on a 2:3 scale) shows the general shape of the tablet:

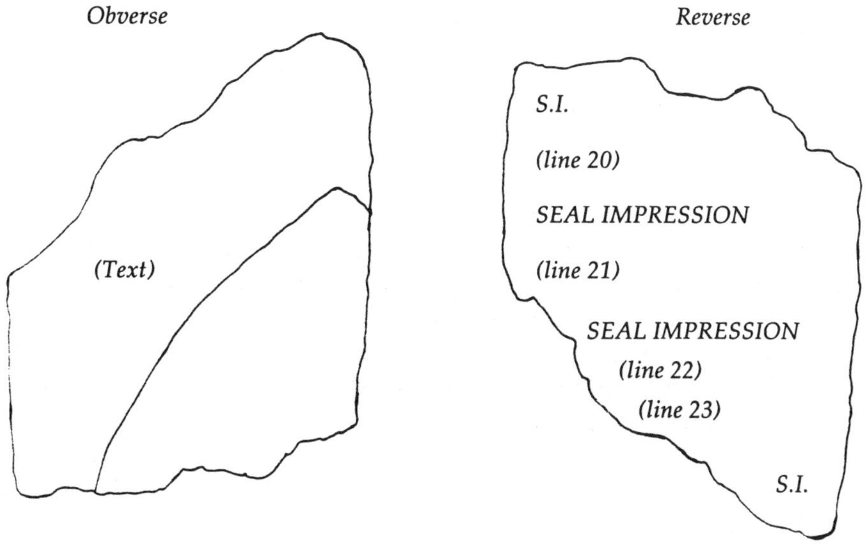

NOTES

l. 1. The signs on this line appear, not as copied, but, rather, as:

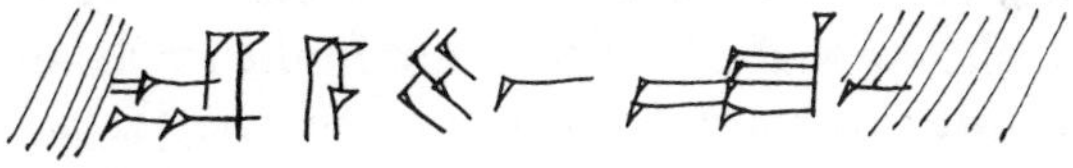

One is tempted to read: [^{m}*Šúk-r*]*a-a-pu* DUMU! ⌜*E*⌝-[*te-ya*]. Šukr-apu son of Eteya adopted Teḫip-tilla elsewhere and ceded land to him in Unap-še. See, for example, *JEN* 770; cf. *JEN* 770:6-7 with *JEN* 709:7-8 for the Unap-še location of this land. The same Šukr-apu had repeated attested contacts with members of the Teḫip-tilla Family. For some further examples, see *NPN*, 136a *sub* ŠUKR-APU 8). However, the witnesses appearing in this text do not appear in those Šukr-apu texts and so it is to be doubted that the son of Eteya is here the adopter. See also below, note to ll. 17-23.

l. 7: 5 BÁN. On the interpretation of these signs, see above, second note to *JEN* 705:8.

l. 9: [Š]À. The sign appears, not as copied, but, rather, as:

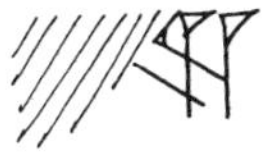

l. 12: [^{m}*Šúk-ra-a-pu*]. This restoration is most probable, but not certain.

l. 13: ⸢*na*⸣-*ši*. Both these signs are rather more typical than depicted in the copy.

l. 14: [+1? MA.NA KÙ.SIG$_{17}$]. Cf., e.g., *JEN* 690:14. On the relevance of *JEN* 690 to this text, see below, note to lines 17-23.

l. 16. Lacheman once read this line as: IGI *Wi-i-r*[*a-*].

ll. 17-23. The identities of the witnesses and sealers in these lines strongly suggest that the real estate involved in this contract is to be located in Unap-še.

The second witness (l. 17) and the third sealer (ll. 22-23) are most likely the same person, very plausibly the ubiquitous Teḫip-tilla witness, Muš-teya son of Ar-šenni. See *NPN*, p. 99b *sub* MUŠ-TEI̯A 4).

The third witness (l. 18) is probably none other than Ḫutip-ukur son of Niš-ḫuḫa, another well attested, if not common, Teḫip-tilla witness. See *NPN*, 66a *sub* ḪUTIP-UKUR 2). "Ḫutip-ukur" appears to be the only name to fit these signs and traces.

The first sealer, Kip-erḫan (l. 20), can hardly be dissociated from the like named son of Ar-tunni, again a well-known witness of Teḫip-Tilla. See *NPN*, 87a *sub* KIP-ERḪAN 2).

The second sealer (l. 21) is the most ubiquitous of Teḫip-tilla's witnesses. See *NPN*, 115 *sub* PIRU 1).

Perusal of the attestations of these four individuals reveals that they either all appear or almost certainly once did all appear as witnesses in a series of twelve texts (including *JEN* 690 and 756 in the present volume) possessing a common witness sequence. Details of this series are given above, note to *JEN* 690:18. It is also noted there that these texts deal with Unap-še real estate (but not in the areas associated with Šukr-apu son of Eteya; see also above, note to line 1).

JEN 732 is thus related to those texts although it is not a part of that cluster. The pattern of witnesses and sealers here is significantly different from the other texts.

l. 19: [*il-mu-ú*]. Or the like.

l. 24: ⸢*x*⸣. The trace appears as:

If the scribe's name appears in this line, and if the same scribe wrote *JEN* 732 as wrote the series of texts mentioned in the immediately preceding note, then one might suggest that [*T*]*a*!-*ya* should be restored. Yet this spelling of this PN is elsewhere unattested.

JEN 733

OBVERSE

1 [*ṭup-p*]*í ma-r*[*u-t*]*i* ⸢*ša*⸣ [^{m}*R*]*i-iš-ké-ya*

\+

---

2 [DUMU *P*]*ur-na-*⸢*ni?-x*⸣(-)[(?)]

---

3 [^{m}]*Te-ḫi-ip-til-*[*la* DUM]U ⸢*Pu*⸣-[*ḫ*]*i-še-en-ni*

---

4 *a-na ma-ru-ti* ⸢*i*⸣-[*p*]*u-uš-*⸢*ma*⸣

---

5 1 ANŠE A.ŠÀ *k*[*i*]*-ma* ḪA.⸢LA⸣

---

6 ^{m}*Ri-iš-ké-ya a-*[*n*]*a* $^{<m>}$⸢*Te*⸣*-ḫi-ip-til-•l*[*a*] SUM

7 *i+na* URU *Kà-ra-an-na ša Pu-ḫi-še-en-ni*

---

8 ⸢*ù*⸣ ^{m}*Te-ḫi-*⸢*ip*⸣*-til-la*

\+

---

9 *a-na* $^{<m>}$*R*[*i-i*]*š-ké-*[*y*]*a* ⸢20⸣ [GÍN? K]Ù.BA[BBAR SUM]

\+

---

10 *ma-an-nu* [*ša* B]AL!-*t*[*u* 2?] MA.⸢NA •KÙ⸣.BABBAR

\+

---

11 •⸢*ù*⸣ 2? MA.•NA KÙ.[S]IG$_{17}$ SU[M-*i*]*n*

---

12 •IGI *U*[*r!-ḫi-y*]*a* DU[MU *M*]*u-•u*[*š-t*]*e-*AŠ

13 •IGI *Še-*⸢*éḫ*⸣-[*l*]*i-*⸢*ya*⸣ DUMU [-RU]

14 IGI *Šu-ur-*⸢*te*⸣*-šup* DUM[U -RU]

15 IGI *Ḫi-in-ti-*⸢*ya*⸣ [DUMU *Te-ḫi-ya*]

16 IGI *A-dá!-še-ya* [DUMU *Tu-uḫ*$_{5}$*-mì-ya*]

17 IGI *Al-*⸢*ki-te*⸣-•[*š*]*up* [DUMU *Tu?-uḫ*$_{5}$*?-mì?-ya?*]

18 IGI ⸢*Ar*⸣-[DUMU *Te?-ḫi-ya*]

REVERSE

19 IGI *A-ki-t*[*e-šup* DUMU *Šu-r*]*i-ša*

20 IGI *Ḫa-iš-*[*te-šup* DUMU *Tu?-u*]*ḫ*$_{5}$*?-mì?-y*[*a*]?

21 IGI *É*[*ḫ-li?*]*-te-*⸢*šup* KI⸣!?.[MIN?]

22 IGI *N*[*a*]*-ni-ya* DUB.SAR DU[MU] *Nu-la-a*[*n*]*-n*[*a*]

S.I. Po 111

23 [^{N}]^{A_4} KI[ŠI]B *Na-ni-ya* ⁺[D]UB.⸢SAR⸣

S.I. Po 982

24 ^{NA_4} KIŠIB *Ḫi-in-<ti>-ya* DUMU *Te-ḫi-ya*

S.I. Po 575

25 [^{NA_4} KIŠIB] ⸢*Ur*⸣-[*ḫ*]*i-ya* DUMU *Mu-uš-te-šu*[*p*]

TRANSLATION

(1-4) Tablet of adoption of Riškeya [son of] Purna-ni(?)-...(?). He adopted Teḫip-tilla son of Puḫi-šenni.

(5-7) Riškeya gave to Teḫip-tilla as an inheritance share a 1 homer field; in the town of Karanna-of-Puḫi-šenni.

(8-9) And Teḫip-tilla [gave] to Riškeya 20 [sheqels?] of silver.

(10-11) He [who] abrogates (this contract) shall give [2?] minas of silver and 2(?) minas of gold.

(12-22) Before Urḫiya son of Muš-tešup; before Šeḫliya son of ...; before Šur-tešup son of ...; before Ḫintiya [son of Teḫiya]; before Addašeya [son of Tuḫmiya]; before Alki-tešup [son of Tuḫmiya?]; before Ar-... [son of Te?-ḫiya]; before Akip-tešup [son of] Šuriša; before Ḫaiš-tešup [son of] Tuḫmiya(?); before Eḫ[li?]-tešup, likewise(?); before Naniya, the scribe, son of Lu-Nanna.

(23-25) (*seal impression*) seal impression of Naniya, the scribe; (*seal impression*) seal impression of Ḫin<ti>ya son of Teḫiya; (*seal impression*) [seal impression of] Urḫiya son of Muš-tešup.

COMMENTS

This tablet has suffered has suffered slight additional damage since it was copied.

The horizontal lines lines dividing the first twelve line of this text (excepting lines 6 and 7) are not represented in the translation since, contrary to usual scribal practice elsewhere, the lines do not serve to divide clauses or other ideational units. (Yet, since these lines end where the witness list starts, it appears that some principle is applied in the employment of these lines, perhaps a principle relating to the relative importance of different sections.) Regular use of horizontal lines to divide lines of text is especially characteristic of older Nuzi texts. See already Purves (1940, 169) who calls them "guide lines."

Restoration of this text, specifically the reconstruction of the witness list, is based largely on *JEN* 578. Where the two texts can be compared, it is clear that they share a practically identical witness sequence, including a common scribe. (Lacheman already notes some connection between these two texts.) The two texts share other common features as well. These include a common purchaser, probably the same location of the land involved (see below, note to line 7), the systematic use of horizontal lines, and the writing of the sealers' names directly over the seal impressions themselves (cf. below, note to lines 23-24). Two other texts have been exploited here as well. *JEN* 8 (presumably written by the same scribe) contains a witness sequence partially overlapping that of the first two texts, a feature helpful in the reconstruction of line 17 here. See below, the note to that line. *JEN* 79, although its witness sequence overlaps that of *JEN* 733 only slightly, was

written by the same scribe (incidentally, that tablet is lined, a characteristic of this scribe's texts; this lining is not indicated in the copy). That text may be relevant in the restoration of line 20 in the present text. See below, the notes to that line and to line 10.

Appeal to these texts is further justified since the scribe of these texts is relatively inactive; see *NPN*, 103a *sub* NANIḪA 12) and 38) for the attestations of his meager output.

NOTES

l. 1. Immediately below this line appears a horizontal line. This is not indicated in the copy.

l. 6: <m>. For this apparent omission, see above, note to *JEN* 730:5-12.

l. 7: URU *Kà-ra-an-na ša Pu-ḫi-še-en-ni*. The same compound toponym is, most likely, to be restored in *JEN* 578:4-5. Cf. the compound, URU GEŠTIN-*na ša* É.GAL-[*lì*] (*JEN* 28:8). Otherwise, Karanna in the Nuzi texts seems not to take a qualifier. For some attestations of this GN in the Nuzi texts, see the partial lists (which themselves partially overlap) in Fisher (1959, 50, no. 354); Astour (1968, 745a *sub* k)); and Fadhil (1983, *passim*; for page references, see p. 358a *sub* Karana).

ll. 8, 9, 10. Immediately below each of these lines appears a horizontal line. They are not indicated in the copy. The horizontal wedge below ⸢*ù*⸣ at the start of line 8 belongs to the start of the first of these three horizontal lines.

l. 8: ⸢*ù*⸣. See above, immediately preceding note.

l. 9: <m>. For this apparent omission, see above, note to *JEN* 730:5-12.

l. 9: [*y*]*a*. The traces do not appear as copied, but, rather, as:

l. 10: [*ša* BAL!-*t*[*u* 2?]. Cf. *JEN* 79:8-9.

l. 12: [*t*]*e*-AŠ. The last sign is an error for /*šup*/. Cf. l. 25. Cf. also below, note to *JEN* 742:15. It is not to be construed as *šup*$_x$. Cf. Gelb in Gelb, Purves, and MacRae (1943, 5) and the fuller treatment referred to there: Gelb (1941, 35-36); and von Soden and Röllig (1976, 1). This class of scribal error has one of two (or a combination of two) causes. It may be due to a mental lapse, where the correct equation RU = /*ru*/, /*šup*/ led to a faulty extrapolation: AŠ = /*ru*/, /*šup*/, the last element in the equation representing the error. A "graphemic pun" (Ann Guinan's happy phrase) results. Alternately, the spelling may be due to a misplaced autonomic motor reflex (where *ru* and *rù* are confused) in a graphically bound environment. In this case, the very specific environment is after TE at the end of a PN. I wish to thank Robert Fink, professor of linguistics

at York University, for the latter suggestion and for discussing this entire issue with me. I intend to treat this phenomenon in greater detail elsewhere.

It has not been possible to collate this last sign from the cast of the tablet.

l. 13: [-RU]. For this restoration, cf. *JEN* 578:12.

l. 14: [-RU]. For this restoration, cf. *JEN* 578:14. *NPN*, 140b *sub* ŠUR-TEŠUP 1), 35a *sub* AR-TEŠUP 41), would restore this lacuna as follows: [*Ar-te-šup*].

l. 16: *dá*!. This interpretation of this peculiarly rendered sign (it might be interpreted as, say, BI) is borne out by the same scribe's TA in *JEN* 79:15. Cf. his ŠA in *JEN* 79:6; 578:19.

l. 16: [*Tu-uḫ*$_5$*-mì-ya*]. This restoration is based on the parallel patronymic in *JEN* 578:16.

l. 17: [DUMU *Tu?-uḫ*$_5$*?-mì?-ya?*]. For this proposed restoration, cf. *JEN* 8:22. The reading of the patronymic there as *Tu-um-ḫi-ya* is established by Purves (1940, 173, n. 51); and *NPN*, 19b *sub* ALKI-TEŠUP 3), 156b *sub* TUḪMIḬA 2). Assuming that the same witness is identified in *JEN* 578:17, the parallel passage to *JEN* 733:17, the patronymic should be restored there as: [*Tu-u*]*ḫ*$_5$*-mì-ya*.

l. 18: [*Te?-ḫi-ya*]. For this restoration, cf. *JEN* 578:18.

l. 19. For the restoration of this line, cf. *JEN* 578:19.

l. 20. This line is correct as copied. For the restoration of this line, cf. *JEN* 79:17. The traces here seem to support this reconstruction. *JEN* 578:20, where we would expect to find the same witness, records a different witness (cf. *JEN* 578:25; 8:21).

l. 21. This line is more or less correct as copied. It was not possible to collate the line from the cast of the tablet. For the restoration of this line, cf. *JEN* 578:21. The rendering of that line should almost certainly be:

[IG]I ⸢*Éḫ*⸣-<*li*>-⸢*te-šup*⸣ DUMU *Tu-uḫ*$_5$-<*mì*>-*ya*

 ⸢*te šup*⸣ DUMU *Tu*  *ya*

See already *NPN*, 42b *sub* E'-TEŠUP (a PN unique to this passage!), 156b *sub* TUḬA 2). (This scribe omits a sign in still another PN in the present text, l. 24.) The restoration there of the patronymic is strengthened by its probable presence here in lines 16, 17, and, especially, 20. The only problem with the restoration of line 21 here is the difficult ⸢KI⸣!?.[MIN]. One would have expected DUMU KI.MIN and less ambiguous traces.

ll. 23-24. These lines are written over their respective sealings.

l. 23. Lacheman identifies the seal impression above this line as, variously, "605" and "111."

l. 23: [D]UB. The traces do not appear as copied, but, rather, as:

l. 24. This line is correct as copied.

JEN 734

OBVERSE

1 *ṭup-pí ma-ru-ti ša* <m>*Te-šu-ya*

2 •⌜DUMU⌝ *Wa-an-ti-ya* ^{m}*Mì-na-a-a*

3 ⌜*a*⌝-[*na m*]*a*-⌜*ru*⌝-*ti* DÙ-*ma*

4 [AN]ŠE A.ŠÀ É.ḪÁ *ù ma-ag-ra-at-tù*

5 [*ki-ma* ḪA].L[A]-*šu* SUM *ù* <m>*Mì-na-a-a*

6 [*ki-ma* NÍG.BA-*š*]*u* 80 <GÍN?> KÙ.BABBAR SUM-*in*

7 [*ma-an-nu* •*š*]*a* BAL 1 MA.NA KÙ.BABBAR 1 MA.NA KÙ.SIG$_{17}$

8 [Ì.LÁ].⌜E⌝

---

9 [IGI *Ḫa-at-ra*]-*ké* DUMU *Te*$_{9}$-*en-te*$_{9}$-*ya*

10 [IGI *Ar-te-šup* •DU]MU •*Ši*!-*in*$_{4}$-*ti-ya*

11 [IGI *Ar-te-ya*] DUMU *Ḫa-ši-ya*

12 [IGI *Ú-na-ap*]-*ta-e*

13 [DUMU *Ši-i*]*n*$_{4}$-*ti-ya-ma*

REVERSE

14 [IGI *A*]*r-na-pu* DUMU *Ki-in*$_{4}$-*tar*

15 [IGI *T*]*ù*-⌜*ul*⌝-*pí-še-en-ni*

16 [DUMU] ⌜*E*⌝-*na-ma-ti*

17 [IGI *Š*]*a-at-tù-ya* DUMU *A-ta-na-aḫ*

18 IGI! *Ḫ*[*a*]-*ni-ku*-$^{+}$*ya* $^{+}$DUMU ^{d}UTU-LUGAL

19 IGI *Pu-un*-$^{+}$*ni*-$^{+}$*ya nu-a-ru*

20 IGI *E-wa*-$^{+}$*ra*-$^{+}$*tù-pí*

21 DUMU ⌜*A*⌝-[*r*]*i-ip*!-*ú-kùr*

TRANSLATION

(1-3) Tablet of adoption of Teššuya son of Wantiya. He adopted Minaya.

(4-5) He gave (to him) [as] his inheritance share a(n) x homer field, structure(s), and a threshing floor.

(5-6) And Minaya gave (to him) [as] his [gift] 80 <sheqels?> of silver.

(7-8) [He] who abrogates (this contract) shall weigh out 1 mina of silver (and) 1 mina of gold.

(9-21) [Before] Ḫatrake son of Tenteya; [before Ar-tešup] son of Šintiya; [before Ar-teya] son of Ḫašiya; [before] Unap-tae also [son of] Šintiya; [before] Arn-apu son of Kintar; [before] Tulpi-šenni [son of] Enna-mati; before Šattuya son of Âtanaḫ; before Ḫanikuya son of Šamaš-šarri; before Punniya, the musician; before Ewara-tupi son of Arip-ukur.

COMMENTS

This tablet is virtually unchanged from the time it was copied.

The text bears a close resemblance, noted already by Lacheman, to *JEN* 566. The two texts have an identical witness sequence; restoration of witness PNs in *JEN* 734 is based on the better preserved equivalent lines of *JEN* 566. Neither text contains the expected seal impressions. There are other parallels as well. Other restorations in the present text are thus also based on *JEN* 566.

Some of the peculiarities of these texts, such as the lack of seal impressions and the absence of the patronymic for the adoptee in *JEN* 734, are possibly related to the fact that Minaya (son of Ipša-ḫalu) may well have acted as agent for Teḫip-tilla son of Puḫi-šenni. In addition to Minaya's presence in *JEN* 566 and 734, see *JEN* 289, 517, 774. On the evidence for possible proxies and other agents in Teḫip-tilla contracts and other contexts, see, for the moment, Maidman (1976, 373-75, n. 475). Note also *JEN* 737, below.

NOTES

l. 1: <m>. For this apparent omission, see above, note to *JEN* 730:5-12.

l. 2: ⸢DUMU⸣. This sign does not appear as copied, but, rather, as:

l. 2: ^{m}*Mì-na-a-a*. He is the son of Ipša-ḫalu. See *JEN* 566:2-3.

l. 4: *ma-ag-ra-at-tù*. For a discussion of this term in the Nuzi texts and its range of meanings, see Maidman (1976, 382, n. 506).

l. 5: <m>. For this apparent omission, see above, note to *JEN* 730:5-12.

l. 10: *Ši*!. The sign appears almost to be a ligature: ŠE+ŠI. Collation of the sign from a cast suggests that all wedges preceding the standard ŠI were erased by the scribe.

ll. 17-20. There is no lacuna in the middle of these lines. I suspect that Lacheman's photograph of this text was faulty or became damaged and he subsequently interpreted that flaw as a gap in the tablet.

JEN 735

OBVERSE

1 *ṭup-pí ma-ru-·ti ša*
2 ^{m}*Mu-*še-ya* DUMU ^{d}XXX-KAM
3 ^{m}*Te-ḫi-ip-til-·la* ·DUMU *Pu-ḫi-še-en-ni*
4 *·a-*na ·ma-ru-t[i] i-pu-us-sú-ma*
5 *A.*ŠÀ.*MEŠ-**šu ·ša ·a-·na* ḪA.LA-*šu*
6 *·i+·na* ·URU *Ḫu-ra-ṣí-·na*-TUR
7 *·ki-ma* ḪA.LA-*šu id-dì-na-aš-šu*
8 *·ma-·an-nu ša* BAL 2 MA.NA KÙ.BABBAR
9 2 *⸢MA⸣.·NA KÙ.SIG$_{17}$ Ì.LÁ.E
10 IGI *·Ma?-ṣí-·⸢ya* ·DUMU *·Ki*⸣*?-·iz-za-al-li*
11 IGI *⸢Ni⸣-íḫ-ri-ya* DUMU *Ik-ku-⸢ya⸣*
12 ⸢IGI⸣ *Ḫi-iš-⸢mi⸣-še-er-ša*
13 DUMU *⸢Šar⸣-ta-an-a-pí*
14 ·IGI *⸢Zi⸣-il$_{5}$-te-eš-šu-⸢up⸣*
15 DUMU *Ar-te-[eš]-šu-up*

LOWER EDGE

16 IGI *·⸢Ki⸣-in$_{4}$-·na-a[n]-ni*
17 *DUM[U] *Nu-la-[za]-ḫi*

REVERSE

18 *IGI *·Ta-a-a* DUMU *·A[r-*]
19 *IGI *·It-ḫa-a-pu* DUMU *Ḫ[u?-ip?-er?-wi?]*
20 [IGI] *·I-ga$_{14}$-ar-še-mi-⸢i⸣?/i[d]?*
21 ^{LÚ}*nu-a-ru ša* LUGAL
22 IGI *Bal-$^{+}$ṭu$_{4}$-ka-ší-id*
23 DUB.SAR-*rù*
24 IGI *·Ma-·an-nu-ki-be-li-ya*
25 x *nu-a-ru*
26 IGI *Mu-uš-še-en-ni*

\+ ———————————————

27 DUMU *Ni-nu-a-tal*
28 ·^{NA_4} KIŠIB
29 DUB.SAR-*ri*

S.I. Po 995

S.I.

LEFT EDGE

30 [N]A$_4$ •Ḫ[i-iš-*m]i-[š]e-er-[ša]

TRANSLATION

(1-4) Tablet of adoption of Mušeya son of Sin-êriš. He adopted Teḫip-tilla son of Puḫi-šenni.

(5-7) He gave to him as his inheritance share his land, which (had been) for his (own) inheritance share, in the town of Ḫurāṣina-ṣeḫru.

(8-9) He who abrogates (this contract) shall weigh out 2 minas of silver (and) 2 minas of gold.

(10-27) Before Ma(?)-ṣīya son of K(?)izzalli; before Niḫriya son of Ikkuya; before Ḫišmi-šerša son of Šartan-api; before Zil-tešup son of Ar-tešup; before Kinnanni son of Nula-zaḫi; before Taya son of Ar-...; before Itḫ-apu son of Ḫuip-erwi(?); before Igārš(u)-êmi(d), the musician of the king; before Balṭu-kašid, the scribe; before Mannu-kī-bêliya, the musician; before Muš-šenni

---

son of Ninu-atal.

(28-30) Seal impression of the scribe (*seal impression*); (*seal impression*) seal impression of Ḫišmi-šerša.

COMMENT

The copy is clear, misrepresenting the current state of preservation of this tablet. It is badly worn, especially on the first part of the obverse. Much that appears in the copy is simply no longer visible.

NOTES

l. 2: *še*. At one point, Lacheman doubted his own copy of this sign. The traces he could see, he supposed, might represent TI.

l. 10: *Ma*?. What remains of this sign is the single vertical wedge. *NPN*, 77b *sub* IZZIḪA 1), 89a *sub* KIZZALLI? 1), hazards *Iz* in place of *Ma*.

l. 10: -⸢*ya* DUMU *Ki*⸣?-. The copy suggests -⸢*ya*⸣ {*ya*} DUMU. Lacheman framed the first two signs by circles, probably to draw attention to what he considered (and copied as) a dittograph. The surviving traces, however, appear as:

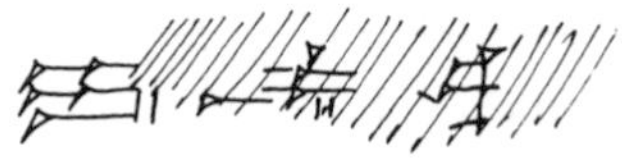

The second sign is a passable DUMU and the third a plausible KI. The same judgment is already implicit in *NPN*. See above, immediately preceding note.

l. 16. This line, not line 15, begins the lower edge.

l. 16: *a*[*n*]-*ni*. The two horizontal wedges of AN survive as well as the entire last sign. The copy is, therefore, incorrect in both these instances. *NPN*, 85b *sub* KINNANNI 1), 108a *sub* NULA-ZAḪI 5), interprets these traces too conservatively as, in effect: ⸢*an-ni*⸣.

l. 19: *Ḫ*[*u*?-*ip*?-*er*?-*wi*?]. The restoration, *Ḫ*[*u-ip-er-wi*], appears in both Lacheman's papers and *NPN*, 62a *sub* ḪUIP-ERWI 1), 75a *sub* ITḪ-APU 6). In *JEN* 69:12 and 762:13 (cf. l. 21), this person appears as a witness together with Muš-šenni son of Ninu-atal (*JEN* 69:16; 762:14). The latter appears in the present text as well (ll. 26-27). The restoration, then, is quite possible.

l. 20: ⸢*i*⸣?. The traces appear, not as copied, but as: 

l. 22: *ṭu*$_4$. The sign is complete and typical, not as copied.

l. 25. The inclusion of this line was an afterthought of the scribe. He squeezed these signs between lines 24 and 26. The horizontal wedge above the ŠE of line 26 is correct as copied. It is neither LÚ nor a typical *Glossenkeil*. It is idiosyncratic.

l. 26. Below this line appears a horizontal line. This is not indicated in the copy.

l. 30. The seal impression (on the reverse) linked to this line is identified as no. 969 by Porada (1947, 138a *ad* no. 969).

The text of the left edge faces the reverse.

JEN 736

OBVERSE

1 *ṭup*-•*pí ma-ru*-[*ti*] *ša*

2 ^{m}*Še*-•*en-na-p*[*è* DUMU] •⸢*Ḫa*⸣-*i-ra*-[*al-la*]

3 ^{m}[*T*]*e*-⸢*ḫi-ip*⸣-[*til-la* DUMU *Pu-ḫi*]-*še*-⸢*en*⸣-[*ni*]

4 *a*-[*n*]*a ma-ru-ti* [*i-te-p*]*u-u*[*š*]

5 *ù* •1+[ ] •ANŠE A.ŠÀ ⸢*i-na*⸣ URU *Ú*-[*na-ap-še-wa*]

6 •⸢*i*⸣-*na* ⸢*il*⸣-*ta-ni*-⸢*šu*⸣ $^{+}$*ša* AN.•Z[A.KÀR]

7 [*š*]*a* ^{m}*A-ka*$_4$-*wa-til* ⸢*i*⸣-*na šu*-[*pa*?-*li*?(-*šu*?)]

8 *ša* AN.ZA.KÀR ^{m}*Ú-lu-li*-•⸢*ya*⸣

9 *i+na mi-in-dá-a*-⸢*ti*⸣ *ša* ⸢É?.GAL⸣?

10 *a-na* ^{m}*Te-ḫi-ip-til*-⸢*la ki*⸣-*ma* [ḪA.LA-*šú* SUM]

11 *ù* ^{m}*Te-ḫi-ip-til-la* 40[+10?/20? MA.NA URUDU.MEŠ]

12 *a-na* ^{m}*Še-en-na-pè* ⸢*ki*⸣-*ma* NÍG.B[A-*šu* SUM]

13 *il-ka*$_4$ *ša* A.ŠÀ ^{m}⸢*Še-en-na-pè-m*[*a na*-(*a*-)*ši*]

14 *šum-ma* A.ŠÀ *pa-qí*-⸢*ra-na*⸣ TUK

15 *ù* ^{m}*Še-en-na-p*[*è*] A.ŠÀ {⸢*ša*⸣-*a*-[*š*]*u*}
16 *š*[*a*]-*a-šu-ma ú*-[*za*]-*ak-ka*$_{4}$-*ma*
17 *a-•na* ^{m}*Te-ḫi-ip-*til-la i-na-an-d*[*in*]
18 *šum-ma* ^{m}*Še*-[*en-n*]*a-pè* KI.B[AL]
19 2 MA.NA [KÙ.SIG$_{17}$] ⸢*nam*⸣-*ra* S[I?.A?-*la*?]
20 *a-na* ^{m}*T*[*e-ḫi-i*]*p-til-la i-na-an-di*[*n*]

---

21 IGI *Tup-ki*-⸢*ya*⸣ DUMU ⸢*Kàr*⸣-*ze*-•⸢*ya*⸣
22 IGI ⸢*A*⸣-•*wi*-⸢*lu*⸣ DUMU [*P*]*u-re-e*-[*a*]
23 [IGI *Ḫa-n*]*a-a-a* DU[MU *A*]*r-te*-⸢*šup*⸣

LOWER EDGE

24 [IGI *In-ka*$_{4}$-*r*]*i* D[UMU *Š*]*e*-⸢*en-na*⸣-[*a-a*]

REVERSE

25 ⸢IGI⸣[DUMU]
26 IGI [DUMU]
27 IGI [DUMU]
28 IGI ⸢X⸣-[DUMU]
29 IGI ⸢X⸣-[DUMU]
30 IGI ⸢X⸣-[DUMU]
31 IGI ⸢*A*?-*x*⸣-[DUMU]
32 IGI ⸢X⸣-[DUMU]
33 IGI •⸢X⸣-[DUMU]
34 IGI *Ḫu*-[DUMU]
.?
.?
.?

S.I.

35 $^{⸢NA_4⸣}$ +KIŠIB ^{m}⸢X⸣-[ ]

S.I.

36 ^{NA_4} KIŠIB [^{m}]

UPPER EDGE

S.I.

37 ^{NA_4} KIŠIB ^{m}*Na*-[*ḫi-iš-še*]-+⸢*ya*⸣

LEFT EDGE

S.I. S.I.

38 ^{NA_4} KIŠIB ^{m}*I*[*n*?-*ka*$_{4}$?-*ri*?] $^{N[A]_4}$ ⸢KIŠIB⸣ ^{m}*Ḫa-na-a-a*

RIGHT EDGE

+39 $^{[N]A_4?}$ KI[ŠIB!?]

TRANSLATION

(1-4) Tablet of adoption of Šennape [son of] Ḫairalla. He adopted Teḫip-tilla [son of] Puḫi-šenni.

(5-10) And [he gave] to Teḫip-tilla as [his inheritance share] a 1+x homer field in the town of Unap-še, to the north of the *dimtu* of Akawatil (and) to the west(?) of the *dimtu* of Ulūliya, (the field measured) by the palace(?) standard.

(11-12) And Teḫip-tilla [gave] to Šennape as [his] gift 40[+10?/20? minas of copper].

(13) And Šennape shall bear the *ilku* of the field.

(14-17) Should the field have claimants, Šennape shall clear {that} that very field and give (it) to Teḫip-tilla.

(18-20) Should Šennape abrogate (this contract), he shall give in payment(?) 2 minas of shiny [gold].

(21-34) Before Tupkiya son of Karzeya; before Awīlu son of Pureya; [before] Ḫanaya son of Ar-tešup; [before] Ikkari son of [Šennaya]; before [... son of ...]; before [... son of ...]; before [... son of ...]; before ... [son of ...]; before ... [son of ...]; before ... [son of ...]; before A(?)-... [son of ...]; before ... [son of ...]; before ... [son of ...]; before Ḫu-... [son of ...]; ...(?).

(35-39) (*seal impression*) seal impression of ...; (*seal impression*) seal impression of ...; (*seal impression*) seal impression of Naḫiššeya; (*seal impression*) seal impression of Ikkari(?); (*seal impression*) seal impression of Ḫanaya; seal(?) impression(?) of(?) ... .

COMMENTS

Regarding this text, the *CAD* Nuzi file records only *JENu* 634. Yet *JEN* 736 consists of two joined fragments, *JENu* 634+690. This join is clear from observation, from the fact that both *JENu* numbers are visible, and from Oriental Institute records.

The tablet has suffered some further deterioration since it was copied.

Restorations in this edition of *JEN* 736, both in the witness section and elsewhere, are based on readings from *JEN* 92 and *JENu* 62a. All three texts share a variety of features including what appears to be a largely common witness sequence. (Owing to breaks in all three texts, certainty regarding the identities of all the witnesses is not possible.) This common witness sequence, the generally similar location of the land involved in these adoptions, the same adoptee in all three cases, and common phraseology (see especially below, note to line 19) all suggest a common scribe for these texts, Waqar-bêli son of Taya (see *JEN* 92:33, 34; *JENu* 62a:33, 35).

Finally, it should be noted that, on the basis of comparison of *JEN* 92, 736, and *JENu* 62a, *JEN* 598 may belong to this group of texts. Partial duplication of *JEN* 598 and 736 proves they are not part of the same tablet.

NOTES

l. 2: ⸢*Ḫa*⸣-*i-ra-*[*al-la*]. This restoration is beyond doubt. Given the traces, it is the only plausible, attested patronymic for Šennape. See *NPN*, 131 *sub* ŠENNAPE; and *AAN*, 125b *sub* ŠENNAPE. Furthermore, in this text, Šennape cedes land to Teḫip-tilla in Unap-še (l. 5). Elsewhere, Šennape son of Ḫairalla is clearly linked to Unap-še. See, for example, *JEN* 58:28, 38.

l. 5: 1+[ ] ANŠE. At one point, Lacheman read: 1 ANŠE.

l. 5: *Ú*-[*na-ap-še-wa*]. This restoration is certain since both the *dimtu* of Akawatil (ll. 6-7) and the *dimtu* of Ulūliya (l. 8) are to be located in this town. For these linkages, see above, respectively, *JEN* 709:7-8; and the note to *JEN* 694:6.

l. 6: *ša*. This sign is complete and typical, not as copied.

l. 7: *šu*-[*pa*?-*li*?(-*šu*?)]. *šu*-[*ta-ni*(-*šu*)] is possible but perhaps less likely since *su*, rather than *šu*, might be expected to begin the latter word.

l. 12: [SUM]. Or the like.

l. 14: TUK. The sign is clear and it is the last sign on the line. The copy is incorrect.

l. 15: {⸢*š*⸣*a-a-*[*š*]*u*}. It appears that the scribe may have made a bad job of this word here and so deliberately repeated it on the next line.

l. 19: ⸢*nam*⸣-*ra* S[I?.A?-*la*?]. This unusual sequence of words is also attested in *JEN* 92:17 and, it seems, *JENu* 62a:17: *nam-r*[*a* (x)]. (The interpretation, *r*[*a*], is absolutely clear; only the two vertical wedges are lost.) The first sign, partially damaged in *JEN* 92 and 736, is perfectly preserved in *JENu* 62a. The last traces here and the succeeding lacuna follow, tentatively, *JEN* 92:17 as interpreted by Fadhil (1983, 306a). Acceptance is tentative because the pertinent section of *JENu* 62a is broken away and the "SI.A" of *JEN* 92:17 is formed in a very peculiar manner (it is correct as copied). The resulting sequence, "*umalla* ... *inandin*" is, as noted in *CAD*, M/1, 183a, an attested hendiadys in these texts.

The sequence of these signs in *JEN* 92:17 has, in the past, been tentatively interpreted as *nam-ra-ak-la* (precise meaning unknown) by Cassin (1938, 142, 143, n. 17); and as *zi-ra-ak-la* (precise meaning unknown) by Koschaker (1928, 14, n.); and Gordon (1936, 64).

ll. 21-34. As noted above, comments, the list of witnesses appears to follow closely those of *JEN* 92 and *JENu* 62a. Lines 21-22 of the present text, themselves clear, parallel *JEN* 92:19, 20 and the less well preserved *JENu* 62a:19, 20. Lines 23-24 follow *JEN* 92:21, 22 and the less well preserved

JENu 62a:21, 22. The traces of witness PNs in lines 28-34 are slight and reconstruction of these names must therefore remain speculative. However, speculations may be hazarded on the basis of the witness lists of *JEN* 92 and *JENu* 62a. The following list of witness PNs attempts to restore *JEN* 736:28-34. The names are followed by the relevant reference(s) to *JEN* 92 and/or *JENu* 62a.

28 IGI DUMU-^{d}[U?] DUMU *Ku*$_8$*-uz-za-ri-ya* (*JEN* 92:26; *JENu* 62a:26)

29 IGI *A-ri-il-lu* DUMU *Ḫa-iš-*[ ] (*JEN* 92:27; *JENu* 62a:27)

30 IGI DUMU-^{d}[U?] DUMU *Ku*$_8$*-uz-za-ri-ya* (*JEN* 92:26; *JENu* 62a:26)

31 IGI *Ḫa-na-ak-ka*$_4$ DUMU *Še-ka*$_4$*-rù* (*JEN* 92:32; *JENu* 62a:30; cf. *JEN* 598:1 and below, note to line 31)

32 IGI *Zi?-ké* DUMU *Še-ka*$_4$*-rù* (*JEN* 92:31)

33 IGI *Wa-qar*-EN DUB.SAR DUMU *Ta-a-a* (*JEN* 92:33; *JENu* 62a:33)

34 IGI *Ḫu-pí-ta* DUMU *Ku-tu-ti-ya* (*JENu* 62a:32; cf. *JEN* 598:3).

Note that lines 28 and 30 cannot both be correct. Also, cf. below, notes to lines 24 and 30.

l. 24: [*r*]*i* D[UMU *Š*]*e-*⸢*en-na*⸣. The traces appear, not as copied, but as:

l. 30: ⸢X⸣. The two horizontal wedges of the copy may be scratches on the surface of the tablet.

l. 31: ⸢*A?-x*⸣. A is more probable than what appears in the copy:

l. 35: ⸢X⸣. Cf., perhaps, l. 22. Porada identifies the seal impression above this line with the witness of line 22.

l. 36. Porada identifies the seal impression above this line as perhaps that of Tupkiya son of Karzeya (cf. l. 21).

ll. 37, 39. The far right side of the upper edge yields the following traces:

l. 37: *Na-*[*ḫi-iš-še*]*-*⸢*ya*⸣. This restoration is based on the name of the sealer identified in *JENu* 62a:38. Cf. also *JEN* 92:23.

l. 38: *I*[*n?-ka*$_4$*?-ri?*]. Porada identifies the seal impression above this line with Ikkari son of Šennaya.

JEN 737

OBVERSE

1 *ṭup-pí ma-ru-ti ša* ^{m}*Zi-ké*
2 *ù ša* ^{m}*Na-ḫi-šal-mu* DUMU.MEŠ *ša*
3 *Ak-ku-ya ù ša* ^{m}*An-•ta-a-a* ÌR!
4 *ša*! ^{m}*Te-ḫi-ip-til-la a-na ma-ru-t[i i-t]e-⸢ep-šu⸣*
5 *ki-ma* ḪA.LA-*šu* É.MEŠ *•i+na* *ŠÀ *U[RU? *Nu*?-z]*i*?
6 17 AŠ *⸢am⸣-ma-ti mu-ra-<ak>-šu-nu*
7 *ù* •9? <AŠ> *am-ma-ti ru-⸢pu⸣-sí-na*
8 *i+na* É.MEŠ ^{d}XXX-*⸢ri⸣?-kí a-na*
9 ^{m}*Ša⸢x-x⸣*[ ] *um-ma* ⸢x x⸣
10 *ù* [ ] ⸢x⸣ IS? ⸢x⸣ *šu-nu-*[*m*]*a*?
11 ⸢x⸣[ ]
12 [ ] ⸢GI⸣[ ] +RI
13 [ ] M[E]Š?

.
.
.

REVERSE

+14 [ ]⸢x⸣[ ]

.
.
.

15 ^{NA_4} KIŠIB ⸢X⸣[(?)]⸢x DUMU⸣? [(?)]
S.I. Po 416
S.I.
16 NA$_4$ *Ut-ḫap-⸢ta⸣-e*
S.I.
17 NA$_4$ ⸢X-•*x-ar*⸣
S.I. Po 387
18 N[A$_4$ *Z*]*i-ké*
S.I.
19 NA$_4$ *Šu-um-mi-⸢ya⸣* <DUMU> •*⸢Eḫ⸣-li-ya*
20 ^{NA_4} KIŠIB *Zi-ni*

LEFT EDGE

S.I.

UPPER EDGE

21 *šum-ma* É *pa-qí-ra-na ir-ta-*[*ši šu-nu-ma*]
22 *ú-za-ku-ma a-na* [^{m}*An*?-*ta*?-*a*?-*a*? SUM]

TRANSLATION

(1-4) Tablet of adoption of Zike and of Naḫiš-šalmu sons of Akkuya and of Antaya slave of Teḫip-tilla. They adopted (him).

(5-9) As his inheritance share, [(they gave to him/)] (to) Ša-...(?) structure(s) in the heart of the town(?) of(?) Nuzi(?), 17 cubits in length and 9(?) cubits <in> width, in (among?) the structures of Sin-riki(?).

(9-13) ... thus ... and ... and(?) they(?) ... -es.

(14) ....

(15-20) seal impression of ... son(?) of(?) ... (*seal impression*); (*seal impression*) seal impression of Utḫap-tae; (*seal impression*) seal impression of ...-ar; (*seal impression*) seal impression of Zike; (*seal impression*) seal impression of Šummiya <son of> Eḫliya; seal impression of Zini (*seal impression*).

(21-22) Should the structure have claimants, [they] shall clear (it) and [give (it)] to [Antaya?].

COMMENTS

This tablet has suffered some additional damage since it was copied.

The scribe of this tablet is guilty of a certain sloppiness and inconsistency. Note the ligature, *ša*$^{+m}$, in lines 1, 2, 3. He has probably included an inappropriate *ša* in line 3. On the other hand, he has omitted signs in lines 6, 7, and 19 (at least); written an incorrect possessive suffix in line 7; written one sign over another (the last signs of lines 19 and 20); and included the clear title clause as an afterthought only (on the upper edge).

NOTES

l. 3: ÌR!. This interpretation follows Lacheman. *JEN* 595 is another text wherein the adoptee is designated as "slave of Teḫip-tilla" (l. 3).

l. 5: U[RU? *Nu*?-*z*]*i*?. Lacheman records these signs as completely preserved.

l. 7: 9?. Although the three right and one lower left wedges are now effaced, I could make out only four others: the upper left "square." I could not make out the bottom center wedge.

l. 8: ⸢*ri*⸣?. Lacheman sees this sign as complete.

ll. 9-13. I can make no sense of these lines. One expects ^{m}*An-ta-a-a* to begin line 9. It does not. A penalty clause is expected afterwards. (The clear title clause appears only in lines 21-22.) Line 11 might start: 2 [MA.NA ...]. However, if it does, then it is difficult to make sense of the traces in line 10. Lines 12 and 13 are no clearer than lines 9-11.

A statement or declaration may have occupied some or all of these lines. Note the possible *um-ma* (l. 9) and the possible *ù* [*u*]*m-ma šu-nu*-[*m*]*a* (l. 10).

In *JEN* 595, a text similar to the present one (see already above, note to line 3), a relatively unusual clause appears, exempting the adoptee from the obligation to mourn (l. 11). See Koschaker (1944b, col. 102).

l. 14: ⸢x⸣. Approximately five lines above line 15, and slightly to the right of the last surviving sign in that line appears:

ll. 15-20. The order in which these line were written is not certain.

l. 15. Seal impression Po 416, which I associate with this line, is tentatively linked to Zini (l. 20) by Porada (1947, p. 131b *ad* no. 416).

l. 15: ⸢X⸣[(?)]⸢x DUMU⸣?. The *CAD* Nuzi file, following Lacheman, reads, at this point: *Ḫu-un-ni-*. If correct, then *Ḫu-un-ni-*[*ya*] is to be restored. Cf. *NPN*, 63a; *AAN*, 60a.

The trace before ⸢DUMU⸣? appears as:

l. 17: ⸢X-*x-ar*⸣. Lacheman, the *CAD* Nuzi file, and *NPN*, 59a *sub* ḪAŠUAR 19), read: ᵐ*Ḫa-šu-ar*. The traces do not support this reading. The sign before ⸢*ar*⸣ is largely effaced. What remains is:

l. 19. Lacheman notes that the seal impression associated with this line does not appear in Porada (1947).

l. 19: ⸢*ya*⸣. The sign appears, not as copied, but, rather, as:

l. 20. The "direction" of the seal impression associate with this line is unclear.

l. 22: [SUM]. Or the like.

JEN 738

OBVERSE

1 [GIŠ?.ŠAR?.M]EŠ ⸢x x x⸣
2 [*i?-na?* ŠÀ? URU] *A-ta-kal*
3 [*i-n*]*a am-ma-ti* [*mu-ra-ak-šu*]
4 [ ]⸢x⸣ 9 *i+na am-ma-*[*ti ru-up-šu* AŠ] *le-et* GIŠ.•⸢ŠAR⸣ *ša* ^{m}*Tar!-mi-*[*ya*]
[:? DU]MU ⸢*Ú*⸣*-na-•ap-•ta-•e ù* ⸢X⸣
[:? *š*]*a* ^{m}*Ḫa-*ši-•ip-•a-•p*[*u* (DUMU *Pá-at-ta*)]
5 [ ]⸢x⸣ x *a-na* ^{m}*Te-ḫi-ip-*[*til-la*]
6 [*ki-ma*] ḪA.LA-*šu id-dì-na-a*[*š-šu*]
7 ⸢*ù*⸣ ^{m}*Te-ḫi-ip-til-la* 1 [+(?) UDU.MEŠ?]
8 [x?+]6 ANŠE ŠE *ki-ma* NÍG.B[A-*šú a-na*]
9 ^{m}*A-ri-ké-*[*e? it-ta-din*]
10 *šum-ma* ^{m}⸢*A*⸣-[*ri-ké-e?* KI.BAL-*at*]
11 1 MA.NA K[Ù.BABBAR 1 MA.NA KÙ.SIG$_{17}$ (*a-na* ^{m}*Te-ḫi-ip-Til-la*)]
12 *i-n*[*a-an-din*]
13 [IG]I? ⸢X⸣-[DUMU]
.?
.?
.?

REVERSE

14 I[GI DUMU]
15 IGI *Nu*?-[DUMU]
.
.
.
S.I.
16 NA$_4$ ^{m}*Ar-t*[*e-*]
S.I.
17 NA$_4$ ^{m}[*Š*]*u-pa-*[*a-a*]
S.I.
18 NA$_4$ ^{m}ÌR!-⸢DINGIR⸣-[*šu*]
[S.I.]

TRANSLATION

....

(1-6) He gave to Teḫip-tilla [as] his inheritance share [an orchard?] ... [in? the? heart? of? the town of] Atakkal, ... cubits [in length], ... 9 cubits [in width], adjacent to (both) the orchard of Tarmiya son of Unap-tae and ...(?) of Ḫašip-apu [(son of Patta)].

(7-9) And Teḫip-tilla [gave] to] Arik-keya as [his] gift 1+x(?) sheep (and) x(?)+6 homers of barley.

(10-12) Should Arik-keya [abrogate (this contract)], he shall give [(to Teḫip-tilla)] 1 mina of silver [(and) 1 mina of gold].

(13-15) Before(?) [... son of ...]; ....(?); before [... son of ...]; before Nu-... [son of ...]; .... .

(16-24) .... (*seal impression*); seal impression of Arte-... (*seal impression*); seal impression of Šupaya (*seal impression*); seal impression of Ward-ilišu [(*seal impression*)]

COMMENTS

This tablet has suffered some additional deterioration on the reverse since it was copied.

Although the tablet is far from complete, much of its sense and wording can be reconstructed from a strikingly parallel text, *JEN* 76. Detailed correspondence exists in the description of real estate. Cf. *JEN* 738:2, 4 with *JEN* 76:8-10. On the basis of this similarity, several restorations have been hazarded. For example, on the basis of *JEN* 76, it may be assumed that four or five lines are missing from the beginning of the obverse. These first lines may be reconstructed as follows:

ṭup-pí ma-ru-ti ša
^{m}*A-ri-ké-e*? DUMU PN
^{m}*Te-ḫi-ip-til-la* DUMU *Pu-ḫi-še-en-ni*
a-na ma-ru-ti i-pu-us-sú-ma

A fifth line may once have been present.

Other, minor, restorations of *JEN* 738 are also based on *JEN* 76.

On the available evidence, it does not appear that *JEN* 76 and 738 share a witness sequence. See below, note to lines 17-18. Note further that, unlike *JEN* 76, *JEN* 738 lacks a clear title clause.

NOTES

l. 1. Cf., perhaps, *JEN* 76:5.

l. 4: *Tar*. This sign is typical, not as copied.

l. 4: *ù* ⌜X⌝. The last horizontal wedge is correct as copied. It cannot represent G[IŠ.ŠAR].

l. 4: [(*Pá-at-ta*)]. For the reading of this PN, attested in *JEN* 76:10, see *NPN*, 57b *sub* ḪAŠIP-APU 7), 112a *sub* PATTA 1).

l. 5: [ ]⌜x⌝ x. The initial traces on this line appear, not as copied, but, rather, as:

Given the surrounding context, one is tempted to render this part of the text: [^{m}*A-ri*]-⸢*ke*⸣!-*e*!. The same PN is spelled with GI (=*ké*) in line 9.

l. 9: [*e*?]. For this possibility, see above, immediately preceding note.

l. 9: [*it-ta-din*]. Or the like. Lacheman once saw, after the lacuna, ZI.

l. 15. The seal impression beneath this line probably *is* right side up.

ll. 17-18. Despite the appearance of these two sealers as witnesses (and, in the latter case, as sealer) in *JEN* 76 (see below, next two notes), on the basis of the surviving evidence, one cannot assume that *JEN* 76 and 738 share a witness sequence. Note, for example, that the sealer identified in line 16 of the present text does not reappear in *JEN* 76.

l. 17: [*Š*]*u-pa-*[*a-a*]. Cf. *JEN* 76:27.

l. 18: ÌR!-⸢DINGIR⸣-[*šu*]. Cf. *JEN* 76:23, 37.

JEN 739

OBVERSE

+1 [*ṭ*]*up-pí ma-ru-ti*
+2 ⸢*ša*⸣ ^{m}*Te-ḫi-ip-til-la*
+3 [DUMU] *Pu-ḫi-še-en-ni* ^{m}*I-ri-*[*r*]*i-*[*til-la*]
+4 [DUMU] *Še-ka$_4$-rù a+na ma-ru-t*[*i i-pu-sú-ma*]
5 [ ]$^{+}$⸢X⸣[ ] $^{+}$⸢*i-*$^{+}$*na* $^{+}$AN⸣!.$^{+}$ZA.$^{+}$⸢KÀR *Ša*⸣*-a*[*k?-ru?-uš?-še?*]
6 [ ]$^{+}$A ⸢x x x⸣[ ]•⸢*x*⸣ *am?* [ ]
7 [ ]⸢x⸣ 1 ANŠE A.•ŠÀ *ši-qí*
8 [^{m}]⸢*I*⸣*-ri-ri-til-*•*la a-na* <m>*Te-ḫi-*⸢*ip*⸣*-*[*til-la*]
9 [ ] ŠU BA.AN.TI *ki-ma* ḪA.LA[*-šú*]
10 •*šum-ma* A.ŠÀ.MEŠ *ši-na pa-qí-ra-na ir-*[*ta-ši*]
11 *ù* ^{m}*I-ri-ri-til-la ú-za-ka$_4$-ma*
12 •*a-na* <m>*Te-ḫi-ip-til-la i+na-di-in*
13 *ù* ^{m}*Te-ḫi-ip-til-la* ⸢10⸣ ANŠE ŠE.MEŠ
14 ⸢*ù*⸣ 50 MA.NA URUDU.MEŠ ⸢*a*⸣*-na* <m>*I-ri-ri-til-*•*la* SUM
15 •*šum-ma* ^{m}*I-*⸢*ri*⸣*-*[*ri*]*-*⸢*til-l*⸣*a* DUMU *Še-ka$_4$-*[*rù*]
16 *⸢*i*⸣*-bá-la-kat* 1 MA.⸢NA⸣ K[Ù].BABBAR 1 MA.NA K[Ù.SIG$_{17}$]
17 *ú-ma-al-*•*la*

---

18 [IGI] ^{m}*Ḫa-na-a-a* DUMU *It-ḫi-til-l*[*a*]
19 [IGI] ^{m}*Ḫu-ti$_4$-ya* DUMU *Eḫ!-li-*[ ]
20 [IGI] ^{m}•*Šúk-*•*ri-ya* DUMU *Al-*⸢*pu*⸣*-*[ ]
21 [IGI] ^{m}*Zi-il$_5$-te-ya*
22 DUMU *Ta-ú-ka$_4$*

REVERSE

.

.

.

S.I.

23 ^{NA_4} KIŠIB ⸢*ša*⸣ ^{m}⸢X⸣[ ]⸢x x⸣

S.I.

24 [^{NA_4} KIŠIB *š*]*a* ^{m}*Zi-il*$_5$-[*te-y*]*a*

25 [DUMU *Ta*]-*ú-ka*$_4$ *sà-s*[*ú-u*]*k*-⸢*ki*⸣

+S.I.

+26 [^{NA_4} K]IŠIB *ša* ^{m}*Ḫa-na-a-a* [(?)]

+27 *ši-bi*

+ ____

TRANSLATION

(1-4) Tablet of adoption of Teḫip-tilla [son of] Puḫi-šenni. Iriri-tilla [son of] Šekaru adopted (him).

(5-9) Iriri-tilla to Teḫip-tilla gave(!) (lit. "took") ... as [his] inheritance share ... in the *dimtu* (of) Šakrušše(?), ..., a 1 homer, irrigated field.

(10-12) Should that land (lit. "those fields") have claimants, then Iriri-tilla shall clear (it) and give (it) to Teḫip-tilla.

(13-14) And Teḫip-tilla gave to Iriri-tilla 10 homers of barley and 50 minas of copper.

(15-17) Should Iriri-tilla son of Šekaru abrogate (this contract), he shall pay 1 mina of silver (and) 1 mina of gold.

(18-22) [Before] Ḫanaya son of Itḫip-tilla; [before] Ḫutiya son of Eḫli-...; [before] Šukriya son of Alpu-...; [before] Zil-teya son of Tauka; .... .

(23-27) ....; (*seal impression*) seal impression of ...; (*seal impression*) [seal impression] of Zil-teya [son of] Tauka, the bookkeeper; (*seal impression*) seal impression of Ḫanaya, witness.

COMMENTS

Since the time when *JENu* 225a was copied as *JEN* 739, a fragment, *JENu* 1141aj, has been added to the tablet. On the obverse, this adds the first four lines of the tablet and all but the last two surviving signs (themselves preserved on *JENu* 225a) of the fifth line (it adds to the partially preserved KÀR of *JENu* 225a). On the reverse, the fragment adds part of the last seal impression (already partially preserved on *JENu* 225a), the last two lines, and a horizontal line after line 27. The rest of the reverse (with room for about one line) and the upper edge are blank.

JENu 225a has suffered some additional damage since it was copied. Also, the appearance of the tablet is somewhat more broken than is indicated in the copy.

Note that the phraseology is not quite typical: ŠU BA.AN.TI (l. 9) and *ši-na* (l. 10) are used. The expected NÍG.BA is not (l. 14; cf. ḪA.LA in l. 9). The payment clause is "misplaced," appearing after the clear title clause rather than before it.

Another peculiarity is the omission of the male determinative in the environment after NA (ll. 8, 12, 14). Perhaps a kind of haplography is at work here. A similar, partial haplography in a Middle Assyrian text is noted in J.N. Postgate (1989a, 2-3). Cf. above, note to *JEN* 730:5-12 and below, comments on *JEN* 742.

For further on this text and on the connections between *JEN* 739 and *JEN* 718, see above, note to *JEN* 718:22.

NOTES

ll. 3-4: ^{m}*I-ri-*[*r*]*i-*[*til-la*] // [DUMU] *Še-ka*$_4$*-rù*. On this individual, see already above, note to *JEN* 718:22. See also below, second note to line 5.

l. 4: [*i-pu-sú-ma*]. Or the like.

l. 5: [ ]˹X˺[ ]. The trace appears as:

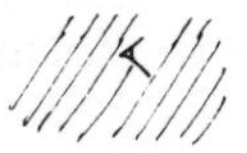

Perhaps, something like [Ḫ]A.[LA-*šu*] is called for, referring to Iriri-tilla's patrimonial share. Cf., for example, *JEN* 735:5. The land itself is described in line 7.

l. 5: ˹AN˺!.ZA.˹KÀR *Ša*˺*-a*[*k*?*-ru*?*-uš*?*-še*?]. ˹AN˺! appears as: 

The tentative restoration of the GN rests on the identification of the vendor here, Iriri-tilla son of Šekaru, with one Iriri-tilla (patronymic not preserved) in *JEN* 411 (l. 2). Both texts are real estate adoptions in which the vendor is "Iriri-tilla" and in which the purchaser is Teḫip-tilla son of Puḫi-šenni. In both texts, the purchase price consists of copper (at least in part). The two texts share two witnesses, Ḫutiya son of Eḫli-... (*JEN* 411:26; 739:19; very likely the same person [cf. below, note to l. 19]) and Zil-teya son of Tauka (*JEN* 411:27; 739:21-22). If these connections are significant, then the fact that land involved in *JEN* 411 is in the *dimtu* of Šakrušše (ll. 5-6) becomes pertinent in the present context. Note further that the presence of Zil-teya son of Tauka as witness in these texts may also be significant. A good half of his other attestations are also linked to transactions involving land in this *dimtu* (*JEN* 40, 49, 401, 614, 763). (The other texts in which he is attested are *JEN* 10, 86, 701, 718, 759.)

On the other hand, if the restoration is correct, one would have expected AN.ZA.KÀR *ša Ša-ak-ru-uš-še* (universal elsewhere) and, moreover, a spelling of the GN with initial ŠÁ (universal except for *JEN* 411:6 which presumably has initial *Ša*! [=TA]).

For further on the *dimtu* of Šakrušše and its possible location in the town of Unap-še, see below, note to *JEN* 758:5-7.

l. 6: Lacheman and the *CAD* Nuzi file read, in effect: A.ŠÀ *i-na* AN.ZA.KÀR *ša* [ ]. See below, next note.

l. 6: A ⸢x⸣. The first traces do not appear as the first three wedges copied, but, rather, as:

l. 7: ⸢*x*⸣. Lacheman and the *CAD* Nuzi file tentatively read *ù* at this point.

l. 9: ŠU BA.AN.TI. Evidently, this complex is meant to represent a form of *nadānu* rather than *leqû*! The syntax of this clause is also unusual; the verb precedes rather than follows *kīma zittišu*. For a similar syntactic juxtaposition, see *JEN* 718:6-7.

l. 10: *šum*. What remains of the sign does not appear as copied, but, rather, as:

l. 10: *qí*. The sign commences with a single *Winkelhaken*, not two as depicted.

l. 12: *Til*. This sign is typical (see the forms directly above and below this sign), not as copied.

l. 13: ⸢10⸣. It appears that "20" was written first. It was then immediately erased. Following the erasure, "10" was written. Part of the last sign survives. On the resulting scale of value, .1 homer of land (l. 7) = 1 homer of barley (l. 13) + 5 minas of copper (l. 14), cf. *JEN* 718: 5, 8, 9 and the comment to *JEN* 718:22. Also, cf., perhaps, *JEN* 650:8, 9, 10, 14, 17, 18, alluding to a transaction involving the very parties mentioned here as principals (but recording a different transaction).

l. 15: [*rù*]. Cf. line 4. Lacheman records RU as preserved.

l. 16: K[Ù.SIG$_{17}$]. Lacheman and the *CAD* Nuzi file record these signs as completely preserved.

l. 19: *Eḫ*!-*li*-[ ]. The first sign does not appear as copied, but, rather, as:

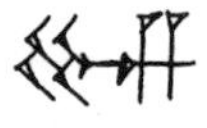

For this patronymic, see *NPN*, 41b *sub* EḪLI, 64b *sub* ḪUTIJA 11). Cf. *AAN*, 40a *sub* EḪLI. The lemmata, EḪLI, should probably be deleted from both *NPN* and *AAN*. It appears this PN results from lacunae and scribal omission.

ll. 21-22, 24-25. On this individual and his function in this context, see above, note to *JEN* 718:22.

l. 23: ⸢X⸣[ ]⸢x x⸣. These traces might represent *Š[úk-ri-ya]* ⸢x x⸣ or *Š[úk-r]i-y[a]*. Cf. l.20.

ll. 24-25. For the seal impression(s) associated with this individual, see above note to *JEN* 718:22. The seal impression above this line is indistinct. It may not have been made by the seal associated with this individual in *JEN* 731 and 759 (also, the sealing is made widthwise here, not lengthwise as in those texts). The impression resembles Porada (1947, pll. VIII-X, nos. 132, 131, 133, 141, 157) but is identical to none of the impressions in her catalogue.

l. 25: *ka*$_4$. The sign does not appear as copied, but, rather, as:

l. 25: *[u]k-⸢ki⸣*. The last part of this line does not appear as copied (i.e., as UŠ), but, rather, as:

JEN 740

OBVERSE

1 *li-ša-an-•š[u] •ša* ^{m}*Ké-e[š-ḫa-a-a]*
2 DUMU *Ki-in-•n[i]-⸢ya⸣ a-na pa-•ni*
3 *ḫal-ṣú-uḫ-[l]e-⸢e⸣ ù* ⸢DI⸣.KU$_5$.ME[Š]
4 *ki-a-⸢am⸣ iq-ta-⸢a⸣-b[i]*
5 ^{m}*Te-ḫi-ip-til-la* ⸢DUMU⸣ *P[u-ḫ]i-š[e-en-ni]*
6 *a-na ma-ru-ti e-⸢te⸣-pu-us-[sú]*
7 *ù* 8 ^{GIŠ}APIN A.ŠÀ *ma-ag-ra-•a[t]-*⸢ti⸣?*
8 *i-na* URU *Nu-zi i-na* KASKAL *ša* URU *[An]-⸢zu-•gal⸣-•lì*
9 *a-na* ^{m}*Te-ḫi-ip-til-la a[t-t]a-•[di]n-mi*
10 *ù* ^{m}*Te-ḫi-ip-til-la* 10 [AN]ŠE ŠE.MEŠ
11 1 TÚG.MEŠ *ù* 10 MA.NA URUDU.MEŠ
12 *ki-mu* NÍG.BA-*ya a-na ⸢ya⸣-a-ši*
13 *it-ta-din-mi šum-ma m[a-a]g-ra-at-tu*$_4$
14 *pa-qí-ra-na i-ra-*aš-[ši]*
15 *ù a-na-ku-ma ú-za-[ak-ka*$_4$*]*
16 *i-na u*$_4$*-mi an-ni-[im]*
17 ^{m}*K[é-e]š-ḫa-⸢a⸣-a aš-[šum]*
18 *ma-[ag-ra-at-ti (an-ni-ti) i-na* EGIR-*ki]*
19 ^{m}*Te-ḫi-i[p-til-la]*
20 *la i-⸢ša⸣-[as-sí]*

21 ŠU ^{md}*A*[*k-dingir-ra* DUB.SAR-*ri*]

REVERSE

S.I. Po 924

22 ^{NA_4} KI[ŠIB ^{m}*Tar-mi-ya* DUM]U *Ú-*⸢*na*⸣*-*[*ap-ta-e*]

S.I. Po 663

23 ^{NA_4} KIŠIB ^{m}*Te-ḫi-ip-til-la*

24 DUMU *Pu-ḫi-še-en-ni*

S.I. Po 492

25 ⸢^{NA_4} KIŠIB ^{m}⸣*Tar-mi-*⸢*te*⸣*-•šu*[*p*]

26 DUMU *Eḫ-*⸢*li-te*⸣*-•šup*

TRANSLATION

(1-4) Declaration of Kešḫaya son of Kinniya before the lands officer and judges; thus he spoke:

(5-15) "I have adopted Teḫip-tilla son of Puḫi-šenni. And I have given to Teḫip-tilla a .8 homer threshing floor in the town of Nuzi, on the road to the town of Anzugalli. And Teḫip-tilla has given to me as my gift 10 homers of barley, 1 garment, and 10 minas of copper. Should the threshing floor have claimants, then it is I who shall clear (it)."

(16-20) From this day forward, Kešḫaya shall not hail Teḫip-tilla (into court) over [(this)] threshing floor.

(21) The hand of Akkadingirra, [the scribe].

(22-26) (*seal impression*) seal impression of [Tarmiya] son of Unap-tae; (*seal impression*) seal impression of Teḫip-tilla son of Puḫi-šenni; (*seal impression*) seal impression of Tarmi-tešup son of Eḫli-tešup.

COMMENTS

This tablet has deteriorated somewhat since the copy was made.

Restorations in the latter part of the text are based on the standard formulary of declaration texts, especially those written by Akkadingirra (l. 21). See, for example, *JEN* 149, 152.

The *CAD* Nuzi file for this tablet was authored by Lacheman. References to the file indicate contributions by Lacheman.

NOTES

l. 5. The *CAD* Nuzi file sees this line as completely preserved.

l. 7: ⸢*ti*⸣?. The *CAD* Nuzi file sees, in effect: [*t*]u_4.

l. 8. The *CAD* Nuzi file sees this line as completely preserved.

l. 18: [(*an-ni-ti*)]. Or the like.

l. 21. Lacheman once saw this line as completely preserved. Both the surviving signs (and trace) and the composition of the rest of the extant text support this restoration.

For the rendering of the PN, see above, first note to *JEN* 689:24.

JEN 741

OBVERSE

1 [*ṭup*]-*pí ma-ru-t*[*i ša* ^{m}*Ta-a-a*]
2 ⸢DUMU⸣ [*Ḫa*]-*pí-a-šu* [^{m}*Te-ḫi-ip-til-la*]
3 DUMU *P*[*u*]-$^{+}$*ḫi-še-en-*$^{+}$*ni* [*a-na ma-ru-ti* DÙ-*ma*]
4 2 ANŠ[E] A.ŠÀ.MEŠ *i-na* ⸢*ta*⸣-*a-a-r*[*i* GAL *š*]*a* [É.GAL(-*lì*)]
5 *i*-⸢*na*⸣ *š*[*u-pa-a*]*l* URU *Ú-na-ap-*$^{+}$*še-*[*w*]*a*
6 *ši-ni*-⸢*šu*⸣ [KASKAL] *ša* URU *Tù-ur-*[*šá*?/*ša*?]
7 *ik-ki-sú k*[*i*]-*m*[*u* ḪA].LA.MEŠ-*šu*
8 ^{m}*Ta-a-a* DUMU *Ḫa-p*[*í*]-*⸢*a*⸣-•*šu* •*a-na*
9 ^{m}*Te-ḫi-ip-til-la* *DUMU **P*[*u-ḫi*]-*še-en*-⸢*ni*⸣ [SUM-*nu*]
10 *ù* ^{m}*Te-ḫi-ip-til*-⸢*la*⸣ [1 GUD 1 GUN URUDU.MEŠ]
11 *ki-mu* NÍG.BA.MEŠ-*šu a-na* ⸢m⸣[*Ta-a-a*]
12 DUMU *Ḫa-pí-a-šu* SUM-*nu šum-m*[*a* A.ŠÀ.MEŠ]
13 *pí-ir-qa ir-ta-ši* ^{m}*Ta-*[*a*]-*a*
14 *ú-za-ak-ka*$_{4}$-*ma a*-•*na* •m**T*[*e-ḫ*]*i-ip-Til*-⸢*la*⸣ [SU]M?
15 *ù il-ka ša* •⸢A.*ŠÀ⸣.[MEŠ]-*ti*
16 ^{m}*Ta-a-a-ma na*-⸢*a*⸣-*š*[*i šu*]*m-ma*
17 ^{m}*Ta-a-a* •KI.BAL-*a*[*t*] *šum-ma*
18 *aš-šum* A.ŠÀ.MEŠ *i-na* ⸢EGIR⸣-*ki* ^{m}*T*[*e-ḫi-ip-til-la*]
19 *i-ša-as-sí* 2 MA.[N]A KÙ.BABBAR 2 M[A.NA KÙ.SIG$_{17}$]
20 *a-na* ^{m}*Te-ḫi-ip-Til-la ú-ma-a*[*l-la*]
21 *ù* EME-*šu* ⸢*ša*⸣ ^{m}*Ta-a-a*

LOWER EDGE

22 *i-na pa-ni* LÚ.MEŠ *ši-bu-tu*$_{4}$
23 *an-nu-tu*$_{4}$ *iq-ta-bi*
24 1 GUD 1 ⸢GUN⸣ URUDU.MEŠ

REVERSE

25 *ki-mu* NÍG.BA.MEŠ-*ya*
26 *a-šar* ^{m}*Te-ḫi-i*[*p*]-*til-l*[*a*] TI.MEŠ
27 IGI *Ḫu-lu-uk-ka*$_{4}$ DU[MU] *Ar-te-šup*
28 IGI *A-ta-na-aḫ*$_{4}$-[DINGIR] DUMU •*Na-a*[*l-te*]-$^{+}$*šup*
29 IGI *Tar-mi-ya* DUMU *A-*[*be-y*]*a*
30 IGI *E-ni-iš-ta-*[*e*]
31 DUMU *A-a-ba-aš* 4 *š*[*i*?-*bu*?]-⸢*tu*$_{4}$⸣?

32 *mu-še-él-mu ša* ⸢A⸣.[ŠÀ.M]EŠ ⸢X⸣
33 IGI *Um-pí-ya* DUMU *T[e-eš-šu]-⸢ya⸣*
34 IGI *Te-ḫi-ip-a-pu* DUMU ⸢*Ni*⸣-[*í*]*ḫ*!-*r*[*i-ya*]
35 IGI *I-ri-ya* DUMU KI.MIN
36 IGI *It-ḫi-iš-ta* DUMU *A-⸢ar-ta-e⸣*
37 IGI *Ut-ḫa-ap-ta-e* DUMU *Z*[*i-k*]*é*
38 IGI *Ḫa-na-ak-ka*$_4$ DUMU *Še-k*[*a*$_4$-*r*]*ù*
39 IGI *Ar-ru-um-ti* DUMU *Ḫ*[*a*]?-⸢*iš*⸣?-[*te*?-*šup*?]
40 IGI DINGIR-*ya* DUB.⸢SAR⸣-*rù*
41 IGI *A-ḫu-um-mì-š*[*a*] DU[MU] *Él-⸢ḫi⸣-ip*-LU[GAL?]

S.I.

42 ^{NA_4} KIŠ[IB ^{m}]
43 ^{NA_4} KIŠIB ^{m}*It-ḫi-iš-ta*

UPPER EDGE

S.I. Po 777

REVERSE

44 ^{NA_4} ⸢KIŠIB⸣ ^{m}*Um-pí-ya*

S.I. Po 477

UPPER EDGE

45 ^{NA_4} KIŠIB ^{m}*Te-ḫ*[*i-i*]*p-pa-pu*

REVERSE

S.I.

LEFT EDGE

S.I. Po 520 S.I.

46 ^{NA_4} KIŠIB ^{m}*I-ri-ya* ^{NA_4} KIŠIB ^{m}DINGIR-*ya* DUB.SAR

TRANSLATION

(1-3) Tablet of adoption [of Taya] son of Ḫapi-ašu. [He adopted Teḫip-tilla] son of Puḫi-šenni.

(4-9) Taya son of Ḫapi-ašu [gave] to Teḫip-tilla son of Puḫi-šenni as his inheritance share a field, 2 homers by the [large] standard of [the palace], to the west of the town of Unap-še; [the road] to the town of Turša(?) cuts (lit. "cut") (the field) in two.

(10-12) And Teḫip-tilla gave to [Taya] son of Ḫapi-ašu as his gift [1 ox (and) 1 talent of copper].

(12-14) Should [the field] have a claim (against it), Taya shall clear (the field) and give (it) to Teḫip-tilla.

(15-16) And it is Taya who shall bear the *ilku* of the field.

(16-20) Should Taya abrogate (this contract)—should he hail Teḫip-tilla (into court) over the field—he shall pay to Teḫip-tilla 2 minas of silver (and) 2 minas [of gold].

(21-23) Declaration of Taya before these witnesses. (Thus) he spoke:

(24-26) "I have received from Teḫip-tilla as my gift 1 ox and 1 talent of copper."

(27-41) Before Ḫulukka son of Ar-tešup; before Âtanaḫ-ilu son of Nan-tešup; before Tarmiya son of Abeya; before Eniš-tae son of Ay-abâš. (These) 4 witnesses(?) are the measurers of the field. Before Umpiya son of Teššuya; before Teḫip-apu son of Niḫriya; before Iriya son of the same; before Itḫišta son of Ar-tae; before Utḫap-tae son of Zike; before Ḫanakka son of Šekaru; before Aril-lumti son of Ḫaiš-tešup(?); before Iluya, the scribe; before Aḫ-ummiša son of Elḫip-ša[rri?].

(42-46) (*seal impression*) seal impression of ...; seal impression of Itḫišta (*seal impression*); seal impression of Umpiya (*seal impression*); seal impression of Teḫip-apu (*seal impression*); (*seal impression*) seal impression of Iriya; (*seal impression*) seal impression of Iluya, the scribe.

COMMENTS

This tablet has suffered little deterioration since it was copied.

The *CAD* Nuzi file for this text was composed by Lacheman. Reference to the file represents a contribution by Lacheman.

NOTES

l. 3: [DÙ-*ma*]. Or the like. See also below, next note.

l. 4: [*š*]*a*. The copy and the *CAD* Nuzi file take this trace as the end of line 3; the file interprets it as [*i-te-pu-u*]*š*. The position of the trace does not accord with the copy. It is lower and somewhat farther to the left than depicted.

l. 6: [KASKAL]. This restoration (or one describing a watercourse) is almost demanded by the surrounding context. Cf. similar descriptions in the Nuzi texts cited in *CAD*, N/1, 174a *sub nakāsu* 1c. See also below, next note.

l. 6: URU *Tù-ur-*[*šá?/ša?*]. This restoration is most likely since the clause would then describe an Unap-še – Turša road (ll. 5-6). Such a road is attested in *JEN* 44:4-5, as most plausibly reconstructed.

Other, more remote possible GNs include (but are not exhausted by) Dūr-ubla (see, e.g., *JEN* 705:6), Dūr-zanzi (see, e.g., *JEN* 339:3), and, possibly, Durdaniya (*JEN* 843:7).

l. 14: [SU]M?. Or the like. Contrary to the copy, after ⌈LA⌉, only the first vertical appears. The three horizontal wedges and the second vertical are not on the tablet. The tablet is well preserved at this point.

l. 15: ⌈A.ŠÀ⌉.[MEŠ]-*ti*. Thus, the plural, *eqlāti*, really is meant although a single field is at issue. Perhaps conceptual plurality derives from the field being split into two by a road (ll. 6-7).

ll. 16-19. The definition of contractual abrogation is here made explicit: raising a claim in court.

l. 20: *a*[*l*]. The horizontal line above the start of this sign in the copy is not present on the tablet.

l. 25. This line begins the reverse.

l. 28. The restoration of the names on this line and the restoration of other witness PNs in this text are based mostly on *JEN* 744. These two texts were written by the same scribe and, where the two texts can be compared, there is a very substantial overlap of witnesses. Not quite a common witness sequence, the lists nevertheless bear such a marked similarity that the extant portions of each text may be used to reconstruct PNs in the other.

Other texts whose witness lists significantly overlap that of *JEN* 741 (and which help restore PNs in this text) are *JEN* 38, 91, 751, and, to a much lesser extent, *JEN* 743, its close parallel, *JEN* 772, and 841. *JEN* 91 and 751 seem to have an identical witness sequence. All the above texts deal with real estate located in Unap-še.

The general relationship among some of these texts has been noted by Weeks (1972, 206-8).

l. 28: *a*[*l*]. The trace of this sign is quite clear. "Nal-tešup," therefore, is a (unique) variant of "Nan-tešup." Cf., e.g., *JEN* 91:21.

l. 28: *šup*. The last sign does not appear as copied, but, rather, as:

l. 31: *š*[*i?-bu?*]-⸢tu_4⸣?. Cf. *JEN* 744:24. *š*[*i-bu-t*]*i* is also possible.

l. 32: ⸢x⸣. The traces is correct as copied. It is not likely to represent TI (cf. l. 15).

l. 34: [*í*]*ḫ*!. The trace consists of two horizontal lines, not three as depicted. The bottom line does not appear on the tablet, which is clear at this point.

l. 42: [^{m}]. Lacheman restores, in the lacuna: ^{m}*Ḫa-na-ak-*ka_4.

l. 43. Contrary to the impression of the copy, S.I. Po 777 should not be associated with line 45 rather than with this line. See already Porada (1947, 136a *ad* no. 777) who associates this impression elsewhere with the Itḫišta of line 43. In fact, the seal impression on the upper edge runs perpendicular to the edge (facing left), not parallel to it as depicted in the copy. It is thus to be linked to Itḫišta.

l. 46. The second seal impression above this line is faint to the point of invisibility.

JEN 742

OBVERSE

1 *ṭup-pí ma-ru-ti ša* ^{m}*Ar-te-šup* DUMU *Ip-šá-ḫa-lu*
2 *ù ša* <m>*Ḫa-na-a-*[*a*] DUMU *Ar-te-šup-ma*
3 ^{m}*Te-ḫi-ip-t*[*il-l*]*a* DUMU *Pu-ḫi-še-en-ni*
4 *a-na ma-ru-*[*ti*] *i-pu-šu-uš*
5 1 ANŠE 8[+1? ^{GIŠ}AP]IN A.ŠÀ *i-na*
6 ^{GIŠ}*ta-a-a-*[*r*]*i* GAL *ša* É.GAL-*lì*
7 *i-na e-l*[*e*]*-en* AN.ZA.KÀR *ša E-ni-ya*
8 *ù* AŠ *i*[*l-t*]*a-na-an* KASKAL *ša*
9 [A]Š? AN.Z[A.KÀR (*ša* ^{m})] *⸢*Ú*⸣-lu-li-ya* DU-*ku* ^{m}*Ar-te-⸢šup⸣*
10 [*ù* ^{m}*Ḫa-na-a-a* DUMU *A*]*r-te-šup-ma*
11 [*a-na* ^{m}*Te-ḫi-ip-til*]*-la it-ta-ad-nu*
12 [1 GUD (*ù*) 1 TÚG.ME]Š!? *ša* 15 *i+na am-m*[*a-ti*]
13 [*mu-ra-ak-šu*] *ù*!? *ša* 5 AŠ *am-*[*ma-ti*]
14 [*ru-pu-us-s*]*ú* <m>*Te-ḫi-ip-til-la*
15 [*a-na* ^{m}*Ar-te-šu*]*p*! *ù a-na* <m>*Ḫa-na-*[*a-a*]
16 [*it-ta-ad-na-aš*]*-šu-nu-ti*
17 [*šum-ma* A.ŠÀ *pa-qí*]*-ra-na* TUK-*ši*
18 [^{m}*Ḫa-na-a-a*] $^{+}$*ù* <m>*Ar-te-šup*
19 [*ú-za-(ak-)ku-m*]*a a-na* ^{m}*Te-ḫi-ip-t*[*il-la*]
20 [*i-na-(an-)di-nu*] ⸢X⸣ *ù*
21 [ ] *šu* [(?)]
22 [*šum-ma* ^{m}*Ar-te-šup ù* ^{m}*Ḫa-n*]*a-⸢a⸣-*[*a*]
23 [K]I.BAL-*t*[*u*$_{4}$ MA.N]A KÙ.SI[G$_{17}$]
24 *a-na* ^{m}*Te-ḫi-•ip-*[*til-l*]*a*
25 *ú-ma-al-lu-ú*

\+ ______________________________________

LOWER EDGE

26 IGI ^{m}*I-lu-ḫa-a-a* DUMU [*N*]*a-*[*ik-ké-mar*]
27 IGI ^{m}*Ši-mi-ku-ya* DU[MU]⸢x⸣[ ]

REVERSE

28 IGI ^{m}*Ú-kùr-a-ta*[*l* DUM]U *Ša-*[ ]
29 IGI ^{m}*Ma-ti-ya* DUMU [ ]*-a-⸢x⸣-*[ ]
30 IGI ^{m}*Šar-ri-ya* DUMU ⸢*Ša*⸣?/⸢*Ta*⸣?*-ri-⸢x⸣-*[(?)]
31 [I]GI ^{m}*Ki-in-nu-uz-•⸢zi⸣*
32 [6 L]Ú.MEŠ *mu-še-el-mu-ú ša* A.Š[À]
33 ⸢*ù*⸣ *na-di-na-nu ša* GUD <*ù*?> TÚG?[.MEŠ?]
34 [IGI] ^{m}*Pal-te-šup* DUMU *Ḫa-li-*[*ip-pa/pá*]
35 [IGI] ^{m}*Ar-ti-ir-wi* D[UMU]
36 [IG]I ^{md}*Uta-an-dùl* DUMU [*Ta-a-a* DUB.SAR-*rù*]
37 [E]ME-*šu* ⸢*ša*⸣ ^{m}*Ḫa-na-⸢a⸣-*[*a*]

38 [A]Š *pa-ni* LÚ.MEŠ *ši-[bu-ti]*
39 *[i]q-ta-a-•bi* A.ŠÀ *[a/ni-ta-din]*
40 ⌜*ù*⌝ *a-na-ku a-•š[ar* ^{m}*Te-ḫi-ip-til-la]*
41 [1 G]UD 1 TÚG.MEŠ ⌜*ù*⌝? [ ]
42 [(?)] *el!-qé* [(?)]

S.I. S.I.

43 ^{NA_4} KIŠIB *I-l[u-ḫa-a-a* ^{NA_4} KIŠIB *Ma]-ti-ya*

S.I. S.I.

44 NA_4 ^{m}*Ú-[k]ùr-a-t[al]* NA_4 *Ši-mi-ku-ya*

UPPER EDGE

S.I.

45 NA_4 $^{md+}$*Uta-an-dùl*

RIGHT EDGE

46 [ ]⌜x⌝[ ]

TRANSLATION

(1-4) Tablet of adoption of Ar-tešup son of Ipša-ḫalu and also of Ḫanaya son of Ar-tešup. They adopted Teḫip-tilla son of Puḫi-šenni.

(5-11) Ar-tešup [and] also [Ḫanaya son of] Ar-tešup gave [to] Teḫip-tilla a field, 1.8[+1?] homers by the large standard of the palace, to the east of the *dimtu* of Eniya and to the north of the road which runs through the *dimtu* of Ulūliya.

(12-16) Teḫip-tilla gave [to] Ar-tešup and to Ḫanaya [1 ox (and) 1 garment] whose [length] is 15 cubits and(!?) whose width is 5 cubits.

(17-20) [Should the field] have claimants, [Ḫanaya] and Ar-tešup [shall clear] (it) and [give (it)] to Teḫip-tilla.

(20-21) … and ….

(22-25) [Should Ar-tešup and] Ḫanaya abrogate (this contract), they shall pay to Teḫip-tilla X mina(s) of gold.

(26-36) Before Iluḫḫaya son of Naik-kemar; before Šimikuya son of …; before Ukur-atal son of Ša-…; before Matiya son of …; before Šarriya son of Ša?-/Ta?-ri-…; before Kinnuzzi. (These) [6] men are the measurers of the field and givers of the ox <and?> garment(?). [Before] Pal-tešup son of Ḫalippa; [before] Ar-tirwi son of …; before Uta-andul son of [Taya, the scribe].

(37-39) Declaration of Ḫanaya before the witnesses. (Thus) he spoke:

(39-42) "[I/We have given] the field and I have received …(?) from [Teḫip-tilla 1] ox (and) 1 garment and(?) … .

(43-45) (*seal impression*) seal impression of Iluḫḫaya; (*seal impression*) [seal impression of] Matiya; (*seal impression*) seal impression of Ukur-atal; (*seal impression*) seal impression of Šimikuya; (*seal impression*) seal impression of Utu-andul.

(46) …

COMMENTS

This tablet has suffered very little damage since it was copied. Yet, part of the tablet may have broken away in modern times before the tablet was first copied. Lacheman notes that the left edge contains a seal impression and, in effect, the following line: [NA$_4$ ^{m}*Ar-t*]*i-ir-wi*. Furthermore, Porada suggests that another seal impression, that of Ḫanakka son of Šekaru, appears on the reverse. However, evidence for neither of these claims is to be found on the tablet or in the copy. It is possible (although clear indications are lacking) that the small fragments, *JENu* 517a and 517b, once stored in the same box with part of this tablet, represent part of a broken off section of the document.

The scribe has omitted the male determinative in lines 2, 14, 15, 18. In each case, the sign immediately preceding the PN ends with a vertical wedge. Thus, haplography may be at work here. Cf. above, comments to *JEN* 739. Note, however, that the male determinative does appear elsewhere in the present text following signs with a final vertical wedge, for example, in line 1. See also above, note to *JEN* 730:5-12.

The location of the real estate described in this text is Unap-še. For this datum, see above, note to *JEN* 723:1.

NOTES

l. 2: *Ar-te-šup-ma*. The AR is typical, not Ù as depicted.

I have interpreted "*-ma*" as an emphasizing copula, stressing the fact that there are two adopters. It is possible perhaps that the enclitic here expresses identification of this Ar-tešup with the Ar-tešup of line 1. This would call for a translations something like: ".... and of Ḫanaya son of the same Ar-tešup." Cf. also the same construction in lines 9-10. However, such a construction is typically employed when the patronymics of two persons are identical, not when the patronymic of one person corresponds to the PN of another. Cf., for example, *JEN* 746:2-3.

This latter interpretation of "*-ma*" apparently underlies the assertion of the father-son-grandson relationship of Ipša-ḫalu, Ar-tešup, and Ḫanaya posited in *NPN*, 52a *sub* ḪANAI̯A 7); 72a *sub* IPŠA-ḪALU 45).

The relationship itself is very probable; its expression by means of the enclitic is less so.

l. 4: *uš*. This sign is typical, not MA as depicted in the copy.

l. 5: 8[+1?]. Both Lacheman and the *CAD* Nuzi file see no lacuna after "8."

l. 8: [*t*]*a*. The trace of this sign does not appear as copied, but, rather, as:

l. 9: [A]Š?. Lacheman once saw this sign as complete.

l. 10. It would be preferable (or at least more symmetrical) for the line to begin: DUMU *Ip-šá-ḫa-lu*. However, there does not appear to be enough room to accommodate these five extra signs.

For further on this line, see above, note to line 2.

ll. 11-12. The dimensions of the garment are standard. See Zaccagnini (1981, 349 and *passim*).

l. 12: [1 GUD (*ù*) 1 TÚG.ME]Š!?. Lacheman records, at this point: ⸢1 GUD 1 TÚG⸣. Yet MEŠ probably belongs after TÚG (cf. l. 41). Lacheman's rendering leaves the following trace unexplained. A problematic sign occurs in a parallel position in the next line. See below, next note.

l. 13: *ù*!?. This sign is a clear DU. See also above, immediately preceding note.

l. 14: [*s*]*ú*. [*sú*] ⸢*ù*⸣ is also possible.

l. 15: [*šu*]*p*!. Perhaps [A]Š is to be preferred. On this sign in place of an expected RU, see above, *JEN* 733:12 and the note thereto.

l. 18. Note that the names in this line appear in reverse order compared to the order in other, similar passages in this text.

l. 21. An abbreviated *ilku* clause might fit in this line. For example: [*il-ka*$_4$ *ša* A.ŠÀ] *šu*-[*nu-ma na-šu-ú*]. The spacing after *šu* would be difficult.

l. 25. Below this line appears a horizontal line. This is not indicated in the copy.

l. 26: [*N*]*a*-[*ik-ké-mar*]. This restoration seems most likely since the individual so defined appears in other Unap-še contexts as well, and in those contexts only. See *JEN* 743:25, 39; 761:38.

l. 27: ⸢x⸣. At this point, Lacheman once saw: RI.

l. 29: [ ]-*a*-⸢*x*⸣-[ ]. Lacheman sees here: ⸢*Ú*⸣-[*a*]-*a*[*r-si-a*]. This is difficult to reconcile with the remaining traces. Perhaps he meant: ⸢*Ú*⸣-*a-a*[*r-si-a*]. Even so, the individual so defined appears elsewhere only in Nuzi contexts. See *JEN* 266:25; 493:13; 748:28.

l. 30: ⸢*Ša*⸣?/⸢*Ta*⸣?-*ri*-⸢*x*⸣-[(?)]. The last traces appear, not as copied, but, rather, as:

The *CAD* Nuzi file and *NPN*, 28b *sub* ARIP-APU 19), 125a *sub* ŠARRIḮA 1), read, in effect, *A*?-*ri-pa-pu*. The sign and traces do not support this interpretation.

l. 31. There is empty space following this line; there is no erasure. Perhaps the scribe left space for Kinnuzzi's patronymic but never succeeded in recording this datum. In any case, the lack of patronymic or other qualifier for a witness is most unusual (if not unique).

l. 33. Following this line there is a crack in the tablet. It is this crack that is depicted in the copy, not a deliberate horizontal line made by the scribe.

l. 35: D[UMU]. Lacheman once saw, at this point: D[UMU *Ta-i-še*]*-en-ni*.

l. 36: *Uta*. Spellings of this name such as *Ú-ta-an-til* (*JEN* 538:15) demonstrate the phonetic value, *uta*, for UD.

l. 36: [*-rù*]. Lacheman once saw this sign as fully preserved.

l. 37: [E]ME. This sign appears as: 

l. 37. One is tempted to restore *ù* ^{m}*Ar-te-šup* following the initial PN. There is certainly room for these signs. However, the singular verbs of lines 39 and 42 and the singular pronoun of line 40 militate against this restoration.

l. 38: *ši-*[*bu-ti*]. IGI.[MEŠ] is also possible. *ki-*(*a-*)*am* or *ki-na-an-na* need not follow. Cf. a parallel context, *JEN* 338:24-26, written by the same scribe. Cf. also above, *JEN* 741:22-23.

l. 39: [*a*/*ni-ta-din*]. Or the like.

l. 43. Traces of seal impressions appear over the first and last parts of this line, contrary to what is indicated in the copy.

l. 46: ⸢x⸣. This trace, between the ends of lines 17 and 18, is clear. It appears to be part of a vertical wedge written on the right edge.

JEN 743

OBVERSE

1 •*ṭup-pí ma-ru-*[*ti*] *š*[*a* ^{m}*A-pa-ak-ké*]
2 DUMU *Pa-li-ya* *^{m}[*Te-ḫi-ip-til-la*]
3 DUMU *Pu-ḫi-še-en-ni* [*a-n*]*a ma-*•*r*[*u-ti i-te-pu-uš*]
4 [x?+]•1 ANŠE A.ŠÀ.MEŠ *i-na* ^{GIŠ}*ta-a-*[*ri* GAL]
5 [*š*]*a* É.GAL *i+na šu-pa-al* A[N.ZA.KÀR]
6 •[*š*]*a* ^{m}*A-ka*$_4$*-wa-til ù i-na* ⸢*x*⸣-[ ]
7 [AN.Z]A.KÀR *ša* ^{m}*Im-bi-li-šu* [*ù*?] KA[SKAL]
8 ⸢*ša*⸣ AN.ZA.KÀR UD-*ḫu-uš-še ši-ni-*[*šu*]
9 *ib-*•*tu*$_4$*-uq* ^{m}*A-pa-ak-ké* DUMU [*Pa-l*]*e-*•⸢*e*⸣
10 *a-na* ^{m}⸢*Te*⸣*-ḫi-ip-til-la* DUMU *Pu-*[*ḫi-še*]*-en-ni*
11 *ki-ma* ḪA.LA.MEŠ-*šú i-din* ⸢*ù*⸣ [^{m}*Te*]*-ḫi-ip-til-la*
12 1 GUD 10[+x? •U]DU.MEŠ *a-na* ^{m}*A-pa-*•*ak-*[*ké k*]*i-ma* NÍG.BA-*šu i-*[*din*]
13 *il-k*[*a*$_4$ •*š*]*a* A.ŠÀ.MEŠ ^{m}*A-pa-a*[*k-k*]*é-ma na-a-ši*
14 *šum-ma* ⸢A⸣.[ŠÀ.MEŠ?] *pa-qí-ra-*•⸢*na*⸣ •*ir-**[*t*]*a-ši*
15 ^{m}*A-pa-*[*ak-k*]*é* ⸢*ú*⸣*-za-*[*ak-ka*$_4$*-ma*]
16 *a-*⸢*na*⸣ ^{m}•*T*[*e-ḫ*]*i-*⸢*ip*⸣*-til-l*[*a i?-n*]*a?-*⸢*an?-din*⸣?
17 *šum-ma* ^{m}*⸢*A*⸣*-pa-ak-ké* •KI.[B]AL-*kat*
18 *aš-šum* A.[ŠÀ.M]EŠ *ša-a-šú* AŠ [EG]IR-*ki*

19 ^{m}*Te-ḫi-*•[*i*]*p-til-*[*l*]*a i-š*[*a-a*]*s-*•⸢*sí*⸣
20 [1? M]A.N[A K]Ù.[BABBAR] ⸢1⸣[+x?] MA.[N]A K[Ù?.SI]G$_{17}$?
21 [*a-na* ^{m}*T*]*e-*$^{+}$*ḫi-i*[*p*]*-t*[*il*]*-*•⸢*la*⸣ *ú-m*[*a-al-la*]
22 I[GI] ⸢*En*⸣*-n*[*a-m*]*a-ti* DUMU *En-*⸢*na-a-***a*⸣
23 IGI *Wa-a*[*n-ti*]*-*•*mu-ša* DUMU *Na-i*[*k-*•*k*]*é-*•*mar*
24 IGI *Ḫa-wi-*[*i*]*š-ta-e* DUMU *Na-an-te-*•*šu*[*p*]
25 IGI *I-lu-*[*u*]*ḫ-ḫa-a-a* DUMU *Na-ik-k*[*é*]*-mar*
26 IGI *A-t*[*a*]*-an-ḫi-lu* DUMU *Na-an-te-*•*šup*
27 5 ⸢LÚ⸣.[M]EŠ *an-nu-*•*tu*$_{4}$ $^{[LÚ].MEŠ}$*mu-še-*[*el*]*-*$^{+}$*mu-ú ša* A.Š[À.MEŠ?]
28 *ù na-di-na-nu* GUD ⸢*ù*⸣ UDU.MEŠ!

LOWER EDGE

29 IGI *Um-pí-ya* DUMU *T*[*e-e*]*š-šu-*•*ya*
30 IGI *Tar-mi-ya* DUMU *Ma-ša-an-te*
31 [I]GI *Pa-a-a* DUMU *Ak-ku*$_{8}$*-ya*

REVERSE

32 IGI *Na-an-te-e* DUMU *Ḫu-ti*$_{4}$*-ya*
33 IGI $^{[d]}$*Iškur*!*-an-dùl* DUMU ^{d}XXX*-né-e* DUB.SAR
34 IGI *T*[*ar*]*-mi-ya* DUMU *A-be-*•*e*
35 IGI $^{+}$⸢X⸣-[ ]-•⸢*x*⸣ DUMU *A-tá-a-a*

S.I. Po 958

36 $^{N[A_4]}$ $^{+}$KIŠIB ^{m}*En-na-ma-ti* DUMU •⸢*En*⸣*-*[*n*]*a-*•*a-*•⸢*a*⸣

S.I.

37 ^{NA_4} KIŠIB $^{m•}$⸢*Wa*⸣*-an-t*[*i*]*-*⸢*mu-ša*⸣ [DUMU *Na-ik*]*-*⸢*ké*⸣*-*[*mar*]

S.I. Po 424

38 ^{NA_4} KIŠIB [^{m}*P*]*a-a-a* [DUMU *A*]*k-*[*ku*$_{8}$*-y*]*a*

S.I. Po 383

39 ^{NA_4} [KIŠI]B ^{m}*I-lu-uḫ-ḫ*[*a-a-a* DUMU] *N*[*a-ik-ké-mar*]

S.I. Po 141

40 ^{NA_4} K[IŠIB] ^{m}*Tar-mi-ya* DUMU *Ma-ša-a*[*n-te*]

UPPER EDGE

S.I.

41 ^{NA_4} KIŠIB $^{m•}$IM?-[ ]

LEFT EDGE

42 S.I. [^{NA_4} K]IŠIB ^{m}*Um-pí-ya*
43 $^{+NA_4}$ $^{+}$KIŠIB $^{md+}$⸢*Iškur*⸣*-*$^{+}$*an-dùl* DUB.SAR S.I. Po 477

TRANSLATION

(1-3) Tablet of adoption of [Apakke] son of Paliya. He adopted [Teḫip-tilla] son of Puḫi-šenni.

(4-11) Apakke son of Paliya gave to Teḫip-tilla son of Puḫi-šenni as his inheritance share a field, x(?)+1 homer(s) by the [large] standard of the palace, to the west of the *dimtu* of Akawatil and to the s[outh?]/n[orth?]/

e[ast?] of the *dimtu* of Inb-ilišu; the road to the *dimtu* of UD-ḫušše divides (lit. "divided") (the field) in two.

(11-12) And Teḫip-tilla gave to Apakke as his gift 1 ox (and) 10+x(?) sheep.

(13) And Apakke shall bear the *ilku* of the field.

(14-16) Should the field have claimants, Apakke shall clear (it) [and] give (it) to Teḫip-tilla.

(17-21) Should Apakke abrogate (this contract)—(should) he hail Teḫip-tilla (into court) over that field—he shall pay [to] Teḫip-tilla [1+x?] mina(s) of silver (and) 1 [+x?] mina(s) of gold ...?.

(22-35) Before Enna-mati son of Ennaya; before Wanti-muša son of Naik-kemar; before Ḫawiš-tae son of Nan-tešup; before Iluḫḫaya son of Naik-kemar; before Âtanaḫ-ilu son of Nan-tešup. These 5 men are the measurers of the field and givers of the ox and sheep. Before Umpiya son of Teššuya; before Tarmiya son of Mašante; before Paya son of Akkuya; before Nan-teya son of Ḫutiya; before Iškur-andul son of Ziniya, the scribe; before Tarmiya son of Abeya; before ... son of Ataya.

(36-43) (*seal impression*) seal impression of Enna-mati son of Ennaya; (*seal impression*) seal impression of Wanti-muša [son of] Naik-kemar; (*seal impression*) seal impression of Paya [son of] Akkuya; (*seal impression*) seal impression of Iluḫḫaya [son of] Naik-kemar; (*seal impression*) seal impression of Tarmiya son of Mašante; (*seal impression*) seal impression of IM(?)-...; (*seal impression*) seal impression of Iškur-andul, the scribe; seal impression of Umpiya (*seal impression*).

COMMENTS

This tablet has suffered considerable additional damage since the copy was made.

In the copy, the left edge is shown after the upper edge. The writing on line 43 faces the obverse, that on line 42 away from the obverse.

The *CAD* Nuzi file for this text was composed by Lacheman. References to the file in the following lines represent contributions by Lacheman.

NOTES

l. 1: [*ti*] *š*[*a*]. The *CAD* Nuzi file sees these signs as completely preserved.

l. 3: [*a-n*]*a*. The *CAD* Nuzi file sees these signs as completely preserved.

l. 3: [*i-te-pu-uš*]. For this restoration, cf. *JEN* 772:2. *JEN* 772 is relevant to *JEN* 743 because the same scribe wrote both and because the witnesses to these two texts are mostly the same. The two texts constitute a cluster. Therefore, restorations in each may be attempted by appeal to parallel passages in the other. See further, below, comments to *JEN* 772. On other texts whose witnesses overlap somewhat those of *JEN* 743, see above,

first note to *JEN* 741:28. Cf. also below, note to *JEN* 761:8 for connections between *JEN* 743 and *JEN* 761.

l. 4: [x?+]1. The *CAD* Nuzi file sees no lacuna at the start of this line. At present, the left margin of this line, including the lower half of the vertical shown in the copy, is broken away.

l. 4: *ta-a-*[*ri*]. For this reconstruction, see above, note to *JEN* 702:6.

l. 6: ⸢*x*⸣-[ ]. The lacuna certainly contains a direction other than west. *s*[*ú-ta-an*], *i*[*l-ta-na-an*], or ⸢*e*⸣*-le-en* (at least) could account for these traces.

l. 8: UD-*ḫu-uš-še*. The first sign is correct as copied. It is tempting to read *Ip*!-*ḫu-uš-še* since the resulting *dimtu* designation is elsewhere well attested. See *JEN* 1:4; 392:3, 19; *HSS*, IX, 104:5; 107:7.

However, *JEN* 392:3-5 suggests (albeit not clearly) a Nuzi locus for that *dimtu*. (Also, the ceder of land in *JEN* 1 has Nuzi interests elsewhere; see *JEN* 258.) Cf., moreover, *HSS*, IX, 107:7, where the town of Puḫi-šenni seems linked to the *dimtu* of Ipḫušše. In the present text, the land is probably located not too far from Unap-še. Cf., e.g., lines 5-6 with *JEN* 709:7-8.

There are three ways out of this dilemma of a wandering *dimtu*, none wholly satisfactory.

First, *ipḫušše* is not a GN, but a descriptive term applicable to more than one *dimtu*. This idea is assumed in *CAD*, D, 146b *sub dimtu* 3. b). Note also that most *dimtu* names are PNs. "Ipḫušše" nowhere appears as a PN. Although this solution would remove the problem of multiple locations for a single toponym, it introduces another difficulty. The use of a term applicable to more than one *dimtu* when describing in a written contract the location of land would appear to inject unnecessary ambiguity where clarity is most desired.

The second solution is that more than one *dimtu* bears the name, Ipḫušše. At least one other name is used for more than one *dimtu*, that of "Teḫip-tilla." See above, note to *JEN* 717:4-5. However, as noted above, "Ipḫušše"—unlike "Teḫip-tilla"—nowhere appears as a PN. Furthermore, as a general dictum, one should avoid the multiplication, without clear evidence, of places bearing the same GN. Clear evidence is wanting in this case.

The third possibility is that, in this Unap-še text, we are dealing with a *dimtu* of *Ut*ḫušše (or *Tam*ḫušše), as written. This solution has the virtues of retaining the text as written and removing the "Ipḫušše" problem from consideration at this point altogether. The difficulty with this solution is that it introduces a *dimtu* name which, until recently, was nowhere else attested, and which remains unattested in texts from Nuzi itself. It is, of course, also a name suspiciously close to "Ipḫušše," well attested itself, as already noted, as a *dimtu* designation.

A *dimtu* of UD-*ḫu-uš-še is* mentioned in three texts from Kurruḫanni. Two are published in al-Rawi (1977). They are IM 70782 (TF_1-136):4 (…

AN.ZA.KÀR UD-*ḫu-uš-še* ...), 8 (... AN.ZA.KÀR UD-*ḫu-uš-še*) (pp. 181-82 [transliteration], 445 [copy]); and IM 73237 (TF_1-511):17 (...AN.ZA.KÀR UD-*ḫu-uš-še*) (p. 467 [copy]; incidentally, this document is remarkable: it appears to record a series of depositions preparatory to a criminal trial). The third is published in Brinkman and Donbaz (1977, 99-104 + 3 pll.); l. 8 (... [A]N.ZA.KÀR UD-*ḫu-uš-še*). K. Deller and B. Eichler *apud* Brinkman and Donbaz (1977, 102) already associated that GN with *JEN* 743:8. Cf. the juxtaposition of all these texts already in Fadhil (1983, 292b-293a; cf. 343a).

Thus, one cannot doubt that a *dimtu* is called UD-*ḫu-uš-še*. However, the problem of this passage remains unresolved. The *dimtu* named in these Kurruḫanni texts can hardly be associated with the *dimtu* in the vicinity of Unap-še. Unap-še, I believe, is not even mentioned in the texts from Kurruḫanni. With these attestations of this GN, we are also thrown back onto a problem noted above: a single designation appears to identify two discrete places, albeit not in the same corpus of texts.

I read here UD-*ḫu-uš-še* because that is what the tablet reads.

ll. 12-13. The *CAD* Nuzi file records both these lines as wholly preserved. According to the file, no sign intervenes between "10" and UDU (l. 12).

l. 14: ⸢A⸣.[ŠÀ.MEŠ?]. The *CAD* Nuzi file records these three signs as wholly preserved.

ll. 17-20. In this fragmented text, the signs at the ends of these lines are lower than the beginnings of these lines.

l. 18: [EG]IR-*ki*. In the copy, there appear, between these two signs, two short parallel lines. These lines do not appear on the tablet. The tablet is satisfactorily preserved at this point.

l. 20: [K]Ù.[BABBAR]. Toward the start of this line, what appears in the copy as [KÙ.SI]G_{17} is actually:

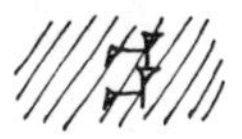

That this represents [K]Ù.[BABBAR] and not [K]Ù.[SIG_{17}] follows from the formula that this scribe employs elsewhere. Cf., for example, *JEN* 38:23; 702:21.

l. 22: ⸢*En*⸣. The one surviving vertical head of this sign is separated from the rest of the sign because of the angle of the join.

l. 22: *ti*. This sign appears rather more typical than depicted in the copy.

l. 22: ⸢*a-a*⸣. One of these signs is now totally effaced. It is not clear which.

l. 24: *Ḫa-wi-*[*i*]*š-ta-e*. The reading of this PN in *JEN* 772:30 points decidedly to the reading adopted here. See below, note to *JEN* 772:30.

NPN, 59b *sub* ḪAWUR-TAE? 1), 104a *sub* NAN-TEŠUP 8), suggests *Ḫa-wu-*[*u*]*r?-ta-e*. Lacheman once proposed *Ḫa-ši!-*[*i*]*p-ta-e*.

l. 28. As indicated in the copy, the signs of this line are smaller and more cramped than those of the neighboring lines.

l. 28: MEŠ!. This sign has but one *Winkelhaken*, not two as depicted. The tablet is clearly preserved at this point.

l. 32. This line begins the reverse.

l. 35: ⸢X⸣-[ ]-⸢x⸣. Between IGI and DUMU appear only the following traces:

See also below, note to line 41.

l. 36: KIŠIB. This sign appears on an unnumbered chip now joined to the tablet.

l. 41. This sealer may be the witness identified in line 35.

l. 42. Seal impression Po 477, associated with Umpiya, has the same orientation as the signs of line 42, not as shown in the copy.

l. 43: ⸢*Iškur*⸣-*an*. The first sign and the start of the second appear on an unnumbered chip now joined to the tablet. ⸢*Iškur*⸣ appears as: 

JEN 744

OBVERSE

+1 [*ṭup-pí ma-r*]*u-ti ša* [^{m}*Ni-íḫ-ri-ya*]
+2 [DUMU] ⸢*E*⸣-[*na*]-*a-a* ^{m}⸢*Te*⸣-[*ḫi-ip-til-la*]
+3 [DUM]U ⸢*Pu*⸣-[*ḫi-še-en*]-⸢*ni*⸣ [*a-na ma-ru-ti* DÙ-*ma*]
4 [ ] +⸢ANŠE⸣ 3 ⸢^{GIŠ}APIN A.ŠÀ.MEŠ x⸣ [(?)]
5 [*i*]-*na e-le-en* AN.•⸢ZA⸣.KÀR *š*[*a*]
6 *ù i-na il-ta-•na-an* ⸢*x*⸣[ ]
7 [*a-š*]*ar* AN.ZA.KÀR *ša Ú-lu-*⸢*li*⸣-[*ya*]
8 *ki-•mu* ḪA.LA.MEŠ-*šu* ^{m}*N*[*i-íḫ*]-*r*[*i-ya*]
9 DUMU [*E-n*]*a-a-a a-na* ^{m}*Te-ḫi-•*⸢*ip*⸣-[*til-la*]
10 DUMU [*Pu-ḫi*]-⸢*še*⸣-*en-ni* SUM-*nu ù* ^{m}*T*[*e-ḫi-ip-til-la*]
11 1[+x? x?+]2 TÚG.ḪÁ.MEŠ 15 MA.NA URUDU.M[EŠ]
12 *ki-mu* NÍG.BA.MEŠ-*šu a-na* ^{m}*Ni-íḫ-•ri-y*[*a*]
13 DUMU *E-na-a-a* SUM-*nu šum-ma* A.ŠÀ.ME[Š]
14 *pí-ir-qa ir-ta-ši* ^{m}*Ni-íḫ-ri-ya*
15 *ú-za-ak-*ka_4*-ma a-na* ^{m}*Te-ḫi-ip-t*[*il*]-•*la* SUM-*nu*
16 ⸢*ù*⸣ *il-ka ša* A.ŠÀ.MEŠ-*ti*
17 [^{m}]*Ni-íḫ-ri-ya-ma na-a-ši*
18 [*š*]*um-ma* ^{m}*Ni-íḫ-ri-ya* KI.BAL-[*at*]
19 [*šu*]*m-ma aš-šum* A.ŠÀ.MEŠ *i+na* EGIR-[*ki*]
20 [^{m}*T*]*e-ḫi-ip-til-la i-ša-as-s*[*í*]
21 [2 M]A.⸢NA⸣ KÙ.BABBAR 2 MA.⸢NA KÙ⸣.[SIG_{17}]

22 [a-na] ^{m}Te-ḫi-˹ip˺-[til-la ú-ma-al-la]

.

.

.

REVERSE

.

.

.

23 IGI ˹Ḫu˺?-[lu?-uk?-ka$_4$? DUMU Ar?-te?-šup?]

24 IGI A-t[a]-˹na-aḫ$_4$-DINGIR DUMU˺ [Na-al-te-šup]

25 IGI Tar!-˹mi˺-ya DUMU A-be-ya

26 •IGI E-•ni-iš-ta-e DUMU A-a-ba-[aš]

27 [4 $^{LÚ.MEŠ}$]*ši-*bu-tu$_4$ mu-še-él-m[u ša A.ŠÀ.MEŠ]

28 [IGI Te-ḫ]i-ip-a-pu DUMU Ni-íḫ-ri-y[a]

29 [IGI *U]m-•pí-ya DUMU Te-eš-šu-ya

30 [IGI I]t-ḫi-iš-ta DUMU A-ar-ta-˹e˺

31 [IGI Ḫa]-na-ak-ka$_4$ DUMU Še-ka$_4$-rù

32 [IGI Ut]-ḫa-ap-ta-e DUMU Zi-ké

33 [IGI]-•še?-ke-er-ri-ya DUMU Pu-ḫi-š[e-en-ni]

34 [IGI]-ka$_4$-[z]i-•ya DUMU DINGIR-˹ya˺

35 [IGI]-pí-•˹ya˺ •DUMU •˹A˺-be-˹ya˺

36 [IGI] Uk-ka$_4$-a-a D[UMU]˹x x˺[ ]

37 [IGI] DINGIR-ya DUB.S[AR-rù]

+38 [^{NA_4} KIŠIB ^{m}]-˹x˺

S.I.

39 ^{NA_4} KIŠIB $^{[m]}$+It-[ḫi]-+˹iš˺-[ta]

+S.I.

UPPER EDGE

+S.I.?

+40 [^{NA_4} KIŠI]B ^{m}˹Te?-ḫi?-ip?-a˺?-[pu?]

LEFT EDGE

+S.I.

+41 [^{NA_4} KIŠIB ^{m}DINGIR-ya D]UB.SAR-rù

TRANSLATION

(1-3) [Tablet of] adoption of [Niḫriya son of] Ennaya. [He adopted] Teḫip-tilla son of Puḫi-šenni.

(4-10) Niḫriya son of Ennaya gave to Teḫip-tilla son of Puḫi-šenni as his inheritance share a(n) x.3 homer … field, to the east of the *dimtu* of … and to the north … where the *dimtu* of Ulūliya is.

(10-13) And Teḫip-tilla gave to Niḫriya son of Ennaya as his gift 1+x(?) … , x(?)+2 garments, (and) 15 minas of copper.

(13-15) Should the field have a claim (against it), Niḫriya shall clear (the field) and give (it) to Teḫip-tilla.

(16-17) And it is Niḫriya who shall bear the *ilku* of the field.

(18-22) Should Niḫriya abrogate (this contract)—should he hail Teḫip-tilla (into court) over the field—[he shall pay to] Teḫip-tilla [2] minas of silver (and) 2 minas of gold.

....

(23-37) Before Ḫulukka(?) [son of Ar-tešup?]; before Âtanaḫ-ilu son of [Nan-tešup]; before Tarmiya son of Abeya; before Eniš-tae son of Ay-abâš. (These) [4] witnesses are the measurers [of the field]. [Before] Teḫip-apu son of Niḫriya; [before] Umpiya son of Teššuya; [before] Itḫišta son of Ar-tae; [before] Ḫanakka son of Šekaru; [before] Utḫap-tae son of Zike; [before] ...-še(?)-kerriya son of Puḫi-šenni; [before] ...-kaziya son of Iluya; [before] ...-piya son of Abeya; [before] Ukkaya son of ...; [before] Iluya, the scribe.

(38-41) [seal impression of] ... (*seal impression*); seal impression of Itḫišta (*seal impression*); (*seal impression*?) seal impression of Teḫip-apu(?); (*seal impression*) [seal impression of Iluya], the scribe.

COMMENTS

This tablet has suffered some additional damage since it was copied. Parts of the tablet are lightly coated with a glue-like substance rendering these parts more difficult to decipher. This encrustation is most apparent on the reverse.

Since the copy was completed, joins to the tablet of one fragment and two chips have been made. These have contributed the first three lines of the text, part of the fourth, line 38, part of line 39, the last seal impression on the reverse, and all the text and impressions of the upper and left edges. These additions are indicated in the transliteration. Collectively, they appear as:

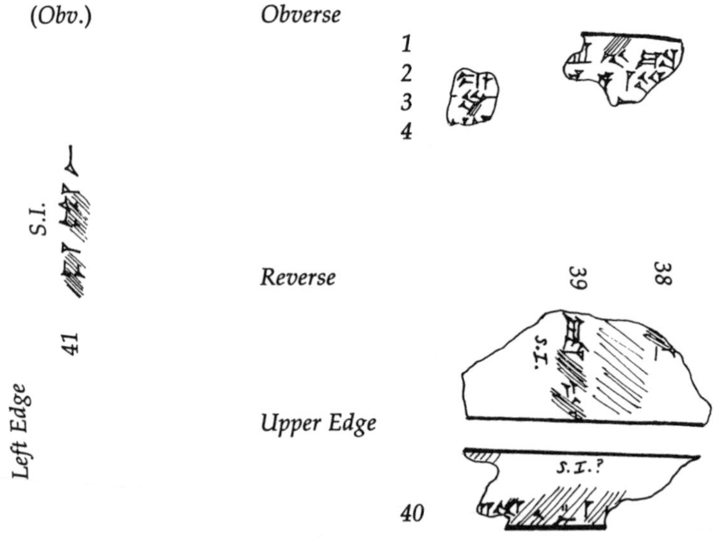

Restorations in *JEN* 744, including names of witnesses, are undertaken by appeal to parallel passages in *JEN* 741. For the relationship of these two texts, see above, first note to *JEN* 741:28.

In this connection, the end of the obverse and the start of the reverse of *JEN* 744, now missing, may have contained a declaration by the adopter. Cf. *JEN* 741:21-26.

NOTES

l. 4: ⌜ANŠE⌝. The sign does not appear as depicted (i.e., as TAB). Rather, the traces derived from both the tablet and a recently effected join (see above, comments) appear as: 

l. 4: ⌜x⌝ [(?)]. The end of line 4 might well have contained a formula describing the standard of measurement used. Cf. *JEN* 741:4.

l. 5: *š*[*a*]. The *dimtu* of Akawatil is a plausible restoration here since Niḫriya elsewhere cedes (with another adopter) to Teḫip-tilla land east of this *dimtu*. See *JEN* 38, especially line 6. However, the *dimtu* of Umpin-api also qualifies since Niḫriya is involved in ceding to Teḫip-tilla land east of this *dimtu* as well. See *JEN* 703, especially lines 11-12.

l. 13: ME[Š]. This sign is a normal MEŠ with the third *Winkelhaken* effaced. It is not BI as copied.

l. 23. For the basis of this restoration and the ones that follow (except in line 33), see above, comments. The restoration of this particular line is grounded in an indistinct trace. Its identification as ḪU is not compelling.

l. 33. Lacheman reads the former PN, [Z]*i-ki-ir-ri-ya*. Regarding the patronymic, no other restoration seems possible.

l. 35: [ ]-*pí*-⌜*ya*⌝. Lacheman reads here: *A-kà-a-a*.

l. 36: ⌜x x⌝. The second of these traces appears, not as copied, but, rather, as:

l. 38. Porada identifies the sealing associated with this line as that of Itḫišta son of Ar-tae. Cf. line 27.

JEN 745

OBVERSE

1 [ṭup]-*pí *ma-*⌜ru⌝-*t[i] *š[a $^{m•}$E]ḫ-•li-i[p-LUGAL]
2 [DUMU] *Tu-*ur-*ru *$^{m•}$Te-•ḫi-ip-til-•l[a DUMU Pu-ḫi-*š]e-*en-*ni
3 *⌜a-*na⌝ *ma-*ru-•ti •i-•pu-•us-•sú
4 *1 *ANŠE •6 a-wi-•ḫa-*ri *A.*ŠÀ
5 [i-na] *le-*et *AN.ZA.*KÀR •⌜ša⌝ •^{m}*[T]e-*ḫi-*i[p-til-*l]a
6 $^{[m]}$*⌜Eḫ⌝-•li-ip-•LUGAL
7 [a-na ^{m}*T]e-*ḫi-•ip-til-•la •ki-*ma •ḪA.•LA-šu
8 [id]-*dì-na-aš-•šu
9 [ù ^{m}*T]e-ḫi-•ip-til-la
10 [ki-ma NÍG.BA-šu] •12 ANŠE ŠE.MEŠ
11 *i[d-dì-n]a?-[aš-šu]
12 ma-a[n-nu] ⌜ša⌝ B[AL i?-na? bi$_{4}$?-r]i?-šu!?-[nu?]
13 1 M[A.NA KÙ.BABBAR 1 MA.NA KÙ.SIG$_{17}$ i-na-an]-⌜din⌝?
14 [šum-ma A.ŠÀ pa-q]í-ra-n[a]
15 [ir-ta-ši ^{m}Eḫ]-⌜li⌝-[i]p-LU[GAL]!

.

.

.

REVERSE

.

.

.

16 [IGI? Mu?-u]š?-⌜te⌝?-š[up? DUMU? Ar?-na?-(a?-)pu?]
17 [IGI] *⌜Pí-•ru⌝ DUMU •Na-•⌜iš-*ke-*el⌝-pé
18 [IGI] ⌜Ḫa⌝-•ma-an-na DUMU •Ar-•ša-•an-t[a]
19 [IGI] ⌜It⌝-ḫi-iš-ta DUMU A-•ar-•ta-e
20 $^{+}$IGI Ik!-ki-ya •DUMU •A-•dá-še-mi
21 $^{+}$IGI Ḫu-lu-uk-ka$_{4}$ •DUM[U *K]u-šu-⌜ḫa⌝-tal
22 $^{+}$[I]GI Ḫe-ša-al-la D[UMU Zu]-⌜ú⌝-me
23 [IG]I Ḫa-ma-[a]n-na DUMU [DUMU-^{UD}X]X$^{KA[M]}$
24 [IGI] ⌜A-ri⌝-ku-šu •DUMU ⌜X⌝-pí-še-•en-•ni
25 [IGI •A]r-te-šup *DU[MU Ta-a]-⌜a⌝ DUB.•SAR
26 [IGI T]a-a-$^{+}$a-ú-kí •DUMU *⌜X⌝-[ ]
27 [^{NA_4} KIŠIB ^{m}]*⌜It?-*ḫi?-*iš?-*ta⌝?
28 [DUMU? A?]-*⌜ar?-*ta⌝?-[e?]

[S.I.]

29 ^{NA_4} KIŠIB $^{m•}$Ar-*T[e-šup DUMU Ta-a-a DUB.SAR]

S.I. Po 107

TRANSLATION

(1-3) Tablet of adoption of Elḫip-šarri [son of] Turru. He adopted Teḫip-tilla [son of] Puḫi-šenni.

(4-8) Elḫip-šarri gave [to] Teḫip-tilla as his inheritance share a 1.6 homer field adjacent to the *dimtu* of Teḫip-tilla.

(9-11) [And] Teḫip-tilla gave [to him as his gift] 12 homers of barley.

(12-13) Whoever between(?) them(?) abrogates (this contract) shall give(?) 1 mina [of silver (and) 1 mina of gold].

(14-15) [Should the field have] claimants, Elḫip-šarri ....

....

(16-26) [Before?] Muš-tešup(?) [son? of? Arn-apu?]; [before] Piru son of Naiš-kelpe; [before] Ḫamanna son of Ar-šanta; [before] Itḫišta son of Ar-tae; before Ikkiya son of Adad-šēmī; before Ḫulukka son of Kušuḫ-atal; before Ḫešalla son of Zume; before Ḫamanna son of Mâr-ešrī; [before] Arik-kušuḫ son of ...-pi-šenni; [before] Ar-tešup son of Taya, the scribe; [before] Tayuki son of ... .

(27-29) [seal impression of] Itḫišta(?) [son? of?] Ar-tae(?) [(*seal impression*)]; seal impression of Ar-tešup [son of Taya, the scribe] (*seal impression*).

COMMENTS

This tablet is in a wretched state of preservation. Most of the obverse is now destroyed; mere patches of surface remain. When the copy was made, the tablet was obviously in much better shape. Moreover, the *CAD* Nuzi file demonstrates that, while in Chicago, the tablet was once in significantly better condition than when Lacheman made his copy. For example, the *CAD* Nuzi file records lines 2, 5, 7-9, 11, 18-19 as being wholly preserved. Other examples of a fuller text recorded in the *CAD* Nuzi file are given below, notes to lines 10, 12, 13, 24, 25, 29. The copy does not reflect this fuller text. Significant content is gained by appeal to the file—more so, perhaps, than in any other instance in *THNT*. The state of this tablet has thus passed through three recorded stages in the last five or six decades, the latter two stages showing progressive deterioration. On the other hand, since the time of Lacheman's original copy, three chips containing text have been glued back onto the surface. These have yielded the signs in the middle of lines 11-12 (one chip) and the first sign (i.e., IGI) in each of lines 20-22 (two chips).

NOTES

ll. 1-2: [*E*]*ḫ-li-i*[*p*-LUGAL] // [DUMU] *Tu-ur-ru*. For the first PN, cf. l. 6. The restoration of the first name and the correctness of the patronymic are confirmed by *JEN* 641:1. *JEN* 641 is a list and the first entry in that list almost certainly is based on the present text. In both instances, 1.6 homers of land (for this figure, see below, next note) in the same area

of Zizza is ceded to Teḫip-tilla. The *dimti piršanni* (*JEN* 641:31) and the *dimtu* of Teḫip-tilla (*JEN* 745:5) refer to the same district. On this issue, see the reference given above, note to *JEN* 692:5-6.

l. 4: 1. Both the *CAD* Nuzi file and Lacheman note that this vertical begins line 4; that is, no number has been lost. See also above, immediately preceding note.

l. 5: ⸢*ša*⸣ m. These signs are visible only as vague impressions beneath the surface of the tablet.

l. 10: [NÍG.BA-*šu*] 12. The *CAD* Nuzi file records these signs as completely preserved; no wedge intervenes between ŠU and the *Winkelhaken* of "12."

l. 12: *ma-a*[*n-nu*] ⸢*ša*⸣ B[AL]. The *CAD* Nuzi file records these signs as wholly preserved.

l. 13: 1 M[A.NA KÙ.BABBAR 1 MA.NA KÙ.SIG$_{17}$]. The *CAD* Nuzi file records these signs as completely preserved.

ll. 14-15. The rest of the clear title clause will have appeared after line 15 and would have read approximately as follows: *ú-za-ak-ka*$_4$*-ma a-na* m*Te-ḫi-ip-til-la i-na-an-din*.

l. 15: [*ir-ta-ši*]. Or the like.

l. 16. This most tentative restoration is based on the presence of this individual in *approximately* this position in parallel texts. See, for example, *JEN* 217:15; 778:11.

l. 24: [IGI]. The *CAD* Nuzi file records this sign as completely preserved.

l. 24 ⸢X⸣. Lacheman suggests, in effect: [*Tú*]*l*. [*Ḫu-u*]*r* is also possible.

l. 25: [IGI *A*]*r*. The *CAD* Nuzi file records these signs as entirely preserved.

l. 25: [*Ta-a*]-⸢*a*⸣. For this restoration, see the next note.

l. 29. The *CAD* Nuzi file records the first PN as entirely preserved. Lacheman agrees and sees part of DUMU as well. Porada (1947, 127b *ad* no. 107) identifies the seal impression associated with this line as that of Artešup son of Taya. The identification is based on the presence of the same impression in another text.

JEN 746

OBVERSE

1 $^{[m]}$W[a-an-ti-iš-še] DUMU Tù-ra-[r]i
2 ša [^{m}Eḫ-]-⸢x⸣-še-li DUMU A-ri-kùr-ri
3 ⸢ša⸣ ^{m}[Ḫa-šu-ma-tal DUMU A-r]i-kùr-ri-ma
4 ù š[a ^{m}Ta-e?]
5 ⸢DUMU X⸣-[ ]-⸢x⸣ 4 LÚ.MEŠ an-nu-ti ŠEŠ.MEŠ
6 [^{m}Te-ḫ]i-ip-til-l[a DUMU Pu-ḫ]i-•še-ni
7 [a-na] ma-ru-ti i-[t]e-ep-šu-šu-ma
8 [1? A]NŠE A.ŠÀ i+na URU Nu-zi
9 [AŠ *A]N.ZA!.⸢KÀR⸣ Šu-ma-ša-wa-al-⸢ḫi⸣
10 [ ]•⸢x ša⸣ AN.ZA.KÀR ša ^{m}⸢Zi⸣?-[ ]
11 [ki]-*m[a] ḪA.⸢LA-šu⸣ a-na ^{m}Te-ḫi-i[p-til-la]
12 [•i]t-⸢ta-ad⸣-n[u] ⸢ù⸣ [^{m}T]e-ḫi-ip-[til-la]
13 [a-na] ^{m}Wa-an-ti-⸢iš⸣-še ^{m}Eḫ-[-x-še-li]
14 [a-na] •^{m}Ḫa-šu-ma-tal ù a-na ^{m}•Ta-•⸢e⸣?
15 [+]•8 ANŠE ŠE.MEŠ ki-ma NÍG.BA-šu-nu
16 [i]t-•ta-din šum-ma A.ŠÀ an-nu-um
17 [di]-na TUK-ši ú-za-ku-ma
18 [a-n]a ^{m}Te-ḫi-ip-til-la i-na-an!-[din]

LOWER EDGE

19 [šum]-ma 4 ŠEŠ.⸢MEŠ an⸣-nu-ti
20 [K]I.BAL-tù ⸢2⸣ MA.NA

REVERSE

21 [K]Ù.BABBAR 2 MA.NA KÙ.SIG$_{17}$
22 ⸢a⸣-+na ^{m}Te-ḫi-ip-til-la ú-ma-a[l-lu-ú]
23 ù re-eḫ-ti A.ŠÀ.MEŠ-šu-<nu?> ki-mu-ú IR BE ŠI
24 ša ^{m}⸢Ke-el⸣-[ ]
25 IGI ⸢Ni⸣-nu-a-ta[l DUMU A]r-•⸢ša⸣-w[u]-uš-ka$_{4}$
26 [IGI] Ta-a-a DUMU A-rip-LUGAL
27 IGI Mu-uš-te-ya DUMU Ar-še-ni
28 IGI Šum-mi-ya DUMU A-[r]i-ka$_{4}$-na-[ri]
29 IGI Ḫa-⸢x-x DUMU⸣? [ ]
30 IGI Pí-ru [DUMU N]a-[i]š-[k]é-[el-pè]
31 IGI Mu-uš-te-šup DU[MU] Ar-[na-pu]
32 [1+]•6 LÚ.MEŠ an-nu-ti [m]u-še-el-[mu-ú]
33 [š]a +A.+ŠÀ IGI Ú-ku-⸢ya⸣ DUMU Šu-pa-a-[a]
34 IGI A[r-š]a-tù-⸢ya⸣ DUMU Še-⸢la⸣-pa-⸢i⸣
35 IGI Ta-⸢a⸣-[a DUB].SAR-rù

S.I. Po 314

36 ^{NA_4} KIŠIB $^{m+}$Mu-⸢uš-•te⸣-šup

37 DUMU •[*A*]*r-na-pu*

.

.

.

LEFT EDGE

S.I.

38 [^{NA_4} KIŠIB ^{m}*Ta*]-⌜*a*⌝-*a* DUB.S[AR]

TRANSLATION

....

(1-7) Wantiš-še son of Turari, of Eḫ-...-šeli son of Ari-kurri, of [Ḫašum-atal], also [son of] Ari-kurri, and of [Tae?] son of ... . These 4 men, brothers, adopted Teḫip-tilla [son of] Puḫi-šenni.

(8-12) They gave to Teḫip-tilla as his inheritance share a [1?] homer field in the town of Nuzi [in] the *dimtu* of Šumaššawalli, ... of the *dimtu* of Zi(?)-... .

(12-16) And Teḫip-tilla gave [to] Wantiš-še, Eḫ-...-šeli, [to] Ḫašum-atal, and to Tae(?) as their gift x+8 homers of barley.

(16-18) Should this field have a case (against it), then they shall clear (the field) and give (it) to Teḫip-tilla.

(19-22) Should these four brothers abrogate (this contract), they shall pay to Teḫip-tilla 2 minas of silver (and) 2 minas of gold.

(23-24) And the rest of his (or: th<eir>) land (remains) as a ... of/for Kel-... .

(25-35) Before Ninu-atal [son of] Ar-šawuška; [before] Taya son of Arip-šarri; before Muš-teya son of Ar-šenni; before Šummiya son of Arik-kanari; before Ḫa-... son(?) of(?) ...; before Piru [son of] Naiš-kelpe; before Muš-tešup son of Arn-apu. These [1+]6 men are the measurers of the field. Before Ukuya son of Šupaya; before Ar-šatuya son of Šellapai; before Taya, the scribe.

(36-38) (*seal impression*) seal impression of Muš-tešup son of Arn-apu; ....; (*seal impression*) seal impression of Taya, the scribe.

COMMENT

This tablet has suffered some additional deterioration since the copy was made.

The tablet is also missing its first line:

ṭup-pí ma-ru-ti ša.

Furthermore, another line appears to be missing. Lacheman notes text on the upper edge:

[ ]-*a-tal*

[ ]-ka_4

In accordance with line 25, this section should probably be restored:

[S.I.]

[^{NA_4} KIŠIB ^{m}*Ni-nu*]-*a-tal*
[DUMU *Ar-ša-wu-uš*]-ka_4

Again, these signs are no longer visible, nor do they appear in the copy.

NOTES

l. 1: $^{[m]}$. Lacheman records this sign as preserved.

l. 4: [^{m}*Ta-e*?]. For this PN, see below, note to line 14.

l. 5: ⌜X⌝. Lacheman sees this sign as A and identifies this patronymic with those of lines 2-3.

l. 6. The *CAD* Nuzi file records this line as completely preserved.

l. 8: [1?]. The proposed restoration is based on *JEN* 140:5. *JEN* 140 may very well be directly related to *JEN* 746. The plots of land appear to be described largely in the same way (cf. *JEN* 140:5-8 with *JEN* 746:8-10) and the recipient of the land there (*JEN* 140:9-10) is one of the ceders in the present instance (*JEN* 746:1). Both tablets stem from room 16 of the house of Teḫip-tilla.

l. 9. For the toponym mentioned in this line, see above, note to *JEN* 711:1. The sign before ⌜KÀR⌝ is a clear A, not ZA as copied. Although [*i-n*]*a* A.⌜GÀR⌝ yields good sense, nowhere else is this GN associated with an *ugāru*. It is elsewhere called a *dimtu*, e.g., *JEN* 140:6, a context already noted as pertinent to the present text. Therefore, the proposed reconstruction of this line is to be preferred.

The last sign is correct as copied.

l. 10: ⌜x⌝. Lacheman and the *CAD* Nuzi file saw, at one point, a completely preserved LI. Lacheman restored: [*i-na ti*]-*li*. Cf., perhaps, *JEN* 140:8. See also next note.

l. 10: ⌜*Zi*⌝?-[ ]. This sign seems to have been a clear ZI according to Lacheman and the *CAD* Nuzi file. It is for this reason that the interpretation, *Zi*, is adopted here, if only tentatively. In fact, a *dimtu* of Zike is attested in *JEN* 279:9. It is probably in the vicinity of the *dimtu* of Kip-tešup (*JEN* 279:5), itself located in Nuzi (see *JEN* 252:9-10). The real estate at issue here is also located in Nuzi (l. 8). At one point, Lacheman, in fact, restored the *dimtu* name here as, in effect: *Zi*-[*ké*]. Cf. also a *dimtu* of *Zi*-..., perhaps located in Nuzi, *JEN* 815:4, 14-15.

However, if the sign appeared decades ago as it appears now, then, in light of *JEN* 140:7, ⌜*A*⌝-*w*[*i-lu*] should probably be restored.

l. 11: -*i*[*p-til-la*]. The *CAD* Nuzi file records these signs as completely preserved.

l. 12. The *CAD* Nuzi file records this line as completely preserved.

l. 13: [*-še-li*]. Lacheman records these signs as completely preserved. The *CAD* Nuzi file notes that the latter sign is preserved.

l. 14: *Ta-*⸢*e*⸣?. Both Lacheman and the *CAD* Nuzi file suggest the PN be restored as: *Ta-*[*a*]*-a*. The spacing would favor the alternative adopted here.

ll. 23-24. The precise sense of these lines eludes me. One is tempted to see here a statement reserving the land remaining after the sale as a gift, possibly to serve as a dowry for a female relative. However, a series of textual difficulties arising from this interpretation cumulatively render this interpretation doubtful.

First, it is questionable that all four vendors are relatives of each other. They are certainly not all brothers. Their fraternity, asserted in lines 5 and 19, consists in their common status as vendors to Teḫip-Tilla, their newfound "son." Thus, the basic premise of the interpretation may be questioned. Next, if this obstacle could be overcome, one would expect A.ŠÀ.MEŠ-*šu-nu*, not A.ŠÀ.MEŠ-*šu*, to appear. To maintain the case, one has to assume a scribal omission of *-nu*. One might also question the presence of *ki-mu-ú* where this scribe elsewhere employs *ki-ma* in this text (ll. 11, 15). Then, one would have to interpret IR BE ŠI as: *ir-bi*$_4$*-ši*, "her gift." This would assume a most unusual context for *irbu* and a grammatical error, "*-ši*" for "*-ša*." Finally, the PN of line 24 appears to be preceded by a male, not female, determinative as would be expected. Together, all these objections seem decisive.

l. 25: [*A*]*r-*⸢*ša*⸣*-w*[*u*]*-uš-//ka*$_4$. The restoration of this PN follows Lacheman who saw these signs as completely preserved. Cf., above, comments, for further support for this restoration.

The assignment of some of these traces to line 25 rather than to line 24 is not self-evident. The appearance of QA below UŠ is also disquieting. If these signs belong to a single name, the scribe should have continued horizontally onto the right edge, as he did with line 23.

l. 27: *Mu*. This sign is typical, not as copied.

l. 29: *Ḫa*. This sign is typical, not A as copied.

l. 32: LÚ. This sign has two verticals, not three as copied.

l. 32: [*m*]*u*. Lacheman and the *CAD* Nuzi file record this sign as preserved.

JEN 747

OBVERSE

1 [*ṭup-p*]*í* •*ma-ru-ti ša* ^{m}⸢*I*⸣*-lu-*⸢*ya*⸣ $^{+}$DUMU *Ḫa-ma-at-ti-ir*
2 [^{m}*T*]*e-ḫi-ip-til-la* DUMU •*Pu-*[*ḫi-še-en-ni*]
3 [*a-n*]*a ma-ru-ti i-te-p*[*u-uš*(*-ma*)]
4 [*ma*]*-la* ^{GIŠ}APIN A.ŠÀ.MEŠ *pa-i-*⸢*ḫu* ***⸢*i*⸣*-*[*na*] *ṣé-ri-ti*^{MEŠ}
5 AŠ URU *Ú-na-ap-še-wa*
6 *i-na e-le-en* A.ŠÀ *ša* ^{m}⸢*Ar*⸣*-*[*te*]*-*•*šup* [DUMU] *Ip-ša-ḫa-lu*
7 ḪA.LA.MEŠ*-šu ša* ^{m}*I-lu-ya* DUM[U] *Ḫa-*[*ma*]*-a*[*t-t*]*i-ir*
8 *ki-mu* ḪA.LA.MEŠ*-*⸢*šu a-na*⸣ ^{m}*Te-ḫi-ip-til-la*
9 DUMU *Pu-ḫi-še-*[*e*]*n-ni i-*[*di*]*n*
10 *ù* ^{m}*Te-ḫi-ip-til-la* ⸢9⸣ [AN]ŠE ŠE.MEŠ *ki-mu* ⸢NÍG⸣.B[A].⸢MEŠ⸣*-šu*
11 *a-na* ^{m}⸢*I*⸣*-lu-y*[*a i-d*]*i*[*n i*]*l-*[*k*]*u-ú ša* A.Š[À]
12 ^{m}*I-lu-ya* [*na-*(*a-*)*ši*]
13 *šum-*⸢*ma*⸣ A.Š[À *pa-qí-r*]*a-na i-ra-aš-*[*ši*]
14 ^{m}*I-lu-*[*ya ú*]*-za-ak-ka*$_4$ *a-na* ^{m}*Te-ḫ*[*i-ip-til*]*-la*
15 *i-na-*⸢*an*⸣*-*[*din šum*]*-ma* ^{m}*I-lu-ya* KI.[B]AL
16 ⸢3 MA⸣.[N]A •KÙ.•BABBAR.*M[EŠ] 3 MA.NA KÙ.SIG$_{17}$.MEŠ
17 •*a-*•*n*[*a* ^{m}•*T*]*e-*•*ḫi-*•*ip-*[*ti*]*l-la ú-ma-al-l*[*a*]

---

18 IGI ⸢*A*⸣*-*[*ka*]*p-*•*ta-*•*e* DUMU *Ku-us-ki-pa*
19 IGI ⸢*Ú*⸣*-*•[*n*]*a-*•*áp-še-en-ni* DUMU *Ar-nu-ur-ḫe*
20 IGI *T*[*ar-mi*]*-ya* DUMU *Šur-ku*$_8$*-ma-tal*
21 IG[I *Ṣa-al*]*-mu* DUMU *A-a-ba-aš*
22 [IGI]*-i-qí-ša* DUMU *Na-*⸢x⸣*-*[ ]*-ya*
23 [(5) LÚ.ME]Š *an-nu-ti* [ ]⸢x⸣[(?)]

LOWER EDGE

24 [*mu-še*]*-*⸢*el*⸣*-mu ša* A.ŠÀ
25 IGI [*-t*]*e-*$^{+}$*šup* $^{+}$DUMU $^{+}$*A-*$^{+}$*ri-*$^{+}$*ik-*$^{+}$*ka*$_4$*-*$^{+}$*na-*$^{+}$*ri*
26 IGI ⸢X⸣*-*$^{+}$*li-*⸢*te*⸣?[-x? DUMU] •*Nu-ri-li-ya*

REVERSE

27 IGI *Na-ḫi-iš-še-*•*ya* *DUMU •*Ki-pè-er-ḫa*
28 IGI *Um-pí-ya* DUMU *Ki-*•*pè-*•*er-ḫa-ma*
29 IGI *Ak-ku-le-en-ni* DUMU *Zi-ka*$_4$*-a-a*
30 IGI *Ur-ḫi-ya* DUMU *Ke-li-ya* DUB.SAR
31 IGI *Ku*$_8$*-tùk-ka*$_4$ DUMU *I-ú-*•*uz*?*-*[z]*i*
32 IGI *E-mu-ya* DUMU *Ka*$_4$*-a-a*

S.I. Po 246

33 ^{NA_4} KIŠIB ^{m}*Na-ḫi-iš-še-*⸢*ya*⸣ [DUMU *Ki-pè-er-ḫa*]

S.I. Po 333

34 ^{NA_4} KIŠIB ^{m}*Tar-mi-*⸢*ya*⸣ [D]UMU *Šur-ku*$_8$*-*⸢*ma*⸣*-*[*tal*]

S.I. Po 138

35 ^{NA_4} KIŠIB ^{m}*Ú-náp-še-en-ni*
36 DUMU *Ar-nu-ur-ḫe*

UPPER EDGE

S.I. Po 192

37 [^{NA_4} KIŠIB ^{m}]•⌈*E*⌉*-mu-ya* DUMU *Ka*$_4$*-a-a*

LEFT EDGE

S.I. Po 39

38 ^{NA_4} K[IŠIB ^{m}]⌈*A*⌉*-kap-ta-e* D[UMU *K*]*u-us-ki-pa*

TRANSLATION

(1-3) Tablet of adoption of Iluya son of Ḫamattar. He adopted Teḫip-tilla son of Puḫi-šenni.

(4-9) Iluya son of Ḫamattar gave to Teḫip-tilla son of Puḫi-šenni as his inheritance share .1 homer (lit.: "a full *awiḫaru*") of *paiḫu*-land in the suburbs, in the town of Unap-še, to the east of the land of Ar-tešup [son of] Ipša-ḫalu, (this land constituting) the inheritance share of Iluya son of Ḫamattar (himself).

(10-11) And Teḫip-tilla gave to Iluya as his gift 9 homers of barley.

(11-12) Iluya [shall bear] the *ilku* of the land.

(13-15) Should the land have claimants, Iluya shall clear (it and) give (it) to Teḫip-tilla.

(15-17) Should Iluya abrogate (this contract), he shall pay to Teḫip-tilla 3 minas of silver (and) 3 minas of gold.

(18-32) Before Akap-tae son of Kuš-kipa; before Unap-šenni son of Arn-urḫe; before Tarmiya son of Šurkum-atal; before Ṣalmu son of Ay-abâš; before ...-iqîša son of Na-...-ya. These ...(?) [5] men are the measurers of the land. Before ...-tešup son of Arik-kanari; before ... [son of] Nûr-iliya; before Naḫiššeya son of Kip-erḫan; before Umpiya also son of Kip-erḫan; before Akkul-enni son of Zikaya; before Urḫiya son of Keliya, the scribe; before Kutukka son of Iuzzi; before Emuya son of Kaya.

(33-38) (*seal impression*) seal impression of Naḫiššeya [son of Kip-erḫan]; (*seal impression*) seal impression of Tarmiya son of Šurkum-atal; (*seal impression*) seal impression of Unap-šenni son of Arn-urḫe; (*seal impression*) [seal impression of] Emuya son of Kaya; (*seal impression*) seal impression of Akap-tae son of Kuš-kipa.

COMMENT

This tablet has suffered considerable additional damage since it was copied.

NOTES

l. 3: *te*. This sign is typical and complete, not PU as copied.

l. 10: ⸢9⸣. "8" is also possible.

l. 11: [*i-d*]*i*[*n*]. Or the like.

l. 15: [*din šum*]. The *CAD* Nuzi file records these signs as wholly preserved.

l. 16. The number "3," twice expressed in this line, is unusual in this context. In the second instance, the form is unusual as well. The wedges are correct as copied.

l. 18: *us*. In light of the spellings of this PN elsewhere (see *NPN*, 92b *sub* KUŠ-KIPA and *AAN*, 88a *sub* KUŠ-KIPA), perhaps this sign ought to be rendered $uš_{10}$.

l. 19: *ḫe*. This sign does not appear as copied. Rather, it is written in the form of ḪE as it appears in line 36.

l. 21: [*Ṣa-al*]-*mu*. This restoration is almost certain since it is the only one reflecting a "...-mu son of Ay-abâš" attested elsewhere at Nuzi. See *NPN*, 11a *sub* AḮ-ABÂŠ. This individual has other Unap-še connections with Teḫip-Tilla. See, for example, *JEN* 254.

l. 22: [ ]-*i-qí-ša*. This PN is probably "Sin-iqîša" (thus *NPN*, 121a *sub* SIN-IQÎŠA 1)) or "Ili-iqîša." See *NPN*, 313a *sub qašu*. If the former be the case, then this individual may also appear in *JEN* 756:16.

l. 22: *Na*-⸢*x*⸣-[ ]-*ya*. On the identity of this PN, see above immediately preceding note.

ll. 23-26. Line 23 is the last line of the obverse. Lines 24-26 appear on the lower edge of the tablet.

l. 23: -*ti* [ ]⸢x⸣[(?)]. The signs after TI may have been effaced deliberately through erasure by the scribe.

l. 26: ⸢*X*⸣-*li*-⸢*te*⸣?[-*x*? DUMU]. The *CAD* Nuzi file and *NPN* suggest, in effect, the restoration: [*E*]*ḫ-li-t*[*e-šup*]. *See NPN*, 42a *sub* EḪLI-TEŠUP 12), 108b *sub* NÛR-ILIḮA 1). However, there may not be enough room to restore [*šup* DUMU].

l. 26: *Nu*. Only the initial wedge of this sign is now missing and what remains appears a typical NU, not as copied.

l. 31. *uz*?. What remains of this sign in this unique PN is: 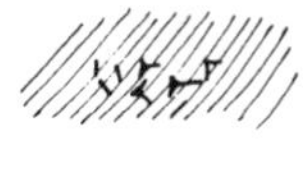

l. 34: *Tar*. This sign is typical, not as copied.

l. 34: ku_8. This sign is typical, not as copied.

JEN 748

OBVERSE

1 [ṭup-pí šu-pé-u]l-ti [ša]

2 [^{m}Te-ḫi-ip-til]-la DUMU ⸢Pu⸣-•[ḫ]i-⸢še⸣-[en-ni]

3 [ù ša] ⸢Ú⸣-na-ap-ta-e [DUMU Na-a-a]

4 [É.ḪÁ] ki-ma É.ḪÁ uš-[te-pè-i-lu]

5 [É.Ḫ]Á i-na ŠÀ URU Nu-•⸢zi⸣

6 [^{m}Ú-n]a-ap-ta-⸢e⸣ a-•na ^{m}⸢Te⸣-[ḫi-ip-til-la] SUM

7 [É.ḪÁ] ⸢i⸣-na ṣe-[r]i-⸢ti⸣ [i-na URU Nu-zi]-ma ù 2 ⸢MA⸣.NA ⸢KÙ⸣.BABBAR ṣa[r-pa]

8 [^{m}Te-ḫi]-⸢ip⸣-til-l[a a-na Ú-na-ap-ta-e] •SUM

9 [ma-an-n]u ša KI.BA[L-tu$_{4}$ (?)]

10 [2 MA.NA] +⸢KÙ!.+BABBAR⸣! 2 MA.NA ⸢KÙ⸣.[SIG$_{17}$ ú-ma-al-la]

11 [ù i-na] ⸢É⸣.ḪÁ qá-as-s[ú e-il-li]

12 [šum-ma É.Ḫ]Á ša ŠÀ URU ⸢pa⸣-[qí-ra-na]

13 [i-ra-aš-šu]-⸢ú⸣ ù ^{m}Ú-[náp-ta-e ú-•z]a-•ak-[ka]

14 [šum-ma É.ḪÁ] ša ṣe-ri-[ti]

15 [pa-qí-ra-n]a i-ra-aš-[ši?]

16 [^{m}Te-ḫi-i]p-til-la [ú-za-ak-ka]

---

17 [IGI M]u-uš-t[e-eš-šu]p •DUM[U Ḫa-ši-y]a

18 [IG]I Ké-li-⸢ya⸣ [DUMU Ka$_{4}$]-⸢ti-•ri⸣

19 •IGI Ki-ip-ta-⸢e⸣ [DUMU] ⸢E⸣-en-na-⸢ma-•a-ti⸣

20 IGI •Tar-mi-ya [DUMU Pa]-i-•ik-ku

21 IGI Ni-íḫ-ri-ya DUMU K[a]-lu-li

22 IGI Ta-•a-⸢a⸣ DUMU É[ḫ-•l]i-•ip-•LUGAL

23 IGI Pí-i-[r]u DUMU ⸢Na⸣-[iš-ké-el-pè]

LOWER EDGE

24 [IGI *Š]e-•éḫ-•li-ya DUMU [Zu-ú-me]

25 *IGI Ši-m[i-ka$_{4}$] +DUMU N[a-iš-ké-el-pè]

26 •IGI Ma-ti-ya [DU]M[U] ⸢Ú⸣-a[r-si-a]

REVERSE

27 IGI Ar-ta-še-en-⸢ni⸣ [DUB.SAR]

28 DUMU IBILA-^{d}XXX

S.I. Po 637

29 [^{NA_4} KIŠIB ^{m}Ú-na-ap-ta-e] DUMU Na-a-a

S.I.

30 +^{NA_4} +KIŠIB $^{+m+}$Mu-uš-te-eš-šup

S.I.

31 [^{NA_4} KIŠIB ^{m}Ta]r-mi-ya ^{LÚ}[ ]

S.I.

32 [^{NA_4} KIŠIB ^{m}Ar-ta-•š]e-⸢en⸣-ni

LEFT EDGE

S.I.

TRANSLATION

(1-4) [Tablet of] exchange [of] Teḫip-tilla son of Puḫi-šenni [and of] Unap-tae [son of Naya]. They exchanged [structures] for structures.

(5-6) Unap-tae gave to Teḫip-tilla structures in the heart of Nuzi.

(7-8) Teḫip-tilla gave [to Unap-tae structures] in the suburbs [of (lit. "in") Nuzi] and, further, 2 minas of refined silver.

(9-11) He who abrogates (this contract) [shall pay 2 minas] of silver (and) 2 minas of gold; [and] he shall forfeit the structures (lit. "his hand [shall rise up from] the structures").

(12-16) [Should] the structures in the heart of town have claimants, then Unap-tae shall clear (the structures). [Should the structures] in (lit. "of") the suburbs have claimants, Teḫip-tilla [shall clear (the structures)].

(17-28) [Before] Muš-tešup son of Ḫašiya; before Keliya [son of] Katiri; before Kip-tae [son of] Enna-mati; before Tarmiya [son of] Paikku; before Niḫriya son of Kalūli; before Taya son of Elḫip-šarri; before Piru son of Naiš-kelpe; [before] Šeḫliya son of [Zume]; before Šimika son of Naiš-kelpe; before Matiya son of Ṷarsia; before Artašenni, [the scribe], son of Apil-sin.

(29-32) (*seal impression*) [seal impression of Unap-tae] son of Naya; (*seal impression*) seal impression of Muš-tešup; (*seal impression*) [seal impression of] Tarmiya, the ...; (*seal impression*) seal impression of Artašenni; (*seal impression*) .... .

COMMENTS

This tablet has suffered additional deterioration since it was copied. As in other copies in Lacheman and Maidman (1989), the reverse is not rendered to scale. The seal impressions are, in reality, of greater height than depicted.

A partially preserved seal impression on the left edge indicates that a further line on the left edge has been entirely effaced. On the basis of *JEN* 266:31, 32, that missing line may have identified the sealer as Kip-tae (cf. *JEN* 748:19) or Keliya (cf. *JEN* 748:18) or even both if another seal impression once appeared on the left edge. On the relevance of *JEN* 266 to the present text, see below, note to line 3.

NOTES

l. 3: [*Na-a-a*]. This restoration follows *JEN* 266:3. (Consequently, cf. *JEN* 748:29 for this PN in the present text.) This interdependence of *JEN* 266

and 748 is not, however, without its complications. The following remarks address this issue. (I presented some of these remarks first in a seminar on the functions of sealing conducted at the Metropolitan Museum of Art on 20 March 1986. I should like to thank Edith Porada for inviting me to address that seminar and the participants for their thoughtful and helpful remarks.)

Wherever *JEN* 748 and 266 can be compared, they are virtually identical with but three exceptions. (They even share a findspot: room 15 of the Teḫip-tilla Family archives.)

The first exception is the description, present only in *JEN* 748 (ll. 7-8), of a payment of mobilia, i.e., two minas of refined silver, made by Teḫip-tilla to Unap-tae. The second exception is that *JEN* 748 contains seal impressions whereas *JEN* 266 lacks them. This particular peculiarity was already noted by Purves (1945, 71, n. 19). A third difference is that the identity of the sealers is not precisely the same in the two documents.

It is possible that these differences and the very fact of the existence of two tablets indicate that two similar but discrete transactions were recorded in very similar ways. The fact that the real estate involved is described in such a vague way—no real landmarks are given for either item—further encourages us to suppose that two different transactions are at stake. Nevertheless, one must question whether the fact of the existence of two tablets and the differences between them are sufficient criteria for positing two transactions, since the similarities between them are so very extensive and thoroughgoing.

These texts are so close to one another that one must, *a priori*, consider that they describe the same transaction. The presence of parallel texts of this sort, describing, often in the very same words, the same course of events, is clearly attested in this family's archives (Maidman 1976, 562-63). If only one transaction *is* involved, then two questions must be asked. Why are there two copies of the text in the same archive? What is the significance of the differences between the texts? The two questions may be interrelated. One is tempted to account for the presence of two texts by the differences between the texts. That is, the description of a supplementary payment and the presence of seal impressions only in *JEN* 748, as well as the partially different list of sealers in each text may be the key to the preservation in the same archive of these "parallel" texts.

We may attack these issues by considering the chronological ordering of these texts. Purves (1945, 71, n. 19) considered the two texts to have referred to the same transaction and that *JEN* 266 is a copy of the earlier *JEN* 748. Thus, the making of a copy, i.e., *JEN* 266, without mention of a supplementary payment might be plausible, e.g., if the copy acted only as an internal memorandum for Teḫip-tilla's real estate archive (although the text is very long for that function). Further, one would not expect seal impressions in an administrative copy of a contract. This

much supports Purves. However, one is hard pressed to account, on the basis of Purves' reconstruction, for the change in the identities of some of the sealers. Abridgement may occur in text copying. Alteration of personal names should not.

It may be, however, that *JEN* 266 was drawn up first. In this case, the following course of events may have obtained. The payment offered by Teḫip-tilla in *JEN* 266 (lacking the supplemental payment of silver) was rejected by Unap-tae as inadequate. In this case, the tablet, of course, would not have been sealed. (Yet, for some reason, the tablet was not destroyed.) *JEN* 748 would then represent a second, better offer by Teḫip-tilla to Unap-tae. Unap-tae would then have accepted the new contract and the document would have been sealed. This would account for the three differences in these texts: amount of payment, sealing, slightly different sealers (the last being insignificant). A variation of this scheme would involve scribal carelessness in omitting mention of the payment of silver in *JEN* 266. This would have forced the writing of a new text, *JEN* 748.

The major weakness of this otherwise logical reconstruction of events is its assumption that, in *JEN* 266, the legends identifying the sealers were all written first, with space between the legends left for subsequent impressing of the seals. But collation of *JEN* 266 does not support this assumption. Between lines 27 and 28, there is indeed blank space the width of the tablet, but only to a height of about an average cuneiform sign, too short for a seal impression. There is no space between lines 28 and 29 at all. After line 29, there is slight space (about half the height of the space between lines 27 and 28) before line 30, itself on the upper edge. No space separates lines 30 and 31, the latter being the last visible line on the upper edge. Thus, although there do exist two small gaps in this section, there is insufficient space for typical seal rollings. The upshot of this is that, although sealers are identified, the tablet appears to have been written from the start with no intention of its being sealed.

Another reconstruction of events overcomes this last problem, albeit not neatly. *JEN* 266 was written first, as a draft. In other words, the text, although containing the names of witnesses and sealers, was never meant to be operative and was never meant to be sealed. Thus, there is no room for seal impressions. *JEN* 748 was written up as the operative contract, based on, and containing the same stipulations as, *JEN* 266. This was rejected by Unap-tae whereupon an additional payment was offered to induce Unap-tae's acceptance. Note that the statement of the payment of silver at the end of line 7 makes that line uniquely long in this text. It may have been added after the rest of the contract's stipulations were written and following Unap-tae's objection. This would account for a host of phenomena involving these two texts: the difference in payment, the lack of seal impressions in *JEN* 266, the difference in sealers (as before, insignificant, based on the difference between

expectations and reality), the lack of space for seal impressions in *JEN* 266, and the uniquely long *JEN* 748:7. Nevertheless, this reconstruction raises problems of its own. Why would a draft have been written? To judge from the few surviving examples of possible drafts, it seems not to have been common practice. If the practice of writing drafts were common, then why have so few survived? If, in response to the latter question, it is suggested that they were routinely destroyed, then why was not *JEN* 266 (and its analogues in these archives) destroyed as well? Forgetfulness or inefficiency might provide answers but they are *ad hoc* answers and therefore not compelling. Finally, assuming that *JEN* 266 is a draft, it is not immediately apparent why names of witnesses and sealers whose identities could be established only on a future occasion (albeit a near future occasion) would have been included.

These nagging questions notwithstanding, it appears that this last reconstruction—*JEN* 266, a draft, first, followed by *JEN* 748, slightly altered—provides the best explanation at present of the relationship of these two texts and the transaction they represent. When all is said and done, the phenomenon of parallel texts here (and elsewhere in the Teḫip-tilla Family archives) is not adequately accounted for. More specifically, the function of *JEN* 266 (with its peculiar form) remains obscure. (If it turns out that two transactions are described in these two texts, some of these problems vanish but other, very serious, issues arise.)

JEN 131 (like the other two texts, from room 15) complicates the issue yet further. There, an additional payment is in fact tendered by Teḫip-tilla to Unap-tae (ll. 10-13). Yet the connection of the received payment of *JEN* 131 with the one described in *JEN* 748 is not a clear one (recall, *JEN* 266 mentions no payment in mobilia). The value of the commodities described in *JEN* 131 almost certainly does not amount to even one mina of silver, much less the two mentioned in *JEN* 748. (For the values in silver of two of the four commodities enumerated in *JEN* 131, see Eichler 1973, 15.)

However, if the same transaction is involved in both cases, then *JEN* 131 could represent partial, perhaps final, payment. It may even represent (if my preferred solution is *not* correct) a compromise settlement between the alternatives posed in the two earlier texts. At this point, though, speculation passes beyond the reasonable bounds imposed on us by the evidence and so must cease.

Whatever the relationship of *JEN* 266, 748, and 131, *JEN* 266 serves as the basis, not only for the restoration of the patronymic, *Na-a-a*, but for other damaged parts of *JEN* 748, including the PNs of witnesses. Dependence upon *JEN* 266 for the restoration of *JEN* 748 is not affected by the order of the two texts or by the possibility that two transactions may be involved.

l. 7. On the length of this line and the possible significance of this feature, see above, note to line 3.

l. 7: *ṣa*[*r-pa*]. The trace appears, not as copied, but, rather, as:

The restoration of this word adopted here is based on an interpretation of Lacheman.

l. 9. Following the last restoration, there is room for an additional phrase, such as: (*ša*) *i-na bi*$_4$*-ri-šu-nu*.

l. 10: ˹KÙ!.BABBAR˺!. The traces appear, not as copied, but, rather, as:

l. 10: ˹KÙ˺.[SIG$_{17}$]. Lacheman once saw these signs as completely preserved.

l. 11: *qá-as-s*[*ú e-il-li*]. On this idiom, see *CAD*, E, 125a *sub elû* 3 b 3′.

l. 13: [*ka*]. Lacheman once saw this sign partially preserved, i.e., as K[A] (and with no sign following).

l. 15: *i-ra-aš-*[*ši?*]. According to Lacheman, the last sign was once completely preserved. Cf. also the same form of the verb in *JEN* 266:14. However, note the different verbal form partially restored above, l. 13.

l. 17. For the restoration of this line, see below, l. 30 and the note thereto. Cf. also *JEN* 266:19.

l. 18: [*Ka*$_4$]-˹*ti-ri*˺. This restoration is most likely. See *NPN*, 81b-82a *sub* KELIḪA. "Katiri" is the only "...-*ti-ri*" father of Keliya attested at Nuzi.

l. 20: [*Pa*]. *NPN*, 148b *sub* TARMIḪA 23), saw P[A] at this point.

l. 24. Contrary to the copy, this line, not line 25, begins the lower edge.

l. 24: *éḫ-li*. The copy does not seem to reflect the remaining traces of these signs. The traces appear as:

l. 25: *m*[*i-ka*$_4$]. The *CAD* Nuzi file saw these signs as completely preserved.

l. 30. Lacheman identifies the seal impression associated with this line as Po 917. Porada (1947, 137b *ad* no. 917) identifies seal impression 917 with Muš-Tešup son of Ḫašiya in another tablet.

l. 31. Lacheman identifies the seal impression associated with this line as Po 635.

l. 32. Lacheman identifies the seal impression associated with this line as Po 17. Porada (1947, 126b *ad* no. 17) identifies seal impression 17 with Artašenni son of Apil-sin in another tablet.

JEN 749

OBVERSE

1 [^{m}Te-ḫi]-⸢ip⸣-til-l[a DUMU Pu-ḫi-še-en-ni]
2 [a-na ma]-ru-ti i-t[e-pu-uš-ma]
3 [ki-ma] ḪA.LA-šu 2 A[NŠE (?) A.ŠÀ i?-na? $^{GIŠ?}$ta?-a?-a?-ri?]
4 [ša?] ⸢É⸣?.GAL i+na [ ]
5 [ ]⸢x x x⸣[ ]•⸢x⸣
6 [i?-na? e]-$^{+}$le-ni [ ]⸢x⸣[ ] KI
7 [i?]-⸢na⸣? [URU] ⸢Ú⸣-na-ap-[še-wa ^{m}T]a-a-⸢a⸣ [ ]⸢x⸣?
8 [a-na ^{m}Te-ḫi]-⸢ip⸣-til-la [S]UM ù ^{m}T[e-ḫi-ip-ti]l-l[a]!
9 [2 GUD.MEŠ k]i-ma NÍG.⸢BA-šu⸣ a-na ^{m}[T]a-•a-•a [SUM]
10 [šum-m]a A.ŠÀ pí-ir-•q[a TU]K.•MEŠ-ši
11 [^{m}]Ta-a-a ú-za-•⸢ak⸣-ka$_4$-ma ù
12 [a-n]a ^{m}Te-ḫi-ip-til!-la ⸢i⸣-[n]a-an-din
13 ⸢ù⸣ il-ku ša A.•ŠÀ ⸢an-ni⸣-i ^{m}⸢Ta-a-a⸣-[ma? na]-ši
14 [^{m}]Te-ḫi-ip-til-la il-ka$_4$ ša A.ŠÀ an-ni-$^{+}$i
15 la na-ši šum-ma ^{m}Ta-a-a KI.BA[L-at?]
16 [1]+1 MA.NA KÙ.BABBAR 2 MA.NA KÙ.SIG$_{17}$ a+na
17 ^{m}Te-ḫi-ip-til-la ú-ma-al-l[a]

---

18 IGI A-•⸢al⸣-te-šup DUMU Šum-mi-ya
19 [I]GI [ ]-⸢ya⸣ [DU]MU ŠU-^{d}[I]M?

LOWER EDGE

20 [IGI DUMU]⸢x RU⸣?

REVERSE

21 [mu-š]e-el-mu-ú
22 [ša A.ŠÀ ù na-di-n]a!?-nu ša GUD.[MEŠ]
23 [IGI A?-kip?-til?]-l[a? DUM]U Ké-li-ya
24 [IGI Ar-t]i-ir-•[w]i [DU]M[U P]a-a-a
25 [IGI En-na]-ma-ti [DUM]U ⸢A-al⸣-te-[š]up
26 [IGI Ta?-(i?-)i]n?-šu-uḫ DUMU Š[u]-ru-pé-ya
27 [IGI Um?-pí?]-ya DUMU Ú-zi-ya
28 [IGI E?-/Še?-ḫe?-el?]-⸢te⸣-šup DUB.SAR DUMU XXX-ib-ni
29 [IGI]⸢x⸣[ ] DUMU Ni-iḫ-ri-ya
30 [IGI A?-kip?-ta?-še?-en?-n]i? DUM[U] •Me-le-ya
31 [IGI DUMU? -t]e?-šup
32 [EME-šu ša] ⸢^{m}⸣Ta-a-⸢a⸣ a+na pa-ni IGI.MEŠ i[q]-ta-bi
: 2 GUD.MEŠ él-[qé]
33 [(?)] ù 2 GUD.[MEŠ]
S.I.
34 [NA$_4$ (KIŠIB)]⸢x⸣[ ]
S.I.

TRANSLATION

....

(1-2) He adopted Teḫip-tilla [son of Puḫi-šenni].

(3-8) [As] his inheritance share, Taya ...(?) gave [to] Teḫip-tilla a 2 homer ...(?) [field by? the? standard? of?] the palace(?) in .... [to?] the east of ... in(?) [the town of] Unap-še.

(8-9) And Teḫip-tilla [gave] to Taya as his gift [2 oxen].

(10-12) Should the field have a claim (against it), Taya shall clear (the field) and then give (it) to Teḫip-tilla.

(13-15) And Taya shall bear the *ilku* of this field; Teḫip-tilla shall not bear the *ilku* of this field.

(15-17) Should Taya abrogate (this contract), he shall pay to Teḫip-tilla 2 minas of silver (and) 2 minas of gold.

(18-31) Before Al-tešup son of Šummiya; before ...-ya son of Gimill-adad(?); [before ... son of] ...; ... measurers [of the field and] givers of the oxen. [Before] Akip-tilla(?) son of Keliya; [before] Ar-tirwi son of Paya; [before] Enna-mati son of Al-tešup; [before] Tain(?)-šuḫ son of Šurupeya; [before Umpi?]ya son of Uziya; [before Eḫli?-/Šeḫel?]-tešup, the scribe, son of Sin-ibnī; [before] ... son of Niḫriya; [before] Akip-tašenni(?) son of Meleya; [before ... son? of? ...]-tešup(?).

(32) [Declaration of] Taya before witnesses; he spoke (as follows):

(33) "I have received 2 oxen ....(?) and 2 oxen ... .

(34) (*seal impression*) [seal impression of] ...; (*seal impression*) ..... .

COMMENTS

This tablet has suffered slight additional damage since it was copied. Two fragments have been attached to the tablet since Lacheman made his copy. These fragments contribute (1) the first trace and *le-ni* respectively to lines 5 and 6; and (2) part of ⸢*Ta*⸣, as well as ⸢*a-a*⸣, and *an-ni* respectively to lines 13 and 14. Furthermore, a fragment containing [*T*]*a-a-a* has been attached to the end of line 10. This appears to represent the last preserved signs of line 9 as copied. That portion of the tablet must have broken away, later to be reattached to the tablet at the wrong spot. There is no [*T*]*a-a-a* currently at the end of line 9.

Two lines appear to be missing at the start of the obverse. These lines would have read:

ṭup-pí ma-ru-ti ša
^{m}*Ta-a-a* DUMU PN

At least one line is missing at the end of the text. It identified the maker of the second seal impression.

NOTES

l. 3: A[NŠE]. Lacheman and the *CAD* Nuzi file record this sign as entirely preserved. ^{G}[^{IŠ}APIN] is another possible interpretation of these traces.

l. 3: [*i*?-*na*? $^{GIŠ?}$*ta*?-*a*?-*a*?-*ri*?]. This restoration is already to be found in Lacheman and the *CAD* Nuzi file.

l. 6: KI. This sign seems indeed to represent KI but does not appear as copied. Rather, it appears as: 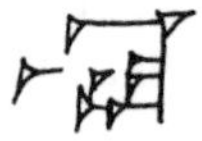

l. 7: [URU] ⸢*Ú*⸣-*na-ap-*[*še-wa*]. This restoration is based on indirect, but convincing, evidence derived from the witness list of this text.

Ar-tirwi son of Paya (l. 24) is attested in only two other texts, *JEN* 761:37 (very likely) and *JEN* 841:31. In both, he is a witness. *JEN* 761 is a Teḫip-tilla adoption tablet dealing with Unap-še land (l. 6, explicitly). *JEN* 841 is also a Teḫip-tilla adoption tablet dealing with Unap-še land (implicitly; cf., e.g., ll. 5-7 with *JEN* 214:7-10 where, in addition to the GNs mentioned in *JEN* 841:5-7, Unap-še is explicitly named).

Enna-mati son of Al-tešup (l. 25) has even stronger ties to Unap-še. Wherever his appearance can be linked to real estate in a given location (*JEN* 38, 91, 375, 653 [=348]; cf. *JEN* 375, *HSS*, XVI, 349), that real estate is in Unap-še. See, for example, *JEN* 653:2-3, 38-39.

Tain(?)-šuḫ son of Šurupeya (l. 26) reappears (most probably) only once elsewhere, in *JEN* 757:25, as a witness. *JEN* 757 is a Teḫip-tilla adoption text dealing with Unap-še land (ll. 3, 6; cf. *JEN* 761:6-8).

No other identifiable witness from *JEN* 749 has clear links with any one town predominantly. (But see below, notes to lines 23, 30.) It thus appears that the witnesses to this text (insofar as their names survive) are linked, to a great extent, with Unap-še real estate interests of the Teḫip-tilla Family. And so the restoration proposed here seems very likely.

The concatenation of texts cited thus far in this note is not a strong one. However, linkages are sufficiently pronounced to allow for some tentative restorations in *JEN* 749. Specifically, *JEN* 757 (the other Tain(?)-šuḫ text) and *JEN* 841 (an Ar-tirwi text) contain witness PNs better preserved than those found in *JEN* 749 and which may overlap with this last text. These restorations are found in lines 23, 28, 30.

On the interconnections between *JEN* 749, 757, and 761, see also below, note to *JEN* 757:13-15.

l. 11: $^{[m]}$. The *CAD* Nuzi file records this sign as preserved.

l. 12. Lacheman and the *CAD* Nuzi file record this line as entirely preserved.

l. 12: *til*!. The sign is correct as copied.

l. 13: [*ma*?]. Lacheman records this sign as completely preserved.

l. 15: KI.BA[L-*at*?]. Lacheman sees KI.BAL-tu_4 completely preserved. However, tu_4 would be quite out of place here. Cf. *JEN* 757:16 for the restoration offered here. On the relevance of *JEN* 757 for this issue, see below, note to line 28.

l. 16: [1]+1. Lacheman and the *CAD* Nuzi file record the number "2" as entirely preserved.

l. 19: ŠU-^{d}[I]M?. This interpretation follows Lacheman who saw all three signs as entirely preserved.

l. 22: [MEŠ]. The *CAD* Nuzi file records this sign as completely preserved.

l. 23: [*A?-kip?-til?*]-*l*[*a*?]. This restoration is based on a witness PN, also son of Keliya, in *JEN* 757:27. See the note to that line. On the bearing of *JEN* 757 and its witness list on the present context, see above, note to line 7.

l. 24: [*Ar*]. This restoration is based on the fact that "Ar-tirwi" is the only "[ ]-tirwi son of Paya" elsewhere attested in the Nuzi texts. See *NPN*, 109b *sub* PAI̯A 18) - 25), especially 18); and *AAN*, 104a *sub* PAIA.

l. 25: [*En-na*]. This restoration is based on the fact that "Enna-mati" is the only "[ ]-mati son of Al-tešup" elsewhere attested in the Nuzi texts. See *NPN*, 20a *sub* AL-TEŠUP 4) - 5), especially 4); and *AAN*, 22b *sub* AL-TEŠUP.

l. 26: [*Ta?-(i?-)i*]*n*?. This restoration is also proposed in the *CAD* Nuzi file and, tentatively, in *NPN*, 141a *sub* ŠURUPEI̯A 3), 144a *sub* TAIN-ŠUḪ 2). [*Ša-ti-i*]*n-šu-uḫ* and [*Ša-n*]*i-šu-uḫ* are also possible, though somewhat less likely. See *NPN*, 258b *sub* šuḫ.

The same person probably appears in *JEN* 757:25 as a witness. The PN is broken in virtually the same place; the patronymic is entirely preserved.

l. 26: *Š*[*u*]. The *CAD* Nuzi file records this sign as entirely preserved.

l. 27: [*Um?-pí?*]. This restoration is suggested by *JEN* 588:2 as restored by Edward Chiera *apud NPN*, 163b *sub* UMPII̯A 22).

No other son of Uziya is attested at Nuzi.

l. 28: [*E?-/Še?-ḫe?-el?*]. This restoration of the scribe's name is based on the surviving part of *JEN* 757:29, supplemented by the reading of that line (presumably when better preserved) in *NPN*, 121b *sub* SIN-IBNĪ 2). (*E* and *Še* are, it seems, the only possible alternatives for the start of this PN; see *NPN*, 265b-66a.)

On the relevance of *JEN* 757 for the present text, see above, note to line 7. *JEN* 841 is relevant for the same reason and so it is interesting to note that the scribe of that text is the only other son of a "Sin-ibnī," Muš-teya (l. 41). (One Sin-ibnī is also known to have been a scribe; see *HSS*, V, 65:23).

l. 30: [*A?-kip?-ta?-še?-en?-n*]*i*?. This restoration is based on *JEN* 841:38. On the importance of that text in the present context, see above, note to line 7.

l. 31: [-*t*]*e?-šup*. [*Še-k*]a_4!-*ru*, or the like, is possible.

l. 34. It is unclear whether one or two seal impressions appear above this line.

JEN 750

OBVERSE

1 [ṭ]up-pí •ma-*ru-•ti •ša
2 ^{m}Ki-pá-•a-*⌜a⌝ *D[UMU] I-•la-*a[p-ri]
3 $^{m•}$⌜En⌝-na-m[a-ti] •DU[MU] •Te-ḫi-*ip-[til-la]
4 *a-•na ma-⌜ru⌝-[t]i ⌜i⌝-•te-*pu-*[u]š[-(ma)]
5 •É.ḪÁ.MEŠ ša URU Nu-•⌜zi⌝ *AŠ [(?)] BI?
6 •EDIN.MEŠ 2 ma-•ti ⌜10⌝?+ 20 <AŠ> a[m]-•ma-⌜ti⌝ [(?)]
7 •ḫu-bá-al-lu •ù i-na •l[e-et]
8 •A.•ŠÀ.MEŠ •tab-•re-•e •ša É.GA[L]-*⌜lì⌝
9 ù •⌜PÚ⌝.MEŠ ša a-gu_5-ra [ ] •AN?
10 ù ^{m}Ki-pá-a-•a a-na
11 ^{m}En-na-ma-ti ki-ma ⌜ḪA⌝.[LA].MEŠ $^{+}$SUM-[di]n?
12 ù ^{m}En-na-ma-•ti a-na
13 ^{m}Ki-pa-a-a 2 TÚG?.MEŠ ⌜x⌝[ ]⌜x⌝
14 12 MA.NA a-na-ku 40 ⌜x⌝[ ]⌜x⌝ ZA? ⌜x⌝
15 •a-na NÍG.BA.MEŠ i-din
16 $^{+}$šum-ma É.ḪÁ.MEŠ pá-qí-[r]a-na
17 ir-ta-ši ^{m}Ki-pá-a-•a
18 ú-za-ak-kà a-na ^{m}En-na-[m]a-[t]i
19 *i-din ma-nu-um-mé-e i-•na

$^{+}$ ———

20 •DAL.BA.NA.MEŠ KI.BAL.$^{+}$MEŠ
21 •5 •MA.NA KÙ.BABBAR 5 •MA.•NA KÙ.•SIG_{17}
22 •ú-ma-al-la [ ]*⌜x⌝ ḪA.•LA
23 •ù [ ]⌜x⌝ •a •ra [ ] •i-na
24 [ ] a •⌜IB⌝? [ ]
25 [ ]*⌜x *x⌝[ ]*⌜x⌝

REVERSE

26 [IGI]-⌜x⌝ DUMU [ ]-⌜ya⌝
27 [IGI Ḫa-na-ak]-•ka_4 •DUMU •Š[e]-•ka_4-rù
28 [IGI A-li-ip-pí]-•ya DUMU *K[i]-•zi-•ḫar-*pè
29 *IGI *⌜Ur⌝-•ḫi-•ya *DUMU [Ú-ṣú-*u]r-•mé
30 •IGI •Ze-•⌜en⌝-*ni [DUMU Ḫa?-ma?-an?-na?]
31 *IGI *⌜X⌝-[ ] *DUMU *⌜X⌝-[ ]
32 *[I]GI *Tu-*ra-•ri •DU[MU] •E-*⌜mu⌝-*y[a]
33 *[IG]I •Ar-te-ya •DUMU A-*ka_4-*a-*a

34 *⸢IGI⸣ •Šu-[m]i-[y]a DUMU Eḫ-•li-*y[a]
35 •IGI Ki-[p]á-[a-a] DUMU A-ka$_4$-•a-[a]
36 IGI Tu-+⸢ra⸣-[ri] DUMU A-ka$_4$-•a-*a-*⸢ma⸣
37 IGI Zi-⸢li⸣-[ya DU]MU •Tu-•up-ki-⸢ya⸣
38 IGI Ša-ma-aš-[ ]-•⸢x⸣ DUMU Ki-•[p]á-a-*⸢a⸣
39 IGI ^{d}Iškur-•an-dù[l DUB].SAR
40 DUMU Zi-•ni-•ya

S.I.

41 *NA$_4$ *^{m}[ ]-*ḫa *D[UMU? (?)]
42 $^{[NA_4]}$ *KIŠIB *^{m}*M[I]?.*⸢NI⸣?-[ya? DUMU? (?)]

S.I.

LEFT EDGE

43 [^{NA_4} *KI]ŠIB ^{m}•Ar-te-ya ^{NA_4} KIŠIB ^{m}Tu-r[a-ri]

S.I. [S.I.]

TRANSLATION

(1-4) Tablet of adoption of Kipaya son of Ilapri. He adopted Enna-mati son of Teḫip-tilla.

(5-11) Now Kipaya gave to Enna-mati as an inheritance share structures in (lit. "of") the town of Nuzi in ...(?) the suburbs, (having) a perimeter (lit. "fence") of 220+10(?) cubits ...(?), adjacent to the *tabru*-land of the palace, and a cistern (or: cisterns) of ... brick(s).

(12-15) And Enna-mati gave to Kipaya for a gift 2 ... garments(?), 12 minas of tin, (and) 40 ... .

(16-19) Should the structures have claimants, Kipaya shall clear (the structures and) give (lit. "gave") (them) to Enna-mati.

(19-22) Who (horizontal line here—M.P.M.) amongst them abrogates (this contract) shall pay 5 minas of silver (and) 5 minas of gold.

(22-25) ... (inheritance) share and ... in .... .

(26-40) [Before] ... son of ...-ya; [before] Ḫanakka son of Šekaru; [before] Alippiya son of Kizzi-ḫarpa; before Urḫiya son of Uṣur-mê; before Zenni [son of Ḫamanna?]; before ... son of ...; before Turari son of Emuya; before Arteya son of Akaya; before Šummiya son of Eḫliya; before Kipaya son of Akaya; before Turari also son of Akaya; before Ziliya son of Tupkiya; before Šamaš-... son of Kipaya; before Iškur-andul, the scribe, son of Ziniya.

(41-43) (*seal impression*) seal impression of ...-ḫa son(?) of(?) ...(?); seal impression of Ziliya(?) [son? of? (if so, then "Tupkiya" follows—M.P.M.)] (*seal impression*); seal impression of Ar-teya (*seal impression*); seal impression of Turari [(*seal impression*)].

COMMENTS

This tablet has deteriorated greatly since the copy was made.

Lacheman's notes indicate, furthermore, that the tablet deteriorated significantly between the time he first studied the text and the occasion he copied it. Therefore, his notes are particularly important for this text, especially for the restoration of witness PNs.

The *CAD* Nuzi file for this text was authored by Lacheman. References below to that file indicate contributions by Lacheman.

The scribe of this text is guilty either of two inadvertent omissions or of two grammatical infelicities. See line 6 (<AŠ>) and below, note to line 19. Cf., also, the note to line 15.

NOTES

l. 2: *I-la-a*[*p-ri*]. No other restoration is even remotely plausible. See *NPN*, 86b *sub* KIPAI̯A 1) - 6), especially 5); and *AAN*, 82b *sub* KIPAIA. Lacheman reads at this point: [*I*]-*la-ap-ri*.

l. 5: BI?. This sign appears in the middle of the reverse. It is depicted in the copy above the second seal impression. It seems to belong either to this line or to line 6. Additional text may be lost at the end of either line—or at the end of neither. For the possible missing context at the end of line 6, cf. *CAD*, Ḫ, 213a-b *sub ḫubballa/i*; L, 191b *sub limītu* 1. a) 1′.
The sign could also represent ⌈*am*⌉, ⌈KÀR⌉, or the like.

l. 6. See above, comments and immediately preceding note.

l. 6: ⌈10⌉?. The *CAD* Nuzi file reads "30" without question. The first *Winkelhaken*, if such it be, is difficult to discern.

l. 7: *l*[*e-et*]. The *CAD* Nuzi file records these signs as wholly preserved.

l. 8: *tab-re-e*. *tabrû* is a term qualifying, not only land, but grain and even people. No satisfactory definition of the lexeme has yet been achieved. Discussion of, and bibliography on, this term are found in Maidman (1976, 404, n. 693). To the references noted there may be added: *AHw*, 1299b; Cassin (1958, 20 with n. 5); Postgate (1973, 84-85; 1976, 23; 1989b, 143a); Zaccagnini (1975, 185-86); and Wilhelm (n.d., 60 [*SMN* 3113 is now published as *EN*, 9/1, 286]).

l. 9. Cf. *JEN* 160:10-11.

l. 11: ⌈ḪA⌉.[LA]. The *CAD* Nuzi file records these signs as entirely preserved.

l. 11: SUM. This sign is a clear and complete SUM, not as depicted.

l. 11: MEŠ SUM-[*di*]*n*?. The position of these signs relative to the rest of line 11 is accurately depicted. Cf., below, note to line 16.

l. 13: TÚG?.MEŠ ⌈x⌉. The *CAD* Nuzi file at this point reads, in effect: UDU.MEŠ QA-*al*-[ ]. If this is correct, then the latter word may represent a form of *qallu*, "young," sometimes used to describe livestock. See *CAD*, Q, 64a-b *sub qallu* 3. c); *AHw*, 894b *sub qallu(m)* 2) d). The word likely does

not represent a form of *kalūmu* which, it appears, is nowhere else spelled this way in the Nuzi texts.

l. 14: 40 ⸢x⸣[ ]⸢x⸣ ZA? ⸢x⸣. Cf. perhaps, *JEN* 38:13; 214:14, written by the same scribe.

l. 15: *a-na* NÍG.BA.MEŠ. This preposition is most unusual in this context. Perhaps the scribe started to write: *a-na* ^{m}*Ki-pá-a-a ki-ma* NÍG.BA.MEŠ. Seeing that he had already expressed the first part of this idea in lines 12 and 13, he simply attached the new element, that of the "gift," to the preposition he had already written.

l. 16: *na*. This sign is as portrayed, higher than the rest of line 16. Cf. above, third note to line 11.

l. 18: *En*. This sign appears rather more typical than it does in the copy. It does not look like AK.

l. 19: *i-din*. This form is unexpected here. Contrast *JEN* 38:17, written by the same scribe. Perhaps these signs should be interpreted as: *i-*<*na*(*-an*)>*-din*.

l. 20. Above this line appears a horizontal line. This is not depicted in the copy.

ll. 22-25. The sense of these lines (after *ú-ma-al-la*) eludes me. The witness list may start with line 24 or even line 23.

l. 27: [*Ḫa-na-ak*]*-ka*$_4$. Lacheman records the restored signs as preserved. The *CAD* Nuzi file (presumably from a later date) records only "*-ak-ka*$_4$" as preserved.

No other "[ ]-ka son of Šekaru" is attested in the Nuzi texts.

l. 28. Lacheman records this line as completely preserved.

l. 29: [*Ú-ṣú-u*]*r-mé*. The *CAD* Nuzi file records UR as completely preserved. No other "Urḫiya son of [ ]-MI" is attested in the Nuzi texts.

l. 30: [*Ḫa?-ma?-an?-na?*]. Lacheman restores this PN. "Ḫamanna" is the only patronymic for a Zenni attested in the Nuzi texts. See *NPN*, 175b *sub* ZENNI; *AAN*, 170a, *sub* ZENNI.

l. 32: *y*[*a*]. Lacheman records this sign as completely preserved.

l. 34: [*m*]*i-*[*y*]*a*. The *CAD* Nuzi file records these signs as completely preserved.

l. 35. The *CAD* Nuzi file records this line as completely preserved.

l. 36: ⸢*ra*⸣-[*ri*]. The *CAD* Nuzi file records these signs as completely preserved. ⸢RA⸣ does not appear as in the copy but, rather, as:

l. 38: [*p*]*á*. The *CAD* Nuzi file records this sign as completely preserved.

l. 41: NA$_4$ ^{m}. On the basis of lines 42 and 43, one would have expected at this point: ^{NA_4} KIŠIB.

l. 41: [ ]-*ḫa* D[UMU?]. Lacheman reads, at this point: *It-ḫa-pí*.

l. 42. Cf. line 37. If all interpretations and restorations here are correct, then the patronymic, *Tu-up-ki-ya*, is to be supplied.

JEN 751

OBVERSE

1 [*ṭu*]*p-pí* [*ma-r*]*u-ti ša*

2 [^{m}*Pa*]-⸢*a-a*⸣ [DUMU] ⸢*I*⸣-*bá-aš*-DINGIR

3 *^{m}[*T*]*e-ḫi-i*[*p-til-l*]*a* DUMU *Pu-ḫi-še-en-ni*

4 •*a+na ma-r*[*u-t*]*i i-pu-uš-ma*

5 1 ANŠE 2 ^{G}[^{IŠ}A]PIN A.ŠÀ.MEŠ *i+na šu-pa-al*

6 AN.ZA.KÀR [ ]⸢*x*⸣-•*ta-ya i-na su-*⸢*ta*⸣-$^{+}$*na-nu*

7 AN.ZA.KÀR [*ša*] ⸢^{m}⸣*A-ka$_{4}$-wa-til i-na* ^{GIŠ}•⸢*ta-a*⸣!?-*a-ri* GAL

8 *a+na* ^{m}*Te-*[*ḫi-*•*i*]*p-til-la* [*k*]*i-*[*m*]*a* ḪA.⸢LA⸣-*šu* SUM-*in*

9 *ù* ^{m}*T*[*e-ḫi*]*-ip-til-la* [*a-na*] ^{m}*Pa-a-*⸢*a*⸣

10 *⸢x⸣[ ] ⸢*ù*⸣ 20 MA.NA [URUD]U.MEŠ

11 *k*[*i-m*]*a* •NÍG.BA-*šu id-*⸢*din*⸣

12 *š*[*um-*•*m*]*a* A.ŠÀ.MEŠ *šu-u$_{4}$ up-*⸢*ta*⸣-[*qar*]

13 [^{m}*Pa-a-a*] *ú-za-ak-ka$_{4}$-*⸢*ma*⸣

14 [*a-na* ^{m}*Te-ḫi-i*]*p*!-⸢*til*⸣-*la i-na-din*

15 [*il-ka$_{4}$* •*š*]*a* •A.[ŠÀ.MEŠ •*š*]*a-a-šu*

16 [^{m}*Pa-a*]-⸢*a*⸣-*ma* [*n*]*a-ši šum-ma* [^{m}*P*]*a-a-a*

17 [KI].BAL-⸢*at*⸣ 2 [MA.N]A KÙ.BABBAR

18 [2 MA.NA] KÙ.S[IG$_{17}$] *ú-*[*m*]*a-*[*a*]*l-la*

---

19 [IGI *Tup-ki-ya* DUMU *Kàr-z*]*e-y*[*a*]

.

.

.

LOWER EDGE

20 [IGI *Tar-mi-ya* DUMU *A-be*]-⸢*ya*⸣

21 [IGI *En-na-ma-ti* DUMU *A-a*]*l-te-š*[*up*]

REVERSE

22 [5 LÚ.MEŠ *an-nu-ti mu-še-e*]*l-*$^{+}$*mu* <*ša*> $^{+}$A.$^{+}$ŠÀ

23 [*ù na-dì-na-nu ša*] URUDU.MEŠ

24 [IGI *Te-ḫu-up-še-en-ni*] $^{+}$DUMU *Pì-ru*

25 [IGI] *M*[*u-uš-te-ya*] DUMU *Te-ḫi-ya*

26 •IGI *Um-*[*pí-ya*] DUMU *Te-eš-šu-ya*

27 IGI *Ut-ḫá*[*p*]*-*•⸢*ta*⸣*-e* DUMU *Zi-ké*

28 IGI *Ḫu-u*[*n*]*-ni-ya* [D]UMU *Ḫa-ma-an-na*

29	IGI •*Šèr-š[i]-ya*	•DUMU *Šúk-ri-ya*
30	IGI *Ur-ḫi-•ya*	DUMU *Še-ka*$_4$*-rù*
31	IGI MU-GÁ[L]-*ši*	DUMU *Ta-a-a* DUB.SAR
32	IGI *It-ḫ[i-i]š-ta*$_5$	DU[MU] *A-•ar!-ta-e*
	S.I.	
33	$^{\mathrm{NA_4}}$ KIŠIB $^{<\mathrm{m}>}$*Um-[pí]-*$^{+}$*ya*	
	S.I.	
34	$^{\mathrm{[N]A_4}}$ KIŠIB ^{m}*Ḫu-*$^{+}$*u[n!-ni]-*$^{+}$*ya*	
	S.I.	
35	$^{⸢\mathrm{NA_4}⸣}$ KIŠIB $^{\mathrm{[m?]}}$*It-ḫi-iš-ta*$_5$	
LEFT EDGE		
36	[$^{\mathrm{NA_4}}$ KIŠIB $^{\mathrm{m+}}$M]U-$^{+}$GÁL-*ši* DUB.SAR	S.I.
37	S.I.	$^{\mathrm{[N]A_4}}$ KIŠIB ^{m}*Šèr-ši-•⸢ya⸣*

TRANSLATION

(1-4) Tablet of adoption of Paya [son of] Ibaššī-ilu. He adopted Teḫip-tilla son of Puḫi-šenni.

(5-8) He gave to Teḫip-tilla as his inheritance share a 1.2 homer field to the west of the *dimtu* of ...-taya, to the south of the *dimtu* [of] Akawatil, (measured) by the large standard.

(9-11) And Teḫip-tilla gave [to] Paya as his gift ... and 20 minas of copper.

(12-14) Should that field be claimed, [Paya] shall clear (it) and give (it) [to] Teḫip-tilla.

(15-16) It is Paya who shall bear [the *ilku*] of that field.

(16-18) Should Paya abrogate (this contract) he shall pay 2 minas of silver (and) [2 minas] of gold.

(19-32) [Before Tupkiya son of] Karzeya; ....; ....; [before Tarmiya son of] Abeya; [before Enna-mati son of] Al-tešup. [These 5 men] are the measurers <of> the field [and the distributors of] the copper. [Before Teḫup-šenni] son of Piru; [before] Muš-teya son of Teḫiya; before Umpiya son of Teššuya; before Utḫap-tae son of Zike; before Ḫunniya son of Ḫamanna; before Šeršiya son of Šukriya; before Urḫiya son of Šekaru; before Šumu-libšī son of Taya, the scribe; before Itḫišta son of Ar-tae.

(33-37) (*seal impression*) seal impression of Umpiya; (*seal impression*) seal impression of Ḫunniya; (*seal impression*) seal impression of Itḫišta; seal impression of Šumu-libšī, the scribe (*seal impression*); (*seal impression*) seal impression of Šeršiya.

COMMENTS

This tablet has suffered some additional deterioration since it was copied.

The last part of the obverse is now totally effaced. Most likely, two lines are now missing, lines which once read:

IGI *A-tá-an-ḫi-lu* DUMU *Na-an-te-šup*
IGI *Ḫu-lu-uk-ka*$_4$ DUMU *Ar-te-šup*

This restoration is based on *JEN* 91:21-22. The witness list of *JEN* 91 (including the identities of the sealers) appears identical to that of *JEN* 751 where the two can be compared. See already, Weeks (1972, 207), and cf. above, note to *JEN* 741:28. The names of witnesses in broken sections of the present text may be restored with confidence on the basis of *JEN* 91. Where *JEN* 91 itself lacks completely preserved PNs, *those* names may be restored from *JEN* 38. Except for the scribe, *JEN* 38 and 91 share identical witnesses, although in a slightly different order.

Other, minor, restorations in *JEN* 751 are also based on forms found in *JEN* 91.

NOTES

l. 3. The *CAD* Nuzi file records this line as entirely preserved.

l. 4: *uš*. This sign is typical, not as copied (i.e., the sign has no lower *Winkelhaken*).

l. 6: [ ]⸢*x*⸣-•*ta-ya. The CAD* Nuzi file records the second sign as NA. This sign is now partially effaced but enough remains to confirm the reading TA, as opposed to NA. Lacheman reads, in effect: [*ša* ᵐ]*Ú-ta-a-a*.

l. 6: *na*. This sign is typical, not AN as copied.

ll. 7-9. The *CAD* Nuzi file records these lines as entirely preserved. Lacheman records line 7 as entirely preserved.

l. 7: AN.ZA.KÀR [*ša*] ⸢ᵐ⸣*A-ka*$_4$*-wa-til*. The land is thus to be located in Unap-še. See, e.g., *JEN* 761:6-7.

l. 7: ⸢*ta-a*⸣!?-*a-ri*. Lacheman and the *CAD* Nuzi file both read: *ta-a-a-ri*. Cf. *ta-a-a-ri* in *JEN* 91:7, written by the same scribe. However, the copy appears to reflect ⸢*ta*⸣-*a-ri*. Unfortunately, the vertical wedge to the left of A is now entirely gone.

l. 10: ⸢x⸣[ ]. The two wedge heads are no longer discernible. In *JEN* 91, where there are other striking similarities to this text (see above, comments), Teḫip-tilla again acquires 1.2 homers of land in Unap-še (for the Unap-še location of the land, cf. *JEN* 91:4-6 with *JEN* 214:7-10). There, he pays (l. 11): 1 GUD *ù* 20 MA.NA URUDU.MEŠ.

l. 12: *šu-u_4 up-⸢ta⸣-[qar]*. This interpretation follows Lacheman and the *CAD* Nuzi file. Lacheman seems to have seen more than is presently visible, noting: *up-t[a-qa]r*. Cf. *G* 30:9; 31:19.

The spelling of the first word appears playful (the scribe employs UD again in lines 32 and 35 with another unusual value), as may be the scribe's choice of phraseology for this clause. Cf. *JEN* 91:13, written by the same scribe, for a more typical expression of this idea.

l. 17: ⸢*at*⸣ 2. The amount of space between these signs suggests missing text. However, cf. *JEN* 91:17-18 for the same penalty as here assumed. As noted above, comments, *JEN* 91 is very close in form to the present text.

l. 19: [*z*]*e-y*[*a*]. The traces do not appear as copied but, rather, as:

l. 21: [*a*]*l*. Lacheman records this sign as completely preserved.

l. 29: *Šèr*. This sign, both here and in line 37, begins with two, then three, *Winkelhakens*, not three and three as drawn.

l. 34. The seal impression above this line is identified by Lacheman as "Po 699."

l. 34: *u*[*n*!]. The trace appears, not as copied, but, rather, as:

l. 35. The seal impression above this line is identified by Lacheman as "Po 777."

l. 36: [M]U. The trace appears as:

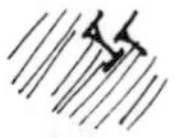

l. 37. The seal impression on this line is identified by Lacheman as "Po 595(?)."

l. 37: *Šèr*. See above, note to line 29.

JEN 752

OBVERSE

1 [*ṭup*]-*pí* •*ma*-•*ru-ti ša*

2 $^{[m]}$⸢*It*⸣-[*ḫa*]-*⸢*a*-•*pu*⸣ DUMU [*I*]*p-šá-ḫa-lu*

3 *^{m}**T*[*e-ḫi-ip-til*]-*la* •D[UM]U *Pu-ḫi-še-en-ni*

4 •*a*-•*na* [*ma-ru-ti*] *i*-⸢*te*⸣-*pu-us-sú*

5 4 •AN[ŠE? (?) A.ŠÀ (?) *i-na* ^{GIŠ}*ta-a-a-ri* (GAL)] ⸢*ša* É⸣.GAL-*lì* AŠ AN.ZA.KÀR $^{+}$*pí*-$^{+}$*ir*-$^{+}$*ša-an-ni*

6 *ša* $^{+m}$*T*[*e-ḫi-i*]*p*-⸢*til-la*⸣ [*i-na sú-/il-t*]*a-na*-•*nu š*[*a*] AN.⸢ZA⸣.KÀR [(?) *ša*?]

7 *a*-$^{+}$⸢*x*⸣ [ ]-ŠI ka_4-*ši-id*

8 *ki-m*[*a*? ḪA.LA-*šu*] *a-n*[*a*]

9 ^{m}*T*[*e-ḫi-ip-Til-l*]*a* DUMU [*P*]*u*-⸢*ḫi*⸣-*š*[*e-e*]*n-ni in*-⸢*din*⸣

10 ⸢*ù*⸣ [^{m}*Te-ḫi-ip-til-la* (?)]

11 [x?+] 6 A[NŠE?] ⸢ŠE⸣!?.[MEŠ?] ŠU?
12 *a-na* ^{m}*It-ḫa-*⸢*a*⸣-[*pu k*]*i-*⸢*ma*⸣ NÍG.⸢BA⸣-[*š*]*u*
13 *in-din il-*[*ka*$_4$ *ša*] ⸢A⸣.•ŠÀ $^{m?}$[*It-ḫ*]*a-a-pu* ⸢*na*⸣*-ši*
14 *šum-ma* A.ŠÀ *pa-*[*qí-ra-na i-r*]*a-*[*aš-ši*]
15 ^{m}*It-ḫa-a-*•*p*[*u ú-za-ak-ka*$_4$*-ma*]
16 •*a-na* ^{m}*Te-*$^{+}$*ḫi-*⸢*ip*⸣-[*til-la i-na-an-din*]
17 *šum-ma* $^{m•}$*I*[*t-ḫa-a-pu* KI.BAL]-⸢*tu*$_4$⸣
18 1 MA.NA KÙ.BAB[BAR 1 MA.NA KÙ.SIG$_{17}$]
19 *ú-ma-*[*a*]*l-l*[*a*]

---

20 [I]GI ⸢*Šúk-ri*⸣*-ip-a-pu* *DUM[U]⸢x⸣
21 [IGI]*-pí-še-en-ni* *DUMU [ ]
22 [IGI *Ḫ*]*u?-ti-ya* •DUMU *WA-[ ]
$^{+}$23 [IGI *Še?*]*-eš-wi-ya*
24 [D]UMU $^{+}$*Ki-ri-ip-a-pu*

LOWER EDGE

25 [IGI *A*]*k-ku-te-šup* DUMU *Ḫu-pí-*$^{+}$*ta-*$^{+}$*aḫ-*$^{+}$*ḫé*

REVERSE

26 [IGI *T*]*úr-še-en-ni*
27 ⸢DUMU *Ḫa*⸣*-ma-an-na*
28 6 LÚ.[ME]Š $^{+}$*mu-*$^{+}$*še-el-mu-ú* $^{+}$⸢*ša* A⸣.ŠÀ
29 *ù na-*$^{+}$*di-na-nu* $^{+}$*ša* Š[E]!?.M[EŠ]?

---

30 [IG]I *Šur-k*[*ip*]-⸢LUGAL⸣ DU[MU *-t*]*e-šu*[*p*]
31 ⸢IGI⸣ *Ar-*⸢*ti*⸣*-ir-*[*wi* DUMU]-•⸢x⸣
32 IGI *Ša-*⸢*ar*⸣*-te-š*[*up* DUMU]-⸢x⸣-AT-TA
33 IGI *Ar-ni-ya* D[UMU] ⸢*Šúk*⸣*-ri-ya*
34 IGI *Er-wi-*LUGAL D[UM]U *Te-eš-šu-ya*
35 IGI *Wa-qar-*EN DUMU *It-ḫi-iš-ta*
36 [I]GI ^{d}*Uta-an-dùl* [D]UMU *Ta-a-a* DUB.S[AR]*-rù*

S.I.

37 ^{NA_4} KIŠIB ^{m}*Ar-ti-ir-wi* ^{NA_4} KIŠIB ^{m}*Er-wi-*LUGAL

S.I.

38 ^{NA_4} ⸢KIŠIB⸣ ^{m}*Šúk-ri-ip-a-pu* ⸢^{NA_4} KIŠIB⸣ ^{m}*Ak-ku-Te-šup*

S.I.

39 ^{NA_4} ⸢KIŠIB⸣ ^{m}*Wa-qar-*EN

UPPER EDGE

S.I.

40 ^{NA_4} KIŠIB ^{d}*Uta-an-*$^{+}$*dùl*

TRANSLATION

(1-4) Tablet of adoption of Itḫ-apu son of Ipša-ḫalu. He adopted Teḫip-tilla son of Puḫi-šenni.

(5-9) He gave to Teḫip-tilla son of Puḫi-šenni as [his inheritance share a ...? field,] 4[+.x? homers? by the large? standard] of the palace in the *piršanni dimtu* of Teḫip-tilla, [to] the south/north of the *dimtu* ..., reaching ... .

(10-13) And [Teḫip-tilla] ...? gave to Itḫ-apu as his gift x(?)+6 homers(?) of barley(?) .... .

(13) Itḫ-apu shall bear the *ilku* [of] the field.

(14-16) Should the field have claimants, Itḫ-apu [shall clear (it) and give (it)] to Teḫip-tilla.

(17-19) Should Itḫ-apu abrogate (this contract), he shall pay 1 mina of silver [(and) 1 mina of gold].

(20-36) Before Šukrip-apu son of ...; [before] ...-pi-šenni son of ...; [before] Ḫu(?)-tiya son of WA-...; [before Š?]ešwiya son of Kirip-apu; [before] Akku-tešup son of Ḫupitaḫḫe; [before] Tur-šenni son of Ḫamanna. (These) 6 men are the measurers of the field and distributors of the barley(?).

Before Šurkip-šarri son of ...-tešup; before Ar-tirwi [son of] ...; before Šar-tešup [son of] ...; before Arniya son of Šukriya; before Erwi-šarri son of Teššuya; before Waqar-bêli son of Itḫišta; before Uta-andul son of Taya, the scribe.

(37-40) (*seal impression*) seal impression of Ar-tirwi (and) seal impression of Erwi-šarri; (*seal impression*) seal impression of Šukrip-apu (and) seal impression of Akku-tešup; (*seal impression*) seal impression of Waqar-bêli; (*seal impression*) seal impression of Uta-andul.

COMMENTS

The condition of this tablet is considerably worse now than when copied. A glue-like substance on the tablet surface has glazed over the signs, rendering them still more difficult to read.

The beginnings and ends of some of the lines of the obverse appear in the copy not to be written on the same "latitude." This alignment reflects accurately the appearance of these lines on the tablet.

The *CAD* Nuzi file for this text was authored by Lacheman. References to the file in the notes to this text indicate contributions by Lacheman.

Finally, in his unpublished notes, Chiera wrote regarding *JEN* 752, "Watch for this." The reason for this laconic admonition escapes me. It is disquieting.

NOTES

l. 1. The *CAD* Nuzi file records this line as completely preserved.

l. 3. The *CAD* Nuzi file records this line as completely preserved.

l. 5: AN[ŠE?]. The *Winkelhaken* is no longer visible. Lacheman once read, in effect: "^{GIŠ}[ ]," implying "^{GIŠ}[APIN]."

l. 5: [*i-na* ^{GIŠ}*ta-a-a-ri* (GAL)]. Or the like.

l. 5: AŠ AN.ZA.KÀR *pí-ir-ša-an-ni*. The land thus defined is to be located in Zizza. See above, note to *JEN* 692:5-6.

l. 7: ⸢*x*⸣. The trace appears, not as copied, but, rather, as:  Lacheman read *a-na* at the start of this line.

l. 8: *n*[*a*]. The *CAD* Nuzi file records this sign as completely preserved.

l. 10. To the line as here restored, Lacheman adds: [*ki-ma* N]ÍG.BA-*šu*, attaching what appears to be ŠU to this line, rather than to line 11, as in the present transliteration. He further notes that, as a result, the [*k*]*i*-⸢*ma*⸣ NÍG.⸢BA⸣-[*š*]*u* of line 12 becomes tautological.

Lacheman's reading is here perhaps the result of confusion resulting from halves of lines lacking clear alignment. The *CAD* Nuzi file fails to note [N]ÍG.BA-*šu*, i.e., any traces or signs at the end of line 10.

The ŠU? of line 11 might even represent [*l*]*a* at the end of line 10.

l. 11: [x?+] 6 A[NŠE?]. No wedge intervenes between these two signs. The tablet is clear at this point.

l. 11: ⸢ŠE⸣!?. This interpretation is dubious. The equivalent trace in line 29 does not remove this doubt. Lacheman (unpublished papers) and the *CAD* Nuzi file read "ŠE" at this point.

l. 11: ŠU?. See above, note to line 10.

l. 12: [*k*]*i*-⸢*ma*⸣ NÍG.⸢BA⸣-[*š*]*u*. See above, note to line 10.

l. 13: *$^{\text{m?}}$[*It-ḫ*]*a*. M[EŠ ^{m}*It-ḫ*]*a* is also possible.

l. 16: ⸢*ip*⸣-[*Til-la*]. The *CAD* Nuzi file records these signs as completely preserved.

l. 17: *I*[*t-ḫa-a-pu*]. The *CAD* Nuzi file records these signs as completely preserved.

l. 20: [ ]⸢x⸣. Only two patronymics are attested for the PN, "Šukrip-apu," Šaḫluya (*JEN* 277:26) and Zuizza-turiya (*JEN* 470:32). See *NPN*, 137a *sub* ŠUKRIP-APU. If the lacuna in line 20 is to be filled by either of these PNs, "Šaḫluya" is to be preferred. The space of the lacuna is more easily bridged by this shorter PN. (Also, the trace is consistent with a final [*y*]*a*—appropriate, to be sure, for either PN.) *JEN* 277, as opposed to *JEN* 470, shares with *JEN* 752 the following features. They reflect activity in the same generation. In both, Teḫip-tilla is involved in acquiring real estate,

and in the same area of the same town, Zizza. The same scribe wrote both texts and "Šukrip-apu" is the initial witness in both documents.

l. 21: [ ]-*pí-še-en-ni*. The first element of this name might be "Ḫurpi-," "Tulpi-," or, perhaps, "Umpi-." See *NPN*, 256a.

l. 26: [*T*]*úr*. The last part of this sign includes one small vertical wedge, not two as copied; the right wedge of the two in the copy does not appear on the tablet.

l. 29: Š[E]!?.M[EŠ]?. The *CAD* Nuzi file records ŠE.MEŠ as completely preserved. See also above, second note to line 11.

l. 30: *k*[*ip*]-⌜LUGAL⌝ DU[MU]. The *CAD* Nuzi file records these signs as completely preserved.

l. 31: ⌜x⌝. The trace consists of the right part of a horizontal wedge only, not a horizontal wedge across three small verticals as depicted.

ll. 37-38. Above each of these two lines, one seal has been rolled continuously across the entire width of the tablet. Each of these rollings is associated with two sealers. This means that, in some cases, not only does the legend under a seal impression not identify the owner of a seal (see above, note to *JEN* 675:45-48), it does not even identify the one who rolled the seal over the wet clay.

l. 38: ⌜KIŠIB⌝. Or: ⌜KIŠIB⌝ ^{m}.

l. 39: ⌜KIŠIB⌝. Or: ⌜KIŠIB⌝ ^{m}.

l. 40. Contrary to the impression of the copy, this line extends down almost to the edge of the obverse.

l. 40: *dùl*. The sign appears, not as copied, but, rather, as:

JEN 753

OBVERSE

1 [*li-ša-an-šu ša*] ^{m}*Ḫu-pí-ta* DUMU *Ké-li-ya*
2 [*a-na pa-ni* DI.KU$_{5}$].MEŠ *ki-a-am*
3 [*iq-ta-bi* x?+2 ANŠE] A.ŠÀ
4 [*i-na ša-pa-at N*]*i*!*-ri-iš-ši*
5 [(?) *i?-na?* URU? *Nu?*]*-zi*
6 [*a-na* ^{m}*Te-ḫi-ip-til-la*] *at-<ta>-din*
7 [*ù?* $^{\mathrm{m?}}$*Te?-ḫi?-ip?-til?-la?* x?+]2 ANŠE A.ŠÀ
8 [*ki?-ma? pu?-uḫ?* A?.Š]À?*-ya*
9 [*ù?* x? ANŠE? ŠE?].MEŠ
10 [*a?-na?* Ú?*-ti?* ^{m}*Te-ḫi*]-•*ip-til-la*
11 [*a-na ya-ši i-/id-d*]*i-na*
12 [*šum?-ma?* A.ŠÀ *p*]*a*!*-qí-ra-na*
13 [*i-ra-aš-ši* / TUK(*-ši*) *ù ú*]*-za-ak-kà*
14 [*iš-tu$_{4}$ u$_{4}$-mi an-ni*]*-i*
15 [*ma-am-ma* AŠ EGIR]*-ki*
16 [*ma-am-ma la i-ša-as*]*-sí*

LOWER EDGE

17 [ŠU ^{m} DUB].SAR
18 [$^{\mathrm{NA_4}}$ KIŠIB ^{m}*Tar-mi*]-*⸢*ya* *DUMU⸣ **Ú*-[*na-ap-*]

REVERSE

[:?]**ta*-[*e*]
S.I. Po 924
19 [$^{\mathrm{NA_4}}$ KIŠIB] ⸢^{m}*Te*⸣*-eš-šu-ya* DUMU •LUGAL
S.I. Po 632
20 [$^{\mathrm{NA_4}}$ KIŠIB] ^{m}⸢*Tar*⸣*-mi-Te-šup* DUMU
21 ⸢*Éḫ*⸣*-li-Te-šup*
S.I. Po 361

TRANSLATION

(1-3) [Declaration of] Ḫupita son of Keliya [before judge]s; thus [he spoke]:

(4-11) "I <have> given [to Teḫip-tilla a 2+x? homer] field [on the bank of] the Nirašši (Canal) [...? in? the? town? of?] Nuzi(?); [and?? Teḫip-Tilla??] Teḫip-Tilla has given (lit. "gave") [to me] a 2[+x?] homer field [as? the? equivalent? of?] my field(?) [and? x? homers? of? barley? as? excess? payment?].

(12-13) [Should? the field (of one) have] claimants, [then] he shall clear (it).

(15-16) [From] this [day] forward, [neither] shall hail [the other] (into court).

(17) [Hand of ...], the scribe.

(18-21) [seal impression of] Tarmiya son of Unap-tae (*seal impression*); [seal impression of] Teššuya son of the king (*seal impression*); [seal impression of] Tarmi-tešup son of Eḫli-tešup (*seal impression*).

COMMENTS

Lacheman copied this tablet twice, as *JEN* 753 and as *JEN* 712, 877. The latter two numbers represent the same copy and appear unaltered in Lacheman and Maidman (1989). *JEN* 753 is the better and more complete copy. However, it should be noted that *JEN* 753:18 (both parts) differs significantly from its counterpart, *JEN* 712 (=877):17-18. Collation of this part of the text proved impossible: the tablet is now totally obliterated at this point. Another important difference in the two copies is the identification of the seal impressions. In *JEN* 753, the first and second seal impressions are identified as S.I. Po 632 and 361 respectively. In the other copy, the second and third seal impressions are thus identified. The version of the other copy is to be preferred. See below, note to lines 18-21.

This tablet has suffered little additional damage since it was copied.

A fairly confident interpretation of this text is made possible by two happy circumstances. First, the surviving text makes it quite likely that the text is a declaration of real estate exchange, close in form, but clearly not identical, to *JEN* 131, 199, 711, to name but three. Second, the name of the principal is fully preserved (l. 1), and he is known to have engaged in another real estate exchange with Teḫip-tilla son of Puḫi-šenni, recorded in *JEN* 805. (The Teḫip-tilla of *JEN* 753:[6], [7?], 10 is certainly the son of Puḫi-šenni; the tablet comes from the family archive.) With these texts at hand, not only does the text yield sense, but some detailed restorations may be hazarded as well.

NOTES

l. 2: [DI.KU$_5$]. The three sealers of this text (ll. 18-21) all bear this title elsewhere. See Maidman (1981, 236-37, n. 15). Considerations of space also suggest this (short) restoration. Cf., however, a different, longer identification of these three officials in *JEN* 176:21-23, 2-3.

l. 3: [x?+2 ANŠE]. This restoration is most likely in light of line 7. Cf. also *JEN* 805:3, 8.

ll. 4-5. Line 4 is restored on the basis of *JEN* 805:3-4. The land described there suggests a Nuzi locus. (For this implication and on the designation "Niraššì" in general, see above, note to *JEN* 699:11.) The probable Nuzi location of the real estate leads, in turn, to the proposed restoration of that GN in line 5 of this text.

l. 4: [*N*]*i*!. The trace is correct as copied and does not appear to reflect a typical *Ni*.

l. 6: *at-<ta>-din*. *at-ta-din* is expected. See, for example, *JEN* 199:8. *ad-din* is possible but, in fact, very rare in such a context. Cf. *JEN* 187:16.

l. 7: [*ù*? ^{m}?*Te*?-*ḫi*?-*ip*?-*til*?-*la*?]. This restoration would be expected. Cf., e.g., *JEN* 141:10. I do not otherwise know how to fill this lacuna.

However, if this restoration is accepted, then the scribe is guilty of inappropriate repetition. Note the same PN in line 10, in conformity with the phraseology of this clause found, for example, in *JEN* 144:11-13.

ll. 8-10. The restorations proposed for these lines mean that the description of both the real estate to be ceded and an excess payment precedes the verb (l. 11). This order finds an analogue in *JEN* 185:11-13.

l. 8. This line is restored on the analogy of *JEN* 137:13; 152:12. A restoration, [*i-na* / AŠ AN.ZA.KÀR (*ša*) ^{m}*Ki-in-z*]*u-ya*, following *JEN* 805:9, is less likely owing to apparent lack of sufficient space.

ll. 9-10. For the restoration of these lines, cf. the form of *JEN* 114:13.

l. 10: [^{m}*Te-ḫi*]-*ip-til-la*. See above, note to line 7.

l. 12: [*šum*?-*ma*?]. This restoration would represent an abbreviated form of the formula found in *JEN* 122:16-21. *ša ma-an-ni-me-e* is expected. See, for example, *JEN* 711:7. There appears to be too little space for that restoration. Perhaps *ša ma-an-ni* was written. Cf. *JEN* 194:13.

l. 17: SAR. This sign, perfectly preserved, is typical. It does not appear as IN, as copied.

ll. 18-21. Collation of the seal impressions associated with these lines shows Lacheman to have been incorrect in his assignment of "Po" numbers to these sealings. His interpretation in *JEN* 712 (=877) is closer to the mark. The first impression is in fact represented as no. 924 in Porada (1947, plate XLV). The second is Po 632, and the third is Po 361. Below the third impression the tablet is preserved and blank.

Po 924 is identified elsewhere with Tarmiya son of Unap-tae (Porada 1947, 137b *ad* no. 924). Po 632 is identified with Teššuya *mār šarri* in another text (Porada 1947, 134a *ad* no. 632). Porada identifies Po 361 from *JEN* 753 itself (1947, 131a *ad* no. 361).

All of this means that, in this text, sealers are identified by means of legends before (i.e., above) their respective impressions rather than after (i.e., below) them. This is a very unusual phenomenon. See also *JEN* 757:30-32.

l. 18. The signs and traces at the equivalent point in *JEN* 712 (=877) are not the same. They yield no appreciable sense. This part of the tablet is now totally effaced. See above, comments.

l. 18: [*na-ap*]. Or the like.

l. 21: ⸢*Éḫ*⸣. This sign appears as: 

JEN 754

OBVERSE

1 [m]Ku$_8$-uš-ši-•ya [DUMU?]

---

2 [(?)]⸢x⸣ DUMU-šu [m]WA-aš?-[ ]
3 [a?]-⸢na⸣? [m?]⸢x x x⸣[ ]-in-•ti
+

---

4 ⸢i?-di⸣?-+in-⸢šu⸣

---

5 ⸢A⸣.ŠÀ.MEŠ-šu +É.+ḪÁ.MEŠ-šu GIŠ.ŠAR.M[EŠ-šu]

---

6 ma-na-ḫa-ti-š[u] ù? [ ].ḪÁ.MEŠ-šu

---

7 •ki?-ma ŠE-šu ⸢x x x⸣ iš-BI-⸢x⸣

---

8 ⸢x⸣-[š]u [m?]⸢Še⸣?-[ḫe?]-⸢el-te-šup⸣ it-⸢ta-din⸣

---

9 [ ] *ša •⸢DUMU [m]⸣Ku$_8$-uš-⸢ši-ya⸣

---

10 [B]I? ⸢la⸣? šu BI ⸢iš!? šu⸣-ni

---

11 [ ] el ⸢LI? KI⸣? [(?)] ⸢i⸣?-na ⸢x⸣ [š]a?

---

12 [ ]⸢x e⸣ BE ⸢x⸣[ ]
+

---

13 [I]K ⸢šu⸣?/⸢ma⸣? WA [Z]I •IK-⸢šu⸣

---

14 [ ] ka-⸢lu il x x-šu⸣?
15 [ ]-⸢šu x x⸣ [(?)] [m]Še-ḫe-⸢el⸣-[t]e-šup
16 [-+W]A?

.
.
.

REVERSE

.
.
.

---

17 [ ] ⸢x DUMU⸣ [ ]
18 [ ]⸢x-te?-šup⸣? [(?)]

S.I. Po 678

TRANSLATION

(1-18) Kuššiya [son? of? ...] gave it/him, (if "it," then: to?; if "him," then: i.e.,?; perhaps neither—M.P.M.) ... his son, Waš(?)-..., to(?) .... Šeḫel-tešup(?) gave his land, his structures, [his] orchards, his property and(?) his ...-s as(?) his barley(?) .... of the son of Kuššiya .... Šeḫel-tešup .... son of .... . *(seal impression)*

COMMENTS

This tablet is in poor condition. Yet it has deteriorated only slightly since the copy was made. Five fragments (unnumbered) have been reattached to the tablet since Lacheman first copied the document. These five fragments contain: (1) the missing part of *in* in line 4; (2) the three wedges after *šu* in line 7 (it is not clear to me that this fragment really belongs here); (3) the adjoining parts of ⌜*te-šup*⌝ in line 8; (4) the traces after *el* in line 11; and (5) the traces of the last three signs of line 14.

Lacheman did not copy the reverse. Collation confirms that the lengthy seal impression is Po 678. Cf. already Porada (1947, 134b *ad* no. 678). The two long vertical lines of the reverse indicate the limits of the seal impression. On this impression, see further below.

The meaning of this document is unclear. More is the pity since what remains suggests an unusual—if not unique—contract in the Nuzi texts. Lines 5-6, relatively well preserved, recall the phraseology in certain Nuzi wills (e.g. *HSS*, XIX, 9:4) and genuine adoptions (e.g., *HSS*, V, 60:5-6; cf. also below, note to line 14). On the other hand, the apparent structure of lines 1-7 is vaguely reminiscent of the antichretic loan context, *JEN* 299:1-6. If *that* comparison is correct, then *JEN* 754 might represent a similar type of loan based on personal service *and* real estate *and* mobilia, a combination of interest-producing types of collateral unique in the Nuzi texts as far as I know.

However, establishment of context in this document is very tenuous and it is very possible that *JEN* 754 deals neither with a bequest nor with a loan.

Nor are we aided by appeal to PNs. "Kuššiya" is a key name in the document (ll. 1, 9). Since the text comes from room 11, it is difficult to dissociate this Kuššiya from the like-named father of Ḫutiya of a family whose archives were, in part, stored in this very room. See, for example, *JEN* 342, 666. Yet the PNs in *JEN* 754 (ll. 2 [possibly a son of Kuššiya], 3?, 8 and 15, 18) are not attested as relatives of *the* Kuššiya. Cf. the useful genealogical chart in Dosch and Deller (1981, 97), a maximalist interpretation, quite possibly including individuals not part of the family at all. Thus either the Kuššiya of lines 1 and 9 is not the individual who sired Ḫutiya, despite the provenience of the tablet, or we are here confronted (in a broken context!) with one or more (adopted?) family members nowhere else attested. Neither solution satisfies. And so the preserved PNs do not advance our understanding of this text.

There are clear indications that *JEN* 754 is one of the earlier Nuzi texts. (This might tell against identifying this Kuššiya with the father of Ḫutiya; the latter does not belong to this early period.) The regularity of scribal lines (these lines are not represented in the translation; see above, comments to *JEN* 733) and the form of ḪA (l. 6) are telltale signs of the tablet's relative age. For characteristics of older Nuzi texts, see Purves (1940, 162-87); cf. above, comments to *JEN* 733 and below, comments to *JEN* 774.)

Now a further feature of older Nuzi texts is the frequent instability of contract formulas, even to the point where the precise definition of the contract type is open to dispute. See, for example, *JEN* 552 in the discussion of Purves (1945, 82-84). In this context, it should be reiterated that the surviving content of *JEN* 754 resembles, at points, several attested contract forms—and none convincingly. If this phenomenon is not illusory, i.e., due to the poor state of the tablet's preservation, then it may be a display of that very instability of form often found in older texts.

Finally, and most intriguingly, the unusual manner of sealing mirrors a most unusual seal impression. It is an early royal legend, not heretofore attested, of a type usually associated with royal land grants (Maidman 1987b, 335, no. 2):

(one line at the start is possibly missing)

1 [ ] ⸢DUMU⸣?
2 ⸢*Ki*⸣?-*pí-te-*
3 *eš-šu-up* LU[GAL KUR?]
4 *Ar-ra-*⸢*ap*⸣-
5 *ḫi* ^{NA_4} KIŠIB *an-*
6 ⸢*na*⸣-*a* ⸢*i*⸣-[*na*?]
7 [ ] ⸢x x⸣ [ ]
8 ⸢*di*⸣?-[*ni*?] ⸢*uš*⸣-[*ga*]-
9 *ra-ar* AŠ
10 [ ] [ ]
11? [ ]

Once again, it is particularly unfortunate that precisely such an atypical text is in such a poor state of preservation.

NOTES

l. 2: [(?)]⸢x⸣. If this document records a bequest of some sort (see above, comments, for this possibility), then "[*a-n*]*a*" would be a plausible restoration.

l. 2: ^{m}WA-*aš*?-[ ]. A "Wantiya son of Kuššiya" is elsewhere attested in the Nuzi texts. See *NPN*, 92b *sub* KUŠŠIḪA 16). ^{m}*Wa-a*[*n-ti-ya*] might be represented here. However, he appears elsewhere in contexts significantly later than the probable time period during which this text was written.

l. 3. A horizontal line may once have been visible above this line.

l. 3: *in-ti*. These signs quite clearly belong to line 3 and not line 4.

l. 4. A horizontal line appears above this line. This is not indicated in the copy.

l. 4: *in*. See above, comments.

l. 7: ⸢x x x⸣. For the first of these traces, see above, comments.

l. 8: ⸢x⸣. Might [DU]M[U] be thus represented?

l. 8: ⸢*el-te-šup*⸣. For the second and third signs, see above, comments. The first trace appears, not as copied, but, rather, as:

l. 11: ⸢LI⸣?. See above, comments. The traces might represent ⸢x⸣ TE or even TE!. If the latter be so, then the start of the line may might perhaps be restored: [^{m}*Še-ḫe*]-*el-te*!-⸢*šup*⸣. Cf. lines 8, 15. A form of the verb, *leqû*, might also be represented.

l. 12: ⸢x⸣ (= last preserved traces). The bottom of the three horizontal lines does not appear on the tablet. The surface is preserved at this point.

l. 13. A horizontal line appears above this line. This is not indicated in the copy.

l. 13: [I]K ⸢*šu*⸣?/⸢*m*⸣*a*? WA. *ik*-⸢*š*⸣*u-ud* ⸢x⸣ is possible.

l. 14. *ka*-⸢*lu-um*!-*ma-nu-ya*⸣ is possible. Cf. *HSS*, V, 60:7. On the possible relevance of *HSS*, V, 60 for this text, see above, comments. On the last three signs of this line, see above, comments.

l. 15: ⸢*šu*⸣. This trace appears, not as copied, but, rather, as:

l. 16: [W]A?. This trace appears, not as copied, but, rather, as:

JEN 755

OBVERSE

1 *ṭup-pí ma-ru-ti ša*
2 ^{m}*Še*-•⸢*ka*$_4$-•⸢*ru*⸣ •DU[MU] •*Ḫu-ti-ya* $^{[m]+}$*Te-ḫi-ip-til-la*
3 [DUMU *Pu-ḫi-še-en-ni*] ⸢*a*⸣-[*n*]*a ma-ru-ti*
4 [*i-pu-us-sú-ma* É?.Ḫ]Á? *i-na*
5 [*i-na le-e*]*t bi-ta-ti*
6 [*ša* *A-r*]*i-ka*$_4$-*ni*
7 [ ]-⸢*a*⸣?
8 [*a-na* ^{m}*Te-ḫi-ip-til-la ki*]-*ma* ḪA.LA-*šu*
9 [SUM-*šu ù* ^{m}*Te-ḫi-i*]*p-til-la*
10 [*ki?-ma?*] ⸢x⸣ AN? SUM-*šu*
.
.
.

REVERSE

.
.
.

S.I.

11 [^{NA_4} KIŠIB ^{m}T]I.LA-KUR ^{LÚ}DUB.•SAR

S.I.

12 [^{NA_4} KIŠIB ^{m}*M*]*u-uš-te-ya* DUMU *Zi-ir-ri*

S.I. S.I.

UPPER EDGE

13 $^{[NA_4]}$ ⸢KIŠIB⸣ ÌR-DINGIR-*šu* | | •NA$_4$ ^{m}*Mu-uš-te-šu-up* DUMU
+14 *Ar-na-a-pu*

TRANSLATION

(1-4) Tablet of adoption of Šekaru son of Ḫutiya. He adopted Teḫip-tilla [son of Puḫi-šenni].

(4-9) [He gave to Teḫip-tilla] as his inheritance share structures(?) in ... adjacent to the structures [of ...] Arik-kani ... .

(9-10) [And] Teḫip-tilla gave [... as?] .... .

....

(11-14) (*seal impression*) [seal impression of] Balṭu-kašid, the scribe; (*seal impression*) [seal impression of] Muš-teya son of Zirri; (*seal impression*) seal impression of Ward-ilišu; (*seal impression*)] seal impression of Muš-tešup son of Arn-apu.

COMMENTS

This tablet has suffered slight additional deterioration since it was copied.

The *CAD* Nuzi file for this text was authored by Lacheman. References to the file in the following notes indicate contributions by Lacheman.

NOTES

l. 2. The *CAD* Nuzi file records this line as completely preserved.

l. 4: [*i-pu-us-sú-ma*]. Or the like.

l. 4: [É?.Ḫ]Á?. This restoration is suggested by what is left of the next line.

ll. 5-6. The juxtaposition of structures and the PN/GN, "Arik-kani," both in a Teḫip-tilla context, recalls *JEN* 392:4 as restored by H. Lewy (1942, 35) on the basis of the related context, *JEN* 382:3. If the two references (i.e., *JEN* 755 and 392) refer to the same area, then a Nuzi locus is probably indicated for this real estate. See *JEN* 392:5 and cf. *JEN* 258:4, 7.

l. 5: [*le-e*]*t*. The *CAD* Nuzi file records these signs as completely preserved.

l. 10: ⸢x⸣ AN?. "*ki-ma* NÍG.BA-*šu*" is expected at this point. Perhaps the scribe erred and what appears is: [Ḫ]A.⸢LA⸣.

l. 12. The seal impression above this line is identified by Lacheman as Po 93.

l. 12: [*M*]*u*. The *CAD* Nuzi file records this sign as completely preserved.

l. 13. The seal impressions above this line are identified by Lacheman as Po 996 and Po 917 respectively.

l. 13: | |. What appears on the copy as a sideways [P]A is, in fact, a pair of parallel lines made by the scribe to indicate that the last three signs of the line are not to be read after the first four signs.

JEN 756

OBVERSE

1 [IGI *A-tal*]-⸢*te*⸣-[*šup* DUMU *Šum-mi-ya*]

2 [IGI *Šum-m*]*i-y*[*a* DUMU *A-ri-ka*$_4$*-na-ri*]

3 [IGI *Mu*]*š-te-y*[*a* DUMU *Ar-še-ni*]

4 I[GI *I*]*t-ḫi-iš-t*[*a* DUMU *Ta-mar-ta-e*]

5 ⸢IGI⸣ •*Ḫu-ti*$_4$*-pu-kùr* [DUMU *Ni-iš-ḫu-ḫa*]

6 IG[I] ⸢*A*⸣*-ri-ké-ya* DUMU [*A-ri-ya*]

7 IGI *It-ḫi-iš-ta* DUMU *A*[*l*]-$^+$⸢*pu*-$^+$*ya*⸣

8 IGI *Ḫu-i-te-šup* DUMU $^+$*Al*-$^+$*pu*-$^+$*ya*

9 IGI *Ta-a-a* DUMU *A-pil*-XXX $^+$DUB.$^+$SAR-$^+$*rù*

LOWER EDGE

10 *an-nu-ti ši-bu-ti ša* $^+$URU $^+$*Nu*-$^+$*zi*

11 IGI *Ki-pè-er-ḫa* DUMU *Ar-*$^{+}$*tù-*$^{+}$*un-*$^{+}$*ni*
12 IGI *Um-pí-ya* DUMU *Ki-pè-e*[*r*]-$^{+}$*ḫa*
REVERSE
13 •IGI *Še-en-na-pè* DUMU *Ḫa-i-*$^{+}$⸢*ra*⸣-$^{+}$*al-*$^{+}$*la*
14 IGI *A-ri-ka*$_4$*-ma-ri* DUMU $^{+}$*Zi-*$^{+}$*li-*$^{+}$*ya*
15 IGI *Ša-an-na-pu* DUMU *Še-*•$^{+}$*eš-wa-a-a*
16 IGI ^{d}XXX-MA.AN.BA DUMU *Na-*$^{+}$[*a*]*š-*$^{+}$*wi-*$^{+}$*ya*
17 IGI *Pu-ut-tù* DUMU *A-*•*ra-an-*•⸢*ta-*$^{+}$*i*⸣
18 *an-nu-ti ši-bu-ti ša* $^{+}$⸢URU $^{+}$*Ú*⸣-$^{+}$*na-*$^{+}$*ap-*$^{+}$*še-*$^{+}$*wa*
19 $^{+}$[*š*]*i-*⸢*bu*⸣*-ti ša ṭup-pí š*[*a-aṭ-rù* (*ù*)] ⸢A.ŠÀ⸣ [*il-mu*]-⸢*ú*⸣

S.I.

TRANSLATION

....

(1-19) [Before] Atal-tešup [son of Šummiya]; [before] Šummiya [son of Arik-kanari; before] Muš-teya [son of Ar-šenni]; before Itḫišta [son of Tamar-tae]; before Ḫutip-ukur [son of Niš-ḫuḫa]; before Arik-keya son of [Ariya]; before Itḫišta son of Alpuya; before Ḫui-tešup son of Alpuya; before Taya son of Apil-sin, the scribe. These are the witnesses of the town of Nuzi. Before Kip-erḫan son of Ar-tunni; before Umpiya son of Kip-erḫan; before Šennape son of Ḫairalla; before Arik-kamari son of Ziliya; before Šann-apu son of Šešwaya; before Sin-iqîša son of Našwiya (*sic*); before Puttu son of Aran-tai. These are the witnesses of the town of Unap-še. Witnesses who wrote (lit. are written) the tablet (and) who encircled the field.

(*seal impression*) ....

COMMENTS

The major part of this tablet, i.e., *JENu* 297, has suffered only slight additional damage since it was copied.

JENu 297, published in Lacheman and Maidman (1989), has now been joined by *JENu* 1167d. The latter fragment, like the former, comes from room 16 of the Teḫip-tilla Family archives. It adds the final signs of lines 7-19. This joined tablet is presented here as *JEN* 756 and supersedes the published copy.

Although the text now consists of only part of a witness list, the contract is easily identified. The surviving PNs are part of a witness sequence shared by perhaps eleven other texts. (Lacheman seems also to have recognized a witness sequence in this text.) These dozen texts are Teḫip-tilla real estate adoption contracts involving land in Unap-še. For further on this series of texts and a possible join to *JEN* 756, see above, note to *JEN* 690:18. On the basis of other texts in this series, restoration of lines 1-6 of the present text can be undertaken with confidence. On that basis also, it may be noted that

the present tablet lacks the text of the contract itself as well as the first two witnesses and, at the end, seal impressions with legends.

Porada's notes indicate that "[ ] BE" may once have appeared on the left edge. This line may have identified Šennape (cf. line 13) as a sealer of the tablet.

NOTES

l. 2: *y*[*a*]. The trace appears, not as copied, but, rather, as:

l. 16: *Na*-[*a*]*š-wi-ya*. These signs are quite clear. [A]Š is represented by a single horizontal stroke; the wedge head is destroyed. This clarity is disturbing since, wherever else this part of the witness sequence appears, the patronymic of this Sin-iqîša appears as Šešwaya, not Našwiya. See *JEN* 51:31; 58:31; 70:33; 582:32; *JENu* 716:25. The appearance of this patronymic is furthermore disturbing since the PN, Našwiya, seems nowhere else attested in the Nuzi texts. Either the scribe has erred here (very likely) or Sin-iqîša was identified by more than one patronymic (less likely).

If the scribe erred, perhaps he "reasoned" or "heard": Šešwaya (cf. line 15) > Šešwiya (well attested) > Našwiya (Našwi is well attested). Such failure of the mind's ear are termed "auto-dictation" errors by Grayson (1991, 265-66). Grayson considers this a type of *Hörfehler* and envisions a process whereby the scribe mutters to himself the text he is copying. The same type of error occurs during silent writing.

If the scribe did not err, then the same son of Našwiya may have appeared as a witness in *JEN* 747:22. See above, first note to *JEN* 747:22. For another possible scribal error, see below, note to line 19.

l. 18: ⸢URU⸣. The restoration is clear although the trace is minimal:

l. 19: *š*[*a-aṭ-rù* (*ù*)] ⸢A.ŠÀ⸣ [*il-mu*]-⸢*ú*⸣. The traces appear as:

The restorations are based on close parallels in *JEN* 51:33-34 and 582:34-35, from texts in the series to which *JEN* 756 belongs. By analogy to those passages, one would expect *šu-nu-ma* to appear here before A.ŠÀ. However, there does not appear to be sufficient room in the first lacuna for three additional signs. It is unclear whether or not this omission represents a scribal lapse. For another possible scribal error, see above, note to line 16.

JEN 757

OBVERSE

1 [^{m}Ni-iḫ-ri-ya DUMU -r]i-ya
2 [a-na ma-ru-ti i(-te)]-pu-uš-ma
3 [x?+1 ^{GIŠ}APIN A].ŠÀ i+na mi-iṣ-ri ša URU A-ki-p[a-/p[á-pu(-wa)]
4 [ù? AN?.ZA?.KÀR?] ⸢ù⸣? ma-QA-ḫu i+na le-et É.ḪÁ ma x ⸢x⸣
5 [x?+]⸢1⸣ ^{GIŠ}APIN A.ŠÀ •an-nu-ú a-šar É.ḪÁ na-du-ú
6 [i-na URU] Ú-na-ap-še
7 ⸢x⸣[ki-ma ḪA.LA]-šu SUM-šu
8 [ù ^{m}]Te-[ḫi-ip-til-la x?+]3 MA.NA URUDU
9 $^{+}$⸢x $^{+}$x⸣ ma AŠ? [a-na ^{m}Ni-iḫ-ri-y]a SUM
10 [šum-ma] A.ŠÀ AN.ZA.KÀR ù tar-bá-ṣú
11 [pí-i]r-qa TUK-ši šu-ú ^{m}Ni-iḫ-ri-ya
12 [ú-z]a-ak-ka$_{4}$-ma ù a-na ^{m}Te-ḫi-ip-til-la i+na-an-din
13 [ù i]l-ku ša A.ŠÀ an-ni-i
14 [^{m}Te]-ḫi-ip-til-la la na-ši
15 [^{m}Ni-i]ḫ-*r[i-y]a [n]a-ši
16 [šum-ma ^{m}Ni-iḫ-ri-ya K]I.BAL -at
17 [2? MA.NA KÙ.BABBAR 2? MA.NA KÙ.SI]G$_{17}$ ú-ma-al-la
18 [IGI DUMU -y]a/]-e

.

.

.

LOWER EDGE

19 [IGI DUMU]-RU
20 [IGI DUMU -n]a?-a-a

REVERSE

21 [IGI DUMU]-PA?-[(?)]-RU
22 [IGI DUMU]-te-šup
23 [mu-še-e]l-wu-ú ša A.ŠÀ ù na
24 [IGI DUMU] ⸢Še⸣?-[k]a$_{4}$?-rù
25 [IGI Ta?-(i?-)$^{+}$i]n-šu-uḫ DUMU Šu-ru-pé-ya
26 [IGI Ul-m]i-a-tal DUMU Šúk-ri-ya
27 [IGI A?-ki]p?-til-la DUMU Ké-li-ya
28 [IGI Ša]-am-ḫa-ri DUMU Tu-ra-ri
29 [IGI E?-/Še?-ḫe]-el-te-šup DUB.SAR DUMU XXX-ib-ni
30 NA$_{4}$ ^{m}A-kip-til-la
S.I. Po 120
31 NA$_{4}$ ^{m}Ul-mi-a-tal
S.I. Po 14

LEFT EDGE

32 NA$_{4}$ ^{m}Ša-am-ḫa-ri

S.I. Po 187

UPPER EDGE

33 [NA$_4$? $^{m?}$]-⸢x⸣-PA-*ni*

[S.I.?]

TRANSLATION

....

(1-2) [Niḫriya son of] ...-riya adopted him.

(3-7) He gave to him (i.e., to Teḫip-tilla) ... [as] his [inheritance share], a [...? .1+x? homer] field within the border of the town of Akip-apu, [a ... tower?], and(?) a (livestock) pen(?) adjacent to the ... structures .... this .1+x(?) homer field is situated by the structures; [... in the town of] Unap-še.

(8-9) [And] Teḫip-Tilla gave [to] Niḫriya ... 3+x(?) minas of copper.

(10-12) [Should] the field, the tower, and the (livestock) pen have a claim (against them), he, Niḫriya, shall clear (them) and then give (them) to Teḫip-tilla.

(13-15) [And] Teḫip-tilla shall not bear the *ilku* of this field. Niḫriya shall bear (it).

(16-17) [Should Niḫriya] abrogate (this contract), he shall pay [2? minas of silver (and) 2? minas of] gold.

(18-29) [Before ... son of] ...; ....; [before ... son of] ...; [before ... son of] ...; [before ... son of] ...; [before ... son of] ...-tešup. ... measurers of the field and gi (*sic;* start of "givers of ...."). [Before ... son of] Šekaru(?); [before] Tain(?)-šuḫ son of Šurupeya; [before] Ulmi-atal son of Šukriya; [before] Akip(?)-tilla son of Keliya; [before] Šamḫari son of Turari; [before Eḫ]li(?)-/[Še]ḫel(?)-tešup, the scribe, son of Sin-ibnī.

(30-33) seal impression of Akip-tilla (*seal impression*); seal impression of Ulmi-atal (*seal impression*); seal impression of Šamḫari (*seal impression*); [seal? impression? of?] ... [(*seal impression*?)].

COMMENTS

This tablet has suffered practically no additional damage since it was copied.

The *CAD* Nuzi file for this text was authored by Lacheman. References below to this file signify contributions by Lacheman.

Probably one line is missing at the start of this tablet: *ṭup-pí ma-ru-ti ša* ^{m}*Te-ḫi-ip-til-la* DUMU *Pu-ḫi-še-en-ni.* Line 1 would then identify the adopter as Niḫriya (cf. line 11) son of ...-riya. Less likely, but still possible, the missing (first) line could be rendered: *ṭup-pí ma-ru-ti ša* ^{m}*Te-ḫi-ip-til-la*. This would be followed by:

1 [DUMU *Pu-ḫi-še-en-ni* ^{m}*Ni-iḫ-r*]*i-ya*

2 [DUMU PN *a-na ma-ru-ti i*(*-te*)]*-pu-uš-ma*

NOTES

ll. 1-2. See comments.

l. 3: URU *A-ki-p*[*a-/p*[*á-pu*(*-wa*)]. For this restoration, cf. lines 3 and 6 with *JEN* 761:8, 6.

l. 4: *ma*-QA-*ḫu*. Cf. *JEN* 631:10. No other occurrence of this term is known to me. If the order, *eqlu-dimtu-tarbaṣu* (*JEN* 757:10), is consistent with the order here suggested for lines 3-4, then *ma*-QA-*ḫu* is equivalent to *tarbaṣu* and may represent its Hurrian language counterpart. The previous literature on this term is predictably sparse and laconic: Goetze (1940, 170 [no translation]); *CAD*, M/1, 121b *sub makaḫu* ("enclosure(?)").

l. 4: x ⸢x⸣. These wedges appear, not as depicted, but, rather, as:

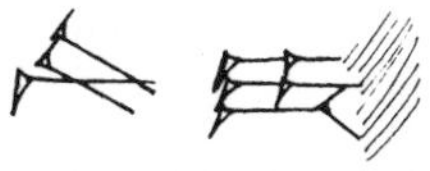

I do not understand the meaning of these wedges or their significance in this context.

l. 5: *na-du-ú*. For the meaning "situated" for *nadû*, see *CAD*, N/1, 91b *sub* b).

l. 6: [*i-na*]. This restoration is based on *JEN* 761:6-8 which bears on *JEN* 757:3-6. Apropos the former text, the *dimtu* of Akawatil is located in Unap-še (cf. *JEN* 736:5-7). For other connections between *JEN* 757 and 761, see below, note to lines 13-15.

l. 6: *še*. This is the last sign on this line. The tablet is well preserved in this area.

l. 8: 3. The tablet, at this point, contains three vertical wedges, not four as depicted.

l. 9: ⸢x x⸣. The first visible traces are not "[Ḫ]A" as depicted, but, rather:

The start of this line may be rendered: ⸢*ki*⸣!-*ma* N[ÍG!.BA-*šu*]. Difficult as this interpretation appears, the space in the lacuna itself seems insufficient for [*ki-ma* NÍG.BA-*šu*] before [*a-na* ^{m}*Ni-iḫ-r*]*i-*.

ll. 13-15. This *ilku* clause is somewhat unusual in its statement of who does not bear this impost as well as who does. Cf., by contrast, *JEN* 752:13. Clauses similar to the present one are found in *JEN* 749:13-14; 761:16-17. Note further that all three of these Teḫip-tilla adoption texts deal with land in Unap-še (*JEN* 749:7; 757:6; 761:6), the latter two texts sharing even more detailed description (see above, note to *JEN* 757:3). Two, perhaps all three, texts were likely written by the same scribe (*JEN* 749:28; 757:29; 761:41?).

Cf. also above, notes to *JEN* 749:7, 23.

l. 13: A.ŠÀ. It is plausible that this term stands here for all three alienated items, field, tower, and (livestock) pen(?), that is, A.ŠÀ here means "real estate." That A.ŠÀ can represent different types of land has already been shown above, note to *JEN* 715:5. See also below, *JEN* 774:6.

l. 17: [2? MA.NA KÙ.BABBAR 2? MA.NA KÙ.SI]G$_{17}$. For this possible restoration, cf. *JEN* 749:16. On the relevance of *JEN* 749 for the present text, see immediately preceding note.

ll. 18-20, 22. For the identity of these witnesses, cf., perhaps, *JEN* 761:29-31, 33, respectively. On the relevance of *JEN* 761 for the present text, see above, note to ll. 13-15.

l. 23: [*e*]*l*. The trace does not appear as copied but, rather, as:

l. 23: *na*. The scribe appears to have ceased writing, at this point, what should have continued as: *-di-na-nu ša* URUDU (*ù*? ...?). See also next note.

l. 24. The *CAD* Nuzi file, in effect, records for this line: [ ] DUMU *Še-ka*$_4$*-rù*. It is possible that this line continues the clause begun in line 23.

l. 25: [*Ta*?-(*i*?-)*i*]*n-šu-uḫ*. For this restored PN, see above, note to *JEN* 749:26. That note applies to this line as well.

l. 25: [*i*]*n*. The trace appears, not as copied, but, rather, as:

l. 26: [*Ul-m*]*i*. Cf. line 31.

l. 27: [*A*?-*ki*]*p*?. This restoration is accepted by the *CAD* Nuzi file and by *NPN*, 16b *sub* AKIP-TILLA 15), 82a *sub* KELIJA 23). This restoration is based, no doubt, on line 30 of the present text. Although, in theory, the "Akip-tilla" of line 30 could be one of the anonymous witnesses of lines 18-22 and the break in the text (or even no witness at all), it is quite possible that he is this witness, the son of Keliya. Note that the sealers in lines 31 and 32 are almost surely the witnesses of lines 26, 28, i.e., the PNs of the sealers (ll. 30-32) seem also to be clustered in lines 26-28.
Cf. *JEN* 749:23.

l. 29: [*E*?-/*Še*?-*ḫe*]. The *CAD* Nuzi file records ḪE as completely preserved. On the restoration of this PN, see above, note to *JEN* 749:28.

ll. 30-32. See above, note to l. 27. Note that these lines, identifying the sealers of the tablet, appear above the seal impressions rather than below, as is usually the case. Cf. above, note to *JEN* 753:18-21.

JEN 758

OBVERSE

1 ṭup-p[í ma-ru-ti •š]a

2 ^{m}Na-*an-*t[e-eš-šu-up] •DUMU Kip-til-la

3 •ù •^{m}•Te-•ḫi-ip-[til-l]a DUMU Pu-ḫi-še-en!-ni

4 a-na ma-ru-t[i] ⸢i⸣-te-pu-uš

5 9 ^{GIŠ}APIN A.ŠÀ i-na ta-a-ri ša É.GAL ⸢ša GAL⸣

6 i-na le-•⸢et⸣ AN.ZA.KÀR

7 ša ^{m}Šá-$^{+}$⸢ak⸣-ru-uš-še-e

8 a-na ^{m}Te-ḫi-ip-til-la SUM

9 ù ^{m}Te-ḫi-ip-til-la 9 BÁN ŠE.MEŠ

10 ki-ma NÍG.BA ⸢a⸣-na ^{m}Na-an-te-eš-šu-up •SUM

11 šum-ma A.ŠÀ pa-qí-ra-an-na ir-ta-⸢ša⸣

12 ù •^{m}Na-an-•te-eš-šu-up ú-za-ak-⸢ku⸣-[ma]

13 a-na ^{m}Te-ḫi-ip-til-la i-na-an-di

14 šum-ma ^{m}Na-an-te-eš-šu-up

15 K[I].•BAL-tu$_4$ 1 MA.NA KÙ.BABBAR 1 MA.NA KÙ.⸢SIG$_{17}$⸣

16 [ú-*m]a-•al-la

17 [il-ku]-⸢ú⸣ ša A.ŠÀ a-na ^{m}Na-an-te-eš-šu-$^{+}$⸢up⸣-[ma na-a-ši]

---

18 [IGI Ur-ḫi-ya DU]MU Še-ka$_4$-rù

19 [IGI Zi-il$_5$-te-y]a DUMU Ta-ú-ka$_4$

LOWER EDGE

S.I.

REVERSE

20 IGI Ú-[na-ap-ta]-⸢e⸣ DUMU Ni-$^{+}$ir-ḫi-te-eš-š[u-up]

21 IGI Ḫu-t[i-ip-ti]l-la DUMU KI.MIN

22 IGI Be-li-⸢ya⸣ DUMU A-ki-a

23 IGI [Ḫ]a-⸢al⸣-[še-en]-ni DUMU Ta-a-a

24 IGI •⸢A-•ri⸣-*ḫ[a!-ar-me-e] ⸢DUMU⸣ [Ḫ]a-na-a-a

25 IGI Ke-[li-ip-LUGAL DUMU] Al-ki-ya

26 DUMU ⸢KI⸣ [ ]⸢x⸣[(?)]

27 IGI Š[e!-eḫ-l]i-⸢ya⸣ D[UMU] Ak-[ku-ya]

S.I. Po 358

28 ^{NA_4} KIŠIB Be-li-ya š[i-b]i

S.I.

29 [^{NA_4} KIŠIB Še]-⸢eḫ⸣-[li]-y[a] [š]i-bi

S.I. Po 199

LEFT EDGE

30 ^{NA_4} KIŠIB Ur-ḫi-ya

REVERSE

31 ^{NA_4} KIŠIB •⸢Ú-•na-•ap-ta-e⸣ ši-bi

S.I. Po 573

32 ^{NA_4} KIŠIB *A-⌜ri⌝-ḫa-ar-me-e*

S.I. Po 175

UPPER EDGE

33 *an-nu-tu*$_4$ ^{LÚ}*ši-bu-tu*$_4$ ⌜*ša*⌝?

34 •*la-mu-ú ša* A.ŠÀ

LEFT EDGE

35 ^{NA_4} KIŠIB *En-na-ma-ti* DUB.SAR-*rù*

TRANSLATION

(1-4) Tablet of [adoption] of Nan-tešup son of Kipi-tilla. Now he adopted Teḫip-tilla son of Puḫi-šenni.

(5-8) He gave to Teḫip-Tilla a field, .9 homers by the large standard of the palace (lit. "the standard of the palace which is large"), adjacent to the *dimtu* of Šakrušše.

(9-10) And Teḫip-tilla gave to Nan-tešup as a gift .9 homers of barley.

(11-13) Should the field have claimants, then Nan-tešup shall clear (it) [and] give (it) to Teḫip-tilla.

(14-16) Should Nan-tešup abrogate (this contract), he shall pay 1 mina of silver (and) 1 mina of gold.

(17) [It is] Nan-tešup [who shall bear] the *ilku* of the field.

(18-27) [Before Urḫiya] son of Šekaru; [before] Zil-teya son of Tauka; (*seal impression* [cf., below, last sealer]); before Unap-tae son of Niḫri-tešup; before Ḫutip-tilla son of the same; before Bêliya son of Akiya; before Ḫalu-šenni son of Taya; before Ariḫ-ḫarpa son of Ḫanaya; before Kelip-šarri [son of] Alkiya; son of (*sic*) ...; before Šeḫliya son of Akkuya.

(28-35) (*seal impression*) seal impression of Bêliya, witness; (*seal impression*) [seal impression of] Šeḫliya, witness; (*seal impression*) seal impression of Urḫiya; seal impression of Unap-tae, witness (*seal impression*); seal impression of Ariḫ-ḫarpa (*seal impression*). These are the witnesses who(?) are(?) the encirclers of the field. Seal impression of Enna-mati, the scribe (cf. above, impression after second witness).

COMMENTS

This tablet has suffered some deterioration since it was copied.

The *CAD* Nuzi file for this tablet was authored by Lacheman. The reference below to this file indicates a contribution by Lacheman.

Interpretation of this text is aided at several points by appeal to a series of tablets very similar to *JEN* 758. For details, see below, note to lines 5-7.

In addition to scribal idiosyncrasies, the writer of this text seems to have had mental lapses. See below, notes to lines 5, 17 and 26.

NOTES

ll. 1-4. The *CAD* Nuzi file records these lines as completely preserved.

l. 3: *en*!. This sign is correct as copied.

ll. 5-7. The real estate described in these lines is perhaps to be located in Unap-še. The key to linking the *dimtu* of Šakrušše (ll. 6-7) to Unap-še is the distinct possibility that a single, infrequently attested scribe appears in connection with both toponyms. Enna-mati son of ᵈUTU-DINGIR-AŠ-KUR is the scribe of *JEN* 614, a text dealing with land near this *dimtu* (for the scribe, see line 30; for the GN, lines 5-6). One "Enna-mati," lacking a patronymic but doubtless the same scribe, appears in seven other texts, similar to *JEN* 614, dealing with land in or near this *dimtu*: *JEN* 40 (l. 28), 49 (l. 35), 401 (l. 30), 758 (the present text; l. 35), 763 (l. 39, very likely), 764 (l. 22), 765 (l. 31; see also note to *JEN* 765:30).

These eight tablets represent all but one or two of the Teḫip-tilla texts mentioning the *dimtu* of Šakrušše; the other such texts are *JEN* 411 and, possibly, 739. These eight tablets also represent all but three of the texts written by Enna-mati son of ᵈUTU-DINGIR-AŠ-KUR; the other such texts are *JEN* 119, 546, 812. None of those texts deals with real estate. But a toponym does appear: *JEN* 546 was written in the town of Ulamme (ll. 29-32). Cf. also below, note to line 19.

The only other texts in the Teḫip-tilla Family archives in which a scribe, "Enna-mati," appears are *JEN* 191 (l. 17) and 379 (l. 35, very likely), both dealing with Unap-še real estate (see *JEN* 191:5-6; 379:5-6). The latter two texts differ from the former eight in several ways. To name but one, Teḫip-tilla is involved in the former eight, a son of his in the latter two. Yet only one other clearly identified "Enna-mati" is known to have been a scribe for this family, a son of one Puḫi-šenni. He is attested but once, *JEN* 403:41-42, in a context two generations removed from Teḫip-tilla.

If all the other texts (excepting *JEN* 403) emanate from the same Enna-mati (i.e., the son of ᵈUTU-DINGIR-AŠ-KUR), then the *dimtu* of Šakrušše and Unap-še real estate locations described in those texts may indicate that this *dimtu* is to be located in the environs of Unap-še. (Note also that Urḫiya son of Šekaru, the most ubiquitous Teḫip-tilla witness to be found in the eight *dimtu* of Šakrušše texts, is several times identified with Unap-še real estate transactions. "Šekaru - Unap-še" texts include, e.g., *JEN* 38, 703, 751.)

Fadhil (1983, 261b-263b, especially 263a) suggests the town of Ulamme as the location of this *dimtu*. Clear evidence is lacking for this suggestion and the circumstantial evidence adduced is at least as weak as that supporting Unap-še. (To the evidence given can be added *JEN* 546, noted above as having been written in Ulamme by the writer of eight of the *dimtu* of Šakrušše texts.)

The common scribe and common GN of *JEN* 40, 49, 401, 614, 758, 763, 764, 765 is noteworthy in another context as well. Weeks (1972, 204) already discerned these two common features linking the eight texts. He further describes other common elements. These include a largely common roster of witnesses. So regular is the reappearance of witnesses in these eight texts that partial lacunae in one (including the present text) may be restored with confidence on the basis of the witness lists of other texts in this cluster.

What is odd about this largely homogeneous group is the lack of a stable witness *sequence*, such as is found in other, similar groupings. Cf., e.g., the Nuzi-Apena witness sequence discussed above, note to *JEN* 674:23. Perhaps this lack of a common sequence is itself a scribal characteristic of Enna-mati. Enna-mati exhibits a number of scribal peculiarities. Weeks (1972, 204) notes several, including characteristic orthography, phraseology, relative positioning of clauses, amount of penalty, and price tendered for land (1 homer of land = 1 homer of barley; Fadhil [1983, 262b] also recognizes this feature; see also below, first note to *JEN* 764:5). Other such peculiarities are noted below, notes to lines 5, 11, 13, 17 (first note), 19, 22. (Features already noted by Weeks are not mentioned below.) Where such scribal peculiarities are effaced in one text, they are, of course, revealed by comparison with its companion texts.

l. 5: *i-na ta-a-ri ša* É.GAL ⌜*ša* GAL⌝. One expects *i-na ta-a-ri ša* É.GAL (cf. *JEN* 49:5?; 614:5; 763:5?, all written by the scribe of this text) or *i-na ta-a-ri* GAL *ša* É.GAL (or the like; an otherwise common formulation, e.g., *JEN* 686:4), or even *i-na ta-a-ri ša* É.GAL GAL (or the like; another common formulation, e.g. *JEN* 700:6), but not *i-na ta-a-ri ša* É.GAL *ša* GAL. Yet, this scribe employs the same peculiar form in *JEN* 764:6

l. 7: ⌜*ak*⌝. The trace appears, not as copied, but, rather, as:

l. 11: *pa-qí-ra-an-na*. For this spelling, cf. *JEN* 764:11, written by the same scribe.

l. 12: *ú*. This sign appears, not as copied, but, rather, as:

l. 12: ⌜*ku*⌝. ka_4 is expected.

l. 13: *i-na-an-di*. There is probably no sign missing at the end of this line, nor may one posit an accidental omission of *in*. For this spelling, see also *JEN* 40:12, 15; 49:13; 763:14, 17; 764:13.

l. 17. For the restoration of this line, cf. *JEN* 40:16. Two oddities deserve note. First, the spelling *il-ku-ú* appears regularly in this group of texts: *JEN* 40:16; 49:17; 614:18; 763:18. Second, the appearance of *a-na* recurs in the same context, *JEN* 40:16. This appears to be a scribal error in both

places (i.e., a mental lapse, perhaps based on the pattern established by *JEN* 40:15; 758:13). The expected word here is *ù*. Cf. *JEN* 49:17; 763:18. If *a-na* is deliberate then a translation such as the following (forced though it be) is called for: "The *ilku* of the field is for Nan-tešup <to> bear."

Below ⸢*ú*⸣ and *ša* in the copy appears a horizontal line. This is a deliberate line made by the scribe.

l. 17: ⸢*up*⸣. The trace does not appear as copied, but, rather, as:

l. 18: [*Ur-ḫi-ya*]. For this restoration, as well as that of other PNs in this witness list, see above, note to lines 5-7.

l. 19. *Below* DUMU *Ta* in the copy appears a wedge. This wedge (and the line of text it implies) does not appear on the tablet. The tablet is well preserved at this point.

Below line 19, on the lower edge, appears a seal impression. The placement of this impression in the midst of the list of witnesses is unexpected. Note that line 35, on the left edge, identifies a seal impression as that of Enna-mati, the scribe. There is no seal impression on the same edge as the legend (*NB*: all other such legends on this tablet can be paired off with impressions). It appears that the impression on the lower edge is that which is identified on the left edge. (Yet the seal impression on the lower edge, though very faint, is clearly not Po 100 [cf. Porada 1947, 127b], an impression identified with Enna-mati in *JEN* 546:27.) For a possibly similar phenomenon, see below, note to *JEN* 765:30.

l. 22: *A-ki-a*. For this spelling (as opposed to the expected *A-ki-ya*), cf. the similar practice of the same scribe in *JEN* 763:28; 764:19; 765:2, 28.

l. 25: *Ke*-[*li-ip*-LUGAL]. If the restoration of this PN is correct—and it appears all but certain—then this is a unique spelling for this scribe. This PN is elsewhere spelled with initial GI (=*ké*).

l. 26. Perhaps one ought to consider DUMU a mental lapse for IGI and render this line: IGI! ⸢*Ki*⸣-[*in-na-a-a* DUMU *A*]*r*-[*Til-la*]. As it stands, the line makes little sense.

l. 31. The seal impression below this line is Po 573, not Po 578 as stated in the copy. Cf. Porada (1947, 133b).

l. 33. ⸢*ša*⸣?. The trace appears, not as copied, but, rather, as:

l. 35. See above, note to line 19.

JEN 759

OBVERSE

1 [ṭup-*p]í •ma-[ru-ti ša]
2 [^{m}*M]i-•na-aš-⸢šu⸣-[uk DUMU]
3 [ù] *^{m}•Te-•ḫi-ip-[til-la DUMU Pu-ḫi-še-en-ni]
4 [a-na] •ma-ru-ti i!-p[u-us-sú]
5 *⸢4⸣? •^{GIŠ}•APIN A.ŠÀ i-na ⸢X⸣[ ]
6 ki-•ma •ḪA.LA-šu ^{m}M[i-na-aš-šu-uk]
7 a-na ^{m}•Te-ḫi-ip-til-la ⁺⸢i-⁺di⸣?-[in?]
8 ù ^{m}Te-ḫi-ip-til-la 4 ⸢ANŠE •5? BÁN? ŠE⸣!?
9 a-na ^{m}Mi-na-aš-šu-uk ki-ma NÍG.BA-šu SUM
10 šum-ma A.ŠÀ •pa-i-iq-ra-⸢na ir⸣-[t]a-ši
11 ^{m}Mi-na-aš-šu-uk ú-za-⸢ak⸣-ka$_{4}$-m[a] •⸢ù⸣
12 a-n[a ^{m}]⸢T⸣e-ḫi-ip-til-la ⸢i⸣-[n]a-din [šu]m-ma
13 ^{m}⸢Mi⸣-na-aš-šu-uk KI.•⸢BAL ⸣-kat
14 1 MA.NA ⸢KÙ⸣.BABBAR 1 MA.NA KÙ.SIG$_{17}$
15 ú-ma-a[l]-la
16 IGI ^{m}Ma-⸢ti-ya⸣ [DUMU Ma-ra?-]
17 IGI ^{m}Zi-il-⸢te-eš⸣-šup *D[UMU T]e-eš-šu-⸢ya⸣
18 IGI ^{m}Eḫ-li-y[a] DUMU Pur-ni-tù-rù

LOWER EDGE

19 IGI ^{m}A-ka$_{4}$-we ⸢DUMU⸣ I-lu-ša
20 IGI ^{m}Zi-il-te-ya DUMU T[a-ú-ka$_{4}$]
21 an-nu-tu$_{4}$ $^{LÚ.ME[Š]}$ mu-še-el-•mu-⸢ú⸣

.

.

.

REVERSE

S.I.

22 [^{NA_4} KIŠIB ^{m}]⁺Mi-na-aš-šu-u[k]

S.I.

23 N[^{A_4} KI]ŠIB ^{m}Zi-il-te-ya

24 ^{L}[^{Ú}s]à-sú-uk-ki S.I. Po 302

25 ^{NA_4} KIŠIB ^{m}Er-wi-LUGAL ⁺DUB.S[AR-ri?]

S.I.

26 ⸢^{NA_4}⸣ KIŠIB ^{m}Eḫ-li-ya DUMU Pur-ni-tù-rù

TRANSLATION

(1-4) Tablet of adoption [of] Minaš-šuk [son of ...]. [Now] he adopted Teḫip-tilla [son of Puḫi-šenni].

(5-7) Minaš-šuk gave to Teḫip-tilla as his inheritance share a .4(?) homer field in .... .

(8-9) And Teḫip-tilla gave to Minaš-šuk as his gift 4.(?)5(?) homers of barley(?).

(10-12) Should the field have claimants, Minaš-šuk shall clear (it) and then give (it) to Teḫip-tilla.

(12-15) Should Minaš-šuk abrogate (this contract), he shall pay 1 mina of silver (and) 1 mina of gold.

(16-21) Before Matiya [son of Ma-ra?-...]; before Zil-tešup son of Teššuya; before Eḫliya son of Purni-turu; before Akawe son of Iluša; before Zil-teya son of Tauka. These are the measurers ....

(22-26) (*seal impression*) [seal impression of] Minaš-šuk; (*seal impression*) seal impression of Zil-teya, the bookkeeper; (*seal impression*) seal impression of Erwi-šarri, the scribe; (*seal impression*) seal impression of Eḫliya son of Purni-turu.

COMMENTS

This tablet has suffered additional deterioration since it was copied. This is especially pronounced on the first lines of the obverse.

JEN 759 shares several significant features with *JEN* 731, including a common witness sequence. For further details regarding these similarities and on Zil-teya son of Tauka, the bookkeeper (cf. ll. 20, 23-24), see above, note to *JEN* 718:22.

There is a line missing after line 21. It will have contained at least: *ša* A.ŠÀ (or the like); and perhaps: *ù na-di-na-nu ša* ŠE? (or the like), as well.

NOTES

l. 4: [*a-na*]. The *CAD* Nuzi file records these signs as completely preserved.

l. 4: *i*!-*p*[*u-us-sú*]. Or the like.

l. 5: ⌜4⌝?. This part of the tablet is now totally gone. The *CAD* Nuzi file reads, at this point: 2. Lacheman sees: 6.

l. 7: ⌜*i-di*⌝?. These traces, after LA, appear, not as copied, but, rather, as:

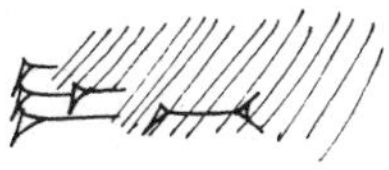

l. 10: *pa-i-iq-ra-na*. Cf. *JEN* 731:10 and the first note thereto. "*pāqirāna*" seems to have been susceptible to scribal quirks of several sorts. Examples of "*paiqrana*" and "*pariqana*" for *pāqirāna*, as well as various spellings of *pāqirāna* itself, are found in Gordon (1936, 111-12).

l. 16: [*Ma-ra*?-]. For this patronymic, see above, *JEN* 731:16 and the note thereto.

ll. 20, 23-24. On this individual, see above, comments.

l. 20: *T[a-ú-ka$_4$]*. For the restoration of this PN, see above, note to *JEN* 718:22.

ll. 23-25. For further on these persons, see above, notes to *JEN* 718:22; 731: 21, 23. The seal impression of line 24 is all but invisible.

JEN 760

OBVERSE

1 *ṭup-pí ma-ru-ti* ⸢*ša*⸣ ^{m}*Ša-ma-ḫu-ul*

2 DUMU *Pa-ḫu-ur ù* $^{<m>}$*Te-ḫi-ip-til-la*

3 DUMU *Pu-ḫi-še-en-ni a-na ma-ru-ti*

4 *i-te-pu-us-sú ù ki-mu*

5 ḪA.LA-*šu* 2 ^{GIŠ}APIN GIŠ.ŠAR.MEŠ

6 *i-na* URU *Pu-ru-ul-li-wa it-ta-din*$^{-in}$*-na-aš-šu*

7 *šum-ma* GIŠ.ŠAR *pa-qí-[r]a-[n]a* ⸢*ir-ta*⸣*-ši*

8 *ù* ^{m}*Ša-ma-ḫu-ul* ⸢*ú*⸣*-[za-ak]-ka-ma ù*

9 *a-*⸢*na* ^{m}*Te-ḫi-ip-til*⸣*-l[a]* ⸢*i*⸣*-•na-din*$^{-in}$

10 *ù šum-ma* ^{m}*Ša-m[a-ḫu]-ul*

11 *i-bá-la-ka-*⸢*at ù*⸣? [GI]Š.ŠAR.MEŠ-*šu*

12 *i+na* ŠU ^{m}*Te-ḫi-i[p-til-la i?-le?-e]q?-[q]è*

13 [*ù*? x MA.N]A KÙ.BABBAR.MEŠ [x MA?.NA? KÙ?.SIG$_{17}$?.MEŠ?]

14 [*a-na* ^{m}*Te-ḫi-i*]*p-[til-la]*

15 [*i-n*]*a-din*$^{-in}$

16 [IGI *W*]*a-an-ti$_4$-ya* DUMU [*Šu-pu-uk-ka$_4$*]

LOWER EDGE

17 [IGI]-⸢*x*⸣*-ip-til-l[a]*

18 $^{+}$DUMU $^{+}$⸢*Ar*⸣!*-te-šup*

REVERSE

19 [IGI] *It-ḫa-pu* DUMU *Še-ri-*⸢*x*⸣-[(?)]

20 [IGI] *Ik-ki-ya* DUMU *Ka$_4$-k]í-[ya]*

21 [IGI *Pu*]*r-ni-ya* DUMU *Ak-ku-ul-e[n?-ni]*

22 [IG]I •*Pu-***ḫi-*•*ya* DUMU *Ar-na-pu*

23 ⸢ŠU⸣ ^{m}*Ḫa-ma-an-na* DUB.SAR

S.I.

24 [N]A$_4$ *Wa-an-*⸢*ti$_4$*⸣*-ya* DUMU *Šu-pu-uk-ka$_4$*

S.I.

25 NA$_4$ *Pur-ni-ya*

S.I.

26 $^{+}$NA$_4$ *Pu-ḫi-ya*

27 NA$_4$ ^{m}*It-ḫa-pu ḫa-za-an-ni*

UPPER EDGE

S.I.

LEFT EDGE
28 [NA_4?]-*ni*?
[S.I.?]

TRANSLATION

(1-4) Tablet of adoption of Šamaḫul son of Paḫur. Now he adopted Teḫip-tilla son of Puḫi-šenni.

(5-6) And as his inheritance share, he (i.e., Šamaḫul) gave to him a .2 homer orchard in the town of Purulli.

(7-9) Should the orchard have claimants, then Šamaḫul shall clear (it) and then give (it) to Teḫip-tilla.

(10-15) And should Šamaḫul abrogate (this contract) and retrieve(?) his (erstwhile) orchard from Teḫip-tilla's possession, [then?] he shall give [to] Teḫip-tilla [x] mina(s) of silver [(and)? x? mina(s)? of? gold?].

(16-23) [Before] Wantiya son of [Šupukka]; [before...]-ip-tilla son of Ar-tešup; [before] Itḫ-apu son of Šeri-...; [before] Ikkiya son of Kakkiya; [before] Purniya son of Akkul-enni; before Puḫiya son of Arn-apu. Hand of Ḫamanna, the scribe.

(24-28) (*seal impression*) seal impression of Wantiya son of Šupukka; (*seal impression*) seal impression of Purniya; (*seal impression*) seal impression of Puḫiya; seal impression of Itḫ-apu, the mayor (*seal impression*); [seal? impression? of?] ... [(*seal impression*?)].

COMMENT

This tablet has suffered slight additional damage since it was copied.

NOTES

l. 2: <m>. For this apparent omission, see above, note to *JEN* 730:5-12.

l. 4: *us*. This sign is typical, not as depicted.

l. 8: ⸢*ú*⸣-[*za-ak*]. The *CAD* Nuzi file records these signs as entirely preserved.

ll. 11-12. According to the interpretation of these lines adopted here, seizure (or retention) of the orchard by Šamaḫul constitutes and defines abrogation of the contract. This would represent a variation on the clearly attested definition of abrogation as raising a false claim to property. Cf. above, *JEN* 741:16-19; 743:17-19; 744:18-20; and below, *JEN* 761:18-20.

The *CAD* Nuzi file, following Lacheman, restores (in effect), after *i-bá-la-ka-*⸢*at*⸣: [2 ^{GIŠ}APIN], and, after ^{m}*Te-ḫi-i*[*p-til-la*]: [*inaddin*]. Thus the statement of abrogation (i.e., the protasis) seems to be followed by a dual penalty (i.e., the apodosis): restoration of the orchard and a fine (ll. 13-15). The first of those penalties is, of course, no penalty at all. (If it is not a penalty, then it is also too self-evident to need stating and, in fact, is

nowhere else attested.) Nor do the text restorations accord with the traces visible on the tablet.

The reverse of the tablet has an erasure of what would have been a continuation of line 12.

l. 13. If the restoration of the second half of the line is correct, then it is to be expected that the number of minas of silver and of gold be the same.

l. 16: [IGI *W*]*a*. The *CAD* Nuzi file records these signs as completely preserved.

l. 18: ⸢*Ar*⸣!. The traces appear, not as depicted, but, rather, as:

⸢UN⸣! is also possible. Both "Ar-tešup" and "Un-tešup" are well attested Nuzi names. See, e.g., *NPN*, 34b-35a *sub* AR-TEŠUP, 165a *sub* UN-TEŠUP.

l. 19: [IGI]. The *CAD* Nuzi file records this sign as completely preserved.

l. 20: [*ya*]. This restoration is based on *JEN* 767:2, 7, 9. This person is here a witness to a Teḫip-tilla real estate acquisition in Purulli. There, he himself cedes Purulli real estate to Teḫip-tilla. He is attested nowhere else.

l. 21. The *CAD* Nuzi file records this entire line, except for the last sign, as completely preserved. *NPN*, 119a *sub* PURNIḪA 1), suggests that the last three signs are completely preserved.

l. 23: ⸢ŠU⸣ ^{m}. As unusual as this interpretation appears in the context of a real estate adoption text (IGI (^{m}) is expected), the traces point in this direction. (Cf. the practice of using "ŠU" to identify the scribe in declaration texts, e.g., *JEN* 150:15; 152:17; 740:21.) The *CAD* Nuzi file records for this line: IGI *Ḫa-ma-an-na* DUB.SAR.

l. 28. Cf., perhaps, line 21.

JEN 761

OBVERSE

1 [*ṭup-p*]*í ma-*[*r*]*u-ti*

2 [*ša*] ^{m}*Ta-a-a-*⸢*ú-ki* DUMU⸣ *A-*⸢*x*⸣-[ ]-•⸢x⸣

3 ⸢*ù*⸣ ^{m}*Te-ḫi-ip-til-l*[*a* DUMU *P*]*u-ḫi-še-en-ni*

4 [*a-na*] *ma-ru-ti i-pu-u*[*š*]-⸢*ma*⸣

5 [*ki*]*-ma* ḪA.⸢LA⸣-*šu* 1 ANŠE [2?+]2 ^{GIŠ}APIN A.ŠÀ *i*+$^{+}$*na mi-in-d*[*á-t*]*i* GAL

6 [*i-na*] URU *ša Ú-na-ap-š*[*e-wa*?]

7 [*i-na šu*]-•*pa-al* AN.ZA.KÀR *ša A-*[ka_4]-⸢*wa*⸣-*til*

8 [*i-n*]*a le-e*[*t m*]*i-iṣ-*•*r*[*i*] ⸢*ša* URU⸣ *A-*⸢*ki*⸣*-pa-pu-*[*wa*?]

9 [^{m}*T*]*a-a-*⸢*a-ú*⸣*-ki a-na* ^{m}*Te-*[*ḫi*]*-ip-til-*⸢*la*⸣ •SUM-*š*[*u*]

10 ⸢*ù*⸣ ^{m}*Te-ḫi-*⸢*ip*⸣*-til-la* 1 UD[U] ⸢*ù*⸣? MA.NA URUDU

11 1 ZAG *ša* 2 MA.⸢NA⸣ ZABAR

12 ù 10 MA.NA Z[A]BAR ki-ma [NÍ]G.BA-šu
13 *a-na ^{m}Ta-a-a-⸢ú⸣-ki SUM-šu [š]um-ma
14 A.ŠÀ pí-ir-qa TUK.MEŠ-ši ^{m}⸢Ta⸣-a-a-ú-ki
15 ⸢ú⸣-za-ak-ka$_{4}$-ma ù a-na ^{m}⸢Te⸣-ḫi-ip-til-la i+na-an-din
16 [i]l-ku ša A.ŠÀ [a]n-ni-i ^{m}Ta-a-a-ú-⸢ki⸣-ma na-ši
17 [^{m}T]e-ḫi-ip-til-[l]a la na-ši
18 [šum]-ma ^{m}Ta-[a]-⸢a⸣-ú-ki KI.BAL-at
19 ⸢ù⸣ aš-šum ⸢A⸣.Š[À] an-ni-i i-na EGIR[-ki?]
20 [^{m}T]e-ḫi-ip-[ti]l-la i-ša-as-⸢sí⸣
21 [2? MA.NA KÙ.BABBAR 1?+]⸢1⸣ MA.NA KÙ.SIG$_{17}$
22 [a-na ^{m}Te-ḫi]-⸢ip⸣-til-la ú-ma-⸢al-la⸣

LOWER EDGE

23 [ ] ⸢Pu⸣-+ḫi-še-en-ni
24 [p]a?-ni $^{LÚ.MEŠ}$⸢IGI⸣.[MEŠ]
25 [ ]⸢x x⸣ PU ⸢x x⸣[ ]-ni-mi

REVERSE

26 [^{m}Ta]-a-a-ú-ki
27 [ ] KI a-na
28 [ ]⸢x x⸣[ ]

+ ____

29 [IGI Tup]-+ki-ya DUMU Kar-ze-ya
30 [IGI I-r]i-+ri-til-la DUMU Še-ḫe-el-te-•šup
31 [IGI En]-na-ma-ti DUMU En-na-a-a
32 [IGI Wa]-•an-ti-mu-ša DUMU Na-ik-ké-mar
33 [IGI Pu-ḫ]i-še-en-ni DUMU Ar-te-šup
34 [an-nu-t]u$_{4}$ LÚ.ME[Š] ⸢ša⸣ A.ŠÀ ú-šal-mu-ú
35 [ù š]a KÙ.BABBAR SUM-⸢nu⸣
36 [IGI Še?-e]r?-ši-ya DUM[U I]t-ḫi-til-la
37 [IGI A]r-ti-i[r-w]i DUMU Pa-a-a
38 [IGI I-lu-uḫ]-•ḫa-a-a DUMU Na-ik-ké-mar
39 [IGI Te]-šup-er-[wi] DUMU Ar-te-šup
40 [IGI +Š]e?-+⸢él?-+wi⸣!?-[ya?] DUMU En-na-+mil-+ki
41 [IGI X?-ḫ]e?-el-t[e- DUMU]⸢x⸣[(?)]
42 [IGI]-+⸢ri⸣-ya DUMU DINGIR-TUK-š[u]

? ____

43 EME-⸢šu ša⸣ ^{m}Ta-a-[a]-⸢ú⸣-+ki
44 *⸢a⸣-na pa-ni $^{[L]Ú.MEŠ}$ IGI.ME[Š i]q-ta-bi
45 KÙ.⸢BABBAR⸣ an-[nu]-ú ša [p]í ṭup-pí il-qú!-mi

S.I.

46 [^{NA_4} KIŠIB I-ri-ri]-til-la
47 ^{NA_4} KIŠIB En-na-ma-t[i]

[S.I.]

UPPER EDGE

S.I.

48 ^{NA_4} KIŠIB *Ar-ti-ir-wi*

TRANSLATION

(1-4) Tablet of adoption [of] Tayuki son of A-.... Now he adopted Teḫip-tilla [son of] Puḫi-šenni.

(5-9) As his inheritance share, Tayuki gave to Teḫip-tilla a field, 1.2 [+.2?] homers by the large standard, [in] the town of Unap-še, [to] the west of the *dimtu* of Akawatil, adjacent to the border of the town of Akip-apu.

(10-13) And Teḫip-tilla gave to Tayuki as his gift 1 sheep and(?) a(?) mina of copper, 1 ZAG (consisting) of 2 minas of bronze, and 10 minas of bronze.

(13-15) Should the field have a claim (against it), Tayuki shall clear (the field) and then give (it) to Teḫip-tilla.

(16-17) And it is Tayuki who shall bear the *ilku* of this field; Teḫip-tilla shall not bear (it).

(18-22) Should Tayuki abrogate (this contract) by hailing Teḫip-tilla (into court) over this field, he shall pay [to] Teḫip-tilla [2? mina(s) of silver (and) 1?+]1 mina(s) of gold.

(23-28) ... Puḫi-šenni ... before(?) witnesses .... Tayuki ... to .... .

(29-42) [Before] Tupkiya son of Karzeya; [before] Iriri-tilla son of Šeḫel-tešup; [before] Enna-mati son of Ennaya; [before] Wanti-muša son of Naik-kemar; [before] Puḫi-šenni son of Ar-tešup. These are the men who measured the field [and] who distributed the money (lit. "silver"). [Before] Šer(?)-šiya son of Itḫip-tilla; [before] Ar-tirwi son of Paya; [before] Iluḫḫaya son of Naik-kemar; [before] Tešup-erwi son of Ar-tešup; [before] Šelwiya(?) son of Enna-milki; [before] ... [son of] ...; [before] ...-riya son of Ila-nîšū.

(?)———————————————————

(43-44) Declaration of Tayuki before the witnesses. (Thus) he spoke:

(45) "I (lit. he/they) have received this money (lit. "silver") as per the tablet.

(46-48) (*seal impression*) [seal impression of] Iriri-tilla; seal impression of Enna-mati [(*seal impression*)]; (*seal impression*) seal impression of Ar-tirwi.

COMMENTS

This tablet has suffered slight additional deterioration since it was copied.

The *CAD* Nuzi file for this tablet was authored by Lacheman. References below to this file signify contributions by Lacheman.

NOTES

l. 3: *ip*. This sign is correct as copied.

l. 3: [DUMU]. The *CAD* Nuzi file records this sign as completely preserved.

l. 5: *d*[*á-t*]*i* GAL. At this point, the *CAD* Nuzi file restores, in effect, *dá*-[ti_4 *ša* É.GAL GAL]. There does not seem to be enough room in the gap to support this restoration.

l. 6: URU *ša*. Grammatical constructions such as this demonstrate that, in the Nuzi texts, URU followed directly by a toponym is to be considered a logogram rather than a determinative. For further discussion of this issue, see Maidman (1976, 355, n. 321).

l. 7: AN. This sign is clear and typical, not as copied.

l. 8. Cf. *JEN* 757:3. *JEN* 761 and 757 have other similarities as well. Both these texts also bear a certain resemblance to *JEN* 749. See above, note to *JEN* 757:13-15 and the other notes cited there. Interpretation of the present text is aided by reference to *JEN* 757 and, to a lesser extent, *JEN* 749.

(*JEN* 761 bears a certain resemblance to *JEN* 743 as well, in the witness list [cf. *JEN* 761:31, 32, 38 with, respectively, *JEN* 743:22, 23, 25; the first two of these witnesses turn up again as witnesses in *JEN* 772:25-27, as perhaps implied already by Lacheman] and the unusual penalty clause [cf. *JEN* 761:18-20 with *JEN* 743:17-19].)

l. 9. The *CAD* Nuzi file records this line as wholly preserved.

l. 9: *š*[*u*]. The *CAD* Nuzi file records this sign as: $^{-nu}$. However, cf. below, line 13, for a parallel to the verb form as restored here.

l. 10: ⌈*ù*⌉?. The *CAD* Nuzi file records Ù as entirely preserved. However, a number is expected before MA.NA. Perhaps the scribe has inadvertently omitted the number.

l. 11. Cf. *G* 26:10. ZAG signifies a weapon or other type of military paraphernalia. See *HSS*, XIV, 264 (=616): 18.

(Cf. the different judgments of Gadd [1926, 103, 104]; Cross, [1937, 45]; and Fadhil [1983, 306a]. Cf. also Lacheman 1939a, 542 ("of doubtful meaning")]; and Wilhelm [1974, 207 *ad HSS*, XIX, 128:2 (left as ZAG, untranslated)].)

ZAG is equated with *imittu* (i.e., spear) in the Nuzi texts by Zaccagnini (1977b, 31). Zaccagnini refers to the *HSS* XIV text. To my knowledge, there is no phonetic spelling of *imittu* in the Nuzi texts and so this identification must remain tentative.

An equation, ZAG = *aḫu*, (i.e., "[bronze] sleeve" as part of body armor) may also be considered. *JEN* 527:5-6 may indicate that the *aḫu*(s?) there weigh approximately the same as here. Yet "1 mina 85" (*JEN* 527:6) is a curious expression. It could represent "2 minas 25 sheqels," perhaps, but the scribe erased the sign(s) at the end of that line and it is likely that an error is somehow involved. On *JEN* 527:5-6, see Zaccagnini

(1979b, 26); and Kendall (1981, 212, n.42). On the weight of bronze armor at Nuzi, see Zaccagnini (1979b, 26-27). On the weight of helmets, see Kendall (1981, 211-14). As with *imittu*, the equation, ZAG = *aḫu*, is not certain in these texts. Also, does one transfer sleeves as part of an economic transaction? It is possible that ZAG refers to neither of the items noted above. (For *aḫu* in the Nuzi texts, see *CAD*, I/J, 208b *sub* c); and Kendall [1981, 202, n. 7, 203, n. 16].)

The sign, ZABAR, appears more distinct than shown in the copy.

l. 15: *ak*. In the copy, this sign is contained within a cartouche-like enclosure. This enclosure does not appear on the tablet.

ll. 16-17. Cf. *JEN* 757:13-15 and the note thereto.

l. 17: [^{m}*T*]*e*. The *CAD* Nuzi file restores: [*ù Te*].

l. 21: [2? ... 1?+] These tentative restorations are based on *JEN* 749:16. On the relevance of *JEN* 749 for the present text, see above, note to line 8.

ll. 23-28. These lines appear to contain a single contractual clause. Although the precise interpretation of the surviving traces is not always clear, the general sense of these lines may not be wholly obscure. Lines 43-45 contain a declaration by the vendor that he has, in fact, received the price of the field. Although parallels from other texts are, to my knowledge, lacking, it is possible that lines 23-28 represent a parallel declaration by the purchaser that he has, in fact, received the field from the vendor. Cf. *JEN* 742:39-42, where the vendor declares, in a contractual context similar to that of *JEN* 761, that he has both transferred a field and received his payment from the purchaser.

Such a supposition would allow for the following interpretation of these lines:

23 [(EME-*šu ša*) ^{m}*Te-ḫi-ip-til-la* DUMU] ˹*Pu*˺-*ḫi-še-en-ni*
24 [(?) *a-na p*]*a-ni* $^{\text{LÚ.MEŠ}}$˹IGI˺.[MEŠ]
25 [*iq-t*]*a-b*[*i*]˹x˺ PU ˹x x˺[ ]-*ni-mi*
26 [A.ŠÀ *ša* ^{m}*Ta*]-*a-a-ú-ki*
27 [^{m}*Ta-a-ú*]-*ki a-na*
28 ˹*ya-ši!*˺[SUM (or the like)]

The *CAD* Nuzi file also restores line 27 as here suggested but line 28 as: [^{m}*Te-ḫi-ip-til-l*]*a*. And, in fact, no sign may be lost after the last trace. Lacheman interprets the end of line 28, in effect, as: [*inandin*].

The second half of line 25, in any case, remains difficult. See below, note to line 25. If one reconstructs the end of line 25 as *iš!-pu*-˹*ra-an*˺-*ni-mi*, then the interpretation proposed here cannot be correct.

l. 23: *en*. This sign is clear and typical, not AN as depicted.

l. 25. The *CAD* Nuzi file reads this line: "- - - zu-pu?-um?." The sign before PU resembles URU (less likely, IŠ) more than it does ZU (as ZU is normally rendered in the Nuzi orthography). It appears as: 

-ni-mi of the right edge belongs to this line. In the copy, it appears twice, with line 25 and on the reverse right edge. Cf. above, note to ll. 23-28.

l. 26: *ki*. This sign is clear and not as depicted.

l. 27: KI. This sign is clear and not as depicted.

l. 28. The *CAD* Nuzi file renders the traces following the horizontal wedges:

Below this line appears a horizontal line. This scribal line is not indicated in the copy.

l. 29: [*Tup*]. This restoration is all but certain. Tupkiya is the only attested son of a Karzeya in the Nuzi texts. See *NPN*, 80b *sub* KARZEḬA 2). In addition, he reappears as a witness in *JEN* 841:30 along with an individual (l. 31) who reappears in the present text as a witness (l. 37). See also below, second note to line 33.

l. 30: *ri*. Lacheman's copy inadvertently omits a complete RI between [R]I and TIL.

l. 30: *šup*. The copy reflects ŠUP. At right angles to this sign appears NI MI from the end of line 25. See above, note to line 25.

What appears after TE is: 

The *CAD* Nuzi file, misinterprets these wedges as YA, as does *NPN*, 127b *sub* ŠEḪEL-TEḬA 2), 73a *sub* IRIRI-TILLA 5).

ll. 31-32. See below, note to line 38.

l. 33. The copy accurately depicts the progressively decreasing size of the signs in this line. Overlap of text from the obverse at this "latitude" forced the scribe to cramp the text at this point.

l. 33: [*Pu-ḫ*]*i*. This seems the most plausible restoration. A Puḫi-šenni son of Ar-tešup appears in *JEN* 91 as vendor to Teḫip-tilla of Unap-še real estate (cf. *JEN* 91:6 with *JEN* 63:5-7 for the location of the real estate), i.e., land in the same vicinity as the real estate at issue in this text. (*JEN* 91:20 records a witness who appears in this text as well [l. 29].)

This restoration appears in The *CAD* Nuzi file. See also *NPN*, 35a *sub* AR-TEŠUP 36), 116a, *sub* PUḪI-ŠENNI 5).

l. 34: *šal*. This sign is typical, not as depicted.

l. 35: KÙ.BABBAR. For the meaning "money" here, see above, note to *JEN* 715:27.

l. 37. See above, note to line 29.

l. 38: [*I-lu-uḫ*]-*ḫa-a-a* DUMU. This restoration is all but certain. See *NPN*, 101b *sub* NAIK-KEMAR 5). The same witness reappears in *JEN* 743:25. On the relation of *JEN* 743 to the present text, see above, note to line 8.

The spacing between A and DUMU is accurately depicted. It is assumed here that no signs occupy this lacuna.

l. 39: [*Te*]-*šup-er*-[*wi*]. This restoration is tentatively adopted in *NPN*, 35a *sub* AR-TEŠUP 43), 155a *sub* TEŠUP-ERWI 2). To my knowledge, this individual is nowhere else attested in the Nuzi texts.

l. 40: [*Š*]*e*?-⸢*él*?-*wi*⸣!?. The traces appear as: 

l. 41. Perhaps this line ought to be interpreted: [IGI *E*?-/*Še*?-*ḫ*]*e-el-te*-[*šup* DUB.SAR DUM]U [XXX-*ib-ni*]. See above, note to *JEN* 757:13-15.

l. 42. Below this line appears a horizontal line which may have been made deliberately by the scribe. This line is not indicated in the copy.

l. 42: ⸢*ri*⸣. The trace appears, not as copied, but, rather, as: 

ll. 43-45. These lines all appear to have been indented relative to the preceding text.

l. 44: $^{[L]Ú}$. The initial trace is not a *Winkelhaken*, as depicted, but the right ends of two horizontal wedges, i.e., from the context, $^{[L]Ú}$.

l. 45: KÙ.⸢BABBAR⸣. The signs are small and quite faint. But this reading is very possible.
See also above, note to line 35.

l. 45: *il-qú*!-*mi*. A 1CS form is expected. The subjunctive (or plural) is unexpected. The second sign does not appear as depicted, but, rather, as:

Perhaps, therefore, these signs should be interpreted as *él*-⸢*qé*⸣-*mi*.

l. 46. Cf. l. 30.

l. 48. The seal impression above this line is identified by Lacheman as Po 993. This accords with Porada (1947, 138 *ad* no. 993).

JEN 762

OBVERSE

1 *ṭup-pí šu*-[*pé-ul-ti*]
2 *ša* ^{m}*Te*-[*ḫi-ip-til-la*]
3 DUMU *Pu*-[*ḫi-še-en-ni*]
4 *it-ti* [^{m}*Na*?- DUMU]-*te*
5 GIŠ.ŠAR *k*[*i-ma* GIŠ.ŠAR *i-na* URU] *Nu-zi*
6 *uš-pè*-⸢*e*⸣-[*lu* (?)]
7 *ù* $^{+}$IB [ ]⸢x⸣
8 *ša* ^{m}*Na*-[ ] *la* ⸢x⸣ [(?)]

9 *ù* 1 ^{GIŠ}⸢x⸣[ ]
10 *ma-an-nu-u*[*m-me-e ša* KI.BAL-tu_4]
11 +2 +MA.+NA +KÙ.[SIG_{17}? *ú-ma-al-la*]
12 IGI *Še-él-la-pá-e* DUMU *A-ar-ta-e*
13 IGI *It-ḫa-pu* DUMU *Ḫu-e-ep-er*!-*wi*
14 IGI *Mu-uš-še-en-ni* DUMU *Ni-nu-a-tal*

LOWER EDGE

15 IGI *Iṣ*-•*ṣú-ur*!-^{d}IM
16 DUMU *In-dì-nu*

REVERSE

17 IGI *Te-tu-a-e* DUMU *Zi-ri-ra*
18 IGI *Zi-k*[*a-a-a*]
19 DUMU *E*[*ḫ*]-⸢*li*⸣-<*ip*>-⸢LUGAL⸣
20 IGI *Ar-t*[*a*]-*še-en-ni* DUB.SAR

S.I. Po 758

21 $^{\text{NA}_4}$ KIŠIB $^{\text{m}+}$*It-ḫa*-[*p*]*u* DUMU *Ḫu-e-e*[*p-er-wi*]

S.I. Po 634

22 $^{\text{NA}_4}$ +KIŠIB [^{m}*Te*]-*⸢*tu*⸣!-[*a-e*]
23 *DUMU •*Zi*-•*ri*-[*r*]*a-aš*

TRANSLATION

(1-6) Tablet of exchange of Teḫip-tilla son of Puḫi-šenni (together) with [Na?-... son of] ...-te. They exchanged orchard [for orchard in the town of] Nuzi.

(7-9) And .... of Na-... ... and .... .

(10-11) Who [abrogates (this contract) shall pay] 2 minas of gold(?).

(12-20) Before Šellapai son of Ar-tae; before Itḫ-apu son of Ḫuip-erwi; before Muš-šenni son of Ninu-atal; before Iṣṣur-adad son of Iddinu; before Tetuae son of Ziriraš; before Zikaya son of Elḫip-šarri; before Artašenni, the scribe.

(21-23) (*seal impression*) seal impression of Itḫ-apu son of Ḫuip-erwi; (*seal impression*) seal impression of Tetuae son of Ziriraš.

COMMENT

Only the last two lines have further deteriorated since the copy was made.

NOTES

l. 1: [*pé*]. Lacheman records this sign as partially preserved.

l. 4: [*Na*?]. This tentative restoration is based on the apparent PN of line 8. See further, next note.

ll. 7-9. The sense of these lines is not transparent. Lacheman restores, in effect:

7 *ù ip-*[*le-ti-šu ša* ^{GIŠ}] (*sic*)
8 *ša* ^{m}*Na-*[*a-na* ^{m}*Te-ḫi-ip-til*]*-la* ⌜*ú*⌝-[*ma-a*]*l-la*
9 *ù* 1 ^{GIŠ}[ ]

Utilizing these ideas, one may expand and modify the restoration as follows:

7 *ù ip-*[*le-ti-šu ša* GIŠ.Š]AR!
8 *ša* ^{m}*Na-*[^{m}*Te-ḫi-ip-til*]*-la ú-*[*ma-al-la*]
9 *ù* 1 ^{GIŠ}⌜X⌝[*a-na* Ú*-ti id-din* (or the like)]

For line 8: *ú-*[*ma-al-la*], note the last traces implicit in Lacheman's transliteration. For the verbal form in this context, cf. e.g., *JEN* 223:8-10; 282:8-9. For l. 9: [*a-na* Ú*-ti id-din*], cf. e.g., *JEN* 223:11-12. (On the basis of this last passage, one might even hazard to restore the start of the line: *ù* 1 AN[ŠE! ŠE *a-na* etc.].)

This proposed restoration of lines 7-9 is not, however, without its difficulties. First, the signs assigned to the end of lines 7 and 8 respectively may belong to lines 6 and 7 respectively. Second, the first of those signs, interpreted as [Š]AR, is not typical in form. Cf. the second sign of line 5. Third, the interpretation, [Š]AR, is rendered more suspect still by another consideration. If *ip-*[*le-ti-šu*] is correct, then that word should be followed by: *ša* PN (cf., e.g., *JEN* 238:8-9), not: *ša* GIŠ.ŠAR/A.ŠÀ/etc. *ša* PN. The formula restored here in lines 7-8 is, to my knowledge, nowhere else attested. These three points make the proposed restoration of line 7 particularly questionable. A fourth difficulty is that, in line 9, what is rendered as 1 ^{GIŠ}⌜X⌝ looks suspiciously like ^{m}*Ut-ḫa*[*p-*]. (Lacheman elsewhere renders the last two elements ^{GIŠ}GIG[IR] and copies the last traces:

This is most unlikely.) Finally, lines 7-9 are followed immediately by a penalty clause. Such a clause in tablets of real estate exchange are typically preceded by a clear title clause.

l. 11. Below this line appears blank space, as depicted.

l. 11: 2 MA.NA KÙ. These signs are clear and complete. The copy, at this point, should be ignored completely.

l. 11: [SIG$_{17}$? *ú-ma-al-la*]. Cf., e.g., *JEN* 223:16. A form of *nadānu* may also be used in this context. See, for example, *JEN* 249:12.

If gold is not involved here, silver is.

l. 17: *ra*. This is the last sign on this line. The tablet is well preserved in this area. Cf. the spelling of this name in line 23.

ll. 18-19. For the restoration of this witness's names, see below, note to lines 22-23. He is a ubiquitous witness in Teḫip-tilla texts. See *NPN*, 175b *sub* ZIKAḬA 1) (the present text is not cited).

l. 20. On this scribe, see above, notes to *JEN* 730:1, 25.

l. 20: *t*[*a*]. The *CAD* Nuzi file records this sign as completely preserved.

ll. 22-23. The *CAD* Nuzi file records these lines as completely preserved.

Lacheman identifies the seal impression above these lines as Po 634. Collation confirms this identification. Porada (1947, 134a *ad* no. 634) identifies this impression elsewhere with Zikaya son of Elḫip-šarri (in a text where Tetuae son of Ziriraš does not appear). Cf. lines 18-19 of the present text. That Zikaya's seal (if it is indeed his) should be used here by a fellow witness (i.e., by Tetuae son of Ziriraš) should occasion no surprise. On seal usage at Nuzi, see above, note to *JEN* 675:45-48 and the further references given there.

JEN 763

OBVERSE

1 •⸢*ṭup*⸣-•*pí* •*ma*-**r*[*u-ti ša*]⸢X X⸣ [*ù*?]
2 ^{m}*Šu-ur-*•*te-*•*eš-*[*šu-up* DUMU.MEŠ? *Te?-ḫi?-ip?*]-*til-la*
3 *ù* $^{<m>}$*Te-ḫi-ip-til-l*[*a* DUMU *Pu-ḫi-še-en-ni*]
4 *a-na ma-ru-ti i-*•*te-pu-*[*uš*]
5 1 ⸢ANŠE⸣ 3 ^{GIŠ}APIN *ku-ma-*⸢*ni*⸣-[*ma* A.ŠÀ *i?-na? ta?-a?-r*]*i*!? •*ša* •É.•GAL
6 *i-n*[*a*] ⸢*le*⸣-*et* AN.ZA.⸢KÀR⸣ *ša Šá-ar-ku-uš-še*$_{20}$
7 *e-*⸢*le*⸣-[*e*]*n*
8 *a-na* ^{m}*Te-*[*ḫ*]*i-ip-til-la ki-ma* ⸢ḪA⸣.LA *i-din*
9 *ù* ^{m}*Te-ḫi-ip-til-la ki-ma* NÍG.BA-*šu-nu*
10 1 ANŠE 3 BÁN [1]+3 SILA$_{3}$ ŠE.MEŠ
11 *a-na* ^{m}*Šu-u*[*r-t*]*e-eš-šu-up i-din*
12 *šum-ma* A.ŠÀ *pa-q*[*í*]-*ra-na ir-ta-ša*
13 *ù* ^{m}*Šu-ur-te-eš-*⸢*šu*⸣-*up ú-za-*$^{+}$*ak-*$^{+}$*ka*$_{4}$-[*m*]*a*
14 *a-na* ^{m}*Te-ḫi-ip-til-la i-na-an-di*
15 *šum-ma* ^{m}*Šu-ur-te-eš-šu-up*
16 KI.BAL-*tu*$_{4}$ 1 MA.NA KÙ.BABBAR 1 MA.NA KÙ.SIG$_{17}$
17 *a-na* ^{m}*Te-ḫi-ip-til-la i-na-an-di*
18 *il-ku-ú ša* A.ŠÀ *ù* ^{m}*Šu-ur-te-eš-šu-up*
19 *na-a-ši*
20 IGI *Ur-ḫi-ya* DUMU *Še-ka*$_{4}$-*rù*
21 IGI *Zi-il*$_{5}$-*te-ya* DUMU *Ta-ú-ka*$_{4}$
22 IGI *Ḫa-al-še-en-ni* DUMU *Ta-a-a*
23 •IGI *A-ri-ḫa-ar-me-e* DUMU *Ḫa-na-a-a*

LOWER EDGE

24 •IGI *Un-nu-ú!-ki* DUMU *Ar-til-la*

25 IGI *Ak-ku-ya*

26 DUMU *Al-ki-til-la*

REVERSE

27 IGI *Ki-in-na-a-a* DUMU *Ar-til-la*

28 IGI *K[é]-li-ip*-LUGAL DUMU *Al-ki-a*

29 IGI *Ú-na-ap-ta-e*

30 DUMU *Ni!-iḫ-ri-te-eš-šu-up*

31 IGI *Ḫu-ti-ip-til-la* DUMU KI.MIN

32 IGI *Be-li-ya* DUMU *Túr-še-en-ni*

33 IGI *Še-eḫ-li-ya* DUMU *Ak-ku-ya*

34 *an-nu-tu_4* ^{LÚ}*pè-ni-⸢ḫu⸣-rù ša* A.ŠÀ

S.I. Po 963

35 $^{\text{⸢NA}_4\text{⸣}}$•KIŠIB •^{m}*Ur-ḫi-[y]a* DUMU *Še-ka_4-rù*

S.I. Po 573

36 $^{\text{NA}_4}$ KIŠIB *Ú-na-⸢ap⸣-ta-e ši-bi*

37 $^{\text{NA}_4}$ KIŠIB *Ki-in-n[a-a-a]*

S.I. Po 217

38 $^{\text{NA}_4}$ KIŠIB *Še-eḫ-[li-ya]*

S.I.

UPPER EDGE

39 $^{\text{[N]A}_4}$ KIŠIB *[En-na]-m[a]-ti*

S.I.?

LEFT EDGE

40 •$^{\text{NA}_4}$ KIŠIB ^{m}*A-ri-ḫa-a[r-m]e-e* $^{\text{NA}_4}$ KIŠIB *⸢Be?-li⸣?-[ya?]*

S.I. Po 175 S.I.

TRANSLATION

(1-4) Tablet of adoption [of] ... [and?] Šur-tešup [son(s) of Teḫip?]-tilla. Now he adopted Teḫip-tilla [son of Puḫi-šenni].

(5-8) He gave to Teḫip-tilla as an inheritance share a [field], 1.35 homers [by?] the palace standard(?), adjacent to the *dimtu* of Šakrušše, east of (*sic*).

(9-11) And Teḫip-tilla gave to Šur-tešup as their (*sic*) gift 1.3375 [+.0125] (i.e., 1.35) homers of barley.

(12-14) Should the field have claimants, then Šur-tešup shall clear (it) and give (it) to Teḫip-tilla.

(15-17) Should Šur-tešup abrogate (this contract), he shall give to Teḫip-tilla 1 mina of silver (and) 1 mina of gold.

(18-19) Now Šur-tešup shall bear the *ilku* of the field.

(20-34) Before Urḫiya son of Šekaru; before Zil-teya son of Tauka; before Ḫalu-šenni son of Taya; before Ariḫ-ḫarpa son of Ḫanaya; before

Unnuki son of Ar-tilla; before Akkuya son of Alki-tilla; before Kinnaya son of Ar-tilla; before Kelip-šarri son of Alkiya; before Unap-tae son of Niḫri-tešup; before Ḫutip-tilla son of the same; before Bêliya son of Tur-šenni; before Šeḫliya son of Akkuya. These are the encirclers of the field.

(35-40) (*seal impression*) seal impression of Urḫiya son of Šekaru; (*seal impression*) seal impression of Unap-tae, witness; seal impression of Kinnaya (*seal impression*); seal impression of Šeḫliya (*seal impression*); seal impression of Enna-mati (*seal impression*?); seal impression of Ariḫ-ḫarpa (*seal impression*); seal impression of Bêliya(?) (*seal impression*).

COMMENT

This tablet has deteriorated slightly since it was copied.

NOTES

l. 1: ⌜X X⌝. These traces may be the remnant of a PN identifying the co-adopter (with Šur-tešup [l. 2]) of Teḫip-tilla. In this connection, note the plural suffix in line 9. (See also next note.) Cf., however, lines 4, 11, 13, 15, 18, all of which imply a single adopter.

If the traces do not reflect a PN, then their presence in line 1 is inexplicable. It is not absolutely certain that the ⌜X X⌝ assigned to line 1 and the *til-la* of line 2 belong to those lines.

l. 2: [*Te*?-*ḫi*?-*ip*?]-*til-la*. On the surviving signs, see the immediately preceding note.

The tentative restoration of the patronymic is based on the fact that the only known "Šur-tešup son of ...-tilla" having connections with members of the Teḫip-tilla family is a son of "Teḫip-tilla." He is attested in *HSS*, V, 48:18; *JEN* 650:30; and probably *JEN* 780:2, 12, 16, 21, 25, 27. (Lacheman already restored [*Te-ḫi-ip*] in *JEN* 763:2.) The first and third of these texts associate Šur-tešup with a brother of his. This may be germane to the present text where more than one adopter may be involved. See above, preceding note.

Another "Šur-tešup son of ...-tilla," a son of Akip-tilla, appears in *HSS*, XVI, 377:11.

l. 3: [*ni*]. At this point, Lacheman reads: [*n*]*i*.

l. 5: *ku-ma-*⌜*ni*⌝. Lacheman and the *CAD* Nuzi file record the last sign as completely preserved. The *kumānu* is one-half of an *awiḫaru*, i.e., 1/20 of a homer. For further on this measurement, see below, second note to *JEN* 764:5.

l. 5: [*ma* A.ŠÀ *i*?-*na*? *ta*?-*a*?-*r*]*i*!? *ša* É.GAL. This restoration is based on forms found in *JEN* 401:6 and 614:5. Those two texts are relevant in the present context since *JEN* 40, 49, 401, 614, 758, 763 (i.e., the present text), 764,

and 765 constitute a cluster of very similar texts. Lacunae in one may be filled by appeal to the others. For details on the similarities linking these texts, see above, note to *JEN* 758:5-7 and the further references there given. Orthographic peculiarities shared by this text and others of this cluster (in the present text, these include, e.g., *ir-ta-ša* [l. 12], *i-na-an-di* [ll. 14, 17], KI.BAL-*tu*$_4$ [l. 16], *il-ku-ú* [l. 18], *Al-ki-a* [l. 28]) are discussed or alluded to above, notes to *JEN* 758:5-7, 11, 13, 17, 22.

The correctness of the proposed restoration is, however, far from certain. There seem to be too many restored signs for the size of the lacuna. Furthermore, the trace preceding ŠA does not reflect a typical RI. (Lacheman reads: [A.ŠÀ].MEŠ, in better conformity with the trace but making dubious contextual sense; the *CAD* Nuzi file reflects: [ ].MEŠ.) One should also note that "*ša* É.GAL" is now almost completely effaced and difficult to discern.

l. 6: *Šá-ar-ku-uš-še*$_{20}$. This spelling contains a unique metathesis for a GN otherwise rendered *Šá-ak-ru-uš-še-e* (*JEN* 758:7), or the like.

All other spellings of this GN have final ŠE except for *JEN* 758:7. Thus ŠI in the present instance appears to represent ŠE$_{20}$.

The *dimtu* of Šakrušše may be located in Unap-še. See above, note to *JEN* 758:5-7.

l. 7. This line is correct as copied. It seems to be a contextual fragment, an incomplete further description of the real estate. Perhaps the scribe, having written *e-le-en*, then realized his failure to begin the line with *i-na*, and so abandoned the line (and the thought) altogether.

l. 10: [1]. The ratio of land area to payment in the eight *dimtu* of Šakrušše texts is very likely uniform. See below, first note to *JEN* 764:5. That ratio is 1 homer of land : 1 homer of barley. Therefore, for this restoration, cf. *JEN* 401:10 where four SILA$_3$ represents the value of 1 *kumānu* of land (l. 6). Thus, in *JEN* 763, 1 *kumānu* of land is likewise to be valued at 4, i.e., [1]+3, SILA$_3$.

l. 13: *ak-ka*$_4$. These signs are complete and typical, not as depicted.

l. 22: *al*. The sign appears, not as copied, but, rather, as: 

l. 24: *ú*!. This sign resembles NI. Cf. l. 30, where NI! resembles Ú.

l. 25: *Ak*. The form of this sign is more typical than depicted.

l. 30: *Ni*!. See above, note to line 24.

l. 32. A "Bêliya son of Tur-šenni" is, to my knowledge, nowhere else attested in the Nuzi texts. On the other hand, a "Bêliya son of Akiya" is attested in other texts of this cluster (*JEN* 40:17, 32; 49:19, 32; 401:26 [probably]; 614:20, 33; 758:22, 28; 765:27?, 32—only the poorly preserved *JEN* 764 fails to reveal his name), but not here. Perhaps the scribe here simply erred in recording this witness's patronymic.

l. 34. Cf. *JEN* 49:36 for the identical phrase. The meaning of *peniḫuru* seems to be supplied by the analogues to these two texts, *JEN* 401:31-32 and *JEN* 758:33-34:

JEN 401: (31) *an-nu-tu*$_4$ ^{LÚ}*ši-bu-tu*$_4$ (32) *la-mu-ú* A.ŠÀ

JEN 758: (33) *an-nu-tu*$_4$ ^{LÚ}*ši-bu-tu*$_4$ ⸢*ša*⸣? (32) *la-mu-ú ša* A.ŠÀ

Thus ^{LÚ}*peniḫuru* appears to be the equivalent of ^{LÚ}*šībūtu* (*ša*?) *lāmû*. Cf. *JEN* 836:7, 10, 11, 13, 18 (cf. l. 11), which identifies four witnesses out of eleven listed as *peniḫuru*. (*JEN* 49, 763, and 836 are the only texts known to me in which this term appears.) Thus *peniḫuru* is a sub-class of witnesses. The term likely means (in Hurrian, presumably), "encirclers," *lāmû*. For similar interpretations (i.e., surveyor, *mušelwû* or the like), see already Koschaker (1928, 15 n.) and Gordon (1936, 111). Cf. Gordon (1938, 55) and Speiser (1941, 130). Note Bush (1964, 113: "overseer(?)").

l. 36: *ši*. The sign is normal, not as depicted.

ll. 37-38. Contrary to the copy, no seal impression appears above line 37. Writing wrapped around from the obverse appears at this spot on the tablet. The seal impressions associated with lines 37-38 are placed *below* those lines. Collation confirms that the first of these impressions, appearing below line 37, is Po 217.

l. 37: *n*[*a-a-a*]. This restoration is based on line 27. There is sufficient room for this reconstruction. The trace appears, not as depicted, but, rather, as:

Lacheman reads at this point: *n*[*a-a-a*].

l. 39. Lacheman saw the PN as: *E*[*n-na-ma*]-*ti*.

Below the start of this line, Lacheman also saw: DUMU. If so, perhaps he saw the start of DUB.SAR(-*rù*). Cf., e.g., *JEN* 758:35. Elsewhere, Lacheman restores, in effect: DUMU [*Pu-ḫi-še-en-ni* DUB.SAR].

A seal impression was once certainly beneath this line. It is now quite indistinct, although traces appear to be preserved.

l. 40. Below this line, the second seal impression faces the legend, not as implied by the copy; that is, it is upside down vis-à-vis S.I. Po 175.

Lacheman found this second seal impression which he identified in the copy as Po 361 peculiar in some way: he wrote "sic!" next to it. Perhaps the peculiarity lies in the fact that this impression is elsewhere linked to an individual not found in the present text at all. See Porada (1947 131a *ad* no. 361). In fact, this impression is not Po 361 though very close to it. Lacheman's error apparently led him to see a nonexistent problem.

JEN 764

OBVERSE

1 *ṭup-pí ma-ru-ti š[a]*
2 ^{m}*Pu-ḫi-ya* DUMU BE-⸢*x*⸣-[ ]
3 *ù* ^{m}*Te-ḫi-ip-til-l[a* DUM]U *P[u-ḫi-še-en-ni]*
4 *a-na ma-ru-ti*! ⸢*i*⸣-[*t*]*e-pu-*⸢*uš*⸣
5 [3]+6 ⸢^{GIŠ}⸣[APIN] ⸢*ḫa*⸣*-ra-ar-*⸢*ni*⸣ [A].⸢ŠÀ⸣!
6 [*i-na ta*]*-a-ri ša* É.GAL *ša* G[AL]
7 [*i-na le-e*]*t* AN.ZA.KÀR *ša* ^{m}*Šá-ak-*[*r*]*u-*[*u*]*š-še*
8 [*a-na* ^{m}*Te-ḫ*]*i-ip-til-la i-din*
9 [*ù* ^{m}]⸢*Te-ḫi*⸣*-ip-til-la* 9 BÁN 2 SILA$_{3}$ ŠE.M[EŠ]
10 [*ki-m*]*a* NÍG.BA *a-na* ^{m}*Pu-ḫ*[*i*]*-ya* SUM
11 [*šum-m*]*a* A.ŠÀ *pa-qí-ra-an-na*
12 [*ir-t*]*a-ša ù* ^{m}*Pu-ḫi-*⸢*ya*⸣ *ú-za-ak-ka*$_{4}$*-*⸢*ma*⸣
13 [*a-na*] ^{m}*Te-ḫi-ip-til-la* ⸢*i*⸣*-na-an-di*
14 [*šum-ma*] ^{m}*Pu-ḫi-ya* K[I.BA]L-*tu*$_{4}$
15 [1 MA.N]A K[Ù.BABBAR 1 MA.NA KÙ.SIG$_{17}$]
16 [*ú*]*-ma-a*[*l-la*]

.
.
.

REVERSE

.
.
.

17 [IGI DUMU]-*til-l*⸢*a*⸣
18 [IGI? DUMU?]-⸢x x x⸣?
*?S.I.
19 [^{NA_4} KIŠIB $^{(m)}$*Š*]*e-eḫ-*⸢*li*⸣*-a*
S.I.
20 ^{NA_4} KIŠIB ^{m}*A-ri-ḫa-a*[*r-me-e*]
S.I.
21 $^{[NA_4]}$ KIŠIB ⸢*Ú*⸣*-na-ap-t*[*a-e*]
S.I.

UPPER EDGE

22 ^{NA_4} KIŠIB ^{m}*En-na-ma-*$^{+}$*ti*$_{4}$

TRANSLATION

(1-4) Tablet of adoption of Puḫiya son of BE... . Now he adopted Teḫip-tilla son of Puḫi-šenni.

(5-8) He gave [to] Teḫip-tilla a field, .625 [+.3] (i.e., .925) homers [by] the large standard of the palace (lit. "the standard of the palace which is large"), adjacent to the *dimtu* of Šakrušše.

(9-10) [And] Teḫip-tilla gave to Puḫiya as a gift .925 homers of barley.

(11-13) Should the field have claimants, then Puḫiya shall clear (it) and give (it) [to] Teḫip-tilla.

(14-16) [Should] Puḫiya abrogate (this contract), he shall pay [1] mina of silver [(and) 1 mina of gold].

....

(17-18) [Before ... son of] ...-tilla; [before? ... son? of?] .... .

(19-22) [(*seal impression*?)] [seal impression of] Šeḫliya; (*seal impression*) seal impression of Ariḫ-ḫarpa; (*seal impression*) seal impression of Unap-tae; (*seal impression*) seal impression of Enna-mati. ....(?)

COMMENTS

The hand copy of this tablet could not be collated against the original before the tablet's return to Baghdad. Prior to the tablet's return, a pair of casts was made, and the copy was checked against these casts. It is very possible that the identity of an additional sealer (or sealers) was once preserved on the left edge.

Between lines 16 and 17 is a gap of some ten to twelve lines containing the *ilku* clause and the names of some eight to eleven witnesses. Some of those names are reflected in lines 19-21 (or 19-22).

NOTES

l. 2: BE-⸢*x*⸣-[ ]. Lacheman reads and restores: *Be-l*[*a-nu*].

l. 4. Lacheman records this line as completely preserved.

l. 5: [3]+6. The cast of this tablet is not clear at this point. What seems to be preserved is: 

"3" is added to the preserved number for the following reasons. *JEN* 764 is part of a cluster of eight closely related texts. These are: *JEN* 40, 49, 401, 614, 758, 763, 764, 765. For details of this relationship, see above, note to *JEN* 758:5-7. These texts are sufficiently closely linked that, frequently, a gap in one may be filled by appeal to parallel passages in the others.

(Orthographic peculiarities shared by this text and others of this cluster [including, here: *pa-qí-ra-an-na* (l. 11); *ir-ta-ša* (l. 12); *i-na-an-di* (l. 13); KI.BAL-tu_4 (l. 14); *Še-eḫ-li-a* (l. 19)] are recognized above, notes to *JEN* 758:5-7, 11, 13, 22.)

One of the characteristic features of these texts is a constant ratio obtaining between the amount of land purchased and the price of that land. The ratio is 1 homer of land : 1 homer of barley. *JEN* 40:4, 8; 49:5, 9; 614:5, 10; 758:5, 9; and 765:8, 11 are unambiguous on this point. *JEN* 401:6, 10 and 763:5, 10 almost certainly describe the same ratio. (A heretofore unresolved question regarding the relative value of the surface measure, *kumānu* [which appears in those texts], means that *JEN* 401 and 763 depend on the other five texts in ascertaining the ratio described in those two cases [See further below, next note.].) Thus, no text attests to other than the 1:1 ratio. In the present instance, the 9 BÁN appearing in *JEN* 764:9 implies (in light of the five clear and two almost certain examples of the 1:1 ratio) a value in line 5 of 9, i.e., [3]+6 *awiḫaru* of land.

Lacheman records, variously, "⌜9⌝" and "⌜7⌝."

l. 5: ⌜*ḫa*⌝-*ra-ar*-⌜*ni*⌝. This text, in conjunction with *JEN* 401 and 763, provides, I believe, the key to the long-standing problem of the values of the Nuzi surface measures, *kumānu* and *ḫararnu*, relative to the *awiḫaru* and, therefore, to each other. The *kumānu* = ½ *awiḫaru* and the *ḫararnu* = ¼ *awiḫaru*, thus confirming Marvin Powell's deductions (1989-90, 485). (For previous studies of this issue, see Maidman [1976, 365, n. 401]; more recent discussions include Zaccagnini [1979a, 849-50 (cf. Zaccagnini [1979c, 120, n. 13])] and Powell [1989-90, 485 ff.].)

The solution is provided by the almost certainly fixed commodity-price ratio of 1 homer of land : 1 homer of barley obtaining in these three texts. (On this determination, see the immediately preceding note.) Since the price in barley is calculated in units whose relative values are known, it should be—and is—easy to calculate the value of the *kumānu* and *ḫararnu* (where these are mentioned) relative to the *awiḫaru*.

The values of the relevant units of dry measure are as follows: 8 SILA$_3$ = 1 BÁN; 10 BÁN = 1 ANŠE (i.e., "homer"). For these values, see Wilhelm (1980, 26-27).

JEN 401:6, 10 relate that 1 homer, 2 *awiḫaru*, and a *kumānu* of land fetch 1 homer, 2 BÁN, and 4 SILA$_3$ of barley. Similarly, *JEN* 763:5, 10 note that 1 homer, 3 *awiḫaru*, and a *kumānu* of land are worth 1 homer, 3 BÁN, and 4 SILA$_3$ of barley. In both cases, a *kumānu* of land is worth 4 SILA$_3$ of barley, i.e., ½ BÁN of barley. Since ½ BÁN is the price of ½ *awiḫaru*, 1 *kumānu* = ½ *awiḫaru*. The present text, lines 5 and 9, almost surely values 9 *awiḫaru* of land at 9 BÁN of barley and a *ḫararnu* of land at 2 SILA$_3$ of barley. The *ḫararnu*, therefore, is worth half as much as the *kumānu* and is to be reckoned as ¼ *awiḫaru* (as 2 SILA$_3$ = ¼ BÁN).

Previous attempts to value the *ḫararnu* as ½ *awiḫaru* (with the *kumānu* = ½ *awiḫaru* as well) or as ⅓ *awiḫaru* (with the *kumānu* = ⅔ *awiḫaru*) should be abandoned accordingly.

According to the values here established, the land areas enumerated in *JEN* 526:1-5 should add up to 4.475 homers. The total is given (l. 7) as 4.5 homers. One must assume a slight upward rounding here, though such an *ad hoc* explanation of a seemingly contrary datum must leave one less than satisfied. Yet, one should note in this connection the observation of Friberg (1990, 537b): "Rounding of numbers occurs fairly frequently in economic texts from all periods." A possibly analogous rounding (this time downward) is discussed below, note to *JEN* 770:5.

l. 7: ᵐ*Šá-ak-*[*r*]*u-*[*u*]*š-še*. The last two signs wrap around well onto the reverse. They are depicted in the copy both on the obverse (l. 7) and, in part, on the reverse, between lines 20 and 21, upside down.

This *dimtu* may be located in Unap-še. See above, note to *JEN* 758:5-7.

l. 9: 9 BÁN 2 SILA₃. The nine wedges of the first number are not distinctly reflected on the cast.

Lacheman reads, in effect: 6 ANŠE (*sic*) 4 SILA₃.

l. 10: *ḫ*[*i*]. This trace appears somewhat more typical of ḪI than depicted in the copy.

l. 13. Lacheman sees this line as completely preserved.

l. 13: *di*. The surface of the tablet is well preserved, and blank, after DI.

l. 14: K[I]. The vertical wedge of the K[I] is not visible on the cast.

l. 17. The witness, part of whose patronymic is here preserved, could be Akkuya son of Alki-tilla or Unnuki or Kinnaya sons of Ar-tilla.

l. 18. The traces do not readily suggest a patronymic from among the standard witnesses of the text series of which *JEN* 764 is a part. Perhaps the traces represent the remnant of a variant form of the formula defining witnesses as field measurers. Cf. above, note to *JEN* 763:34.

Lacheman reads, in effect: [ ] DUMU *A*-[ ], suggesting perhaps, Bêliya son of Akiya (cf. *JEN* 40:17; 49:19; 614:20; 758:22).

l. 19. On the cast, the seal impression above this line is not visible to me.

ll. 20-21. See above, note to line 7.

JEN 765

OBVERSE

1 ṭup-pí ma-ru-ti ša

2 ^{m}Wa-an-ti$_4$-ya DUMU Pur-ni-a

3 ù ša ^{m}Ḫa-šu-ar DUMU KI.*MIN

4 ù ^{m}Te-ḫi-ip-til-la DUMU Pu-ḫi-*še-[en-ni]

5 a-na ma-ru-ti i-te-pu-uš

6 1 ANŠE A.ŠÀ ša ^{m}Wa-an-ti$_4$-ya

7 2 ANŠE A.ŠÀ ša ^{m}Ḫa-šu-ar

8 ŠU.NIGIN$_2$! 3 ANŠE A.ŠÀ i-na AN.ZA.KÀR ša ^{m}⸢Šá⸣-ak-ru-uš-•še

9 i-na le-et A.ŠÀ ša ^{m}Ú-ur-za-[a]z?-⸢zi⸣

10 a-na ^{m}Te-ḫi-ip-til-la i-din

11 ù ^{m}Te-ḫi-ip-til-la 3 ANŠE ŠE.MEŠ

12 ki-ma NÍG.BA a-na ^{m}Ḫa-šu-ar ù

13 a-na ^{m}Wa-an!-ti$_4$-•⸢ya i⸣-d[in]

14 šum-ma A.ŠÀ an-nu-t[u$_4$ pa-qí-ra(-an)]-⸢na⸣

15 •ir-ta-ša ù $^{[m]}$W[a-an-ti$_4$-ya]

16 •ù ^{m}Ḫa-šu-ar [ú-za-ak-ku-ma]

17 •a-na ^{m}Te-ḫi-ip-[til-la i-na-an-di-nu]

18 •šum-•ma ^{m}Ḫa-šu-[ar ù]

19 •^{m}Wa-an-ti$_4$-y[a KI.BAL-tu$_4$]

20 1 MA.NA ⸢KÙ.BABBAR⸣ [1 MA.NA KÙ.SIG$_{17}$]

LOWER EDGE

21 ⸢i⸣!?-n[a?-an?-di?-nu?]

.

.

.

REVERSE

22 $^{+}$IG[I Ki-i]n-⸢na-a⸣-[a DUMU Ar-til-la]

23 $^{+}$IG[I Ur-ḫi]-ya DUMU Še-[ka$_4$-rù]

24 $^{+}$IG[I Ké-/Ke-l]i-ip-LU[GAL DUMU Al-ki-ya/-a]

25 $^{+}$IG[I Zi-i]l$_5$-te-•⸢ya⸣ [DUMU Ta-ú-ka$_4$]

26 $^{+}$IG[I A-ri]-ḫa-ar-me-[e DUMU Ḫa-na-a-a]

27 [IGI Še]-*⸢eḫ⸣-li-ya DUMU ⸢Ak⸣-[ku-ya]

S.I.

28 ^{NA_4} KIŠIB Še-eḫ-li-a

S.I. Po 573 S.I. Po 175

29 •^{NA_4} KIŠIB Ú-[na-ap-*t]a-*e [^{NA_4} KIŠI]B •A-ri-ḫa-ar-me-⸢e⸣

*S.I. S.I. Po 358

LEFT EDGE

30 [$^{NA_4?}$ KIŠIB? ^{NA_4}] ⸢KIŠIB⸣ Be-li-ya

REVERSE

31 $^{[NA_4]}$ KIŠIB En-na-ma-[ti/ti$_4$]

UPPER EDGE

[S.I.?]

TRANSLATION

(1-5) Tablet of adoption of Wantiya son of Purniya and of Ḫašuar son of the same. Now he (*sic*) adopted Teḫip-tilla son of Puḫi-šenni.

(6-10) He (*sic*) gave to Teḫip-tilla a 1 homer field of Wantiya (and) a 2 homer field of Ḫašuar; total: 3 homers of land in the *dimtu* of Šakrušše, adjacent to the field of Ur-za[z?]zi.

(11-13) And Teḫip-tilla gave to Ḫašuar and to Wantiya as a gift 3 homers of barley.

(14-17) Should these fields have claimants, then Wantiya and Ḫašuar [shall clear (the fields) and give (them)] to Teḫip-tilla.

(18-21) Should Ḫašuar [and] Wantiya [abrogate (this contract)], they(?) shall(?) give(?) 1 mina of silver [(and) 1 mina of gold].

....

(22-27) Before Kinnaya [son of Ar-tilla]; before Urḫiya son of Šekaru; before Kelip-šarri [son of Alkiya]; before Zil-teya [son of Tauka]; before Ariḫ-ḫarpa [son of Ḫanaya; before] Šeḫliya son of Akkuya.

(28-31) (*seal impression*) seal impression of Šeḫliya; (*seal impression*) seal impression of Unap-tae; (*seal impression*) seal impression of Ariḫ-ḫarpa; (*seal impression*) [seal? impression? of? ...]; (*seal impression*) seal impression of Bêliya; seal impression of Enna-mati [(*seal impression*?)].

COMMENTS

This tablet has suffered slight additional deterioration since it was copied.

Since the copy was made, a fragment (unnumbered) has been joined to the upper left of the reverse. It contributes to the text the first sign to each of lines 22-26.

Between lines 21 and 22, perhaps one line is missing. If so, it contained the *ilku* clause.

The scribe may accidentally have omitted witness names. Cf. the texts analogous to this one. Four (of six?) such omissions appear reflected in the sealer names in lines 29-31.

NOTES

l. 2: *Pur-ni-a*. For this spelling, see above, note to *JEN* 758:22.

JEN 765 may be compared to *JEN* 758 because both are part of a largely homogeneous series of eight tablets: *JEN* 40, 49, 401, 614, 758, 763, 764, 765. For common features of these texts, see further, above, note to *JEN*

758:5-7. Amongst these features is a largely common repertoire of witnesses. This allows restoration of witness PNs in the present text. Other restorations are also made, based on preserved passages in the other texts of this series. Other orthographic peculiarities in the present text (these include a possible *pa-qí-ra-an-na* [l. 14]; *ir-ta-ša* [l. 15]; *Še-eḫ-li-a* [l. 28]) are discussed or mentioned above, notes to *JEN* 758:11, 5-7, 22.

l. 4. The *CAD* Nuzi file records this line as completely preserved.

l. 8: NIGIN$_2$!. The sign appears, not as copied, but, rather, as:

l. 8: AN.ZA.KÀR *ša* m⌈*Šá*⌉*-ak-ru-uš-še*. This *dimtu* may be located in Unap-še. See above, note to *JEN* 758:5-7.

l. 10: *i*. This sign is a typical I, not DUMU as copied. Therefore, Lacheman's marginal "SIC!" is to be ignored.

l. 12: *Ḫa*. This sign appears, not as copied, but, rather, as:

l. 13: *an*!. This sign has but one horizontal wedge (i.e., MAŠ), not two as copied.

l. 20: MA. This sign is normal, not as depicted.

l. 21. Lacheman restores this line: [*ú-ma-al-lu*].

l. 22. Lacheman at one point saw this line as: [ ]*-in-na-a-*[ ].

l. 24: LU[GAL]. Lacheman sees this sign as completely preserved.

l. 28. The seal impression above this line faces away from the line, not toward it, as implied by the copy.

l. 29: *Ú*-[*na*]. The *CAD* Nuzi file records these signs as completely preserved.

l. 30. Lacheman notes, regarding the first of the seal impressions above this line: "Po 100 (?)." Porada (1947, 127b *ad* no. 100) identifies that impression with the scribe, Enna-mati son of dUTU-DINGIR-AŠ-KUR in *JEN* 546 (l. 27; cf. l. 15). The same scribe wrote this text. See line 31 and the note to *JEN* 758:5-7. If this seal impression is indeed here to be identified with Enna-mati—the impression is now totally effaced—it appears unusually distant from the legend itself and on a different axis as well. For a similar phenomenon involving the same scribe, see above, note to *JEN* 758:19.

l. 31: *En*. This sign is correct as copied.

JEN 766

OBVERSE

1 [ ]⸢x⸣[(?)]

2 [AŠ/*i-na* URU] *Ši-*⸢*ni-na*⸣

3 [*ki-ma* ḪA.LA-*šu*] ⸢*a*⸣-[*n*]*a* ^{m}*Te-ḫi-ip-til-la*

4 [*it-ta-din ù*] ^{m}⸢*Te*⸣!-[*ḫi-ip-til-l*]*a*

5 [ANŠE? ŠE.MEŠ] *k*[*i-m*]*a* NÍG.BA-*šu*

6 [*a-na* $^{m?}$ -x *it?*]-⸢*ta?-din*⸣?

7 [*šum-ma* A?.ŠÀ? *di-n*]*a i-ra-aš-ši*

8 [$^{m?}$ -x *ú*]-*za-ak-ka*$_4$-*ma*

9 [*a-na* ^{m}*Te-ḫi-ip-til-l*]*a i+na-a*[*n-din*]

10 [*šum-ma* $^{m?}$]-⸢x⸣ KI.BAL-*a*[*t*]

11 [2 MA.NA KÙ.SIG$_{17}$ *a-na*] ^{m}*Te-ḫi-i*[*p-til-l*]*a* [*ú-ma-al-la*]

12 [IGI *Mu-uš-te-šup* DUMU *A*]*r-na-p*[*u*]

13 [IGI *Pí-ru* DUMU *Na-iš-k*]*é-el-p*[*è*]

14 [IGI *Te-ḫi-ya* DUMU *A-ka*$_4$]-*a-a*

15 [IGI *Še-el-wi-ya*] $^{+}$DUMU *Ar-zi-ka*$_4$-*ri*

LOWER EDGE

16 [IGI *Ḫa-ra-pa-tal* DUMU *A-rip*-LUGA]L

REVERSE

17 [IGI *Túr-še-(en-)ni* DUMU *A-ri-p*]*a-ap-ni*

18 [IGI *A-wi-iš/šu-uš-še* DUMU *Pa-li-y*]*a*

.

.

.

19 [IGI *Nu-la-za-ḫi* DUMU *E-ri-i*]*š*-⸢*x*⸣-[*x*]

.

.

.

20 [5? (LÚ.MEŠ) *ši-bu-ti/an-nu-ti ša* URU] *Ši-ni-*[*na*]

21 [IGI *Ta-a-a* DUMU *A-pil*]-XXX DUB.SAR-[*rù*]

22 [14? $^{LÚ.MEŠ}$ *ši-bu-ti an-nu-ti*] ⸢*ù*⸣ <*šu?-nu?-ma?*> *mu-še-*[*el*]
:-*mu-*⸢*ú*⸣

S.I.

23 [^{NA_4} KIŠIB ^{m}*Mu-uš-t*]*e-šup* DUMU *Ar-n*[*a-pu*]

S.I.

TRANSLATION

....

(1-4) [He? gave] to Teḫip-tilla [as his inheritance share] .... [in the town of] Šinina.

(4-6) [And] Teḫip-tilla gave [to ...] as his gift [X homers? of barley].

(7-9) [Should the field?] have a case (against it), ...] shall clear (the field) and give (it) [to] Teḫip-tilla.

(10-11) [Should] ... abrogate (this contract), [he shall pay to] Teḫip-tilla [2 minas of gold].

(12-22) [Before Muš-tešup son of] Arn-apu; [before Piru son of] Naiš-kelpe; [before Teḫiya son of] Akaya; [before Šelwiya] son of Ar-zikari; [before Ḫarap-atal son of] Arip-šarri; [before Tur-šenni son of] Arip-papni; [before Awiš-ušše son of] Paliya; ....; [before Nula-zaḫi son of] Êriš-...; ....—[these 5? witnesses (or the like—M.P.M.) are of the town of] Šinina—[before Taya son of] Apil-sin, the scribe. [These are the 14? witnesses] and <as? well?, they? are?> the measurers.

(23) (*seal impression*) [seal impression of] Muš-tešup son of Arn-apu; (*seal impression*) .... .

COMMENTS

The surface of this tablet is very worn. Some signs of the upper left part of the surviving obverse are extremely faint. Furthermore, few signs at all are discernible on the obverse.

The reconstruction of this text may be undertaken (and the extent of the damage deduced) with considerable confidence. This is because key data survive. These include the location of the real estate, Šinina (ll. 2, 20); the genre of the text, a tablet of real estate adoption (l. 5 especially); and the name of the adoptee, Teḫip-tilla (ll. 3, 11 clearly). Amongst the five other texts sharing these features, *JEN* 10, 21, 74, 684, 685, four (all but *JEN* 10) have many other characteristics in common and may be considered part of the same series. For details, see above, note to *JEN* 684:18. Comparison of the texts of this series with the surviving parts of *JEN* 766 demonstrates that the present text is likewise to be considered part of this series. This is especially apparent upon consideration of the witness and sealing sequences. *JEN* 766:12-21 appear to reflect the same sequence as *JEN* 21, 74, 685, and a sequence similar to *JEN* 684.

It is, therefore, reasonable to reconstruct the missing parts of the witness list of *JEN* 766, as well as unambiguous parts of the remaining text, on the basis of the other four texts of this series. On these grounds also, one may deduce how many lines are now totally missing.

Perhaps four or five lines are missing at the start. These will have read somewhat as follows:

ṭup-pí ma-ru-ti ša
PN_1 DUMU PN_2
^{m}*Te-ḫi-ip-til-la* DUMU *Pu-ḫi-še-en-ni*
a-na ma-ru-ti DÙ-*ma*

(amount and, perhaps, more precise location of the real estate to be ceded).

To judge from *JEN* 74:27-29 and 685:24-26, an additional three lines identifying three witnesses are now missing between lines 18 and 19. These will have read, approximately:

IGI *A-kip*-LUGAL DUMU *Ar-zi-iz-za*
IGI *Šur-ki-til-la* DUMU NÍG.BA-*ya*
IGI *Pu-ḫi-še-ni* DUMU KI.MIN

It appears, however, that there may not be enough room for three lines between lines 18 and 19. Perhaps one of these names belongs after line 19 rather than before it (there seems to be enough room there) or perhaps the present restoration of line 19, though reasonable, is simply wrong.

Two more lines (at least) identifying still other witnesses will have followed line 19. At any rate, this is the pattern of the other texts of this series, although they diverge among themselves regarding the identity of these two witnesses.

Finally, at the end of the text, about four additional seal impressions and five lines of text identifying the sealers will have followed the last surviving seal impression. Porada identifies this last surviving impression with Šurki-tilla son of Qîšteya.

The location of the signs on the obverse is not indicated in the copy. The left side of the obverse is totally missing. The right edge can be represented by two imaginary vertical lines in the copy, dropping from the start and end of the word, "destroyed." The remaining signs at the end of the obverse wrap around onto the reverse.

NOTES

l. 1: ⌜x⌝. Perhaps [É].GA[L] ought to be restored. Cf. *JEN* 21:5; 74:6. On the relevance of *JEN* 21 and 74 to the present text, see above, comments.

l. 4: [*it-ta-din*]. Or the like.

l. 6: [*it*?]-⌜*ta*?-*din*⌝?. Or the like.

l. 17: [*A-ri-p*]*a-ap-ni*. Or a similar spelling of this PN. The last sign is a clear NI, not RU as depicted.

ll. 18-20. On the missing text in this part of the tablet, see above, comments.

l. 22. For the restoration of this line, cf. the formulation in *JEN* 21:31-32. On the relevance of *JEN* 21 to the present text, see above, comments.

JEN 767

OBVERSE

1 [^{m}*E-ki-ya* DUMU *Ka*$_4$]-⸢*ki-ya*⸣!

2 [^{m}*Te-ḫi-ip-til-l*]*a* DUMU *Pu-ḫ*[*i-še-en-ni*]

3 [*a-na ma-ru*]-$^{+}$⸢*ti*⸣ *i-pu-sú*

4 [ ] ⸢A⸣.ŠÀ *i+na ú-šal-l*[*i*]

5 [*i-na le-e*]*t a-ta-pí ša* [ ]

6 [*i-na* URU] *Pu*!-*ru-li*-⸢*wa*⸣

7 [^{m}*E-ki-y*]*a* •DUMU *Ka*$_4$-*ki*-⸢*ya*⸣ [*ki-ma* ḪA.LA(-*šu*/*šú*)]

8 [*a-na* ^{m}*T*]*e-ḫi-ip-til-la i*-[*din*]

9 [*šum-ma* ^{m}]⸢*E*⸣-*ki-ya*! *i-bala-k*[*a*$_4$-*at*]

10 [1 MA.N]A KÙ.BABBAR 1 MA.NA KÙ.S[IG$_{17}$ *ú-ma-al-la*]

11 [IGI *Wa*]-*an-ti-ya* DUMU *Ki*-⸢*x*⸣-[ ]

12 [I]G[I *M*]*u-uš-te-šup* DUMU *Ar-na*-⸢*pu*⸣

13 [IGI Ì]R-DINGIR-*šu* DUMU BÀD!-LUGAL

14 [IGI] ⸢*Pí*⸣-*i-ru* DUMU *Na-i-iš-ké-el-pè*

15 [IGI]-⸢*a*⸣?-*a* DUMU! *Mu*-$^{+}$*ra-ni-ya*

16 [IGI -R]I? DUMU *Ar-ḫ*[*i*?-]

17 [IGI]-*nu* DUMU *A*-RI-[ ]

LOWER EDGE

18 [IGI DUMU]-ME?

REVERSE

19 [IGI DUMU]-*ri-ké*

S.I. Po 1007

20 $^{[N]A_4}$ KIŠIB ^{m}*Ka*$_4$-*ri-šu-uḫ* DUMU ⸢*Ar*⸣-*t*[*e*-(*eš*-)*še*]

S.I.

21 ^{NA_4} KIŠIB [ ]

S.I.

TRANSLATION

....

(1-3) Ikkiya son of Kakkiya. He adopted Teḫip-tilla son of Puḫi-šenni.

(4-8) Ikkiya son of Kakkiya gave [to] Teḫip-tilla [as (his) inheritance share a ...] field, in the meadow, adjacent to the ... Canal, [in the town of] Purulli.

(9-10) [Should] Ikkiya abrogate (this contract), [he shall pay 1] mina of silver (and) 1 mina of gold.

(11-19) [Before] Wantiya son of Ki-...; before Muš-tešup son of Arnapu; [before] Ward-ilišu son of Dûr-šarru; [before] Piru son of Naiš-kelpe; [before] ...-aya son of Mûrāniya; [before] ... son of Ar-ḫi(?)-...; [before] ...-nu son of A-RI-...; [before ... son of] ...-ME(?); [before ... son of] ...-rike.

(20-21) (*seal impression*) seal impression of Kari-šuḫ son of Ar-tešše; (*seal impression*) seal impression of ...; (*seal impression*) ....

COMMENTS

This tablet has suffered almost no deterioration since it was copied.

One line is missing at the start of the obverse. It will have read: *ṭup-pí ma-ru-ti ša*.

This real estate adoption text is quite unusual in that it lacks a clear title clause. Note also that the scribe sometimes employs idiosyncratic signs: YA (l. 1; perhaps), PU (l. 6; see below, note to line 6), YA (l. 9), BÀD (l. 13), DUMU (l. 15; see below, note to line 15).

NOTES

l. 1. The restoration of this line is based on lines 9 and 7. For further on this individual, see above, note to *JEN* 760:20. The suggestion of *NPN*, 81b *sub* KELIJA 9), 78b *sub* KAKKIŠU 2), that the adopter is Keliya son of Kakkišu is to be rejected.

l. 3: ⸢*ti*⸣. This sign does not appear as depicted, but, rather, as:

l. 5: [*i-na*]. The real estate involved is most likely in Purulli rather than, for example, on the road to this town. See above, note to *JEN* 760:20.

l. 5: *a-ta-pí*. This interpretation is not absolutely certain. This spelling of *atappi*, assuming it is deliberate and not itself defective, is rare, if not unique, in the Nuzi texts; the doubled /p/ is most usually expressed orthographically.

l. 6: *Pu*!. The sign appears, not as copied, but, rather, as:

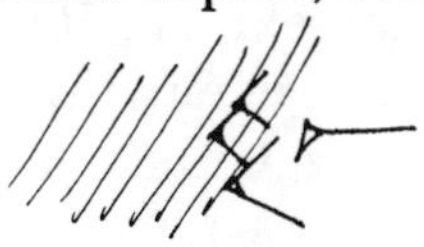

l. 8: [*din*]. Or the like.

l. 9: *k*[a_4-*at*]. Or the like.

l. 10: [*ú-ma-al-la*]. Or the like.

l. 12: ⸢*pu*⸣. Lacheman sees this sign as completely preserved.

l. 15. The first trace appears, not as depicted, but, rather, as:

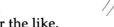

The third sign appears, not as depicted, but, rather, as:

The PN, Mûrāniya, is a rare one. Aside from this line, it is attested only three times. See *NPN*, 99a *sub voce*. One of those attestations (and only one) is consistent with the traces of this line: *Ta-a-a* DUMU *Mu-ra-ni-ya* (*JEN* 95:19). In *JEN* 95, this person acts as witness to a Teḫip-Tilla real estate adoption contract.

Although the locations of the real estate in *JEN* 95 and *JEN* 767 are in different areas (cf. *JEN* 95:1, 4-6 and *JEN* 641:6, 30-31 [a Zizza locus, as proved by *JEN* 244:5-6] with *JEN* 767:6), the two texts share at least three witnesses (*JEN* 767:12-14 // *JEN* 95:13, 12, 11), all, to be sure, ubiquitous in the Teḫip-tilla corpus. If Taya son of Mûrāniya appears in both, the link between these two texts becomes considerably stronger. Note that the scribe of *JEN* 95 is Itḫ-apiḫe son of Taya (ll. 20, 23). It is characteristic of Itḫ-apiḫe to render forms of *nabalkutu* syllabically rather than to employ (KI.)BAL as is otherwise frequent in these texts. See, e.g., *JEN* 95:9. The same verb is rendered here (l. 9) syllabically as well. Perhaps, then, this text was written by Itḫ-apiḫe son of Taya.

l. 19: *ké*. No sign appears after this one. The tablet is well preserved here. The trace below GI might represent a following line. If so, the numbering of the lines after line 19 is to be altered accordingly.

ll. 20-21. Collation reveals that Lacheman erred in assigning the number, "Po 1007," to the seal impression below line 20. It belongs to the impression above this line. Cf. also Porada (1947, 138b *ad* no. 1007). In her unpublished papers, Porada identifies the second seal impression with Muš-tešup son of Arn-apu (cf. l. 12).

l. 20: ⌜*Ar*⌝-*t*[*e-*(*eš-*)*še*]. The *CAD* Nuzi file records AR as entirely preserved. The only other "Kari-šuḫ" attested in the Nuzi texts is the son of Ar-tešše, in *JEN* 14:13, 21. That text, like *JEN* 767, is a Teḫip-tilla real estate adoption text (*NB*: real estate in Nuzi is involved there). The restoration of the same patronymic here is thus very plausible. See already *NPN*, 80b *sub* KARI-ŠUḪ 1), 34b *sub* AR-TEŠŠE 12); and Porada (1947, 138b *ad* no. 1007).

JEN 768

OBVERSE

1 [^{m}*Te-ḫi-ip-til*]-*la* DUMU *P*[*u-ḫi-še-en-ni*]

2 [^{m}*Tu-ra-r*]*i* DUMU *Pu*-⸢*x*⸣-[*a-nà ma-ru-ti i-te-pu-uš*]

3 [*a-w*]*i-ḫa-ri* A.ŠÀ *i-n*[*a* AN.ZA.KÀR (*ša*)] •*pí-ir-ša-an-ni*

4 [*ša* ^{m}*Te-ḫi*]-*ip*-•*til*-•*la* <*a-na*> ^{m}*T*[*e-ḫi-i*]*p-til-la ki-ma* ḪA.LA-*šu* <SUM>

5 [*ù* ^{m}*Te-ḫi*]-*ip*-•*til*-**la* •3 [ANŠE? ŠE?]

6 ⸢*a-na* ^{m}⸣[*Tu*]-⸢*ra*-•*ri*⸣ **ki*-[*ma* NÍG.BA-*šu* SUM]

7 *ma-an*-[*nu-m*]*é ša* *⸢*i*-**na*⸣ •*bi-r*[*i-šu-nu* (*ša*) KI.BAL-*tu*$_4$]

8 1 MA.N[A K]Ù.[BABBAR 1] ⸢MA⸣.•[N]A ⸢KÙ.SIG$_{17}$⸣ [*i-na-din*]

9 IGI *Él*-[*ḫi-ip*-LUGAL DUMU] •*Šu-ul-ma-ad-d*[*á*]

10 IGI ÌR-DINGI[R-*š*]*u* ⸢DUMU⸣ *Du-ur*-LUGAL

11 IGI *Pí-i*-[*r*]*u* DUMU *Na-iš-ké-é*[*l*]-*pè*

12 IGI *Zi*-⸢*kà*⸣-*a-a* DUMU *Él-ḫi-ip*-[LUG]AL

13 IGI *Še-kà-ru* DUMU *Šúk-ri-til-la*

14 IGI *Ḫa-ma-an-na* DUMU DUMU-^{UD}XX^{KAM}

15 IGI *It-ḫi-iš-ta* DUMU *A-ar-ta-e*

16 IGI *Ḫa-ma-a*[*n*]-*na* DUMU *Ar-ša-an-tá*

LOWER EDGE

17 IGI *E*-•*w*[*i-n*]*a-an-ni* DUMU *Še-en-n*[*a-a-a*]

18 IGI *Gi*-⸢*mil*⸣-$^{+\text{d}}$IM DUMU *Zu-mé*

REVERSE

19 IGI *Wa*-[*qar*]-EN DUB.SAR DUMU *Ta-a-a* DUB.⸢SAR⸣

---

20 ⸢*šum*⸣-*ma* ⸢A⸣.ŠÀ *pa-ri-qa-na*

21 ⸢*ir*⸣-[*t*]*a-ši* ^{m}*Tu-ra-ri ú-za-ak-ka*$_4$

S.I. Po 637

22 ^{N}[$^{\text{A}_4}$ KIŠIB ^{m}*Tu-r*]*a-ri ša be*-**é*[*l*] *⸢A⸣.*ŠÀ

S.I. Po 231

23 [$^{\text{NA}_4}$ KIŠIB ^{m}*Še*]-*kà-ru* *[DU]MU *Šúk-ri-til*-•⸢*la*⸣

S.I.

TRANSLATION

....

(1-2) Teḫip-tilla son of Puḫi-šenni. Turari son of Pu-... [adopted him].

(3-4) <He gave to> Teḫip-tilla as his inheritance share a .x homer field in the *piršanni* [*dimtu* of] Teḫip-tilla.

(5-6) [And] Teḫip-tilla [gave] to Turari as [his gift] 3 [homers? of? barley?].

(7-8) Whoever amongst them [abrogates (this contract) shall give] 1 mina of silver (and) [1] mina of gold.

(9-19) Before Elḫip-šarri [son of] Šulm-adad; before Ward-ilišu son of Dûr-šarru; before Piru son of Naiš-kelpe; before Zikaya son of Elḫip-šarri; before Šekaru son of Šurki-tilla; before Ḫamanna son of Mâr-ešrī; before Itḫišta son of Ar-tae; before Ḫamanna son of Ar-šanta; before Ewinnanni son of Šennaya; before Gimill-adad son of Zume; before Waqar-bêli, the scribe, son of Taya, the scribe.

(20-21) Should the field have claimants, Turari shall clear (it).

(22-23) (*seal impression*) seal impression of Turari, (i.e.,) of the (erstwhile) owner of the field; (*seal impression*) [seal impression of] Šekaru son of Šurki-tilla; (*seal impression*) ....

COMMENTS

The copy could not be collated against the original before the tablet was returned to Baghdad. A pair of casts of the tablet was made prior to the return, and collation of the copy against these casts was undertaken.

The tablet has suffered some additional deterioration since it was copied. But, except for the examples in lines 3-7, 9, my failure to discern signs may be due to the quality of the casts rather than to a deteriorated original.

The tablet is now missing one line at the start of the obverse. This line will have read: *ṭup-pí ma-ru-ti ša*. Another line is missing at the end of the reverse. This line will have identified the third sealer. For these two missing lines, cf. *JEN* 215:1, 28.

The relevance of *JEN* 215 to *JEN* 768 is immediate and substantial. The two may be considered to form a "cluster" unto themselves. Both of these Teḫip-tilla real estate adoption tablets locate the land to be ceded in the same *dimtu*. They share a common group of witnesses. All witnesses in *JEN* 215 reappear in *JEN* 768. Only one witness in *JEN* 768 (l. 18) fails to appear in *JEN* 215. The sequence of witnesses is similar, though not identical. The two texts share a common scribe and, therefore, the idiosyncrasies of spelling and formulation of clauses which that implies (especially if both texts were written on the same occasion). Obvious in this regard are the metathetical spelling shared by both texts, *pa-ri-qa-na* (*JEN* 215:12; 768:20; cf. also above, note to *JEN* 759:10) representing "*pāqirāna*" and the additional metathetical *Šúk-ri-til-la* (*JEN* 768:13, 23) representing "Šurki-tilla," only partially realized in *Šúk-ki-til-la* (*JEN* 215:19). Note also the *mutual* penalty clause (*JEN* 215:14-16; 768:7-8), unusual in real estate adoption texts. (In *JEN* 768 only, the scribe has exhibited other peculiarities. He has omitted at least two words [*a-na* (l. 4) and SUM (l. 4)] and has placed the clear title clause between the witness list and the list of sealers. He probably forgot to place this clause

immediately after the statement of purchase price [cf. *JEN* 215:12-13] where it more appropriately belongs.)

Therefore, the definition of missing lines at the start and end of *JEN* 768, based on the pattern of *JEN* 215, seems secure. In similar fashion, other restorations in *JEN* 768 may reasonably be posited, based on the better preserved parallel portions of *JEN* 215.

NOTES

ll. 3-4: [AN.ZA.KÀR (*ša*)] *pí-ir-ša-an-ni* / / [*ša* ^{m}*Te-ḫi*]-*ip-til-la*. On this GN and its location in Zizza, see above, note to *JEN* 692:5-6. Cf. *JEN* 215:6-7 for a variation on the same toponymic theme.

l. 4: <SUM>. Or the like. Cf. *JEN* 215:9, 11, 27.

l. 6: [SUM]. Or the like. Cf. *JEN* 215:9, 11, 27.

l. 7: [*m*]*é*. Lacheman once saw this sign as wholly preserved.

l. 8: [N]A. This trace appears, not as copied, but, rather, as:

l. 9: *Él*-[*ḫi-ip*-LUGAL]. The remaining sign appears, not as copied, but, rather as:

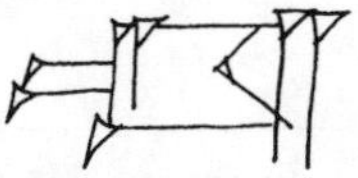

The restoration of this PN is based on *JEN* 215:21. On the relevance of that line for the elucidation of this one, see above, comments. See also *NPN*, 137b *sub* ŠULM-ADAD: in the Nuzi texts, this PN serves as a patronymic for Elḫip-šarri alone.

l. 11: *é*[*l*]. This trace appears, not as copied, but, rather, as:

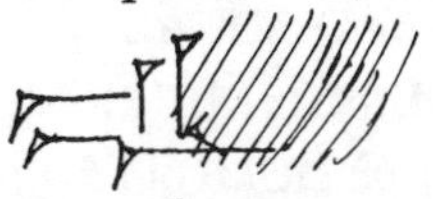

l. 13: *Šúk-ri-til-la*. For this spelling, see above, comments.

l. 17: *n*[*a-a-a*]. Lacheman records these signs as complete.

l. 18: ^{d}. This sign is complete and typical, not as depicted.

l. 19: [*qar*]. Lacheman once saw this sign as completely preserved.

l. 20: *pa-ri-qa-na*. For this spelling, see above, comments.

l. 22. Contrary to the copy, collation reveals that the seal impression above this line is not Po 180 but contains a similar motif. It is elsewhere correctly identified by Lacheman as Po 637. (Regarding S.I. Po 180, Porada [1947, 128b *ad* no. 180] links this impression to *JENu* 793 [=*JEN* 785]. This is correct.)

In her papers, Porada notes that the seal of Piru son of Naiš-kelpe (cf. l. 11) is here used by Turari. For parallels to this phenomenon and its significance, see above, note to *JEN* 675:45-48.

l. 23. The seal impression above this line is identified by Lacheman in other copies of this tablet and in other papers as "No. Po 234." In one instance, he identifies—and collation confirms—the impression as "Po 231."

Porada identifies the seal impression below this line as that of Waqar-bêli son of Taya, the scribe (cf. l.19 and *JEN* 215:26, 28). See also above, comments.

l. 23: *Šúk-ri-til-la*. For this spelling, see above, comments.

JEN 769

OBVERSE

1 [DUMU *Pu-ḫi-še*]-⸢*en-ni a-na*⸣ [ÌR-*du-ti*]
2 ⸢*i*⸣-*te-ru-ub* ᵐ*Te-ḫi-i*[*p-til-la*]
3 ᵐ*A-bu-te-ya aš-ša-t*[*a*]
4 *ú-ša-ḫa-*⁺*as-sú šum-ma* ᵐ⸢*A*⸣-[*bu-te-ya*]
5 *ú-uṣ-ṣí pu-uḫ-šu i-n*[*a-din-ma*]
6 *ù* ⸢*i*⸣-*ta-la-ak*

---

7 •IGI ⸢*Ze*⸣-*e-tu*$_4$ DUMU *I-ri-š*[*a-bi*]
8 IGI ⸢*Ki*⸣-*ip-ta-e* DUMU *E-na-*[*ma?-ti?*]
9 IGI *Zi-li-ya* DUMU *Te-en-t*[*e-ya*]
10 IGI *Pí-*•*i-*[*r*]*u* DUMU *Na-i-iš-k*[*é-el-pè*]
11 IGI *Zi-ké* DUMU *Ka*$_4$*-ku-zi*
12 IGI *Ta-a-a* DUMU BÀD-LUGAL
13 IGI *Ké-*⸢*li*⸣-[*y*]*a* ⸢DUMU⸣ *Mi-*⸢RI⸣?-[ ]
14 [I]GI *A-ri-*⸢*ké*⸣*-e*[*l*]*-pè* DUMU [*Tù-up-ki-ya*]
15 [IG]I [ ]-KI-⸢x⸣-[DUMU]

REVERSE

16 [IGI *It*]-⁺⸢*ḫa*⸣*-p*[*í-ḫé*] ⸢DUB⸣.[SAR]
S.I. Po 408
17 IGI *Ki-i*[*p*]*-ta-e* DUMU *E-n*[*a-ma?-ti?*]
S.I. Po 123
18 [N]A$_4$ [KIŠ]IB [ᵐZ]*e-e-*[*tu*$_4$ DUMU *I-ri-ša-bi*]
S.I.?

TRANSLATION

....

(1-2) entered into [slavery] .... [son of] Puḫi-šenni.

(2-4) Teḫip-tilla shall procure a wife for Abutteya.

(4-6) Should Abutteya wish to leave (the household of Teḫip-tilla), he shall supply a substitute for himself [and] then he may go out.

(7-16) Before Zetu son of Irîš-abi; before Kip-tae son of Enna-[mati?]; before Ziliya son of Tenteya; before Piru son of Naiš-kelpe; before Zike son of Kakkuzzi; before Taya son of Dûr-šarru; before Keliya son of Mi-...; before Arik-kelpe son of [Tupkiya]; before ... [son of ...]; ....(?); [before] Itḫ-apiḫe, the scribe.

(17-18) (*seal impression*) Before (*sic*) Kip-tae son of Enna-[mati?]; (*seal impression*) seal impression of Zetu [son of Irîš-abi]; (*seal impression*)? .... [(*seal impression*)?]

COMMENTS

This tablet has suffered practically no additional damage since it was copied.

Most likely, two lines of text are now missing from the start of the obverse. These lines will have read:

ᵐ*A-bu-te-ya* DUMU PN
i-na É ᵐ*Te-ḫi-ip-til-la*

or the like. Cf. *JEN* 611:1-2.

JEN 611 is relevant to *JEN* 769 because, where both texts are clear (i.e., relatively undamaged), the content is practically identical. The clauses are the same, the difference in phraseology insignificant. The two texts clearly share a common witness (cf. *JEN* 769:11 with *JEN* 611:21). On these grounds, one may restore damaged passages in one by appeal to the better preserved counterparts in the other. Based on such appeals, it emerges that the two texts form a cluster. They share, not just one witness, but at least eight. Cf. *JEN* 769:8 (and 17), 9, 10, 11, 12, 13, 14, 16 with, respectively, *JEN* 611:16 (and 23), 14, 12 (and 24), 21, 20, 17, 18, 22. Cf., perhaps, *JEN* 769:7 with *JEN* 611:17 as well (a possible ninth correspondence). In addition to the retrieval of personal names, another restoration, in *JEN* 769:5, results as well.

Therefore, *JEN* 769 appears to lack the first two lines of the obverse. On the other hand, the lower edge is a blank, contrary to the impression of the copy. Therefore, no gap representing the names of two witnesses intervenes between lines 15 and 16. A third seal impression and its legend may be missing from the bottom of the reverse. In fact, a faint trace of a seal impression may be visible below line 18.

NOTES

l. 5: *i-n*[*a-din-ma*]. For this restoration, see above, comments.

l. 7: *I-ri-š*[*a-bi*]. This restoration follows *NPN*, 175b *sub* ZETU 1), 73b *sub* IRÎŠ-ABI 1). No other patronymic is attested for a Nuzi "ZETU."

l. 8: *E-na-*[*ma*?-*ti*?]. This restoration tentatively follows *NPN*, 87b *sub* KIP-TAE 2), 45b *sub* ENNA-MATI 60). No other "Kip-tae son of En(n)a..." is, to my knowledge, attested at Nuzi. It should be noted, however, that nowhere else is this Kip-tae's patronymic spelled with initial *E-na-*.

l. 9: *Te-en-t*[*e-ya*]. This restoration is most plausible. It yields the identity of a well attested witness in Teḫip-tilla texts. See *NPN*, 178a *sub* ZILIJA 22).

l. 13: *Mi-*⸢RI⸣?-[ ]. Lacheman (in effect) and *NPN*, 98a *sub* MILKI-TEŠUP 4), 82a *sub* KELIJA 13) (explicitly), interpret the patronymic as *Mi-i*[*l-ki-te-šup*]. The trace after MI does not support this restoration.

It should be noted that no attested Nuzi PN known to me seems to have started: *Mi-*RI-. (Cf. *NPN*, 98b *sub* Mi-*ri-im-si*.)

l. 14: [*Tù-up-ki-ya*]. Cf. *JEN* 611:19: DUMU *Tù-up-*[ ]. The only attested patronymic for an "Arik-kelpe" at Nuzi is "Tupkiya." See *NPN*, 26b *sub* ARIK-KELPE.

ll. 15-16. See above, comments.

Contrary to the copy, line 15 appears at the bottom of the obverse.

l. 16: ⸢*ḫa*⸣-*p*[*í*]. The traces appear, not as copied, but, rather, as:

l. 17: IGI. The sign is correct as copied. The scribe has erred by starting the line, not with ^{NA_4} KIŠIB, but with the same sign he had used at the start of every line since line 7. Cf. line 18.

JEN 770

OBVERSE

1 [*ṭup-pí ma-ru-ti š*]*a*

2 [^{m}*Šúk-ra-a-pu* DUMU] *E-te-*[*ya*]

3 [^{m}*Te-ḫi-ip-ti*]*l-la* DUMU *Pu-ḫi-*[*še-en-ni*]

4 [*a-na ma*]-⸢*ru*⸣-*ti* DÙ-*uš*

5 [2 ANŠE 1 ^{GIŠ}APIN] ⸢A⸣.ŠÀ *i-na* ⸢^{GIŠ}⸣ *ta-a-a-ri*

6 [GAL *š*]*a* +É.GAL-*lì i-na e-le-en*

7 [AN.Z]A.KÀR ⸢*ša*⸣ *^{m}•*A-ka$_4$-wa-til*

8 ⸢*i*⸣-*na su-ta-na-an* KASKAL *ša* URU *Ú-náp-še*

9 *ša a-na* AN.ZA.KÀR ⸢*Ú*⸣-*lu-li-ya* DU-*ku*

10 ˹ki˺-mu ḪA.LA-šu ^{m}Šúk-ra-a-pu
11 ˹a˺-na ^{m}Te-ḫi-ip-til-la in-din
12 $^{+}$ù ki-mu NÍG.BA-šu
13 1 ANŠE 5 BÁN ŠE ^{m}Te-ḫi-ip-til-la
14 [a-n]a ^{m}Šúk-ra-a-pu it-ta-din
15 •[i]l-ka$_{4}$ ša A.ŠÀ ^{m}Šúk-ra-a-pu-ma •na-ši
16 [šum-m]a A.ŠÀ.MEŠ pa-qí-ra-na i-ra-aš-•ši
17 [^{m}Šú]k-ra-a-pu ú-za-ak-ka$_{4}$-ma
18 [a-na ^{m}Te-ḫ]i-ip-til-la
19 [ú-ma-a]l-la
20 [šum-ma ^{m}Šúk]-ra-a-pu
21 [KI.BAL 10? M]A.NA KÙ.SIG$_{17}$
22 [a-na ^{m}Te-ḫi-ip-til-la i]-˹na-di?-in˺?

REVERSE

23 [IGI DUMU]˹x˺[ ]
24 [IGI Ze?-en?-ni? DUMU Ḫa?-ma?-an?]-na!?
25 [IGI Z]i?-[ka$_{4}$?-a?-a?] D[UMU!?] ˹Ku˺?-•[tù]k?-ka$_{4}$
26 [IGI Ur?-ḫi?-ya?] D[UMU? Še?]-•ka!?-rù
27 [IGI]˹X-X˺ D[UMU?]
28 ˹IGI˺ [E?]-˹ni?-iš˺?-t[a?-e? DUMU] ˹Ak?-ka$_{4}$˺?-[pa?]
29 IGI [ ]-PU-ni-[ ]-˹x˺-[ ]
30 ˹DUMU˺ I[p]-šá-ḫa-˹lu x˺ [ ]˹x˺ an-nu-TE
31 ˹x˺? IGI ˹x˺ [ ] ˹x˺ BE [ ] ˹ù˺?
32 ^{m}˹Te˺-ḫi-ip-til-l[a] ˹x˺-mu

S.I.

33 [^{NA_4} KIŠ]IB ˹DUB!?.SAR˺!?

S.I.

.
.
.

S.I.

34 [^{NA_4} KIŠI]B? ˹X-x-e˺

UPPER EDGE

S.I.

.
.
.

LEFT EDGE

35 [^{NA_4} KIŠIB?] ˹E-li˺?-ar-AN?-BE?

$^{+}$S.I.

TRANSLATION

(1-4) [Tablet of adoption] of [Šukr-apu son of] Eteya. He adopted Teḫip-tilla son of Puḫi-šenni.

(5-11) Šukr-apu gave to Teḫip-tilla as his inheritance share a field, [2.1 homers] by the [large] standard of the palace, to the east of the *dimtu* of Akawatil (and) to the south of the Unap-še road which goes to the *dimtu* of Ulūliya.

(12-14) And, as his gift, Teḫip-tilla gave to Šukr-apu 1.5 homers of barley.

(15) It is Šukr-apu who shall bear the *ilku* of the field.

(16-19) Should the field have claimants, Šukr-apu shall clear (it) and pay (it) [to] Teḫip-tilla.

(20-22) [Should] Šukr-apu [abrogate (this contract)], he shall give(?) [to Teḫip-tilla 10?] minas of gold.

(23-30) [Before ... son of] ...; [before Zenni? son of] Ḫamanna(?); [before] Zikaya(?) son(?) of(?) Kutukka(?); [before Urḫiya?] son(?) of(?) Šekaru(?); [before ... son(?) of(?) [...]; before Eniš-tae(?) [son of] Akkapa(?); before ... son of Ipša-ḫalu.

(30-32) .... and(?) Teḫip-tilla ... .

(33-35) (*seal impression*) seal impression of the(?) scribe(?); (*seal impression*) ....; (*seal impression*) seal impression of ...; (*seal impression*) ....; [seal impression of] .... (*seal impression*).

COMMENTS

This tablet has suffered some additional deterioration since it was copied. One line is missing after line 33 and one line is missing on the upper edge. Note that the copy mistakenly identifies the left edge as the lower edge.

The lines appear straighter on the obverse than indicated in the copy. The distortion is due to a pronounced convexity of the obverse face.

NOTES

l. 2: [*ya*]. The *CAD* Nuzi file records this sign as completely preserved.

l. 3: [*še-en-ni*]. The *CAD* Nuzi file records *še-ni* as completely preserved.

ll. 5-7. The real estate described here is to be located in Unap-še. See, for example, *JEN* 709:7-8.

l. 5: [2 ANŠE 1 ^{GIŠ}APIN]. These signs are restored on the basis of *JEN* 365:5. *JEN* 365 is a record of litigation almost certainly based on the transaction described in *JEN* 770. The principal parties in these texts and in the closely related *JEN* 652, as well as the description of the real estate in

these contexts, make the restoration of the amount of the land a reasonable undertaking.

In fact, however, *JEN* 365:5 defines the amount as: 2 ANŠE 1 ^{GIŠ}APIN *ù ku-ú-ma-nu*. The restoration of the entire amount, already present in the *CAD* Nuzi file, seems to be precluded here unless "2 ANŠE" already appears at the end of line 4. (Cf. the present reconstruction with that of Fadhil [1983, 286b] who restores: 1 ANŠE.)

If there is a fractional reduction here of the entire amount of land to be ceded (difficult to understand in a text of this type!), then compare a possibly analogous phenomenon in *JEN* 526:1-7, cited above, note to *JEN* 764:5.

l. 6: É. The sign appears, not as copied, but, rather, as: 

l. 7. The *CAD* Nuzi file records this line as completely preserved.

l. 8: KASKAL. The sign appears, not quite as copied, but, rather, as: 

l. 8: *náp-še*. These signs appear as copied.

l. 13: 1. The space to the left of the vertical wedge is well preserved—and blank.

l. 19. *i-na-an-din*, or the like, is expected here. Cf., for example, *JEN* 586:20; 703:22. (Perhaps the scribe has inadvertently transposed *mullû* and *nadānu*, if a form of *nadānu* indeed appears in line 22 where *umalla* would be expected.) *JEN* 586 and 703 share with *JEN* 770 a common text genre and two principal parties. The contents of *JEN* 703 and 770 probably find a common later reflex in *JEN* 384.

A horizontal line seems to appear before LA. In fact, it is a crack on the tablet's surface.

l. 21: [KI.BAL]. Or the like.

l. 21: [10?]. Cf. *JEN* 703:25. On the relevance of *JEN* 703 to the present text, see above, note to line 19.

l. 22: [*i*]-⌈*na-di?-in*⌉?. See above, note to line 19.

l. 24. Cf. *JEN* 703:27. This restoration is most tentative. It is based on similarities between *JEN* 703 and 770. See above, note to line 19. Restorations of lines 25, 26, and 28 are similarly based on *JEN* 703:28, 30, and 31 respectively. (Also, cf. the PN of *JEN* 770:30 with the first PN of *JEN* 703:35.)

It must be stressed that support for these restorations is weak: not a single common witness is clearly attested in these texts.

l. 26. Lacheman once saw, at this point: *Ki-in-nu-zi*. In this he was followed, it seems, by *NPN*, 86a *sub* KINNUZZI 5). (Cf. the like named son of Eteya in lines 29 and 38 of *JEN* 52, a text indirectly related to *JEN* 770.)

See also below, note to line 34.

The second last sign is now almost completely obliterated.

ll. 30-32. It is possible that these lines contain a clause identifying the witnesses as surveyors. If ⸢*ù*⸣? (l. 31) is incorrect, then the sense of these lines might be as follows: "These (*an-nu-ti*$_{7}$ [l. 30]) men are the witnesses (IGI or *ši-b*[*u-ti*] [l. 31]) and they are the ones who encircled ([*i*]*l-mu* l. 32) the (new) field of Teḫip-tilla (⸢*Te*⸣-*ḫi-ip-til-l*[*a*] [l. 32]; see also below, note to line 32)." Not only is this reconstruction tentative, it results in a rare, if not unique, identification of a newly acquired field by the name of its purchaser rather than its vendor.

l. 30. This line is slightly indented. The indentation is not represented in the copy.

l. 32: ^{m}⸢*Te*⸣-*ḫi-ip-til-l*[*a*]. The *CAD* Nuzi file records, at this point: IGI *Te-ḫi-ip-til-la*. The fourth sign is a typical IP, not AR as depicted.

l. 33. Lacheman once saw here: NA$_{4}$ *Ni-im-ta-kal*. This PN seems not to be attested elsewhere at Nuzi (if Lacheman indeed meant to write this).

l. 34. Lacheman once saw here: NA$_{4}$ ^{m}*Ki-in-nu-zi*. The *CAD* Nuzi file saw NA$_{4}$ ^{m}*Ki-in-nu?-zi?*. Cf. above, note to line 26.

JEN 771

OBVERSE

1 [2 ANŠE A.ŠÀ.MEŠ AŠ] *ta-a-a-r*[*i* GAL]
2 [*ša* ^{m}*T*]*a-a*[*n*]-•*ta-ka*$_{4}$*-a-a* DUMU *A*-[*kap-tùk-ké*]
3 [*i-na ša*]-⸢*pá*⸣-*at a-tap-pí* [(?)]
4 [*i-na l*]*e-et* A.ŠÀ *ša* ^{m}*A-ḫ*[*i*]?-⸢*i*⸣?-[*li?-ka*$_{4}$?]
5 [*i-na*] •AN.ZA.KÀR *ma-ḫa*-Z[I]
6 [3 AN]ŠE A.ŠÀ.MEŠ AŠ *ta-a*-⸢*ri*⸣ [GAL]
7 [*ša* ^{m}]•*Ḫa-ni-ú ù ša*
8 [^{m}(*E*)-*eḫ*]-*li-pa-pu* DUMU!.MEŠ *Ar-pí*-•*iš*-•*šu-uḫ-ri*
9 [*i?-na? le?-et?*] A.ŠÀ *ša* ^{m}*A*-RI-[ ]-•⸢*x*-•*x*⸣
10 [DUMU? *A-ka*]*p-tùk-ké* ŠU.•⸢NIGIN$_{2}$⸣ ⸢5⸣ ANŠE A.ŠÀ
11 [*i-na* AN.ZA].KÀR *ša ma-ḫa*-ZI
12 [ANŠE] ⸢A⸣.ŠÀ *ša* ^{m}*Ḫa-ni-ú* DUMU *A-ri-pa-p*[*u*] ⸢*ù*⸣
13 ⸢*ša*⸣ [^{m}*Ku*]-*uš-ši-ya* DUMU *A-ka*$_{4}$*-la-a-a*
14 *ù* ⸢*ša*⸣ ^{m}*K*[*é?-et?*]-*tu*$_{4}$ DUMU •X *Ké*-[*e*]*n-ni*[*-wa?*]
15 [x?+]$^{+}$1 $^{+}$ANŠE $^{+}$A.$^{+}$ŠÀ *š*[*a* ^{m}]-*ta?-ti* DUM[U]
16 $^{+}$*i-na qí-in*-[*na-at* GIŠ].⸢ŠAR⸣ *ša* $^{m?}$
:*Šá-a*[*t?-tù?-ya?*]
17 [*ša?* $^{m?}$]*Ar*-⸢*zi*⸣?-[*iz?-za?*]-•⸢*ya*⸣
18 [ ]⸢x⸣[ ]

TRANSLATION

(1-5) [A field, 2 homers by the large] standard, [of] Tantakaya son of Akap-tukke, [on] the bank of the ...(?) canal, adjacent to the field of Aḫi-illika(?), [in] the *dimti* maḫaZI;

(6-10) A field, [3] homers by the [large] standard, of Ḫaniu and of Eḫlip-apu sons of Arp-iššuḫri, [adjacent? to?] the field of A-RI-... [son? of?] Akap-tukke.

(10-11) Total: 5 homers of land [in] the *dimti* maḫaZI.

(12-14) [A ... homer] field, of Ḫaniu son of Arip-apu and of Kuššiya son of Akalaya and of Kettu(?) son of ...(?) Kenni;

(15-17) A 1+x(?) homer field, of ... son of [...], in the *qinnatu* of the orchard of Šattuya(?) (and?) [of?] Ar-zizza(?) ... .

(18) ....

COMMENTS

A general overview of the contents and structure of this text is in order, and this for two reasons. First and foremost, this document is unusual in its contents. Second, only part of the obverse is preserved (and none of the reverse) and the tablet has suffered additional deterioration since it was first copied. Since restoration of broken passages is attempted, an understanding of the text's outline is desirable.

The text contains, at present, a catalogue of at least four plots of land, described in lines 1-5, 6-10a, 12-14, and 15-17. These are hereafter designated plots I, II, III, and IV, respectively. (Line 1 is the first line of the tablet; contrary to the copy, nothing is missing before this.) Each plot is defined by amount, (erstwhile) ownership, and, except for plot III, location. Line 18 may have begun a fifth real estate entry. Lines 10b-11 represent a sub-total of the amount of land from the *dimti ma-ḫa*-ZI. This reflects plots I and II, at least. Line 5 proves this, containing the same GN as line 11.

As is demonstrated below, notes to ll. 1-11, 12-14, and 16-17, these four plots of land likely represent Teḫip-tilla acquisitions by means of real estate adoption. Furthermore, it is very likely that these plots are to be located in the same general vicinity, i.e., the town of Artiḫi. For plot III, see below, note to ll. 12-14. For plot IV the evidence is weaker. See below, note to ll. 16-17. For plots I and II, there are two kinds of evidence, both circumstantial. First, real estate catalogues in these archives seem to list holdings by general locus. See, for example, *JEN* 641. Thus, if plots III and IV are to be located in Artiḫi, plots I and II may well be located there as well. Second, Karlheinz Deller has correctly noted (private communication, 4 June 1977) strong prosopographical links connecting the *dimti ma-ḫa*-ZI and town of Artiḫi texts. Some of these links are recapitulated below in the notes. (I should like to express my thanks to Professor Deller for his comments to me on this text.) The connection between these two GNs, therefore, is, on prosopographical

grounds, most likely. Maidman (1976, 169), linking the *dimti ma-ḫa-*ZI with Nuzi, is to be corrected accordingly. For other discussions of *JEN* 771 and related texts, see Maidman (1979, 2, n.3) and Fadhil (1983, 43a-45a).

JEN 771, then, expresses a series of Teḫip-tilla real estate acquisitions in Artiḫi by means of adoption This tablet is a summary of those acquisitions, not a series of written contracts effecting acquisition (cf., by contrast, *JEN* 560 and 561, for example.)

Texts cataloguing Teḫip-tilla real estate holdings appear in a variety of forms, attesting, no doubt, to a variety of archival or administrative functions. Perhaps the closest parallel to *JEN* 771 is *JEN* 524. The latter text describes three transactions and contains all the elements noted for *JEN* 771 except the sub-total, albeit in different order. In addition, it notes the recipient of the land (Teḫip-tilla) and the legal form in which it was acquired (as *zittu*, "inheritance share"). Finally, it contains a subscript defining the principle underlying the inclusion of the three plots in one list: these are properties acquired by real estate adoption. Thus, *JEN* 524 appears to be an expanded, more explicit form of the kind of list appearing in *JEN* 771 (unless these types of additional elements appeared in a part of *JEN* 771 now destroyed).

NOTES

ll. 1-11. This section, describing plots I and II and containing a sub-total, deals with real estate in the *dimti ma-ḫa-*ZI. Three extant texts, *JEN* 3, 328, and 426, describe Teḫip-tilla acquisitions of land by means of real estate adoption in this *dimtu*. (No other Nuzi text, to my knowledge, mentions this *dimtu*.) Plot II seems actually to reflect the transaction of *JEN* 3. (The mention of *ma-ḫa-*ZI in *JEN* 3:6 neatly compensates for its absence in *JEN* 771:9-10a.) The other two transactions (i.e., *JEN* 328, 426) are not directly reflected in *JEN* 771 as now preserved. Indirect connections between plot I and *JEN* 426 and 3, however, are apparent and are detailed below, notes to lines 2 and 4.

Restorations of signs and of contextual data are proposed below with varying degrees of confidence. See especially notes to lines 2, 4, 6 (first note), 9, 10. *If* all these proposals prove correct, then a pattern emerges of real estate acquisition in the *dimti ma-ḫa-*ZI.

Teḫip-tilla obtains plot I from Tantakaya son of Akap-tukke, a plot adjacent to land of Aḫi-illika (probably; see below, note to line 4). Now Teḫip-tilla obtains land of Aḫi-illika (by real estate adoption) adjacent to plot I (*JEN* 426:1-6; cf. *JEN* 3:6). He further obtains yet more land adjacent to that of Aḫi-illika from Ḫaniu and Eḫlip-apu sons of Arp-iššuḫri, also by means of real estate adoption (*JEN* 3:1-7; cf. *JEN* 771:6-8). Thus, Teḫip-tilla obtains land of Aḫi-illika (*JEN* 426) and, it seems, two plots adjoining the land of Aḫi-illika (plot I and plot II = *JEN* 3). Furthermore, plot II, the land formerly belonging to Ḫaniu and Eḫlip-

apu, lies adjacent to that of A-RI-... son of Akap-tukke (*JEN* 771:7-10a). Teḫip-tilla might well have acquired *that* land, once again by means of real estate adoption (*JEN* 328:4, 7-10). The pattern emerging from the two transactions resulting in the acquisition of plots I and II and by the other three Teḫip-tilla *dimti ma-ḫa*-ZI texts known to us (*JEN* 3, 328, 426) is that Teḫip-tilla obtained at least four contiguous plots of land in this *dimtu*, all, it would seem, by means of real estate adoption. (The "owners'" names in *JEN* 771, then, would be the names of the vendors of the land to Teḫip-Tilla.) If this supposition (itself based on suppositions) is correct, then we may further deduce that the *raison d'être* of this part of *JEN* 771 was to record just such a tight cluster of acquisitions. (The sub-total [lines 10b-11] would seem to bear this out. Regarding the sub-total, see also below, next note.)

l. 1: [2 ANŠE A.ŠÀ.MES AŠ]. The *CAD* Nuzi file in effect records the following as entirely preserved: [ ] ANŠE A.ŠÀ.MEŠ *ša*? AŠ.

The restoration of "2" follows from the amounts of land noted in lines 6 and 10. The grounds for restoring "3" in line 6 are spelled out below, first note to line 6.

l. 1: [GAL]. This restoration is based on the [GAL] of line 6. For that restoration, see below, second note to line 6. Cf. also *JEN* 3:5; 328:19; 426:4 from the other *dimti ma-ḫa*-ZI texts.

l. 2. This line is restored on the basis of the following considerations. The restoration of the first PN is fairly certain. This PN occurs only once again in the Nuzi texts, *JEN* 426:5. There, his patronymic is Akap-tukke (l. 6). The last sign of *JEN* 771:2 allows for the restoration of the same patronymic here. The restorations are buttressed by the additional coincidence that the land, in both contexts, is located in the *dimti ma-ḫa*-ZI (*JEN* 426:4-6; 771:1-2, 5).

It is indeed most likely that plot I itself is described (but not acquired) in *JEN* 426:5-6. As suggested above, note to lines 1-11, these two passages attest to Teḫip-tilla's acquisition of adjoining properties.

ll. 3, 4, 5: [*i-na*]. [AŠ] is also possible.

l. 4: ^{m}*A-ḫ*[*i*]?-⌜*i*⌝?-[*li*?-ka_4?]. This restoration is tentatively hazarded on the basis of the following considerations. *JEN* 426 notes that, in the *dimti ma-ḫa*-ZI, land of Tantakaya son of Akap-tukke lies adjacent to land sold by Šamaḫul son of Aḫi-illika (ll. 1-6). It is possible that the latter plot was known by the name of Šamaḫul's father. Note that a plot of land in the *dimti ma-ḫa*-ZI is in fact known by the name "Aḫi-illika": *JEN* 3:6. If the land of Aḫi-illika of *JEN* 3 may be identified with the land sold by Šamaḫul in *JEN* 426, then *JEN* 426 records, in effect, the adjacency of land of Aḫi-illika and that of Tantakaya son of Akap-tukke in the *dimti ma-ḫa*-ZI. The restoration proposed here would result in the statement of the same adjacency.

Another factor: recent collation shows that the sign fragments appear as:

traces which could actually be interpreted as: ^{m}⌈*Šá-ma-ḫul*⌉.

l. 5: *ma-ḫa*-Z[I]. For the restoration, cf. line 11.

The question of the spelling of this toponym, *ma-ḫa-zi* or *ma-ḫa-ṣí*, is bound up with the issue of the meaning of the term.

(Unlike most *dimtu* names, *ma-ḫa*-ZI appears not to be a PN. No male determinative ever precedes it.)

H. Lewy (1942, 317 with n. 3) identified this lexeme with Akkadian *maḫāṣu*, "to weave." Cf. Koschaker (1944a, 176-77). Lewy (1942, 317) viewed the district of the weavers as a royal donation to professionals for them to use as a base of operations for the benefit of the crown. (On districts or urban quarters set apart for professionals in the Old Babylonian period and before, see Leemans [1950, 67].) She further notes a "royal" weaving industry employing *ušparātu*. She does not explain, however, why two different terms were used. Cf. *C* 1:8 for a *dimtu* called UŠ.BAR.MEŠ, an indisputable *dimtu* name deriving from a profession. (In discussing districts set apart for different professions at Nuzi, Zaccagnini [1977a, 174 with note 17] accepts AN.ZA.KÀR UŠ.BAR.MEŠ as "district of the weavers" and rejects Lewy's AN.ZA.KÀR *ma-ḫa-ṣí* as a second such district.) Furthermore, *ma-ḫa-ṣí* would represent a nominal form of *mḫṣ* apparently otherwise unattested. Such an industrial quarter is also inconsistent with the agricultural contexts in which this *dimtu* appears, i.e., *JEN* 3, 328, 426, and, especially, the present text.

If this toponym has anything to do with weavers, then it might represent agricultural land once allotted to these professionals. Cf., for the Old Babylonian period, Ellis (1976, 16 with n. 27, 20 with n. 49).

Chiera and Speiser (1927, 38) seem to identify this *dimtu* with *māḫāzu*, i.e., a settlement of some sort. See also Astour (1981, 17, no. 35); *AHw*, 582a; and *CAD*, M/I, 88b 5. On this term in Akkadian and cognate languages with this meaning and as "port" or "market" center, "cult place," etc., see *CAD*, M/I, 85a-88b, the literature cited, *ibid*., 88b-89a, and, in addition, Y. Kutscher (1937, 136-45); Goetze (1953, 59, n. 45); Astour (1970, 118-19); R. Kutscher (1969-70, 267-69); Cogan (1974, 38, n. 98); Cooper (1974, 83-86); Cohen (1978, 70, n. 127); Eph'al (1982, 102, n. 340). Cf. also the discussion of the term in Fadhil (1983, 44a-45a).

This range of meanings, however, seems as ill-suited to the present context as H. Lewy's suggestion of "weavers."

Perhaps the term is not Akkadian at all.

l. 6: [3]. The restoration of this number is based on *JEN* 3:5. The vendors of *dimti ma-ḫa*-ZI land in *JEN* 3 (lines 1-2) reappear in this part of *JEN* 771 (lines 7-8), implicitly in connection with *dimti ma-ḫa*-ZI real estate (see lines 10b-11). Plot II (i.e., *JEN* 771:6-10a), therefore, may well reflect

the real estate adoption recorded in *JEN* 3 and so the amount of land recorded would be 3 homers. (The connection of *JEN* 3 with this section of *JEN* 771 is the clearest indicator that the principal PNs of this text are vendors of real estate to Teḫip-tilla.) Note, however, that the description of the adjacent land in *JEN* 3 (line 6) does not correspond to the parallel description here (lines 9-10a). This is inconvenient for the restoration but not fatal: the same field could well have adjoined more than one property.

l. 6: [GAL]. The *CAD* Nuzi file records this sign as preserved.

l. 7: ${}^{[m]}$. The *CAD* Nuzi file records this sign as preserved.

l. 7: *ša*. The space after this sign is well preserved, and blank, i.e., the line ends with ŠA.

l. 9: [*i*?-*na*?]. [AŠ?] is also possible.

l. 9: ^{m}*A*-RI-[ ]-⸢x x⸣. The last traces of this line now appear as:

This does not appear to reflect a deteriorated version of what is depicted in the copy. (One is tempted to read: ⸢*te*⸣-[*šup*], or the like.)

It is tempting to associate the *dimti ma-ḫa*-ZI land of this person with the similarly located land of Ariya father of Šupa-ḫali, obtained by Teḫip-tilla through real estate adoption, according to *JEN* 328:4, 7-10.

l. 10: [*A-ka*]*p-tùk-ké*. DUG appears, not as copied, but, rather, as:

The restoration, [*A-ka*]*p* appears inevitable: no other "-tukke" PN seems attested at Nuzi. See *NPN*, 269b *sub* -tukke.

It is difficult not to link this possible patronymic with the like-named father of Tantakaya (line 2) from the same general area.

l. 11: [*i-na*]. [AŠ] is also possible.

ll. 12-14. The land described in these lines, plot III, is almost certainly to be located in Artiḫi.

The individuals named in lines 12 and 13 doubtlessly reappear in *JEN* 654:22, 21 as expert witnesses regarding certain Ḫušri real estate (ll. 6-8). Ḫušri is known to have been linked closely to Artiḫi. See Maidman (1976, 194, 407-8, n. 706). On the basis of the similarity of *JEN* 771:12, 13 to *JEN* 654:22, 21, the badly broken *JEN* 771:14 is tentatively restored on the basis of *JEN* 654:20.

In addition, the individuals named in lines 12 and 13 reappear again in *JEN* 521:11, 9-10. (Note, however, that *JEN* 521:9 reads ^{m}*Ḫa-ši-ya* where ^{m}*Ku-uš-ši-ya* is expected. It seems reasonable to suppose that the same individual is meant in all three cases: *JEN* 521:9-10; 654:21; 771:13. Karlheinz Deller (personal communication, 4 June 1977) likewise assumes

this identity, attributing the difference in spelling of this PN to a probable scribal "*Hörfehler.*") *JEN* 521 is a catalogue of tablets taken by Tarmi-tilla son of Šurki-tilla (himself the son of the Teḫip-tilla). These tablets are identified by PNs. By comparing those PNs with their attestations elsewhere in the Teḫip-tilla corpus, it emerges that the tablets taken by Tarmi-tilla seem all to have recorded Teḫip-tilla's acquisition (by real estate adoption) of land in Artiḫi or Ḫušri (and the PNs of *JEN* 521 are the vendors of that land). For example, cf. *JEN* 521:5 with *JEN* 425. For further details of this extended prosopographical correspondence amongst the various texts, see Maidman (1976, 583 *sub N* 521). Thus it is reasonable to assume that the tablet of "Ḫašiya" son of Akalaya and of Ḫaniu son of Arip-apu (*JEN* 521:8-11) also represent Artiḫi real estate.

Therefore, plot III, in light of *JEN* 654 and 521, is very likely to have been located in the area of Artiḫi.

l. 12: [ANŠE]. [^{GIŠ}APIN] appears far less likely a possibility.

l. 14: ^{m}*K*[*é*?-*et*?]-*tu*$_4$ DUMU X *Ké*-[*e*]*n*-*ni*[-*wa*?]. Cf. *JEN* 654:20 and the immediately preceding note. The sign trace after NI in *JEN* 654:20 is not considered part of the patronymic by *NPN*, 83b *sub* KENNI 10) but is so considered by *NPN*, 84a *sub* KETTU 1). *NPN*, 83b *sub* KENNI 10), 84a *sub* KETTU 1), implies that the first name is here preserved.

The undecipherable sign immediately after DUMU appears, not as copied, but, rather, as:

The *CAD* Nuzi file reads, after DUMU: *Ar*-*še*-*en*-*ni*.

l. 15: [x?+] 1 ANŠE A.ŠÀ. The preserved signs are quite clear. The TA-like sign of the copy at the start of this line does not appear on the tablet.

The *CAD* Nuzi file recognizes no lacuna before "1."

l. 15: *š*[*a* ^{m}]-*ta*?-*ti* DUM[U]. This part of the line is restored on the analogy of lines 1-2, 6-8, and, especially, 12. The context seems here to require the names of the (erstwhile) owner of the field. Establishment of the owner's identity is hindered, not only by textual lacunae, but by the unclarity of TA. The lower *Winkelhaken* is by no means clear. Therefore, the sign might represent UŠ rather than TA. See, however, the following note regarding real estate of one Urḫa-tati.

Lacheman restores, in effect: [*mi*-*in*]-*dá*-*ti*. One might follow this reasoning further by reading the following sign: ⸢GAL⸣. However, the wording of this phrase is suspect here in light of the use of *tay*(*y*)*āri* in the parallel contexts, lines 1 and 6.

The *CAD* Nuzi file reads, in effect: *i*-*na* [ ] É-*ti* (with no sign following).

ll. 16-17. The state of preservation of these lines is poor. The restorations are most tentative, representing barely more than a reasonable guess.

The surviving signs and traces, coupled with the fact that plot III is most likely to have been located in the area of Artiḫi (see above, note to lines 12-14), leads to the possibility that the land described here, i.e., plot IV, lies near that described in *JEN* 346:6-8:

6 1 ANŠE A.ŠÀ *i-na ta-a-a-ri* GAL *ša* É.GAL
7 *i-na qí-in-na-at* GIŠ.ŠAR
8 *ša* ^{m}*Ša-at-tù-ya i-na* URU *Ar-[ti/ti*$_4$*]-ḫi*

That land was acquired by Teḫip-tilla by means of real estate adoption from Ar-zizza and Šukr-apu sons of Zilip-tarta (ll. 5, 9-11).

JEN 771:16-17 would represent the location of real estate relative to orchard land of both Šattuya and Ar-zizza. (It may be no more than a curiosity that one Urḫa-tati [or even two] possesses orchard land [*JEN* 29:6; 526:18]. Cf. the proposed PN above, line 15.)

The ⌈YA⌉ of line 17, now even more effaced than the copy indicates, would remain unexplained by the proposed restorations.

l. 17: [*ša*?]. [*ù ša*] might be expected. Yet, if "^{m}*Šá-a[t-tù-ya]*" is an afterthought of the scribe, as it appears to be, then the copula would not have been supplied.

JEN 772

OBVERSE

1 [^{m}*Te-ḫi-ip-til-la* DUMU *Pu]-ḫi-š[e-e]n-n[i]*
2 ⌈*a*⌉*-n[a ma-ru-ti i-te-pu-*$^{+}$*u]š*
3 [ ] AN[ŠE A.ŠÀ]*i-na* ⌈x⌉ [*y*]*a* ⌈x⌉
4 *i-na* ⌈x⌉ [ ] *i-na le-[et]*
5 A.ŠÀ *š[a*]⌈x⌉[ ]-⌈*še*⌉?*-en-ni*
6 *i-na* ⌈*il?-ta*⌉?*-a-ni* AN.ZA.•KÀR
7 •*š[a?* ^{m}?]⌈x⌉[ ]⌈*x*⌉-•*ur?-še-e[n]-ni* $^{+}$*ki-*$^{+}$*ma* [ḪA.LA.MEŠ-*šú*]
8 ^{m}*[Pa]l-[t]e-eš-šup a-na* ^{m}*Te-ḫi-[ip-til-la]*
9 *i-dì-*•*na-aš-šu ù*
10 •^{m}*Te-ḫi-ip-til-la a-na*
11 $^{[m]}$⌈*Pal*⌉*-[t]e-[eš]-*⌈*šup*⌉ 1⌉[+x?] ⌈TÚG⌉.MEŠ ⌈43⌉? [MA?.NA?] URUDU!
12 ⌈*ki*⌉*-ma* NÍG.BA-[*šu*] ⌈*a-na*⌉ [^{m}*Pal-te-(eš-)šup i-dì-n]a-aš-*⌈*šu*⌉
13 *š[u]m-ma* A.⌈ŠÀ⌉ *pá-*⌈*qí-ra*⌉*-na [ir-ta-ši]*
14 $^{[m]}$*Pal-te-eš-*⌈*šup*⌉ *ú-za-a[k-ka*$_4$*]-*⌈*ma*⌉
15 [*a*]*-na* ^{m}*Te-ḫi-*⌈*ip*⌉*-til-l[a]* SUM-*nu*
16 [*š*]*um-ma* ^{m}*Pal-t[e-eš-šup* KI.$^{+}$B]AL
17 [x?+]⌈1⌉ MA.N[A KÙ.BABBAR x?+1? MA.NA K]Ù.SIG$_{17}$
18 ⌈*a-na*⌉ ^{m}*[Te-ḫi-ip]-til-[la]* ⌈*ú*⌉*-[ma-a]l-*⌈*la*⌉
19 ⌈*ù*⌉ *i[l-ka*$_4$ *š]a* A.Š[À ^{m}*Pal-te-eš-šup*]

20 *na-*⸢*a*⸣*-[ši ù?]* ^{m}*Te-ḫi-i[p-til-la]*
21 *u[l? na?-a?-š]i?*

LOWER EDGE

---

22 ⸢EME⸣*-šu* ⸢*ša*⸣ $^{[m]}$⸢*Pal*⸣*-te-šup*
23 *[a-na] pa-ni* IGI.MEŠ *iq-ta-bi*
24 [(?)] TÚG.MEŠ *ù* URUDU.MEŠ *él-q[è]*

\+ ---

REVERSE
25 IGI *En-na-ma-t[i]* DUMU *En-n[a-a-a]*
26 IGI *Wa-an-ti-[m]u-ša*
27 DUMU *Na-i-ké-[mar]*
28 IGI X-⸢*x*⸣-**ni-iḫ-[ ]*
29 [DUMU?]⸢x⸣
30 ⸢IGI +*Ḫa-wi!-*•*iš*⸣*-*•*ta-*•*e* [DUMU *N]a-an-te-šup*
31 [IGI] *A]-*•*ta-na-ḫi-*DINGIR +DUMU ⸢KI⸣.MIN
32 •5 $^{⸢LÚ⸣.MEŠ}$IGI.MEŠ *mu-še-*⸢*el*⸣*-mu-*⸢*ú*⸣ *ša* A.ŠÀ
33 *ù na-dì-na-nu ša* [K]Ù.BABBAR
34 IGI ⸢*Na*⸣*-an-te*$_9$*-ya* DUMU *Ḫu-[ti*$_4$*-y]a*
35 IG[I *Pa]-*⸢*a-a*⸣ DUMU *Ak-ku*$_8$*-*⸢*ya*⸣
36 IGI *Tar-*•*mi-*⸢*ya*⸣ DUMU *A-b[e-ya]*
37 IGI *Um-[p]í-[y]a* DUMU *Te-[e]š-š[u-ya]*
38 ŠU ^{md}*Išk[ur-an-dùl]*
39 ⸢DUMU ^{d}⸣X[XX-*n]é-e!* ⸢DUB⸣.[SAR]
40 ^{NA_4} [KIŠIB ^{m}] S.I.
41 [S.I.] $^{⸢NA_4⸣}$ KIŠIB ^{m}[ ]

.
.
.

LEFT EDGE
42 $^{⸢NA_4⸣}$ KIŠIB DUB.S[AR]
[S.I.]

TRANSLATION

....

(1-2) He adopted [Teḫip-tilla son of] Puḫi-šenni.

(3-9) Pal-tešup gave to Teḫip-tilla as [his inheritance share] [a ...] homer [field ...] in/by ... in ... adjacent to the field of ...-šenni(?), to the north(?) of the *dimtu* of(?) ...-šenni.

(9-12) And Teḫip-tilla to Pal-tešup gave to [Pal-tešup] (*sic*) as [his] gift 1+x(?) garments (and) 43(?) [minas?] of copper.

(13-15) Should the field [have] claimants, Pal-tešup shall clear (it) and give (it) to Teḫip-tilla.

(16-18) Should Pal-tešup abrogate (this contract), he shall pay to Teḫip-tilla 1+x(?) mina(s) [of silver (and) x?+1 mina(s) of] gold.

(19-21) And [Pal-tešup] shall bear the *ilku* of the field [and?] Teḫip-tilla(?) shall(?) not(?) bear(?) (it).

(22-23) Declaration of Pal-tešup before the witnesses. (Thus) he spoke:
(24) "I have received the ...(?) garments and the copper."

(25-39) Before Enna-mati son of Ennaya; before Wanti-muša son of Naik-kemar; before ... [son? of?] ...; before Ḫawiš-tae [son of] Nan-tešup; [before] Âtanaḫ-ilu son of the same. (These) 5 witnesses are the measurers of the field and distributors of the money (lit. "silver"). Before Nan-teya son of Ḫutiya; before Paya son of Akkuya; before Tarmiya son of Abeya; before Umpiya son of Teššuya. Hand of Iškur-andul son of Ziniya, the scribe.

(40-42) seal impression [of ....] [(*seal impression*)]; (*seal impression*) seal impression of [....]; ....; seal impression of the scribe [(*seal impression*)].

COMMENTS

The surface of this tablet is contorted. This is manifested in the copy where the beginnings of lines (especially toward the start of the text) appear far higher than the ends. Nevertheless, the reading of these lines on the tablet itself poses no real difficulty on that count. The text is somewhat difficult to decipher because the surface is both crazed and coated with a glue-like substance. The tablet has also suffered further deterioration since it was copied.

The first two lines of the tablet are missing. These will have read:
ṭup-pí ma-ru-ti ša
^{m}*Pal-te-eš-šup* DUMU PN

The patronymic and, therefore, the identity of this Pal-tešup are uncertain. Perhaps he is the son of Puḫi-šenni, who, according to *JEN* 191:5-9, adopted Teḫip-tilla and ceded to him land in Unap-še. He might be the Pal-teya son of Adaššeya who, amongst other dealings with members of the Teḫip-tilla Family, once co-adopted Teḫip-tilla and ceded to him land in Unap-še, according to *JEN* 408:1-9. He might also be Pal-teya father of Ammarša who likewise had Unap-še real estate dealings with Teḫip-tilla, according to *JEN* 399:5-12 (cf. *JEN* 668:5-8). (This last might well be the Pal-teya son of Kubbutu of *JEN* 98:1-2 [cf. *JEN* 107:1-2]—a Teḫip-tilla Family context involving Unap-še real estate.)

That the Pal-tešup of *JEN* 772 was one of these individuals (no other possibly relevant Pal-tešups or Pal-teyas are known to me) is rendered an attractive possibility for the following reason. All the noted candidates have

Unap-še real estate connections (itself a curious coincidence). And, although a clearly preserved major GN is lacking in *JEN* 772, the witnesses to this text are practically identical to those of *JEN* 743. *JEN* 743 clearly deals with Unap-še real estate. See above, note to *JEN* 743:8.

Thus, *JEN* 743 and 772 constitute a cluster, and broken or missing witness PNs, as well as other items, in one may be restored by appeal to the other. (To a [significantly] lesser extent, *JEN* 772 shares witnesses with several other texts, all dealing with Unap-še real estate. See above, first note to *JEN* 741:28.)

After line 41, one or more lines at the bottom of the reverse may be destroyed. Cf. the parallel section in *JEN* 743. (The latter text, it should be noted, devotes more space to sealings and sealers than does the former.)

NOTES

l. 2: [*u*]*š*. The trace does not appear as copied (i.e., with two wedges only, the topmost wedge being part of the ḪI of line 1), but, rather, as:

l. 3: ⸢*x*⸣ [*y*]*a* ⸢x⸣. One is tempted to restore here: ^{G}[^{IŠ}*t*]*a*!!-*a*-*r*[*i* GAL]. Cf. *JEN* 743:4.

l. 5: -⸢*še*⸣?-*en-ni*. Or $^{[\mathrm{m}]}$⸢*Še*⸣?-*en-ni*. See also below, second note to line 7.

l. 6: ⸢*il*?-*ta*⸣?-*a-ni*. This restoration remains tentative because more signs seem to be required of this damaged space than are supplied and because of the unusual spelling of this term resulting from the restoration.

l. 7: *š*[*a*]. Only traces of the first three horizontals remain.

l. 7: ⸢*x*⸣-*ur*?-*še-e*[*n*]-*ni*. One is tempted to identify this part of the line with the *dimtu* of Tur-šenni, an Unap-še GN and focus of Teḫip-tilla real estate interests. See *JEN* 91:5; 214:9-10; 841:6-7. (*JEN* 841:6-8 juxtapose this *dimtu* with the land of Tur-šenni. The same may occur here, lines 5-7.) However, the position of the GN (if such it be) on this line and the spacing and shape of the surviving traces do not seem to support this interpretation.

l. 8: *eš*. This sign is clear and typical, not ŠE as copied.

ll. 10-12. Note that the scribe seems twice to have inserted: *a-na* ^{m}*Pal-te-*(*eš-*) *šup*. (In the second instance [l. 12], no other restoration seems possible.)

l. 11: ⸢43⸣?. The last vertical wedge is no longer present. It is unclear whether it ever was.

Lacheman once read, at this point: 22.

l. 11: [MA?.NA?] URUDU!. Cf. line 24. The space seems cramped for MA.NA. Lacheman reads: MA.NA [URUDU].

l. 12: [*šu*]. Lacheman saw this sign as preserved.

l. 12: [^{m}*Pal-te-(eš-)šup i-dì-n*]*a*-. Or the like. The lacuna appears inadequate for all these signs.

l. 15: *-nu*. This sign is clear and typical, not as depicted.

l. 16: [B]AL. The last trace appears, not as depicted, but, rather, as:

l. 18: ⸢*la*⸣. This trace does not appear as depicted. Only one horizontal (not two) is visible at the start of this line. I.e., it appears to have been a typical *la*.

ll. 22-23. Line 22 begins the lower edge, not line 23 as depicted.

l. 24. Below this line, on the lower edge, appears a horizontal line. This scribal line does not appear on the copy.

ll. 28-29. In light of *JEN* 743:25 and 761:38 (and cf. line 26 of *JEN* 742, another Unap-še text; for the relevance of *JEN* 743 and 761 to the present text, see above, comments), one is tempted to restore:

IGI *I*!-⸢*lu*⸣!-*uḫ*-[*ḫa-a-a*]
[DUMU KI.MI]N

However, the spacing throughout seems difficult. It should be emphasized that the NI is now totally effaced.

l. 30: ⸢*Ḫa-wi*!-*iš*⸣-*ta-e*. The witness represented in this line is surely to be identified with the "Ḫawiš-tae" son of Nan-tešup proposed for *JEN* 743:24. For suggestions of *NPN* and Lacheman on the PN of that line, see above, note to *JEN* 743:24. The restoration, ⸢*wi*⸣!, adopted here, is based on that line. There, ḪA WA appears clearly. As for the next sign there, it appears as depicted, two surviving verticals. Here, the traces of the first three signs appear as:

Therefore, the IP of the copy here is not correct. Lacheman reads the start of this line: [*Ḫa*]-*ši-ip-ta-e*. Cf. above, note to *JEN* 743:24.

l. 33: [K]Ù.BABBAR. The term represents the commodities listed in lines 11 and 24. For this usage, see above, note to *JEN* 715:27.

l. 39: ⸢DUB⸣. The trace appears, not as copied, but, rather, as:

JEN 773

OBVERSE

1 *ṭup-[pí ma-ru-ti ša]*
2 ^{m}GA-[-x-]
3 *ù š[a* ^{m} -x-x-]
4 DUMU!?.[M]EŠ? ⸢X⸣-[ ]-*⸢x⸣-[ ]
5 ^{m}*[Te-ḫi]-*ip-*til-[l]a* DU[MU *P]u-ḫi-še-en-ni*
6 *[a-na ma]-*ru-•⸢ti⸣ i-p[u]-uš*
7 [ ]*⸢x⸣[ ] ⸢*ù*⸣ *ku-⸢ma⸣-a-nu* •A.•ŠÀ
8 *[i-na]* ⸢*e*⸣-*[le-en/-ni]* AN.ZA.[K]ÀR
9 *[ša?* $^{m?}$]KI-⸢*x*⸣-[ ]-⸢*x*⸣-[ ]-$^{+}$⸢*x*⸣-*ma? i+na le-et*
10 [ ]⸢*i*⸣?-*na* ⸢*ú*⸣-[ ]
11 [^{m}GA-]-⸢x⸣-[ ] •*ù*
12 [^{m}]-⸢x-x⸣-[*a-na* ^{m}]*Te-ḫi-ip-til-la*
13 *[ki-m]a* ḪA.[LA-*šu id-d]i-na-aš-šu ù* [^{m}*T]e-ḫi-ip-ti[l-la a-na]*
14 *[šum-ma]* ⸢A⸣.ŠÀ *p[í-ir-qa ir?-t]a?-⸢ši⸣* : 2 ⸢LÚ⸣.MEŠ *an-[nu-tu$_{4}$]*
15 [ ]⸢x⸣[L]Ú.MEŠ *an-nu-tu$_{4}$*
16 ⸢*ú-za-ak*⸣-*[ka$_{4}$-m]a a-na* ^{m}*Te-ḫi-ip-til-la* : 1 GUD S[UM?]
17 *[i-n]a-an-⸢din⸣ ù il-ki* A.ŠÀ
18 [2? L]Ú.MEŠ *an-nu-tu$_{4}$ [n]a-šu*
19 *[šu]m-ma* LÚ.MEŠ ⸢*an*⸣-*nu-[tu$_{4}$]*
20 [K]I.BAL 1 MA.NA <KÙ.BABBAR> 1 M[A.NA KÙ.SIG$_{17}$]
21 ⸢*a*⸣-*na* ^{m}*Te-ḫi-ip-til-[la]*
22 ⸢*ú*⸣-*ma-al-la*

---

23 IGI *It-ḫi-⸢iš⸣-[ta* DUMU]
24 IGI *Ut-ḫa-[ap-* DUMU]
25 [IG]I ⸢X⸣-[DUMU]

.
.
.

REVERSE

.
.
.

*S.I.

26 [ ]⸢x x x⸣
27 [ ] ⸢*x*⸣ •*še-el*-WA [(?)]

S.I.

28 [ ] *ši!-bi*

29 [ ] •*ši-bi*

S.I.

30 [^{NA_4} KIŠIB ^{m}*I*]*t-ḫi-iš-ta*

LEFT EDGE

31 + $^{[N]A_4}$ KIŠIB ^{m}[ ]

[S.I.?]

TRANSLATION

(1-6) Tablet [of adoption of] GA-... and of [...] sons(?) of(?) .... He (*sic*) adopted Teḫip-tilla son of Puḫi-šenni.

(7-13) GA-... and ... gave [to] Teḫip-tilla as [his] inheritance share a(n) ...x+.05 homer field [to] the east of the *dimtu* [of?] KI-..., adjacent to .... .

(13) And Teḫip-tilla gave [to] these 2 men 1 ox.

(14-17) [Should] the field have a claim (against it), these ... men shall clear (the field) and give (it) to Teḫip-tilla.

(17-18) And these [2?] men shall bear the field's *ilku*.

(19-22) Should these men abrogate (this contract), he (*sic*) shall pay to Teḫip-tilla 1 mina of <silver> (and) 1 mina [of gold].

(23-29) Before Itḫišta [son of ...]; before Utḫap-... [son of ...]; before ... [son of ...];..... (*seal impression*) .... measurers(?) / measured(?) [...?]. (*seal impression*) ...., witness; ...., witness.

(30-31) (*seal impression*) [seal impression of] Itḫišta; seal impression of ... [(*seal impression*)].

COMMENTS

For the most part, this tablet has suffered but minor additional deterioration since it was copied. However, a fragment, formerly attached, is now entirely missing. The effaced signs indicated in the transliteration of lines 4-7 (excluding A.ŠÀ in line 7) reflect that loss.

On the other hand, two additional fragments, unnumbered and now attached, were not present when the original copy was made. The first fragment contributes what remains of lines 1-3, traces of the first three signs of line 4, the first sign of line 5, and the surviving text of the left edge. The second fragment joins the obverse at lines 5-9, contributing the surviving middle of those lines.The following should be kept in mind when consulting the copy. First, the lines are not perfectly straight but tend to curve down toward the middle of the lines. Second, the reverse of the tablet is represented only by the far right side.

The scribe of this text is guilty of at least two omissions. First, he initially failed to include mention of Teḫip-tilla's purchase price for the

land. He corrected this failure by subsequent additions to lines 13, 14, and 16. (*NB*: The scribe does not bother to call this price NÍG.BA, "gift." It is unclear if this failure is due to lack of space or to the relative insignificance of that terminological nicety [probably both].) Second, the scribe omitted mention of the first metal constituting the fine for abrogating the contract (l. 20).

This scribe also regularly writes a singular form of a verb for a required plural. See lines 6, 13, 17, 22. Cf., however, the stative plural in line 18.

NOTES

ll. 2-4. The restoration of these lines assumes that the adopters are named in lines 2 and 3 and that their shared patronymic appears in line 4.
It is possible that line 2 contains the PN and patronymic of the first adopter and line 3 names the second adopter with his patronymic appearing in line 4.

l. 6: [*ma*]. Lacheman records this sign as preserved.

l. 7: [ ] ⸢*ù*⸣. "x ^{GIŠ}APIN" might well be contained in the lacuna.

l. 7: *ku-*⸢*ma*⸣*-a-nu*. The *kumānu* = 1/20 homer. See above, second note to *JEN* 764:5.

l. 7: ŠÀ. Contrary to the copy, the space after this sign is clear; and it is blank.

l. 9: KI-⸢*x*⸣-[ ]-⸢*x*⸣-[ ]-⸢*x*⸣-*ma*?. The name of a *dimtu*, probably a PN, is expected at this point. The trace immediately before MA? appears, not as copied, but, rather, as: 

l. 12: ⸢x-x⸣. These traces are correct as copied.

l. 12: [^{m}]. The *CAD* Nuzi file records this sign as preserved.

l. 13: [^{m}*T*]*e-ḫi-ip-ti*[*l-la*]. The *CAD* Nuzi file records this part of the line as completely preserved.

l. 15: [ ]⸢x⸣[L]Ú. A reading, [*ù*] 2 [L]Ú, would fit the context well (cf. line 18) but too much space after "2" would be left unaccounted for.

l. 16: GUD S[UM?]. The *CAD* Nuzi file reads, at this point: ANŠE.

l. 20: <KÙ.BABBAR> ... [KÙ.SIG$_{17}$]. A reading <KÙ.SIG$_{17}$> ... [KÙ.BABBAR] is also possible, if less likely.

l. 23. See below, note to line 30.

l. 24: [*ap*]. Utḫa-... is most likely to have been Utḫap-..., although there is a slight possibility that the PN is *Ut-ḫa-*[*a-a*]. See *NPN*, 168a-69a; *AAN*, 162a-63a.

ll. 26-29. The precise context of these lines—whether identifying sealers (note the seal impressions above lines 26 and 28) or witnesses (note lines

28 and 29) or measurers (note line 27; possibly ⌜*mu*⌝-*še-el-wu*(-*ú*) or ⌜*ú*⌝-*še-el-wu*(-*ú*)) or a combination of these—eludes me.

The first of the seal impressions is not only effaced, at this point there is no surface at all.

l. 26. This line appears about one-third down the reverse side of the tablet.

ll. 29-30. The space between lines 29 and 30 with its seal impression is occupied, on the right, by the ends of lines 13, 14, and 16 from the obverse.

l. 30. Porada identifies this Itḫišta as the son of Ar-tae.

l. 31. The seal impression associated with this legend might have been located beside the legend or underneath it.

Porada reads the PN of this line: "[ ]-teššup."

l. 31: $^{[N]A_4}$. The trace appears, not as copied, but, rather, as: 

JEN 774

OBVERSE

1 *ṭup-pí ma-ru-ti ša*
2 ^{m}*Šu-ru-uk-ka*$_4$ DUMU *Ta-ú-uḫ-ḫe*
3 ^{m}*Mì-na-a-a* DUMU *Ip-ša-ḫa-l*[*u*]
4 *a-na ma-ti*-ŠU DÙ-*ma* 1 É.ḪI<.A?>-*šu*
5 A.ŠÀ.MEŠ-*šu* AN.ZA.KÀR *ù ma-ag-ra-a*[*t-tù*]
6 *ša li-wi-it* AN.ZA.KÀR A.ŠÀ.MEŠ
7 *ma-la i-ba-aš-ša-a ša* $^{<m?>}$*Mì-na-*[*a-a*]
8 *ma-an-nu ša* BAL 1 MA.NA KÙ.BABBAR 1 MA.N[A KÙ.SIG$_{17}$]
9 Ì.LÁ.E <*a?-na?*> IGI.MEŠ *ú-ba-l*[*a*]?

---

10 IGI *Ḫa-an-ku-ya* DUMU *Ki-in*$_4$*-ni-ya*
11 IGI *Wa-an-*˹*ti-ya* DUMU *Na-ḫi-a-šu*
12 IGI *Zi-li*!*-ya* DUMU *A-ri-ip-*˹*a-*˹*pu*
13 IGI *Um-pu-ur-tù* DUMU *Ar-še-ni*
14 IGI *Ar-ša-tù-ya* DUMU *Še-el-la-p*[*á-i*]

.
.
.

REVERSE

15 [-*l*]*i*?

.
.
.

16 [ ]-*ú*

.

.

.

S.I.

17 IGI *Bal-ṭù-*ka_4*-ši-id*

18 DUB.SAR

TRANSLATION

(1-4) Tablet of adoption of Šurukka son of Tauḫḫe. He adopted Minaya son of Ipša-ḫalu.

(4-7) His (i.e., Šurukka's) one house, his land, the tower, and the threshing floor which abuts the tower, (i.e.,) as much real estate as there is, (all this) is Minaya's.

(8-9) He who abrogates (this contract) shall weigh out 1 mina of silver (and) 1 mina [of gold] (and?) deliver(?) (this? sum?) <to?> the witnesses.

(10-14) Before Ḫankuya son of Kinniya; before Wantiya son of Naḫi-ašu; before Ziliya son of Arip-apu; before Impurtu son of Ar-šenni; before Ar-šatuya son of Šellapai ....

(15-16) ....

(17-18) ....; (*seal impression*) Before Balṭu-kašid, the scribe.

COMMENTS

This text has been transliterated and translated by Purves (1945, 81). Except where otherwise noted, references to Purves in the following comments and notes indicate this page.

But for parts of three signs (see lines 11 and 12), the tablet has not deteriorated since it was copied.

Note that lines 15 and 16 of the reverse survive only in a trace and a single sign respectively. In the copy, these are represented, upside down, at the ends of lines 13 and 11 respectively.

Lacheman notes that the reappearance of Ḫankuya son of Kinniya (l. 10) in *JEN* 82:21 marks this witness as a member of a relatively early Nuzi generation (since *JEN* 82, a text of Teḫip-tilla's mother, is one of the earlier Nuzi texts). See also the presence of this witness in *JEN* 567:15, 45, a context also relatively old. On *JEN* 82 and 567 and their relative antiquity, see Maidman (1979, 4, n. 13). The present text also would appear to be one of the early texts from the Teḫip-tilla Family archives. Cf., for example, the formula in lines 8-9 with *JEN* 82:12-13—both relatively archaic formulations. This would account for the somewhat idiosyncratic phraseology of this text.

Complete standardization of contract language had not yet been achieved for real estate adoption texts. See already above, comments to *JEN* 754.

One of the principal parties in this text, Minaya son of Ipša-ḫalu (l. 3), is known from four other texts, *JEN* 289, 517, 566, 734. All five "Ipša-ḫalu" texts stem from room 16 of the Teḫip-tilla Family archives. (*JEN* 774 appears to be a later stage of an economic process whose anterior stages are chronicled in *JEN* 289 and then *JEN* 517; for *JEN* 289 and 774, cf., already, Purves [1945, 81-82].) In all the other four instances, Minaya either receives real estate or acts in consequence of such receipt. Therefore, in the present text, where it is not clear *a priori* who is adopting whom, we may deduce that Minaya is the adoptee and recipient of the real estate. This becomes certain if we accept the link between *JEN* 289 and 517, on the one hand, and *JEN* 774, on the other.

For a discussion of the presence of these five texts in the Teḫip-tilla Family archives, see above, comments to *JEN* 734 and the reference cited there.

NOTES

l. 4: *ma-ti-*ŠU. This is an aberration. *ma-ru-ti* is, of course, expected (cf. line 1) and somehow meant. Lacheman interprets the scribe's intent as: *ma-<ru>-ti-šu*. (The *CAD* Nuzi file and Purves incorrectly transliterate: *ma-ru-ti-šu*.) However, this construction of *mārūtu* with possessive suffix is, I believe, nowhere else attested in the Nuzi texts.

ma-ri!*-šu* might be meant but this usage is likewise unknown elsewhere at Nuzi.

A third possibility is that the scribe transposed *ma-ru-ti* into *ma-ti-ru*! in a kind of visual metathesis. Delitzsch (1920, v) cites several examples of this phenomenon in cuneiform scribal practice and dubs this class of error: "*Umstellung von Buchstaben*." The difficulty with this interpretation here is that it assumes *two* errors: metathesis and faulty rendering of a misplaced sign.

l. 4: ḪI<.A?>. It is uncertain whether or not the scribe intended to omit "A." Cf. line 7, where the missing male determinative might also not be a true error. See below, second note to line 7.

ll. 4b-7. I interpret these lines, beginning with "1 É ...," as a nominal sentence, describing the extent of Minaya's newly acquired possessions. See already Purves. It is an unusual way of rendering this idea (no verb, no mention of an inheritance share), but unusual phraseology is not unexpected in this text. See above, comments.

The crux appears at the end of line 7. *Mi-na-*[ ] potentially allows for a verb at the end of this section. Lacheman restores, in effect: *iddin*. However, this means that Minaya is the ceder and that would be problematic on contextual grounds. See above, comments. The *CAD* Nuzi file,

besides *iddin*, entertains the possibility of *il-te-qè*. This sidesteps the contextual problem but, along with *iddin* (or any form of any verb), runs into a grammatical roadblock: the verb with *ša* would represent the subordinate clause of a sentence left incomplete.

Therefore, line 7 ends with *Mì-na-*[*a-a*] and the properties are to be construed in the nominative case. See also below, note to line 5.

ll. 5-6. If *JEN* 774 is to be linked to *JEN* 289 (see above, comments) then the real estate described in these lines is to be located in the *dimtu* of Eniya (*JEN* 289:3-4). That *dimtu* is located in Unap-še (see above, note to *JEN* 723:1).

l. 5: [*tù*]. For grammatical reasons, this restoration—already proposed by Lacheman (inconsistent with his interpretation of line 7: *Mì-na-*[*a-a iddin*]; cf. above note to ll. 4b-7)—is to be preferred to [*ta*] as restored by the *CAD* Nuzi file, Purves, and *CAD*, L, 193a. See above, note to lines 4b-7. The restoration, [*ta*], apparently is made because of *ma-ag-ra-at-ta* in *JEN* 289:3. However, there, the noun is the object of the verb, SUM (l. 6). (In view of *JEN* 774:7, it might be noted that the verb in *JEN* 289:6 is *not* associated with the relative particle, *ša*.)

l. 6: A.ŠÀ.MEŠ. For *eqlu* as meaning real estate in general, see above, note to *JEN* 757:13.

Purves and the *CAD* Nuzi file recognize no lacuna after A.ŠÀ.MEŠ. Lacheman posits a gap containing perhaps three signs.

l. 7: *i-ba-aš-ša-a*. For this form, cf. *CAD*, B, 150b k), first example.

l. 7: <m?>*Mì-na-*[*a-a*]. On the lack of the male determinative preceding this PN, see above, note to line 4: ḪI.<A?>. But see also above, note to *JEN* 730:5-12.

On the restoration, [*a-a*], see above, note to ll. 4b-7.

l. 8: N[A KÙ.SIG$_{17}$]. The *CAD* Nuzi file and Purves record these signs as wholly preserved. Lacheman sees "[S]IG$_{17}$" as preserved.

l. 9: IGI.MEŠ *ú-ba-l*[*a*]?. Purves transliterates "*îni*^{MEŠ} *ú-ba-t*[*ù*]" and translates: "and (his) eyes they shall destroy." In support of this rendering, he cites *JEN* 449:13; 452:7-8; 457:11-12 as parallel penalties (1945, 81, n. 64). However, in those instances the verb is *napālu*, not *abātu*. The contexts are also quite different. (To read here *ú-pá-l*[*a*] from *napālu* would yield a nonsensical verbal form which could only be salvaged by assuming that the scribe conjugated the verb as if it were (*w*)*abālu*.) More serious, Purves (1945, 81, n. 63) asserts that, though partially effaced, the last sign is clearly DU. In fact, it is not. Cf. the trace of the last sign with the DUs of lines 13, 14, and 17. My own collation as well as that of Lacheman (unpublished papers) confirm that the trace appears as copied.

The sign could be L[A]. If so, then perhaps one ought to supply *a-na* before IGI.MEŠ. The meaning would be that payment is to be delivered (for eventual redistribution) to the witnesses whose names appear next

in this tablet. Although clear analogues to this procedure in the Nuzi texts are not known to me, compare the function of witnesses as distributors of goods in these texts (classified, in this role, as *nadinānu*), summarized by Hayden (1962, 19).

The difficulty with this interpretation is twofold. It *does* assume a procedure nowhere else attested. And it requires the assumption of a scribal omission. (However, note such possible omissions in lines 4 and 7.)

Alternately, if one does not assume a scribal omission, this sentence might be rendered: "he shall bring witnesses." Following the penalty clause, this sentence would direct the alleged victim to supply witnesses to support his claim that the other party abrogated the terms of the contract. Compare the wording and, in a very general way, the circumstances of *JEN* 191:9-12. On the ubiquity and importance of this process of summoning witnesses in the legal life of Nuzi, see Hayden (1962, 16-19 and the notes thereto, pp. 196-97). Cf. *CAD*, A/1, 14b *sub* 4′.

The difficulty with this interpretation is a sudden and disquieting shift in subject. The subject of the previous verb (i.e., *mannu*) is the offender, yet the *implied* subject of this verb is the victim.

Retaining the same reading, perhaps one should consider a third alternative, namely, the alleged offender shall *either* pay a fine *or* bring witnesses (presumably to attest to his innocence). This procedure, unfortunately, is also unattested but at least no change of subject is required by this interpretation.

l. 14: *p*[*á-i*]. This restoration is buttressed by *JEN* 746:34 and *HSS*, XIX, 9:1-2. Šellapai is a common PN. See *NPN*, 129b *sub* ŠELLAPAI; *AAN*, 124b *sub* ŠELLAPAI. The only other possible restoration of "*Še-el-la*-⸢*x*⸣-[ ]" seems to be *Še-el-la*-⸢*a*⸣!-[*a*]. It is a PN clearly attested only once: *HSS*, XIX, 9:21.

PERSONAL NAMES

The name list in *NPN* includes, not only the Chicago Nuzi texts published to that time, but the unpublished (i.e., "*JENu*") material as well. Nevertheless, *THNT* requires its own name list because *NPN*'s treatment of the unpublished material is defective: most—but far from all—tablets are included, and few of the major fragments are treated. Among those texts edited in this volume, *NPN* fails to deal at all with *JEN* 698, 704, 713, 732, 733, 736, 754, 764, 768, and 772. Other texts are treated only partially, e.g., *JEN* 679, 719, and 771.

In addition to filling in *NPN*'s gaps, the present list supplies line numbers in texts covered by *NPN*, which cites these by tablet only. Gelb exercised good judgment, noting that the "numbering of lines ..... [is] considered unreliable" (*NPN*, 8). This list also corrects faulty readings in *NPN*. However, additions and corrections to *NPN* are not usually noted and no systematic notation of *NPN*'s errors or correction of those errors has been undertaken. Isolated corrections are noted where deemed appropriate. See, for example, the note to *JEN* 767:1. (*NPN* is mostly based on the *CAD* Nuzi file.)

For consistency, the name list presented here follows as closely as possible the pattern of *NPN*. Thus, the order of spellings of PNs in rubrics follows *NPN*, and then *AAN*. New spellings appear only afterwards. For example, three spellings of KENNI are attested in *THNT*. The first two listed correspond to *NPN*'s prime spelling and fourth spelling (p. 83b). The third corresponds to *AAN*'s sixth spelling (p. 80b; itself building on *NPN*). For convenience sake, all these numbers are preserved in the present list. The two spellings of NAN-TEYA offer a similar example. The first spelling is designated "(2)" after *NPN*'s second variation (p. 104a) while the second one is unattested elsewhere and designated "(6; new)" following the four *NPN* spellings and a fifth from *AAN*. Names nowhere else attested are so designated, e.g., "NAŠWIYA (new PN)."

There are some differences between the present list and *NPN*. Perhaps the most conspicuous one involves the "pronunciation" of the spellings. *NPN* tends to retain primary sign values in transliterating personal names while the present list attempts as much as possible to interpret spellings in light of their paradigmatic (i.e., rubric) form. For example, for the name ZIKE *NPN* will render a particular spelling, *Zi-gi*, while this list renders those

same signs, *Zi-ké*. In a sense, the present list opts for the "morphophonemic" principle where *NPN* adopts the "phonological."

Other spelling differences are: substitution of XXX for *NPN*'s Sin and *šúk* for *NPN*'s *šuk*.

Another difference between the two lists is more arcane. Within the numbered sub-rubrics (i.e., rubrics of individual persons), *NPN* orders spellings of patronymics (or other identifiers) according to which text mentions this name first. The spelling appearing there then becomes the first spelling cited. In the present list, the order of spellings is based first on the frequency numbers as established in *NPN* and *AAN*.

Other differences are minor. In this list, *šibu* is not listed as a profession. *NPN*'s "(witness sequence)" notation is not included here. See, instead, notes regarding witness sequences and the catalogue of interrelated texts.

This list employs "Y" for "I̯" and "W" for "U̯." As a result of this, there is some minor deviation from *NPN* of the order in which PNs appear in the list.

As a general dictum, with regard to the normalization of names spelled in Sumerian, where there is evidence (i.e., alternate phonetic realizations) that such names were pronounced in Sumerian, this is indicated in the name list and in the text editions. Such names are not translated into Akkadian. Where there is evidence (again by phonetic spellings) that such names were pronounced in Akkadian, the names are translated in the name list and in the editions. Where there is no such evidence one way or another, Sumerograms are retained. (The order in which such names appear is not affected: all cases follow *NPN*. For example, in the case of ^{d}UTU-DINGIR-AŠ-KUR, the name nevertheless appears in the name list as Šamaš-ilu-ina-māti in conformity with *NPN*.)

An example of the first case is *NPN*'s ^{d}AK.DINGIR.RA. This represents phonetic "Ak(ka)dingirra" and is indicated as such. The same obtains with Iškur-andul. In the second case, NÍG.BA-*ya* represents Akkadian Qîšteya, and that is how the name is rendered. ^{d}UTU-ma.an.sì and ^{d}UTU-DINGIR-AŠ-KUR remain in these forms since we have no clearly phonetic writing of this name.

A

A....

A?-[....], var. (2) *A?-*[....]-⸢X X⸣-[....], var. (3) *A-*⸢*x*⸣-[....]-⸢x⸣
s. of *Na-an-te-šup*, (2) *JEN* 723:24
f. of *Ta-a-ú-ki*, (3) *JEN* 761:2
JEN 707:30

A....A

A-[....]*-a*
f. of ....*-ti-ya*, *JEN* 696:16

A....AYA

A-⸢*x-x*⸣*-a-a*
f. of *Ši-il-wa-te-šup*, *JEN* 727:2

A....RI

A-[ ]-⸢x⸣-RI

f. of *Ḫa-ma-an-na, JEN* 695:18

A....ŠU

A-⌜*x*⌝-[ ]-*°šu*

f. of *Ta-i-še-en-ni, JEN* 684:2

AḪI-ILLIKA

var. (3) *A-ḫi-i-li-ka*$_4$

JEN 771:4?

AḪIU?

A?-ḫi-i-ú?

f. of *I-ri-ya, JEN* 729:23

AḪIYA

A-ḫi-ya

f. of *Ú-na-ap-še, JEN* 702:29

AḪ-UMMIŠA

var. (4) *A-ḫu-um-mì-ša*

s. of *Él-ḫi-ip*-LU[GAL?], *JEN* 741:41

AḪUŠINA

A-ḫu-ši-na

f. of *Ta-i-še-en-ni, JEN* 689:2, 28

AḪU-WAQAR

Aḫ-wa-qar

s. of *A-pil-...., JEN* 695:1, 6, 20 (only line 20 is clear "s. of A.")

AK....KAENIYA

Ak-[(?)]-*kà-e-ni-a*

f. of [....]-*til-la, JEN* 719:32

AKALAYA

A-ka$_4$*-la-a-a*

f. of *Ku-uš-ši-ya, JEN* 771:13

AKKAPA

Ak-ka$_4$*-pa*

f. of *E-ni-iš-ta-e, JEN* 703:31; *E?-ni?-iš?-ta?-e?, JEN* 770:28?

AKAP-TAE

A-kap-ta-e

s. of *Ku-us-ki-pa, JEN* 747:18, 38

AKAP-TUKKE

A-kap-tùk-ké, var. (2) *A-kap-tùk-ke*

f?. of *A*-RI-[....]-⌜x-x⌝, *JEN* 771:10

f. of *Še-el-wi-na-tal*, (2) *JEN* 705:27

f. of *Ta-i-še-en-ni* and *Ta-i-še-ni*, (2) *JEN* 718:3

f. of *Ta-an-ta-ka*$_4$*-a-a, JEN* 771:2

AKAWATIL

A-ka$_4$*-wa-til*

name of a *dimtu, JEN* 703:10 (no ^{m}); 709:7; 736:7; 743:6; 751:7; 761:7 (no ^{m}); 770:7

AKAWE

A-ka$_4$*-we*

s. of *I-lu-ša, JEN* 731:[19]; 759:19

AKAYA

A-ka$_4$*-a-a*, var. (3) *A-ka-a-a*

f. of *Ar-te-ya, JEN* 722:[26], 36; 750:33

f. of *Ḫu-ti-ya, JEN* 704:20; 722:23, 35

f. of *Ki-pá-a-a, JEN* 750:35

f. of *Še-eḫ-li-ya*, (3) *JEN* 699:1?

f. of *Ta-an-te-ya, JEN* 683:32; *Ta-a-an-te-ya, JEN* 714:[25]

f. of *Te-ḫi-ya, JEN* 684:[20]; 685:19; 689:19; 766:14

f. of *Ti-in-ti-ya, JEN* 674:34; 675:38; 676:31; 677:32; 678:31; 679:32; 680:31

f. of *Tu-ra-ri, JEN* 750:36

AKIP-APU

A-kip-a-pu, var. (2) *A-ki-pá-pu*, (3) *A-ki-pa-pu*
- f. of *Ḫa-ši-pa-pu*, *JEN* 704:25
- name of a town, (2) or (3) *JEN* 757:3 (no ^{m}); (3) 761:8 (no ^{m})

AKIP-ŠARRI

A-kip-LUGAL
- s. of *Ak-ku-te-šup*, *JEN* 698:30?
- s. of *Ar-zi-iz-za*, *JEN* 684:23; 685:24

AKIP-ŠENNI

A-kip-še-en-ni
- s. of *Ni-iḫ-ri-ya*, *JEN* 729:15

AKIP-TAŠENNI

A-kip-ta-še-en-ni
- s. of *Me-le-ya*, *JEN* 749:30?
- *JEN* 691:7; 692:7; 724:7?

AKIP-TEŠUP

var. (2) *A-ki-te-šup*
- s. of *Šu-ri-ša*, (2) *JEN* 733:19

AKIP-TILLA

A-kip-til-la
- s. of *Ké-li-ya*, *JEN* 749:23?; 757:27?, 30 (the latter may not be s. of *Ké-li-ya*)
- s. of *Tù-ra-ri*, *JEN* 686:16; 687:18; 700:23, 31; 705:15; 710:17; 716:20; 728:15; *Tu-ra-ri*, *JEN* 702:26; 707:27

AKIYA

A-ki-ya, var. (3) *A-ki-a*
- s. of *Mu-uš-te-šup*, *JEN* 719:23, 37
- f. of *Ki-iz-zi-ḫar-pá*, *JEN* 727:13
- f. of *Be-li-ya*, (3) *JEN* 758:22

^{d}AK.DINGIR.RA (=Ak(ka)dingirra)

^{d}*Ak-dingir-ra*
- s. of ^{d}XXX-*na-ap-šìr*, *JEN* 689:24
- scribe, *JEN* 740:21

AKKUL-ENNI

Ak-ku-le-en-ni, var. (5) *Ak-ku-ul-en-ni*
- s. of *Zi-ka*$_4$*-a-a*, *JEN* 747:29
- f. of *Eḫ-li-ya*, *JEN* 699:7
- f. of *Pur-ni-ya*, (5?) *JEN* 760:21
- f. of *Ta-a-a*, *JEN* 678:2

AKU-ŠENNI

A-ku-še-en-ni
- f. of *Te-ḫi-ya*, *JEN* 689:21

AKKU-TE....

Ak-ku-te-[....]
- s. of *Ḫa-ši-ya*, *JEN* 698:29

AKKU-TEŠUP

Ak-ku-te-šup
- s. of *Ḫu-pí-ta-aḫ-ḫé*, *JEN* 752:25, 38
- f. of *A-kip*-LU[GAL?], *JEN* 698:30

AKKUYA

Ak-ku-ya, var. (2) *Ak-ku*$_8$*-ya*
- s. of *Al-ki-til-la*, *JEN* 763:25
- f. of *Na-ḫi-šal-mu*, *JEN* 737:3
- f. of *Pa-a-a*, (2) *JEN* 743:31, 38; (2) 772:35
- f. of *Še-eḫ-li-ya*, *JEN* 758:27; 763:33; 765:27
- f. of *Zi-ké*, *JEN* 737:3

ALIPPIYA

A-li-ip-pí-ya
- s. of *Ki-zi-ḫar-pè*, *JEN* 750:28

ALKI-TEŠUP

Al-ki-te-šup

s. of *Tù-uḫ-mì-ya*, *JEN* 720:25; [*Tu*?-*uḫ*$_5$?-*mì*?-*ya*?], *JEN* 733:17

ALKI-TILLA

Al-ki-til-la

s. of *A-r*[*i*?]-⸢*x-x*⸣-*la*-⸢*x*⸣, *JEN* 701:23?

f. of *Ak-ku-ya*, *JEN* 763:26

ALKIYA

Al-ki-ya, var. (3; new) *Al-ki-a*

s. of *Mil-ki-te-šup*, *JEN* 707:2, 7, 13, 18

f. of *Ke-li-ip*-LUGAL, *JEN* 758:25; *Ké-li-ip*-LUGAL, (3) *JEN* 763:28;(1) or (3) 765:24

ALPU....

Al-pu-[....]

f. of *Šúk-ri-ya*, *JEN* 739:20

ALPUYA

Al-pu-ya

s. of *A-ri-ya*, *JEN* 719:26, 36

s. of *Ḫa-ši-ya*, *JEN* 674:33; 675:37; 676:30; 677:31; 678:30; 679:31; 680:30

f. of *Ḫu-i-te-šup*, *JEN* 756:8

f. of *It-ḫi-iš-ta*, *JEN* 756:7

f. of *Um-pi-ya*, *JEN* 723:33

AL-TEŠUP

A-al-te-šup

s. of *Šum-mi-ya*, *JEN* 749:18

f. of *En-na-ma-ti*, *JEN* 749:25; 751:21

AMMAKKA [= Arim-matka?]

Am-ma-ak-ka$_4$

f. of *Ar-nu-zu*, *JEN* 694:18; 709:26

AMINIPE

A-mi-ni-pè

s. of *Wa-an-ti*$_4$-*ya*, *JEN* 719:6, 15

AN....

AN-[....]

JEN 683:24

ANITA

var. (2) *A-ni-i-ta*

name of a *dimtu*, (2) *JEN* 697:9 [no ^{m}]

ANTAYA

An-ta-a-a

slave of *Te-ḫi-ip-til-la*, *JEN* 737:3, [22?]

AP....UŠ/TA

Ap-x-uš/ta

s. of ^{d}IM-LUGAL(=Adad-šarri), *JEN* 721:11; 726:12

APAKKE

A-pa-ak-ké

s. of *Pa-li-ya* and *Pa-le-e*, *JEN* 743:[1], 9, 12, 13, 15, 17

APAYA

A-pa-a-a

s. of *Ḫa-na-a-a*, *JEN* 723:19

ABEYA

A-be-ya, var. (5) *A-be-e*

s. of *Ki-pa-a-pu*, *JEN* 675:[2], 14

s. of *Na-iš-ké-el-pè*, *JEN* 692:27

s. of *Pa-az-zi-ya*, *JEN* 674:30; 675:34; 676:27; 677:28; 678:27; 679:28; 680:27

f. of *Tar-mi-ya*, *JEN* 741:29; (5) 743:34; 744:25; 751:20; 772:36

f. of [....]-*pí-ya*, *JEN* 744:35

APIL-....

A-pil-[....]

f. of *Aḫ-wa-qar*, *JEN* 695:[1]?, 20

APIL-SIN

*A-pil-*XXX, var. (2) IBILA-^{d}XXX, (3) IBILA-XXX, (4) *A-pil-*^{d}XXX

f. of *Ar-ta-še-en-ni*, (2) *JEN* 729:25; (2) *JEN* 748:28

f. of *Ki-an-ni-pu*, (2) *JEN* 692:22

f. of TI.LA-KUR (i.e., Balṭu-kašid), *JEN* 682:17

f. of *Ta-a-a*, *JEN* 674:36; 680:33; (3) 683:34; 684:30; (2) 688:22; (4) *JEN* 689:27; (2) 692:32; (2) 693:39; 695:19; 696:[20]; 697:24; 703:36; 704:28; 723:38; 725:24;756:9; 766:21

(2) *JEN* 692:23

ABI-ILU

*A-bi-*DINGIR

s. of *Ša-ri-iš-še*, *JEN* 702:34

APLIYA

Ap-li-a

name of a *dimtu*, *JEN* 709:6(^{m}?)

ABUTTEYA

var. (2) *A-bu-te-ya*

(2) *JEN* 769:3, 4

APUZI

A-pu-zi

f. of *Mil-ki-ya*, *JEN* 719:7

f. of *Na-i-še-ri*, *JEN* 719:5

f. of *Ni-nu-a-tal*, *JEN* 719:8

AR....

Ar-[....]

s. of [*Te?-ḫi-ya*], *JEN* 733:18

f. of *Ta-a-a*, *JEN* 735:18

f. of *Tup-*ka_4*-a-pu*, *JEN* 677:2?

ARAN-TAI

A-ra-an-ta-i

f. of *Pu-ut-tù*, *JEN* 756:17

ARḪI....

Ar-ḫ[*i?-....*]

f. of [....-R]I?, *JEN* 767:16

ARI....

*A-*RI-[....], var. (2) *A-*RI-[....]-⸢x-x⸣

s.? of *A-kap-tùk-ké*, (2) *JEN* 771:9

f. of [....]*-nu*, *JEN* 767:17

ARI...LA...

A-r[*i?*]-⸢*x-x*⸣*-la-*⸢*x*⸣

f. of *Al-ki-til?-la?*, *JEN* 701:23

ARIḪ-ḪAMANNA

A-ri-ḫa-ma-an-na

s. of *Ḫa-tar-te*, *JEN* 721:16; 726:19

s. of *Tù-ri-ki-in-tar*, *JEN* 725:28

ARIḪ-ḪARPA

A-ri-ḫar-pa, var. (2) *A-ri-ḫa-ar-me-e*, (4) *A-ri-ḫa-ar-me*, (5)*A-ri-ḫar-pá*, (6) *A-ri-ḫa-ar-pa*, (8) *A-ri-ḫar-*pa_{12}

s. of *E-en-na-mil-ki*, *JEN* 700:16, 29; (4) 710:30; (6?) 728:27; *E-na-mil-ki*, (8) *JEN* 707:19, 24; s. of *E-en-na-mil-ki*, br. of *Ki-ip-ta-li-li*, (4)(6) *JEN* 716:30, 39; s. of *E-en-*<*na*>*-mil-ki*, br. of *Ki-ip-ta-li-li*, (4) *JEN* 686:28; *En-na-mil-ki*, (5)(1) *JEN* 702:35, 39

s. of *Ḫa-na-a-a*, (2) *JEN* 758:24, 32; (2) 763:23, 40; (2) 765:25,29

(2) *JEN* 764:20

ARIK-KAMARI

A-ri-ka_4*-ma-ri*

s. of *Zi-li-ya*, *JEN* 756:14

ARIK-KANARI

A-ri-ka₄-na-ri, var. (2) *A-ri-ik-ka₄-na-ri*, (4) *A-ri-ké-na-ri*
s. of *Mil-ka₄-pu*, (4) *JEN* 681:[22?]
f. of *Šum-mi-ya*, *JEN* 674:21; 675:28; 677:23; 678:18; 679:22; 680:21; 690:19; 725:18; 746:28; 756:[2]; *Šu-um-mi-ya*, *JEN* 676:19; *Šu-um-mì-ya*, *JEN* 688:15
f. of [....]-*te-šup*, (2) *JEN* 747:25

ARIK-KANI

var. (2) *A-ri-ka₄-ni*
(2) *JEN* 755:6

ARIK-KELPE

A-ri-ké-el-pè
s. of *Tù-up-ki-ya*, *JEN* 769:14

ARIK-KEYA

A-ri-ké-ya, var. (2) *A-ri-ik-ké-e-a*, (3; new) *A-ri-ké-*[*e*?]
s. of *A-ri-ya*, *JEN* 690:[23]; 756:6
s. of *Ši-il-wa-a-a*, *JEN* 698:22, 36
(3) *JEN* 738:9, 10

ARI-KURRI

A-ri-kùr-ri
f. of *Eḫ-...-x-še-li*, *JEN* 746:2
f. of *Ḫa-šu-ma-tal*, *JEN* 746:3

ARIK-KUŠUḪ

var. (2) *A-ri-ku-šu*
s. of *X-pí-še-en-ni*, *JEN* 745:24

ARIL-LUMTI

Ar-ru-um-ti
s. of *Ḫa?-iš?-*[*te?-šup?*], *JEN* 741:39

ARIM-MATKA

var. (2) *A-ri-ma-at-ka₄*
s. of DINGIR-*a-ḫi*, (2) *JEN* 703:32
f. of *Ḫu-ti-ya*, (2) *JEN* 703:33

ARIP-PAPNI

A-ri-pa-ap-ni
f. of *Túr-še-ni*, *JEN* 685:22, 38; [*Túr-še-*(*en-*)*ni*], *JEN* 766:17

ARIP-APU

A-ri-pa-pu, var. (2) *A-ri-ip-a-pu*, (3) *A-ri-pa-a-pu*
s. of *Ké-en-ni*, (3) *JEN* 687:28
s. of [....]-*uz-zi*, br. of *Ku-uš-ši-ya* and *Te-ḫi-pa-pu*, *JEN* 674:2, [10], 12, [15]
f. of *Ḫa-ni-ú*, *JEN* 771:12
f. of *Zi-li-ya*, (2) *JEN* 774:12

ARIP-ENNI

A-ri-pè-en-ni
f. of *Šu-mu-li*, *JEN* 686:2

ARIP-ŠARRI

var. (2) *A-ri-ip-šar-ri*, (3) *A-rip-*LUGAL
f. of *Ḫa-ra-pa-tal*, (3) *JEN* 685:21; (3) 766:16
f. of *Ta-a-a*, *JEN* 746:26
(2) *JEN* 701:20

ARIP-ŠELLI

A-ri-ip-še-el-li
f. of *Ké-el-te-šup*, *JEN* 695:14

ARIP-UKUR

var. (2) *A-ri-ip-ú-kùr*
f. of *E-wa-ra-tù-pí*, *JEN* 734:21

ARIP-URAŠŠE

A-ri-ip-ú-ra-aš-še
f. of *Ta-ú-ka₄*, *JEN* 683:30

ARIYA

A-ri-ya

f. of *Al-pu-ya*, *JEN* 719:26, 36
f. of *A-ri-ké-ya*, *JEN* 690:23; 756:[6]
f. of *Ḫa-ni-a-aš-ḫa-ri*, *JEN* 686:27; 707:25; 710:29; 716:29; 728:26
f. of *Še-la-pa-i*, *JEN* 714:17
f. of *Te-šu-up-er-wi*, *JEN* 716:28 (see also below, TEŠUP-ERWI s. of *A-ri-ya*)
f. of *Ú-kùr*-LUGAL, *JEN* 698:33
f. of [....]-⌜*x*⌝-*i*, *JEN* 723:37
naggāru, *JEN* 722:8

ARN-APU

Ar-na-pu, var. (2) *Ar-na-a-pu*
s. of *Ki-in₄-tar*, *JEN* 734:14
f. of *Ka-ta-a-a*, *JEN* 683:26
f. of *Mu-uš-te-šup*, *JEN* 683:33, 36; 684:18; 708:15, 25 (or *Muš*); 714:16; (1) or (2) 745:[16?]; 746:31, 37; 766:12, 23; 767:12; *Muš-te-šup*, *JEN* 674:18, 38; 675:23, 43; 676:16, 36; 677:17, 35; 678:15,35; 679:17, 37; 680:16, 35; 681:17, 30; 683:33, 36; 684:18; 685:17,35; *Mu-uš-te-šu-up*, (2) *JEN* 755:14
f. of *Pu-ḫi-ya*, *JEN* 760:22

ARNIYA

Ar-ni-ya
s. of *Šúk-ri-ya*, *JEN* 752:33

ARN-URḪE

Ar-nu-ur-ḫe
f. of *Ú-na-ap-še-en-ni* and *Ú-nàp-še-en-ni*, *JEN* 747:19, 36

AR-NUZU

Ar-nu-zu
s. of *Am-ma-ak-ka₄*, *JEN* 694:18 [=Arim-matka?]; 709:26
JEN 723:22

ARP-IŠŠUḪRI

Ar-pí-iš-šu-uḫ-ri
f. of [(*E*)-*eḫ*]-*li-pa-pu*, *JEN* 771:8
f. of *Ḫa-ni-ú*, *JEN* 771:8

AR-ŠALI

Ar-ša-lim
s. of *Šúk-ri-ya*, *JEN* 721:[1], 5, 8, 9, 25, 29; 726:14
s. of *Tam-pu-uš-til*, *JEN* 681:23; 730:21

AR-ŠALIPE

var. (2) *A-ar-ša-li-ip*
f. of *Še-el-wi-na-tal*, (2) *JEN* 702:2

AR-ŠANTA

Ar-ša-an-ta, var. (2) *Ar-ša-an-tá*, (5) *Ar-ša-at-na*
s. of *Ša-am-pí-ya*, (5) *JEN* 698:31
f. of *Ḫa-ma-an-na*, *JEN* 692:26; 745:18; (2) 768:16
f. of *Ni-nu-a-tal*, *JEN* 717:15
f. of *Um-pí-ya*. *JEN* 693:37

AR-ŠATUYA

Ar-ša-tù-ya, var. (4) *Ar-ša-tù-a*
s. of *Še-la-pa-i*, *JEN* 746:34; *Še-el-la-pá-i*, *JEN* 774:14
f. of *Ḫa-na*?-[....], *JEN* 727:15
f. of *Ur-ḫi-ya*, *JEN* 674:25; 675:30; 676:23; (4) 677:24; 678:22; 679:24; 680:23
JEN 696:19

AR-ŠAWUŠKA

Ar-ša-wu-uš-ka₄
f. of *Ni-nu-a-tal*, *JEN* 727:11; 746:25-26

AR-ŠENNI

Ar-še-en-ni, var. (2) *Ar-še-ni*
f. of *Muš-te-šup*, (2) *JEN* 675:29 (see also following item)

f. of *Mu-uš-te-ya*, *JEN* 725:19; 732:[17], 23; *Muš-te-ya*, (2) *JEN* 674:22; (2) 676:20; (2) 678:19; (2) 677:22; (2) 679:23; (2) 680:20; (2) 690:20; (2) 746:27; (2) 756:[3] (see also preceding item)
f. of *Um-pu-ur-tu*, (2) *JEN* 774:13

ARTA....

Ar-t[a?-....
s. of ....*-ri-te*, *JEN* 692:31

AR-TAE

A-ar-ta-e, var. (2) *Ar-ta-e*
f. of *Ar-te-ya*, (2) *JEN* 689:20
f. of *It-ḫi-iš-ta*, (2) *JEN* 688:16; (2) 689:18; ; (1)(2) 693:26 (wr. *A-ar-ta-*<*e*>, 43; 694:25, 37; (2) 695:13;(1)(2) 696:3, 22 (prob. f. of I.); (2) 708:21; 714:19; (2) 715:23;729:20;741:36;744:30; 745:19, 28?; 768:16; *It-ḫi-iš-ta*$_5$, *JEN* 751:32
f. of *Ké-li-ya*, *JEN* 704:23
f. of *Še-el-la-pa-i*, (2) *JEN* 683:[22]; *Še-él-la-pá-e*, *JEN* 730:24;762:12

ARTAŠENNI

Ar-ta-še-en-ni
scribe, s. of IBILA-^{d}XXX, *JEN* 729:24, 26; 748:27, 32
scribe, *JEN* 730:25, 26; 762:20

ARTA-ATAL

Ar-ta-tal
f. of *Šu-pa-a-a*, *JEN* 683:25

ARTE-....

Ar-te-[....]
JEN 738:16

AR-TEŠŠE

Ar-te-eš-še, var. (2) *Ar-te-še*
f. of *Ka*$_4$*-ri-šu-uḫ*, (1) or (2) *JEN* 767:20

AR-TEŠUP

Ar-te-šup, var. (4) *Ar-te-eš-šu-up*
s. of *Ip-šá-ḫa-lu*, *JEN* 742:1, 9, 10, 15, 18, [22]; 747:6; [*Ip?-ša?-ḫa?-lu?*], *JEN* 723:1, 8, 11, 14, 16
s. of *It-ḫi-iš-ta*, *JEN* 686:[23]; 710:25; 716:26; 728:22
s. of *Ši!-in*$_4$*-ti-ya*, br. of *Ú-na-ap-ta-e*, *JEN* 734:[10]
scribe, s. of *Ta-a-a*, *JEN* 745:25, 29
f. of *Ḫa-na-a-a*, *JEN* 694:21; 736:23; 742:2
f. of *Ḫu-lu-uk-ka*$_4$, *JEN* 741:27; 744:[23?]
f. of *Pu-ḫi-še-en-ni*, *JEN* 761:33
f. of *Še-ḫa-la*, *JEN* 705:2
f. of *Te-šup-er-wi*, *JEN* 761:39
f. of *Zi-il*$_5$*-te-eš-šu-up*, (4) *JEN* 735:15
f. of [....]-⌈x⌉*-ip-til-la*, *JEN* 760:18

AR-TEYA

Ar-te-ya
s. of *A-ka*$_4$*-a-a*, *JEN* 722:26, 36; 750:33, 43
s. of *Ar-ta-e*, *JEN* 689:20
s. of *Ḫa-ši-ya*, *JEN* 734:[11]
s. of *Ta-mar-ta-e*, br. of *Ḫu-ti-ya*, *Zi-ké*, [*A-ta-a-a*], and *Ki-pí-ya*, *JEN* 699:[2]
f. of *Ḫa-ši-ip-a-pu*, *JEN* 697:25
f. of *Ip-ša-ḫa-lu*, *JEN* 703:35
f. of *Tar-mi-te-šup*, *JEN* 686:25, 36; 700:18; 710:27; 728:24, 35

AR-TILLA

Ar-til-la

f. of *Ki-in-na-a-a*, *JEN* 763:27; 765:[22]
f. of *Un-nu-ú-ki*, *JEN* 763:24

AR-TIRWI

Ar-ti-ir-wi
s. of *Ḫa-na-a-a*, *JEN* 694:19
s. of *Pa-a-a*, *JEN* 749:24; 761:37, 48
s. of [....]-x, *JEN* 752:31, 37
JEN 742:35

AR-TUKI

var. (2) *Ar-tu-ki*
s. of SILIM-*pa-li-iḫ*-^{d}IM (=Šalim-pāliḫ-Adad), (2) *JEN* 688:21

AR-TUNNI

Ar-tù-un-ni, var. (2) *Ar-tù-ni*
f. of *Ki-pè-er-ḫa*, *JEN* 756:11; *Ki-pé-er-ḫa*, (1) or (2) *JEN* 732:20

ARRUMPA

Ar-ru-um-pa, var. (3) *Ar-ru-pa*, (4) *A-ru-um-pa*$_{12}$, (6) *A-ru-pa*$_{12}$, (7) *Ar-ru-*<*pa*$_{12}$?>
f. of *Ur-ḫi-ya*, (6)(7) *JEN* 686:33, 34; (4) 707:20, 23; (6) 710:35; (1)(3) 716:33, 36; (3) 728:32

AR-ZIKARI

Ar-zi-ka$_4$*-ri*
f. of *Še-el-wi-ya*, *JEN* 685:20; 766:15

AR-ZIZZA

Ar-zi-iz-za
s. of *Mil-ku-ya*, *JEN* 705:21, 29; 707:21
s. of *Ni-ki*, *JEN* 674:32; 675:36; 676:29; 677:30; 678:29; 679:30; 680:29
f. of *A-kip*-LUGAL, *JEN* 684:23; 685:24
JEN 771:17?

ATAL-TEŠUP

A-tal-te-šup
s. of *Šum-mi-ya*, *JEN* 674:23; 675:26; 676:21; 677:21; 678:20; 679:20; 680:21; 690:18; 756:1

ÂTANAḪ

A-ta-na-aḫ
f. of *Ša-at-tù-ya*, *JEN* 734:17

ÂTANAḪ-ILU

A-ta-na-aḫ-DINGIR, var. (2) *A-ta-na-ḫi*-DINGIR, (3) *A-ta-an-ḫi-lu* (7) *A-ta-na-aḫ*$_4$-DINGIR
s. *of Ip-ša-ḫa-lu*, *JEN* 694:22
s. of *Na-an-te-šup*, *JEN* 694:20; (3) 743:26; br. of *Ḫa-wi-iš-ta-e*, (2) *JEN* 772:31 (cf. l.30); *Na-al-te-šup*, (7) *JEN* 741:28; [*Na-al-te-šup*], (7) *JEN* 744:24

ADAŠŠEYA

var. (5; new) *A-dá-še-ya*
s. of [*Tu-uḫ*$_5$*-mì-ya*], (5) *JEN* 733:16

ADATTEYA

^{d}IM-*te-ya*, var. (5) *A-ta-a-te*
s. of *Im-bi*-^{d}UTU, *JEN* 703:37
f. of *Pu-ḫi-še-en-ni*, (5) *JEN* 686:24; (5) 710:26; (5) 716:27; (5) 728:23

ADAD-ŠARRI

^{d}IM-LUGAL
f. of *Ap-x-uš/ta*, *JEN* 721:11; 726:12

ADAD-ŠĒMĪ

^{d}IM-*še-mi*, var. (2) *A-dá-še-mi*
f. of *Ik-ki-ya* (2) *JEN* 696:17; *JEN* 745:20

ATAYA

A-ta-a-a, var. (2) *A-tá-a-a*

- s. of *Ta-mar-ta-e*, br. of *Ḫu-ti-ya*, [*Ar-te-ya*], *Zi-ké*, and *Ki-pí-ya*, *JEN* 699:[3]
- s. of *Tù-ra-ri*, *JEN* 721:18, 24; 726:20, 27
- s. of *Wa-ti*$_4$*-mu-ša*, *JEN* 687:25, 31
- f. of X-[....]-x, *JEN* 743:35
- f. of *Šur-kip*-LUGAL, *JEN* 697:17

ATTILAMMU

var. (12; new) *At-ti*$_4$*-la-am-mu*

- f. of *Wi-ir-ra-aḫ-ḫe*, (12) *JEN* 726:16; *Wi-ra-aḫ-ḫe*, (12) *JEN* 721:14

AWĪLU

A-wi-lu

- s. of *Pu-re-e-a*, *JEN* 736:22
- (name of a *dimtu*, see second note to *JEN* 746:10)

AWIŠ-UŠŠE

A-wi-iš-uš-še, var. (2) *A-wi-šu-uš-še*

- s. of *Pa-li-ya*, *JEN* 684:21; (2) 685:23; (1) or (2) 766:[18]

AY-ABÂŠ

var. (2) *A-a-ba-aš*

- f. of *E-ni-iš-ta-e*, *JEN* 741:31; 744:26
- f. of *Ṣa-al-mu*, *JEN* 747:21

E

EḪ....X-ŠELI

Eḫ-....-x-še-li

- s. of *A-ri-kùr-ri*, br. of *Ḫa-šu-ma-tal*, *JEN* 746:2, 13

EḪLI....

Eḫ-li-[....]

- f. of *Ḫu-ti*$_4$*-ya*, *JEN* 739:19

EḪLIP-APU

Eḫ-li-pa-pu, var. (6) *E-eḫ-li-pa-pu*

- s. of *Ar-pí-iš-šu-uḫ-ri*, br. of *Ḫa-ni-ú*, (1) or (6) *JEN* 771:8
- f. of *Še-e-mi*, (6) *JEN* 724:1

EḪLI-TEŠUP

Eḫ-li-te-šup, var. (2) *E-ḫe-el-te-šup*, (6) *Éḫ-li-te-šup*, (11; new) *Éḫ-ḫe-él-te-šup*

- s. of *La-al-lu-ta-ri*, (2) *JEN* 725:27, 33
- scribe, s. of XXX-*ib-ni*, *JEN* 749:28? (see also ŠEḪEL-TEŠUP); 757:29 (see also ŠEḪEL-TEŠUP)
- s. of [*Tu?-uḫ*$_5$*?-mì?-ya?*], (6) *JEN* 733:21? (cf. l. 20)
- f. of *Tar-mi-te-šup*, *JEN* 682:18; (2) 711:12; 740:26; (6) 753:21
- f. of *Tar-mi-ya*, *JEN* 695:16
- f. of *Te-ḫi-ip-a-pu*, *JEN* 697:19
- (11) *JEN* 691:34

EḪLIYA

Eḫ-li-ya, var. (2) *E-eḫ-li-ya*

- s. of *E-*[*ké?*]*-*⸢*ké*⸣*?*, *JEN* 701:22
- s. of *Ak-ku-le-en-ni*, *JEN* 699:7
- s. of *Pur-ni-tù-rù* and *Pur-ni-tù-ru*, *JEN* 759:18, 26; *Pur-ni-tù-ru/rù*, *JEN* 731:18, 22
- f. of *Ša-aš-ta-e*, (2) *JEN* 686:32; (2) 700:19
- f. of *Šu-um-mi-ya*, *JEN* 737:19; *Šu-mi-ya*, *JEN* 750:34
- f. of *Ta-a-a*, *JEN* 688:17 (see also ŠEḪLIYA f. of *Ta-a-a*)

EKEKE

E-ké-ké

f. of *Eḫ-li-ya*, *JEN* 701:22?
f. of ⸢*Ni-x-x*⸣, *JEN* 698:34
f. of ⸢X⸣[....]⸢X X⸣, *JEN* 698:24?

ELḪIP-....

El-ḫi-ip-....

JEN 717:1, 5

ELḪIP-ŠARRI

El-ḫi-ip-LUGAL, var. (2) *Él-ḫi-ip*-LUGAL, (4) *Eḫ-li-ip*-LUGAL, (7) *Éḫ-li-ip*-LUGAL

s. of *Gi$_5$-mi-li-ya*, *JEN* 702:25, 40
s. of SILIM-^{d}IM (=Šulm-adad), *JEN* 708:22; *Šu-ul-ma-dá*, *JEN* 717:12; *Šu-ul-ma-ad-d*[*á*] (9) *JEN* 768:9
s. of *Tu-ur-ru*, (4) *JEN* 745:1, 6, 15
f. of *A-ḫu-um-mì-ša*, (2) *JEN* 741:41
f. of *Ta-a-a*, (7) *JEN* 748:22
f. of *Zi-ka$_4$-a-a*, *JEN* 688:14; 693:31; 723:27; *Zi-kà-a-a*, *JEN* (7) 729:21; (2) 768:12; *Zi-ka-a-a*, (4) *JEN* 762:19 (wr. *Eh-li-*<*ip*>-LUGAL)

E-LI?-AR-AN?-BE?

E-li?-ar-AN?-BE?

JEN 770:35

EMUYA

E-mu-ya

s. of *Ip-ša-ḫa-lu*, *JEN* 683:21, 37; 704:21; 714:15, 26
s. of *Ka$_4$-a-a*, *JEN* 747:32, 37
f. of *Tu-ra-ri*, *JEN* 750:32

EN....

E[*n-....*]

f. of Z[*i?-l*]*i?-ip-til-la*, *JEN* 697:26

ENNA-MATI

En-na-ma-ti, var. (3) *E-na-ma-ti*, (4) *En-na-ma-ti$_4$*, (5) *E-en-na-ma-ti$_4$*, (10) *E-en-na-ma-a-ti*

s. of *A-al-te-šup*, *JEN* 749:25; 751:[21]
s. of *En-na-a-a*, *JEN* 743:22, 36; 761:31, 47; 772:25
s. of *Ḫa-ni-ku-ya*, *JEN* 688:18
s. of *Ka$_4$-am-pu-tu$_4$*, (5) *JEN* 725:2, 7, 10, 13, 15, 16
s. of *Te-ḫi-ip-til-la*, *JEN* 750:3, 11, 12, 18
f. of *Kip-ta-e*, *JEN* 681:18; 683:31; 697:18; *Ki-ip-ta-e*, (10) *JEN* 748:19; (3) 769:8?, 17?
f. of *Tù-ul-pí-še-en-ni*, (3) *JEN* 734:15
scribe, *JEN* 758:35
JEN 699:31; 763:39; (4) 764:22; (1) or (4) 765:31

ENNA-MILKI

E-en-na-mil-ki, var. (2) *En-na-mil-ki*, (3) *E-na-mil-ki*

f. of *A-ri-ḫar-pa*, *JEN* 700:16, 29; *A-ri-ḫar-pá* and *A-ri-ḫar-pa*, (2) *JEN* 702:35; *A-ri-ḫa-ar-me*, *JEN* 686:28 (wr. *E-en-*<*na*>*-mil-ki*), 710:30; 716:30; *A-ri-ḫa-ar-pa?*, *JEN* 728:27; *A-ri-ḫar-pa$_{12}$*, (3) *JEN* 707:24
f. of *It-ḫi-zi-iz-za*, (3) *JEN* 707:26
f. of *Ki-ip-ta-li-li*, *JEN* 686:28 (wr. *E-en-*<*na*>*-mil-ki*; cf. l. 29); 710:33; 716:30 (cf. l. 31); 728:29
f. of *Še?-el?-wi!?-ya?*, (2) *JEN* 761:40
f. of *Zi-li-ip*-LUGAL, *JEN* 687:29

ENNAYA

En-na-a-a, var. (3) *E-na-a-a*

f. of *En-na-ma-ti*, *JEN* 743:22, 36; 761:31; 772:25

f. of *Ni-iḫ-ri-ya*, *JEN* 703:[3]; *Ni-íḫ-ri-ya*, (3) *JEN* 744:2, 9, 13

ENIŠ-TAE

E-ni-iš-ta-e

s. of *Ak-ka$_4$-pa*, *JEN* 703:31; *Ak?-ka$_4$?-pa?*, *JEN* 770:28?
s. of *A-a-ba-aš*, *JEN* 741:30; 744:26

ENIYA

E-ni-ya

name of a *dimtu*, *JEN* 742:7 (no ^{m})

EN-ŠAKU

var. (2) *E-en-ša-ku*

f. of *Mu-uš-te-ya*, (2) *JEN* 731:2

EN-ŠUKRU

En-šúk-rù, var. (2) *En-na-šúk-rù*

s. of *Ta-a-a*, (2) *JEN* 674:26; (2) 675:31; (2) 676:24; (2) 677:25; (2) 678:23; (2) 679:25; 680:24 (contra *NPN*, 47b, 143a; however, *na* is probably omitted inadvertently)

EPUZI

E-pu-zi

s. of *Ḫa-na-ak-ka$_4$*, *JEN* 680:2, 9, 11, 13

ERATI

E-ra-ti

f. of *Ip-pa-a-a*, *JEN* 693:38 (cf. l. 37)
f. of *Ta-i-na*, *JEN* 693:37

ÊRIŠ-....

E-ri-iš-x-x

f. of *Nu-la-za-ḫi*, *JEN* 684:26; 685:27; 766:19

ERWI-ŠARRI

Er-wi-LUGAL

s. of *Te-eš-šu-ya*, *JEN* 752:34, 37
s.? of [....]-*ma*-RI, *JEN* 731:20 (see note to *JEN* 718:22)
scribe, *JEN* 759:25

ETEŠ-ŠENNI

var. (4) *E-te-eš-še-ni*, (5) *E-te-še-en-ni*

f. of *Pu-i-ta-e*, (5) *JEN* 687:2
s. of Z[*i*]/*K*[*é*]-....-*a-a*, (4) *JEN* 675:[5], 15

ETEYA

E-te-ya

f. of *Šúk-ra-pu*, *JEN* 703:[2]; *Šúk-ra-a-pu*, *JEN* 770:2

EWARA-TUPI

E-wa-ra-tù-pí

s. of *A-ri-ip-ú-kùr*, *JEN* 734:20

EWINNANNI

E-wi-in$_4$-na-an-ni, var. (3) *E-wi-na-an-ni*

s. of *Še-en-na-a-a*, *JEN* 729:18; (3) 768:17

Ḫ

ḪA....

Ḫa-[....], var. (2) *Ḫa*-⸢*x*⸣-[....], (3) *Ḫa*-⸢*x-x*⸣

s. of *It-ḫi-til-la*, (2) *JEN* 730:8
f. of *Wi-ir-ra-aḫ-ḫe*, *JEN* 702:32
JEN 693:45; (3) 746:29

ḪAI....

Ḫa-i-⸢*x*⸣-[....]

s. of *Su-um-mi*-[....], *JEN* 715:31

ḪAIP-ŠARRI

Ḫa-ip-LUGAL

s. of *Ma-li-ya*, br. of *Šúk-ri-ya*, *JEN* 699:6

f. of *Wa-an-ti*$_4$*-ya*, *JEN* 700:24

JEN 689:30?

ḪAIRALLA

Ḫa-i-ra-al-la

f. of *Še-en-na-pè*, *JEN* 736:2; 756:13

ḪAIŠ-TEŠUP

Ḫa-iš-te-šup

s. of [*Tu*?-*u*]*ḫ*$_5$?-*mi*?-*y*[*a*]?, *JEN* 733:20

f. of *Ar-ru-um-ti*, *JEN* 741:39?

ḪALIPPA

Ḫa-li-ip-pa, var. (2) *Ḫa-li-ip-pá*

f. of *Pal-te-šup*, (1) or (2) *JEN* 742:34

ḪALU-ŠENNI

Ḫa-al-še-en-ni, var. (2) *Ḫa-lu-še-en-ni*

s. of *Ta-a-a*, *JEN* 758:23; 763:22

(2) *JEN* 697:2, [4], [8], 13

ḪAMANNA

Ḫa-ma-an-na

s. of *A*-[....]-⌜x⌝-RI, *JEN* 695:18

s. of *Ar-ša-an-ta*, *JEN* 692:26; 745:18; *Ar-ša-an-tá*, *JEN* 768:16

s. of DUMU-^{UD}XX^{KAM} (=Mâr-ešrī), *JEN* 745:23; 768:14; DUMU-*eš*$_{15}$*-ri*, *JEN* 697:21

s. of *Šu-ru-uk-ka*$_4$, *JEN* 689:25; 717:17; *Šu-ru-uk-ka*, *JEN* 727:14

f. of *Ḫu-un-ni-ya*, *JEN* 715:28; 720:28 (wr. *Ḫa-ma-<an>-na*); 722:21; 723:32; 751:28; see ŠEKARU f. of *Ḫu-un-ni-ya*

f. of *Túr-še-en-ni*, *JEN* 752:27; *Tu-ur-še-en-ni*, *JEN* 692:29

f. of *Ze-en-ni*, *JEN* 703:27; 750:[30?]; [*Ze*?-*en*?-*ni*?], *JEN* 770:24?

scribe, *JEN* 760:23

JEN 692:24

ḪAMATTAR

var. (2) *Ḫa-ma-at-ti-ir*

f. of *I-lu-ya*, (2) *JEN* 747:1, 7

ḪANA....

Ḫa-na-[....]

s. of *Ar-ša-tù-ya*, *JEN* 727:15?

f. of ^{f}*Pu-ḫu-mé-ni*, *JEN* 722:2

ḪANAKKA

Ḫa-na-ak-ka$_4$, var. (2) *Ḫa-na-ak-kà*

s. of *Še-ka*$_4$*-rù*, *JEN* 693:29; (2) 699:33, 51?; 715:21, 36; 741:38; 744:31; 750:27 *Še-kà-rù*, *JEN* 694:33; 722:22, 34; (2) 724:20

f. of *E-pu-zi*, *JEN* 680:2

ḪANANNAYA

var. (5; correct *NPN*'s "4") *Ḫa-na-*[*an-ni-y*]*a*

f. of *I-li-ma-ḫi*, (5) *JEN* 700:28

ḪANAYA

Ḫa-na-a-a

s. of *Ar-te-šup*, *JEN* 694:21; 736:23, 38

s. of *Ip-šá-ḫa-lu*, *JEN* 742:2, [10], 15, [18], 22, 37

s. of *It-hi-til-la*, *JEN* 739:18, 26 [for all references, cf. note to *JEN* 730:8]

s. of *Na-al-tùk-ka*$_4$, *JEN* 699:41

s. of *Ta-e*, *JEN* 693:36; 699:39

f. of *A-pa-a-a*, *JEN* 723:19

f. of *A-ri-ḫa-ar-me-e*, *JEN* 758:24; 763:23; 765:[26]
f. of *Ar-ti-ir-wi*, *JEN* 694:19
f. of *Šu-um-mi-ya*?, *JEN* 675:4
f. of ....*-ya*, *JEN* 675:3

ḪANIAŠḪARI

Ḫa-ni-a-aš-ḫa-ri

s. of *A-ri-ya*, *JEN* 686:27; 707:25; 710:29; 716:29; 728:26

ḪANIKUYA

Ḫa-ni-ku-ya, var. (2) *Ḫa-ni-ku-ú-a*

s. of ^{d}UTU-LUGAL (=Šamaš-šarri), *JEN* 734:18
f. of *En-na-ma-ti*, *JEN* 688:18
f. of *Ik-ka-ri-ya*, (2) *JEN* 730:23

ḪANIKUZZI

Ḫa-ni-ku-uz-zi

f. of *Šu-un-ta-ri*, *JEN* 719:4

ḪANIU

Ḫa-ni-ú

s. of *A-ri-pa-pu*, *JEN* 771:12
s. of *Ar-pí-iš-šu-uḫ-ri*, br. of [(*E*)-*eḫ*]*-li-pa-pu*, *JEN* 771:7

ḪANKUYA

Ḫa-an-ku-ya

s. of *Ki-*in_4*-ni-ya*, *JEN* 774:10

ḪAPI-AŠU

Ḫa-pí-a-šu

f. of *Ta-a-a*, *JEN* 741:2, 8, 12

ḪAPIRA

Ḫa-pí-ra

f. of *Ik-ki-ú*, *JEN* 684:27

ḪARAP-ATAL

Ḫa-ra-pa-tal

s. of *A-rip*-LUGAL, *JEN* 685:21; 766:[16]

ḪAŠ-ḪARPA

Ḫa-aš-ḫar-pá

s. of *Mil-ku-ya*, *JEN* 699:38

ḪAŠI....

Ḫa-ši-[....]

JEN 713:12

^{f}ḪAŠIL-LUMTI

var. (2) ^{f}*Ḫa-ši-il-lu-um-ti*

JEN 708:1?, 9

ḪAŠ-ŠIMIKA

Ḫa-aš-ši-mi-ka_4

s. of *Ša-tù-ké-*...., *JEN* 684:28

ḪAŠIN-NA

Ḫa-ši-in-na

f. of *Še-en-na-ya*, *JEN* 702:33

ḪAŠIP-APU

Ḫa-ši-pa-pu, var. (2) *Ḫa-ši-ip-a-pu*, (4) *Ḫa-ši-pa-a-pu*

s. of *A-kip-a-pu*, *JEN* 704:25
s. of *Ar-te-ya*, (2) *JEN* 697:25
s. of [(*Pá-at-ta*)], (2) *JEN* 738:4
f. of *Mu-ša-pu*, (2) *JEN* 683:20
f. of *Za-zi-ya*, (4) *JEN* 726:[1?]
(4) *JEN* 726:6 (see also ḪAŠIP-APU f. of *Za-zi-ya*)

ḪAŠIP-PARALLA

Ḫa-ši-pár-al-la

s. of *Pa-li-ya*, *JEN* 681:26; 690:17, 26

ḪAŠIUKI

Ḫa-ši-ú-ki

s. of *Na-al-tù-ya*, *JEN* 697:15, 27

ḪAŠIYA

Ḫa-ši-ya

f. of *Ak-ku-te-*[....], *JEN* 698:29

f. of *Al-pu-ya*, *JEN* 674:33; 675:37; 676:30; 677:31; 678:30; 679:31; 680:30
f. of *Ar-te-ya*, *JEN* 734:11
f. of *In-ni-ki*, *JEN* 681:[1]; 683:2
f. of *Mu-uš-te-šup*, *JEN* 688:12, 24;689:17,29;700:26,[30];*Mu-uš-te-eš-šup*, *JEN* 729:14, 29; 748:17
f. of *Te-ḫi-ip-til-la*, *JEN* 687:27, 33; 700:21

ḪAŠUAR

Ḫa-šu-ar
s. of *Pur-ni-a*, br. of *Wa-an-ti*$_4$*-ya*, *JEN* 765:3 (cf. l. 2), 7, 12, 16, 18

ḪAŠUM-ATAL

Ḫa-šu-ma-tal
s. of *A-ri-kùr-ri*, br. of *Eḫ-...-x-še-li*, *JEN* 746:[3], 14

ḪATAPI-AŠU

Ḫa-ta-pí-a-šu
s. of *Te-ḫi-ip-til-la*, *JEN* 725:25, 34

ḪATARTE

Ḫa-tar-te
f. of *A-ri-ḫa-ma-an-na*, *JEN* 721:16; 726:19

ḪATRAKE

Ḫa-at-ra-ké
s. of *Te*$_9$*-en-te*$_9$*-ya*, *JEN* 734:9

ḪAWIŠ-TAE

Ḫa-wi-iš-ta-e
s. of *Na-an-te-šup*, *JEN* 743:24; br. of *A-ta-na-ḫi*-DINGIR, *JEN* 772:30

ḪELLAKAL? (new PN)

Ḫe-el?-la-kál?
f. of *Zi-li-ya*, *JEN* 721:13; 726:15 (*kál* is clear)

ḪERPUYA (new PN)

Ḫe-er-pu?-[ya?]
f. of *Pal-te-šup*, *JEN* 721:20; 726:22?

ḪEŠALLA

Ḫé-šal-la, var. (2) *Ḫe-šal-la*, (3) *Ḫe-ša-al-la*, (4) *Ḫé-ša-al-la*
s. of *Zu-me*, (3) *JEN* 692:28 (4) 715:22; (2) 722:27; (2) 724:19; *Zu-ú-me*, *JEN* 699:37; 723:38; (3) 745:22

ḪINTIYA

Ḫi-in-ti-ya, var. (2) *Ḫi-in-ti*$_4$*-ya*
s. of [*Te-ḫi-ya*], *JEN* 733:15, 24 (wr. *Ḫi-in-<ti>-ya*)
f. of *Šur-ki-til-la*, (2) *JEN* 725:29, [35]

ḪIŠMI-ŠERŠA

Ḫi-iš-mi-še-er-ša
s. of *Šar-ta-an-a-pí*, *JEN* 735:13, 30

ḪIŠMI-TEŠUP

Ḫi-iš-mi-te-šup, var. (2) *Ḫi-iš-mì-te-šup*
(2) *JEN* 693:11; 715:9

ḪU....

Ḫu-x-x-[....]
JEN 714:21

ḪUIP-....

Ḫu-i-ip-⌜X⌝-[....]
JEN 724:4

ḪUIP-ERWI

Ḫu-ip-er-wi, var. (4) *Ḫu-e-ep-er-wi*

f. of *It-ḫa-a-pu*, *JEN* 735:19?; *It-ḫa-pu*, (4) *JEN* 762:13, 21

ḪUIŠŠA

Ḫu-iš-ša

s. of *Ḫur-pí-še-en-ni*, *JEN* 688:20; 713:2, 7

ḪUI-TE

Ḫu-i-te

s. of *Ma-li-ya*, *JEN* 723:30; br. of *Šúk-ri-ya*, *JEN* 722:29 (cf. l. 28)

ḪUI-TEŠUP

Ḫu-i-te-šup

s. of *Al-pu-ya*, *JEN* 756:8

s. of *Na-ni-ya*, *JEN* 720:3, 7, [10], 13, 15, 16

ḪULUKKA

Ḫu-lu-uk-ka$_4$

s. of *Ar-te-šup*, *JEN* 741:27; 744:23?

s. of *Ku-ra-sú*, *JEN* 709:21

s. of *Ku-šu-ḫa-tal*, *JEN* 692:30; 745:21

ḪUNNIYA

Ḫu-un-ni-ya

s. of *Ḫa-ma-an-na*, *JEN* 715:28, 38; ; 722:21, 33 (see ŠEKARU f. of *Ḫu-un-ni-ya*); 723:32; 751:28; *Ḫa-ma-*<*an*>*-na* 720:28, 34

ḪUMPAPE

var. (7; new) *Ḫu-pa-pè-e*

f. of *Zi-ké*, (7) *JEN* 724:29

ḪUPITA

Ḫu-pí-ta

s. of *Ké-li-ya*, *JEN* 753:1

f. of *Ma-li-ya*, *JEN* 709:25

JEN 698:37

ḪUPITAḪḪE

Ḫu-pi-ta-aḫ-ḫe

f. of *Ak-ku-te-šup*, *JEN* 752:25

ḪURPI-ŠENNI

var. (3) *Ḫur-pí-še-en-ni*

f. of *Ḫu-iš-ša*, (3) *JEN* 688:20; (3) 713:3

ḪUTIP-ŠARRI

Ḫu-ti-ip-LUGAL

s. of *Te-*[....], *JEN* 699:36

ḪUTIP-TILLA

Ḫu-ti-ip-til-la

s. of *Ni-ir-ḫi-te-eš-šu-up*, br. of *Ú-na-ap-ta-e*, *JEN* 758:21 (cf. l. 20); s. of *Ni-iḫ-ri-te-eš-šu-up*, br. of *Ú-na-ap-ta-e* (cf. ll. 30-31), *JEN* 763:31

ḪUTIP-UKUR

Ḫu-ti-pu-kùr, var. (2) *Ḫu-ti*$_4$*-pu-kùr*

s. of *Ni-iš-ḫu-ḫa*, *JEN* 690:[22]; (2) 732:18; (2) 756:5

ḪUTIYA

Ḫu-ti-ya, var. (2) *Ḫu-ti*$_4$*-ya*

s. of *A-ka*$_4$*-a-a*, *JEN* 704:20; 722:23, 35

s. of *A-ri-ma-at-ka*$_4$, *JEN* 703:33

s. of *Eḫ-li-*[....], (2) *JEN* 739:19

s. of *Me-le-ya*, *JEN* 699:12

s. of *Ta-mar-ta-e*, br. of [*Ar-te-ya*], *Zi-ké*, [*A-ta-a-a*], and *Ki-pí-ya*, *JEN* 699:2

s. of *Ul-lu-ya*, *JEN* 685:29

scribe, s. of ^{d}UTU-ma.an.sì, *JEN* 701:26 (, 27: probably not)

s. of WA-[....], *JEN* 752:22?

s. of *Zi-li-ḫar-pè*, *JEN* 699:44

s. of ⸢*X*⸣*-at-tù-*[....], *JEN* 701:19, 27 (probably)

[f. of *Ma?-....*], *JEN* 679:1 (see l. 12)
[f. of *Me-le-ya*], *JEN* 679:1 (see l. 14)
f. of *Na-an-te-e*, (2) *JEN* 743:32; *Na-an-te*$_9$*-ya*, (2) *JEN* 772:34
f. of *Pa-li-ya*, (2) *JEN* 714:18
f. of *Še-ka*$_4$*-ru*, *JEN* 695:12, 24; 755:2
(2) *JEN* 694:[1], [8], [11], 12, 14, 16; 722:24

I

IGĀRŠ(U)-ÊMI(D)

var. (4; corrects *NPN*'s 4) *I-ga*$_{14}$*-ar-še-mi-*⌜*i*⌝?/*i*[*d*]?
^{LÚ}*nu-a-ru ša* LUGAL, (4) *JEN* 735:20

IKKARI

var. (3) *In-ka*$_4$*-ri*
s. of [*Š*]*e-*⌜*en-na*⌝*-*[*a-a*], (3) *JEN* 736:24, 38?

IKKARIYA

Ik-ka-ri-ya
s. of *Ḫa-ni-ku-ú-a*, *JEN* 730:23

IKKIN

Ik-ki-in
f. of *Šu-um-ma-i-il*, *JEN* 714:3

IKKIU

Ik-ki-ú
s. of *Ḫa-pí-ra*, *JEN* 684:27

IKKIYA

Ik-ki-ya, var. (4) *E-ki-ya*
s. of *A-dá-še-mi*, *JEN* 745:20; *nappāḫu*, s. of ^{d}IM*-še-mi*, *JEN* 696:17, 23 (probably the same person as line 17)
s. of *Ka*$_4$*-kí-ya*, *JEN* 760:20; (4) *Ka*$_4$*-ki-ya*, *JEN* 767:[1], 7, 9
s. of *Ni-nu-a-tal*, *JEN* 674:31; 675:35; 676:28; 677:29; 678:28; 679:29; 680:28

IKKUYA

Ik-ku-ya
f. of *Ni-íḫ-ri-ya*, *JEN* 735:11
f. of [....]-⌜*x*⌝*-ya*, *JEN* 708:14

ILA-NÎŠŪ

DINGIR*-ni-šu*, var. (2) DINGIR-TUK*-šu*
scribe, s. of ^{d}XXX*-nap-šìr*, *JEN* 691:30, 35
f. of [....]*-ri-ya*, *JEN* 761:42

ILAPRI

I-la-ap-ri
f. of *Ki-pa-a-a*, *JEN* 694:31; *Ki-pá-a-a*, *JEN* 715:30; 750:2

ILI-AḪI

DINGIR*-a-ḫi*, var. (2) DINGIR-ŠEŠ
f. of *A-ri-ma-at-ka*$_4$, *JEN* 703:32
f. of *Še-ka*$_4$*-rù*, (2) *JEN* 699:40

ILI-ITTIYA

var. (3) DINGIR-KI*-ya*
s. of *Ki-pè-er-ḫa*, (3) *JEN* 709:29

ILI-MA-AḪI

var. (3) *I-li-ma-ḫi*
s. of *Ḫa-na-*[*an-ni-y*]*a*, (3) *JEN* 700:28

ILUḪḪAYA

I-lu-uḫ-ḫa-a-a, var. (2) *I-lu-ḫa-a-a*
s. of *Na-ik-ké-mar*, (2) *JEN* 742:26, 43; 743:25, 39; 761:38

ILU-MĀLIK

I-lu-ma-lik

f. of *Ib-na-ša-ru*, *JEN* 725:20

ILU-NAMER

I-lu-na-mé-er

s. of *Pu-re-ya*, *JEN* 723:20

ILUŠA

I-lu-ša

f. of *A-ka$_4$-we*, *JEN* 731:19; 759:19

ILUYA

DINGIR-*ya*, var. (2) *I-lu-ya*

s. of *Ḫa-ma-at-ti-ir*, *JEN* 747:1, 7, 11, 12, 14, 15
f. of [....]-*ka$_4$-zi-ya*, *JEN* 744:34
scribe, *JEN* 741:40, 46; 744:37, [41]

IM?....

IM?-[....]

JEN 743:41

IMPURTU

var. (6) *Um-pu-ur-tù*

s. of *Ar-še-ni*, (6) *JEN* 774:13

INNIKI

In-ni-ki

s. of *Ḫa-ši-ya*, *JEN* 681:1, 9, 11, 13, 16; 683:2, 11, 14, 16

INIYA

I-ni-ya

scribe (i.e., "ŠU"), s. of *Ki-an-ni-pu*, *JEN* 699:52

INB-ILIŠU

Im-bi-li-šu

s. of ŠU-*ma*-^{d}IM, *JEN* 704:2, 10, 13, 16, 17
name of a *dimtu*, *JEN* 743:7

INBI-ŠAMAŠ

Im-bi-^{d}UTU

f. of ^{d}IM-*te-ya* (=Adatteya), *JEN* 703:37

IPPARI

I-ip-pa-ri

f. of *Pí-ri-ku*, *JEN* 687:19; 705:[16]

IBAŠŠĪ-ILU

var. (3) *I-bá-aš*-DINGIR

f. of *Pa-a-a*, *JEN* 751:2

IPPAYA

Ip-pa-a-a

s. of *E-ra-ti* and br. of *Ta-i-na*, *JEN* 693:38

IBNĀ-ŠARRU

Ib-na-ša-ru

s. of *I-lu-ma-lik*, *JEN* 725:20

IPŠA-ḪALU

Ip-ša-ḫa-lu, var. (2) *Ip-šá-ḫa-lu*

s. of *Ar-te-ya*, *JEN* 703:35
s. of *It-ḫi-iš-ta*, *JEN* 708:19
s. of *Šu-ur-ku-ma-tal*, *JEN* 729:1, 5, 8, 10, 12, 27
f. of *Ar-te-šup*, *JEN* 723:[1?]; (2) 742:1; 747:6
f. of *A-ta-na-aḫ*-DINGIR, *JEN* 694:22
f. of *E-mu-ya*, *JEN* 683:21, 38; 704:21; 714:15, 26
f. of *It-ḫa-a-pu*, (2) *JEN* 752:2
f. of *It-ḫi-til-la*, *JEN* 721:21; 726:23
f. of *Mì-na-a-a*, *JEN* 774:3
f. of *Ta-a-a*, *JEN* 709:2
f. of *Zi-li-ip-a-pu*, see note to *JEN* 703:5-6
f. of [....]-PU-*ni*-[....]-⌜x⌝-[....], (2) *JEN* 770:30

IPŠAYA

Ip-ša-a-a

s. of *Ke-li-ya*, *JEN* 728:1, 8, 11, 13

IRIRI-TILLA

I-ri-ri-til-la

s. of *Še-ḫe-el-te-šup*, *JEN* 761:30, 46

s. of *Še-ka₄-rù*, *JEN* 739:3, 8, 11, 14, 15; *Še-ka₄-ru?/-rù?*, *JEN* 718:23?

IRÎŠ-ABI

I-ri-iš-a-bi, var. (2) *I-ri-ša-bi*

f. of *Ze-e-tu₄*, *JEN* 693:35; (2) 769:7, [18]

IRIYA

I-ri-ya

s. of *A?-ḫi-i-ú?*, *JEN* 729:23

s. of *Ni-íḫ-ri-ya*, br. of *Te-ḫi-ip-a-pu*, *JEN* 741:35 (cf. l. 34), 46

IŠKARPA

var. (2) *Iš-ka₄-ar-pa*

f. of *Túl-pí-še-en-ni*, (2) *JEN* 724:27

f. of *Zi-ké*, (2) *JEN* 724:24, 32

IŠKUR-ANDUL

dIškur-an-dùl (see note to *JEN* 702:36)

scribe, s. of *Zi-ni-ya*, *JEN* 702:36, 41; 750:39; *d*XXX-*né-e*, *JEN* 743:33, 43; 772:38

ITḪ-APIḪE

It-ḫa-pí-ḫe, var. (2) *It-ḫa-pí-ḫé*

s. of *Ta-a-a*, *JEN* 703:34, 45; 704:27; 709:27, 34; scribe, s. of *Ta-a-a*, *JEN* 686:31; 694:34, 40; 710:32; 716:34; 720:23; 721:22, 27; 722:30?, 37; 723:31; 725:32, 36; 726:24

scribe, *JEN* 687:30, 35; 700:27, 33; 705:31 (also, see note to *JEN* 705:26); 711:14; 714:24; 717:19; 719:35; 724:25, 35; (2) 769:16

ITḪ-APU

It-ḫa-pu, var. (2) *It-ḫa-a-pu*

s. of *Ḫ[u?-ip?-er?-wi?]*, (2) *JEN* 735:19; *Ḫu-e-ep-er-wi*, *JEN* 762:13, 21

s. of *Ip-šá-ḫa-lu*, (2) *JEN* 752:2, 12, 13, 15, 17

ḫazannu, s. of *Še-ri-*⌜*x*⌝-[(?)], *JEN* 760:19, 27

(2) *JEN* 697:[1], 4, 8, 13

ITḪI....

It-ḫi-⌜*x*⌝-[(?)]-X

s. of ⌜X⌝-[....]-IT-[....?], *JEN* 724:21

ITḪIP-....

It-ḫi-ip-⌜X⌝-[....]

JEN 722:25

ITḪIP-TILLA

It-ḫi-til-la, var. (2) *It-ḫi-ip-til-la*, (3) *Ut-ḫi-ip-til-la*

s. of *Ip-ša-ḫa-lu*, *JEN* 721:21; 726:23

s. of *Tup-ki-ya*, (3) *JEN* 686:19; (3) 687:20; (2) 700:17, 32; (2) 705:17;(3) 710:20; (3) 716:23; (3) 720:20?; (3) 728:18; *Tu-up-ki-ya*, (3) *JEN* 702:24;

f. of *Ḫa-*⌜*x*⌝-[....], *JEN* 730:9

f. of *Ḫa-na-a-a*, *JEN* 739:18

f. of *Še?-er?-ši-ya*, *JEN* 761:36

f. of *Tup-ki-til-la*, *JEN* 718:16

ITḪIŠTA

It-ḫi-iš-ta, var. (2) *It-ḫi-iš-ta₅*

s. of Al-pu-ya, *JEN* 756:7

s. of *A-ar-ta-e*, *JEN* 694:25, 37; 696:2, 8; 714:19; 729:20; 741:36, 43; 744:30, 39; 745:19, 27?;(2) 751:32, 35; 768:15; *Ar-ta-e*, *JEN* 688:16; 689:18; 695:13; 708:21; 715:23, 34; *A-ar-ta-e* and *Ar-ta-e*, *JEN* 693:26 (written *A-ar-ta-*<*e*>), 42
s. of *Ta-mar-ta-e*, *JEN* 690:21, 29; 756:4
s. of *Ta-an-....*, *JEN* 717:14
f. of *Ar-te-šup*, *JEN* 686:23; 710:[25]; 716:26; 728:22
f. of *Ip-ša-ḫa-lu*, *JEN* 708:19
f. of *Wa-qar*-EN, *JEN* 752:35
JEN 773:23, 30

ITḪI-ZIZZA

It-ḫi-zi-iz-za
s. of *E-na-mil-ki*, *JEN* 707:26

IDDINU

var. (3) *In-dì-nu*
f. of *Iṣ-ṣú-ur-*^{d}IM, (3) *JEN* 762:16

IUZZI?

I-ú-uz?-zi
f. of *Ku*$_8$*-tùk-ka*, *JEN* 747:31

IṢṢUR-ADAD

Iṣ-ṣú-ur-^{d}IM
s. of *In-dì-nu*, *JEN* 762:15

K

GA....

GA-[....]-x-[....]
s.? of X-[....]-x-[....], br.? of [....]-x-x-[....], *JEN* 773:2, 11

KAKKIYA

var. (2) *Ka*$_4$*-ki-ya*, (3; new) *Ka*$_4$*-kí-ya*
f. of *Ik-ki-ya*, (3) *JEN* 760:20; *E-ki-ya*, (2) *JEN* 767:1, 7

KAKKU

var. (3) *Ka*$_4$*-an-ku*
(3) *JEN* 685:5

KAKKUZZI

var. (3) *Ka*$_4$*-ku-zi*
f. of *Zi-ké*, (3) *JEN* 769:11

KALMAŠ-ŠURA

Kál-ma-aš-šu-ra
f. of *Ur-ḫi-te-šup*, *JEN* 699:42

KALULI

Ka$_4$*-lu-li*, var. (2) *Ka-lu-li*
f. of *Na-aš-wi*, (2) *JEN* 674:19, 39; 675:24, 44; 676:17, 37; 677:18, [36]; (2) 678:16, 36; 679:18, 38; 680:17, 36
f. of *Ni-íḫ-ri-ya*, *JEN* 748:21
f. of *Šur-kip*-LUGAL, *JEN* 704:24

KALŪMU

var. (3) *Ka*$_4$*-lu-mi*
f. of *Nu-i-še-ri*, (3) *JEN* 697:22 (wr. *Nu-i-*<*še*>*-ri*)

KAMPATU

var. (7) *Ka*$_4$*-am-pá-tu*$_4$
f. of *Ta-a-ú-ki?*, (7) *JEN* 727:12

KAMPUTTU

Ka$_4$*-am-pu-tu*$_4$
f. of *E-en-na-ma-ti*$_4$, *JEN* 725:3

KANI

Ka$_4$*-ni*
f. of *Pa-ak-la-pí-ti*, *JEN* 675:40; 676:33; 679:36

KAPATTA

Ka-pá-at-ta, var. (2) *Ka*$_4$*-pá-at-ta*

s. of ⸢X⸣-[....], (1)(2) *JEN* 701:2, 11, 13

KARI-ŠUḪ

Ka$_4$-ri-šu-uḫ

s. of *Ar-te-eš-še* or *Ar-te-še*, *JEN* 767:20

KARZEYA

var. (2) *Kàr-ze-ya*, (6) *Kar-ze-ya*

f. of *Tup-ki-ya*, (2) *JEN* 736:21; (2) 751:19; (6) 761:29

KATAYA

Ka-ta-a-a

s. of *Ar-na-pu*, *JEN* 683:26

KATIRI

Ka$_4$-ti-ri

f. of *Ké-li-ya*, *JEN* 748:18

KAYA

Ka$_4$-a-a

f. of *E-mu-ya*, *JEN* 747:32, 37

JEN 696:18; 719:28

KE?....AYA

Z[i]/K[é]-....-a-a

f. of *E-te-eš-še-ni*, *JEN* 675:5

KEL....

var. (2) *Ke-el-....*

(2) *JEN* 746:24

KELIP-ŠARRI

Ké-li-ip-LUGAL, var. (2) *Ke-li-ip*-LUGAL

s. of *Al-ki-ya*, (2) *JEN* 758:25; *Al-ki-a*, *JEN* 763:28; [*Al-ki-ya/-e*], (1) or (2) *JEN* 765:24

KELIYA

Ké-li-ya, var. (4) *Ke-li-ya*

s. of *A-ar-ta-e*, *JEN* 704:23, 32

s. of *Ka$_4$-ti-ri*, *JEN* 748:18

s. of *Mi*-RI?-[....], *JEN* 769:13

s. of *Un-te-šup*, *JEN* 699:20

f. of [*A?-kip?-til?*]-*l*[*a*]?, *JEN* 749:23; [*A?-ki*]*p?-til-la*, *JEN* 757:27

f. of *Ḫu-pí-ta*, *JEN* 753:1

f. of *Ip-ša-a-a*, *JEN* 728:2

f. of *Pa-i-til-la*, *JEN* 721:17, 26; 726:18, 26

f. of *Ur-ḫi-ya*, (4) *JEN* 747:30

JEN 691:32

KEL-TEŠUP

Ké-el-te-šup

s. of *A-ri-ip-še-el-li*, *JEN* 695:14

KENNI

Ké-en-ni, var. (4) *Ke-en$_6$-ni*, (6) *Ké-en-ni-wa*

f. of *A-ri-pa-a-pu*, *JEN* 687:28

f. of *Ké?-et?-tu$_4$*, (6?) *JEN* 771:14

(4) *JEN* 691:22

KEŠḪAYA

Ké-eš-ḫa-a-a

s. of *Ki-in-ni-ya*, *JEN* 683:28; 740:1, 17

KETTU

Ké-et-tu$_4$

s. of *Ke-en-ni-*[*wa?*], *JEN* 771:14?

KI....

⸢*Ki*⸣/⸢*Ti$_4$*⸣-*x*-[....], var. (2) ⸢KI⸣-[....]-⸢x⸣-[....?], (3) *Ki*-⸢*x*⸣-[....]

f. of *Wa-an-ti-ya*, *JEN* 767:11

f. of [....?]-*x-pá-ya*, *JEN* 718:17

(2) *JEN* 758:26

KIANNIPU

Ki-an-ni-pu

s. of IBILA-^{d}XXX, *JEN* 692:22, 33

f. of *I-ni-ya*, *JEN* 699:53

KIKKIYA

var. (5) *Ki-in-ki-ya*

s. of *Ši-mi-ka₄-tal*, *JEN* 694:26, 38; 699:45

KILLI

Ki-il-li

name of a canal, *JEN* 707:[6]

KILĪLIYA

Ki-li-li-ya

s. of *Šur*!-*ri*-[....], *JEN* 707:22

GIMILL-ADAD

ŠU-^{d}IM, var. (2) *Gi₅-mi-la-dá*, (11) *Gi₅-mil-li-*^{d}IM, (14; new) *Gi-mil-*^{d}IM

s. of *Zu-me*, (2) *JEN* 694:32; 695:15; 697:23, 29?; *Zu-ú-me*, *JEN* 699:34; (11) 729:19; *Zu-mé*, *JEN* 768:18

f. of [....]-*ya*, *JEN* 749:19?

GIMILLIYA

var. (3) *Gi₅-mi-li-ya*

f. of *El-ḫi-ip*-LUGAL, (3) *JEN* 702:25

KINNANNI

var. (2) ⌜*Ki*⌝-*in₄-na-a*[*n*]-*ni*

s. of *Nu-la-za-ḫi*, *JEN* 735:16

KINNAYA

Ki-in-na-a-a

s. of *Ar-til-la*, *JEN* 763:27, 37; 765:22

KINNIYA

Ki-in-ni-ya, var. (2) *Ki-in₄-ni-ya*

s. of *Ta-ú-uḫ-ḫe*, *JEN* 698:32

f. of *Ḫa-an-ku-ya*, (2) *JEN* 774:10

f. of *Ké-eš-ḫa-a-a*, *JEN* 683:28; 740:2

f. of *Te-eš-šu-ya*, *JEN* 681:25

KINTAR

Ki-in-tar, var. (2) *Ki-in₄-tar*

f. of *Ar-na-pu*, (2) *JEN* 734:14

f. of *Na*-⌜*x*⌝-[*x*?]-*ya*?, *JEN* 719:3

KINNUZZI

Ki-in-nu-uz-zi

JEN 742:31

KIPANTIL

var. (2) *Ki-pá-an-til*, (3) *Ki-pá-an-ti-il*

s. of X-...., (3) *JEN* 717:16

name of a *dimtu*, (2) *JEN* 727:4 (no ^{m})

KIP-APU

Ki-pa-a-pu

f. of *A-be-ya*, *JEN* 675:2

KIPA-ŠENNI

Ki-pa-še-ni

JEN 718:35

KIPAYA

Ki-pa-a-a, var. (2) *Ki-pá-a-a*

s. of *A-ka₄-a-a*, br. of *Tu-ra-ri*, (2) *JEN* 750:35

s. of *I-la-ap-ri*, *JEN* 694:31; (2) 715:30; (2)(1) 750:2, 10, 13, 17

f. of *Ša-ma-aš*-[....]-⌜x⌝, (2) *JEN* 750:38

KIP-ERḪAN

Ki-pè-er-ḫa, var. (3) *Ki-pé-er-ḫa*

s. of *Ar-tù-un-ni*, *JEN* 756:11; *Ar*-[*tù*-(*un*-)*ni*], (3) *JEN* 732:20

f. of DINGIR-KI-*ya* (=Ili-ittiya), *JEN* 709:29

f. of *Na-ḫi-iš-še-ya*, *JEN* 747:27, [33]; *Na-ḫi-še-ya*, *JEN* 709:28

f. of *Um-pí-ya*, *JEN* 703:40; 747:28; 756:12

KIPI-TILLA

var. (2) *Kip-til-la*

f. of *Na-an-te-eš-šu-up*, (2) *JEN* 758:2

KIPIYA

Ki-pí-ya

s. of *Ta-mar-ta-e*, *JEN* 724:23, 31; br. of *Ḫu-ti-ya*, [*Ar-te-ya*], *Zi-ké*, and [*A-ta-a-a*], *JEN* 699:4

KIP-TAE

Kip-ta-e, var. (2) *Ki-ip-ta-e*

s. of *En-na-ma-ti*, *JEN* 681:18; 683:31; 697:18; *E-en-na-ma-a-ti*, (2) *JEN* 748:19; *E-na-*[*ma?-ti?*], (2) *JEN* 769:8, 17

KIP-TALILI

Ki-ip-ta-li-li

s. of *E-en-na-mil-ki*, *JEN* 710:33; 728:29; br. of *A-ri-ḫa-ar-me*, *JEN* 716:31 (cf. l. 30); s. of *E-en-*<*na*>*-mil-ki*, br. of *A-ri-ḫa-ar-me*, *JEN* 686:29 (cf. l. 28); *JEN* 702:8

KIP-TEŠUP

Kip-te-šup

name of a *dimtu*, *JEN* 706:9

KIRIP-APU

Ki-ri-ip-a-pu

f. of [*Še?*]*-eš-wi-ya*, *JEN* 752:24

QÎŠTEYA

var. (3) NÍG.BA-*ya*

f. of *Pu-ḫi-še-ni*, (3) *JEN* 684:24 (see l. 25); (3) 685:25 (see l. 26)

f. of *Šur-ki-til-la*, (3) *JEN* 684:24, 34; 685:25, 40

KITTAYA

Ki-it-ta-a-a

s. of MI.NI-*a-bi* (=*Ṣill-abi*), *JEN* 710:[1], 10, 14

KIZZALLI

Ki?-iz-za-al-li

f. of *Ma?-ṣí-ya*, *JEN* 735:10

KIZZI-ḪARPA

var. (3) *Ki-zi-ḫar-pè*, (5) *Ki-iz-zi-ḫar-pá*

s. of *A-ki-ya*, (5) *JEN* 727:13, 21

f. of *A-li-ip-pí-ya*, (3) *JEN* 750:28

KIZZIRI

Ki-iz-zi-ri

s. of *Še-en-na-a-a*, *JEN* 725:30

KUNATU

Ku-na-tù

name of a *dimtu*, *JEN* 674:7; 679:5

KUPPATIYA

K[*u?-pa?-ti?-ya?*]

f. of *Pí-im-pí-li*, *JEN* 701:18

KURASU (new PN)

Ku-ra-sú

f. of *Ḫu-lu-uk-ka*$_4$, *JEN* 709:21

KURIŠNI

Ku-ri-iš-ni

f. of *Pè-ti*$_4$*-ya*, *JEN* 720:27

f. of *Še-er-pa-taš-ši*, *JEN* 697:16

JEN 699:30

KUŠŠIYA

Ku-uš-ši-ya

s. of *A-ka*$_4$*-la-a-a*, *JEN* 771:13

KUŠ-KIPA

var. (4) *Ku-us-ki-pa*

f. of *A-kap-ta-e*, (4) *JEN* 747:18, 38

KUTUKKA

Ku-tùk-ka$_4$, var. (7) *Ku*$_8$*-tùk-ka*$_4$

s. of *I-ú-uz?-zi*, (7) *JEN* 747:31

f. of *Zi-ka*$_4$*-a-a*, *JEN* 703:28

KUŠŠI-ḪARPE

var. (5) *Ku*$_8$*-uš-ši-ḫar-pè*

ḫazannu, (5) *JEN* 693:46

KUŠŠIYA

Ku-uš-ši-ya, var. (2) *Ku*$_8$*-uš-ši-ya*

s. of [....]*-uz-zi*, br. of *A-ri-pa-pu* and *Te-ḫi-pa-pu*, *JEN* 674:2, 10, 12, 15

f. of *Wa-an-ti-ya*, *JEN* 689:23

(2) *JEN* 754:1, 9

KUŠUḪ-ATAL

Ku-šu-ḫa-tal

f. of *Ḫu-lu-uk-ka*$_4$, *JEN* 692:30; 745:21

KUTUKKA

Ku-tùk-ka$_4$

f.? of *Zi?-*[*ka*$_4$*?-a?-a?*], *JEN* 770:25?

KUZZARIYA

Ku-uz-za-ri-ya, var. (2) *Ku-za-ri-ya*

f. of DUMU-^{d}X (=Mâr-ištar), *JEN* 695:17; (2) 703:29, 42; DUMU-^{d}INNIN, *JEN* 708:20

L

LALLU-TARI

La-al-lu-ta-ri

f. of *E-ḫe-el-te-šup*, *JEN* 725:27, [33]

LU-NANNA

Nu-la-an-na

f. of *Na-ni-ya*, *JEN* 733:22

M

MA?....

Ma?-[....]

s. of *Ḫu-ti-ya*, [br. of *Me-le-ya*], *JEN* 679:[1], [10], 12, [14]

MAITTA

Ma-i-it-ta

JEN 699:35

MALIYA

Ma-li-ya

s. of *Ḫu-pí-ta*, *JEN* 709:25

f. of *Ḫa-ip-*LUGAL, *JEN* 699:6

f. of *Ḫu-i-te*, *JEN* 722:29 (cf. l. 28); 723:30

f. of *Šúk-ri-ya*, *JEN* 694:30; 699:6; 722:28

f. of *Um-pí-ya*, *JEN* 694:28

f. of *Wu-ur-tù-ru-uk*, *JEN* 686:17; 707:28; 710:18; 716:21; 728:16

MANNU-KĪ-BÊLIYA

Ma-an-nu-ki-be-li-ya

nu-a-ru, *JEN* 735:24

MARA....

Ma-ra?-[....]

f. of *Ma-ti-ya*, *JEN* 731:16; 759:[16]

MÂR-EŠRĪ

DUMU-^{UD}XX^{KAM}, var. (2) DUMU-*eš*$_{15}$*-ri*

f. of *Ḫa-ma-an-na*, (2) *JEN* 697:21; 745:23; 768:14

MÂR-IŠTAR

DUMU-^{d}X, var. (8) DUMU-^{d}INNIN

s. of *Ku-uz-za-ri-ya*, *JEN* 695:17; (8) 708:20; *Ku-za-ri-ya*, *JEN* 703:29, 42

MAŠANTE

Ma-ša-an-te, var. (2; new) *Ma-ša-an-ta*

f. of *Tar-mi-ya*, *JEN* 686:30; (2)(1) 709:23, 33; 710:34; 716:32; 728:30; 743:30, 40

MATIYA

Ma-ti-ya

s. of *Ma-ra*?-[....], *JEN* 731:16; 759:16

s. of *Ú-ar-si-a*, *JEN* 748:26

s. of [....]-*a-x*-[....], *JEN* 742:29, 43

MAṢĪYA

Ma-ṣí-ya

s. of *Ki?-iz-za-al-li*, JEN 735:10?

MELEYA

Me-le-ya

[s. of *Ḫu-ti-ya*, br. of *Ma*?-....], *JEN* 679:9, [11], 14

f. of [*A?-kip?-ta?-še?-en?-n*]*i*?, *JEN* 749:30

f. of *Ḫu-ti-ya*, *JEN* 699:13

MILK-APU

var. (2)*Mil-ka$_4$-pu*

f. of *A-ri-ké-na-ri*?, (2) *JEN* 681:22

MILKIYA

Mil-ki-ya

s. of *A-pu-zi*, *JEN* 719:7, 15

MILKI-TEŠUP

Mil-ki-te-šup

f. of *Al-ki-ya*, *JEN* 707:2

MILKUYA

Mil-ku-ya

f. of *Ar-zi-iz-za*, *JEN* 705:21, 30; 707:21

f. of *Ḫa-aš-ḫar-pá*, *JEN* 699:38

f. of *Mu-ḫu-ur-sú*, *JEN* 687:24; 705:20

f. of *Ša-ma-ḫul*, *JEN* 687:26

MINAŠ-ŠUK

Mi-na-aš-šúk, var. (2) *Mi-na-aš-šu-uk*

s. of *Za-zi-ya*, *JEN* 699:10

(2) *JEN* 759:2, 6, 9, 11, 13, 22

MINAYA

var. (2) *Mì-na-a-a*

s. of *Ip-ša-ḫa-lu*, (2) *JEN* 774:3, 7

(2) *JEN* 734:2, 5

MI-RI?....

Mi-RI?-[....]

f. of *Ké-li-ya*, *JEN* 769:13

MUḪUR-SIN

Mu-ḫu-ur-sú

s. of *Mil-ku-ya*, *JEN* 687:24; 705:20

MÛRĀNIYA

Mu-ra-ni-ya

f. of [....]-⸢*a*⸣?-*a*, *JEN* 767:15

MUŠ-....

Mu-uš-[....]

JEN 694:27

MUŠ-APU

Mu-ša-pu

s. of *Ḫa-ši-ip-a-pu*, *JEN* 683:20

MUŠ-ŠENNI

Mu-uš-še-en-ni

s. of *Ni-nu-a-tal*, *JEN* 729:17; 730:19; 735:27; 762:14

MUŠEYA

Mu-še-ya

s. of ^{d}XXX-KAM (=Sin-êriš), *JEN* 735:2

MUŠ-TEŠUP

Mu-uš-te-šup, var. (2) *Muš-te-šup*, (3) *Mu-uš-te-eš-šup*, (4) *Mu-uš-te-šu-up*, (5; new) *Mu-uš-te-*AŠ

s. of *Ar-na-pu*, (2) *JEN* 674:18, 38; (2) 675:23, 43; (2) 676:16, 36; (2) 677:17, 35; (2) 678:15, 35; (2) 679: 17, 37; (2) 680:16, 35; (2) 681:17, 30; 683:33, 36; 684:18; 685:17, 34; 708:[15], 25 (or (2)); 714:16; 746:31, 36; 766:[12], 23; 767:12; *Ar-na-a-pu*, *JEN* 755:13; [*Ar?-na?-(a?-)pu?*], *JEN* 745:16?

s. of *Ar-še-ni*, (2) *JEN* 675:29 (see also Muš-teya, s. of *idem*)

s. of *Ḫa-ši-ya*, *JEN* 688:12, 24; 689:17, 29; 700:26, 30; (3) 729:14,29; (3) 748:17, 30

f. of *A-ki-ya*, *JEN* 719:23, 37

f. of *Šu-ri-ša*, *JEN* 700:22

f. of *Ur-ḫi-ya*,(5)(1) *JEN* 733:12, 25

MUŠ-TEYA

Mu-uš-te-ya, var. (2) *Muš-te-ya*, (6) *Muš-te-e*

s. of *Ar-še-en-ni*, *JEN* 725:19; 732:17, 22; *Ar-še-ni*, (2) *JEN* 674:22; (2) 676:20; (2) 677:22; (2) 678:19; (2) 679:23; (2) 680:20; (2) 690:20; 746:27; (2) 756:3 (see also Muš-tešup, s. of *idem*)

s. of *E-en-ša-ku*, *JEN* 731:2, 7, 9, 11, 13, 20?

s. of *Be-la-a-a*, (2)(6) *JEN* 693:40, 49

s. of *Te-ḫi-ya*, *JEN* 715:29, 35; 751:25

s. of *Zi-ir-ri*, *JEN* 755:12

MUŠUYA

Mu-šu-ya

JEN 721:4

N

NA....

Na-[....]

s.? of? [....]-*te*, *JEN* 762:[4?], 8

NA....YA

Na-⌜*x*⌝-[*x*?]-*ya*?, var. (2) *Na-*⌜*x*⌝-[....]-*ya*

s. of *Ki-in-tar*, *JEN* 719:2, 13

f. of [....]-*i-qí-ša*, (2) *JEN* 747:22

NAḪIŠ-ŠALMU

var. (2) *Na-ḫi-šal-mu*

s. of *Ak-ku-ya*, br. of *Zi-ké*, (2) *JEN* 737:2

NAḪI-AŠU

Na-ḫi-a-šu

f. of *Wa-an-ti-ya*, *JEN* 674:20; 675:25; 676:18; 677:19; 678:17; 679:19; 680:18; 774:11

NAḪIŠŠEYA

Na-ḫi-iš-še-ya, var. (2) *Na-ḫi-še-ya*

s. of *Ki-pè-er-ḫa*, (2) *JEN* 709:28;

br. of *Um-pí-ya*, *JEN* 747:27, 33

JEN 736:37

NAḪŠIYA (new PN)

Na-aḫ-ši-ya

s. of *Še-ḫu-ur-x?*, *JEN* 721:19; 726:21

NAIK-KEMAR

Na-i-ké-mar, var. (2) *Na-ik-ké-mar*

f. of *I-lu-uḫ-ḫa-a-a*, (2) *JEN* 743:25, 39; (2) 761:38; *I-lu-ḫa-a-a*, (2) *JEN* 742:26

f. of *Wa-an-ti-mu-ša*, (2) *JEN* 743:23, 37; (2) 761:32; 772:27

NAI-ŠERI

Na-i-še-ri

s. of *A-pu-zi*, *JEN* 719:5, 14

NAIŠ-KELPE

Na-iš-ké-el-pè, var. (2) *Na-i-iš-ké-el-pè*, (3) *Na-iš-ké-el-pé*, (4) *Na-i-iš-ké-el-pé*, (6) *Na-iš-ke-el-pé*, (11) *Na-iš-ké-él-pè*, (16; new) *Na-i-iš-ké-él-pè*, (17; new) *Na-iš-k*[*e-el?-pè?*]

f. of *A-be-ya*, *JEN* 692:27

f. of *Pí-ru*, *JEN* 681:19; 684:[19]; 685:18; 688:13; 689:26; 690:16, 27; (11) 691:28; 692:25; 695:11; 697:20; 704:26; 727:9, 19; (6) 745:17; 746:30; 766:13; *Pí-i-ru*, (4) *JEN* 714:14, 27; (16) 717:11; 729:16, 30; 748:23; (2) 767:14; (11) 768:11; (2) 769:10; *Pí-i-rù*, *JEN* 732:21; (17) *Pí-e-ru*, *JEN* 730:20

f. of *Ši-mi-ka*$_4$, *JEN* 748:25

NALTUKKA

Na-al-tùk-ka$_4$

f. of *Ḫa-na-a-a*, *JEN* 699:41

NALTUYA

Na-al-tù-ya

f. of *Ḫa-ši-ú-ki*, *JEN* 697:15, 27

f. of *Zi-li-pa-a-pu*, *JEN* 719:33, 38

NANNA-MANSI

^{d}ŠEŠ.KI-ma.an.sì

scribe, s. of *Ta-a-a*, *JEN* 715:32, 37?

NANIYA

Na-ni-ya

scribe, s. of *Nu-la-an-na*, *JEN* 733:22, 23

s. of *Šu-ru-ka*$_4$*-a-a*, *JEN* 703:5, 13, 20

f. of *Ḫu-i-te-šup*, *JEN* 720:3

name of a *dimtu*, *JEN* 683:6

NAN-TEŠUP

Na-an-te-šup, var. (2) *Na-an-te-eš-šu-up*, (3; new) *Na-al-te-šup*

s. of *Kip-til-la*, (2) *JEN* 758:2, 10, 12, 14, 17

f. of ⸢*A*⸣?-[....]-⸢X-X⸣-[....], *JEN* 723:24

f. of *A-ta-na-aḫ*-DINGIR, *JEN* 694:20; *A-ta-na-aḫ*$_4$-DINGIR, (3) 741:28; (3) 744:[24]; *A-ta-an-ḫi-lu*, *JEN* 743:26; *A-ta-na-ḫi*-DINGIR, *JEN* 772:30 (cf. l. 31)

f. of *Ḫa-wi-iš-ta-e*, *JEN* 743:24; 772:30

NANTEYA

var. (2) *Na-an-te-e*, (6; new) *Na-an-te*$_9$*-ya*

s. of *Ḫu-ti*$_4$*-ya*, (2) *JEN* 743:32; (6) 772:34

NAŠWI

Na-aš-wi

s. *Ka*$_4$*-lu-li*, *JEN* 675:24, 44; 676:17, 37; 677:18, 36; 679:18, 38; 680:17, 36; *Ka-lu-li*, *JEN* 674:19, 39; 678:16, 36

NAŠWIYA (new PN)

Na-aš-wi-ya

f. of ^{d}XXX-MA.AN.BA (=Sin-iqîša), *JEN* 756:16 (most likely an error for *Še-eš-wa-a-a*; see note to *JEN* 756:16)

NAYA

Na-a-a

f. of *Ú-na-ap-ta-e*, *JEN* 748:[3], 29

NI-[....]-X-[....]

⸢*Ni*⸣-[ ]-⸢x⸣-[ ]

JEN 691:24

NI....

⸢*Ni-x-x*⸣

s. of *E-ké-ké*, *JEN* 698:34

NIḪRI-TEŠUP

var. (3) *Ni-iḫ-ri-te-eš-šu-up*, (5) *Ni-ir-ḫi-te-eš-šu-up*

f. of *Ḫu-ti-ip-til-la*, (5) *JEN* 758:20 (cf. l. 21); (3) 763:30 (cf. l. 31)
f. of *Ú-na-ap-ta-e*, (5) *JEN* 758:20; (3) 763:30

NIḪRIYA

Ni-iḫ-ri-ya, var. (2) *Ni-íḫ-ri-ya*

s. of [*En-na-a-a*], *JEN* 703:3, 12, 19; *E-na-a-a*, (2) *JEN* 744:[1], 8, 12, 14, 17, 18
s. of *Ik-ku-ya*, (2) *JEN* 735:11
s. of *Ka-lu-li*, (2) *JEN* 748:21
s. of [....]-*ri-ya*, *JEN* 757:[1], 9, 11, 15, [16]
f. of *A-kip-še-en-ni*, *JEN* 729:15
f. of *I-ri-ya*, (2) *JEN* 741:34 (cf. l. 35)
f. of *Te-ḫi-ip-a-pu*, (2) *JEN* 741:34; (2) 744:28
f. of [....]-⸢x⸣-[....], *JEN* 749:29

NIKI

Ni-ki

f. *Ar-zi-iz-za*, *JEN* 674:32; 675:36; 676:29; 677:30; 678:29; 679:30; 680:29

NIKIYA

Ni-ki-ya

s. of *Tar-mi-te-šup*, *JEN* 725:31

NINU-ATAL

Ni-nu-a-tal

s. of *A-pu-zi*, *JEN* 719:8, [15]
s. of *Ar-ša-an-ta*, *JEN* 717:15
s. of *Ar-ša-wu-uš-ka*$_4$, *JEN* 727:11; 746:25
f. of *Ik-ki-ya*, *JEN* 674:31; 675:35; 676:28; 677:29; 678:28; 679:29; 680:28
f. of *Mu-uš-še-en-ni*, *JEN* 729:17; 730:19; 735:27; 762:14

NIŠ-ḪUḪA

Ni-iš-ḫu-ḫa

f. of *Ḫu-ti-pu-kùr*, *JEN* 690:22; *Ḫu-ti*$_4$*-pu-kùr*, *JEN* 732:[18]; 756:[5]

NU?....

Nu?-[....]

JEN 738:15

NUI-ŠERI

Nu-i-še-ri

s. of *Ka*$_4$*-lu-mi*, *JEN* 697:22 (wr. *Nu-i-*<*še*>*-ri*)

NULA-ZAḪI

Nu-la-za-ḫi

s. of *E-ri-iš-x-x*, *JEN* 684:26; 685:27; 766:[19]
f. of ⸢*Ki*⸣-*in*$_4$*-na-a*[*n*]*-ni*, *JEN* 735:17

NÛR-....

IZI-^{d}x

f. of *Še-eḫ-li-ya*, *JEN* 698:25

NÛR-ILIYA

Nu-ri-li-ya

f. of ⌜X⌝-*li-te*?-[....?], *JEN* 747:26

NUZZA

Nu-uz-za

f. *Pu-i-ta-e*, *JEN* 674:24; 675:27, 46; 676:22, 38; 677:20, [37?]; 678:21, 37; 679:21, 39; 680:22, 38

f. of *Pu-un-ni-ya*, *JEN* 681:29, 32

P

PAḪUR

Pa-ḫu-ur

f. of *Ša-ma-ḫu-ul*, *JEN* 760:2

PAIKKU

var. (3) *Pa-i-ik-ku*

f. of *Tar-mi-ya*, *JEN* 748:20

PAI-ŠENNI (new PN)

Pá-i-še-en-ni

s. of *Še*?-*el-la*, *JEN* 719:34

PAI-TILLA

Pa-i-til-la

s. of *Ké-li-ya*, *JEN* 721:17, 26; 726:18, 26

PAKLA-PITI

Pa-ak-la-pí-ti

s. of *Ka₄-ni*, *JEN* 675:40; 676:33; 679:36

PALIYA

Pa-li-ya, var. (4; new) *Pa-le-e*

s. of *Ḫu-ti₄-ya*, *JEN* 714:18

s. of [ ]-⌜x-x⌝-[ ], *JEN* 690:2, 7, 10, 12, 14

f. of *A-pa-ak-ké*, (1)(4) *JEN* 743:2,9

f. of *A-wi-iš-uš-še*, *JEN* 684:22; *A-wi-šu-uš-še*, *JEN* 685:23; [*A-wi-iš/šu-uš-še*], *JEN* 766:18

f. of *Ḫa-ši-pár-al-la*, *JEN* 681:27; 690:17, 26

PAL-TEŠUP

Pal-te-šup, var. (5) *Pal-te-eš-šup*

s. of *Ḫa-li-ip-pa/pá*, *JEN* 742:34

s. of *Ḫe-er-pu*?-[*ya*?], *JEN* 721:20; 726:22?

(2)(1) *JEN* 772:8, 11, [12], 14, 16, [19], 22

BALṬU-KAŠID

TI.LA-KUR, var. (2) *Bal-ṭù-ka₄-ši-id*, (9) *Bal-ṭu₄-ka-ší-id*

scribe, s. of *A-pil*-XXX, *JEN* 682:17

scribe, *JEN* 735:22; 755:11; (2) 774:17

PARTASUA

Pár-ta-su-a

mār šarri, *JEN* 720:26

PATTA

Pá-at-ta

f. of *Ḫa-ši-ip-a-pu*, *JEN* 738:[4?]

PAYA

Pa-a-a

s. of *Ak-ku₈-ya*, *JEN* 743:31, 38; 772:35

s. of *I-bá-aš*-DINGIR, *JEN* 751:2, 9, [13], 16 (twice)

s. of *Pu-i-ta-e*, *JEN* 720:24

f. of *Ar-ti-ir-wi*, *JEN* 749:24; 761:37

PAZZIYA

Pa-az-zi-ya

f. of *A-be-ya*, *JEN* 674:30; 675:34 676:27; 677:28; 678:27; 679:28; 680:27

PE?....

Pè?-[....], var. (2) BE-⸢*x*⸣-[....]

f. of *Pu-ḫi-ya*, *JEN* 764:2

f. of [....]-LI-*x-ni*, *JEN* 718:18

BÊLAYA

Be-la-a-a

f. of *Muš-te-ya* and *Muš-te-e*, *JEN* 693:40 (the former spelling only)

BÊLIYA

Be-li-ya

s. of *A-ki-a*, *JEN* 758:22, 28 (See note to *JEN* 763:32)

s. of *Túr-še-en-ni*, *JEN* 763:32, 40? (See note to *JEN* 763:32)

JEN 765:30

PETIYA

Pè-ti_4*-ya*

s. of *Ku-ri-iš-ni*, *JEN* 720:[27]

PILMAŠŠE

Pil-maš-še

f. of [....]-⸢*x*⸣-*im-pa*, *JEN* 719:27

PIMPILI

Pí-im-pí-li

s. of *K*[*u?-pa?-ti?-ya?*], *JEN* 701:18, 31

PIRIKU

Pí-ri-ku

s. of *I-ip-pa-ri*, *JEN* 687:19; 705:16

(PIRŠANNI. Probably not a PN. See GN list)

PIRU

Pí-ru, var. (2) *Pí-i-ru*, (3) *Pí-i-rù*, (5) *Pí-e-ru*, (6) *Pí-i-ru-ú*, (8) *Pì-ru*

s. of *Na-iš-ké-el-pè*, *JEN* 681:19, 31; 684:19, 35; 685:18, 36; 688:13; 689:26; 690:[16], 27; 692:25; 695:11; 697:20; 704:26, 29; (2) 729:16, 30; (3) 732:21; 746:30; (2) 748:23; 766:[13] *Na-iš-ké-el-pé*, *JEN* 727:9, 19; *Na-i-iš-ké-el-pé*, (2) *JEN* 714:14, 27; *Na-iš-ke-el-pé*, *JEN* 745:17; *Na-iš-ké-él-pè*, *JEN* 691:28; (2) 768:11; *Na-i-iš-ké-él-pè*, (1)(6) *JEN* 717:11, 20; *Na-iš-k*[*e-el?-pè?*], (5) *JEN* 730:20; *Na-i-iš-ké-el-pè*, (2) 767:14; (2) 769:10

f. of *Te-ḫu-up-še-en-ni*, *JEN* 688:19; (8) 751:24; *Te-ḫu-up-še-ni*, (3) *JEN* 723:28, 34

PISI-....?

Pí-si?-[....]

f. of ^{f}*Ša-áš-ku-li*, *JEN* 708:24

PU....

Pu-⸢*x*⸣-[....]

f. of *Tu-ra-ri*, *JEN* 768:2

PUḪI-ŠENNI

Pu-ḫi-še-en-ni, var. (2) *Pu-ḫi-še-ni*

s. of *Ar-te-šup*, *JEN* 761:33

s. of *A-ta-a-te*, *JEN* 686:[24]; 710:26; 716:27; 728:23

s. of NÍG.BA-*ya* (=Qîšteya), br. of *Šur-ki-til-la*, (2) *JEN* 684:25; (2) 685:26

f. of *Te-ḫi-ip-til-la*, *JEN* 674:[4]; 675:7; 676:3; 677:3; (2) 678:3;

(2) 679:2; 680:3; 681:2; 682:21; 683:3; 684:3; 685:2; 686:3; 687:3; 688:4; 689:3; 690:3; 691:3; 692:3; 693:[3], 15; 694:2; 695:3; 698:[3]; 699:15; 700:3; 701:4; 702:3; 703:7; (2) 704:3; 705:3; 706:[(22)]; 709:3; 710:3; 714:2; 715:[3]; (re *JEN* 716:3, see below, TEḪIP-TILLA, f. of *Te-ḫi-ip-til-la*); 717:2; (2) 718:2; 719:2; 720:2; 721:2; 722:1; 723:[2]; 725:2; 726:2; 727:2; 728:3; 729:2; 730:3; 731: 3; 732:2; 733:3; 735:3; 736:3; 739:3; 740:5, 24; 741:3, 9; 742:3; 743:3, 10; 744:3, 10; 745:2; (2) 746:6; 747:2, 9; 748:2; 749:[1]; 751:3; 752:3, 9; 755:[3]; 758:3; 759:[3]; 760:3; 761:3, 23; (probably); 762:3; 763:[3]; 764:3; 765:4; 767:2; 768:1; 769:1; 770:3; 772:1; 773:5

f. of [....]-*še?-ke-er-ri-ya*, *JEN* 744:33

JEN 733:7

PUḪIYA

Pu-ḫi-ya

s. of *Ar-na-pu*, *JEN* 760:22, 26

s. of BE-⸢*x*⸣-[....], *JEN* 764:2, 10, 12, 14

f. of *Ú-zi-ya*, *JEN* 695:[10]

f. of ⸢x x⸣ [....], *JEN* 699:29

ᶠPUḪU-MENNI

var. (2) *ᶠPu-ḫu-mé-ni*

d. of *Ḫa-na-....*, (2) *JEN* 722:2, 11, 17

PUI-TAE

Pu-i-ta-e

s. of *E-te-še-en-ni*, *JEN* 687:1, 9, 12, 15

s. of *Nu-uz-za*, *JEN* 674:24; 675:27, 45; 676:22, 38; 677:20, 37; 678:21, 37; 679:21, 39; 680:22, 37

f. of *Pa-a-a*, *JEN* 720:24

f. of *Ta?-a-*[*a?*], *JEN* 719:24

PUNNIYA

Pu-un-ni-ya

s. of *Nu-uz-za*, *JEN* 681:29, 32

nu-a-ru, *JEN* 734:19

JEN 698: 2, 10, 13, 15, 17

PUREYA

Pu-re-e-a, var. (2) *Pu-re-ya*

f. of *A-wi-lu*, *JEN* 736:22

f. of *I-lu-na-mé-er*, (2) *JEN* 723:20

PURNA-NI?-....

Pur-na-ni?-x(-)[....?]

f. of *Ri-iš-ké-ya*, *JEN* 733:2

PURN-APU

Pur-na-pu

f. of *Zi-zi-ya*, *JEN* 694:23; 723:21

PURNI-TURU

Pur-ni-tù-ru, var. (2) *Pur-ni-tù-rù*

f. of *Eḫ-li-ya*, (1) or (2) *JEN* 731:18, [22]; (2)(1) 759:18, 26

PURNIYA

Pur-ni-ya, var. (2; new) *Pur-ni-a*

s. of *Ak-ku-ul-e*[*n?-ni*], *JEN* 760:21, 25

f. of *Ḫa-šu-ar*, (2) *JEN* 765:2 (see l. 3)

f. of *Wa-an-ti₄-ya*, (2) *JEN* 765:2

PUTTU

Pu-ut-tù

s. of *A-ra-an-ta-i*, *JEN* 756:17

PUYA

Pu-ya

f. of *Šu-ul-mi-ya*, *JEN* 674:35; 675:39; 676:32; 677:33; 678:32; 679:33; 680:32

R

RIŠKEYA

Ri-iš-ké-ya

s. of *Pur-na-ni?-x*(-)[....?], *JEN* 733:1, 6, 9

RUSA (new PN)

Ru-ú-sa

f. of [....]-*a?-a*, *JEN* 719:30

S

SIN-NA....ANU?

^{d}XXX-*na*-⌜*x*⌝-[(*x*-)*a-nu?*], var. (2) ⌜*Sí*⌝*?*-[*in?-n*]*a?-a-nu?*

f. of *Wa-at-wa*, *JEN* 721:12; (2) 726:13

SIN-NAPŠIR

^{d}XXX-*nap-šìr*, var. (4) ^{d}XXX-*na-ap-šìr*

f. of ^{d}*Ak-dingir-ra*, (4) *JEN* 689:24

f. of DINGIR-*ni-šu*, *JEN* 691:30

SIN-ÊRIŠ

^{d}XXX-KAM

f. of *Mu-še-ya*, *JEN* 735:2

SIN-IQÎŠA

^{d}XXX-*i-qí-ša*, var. (5) ^{d}XXX-MA.AN.BA

s. of *Na-aš-wi-ya* (most likely an error for *Še-eš-wa-a-a*), *JEN* 756:16 (see note, *ad loc.*)

scribe, *JEN* 698:26

SIN-IBNĪ

var. (2) XXX-*ib-ni*

f. of [*E?-*/*Še?-ḫ?-el?*]-⌜*te*⌝-*šup*, (2) *JEN* 749:28; [*E?-*/*Še?-ḫe*]-*el-te-šup*, (2) *JEN* 757:29

SIN-RI?KI (PN?)

^{d}XXX-*ri?-ki*

JEN 737:8

SUMMI....

Su-um-mi-[....]

f. of *Ḫa-i*-⌜*x*⌝-[....], *JEN* 715:31

Š

ŠA....

Ša-⌜*x-x*⌝, var. (2) *Ša*-[....]

f. of *Ú-kùr-a-tal*, (2) *JEN* 742:28

JEN 737:9 (PN?)

ŠAKARAYA

Ša-ka$_4$-ra-a-a

s. of *Ta-an-ta-ú-a*, *JEN* 674:29; 675:33, 47; 676:26, 40; 678:26, 39; 679:27, 40; 680:[26], 40; *Ta-ta-ú-a*, *JEN* 677:27, 39

(ŠAKRUŠŠE. Probably not a PN. See GN list)

ŠALIM-PĀLIḪ-ADAD

var. (2) SILIM-*pa-li-iḫ*-^{d}IM

f. of *Ar-tu-ki*, (2) *JEN* 688:21

ŠALIM-PÛTI

var. (2) *Ša-li-pu-ti*$_5$

s.? of ⸢*x*⸣*-un-na-an-ni*, *JEN* 691:1, 12, 14, 16

ŠAMAḪUL

Ša-ma-ḫul, var. (2) *Ša-ma-ḫu-ul*

s. of *Mil-ku-ya*, *JEN* 687:26

s. of *Pa-ḫu-ur*, (2) *JEN* 760:1, 8, 10

ŠAMAŠ-....

Ša-ma-aš-[....]-⸢x⸣

s. of *Ki-pá-a-a*, *JEN* 750:38

ŠAMAŠ-ŠARRI

^{d}UTU-LUGAL

f. of *Ḫa-ni-ku-ya*, *JEN* 734:18

ŠAMAŠ-ILU-INA-MÂTI

^{d}UTU-DINGIR-AŠ-KUR

scribe?, *JEN* 718:31, 36

ŠAMḪARI

var. (4) *Ša-am-ḫa-ri*

s. of *Tu-ra-ri*, (4) *JEN* 757:28, 32

ŠAMPIYA

Ša-am-pí-ya

f. of *Ar-ša-at-na*, *JEN* 698:31

ŠANN-APU

Ša-an-na-pu

s. of *Še-eš-wa-a-a*, *JEN* 756:15

ŠA?-RI-....

⸢*Ša*⸣?/⸢*Ta*⸣?*-ri-*⸢*x*⸣-[(?)]

f. of *Šar-ri-ya*, *JEN* 742:30

ŠARIŠŠE

Ša-ri-iš-še

f. of *A-bi*-DINGIR, *JEN* 702:34

ŠARRIYA

Šar-ri-ya

s. of ⸢*Ša*⸣?/⸢*Ta*⸣?*-ri-*⸢*x*⸣-[....?], *JEN* 742:30

ŠARTAN-API (new PN)

Šar-ta-an-a-pí

f. of *Ḫi-iš-mi-še-er-ša*, *JEN* 735:13

ŠAR-TEŠUP

Ša-ar-te-šup

s. of [....]-⸢x⸣-AT-TA, *JEN* 752:32

^{f}ŠAŠ-KULI

^{f}*Ša-áš-ku-li*

d. of *Pí-si*?-[....], *JEN* 708:11, 12, 24

ŠAŠ-TAE

Ša-aš-ta-e

s. of *E-eḫ-li-ya*, *JEN* 686:32; 700:19

ŠATUKE-....

Ša-tù-[*ké-x*]

f. of *Ḫa-aš-ši-mi-ka*$_4$, *JEN* 684:28

ŠATUŠA

Ša-tù-ša, var. (2) *Ša-tu-ša*

s. of *Tù-ra-ri*, *JEN* 686:18; 720:18; *Tu-ra-ri*, (2) *JEN* 702:23, 42; 710:19; 716:22; 728:17

ŠATTUYA

Ša-at-tù-ya (*NPN*, incorrectly: *Ša-at-tu-ya*), var. (2) *Šá-at-tù-ya*

s. of *A-ta-na-aḫ*, *JEN* 734:17

(2) *JEN* 771:17?

ŠE?....

Še?-⸢*x-x*⸣-[....]

f. of *Šúk-ra-pu*, *JEN* 694:35

ŠEḪALA

Še-ḫa-la

s. of *Ar-te-šup*, *JEN* 705:2, 9, 13

ŠEḪEL-TEŠUP

var. (2) *Še-ḫe-el-te-šup*

scribe, s. of XXX-*ib-ni*, (2) *JEN* 749:28? (see also EḪLI-TEŠUP); (2) *JEN* 757:29? (see also EḪLI-TEŠUP)

f. of *I-ri-ri-til-la*, (2) *JEN* 761:30

(2) *JEN* 754:8?, (see note to l. 11), 15

ŠEḪIRU

Še-ḫi-rù

s. of *Te-eš-šu-ya*, *JEN* 700:20

ŠEḪLIYA

Še-eḫ-li-ya, var. (2) *Še-éḫ-li-ya*, (3) *Še-eḫ-li-a*

s. of *A!?-k[a?-a-a]*, *JEN* 699:1

s. of *Ak-ku-ya*, *JEN* 758:27, 29; 763:33, 38; (1)(3) 765:27, 28

s. of IZI-^{d}x (= *Nûr-*^{d}x), *JEN* 698:25

s. of *Zi-li-ya*, *JEN* 725:26

s. of *Zu-ú-me*, (2) *JEN* 748:24

s. of *Zu-zu*, *JEN* 683:27

s. of [[....]-RU], *JEN* 733:13

f. of *Ta-a-a?*, *JEN* 688:17 (wr. [(*Še?*)-*e*]*ḫ-li-ya*)

(3) *JEN* 764:19

ŠEḪUR-X?

Še-ḫu-ur-[....]

f. of *Na-aḫ-ši-ya*, *JEN* 721:19; 726:21

ŠEKARU

Še-ka₄-rù, var. (2) *Še-kà-rù*, (3) *Še-ka₄-ru*, (6) *Še-ka-rù*

s. of *Ḫu-ti-ya*, *JEN* 695:12, 24; (3) 755:2

s. of DINGIR-ŠEŠ (=Ili-aḫi), *JEN* 699:40

s. of *Šúk-ri-til-la*, *JEN* 768:13, 23

f. of *Ḫa-na-ak-ka₄*, *JEN* 693:29; 715:21; 741:38; 744:31; 750:27 *Ḫa-na-ak-kà*, (2) *JEN* 694:33; 699:[33]; (2) 722:22, 34; (2) 724:20

f. of *Ḫu-un-ni-ya*, (2) *JEN* 722:33 (Š. mistake for *Ḫa-ma-an-na*)

f. of *I-ri-ri-til-la*, *JEN* 739:4, 15; [*I?-ri?-r*]*i?-til-la*, (1)/(3) *JEN* 718:23?

f. of *Ta-i-šu-uḫ*, (2) *JEN* 723:29

f. of *Ur-ḫi-ya*, *JEN* 693:27; 699:43; 703:30; 709:22, 36; 751:30; 758:18; 763:20, 35; 765:23; [*Ur?-ḫi?-ya?*], (6) *JEN* 770:

f. of *Zi-ké*, *JEN* 693:32; *Zi-ke*, *JEN* 715:24

f. of [....]-⌜X⌝, *JEN* 723:39

JEN 757:24?

ŠELLA? (new PN)

Še?-el-la

f. of *Pa-i-še-en-ni*, *JEN* 719:34

ŠELLAPAI

Še-el-la-pa-i, var. (2) *Še-la-pa-i*, (5) *Še-él-la-pá-e*

s. of *A-ri-ya*, (2) *JEN* 714:17

s. of *A-ar-ta-e*, (5) *JEN* 730:24; (5) 762:12; *Ar-ta-e*, *JEN* 683:22

f. of *Ar-ša-tù-ya*, (2) *JEN* 746:34; 774:14

JEN 708:18

ŠELWIN-ATAL

Še-el-wi-na-tal

s. of *A-kap-tùk-ke*, *JEN* 705:27

s. of *A-ar-ša-li-ip*, *JEN* 702:2, 9, 12, 15, 18, 20

ŠELWIYA

Še-el-wi-ya

s. of *Ar-zi-ka*$_4$*-ri*, *JEN* 685:20; 766:[15]

s. of *En-na-mil-ki*, *JEN* 761:40?

ŠEMI

Še-e-mi, var. (2) *Še-e-mì*

s. of *E-eḫ-li-pa-pu*, (1)(2) *JEN* 724:1, 11, 12, 14, 17, 33

ŠENNAPE

Še-en-na-pè

s. of *Ḫa-i-ra-al-la*, *JEN* 736:2, 12, 13, 15, 18; 756:13

ŠENNAYA

Še-en-na-a-a, var. (4) *Še-en-na-ya*

s. of *Ḫa-ši-in-na*, (4) *JEN* 702:33

f. of *E-wi-in*$_4$*-na-an-ni*, *JEN* 729:18; *E-wi-na-an-ni*, *JEN* 768:17

f. of *In-ka*$_4$*-ri*, *JEN* 736:24

f. of *Ki-iz-zi-ri*, *JEN* 725:30

ŠENNEYA

var. (2) *Še-né-ya*

s. of *Tu-ra-ri*, (2) *JEN* 676:2, 9, 10, 13

ŠERI....

Še-ri-⸢*x*⸣-[(?)]

f. of *It-ḫa-pu*, *JEN* 760:19

ŠERPA-TAŠŠI

Še-er-pa-taš-ši

s. of *Ku-ri-iš-ni*, *JEN* 697:16, 28

ŠERŠIYA

Še-er-ši-ya, var. (2) *Šèr-ši-ya*

s. of *It-ḫi-til-la*, *JEN* 761:36?

s. of *Šúk-ri-ya*, *JEN* 719:25; (2) 751:29, 37

ŠERWI

Še-er-wi

f. of *U-na-ap-ta-<e>*, *JEN* 730:22

ŠEŠWAYA

Še-eš-wa-a-a

f. of ^{d}XXX-MA.AN.BA (=Sin-iqîša), see NAŠWIYA

f. of *Ša-an-na-pu*, *JEN* 756:15

JEN 680: [2], 9, 11, 13

ŠEŠWIKKA

Še-eš-wi-ka$_4$

s. of *Tù-ra-ri*, br. of *Wa-an-ti*$_4$*-pu-ku-ur*, *JEN* 722:3, 12, 18

ŠEŠWIYA

Še-eš-wi-ya

s. of *Ki-ri-ip-a-pu*, *JEN* 752:23?

ŠILWA-TEŠUP

Ši-il-wa-te-šup

s. of *A-*⸢*x-x*⸣*-a-a*, *JEN* 727:1, 6

ŠILWAYA

Ši-il-wa-a-a

f. of *A-ri-ik-ké-e-a*, *JEN* 698:23

ŠIMIKA

Ši-mi-ka$_4$

s. of *Na-iš-ké-el-pè*, *JEN* 748:25

ŠIMIKA-ATAL

Ši-mi-ka$_4$*-tal*

s. of *Ta-ku*, *JEN* 681:20

f. of *Ki-in-ki-ya*, *JEN* 694:26; 699:45

ŠIMIKUYA

Ši-mi-ku-ya

s. of [....]-x-[....], *JEN* 742:27, 44

ŠINTIYA

Ši-in$_4$*-ti-ya*

f. of [*Ar-te-šup*], *JEN* 734:10
f. of *Ú-na-ap-ta-e*, *JEN* 734:13

ŠUKR-APU

Šúk-ra-pu, var. (2) *Šúk-ra-a-pu*
s. of [*E-te-ya*], *JEN* 703:2, 12, 19; *E-te-*[*ya*], *JEN* 770:[2], 10, 14, 15, 17, 20
s. of *Še*?-⌜*x-x*⌝-[....], *JEN* 694:35
s. of *Tù-un-tù-ya*, *JEN* 674:28; 675:32; 676:25; 677:26; 678:25; 679:26; 680:[25]
s. of ⌜X⌝-[....], (2) *JEN* 732:1, 5, 8, 10, [12], [13]

ŠUKRI....

Šúk-ri-[....]
JEN 715:2, [11?], 15, [17]

ŠUKRIP-APU

Šúk-ri-ip-a-pu
s. of [....]-x, *JEN* 752:20, 38

ŠUKRIYA

Šúk-ri-ya
s. of *Al-pu-*[....], *JEN* 739:20
s. of *Ma-li-ya*, *JEN* 694:30; br. of *Ḫa-ip-*LUGAL, *JEN* 699:6; br. of *Ḫu-i-te*, *JEN* 722:28
s. of X-*li-ya*, *JEN* 710:31; 728:28
f. of *Ar-ni-ya*, *JEN* 752:33
f. of *Ar-ša-lim*, *JEN* 721:1; 726:14
f. of *Še-er-ši-ya*, *JEN* 719:25; *Šèr-ši-ya*, *JEN* 751:29
f. of *Ṭá-ab-til-la*, *JEN* 685:1
f. of *Te-šu-up-er-wi*, *JEN* 686:26; 710:28; (re *JEN* 716:28, see TEŠUP-ERWI s. of *A-ri-ya*); 728:25
f. of *Ul-mi-a-tal*, *JEN* 757:26

ŠULM-ADAD

Šu-ul-ma-ad-dá, var. (2) SILIM-^{d}IM, (3) *Šu-ul-ma-dá*
f. of *El-ḫi-ip-*LUGAL, (2) *JEN* 708:22; (3) 717:12; *Él-ḫi-ip-*LUGAL, *JEN* 768:9

ŠULMIYA

Šu-ul-mi-ya
s. of *Pu-ya*, *JEN* 674:35; 675:39; 676:32; 677:33; 678:32; 679:33; 680:32
name of a *dimtu*, *JEN* 675:10?; 676:6; 680:6

ŠUMMA-ILU

var. (2) *Šu-um-ma-i-il*
s. of *Ik-ki-in*, *JEN* 714:2, 6, 9, 11

ŠU-MA-^{d}IM

ŠU-*ma*-^{d}IM
f. of *Im-bi-li-šu*, *JEN* 704:2

ŠUMMIYA

Šum-mi-ya, var. (2) *Šu-um-mi-ya*, (3) *Šu-um-mì-ya*, (4) *Šu-mi-ya*
s. of *A-ri-ka*$_4$*-na-ri*, *JEN* 674:21; 675:28; (2) 676:19; 677:23; 678:18; 679:22; 680:19; (3) 688:15; 690:19; 725:18; 746:28; 756:2
s. of *Eḫ-li-ya*, (2) *JEN* 737:19 (<s. of>); 750:34
s. of *Ḫa-na-a-a*, (2) *JEN* 675:[4]?, 15?
f. of *A-al-te-šup*, *JEN* 749:18
f. of *A-tal-te-šup*, *JEN* 674:22; 675:26; 676:21; 677:21; 678:20; 679:20; 680:21; 690:18; 756:[1]

ŠUMULI

Šu-mu-li
s. of *A-ri-pè-en-ni*, *JEN* 686:1, 8, 11, 14

ŠUMU-LIBŠĪ

MU-GÁL-*ši*, var. (5) MU-*lib-ši*

scribe, s. of *Ta-a-a*, (5) *JEN* 694:29, 40 (wr. MU-*lib*-<*ši*> both times); 751:31, 36

ŠUN-TARI

Šu-un-ta-ri

s. of *Ḫa-ni-ku-uz-zi*, *JEN* 719:3, 14

ŠUPAYA

Šu-pa-a-a

s. of *Ar-ta-tal*, *JEN* 683:25
f. of *Ú-ku-ya*, *JEN* 746:33
JEN 738:17

ŠUPUKKA

Šu-pu-uk-ka$_4$

f. of *Wa-an-ti*$_4$*-ya*, *JEN* 760:[16], 24

ŠURRI....

Šur!*-ri-*[....] (cf. *NPN*, *s.v.*)

f. of *Ki-li-li-ya*, *JEN* 707:22

ŠURIŠA

Šu-ri-ša

s. of *Mu-uš-te-šup*, *JEN* 700:22
f. of *A-ki-te-šup*, *JEN* 733:19

ŠURKIP-ŠARRI

Šur-kip-LUGAL

s. of *A-ta-a-a*, *JEN* 697:17
s. of *Ka*$_4$*-lu-li*, *JEN* 704:24
s. of [....]*-te-šup*, *JEN* 752:30

ŠURKI-TILLA

Šur-ki-til-la, var. (3) *Šúk-ri-til-la*

s. of *Ḫi-in-ti*$_4$*-ya*, *JEN* 725:29, 35
s. of NÍG.BA-*ya* (=*Qîsteya*), br. of *Pu-ḫi-še-ni*, *JEN* 684:24, 33; 685:25, 39
f. of *Še-kà-ru*, (3) *JEN* 768:13, 23

ŠURKUM-ATAL

Šur-ku-ma-tal, var. (4) *Šur-ku*$_8$*-ma-tal*

f. of *Ip-ša-ḫa-lu*, *JEN* 729:1, 28
f. of *Tar-mi-ya*, (4) *JEN* 747:20, 34
JEN 700:5

ŠUR-TEŠUP

Šu-ur-te-šup, var. (2) *Šu-ur-te-eš-šu-up*

s. of [*Te*?*-ḫi*?*-ip*?]*-til-la*, br.? of [....]⸢XX⸣, (2) *JEN* 763:2, 11, 13, 15, 18
s. of [[....]-RU], *JEN* 733:14

ŠURUKKA

Šu-ru-uk-ka$_4$, var. (4) *Šu-ru-uk-ka*

s. of *Ta-ú-uḫ-ḫe*, *JEN* 774:2
f. of *Ḫa-ma-an-na*, *JEN* 689:25; 717:17; (4) 727:14

ŠURUKKAYA

Šu-ru-ka$_4$*-a-a*

f. of *Na-ni-ya*, *JEN* 703:5

ŠURUPEYA

var. (3) *Šu-ru-pé-ya*

f. of [*Ta*?*-*(*i*?*-*)*i*]*n*?*-šu-uḫ*, (3) *JEN* 749:26; [*Ta*?*-*(*i*?*-*)*i*]*n-šu-uḫ*, (3) *JEN* 757:25

T

TA....

Ta-a-[....]

JEN 727:18

TAE

Ta-e

s. of *Ta-i-šu-uḫ*, *JEN* 700:[1], 7, 11, 12, 14
s. of X....x, *JEN* 746:[4?], 14?
f. of *Ḫa-na-a-a*, *JEN* 693:36; 699:39

TAENA

var. (2) *Ta-i-na*
s. of *E-ra-ti* and br. of *Ip-pa-a-a*, (2) *JEN* 693:37

TAIN-ŠUḪ

Ta-i-in-šu-uḫ, var. (2) *Ta-in-šu-uḫ*, (4) *Ta-i-šu-uḫ*
s. of *Še-kà-rù*, (4) *JEN* 723:29
s. of *Šu-ru-pé-ya*, (1) or (2) *JEN* 749:26?; (1) or (2) 757:25?
f. of *Ta-e*, (4) *JEN* 700:2

TAI-ŠENNI

Ta-i-še-en-ni, var. (2) *Ta-i-še-ni*
s. of *A-⸢x⸣-...-šu*, *JEN* 684:2, 11, 13, 15
s. of *A-kap-tùk-ke*, (1)(2) *JEN* 718:3, 6, 9, 11, 13, 33
s. of *A-ḫu-ši-na*, *JEN* 689:2, 7, 11, 13, 28
s. of *Ti-x-*[....], *JEN* 717:13

TAI-TILLA

Ta-i-til-la
s. of *Wa-an-ti-ya*, *JEN* 692:2, 12, 15, [18]

TAKKU

var. (3) *Ta-ku*
f. of *Ši-mi-ka₄-tal*, *JEN* 681:20

TAMAR-TAE

Ta-mar-ta-e
f. of [*Ar-te-ya*], *JEN* 699:4
f. of [*A-ta-a-a*], *JEN* 699:4
f. of *Hu-ti-ya*, *JEN* 699:4
f. of *It-ḫi-iš-ta*, *JEN* 690:21, 29; 756:[4]
f. of *Ki-pí-ya*, *JEN* 699:4; 724:23, 31
f. of *Zi-ké*, *JEN* 699:4
f. of [....-*u*]*š*?-⸢*x*⸣-*e*

TAMPUŠTIL

Tam-pu-uš-til
f. of *Ar-ša-lim*, *JEN* 681:23; 730:21

TAN....

Ta-an-[....]
f. of *It-ḫi-iš-ta*, *JEN* 717:14

TANNA-TAŠŠI

Ta-an-na-taš-ši
name of a *dimtu*, *JEN* 681:6
JEN 683:7 (probably also the name of a *dimtu*)

DAN-RIGIMŠU

KALAG.GA-KA-*šu*
s. of ....-AN, *JEN* 685:28

TANTAKAYA

Ta-an-ta-ka₄-a-a
s. of *A-kap-tùk-ké*, *JEN* 771:2

TANTAWA

Ta-an-ta-ú-a, var. (2) *Ta-ta-ú-a*
f. of *Ša-ka₄-ra-a-a*, *JEN* 674:29; 675:33; 676:26; (2) 677:27; 678:26; 679:27; 680:26

TANTEYA

Ta-an-te-ya, var. (7) *Ta-a-an-te-ya*
s. of *A-ka₄-a-a*, *JEN* 683:32; (7) 714:25

ṬÂB-TILLA

var. (2) *Ṭá-ab-til-la*

s. of *Šúk-ri-ya*, (2) *JEN* 685:1, 9, 12, 14

TA?-RI-....

⌜*Ta*⌝?/⌜*Ša*⌝?-*ri*-⌜*x*⌝-[(?)]

f. of *Šar-ri-ya*, *JEN* 742:30

TARMI....

Tar-mi-[....]

JEN 701:29?

TARMI-TEŠUP

Tar-mi-te-šup

s. of *Ar-te-ya*, *JEN* 686:25, 35; 700:18; 710:27, 37; 728:24, 34

s. of *Eḫ-li-te-šup*, *JEN* 682:18; 740:25; *E-ḫe-el-te-šup*, *JEN* 710:11; *Éḫ-li-te-šup*, *JEN* 753:20

f. of *Ni-ki-ya*, *JEN* 725:31

TARMIYA

Tar-mi-ya

s. of *A-be-ya*, *JEN* 741:29; 744:25; 751:20; 772:36; *A-be-e*, *JEN* 743:34

s. of *Eḫ-li-te-šup*, *JEN* 695:16

s. of *Ma-ša-an-te*, *JEN* 686:30; 710:34; 716:32; 743:30, 40; *Ma-ša-an-ta* and *Ma-ša-an-te*, *JEN* 709:23, 33; 728:30

s. of *Pa-i-ik-ku*, *JEN* 748:20, 31

s. of *Šur-ku$_8$-ma-tal*, *JEN* 747:20, 34

s. of *Ta-a-a*, *JEN* 724:28

s. of *Ú-na-ap-ta-e*, *JEN* 682:19; 706:20; 738:4; 740:[22]; 753:18; *Ú-nap-ta-e*, *JEN* 710:10

f. of *Wu-un-nu-ki-ya*, *JEN* 709:24

TAUḪḪE

var. (2) *Ta-ú-uḫ-ḫe*

f. of *Ki-in-ni-ya*, (2) *JEN* 698:32

f. of *Šu-ru-uk-ka$_4$*, (2) *JEN* 774:2

TAUKA

Ta-ú-ka$_4$

s. of *A-ri-ip-ú-ra-aš-še*, *JEN* 683:30

f. of *Zi-il-te-ya*, *JEN* 701:25; 759:20; *Zi-il$_5$-te-ya*, *JEN* 739:22, 25; 758:19; 763:21; 765:[25]

TAYA

Ta-a-a

s. of *Ak-ku-le-en-ni*, *JEN* 678:2, 9, 10, 12

s. of *A-pil*-XXX, *JEN* 723:38; 725:24; scribe, *JEN* 674:36; 680:33, 39; 684:30, 35; 695:19, 22; 696:[20], 21; 697:24, 30; 703:36, 45; 704:28; 756:9; 766:[21] scribe, s. of IBILA-^{d}XXX, *JEN*688:22, 25; 692:32, 34; 693:39, 43; scribe, s. of IBILA-XXX, *JEN* 683:34, 39; scribe, s. of *A-pil*-^{d}XXX, *JEN* 689:27

s. of *Ar*-[....], *JEN* 735:18

s. of *A-rip*-LUGAL, *JEN* 746:26

s. of *Eḫ-li-ya*, *JEN* 688:17 (or s. of [*Še*]-*eḫ-li-ya*)

s. of *Éḫ-li-ip*-LUGAL, *JEN* 748:22

s. of *Ḫa-pí-a-šu*, *JEN* 741:[1], 8, [11], 13, 16, 17, 21

s. of *Ip-ša-ḫa-lu*, *JEN* 709:2, 9, 13, 15, 17, 18

s. of *Pu-i-ta-e*, *JEN* 719:24?

s. of [*Še*]-*eḫ-li-ya*, *JEN* 688:17 (or s. of *Eḫ-li-ya*)

s. of BÀD-LUGAL (=Dûr-šarru), *JEN* 769:12

f. of *Ar-te-šup*, *JEN* 745:25, [29]

f. of *En-na-šúk-rù*, *JEN* 674:26; 675:31; 676:24; 677:25; 678:23; 679:25

f. of *Ḫa-al-še-en-ni*, *JEN* 758:23; 763:22

- f. of *It-ḫa-pí-ḫe*, *JEN* 686:31; 694:34; 703:34, [45?]; 704:27; see note to *JEN* 705:26; 709:27, 34; 710:[32]; 716:34; 720:[23]; 721:23; 722:[30?]; 723:31; 725:32; 726:25
- f. of ^{d}ŠEŠ.KI-ma.an.sì (=Nanna-mansi), *JEN* 715:33
- f. of MU-GÁL-*ši* (=Šumu-libšī), *JEN* 751:31; MU-*lib*-<*ši*>, *JEN* 694:29, 40
- f. of *Tar-mi-ya*, *JEN* 724:28
- f. of *Uta-an-dùl*, *JEN* 742:[36]; 752:36
- scribe, f. of *Wa-qar*-EN, *JEN* 768:19
- scribe, *JEN* 675:41; 676:34, 39; 677:38; 678:33, 38; 679:34; 681:28, 33; 685:31, 39; 690:28; 708:23; 709:30; 746:35, 38
- *JEN* 749:7, 9, 11, 13, 15, 32

TAYUKI

Ta-a-a-ú-ki, var. (3) *Ta-a-ú-ki*?

- s. of *A*-⌜*x*⌝-[....]-⌜x⌝, *JEN* 761:2, 9, 13, 14, 16, 18, 26, 43 (see also note to ll. 23-28)
- s. of *Ka*$_4$-*am-pá-tu*$_4$, (3) *JEN* 727:12
- s. of X-[....], *JEN* 745:26

TE....

Te-[....]

- f. of *Ḫu-ti-ip*-LUGAL, *JEN* 699:36

TEḪIP?-....

Te-ḫ[*i*?]-⌜*ip*?-*x*⌝[-*x*?]

- *JEN* 706:2

TEḪIP-APU

Te-ḫi-pa-pu, var. (2) *Te-ḫi-ip-a-pu*, (5) *Te-ḫi-ip-pa-pu*

- s. of *Eḫ-li-te-šup*, (2) *JEN* 697:19
- s. of *Ni-íḫ-ri-ya*, (2)(5) *JEN* 641:34, 45; (2) 644:28, 40?
- s. of [....]-*uz-zi*, br. of *Ku-uš-ši-ya* and *A-ri-pa-pu*, *JEN* 674:3, 11, 13, 15

TEḪIP-ŠARRI

Te-ḫi-ip-LUGAL

- f. of MI.NI-*ya* (=Ziliya), *JEN* 705:28

TEḪIP-TILLA

Te-ḫi-ip-til-la, var. (5; new) *Te-ḫi-ip-til-a*

- s. of *Ḫa-ši-ya*, *JEN* 687:27, 32; 700:21
- s. of *Pu-ḫi-še-en-ni*, *JEN* 674:4, 8, 9, 14, 17; 675:7, 12, 13, [19], 22; 676:3, 7, 8, 12, 14; 677:3, 7, 8, 13, 16; 680:3, 7, 8, 12, 14; 681:2, 7, 8, 12, 14; 682:7, 9, 12, 15, 20 (all these citations are placed under this rubric by analogy to *NPN*'s treatment of Teḫ. in *JEN* 187); 683:3, 8, 9, 15, [18]; 684:3, 8, 9, 14, 17; 685:2, 7, 8, 13, 15; 686:2, 6, 7, 12; 687:3, 7, 8; 688:4, 8, 11; 689:3, 8, 12, 16; 690:3, 8, 9, 13, 15; 691:2, 10, 11, 17; 692:3, 8 (as GN, no patr.), 9, 10, 16, 20; 693:3, 15, 16, 23, 48; 694:2, 9, 11, 15; 695:[3], 7; 698: 3, 11 (wr. *Še-ḫi-ip-til-la*), 12, 18; 699:15, 19, 24, 25, 27; 700:3, 7, 9; 701:3, 7, 8, 14; 702:3, 10, 11, 16, 19, 22; 703:7, 15, 16, 22, 25; 705:3, 7, 8; 706: 6, 10, 11, 22; 709:3, 10, 11, 16, 19; 710:2, 8, 9; 714:1, 7, 8; 715:3, [12], 14; 717:2, 6, 7 (see also name of a *dimtu*); 719:1, 9, 12, 13, 22?; 720:2, 7, 9, 14, 18; 721:2, 5, 7; 722:1, 4, 7 (as GN, = s. of P.), 9, 10, 15; 723:2, 8, 10, 15, 18; 724:2, 8, 9, 16; 725:1, 7, 9, 14;

726:2, 7, 8, 32; 727:2, 5, 8; 728:2, 6, 7; 729:2, [5], 7, 11; 730:2, 11, 14; 731:3, 5 (as GN, = s. of P.), 8 (twice), 12; 732:[2], 6, 7, 11, [14?]; 733: 3, 6, 8; 735:3; 736:3, 10, 11, 17, 20; 739:2, 8, 12, 13; 740:5, 9, 10, 19, 23; 741:[2], 9, 10, 14, 18, 20, 26; 742:3, 11, 14, 19, 24, [40]; 743:[2], 10, 11, 16, 19, 21; 744:2, 9, 10, 15, 20, 22; 745:2, 7, 9; 747:2, 8, 10, 14, 17; 748:2, 6, 8, 16; 749:1, 8 (twice), 12, 14, 17; 751:3, 8, 9, 14; 752:3, 9, 10, 16; 755:2, [8], 9; 758:3, 8, 9, 13; 759:3, 7, 8, 12; 760:2, 9, 12, 14; 761:3, 9, 10, 15, 17, 20, 22; 762:2; 763:3, 8, 9, 14, 17; 764:3, 8, 9, 13; 765:4, 10, 11, 17; 767:2, 8; 768:1, 4, 5; 769:2; 770:3, 11, 13, 18, [22], 32; 772:[1], 8, 10, 15, 18, 20; 773: 5, 12, 13, 16, 21; *Pu-ḫi-še-ni*, *JEN* 678:3, 7, 8, 11, 13; 679:2, 7, 8, 13, 16; 704:3, 7, 8, 14, 19; 718:2 (wr. *Ut-ḫi-ip-til-la*), 6, 8, 12, 15; 746:6, 11, 12, 18, 22

s. of *Te-ḫi-ip-til-la*, *JEN* 716:2, 7, 9, 15 (scribal error: s. of Puḫi-šenni is meant in l. 3)

f. of *En-na-ma-ti*, *JEN* 750:3

f. of *Ḫa-ta-pí-a-šu*, *JEN* 725:25, [34]

f. of *Šu-ur-te-eš-šu-up*, *JEN* 763:2?

f. of *Te-ḫi-ip-til-la*, *JEN* 716:3 (scribal error: Puḫi-šenni f. of Teḫip-tilla is meant in l. 3)

f.? of [....]⌜X X⌝, *JEN* 763:2?

name of a *dimtu*, (5) *JEN* 717:5; 745:5; 752:6 (*d. p. ša T.*); 768:4 (*d. p. ša T.*)

JEN 697:6, 7, 12; 708:3, [9], 12; 711:3, 4; 713:1, 5, 9; 737:4; 738:5, 7, [11?]; 753:[6], [7?], 10; 757:8, 12, 14; 766:3, 4, 9, 11

TEḪIYA

Te-ḫi-ya

s. of *A-ka$_4$-a-a*, *JEN* 684:20; 685:19; 689:19; 766:[14]

LÚ*sà-sí-in-nu*, s. of *A-ku-še-en-ni*, *JEN* 689:21

f. of *Ar-....*, *JEN* 733:18

f. of *Ḫi-in-ti-ya* and *Ḫi-in-<ti>-ya*, *JEN* 733:[15], 24

f. of *Mu-uš-te-ya*, *JEN* 715:29; 751:25

TEḪUP-ŠENNI

Te-ḫu-up-še-en-ni, var. (2) *Te-ḫu-up-še-ni*

s. of *Pí-ru*, *JEN* 688:19; *Pí-i-rù*, (2) 723:28, 34; *Pì-ru*, *JEN* 751:[24]

TENTEYA

Te-en-te-ya, var. (2) *Te$_9$-en-te$_9$-ya*

f. of *Ḫa-at-ra-ké*, (2) *JEN* 734:9

f. of *Zi-li-ya*, *JEN* 682:2; 769:9

TEŠUP-ERWI

Te-šup-er-wi, var. (2) *Te-šu-up-er-wi*

s. of *A-ri-ya*, (2) *JEN* 716:28, 38 (see note to *JEN* 716:3)

s. of *Ar-te-šup*, *JEN* 761:39

s. of *Šúk-ri-ya*, (2) *JEN* 686:26, 37; (2) 710:28 (see also T. s. of *A-ri-ya*); (2) 728:25, 36

TEŠŠUYA

Te-eš-šu-ya, var. (2) *Te-šu-ya*, (9; new) *Te-eš-šu-a-a*

s. of *Ki-in-ni-ya*, *JEN* 681:24

s. of *Wa-an-ti-ya*, (2) *JEN* 734:1

f. of *Er-wi*-LUGAL, *JEN* 752:34

f. of *Še-ḫi-rù*, *JEN* 700:20

f. of *Um-pí-ya*, *JEN* 741:33; 743:29; 744:29; 751:26; 772:37

f. of *Zi-il-te-eš-šup*, *JEN* 731:[17]; 759:17

mār šarri, *JEN* 710:13; 713:13; 753:19
(9) *JEN* 707:[1], 7, 12, 15, 16

TETUAE

var. (2) *Te-tu-a-e*
s. of *Zi-ri-ra* and *Zi-ri-ra-aš*, *JEN* 762:17, 22

TI....

Ti-x-[....], var. (2) ⸢*Ti*$_4$⸣/⸢*Ki*⸣*-x-*[....]
f. of *Ta-i-še-en-ni*, *JEN* 717:13
f. of [....?]*-x-pá-ya*, *JEN* 718:17

TINTIYA

Ti-in-ti-ya
s. of *A-ka*$_4$*-a-a*, *JEN* 674:34, 40; 675:38, 47; 676:31, 40; 677:32, 39; 678:31, 39; 679:32; 680:31, 40

TU....

Tù-⸢*x*⸣*-*[....]*-*⸢*x-x*⸣
s. of ⸢X X⸣[....], *JEN* 724:22

TU....NI?/RU?

TU-[....]*-ni*?/RU?
JEN 718:26

TUḪMIYA

var. (2) *Tù-uḫ-mì-ya*, (6) *Tu-uḫ*$_5$*-mì-ya*
f. of *Al-ki-te-šup*, *JEN* 720:25; (6) 733:[17?]
f. of *A-dá-še-ya*, (6) *JEN* 733:[16]
f. of *Ḫa-iš-*[*te-šup*], *JEN* 733:20?

TULPI-ŠENNI

Túl-pí-še-en-ni, var. (3) *Tù-ul-pí-še-en-ni*, (6; new) *Tù-ul-pí-še-ni*
s. of *E-na-ma-ti*, (3) *JEN* 734:15
s. of *Iš-ka*$_4$*-ar-pa*, *JEN* 724:27
s. of *Tù-ra-ri*, (1)(6) *JEN* 716:1, 7, 10, 12, 14, 17

TUNTUYA

Tù-un-tù-ya
f. of *Šúk-ra-pu*, *JEN* 674:28; 675:32; 676:25; 677:26; 678:25; 679:26; 680:25

TUPK-APU

Tup-ka$_4$*-a-pu*
s. of *Ar?....*, *JEN* 677:2, 10, 12, 14

TUPKI-TILLA

Tup-ki-til-la, var. (2) *Tup*$^{-up}$*-ki-til-la*
s. of *It-ḫi-til-la*, *JEN* 718:16
(2) *JEN* 730:1, 7, 10, 15

TUPKIYA

Tup-ki-ya, var. (3) *Tù-up-ki-ya*, (4) *Tu-up-ki-ya*
s. of *Kàr-ze-ya*, *JEN* 736:21; 751:19; *Kar-ze-ya*, *JEN* 761:29
f. of *A-ri-ké-el-pè*, (3) *JEN* 769:[14]
f. of *It-ḫi-ip-til-la*, *JEN* 700:17, 32; 705:[17]; *Ut-ḫi-ip-til-la*, *JEN* 686:19; 687:20; (4) 702:24; 710:20;716:23; 720:[20?]; 728:18
f. of *Zi-li-ya*, (4) *JEN* 750:37

TURARI

Tù-ra-ri, var. (2) *Tu-ra-ri*
s. of *A-ka*$_4$*-a-a*, br. of *Ki-pá-a-a*, (2) *JEN* 750:35, 43 (43: or s. of Emuya)
s. of *E-mu-ya*, *JEN* 750:32, 43 (43: or s. of Akaya)
s. of *Pu-*⸢*x*⸣*-*[....], (2) *JEN* 768:2, 6, 21, 22
f. of *A-kip-til-la*, *JEN* 686:16; 687:18; 700:23, 31; (2) 702:27; 705:[15]; (2) 707:27; 710:17; 716:20; 728:15
f. of *A-ta-a-a*, *JEN* 721:18, 24; 726:20, [27]

f. of *Ša-am-ḫa-ri*, (2) *JEN* 757:28
f. of *Ša-tù-ša*, *JEN* 686:18; 710:19; 716:22; *Ša-tu-ša*, (2) *JEN* 702:23; 720:19; 728:17
f. of *Še-né-ya*, (2) *JEN* 676:2
f. of *Še-eš-wi-ka*$_4$, *JEN* 722:4
f. of *Túl-pí-še-en-ni* and *Tù-ul-pí-še-ni* , *JEN* 716:2
f. of *Wa-an-ti*$_4$*-pu-ku-ur* and *Wa-an-ti*$_4$*-pu-kùr*, *JEN* 722:4
f. of *Wa-an-ti-iš-še*, *JEN* 746:1
f. of [....]-⌜*x*⌝-*ú-ša*, *JEN* 719:29
itinnu (=ŠITIM), (2) *JEN* 729:22

TURI-KINTAR

Tù-ri-ki-in-tar
f. of *A-ri-ḫa-ma-an-na*, *JEN* 725:28

TUR-MARTI

Túr-mar-ti, var. (2) *Tu-ur-mar-ti*
f. of *Wa-an-ti-ya*, (1)(2) *JEN* 688:3, 23

DÛR-ŠARRU

BÀD-LUGAL, var. (2) *Du-ur-*LUGAL, (3) *Du-ur-šar-ru*, (9; new) BÀD-LUGAL-[*r*]*u*?
f. of *Ta-a-a*, *JEN* 769:12
f. of ÌR-DINGIR-*šu*, (9) (1) *JEN* 683:29, 35; 691:31; 704:22; 717:10; (3) *JEN* 727:10, 20; 767:13; (2) 768:10

TUR-ŠENNI

Túr-še-en-ni, var. (3) *Tu-ur-še-en-ni*, (4) *Túr-še-ni*
s. of *A-ri-pa-ap-ni*, (4 both) *JEN* 685:22, 37; (1) or (4) 766:[17]
s. of *Ḫa-ma-an-na*, (3) *JEN* 692:29; 752:26
s. of *Zi-li-ip-ka*$_4$*-na-ri*, *JEN* 703:4, 13, [20]

f. of *Be-li-ya*, *JEN* 763:32 (see note to *JEN* 763:32)

TURRU

Tu-ur-ru
f. of *Eḫ-li-ip-*LUGAL, *JEN* 745:2

U

U-[X?]-KUR-X

Ú-[....?]-*kùr*!-⌜X⌝
s. of [....]-⌜*a*⌝?, *JEN* 723:23

ỤARSIA

Ú-ar-si-a
f. of *Ma-ti-ya*, *JEN* 748:26

UKKAYA

Uk-ka$_4$*-a-a*
s. of [....]-x-x-[....], *JEN* 744:36

UKIN-ZAḪ

Ú-ki-in-za-aḫ
name of a *dimtu*, *JEN* 698:6, 7 (no ^{m})

UKUR-ATAL

Ú-kùr-a-tal
s. of *Ša-*[....], *JEN* 742:28, 44

UKUR-ŠARRI

*Ú-kùr-*LUGAL
s. of *A-ri-ya*, *JEN* 698:33

UKUYA

Ú-ku-ya
s. of *Šu-pa-a-a*, *JEN* 746:33

ULMI-ATAL

Ul-mi-a-tal
s. of *Šúk-ri-ya*, *JEN* 757:26, 31

ULŪLIYA

Ú-lu-li-ya

name of a *dimtu*, *JEN* 694:6 (probably); 736:8; 742:9; 744:7 (no ^{m}); 770:9 (no ^{m})

ULLUYA

Ul-lu-ya

f. of *Ḫu-ti-ya*, *JEN* 685:29

UMPIN-API

Um-pí-na-pí

name of a *dimtu*, *JEN* 703:12

UMPIYA

Um-pí-ya

s. of *Al-pu-ya*, *JEN* 723:33

s. of *Ar-ša-an-ta*, *JEN* 693:36

s. of *Ki-pè-er-ḫa*, *JEN* 703:40; 756:12; br. of *Na-ḫi-iš-še-ya*, *JEN* 747:28

s. of *Ma-li-ya*, *JEN* 694:28

s. of *Te-eš-šu-ya*, *JEN* 741:33, 44; 743:29, 42; 744:29; 751:26, 33; 772:37

s. of *Ú-zi-ya*, *JEN* 749:27?

UNAP-ŠE

Ú-na-ap-še

s. of *A-ḫi-ya*, *JEN* 702:28

(name of a town; see GN list)

UNAP-ŠENNI

var. (2; corrects *NPN*'s 2) *Ú-náp-še-en-ni*, (6) *Ú-na-áp-še-en-ni*

s. of *Ar-nu-ur-ḫe*, (6)(2) *JEN* 747:19, 35

UNAP-TAE

Ú-na-ap-ta-e, var. (3) *Ú-náp-ta-e*

s. of *Na-a-a*, (1)(3) *JEN* 748:3, 6, [8], 13, [29]

s. of *Ni-ir-ḫi-te-eš-šu-up*, br. of *Ḫu-ti-ip-til-la*, *JEN* 758:20, 31; s. of *Ni-iḫ-ri-te-eš-šu-up*, br. of *Ḫu-ti-ip-til-la*, *JEN* 763:29, 36

s. of *Še-er-wi*, *JEN* 730:22 (wr. *Ú-na-ap-ta-*<*e*>)

s. of *Ši-in$_4$ti-ya*, br. of [*Ar-te-šup*], *JEN* 734:12

f. of *Tar-mi-ya*, *JEN* 682:19; 706:21; (3) 711:10; 738:4; 740:22; 753:18

JEN 764:21; 765:29

UN-TEŠUP

Un-te-šup

f. of *Ké-li-ya*, *JEN* 699:21

UNNUKI

var. (2) *Un-nu-ú-ki*

s. of *Ar-til-la*, (2) *JEN* 763:24

UR?....

Ur?-....

s. of *Wa-an-ti-....*, *JEN* 675:[6], [16]

URḪI-TEŠUP

Ur-ḫi-te-šup

s. of *Kál-ma-aš-šu-ra*, *JEN* 699:42

URḪIYA

Ur-ḫi-ya

s. of *Ar-ru-um-pa* and *Ar-ru-pa*, *JEN* 716:33, 35; *Ar-ru-pa*, *JEN* 728:31; *A-ru-um-pa$_{12}$*, *JEN* 707:20, 23; *A-ru-pa$_{12}$*, *JEN* 710:35, 36; *A-ru-pa$_{12}$* and *Ar-ru-*<*pa$_{12}$*?>, *JEN* 686:33, 34

s. *Ar-ša-tù-ya*, *JEN* 674:25; 675:30; 676:23; *Ar-ša-tù-a*, *JEN* 677:24; 678:22; 679:24; 680:23

scribe, s. of *Ke-li-ya*, *JEN* 747:30

s. of *Še-ka$_4$-rù*, *JEN* 693:27, 50; 699:43; 703:30, 41; 709:22, 36; 751:30; 758:[18], 30; 763:20, 35;

765:23; [*Še*?]-*ka*?-*ru*, *JEN* 770:[26?]
s. of *Ú-ṣú-ur-mé*, *JEN* 750:29
f. of *Mu-uš-te*-AŠ and *Mu-uš-te-šup*, *JEN* 733:12, 25
JEN 699:49

ŲUR-ZAZZI?

Ú-ur-za-az?-zi
JEN 765:9

UTA-MANSI

^{d}UTU-ma.an.sì
f. of *Ḫu-ti-ya*, *JEN* 701:26

UTA-ANDUL

^{d}*Uta-an-dùl*
scribe, s. of *Ta-a-a*, *JEN* 742:36, 45; 752:36, 40

UTḪAP-....

Ut-ḫa-[*ap-*....]
JEN 773:24

UTḪAP-TAE

Ut-ḫap-ta-e, var. (2) *Ut-ḫa-ap-ta-e*, (4) *Ut-ḫáp-ta-e*
s. of *Zi-ké*, *JEN* 681:21; (4) 693:28; (2) 741:37; (2) 744:32; (4) 751:27; *Zi-ke*, *JEN* 715:20
JEN 737:16

Ut-ḫi-ip-til-la, see Itḫip-tilla

(UTḪUŠŠE see GN list)

UZIYA

Ú-zi-ya
s. of *Pu-ḫi-ya*, *JEN* 695:10, 21
f. of [*Um*?-*pí*?]-*ya*, *JEN* 749:27

UṢUR-MÊ

var. (2) *Ú-ṣú-ur-mé*
f. of *Ur-ḫi-ya*, (2) *JEN* 750:29

W

WA....

WA-[....]
f. of [*Ḫ*]*u*?-*ti-ya*, *JEN* 752:22

WAQAR-BÊLI

Wa-qar-EN
s. of *It-ḫi-iš-ta*, *JEN* 752:35, 39
scribe, s. of *Taya*, the scribe, *JEN* 768:19

WANTI....

Wa-an-ti-....
f. of *Ur*?-...., *JEN* 675:6

WANTI-MUŠA

Wa-an-ti-mu-ša, var. (3) *Wa-ti*$_4$-*mu-ša*
s. of *Na-ik-ké-mar*, *JEN* 743:23, 37; 761:32; *Na-i-ké-mar*, *JEN* 772:26
f. of *A-ta-a-a*, (3) *JEN* 687:25, 31

WANTIP?-....

Wa-[*an*?-*t*]*i-i*[*p-*....]
JEN 715:11

WANTIP-UKUR

Wa-an-ti$_4$-*pu-ku-ur*, var. (2) *Wa-an-ti*$_4$-*pu-kùr*
s. of *Tù-ra-ri*, br. of *Še-eš-wi-ka*$_4$, (1)(2) *JEN* 722:3, 12, 18

WANTIŠ-ŠE

Wa-an-ti-iš-še
s. of *Tù-ra-ri*, *JEN* 746:1, 13

WANTIYA

Wa-an-ti-ya, var. (2) *Wa-an-ti*$_4$-*ya*
s. of *Ḫa-ip*-LUGAL, (2) *JEN* 700:24
s. of *Ki-*⌜*x*⌝-[....], *JEN* 767:11

s. of *Ku-uš-ši-ya*, *JEN* 689:23
s. of *Na-ḫi-a-šu*, *JEN* 674:20; 675:25; 676:18; 677:19; 678:17; 679:19; 680:18; 774:11
s. of *Pur-ni-a*, br. of *Ḫa-šu-ar*, (2) *JEN* 765:2, 6, 13, 15, 19
s. of *Šu-pu-uk-ka*$_4$, *JEN* 760:16, 24
s. of *Tu-ur-mar-ti* and *Túr-mar-ti*, *JEN* 688:3 [first], 7, 9, 23 [second]
f. of *A-mi-ni-pè*, (2) *JEN* 719:6
f. of *Ta-i-til-la*, *JEN* 692:2
f. of *Te-šu-ya*, *JEN* 734:2
JEN 701:21

WARATTEYA

var. (4) *Wa-ra-at-te-ya*, (13; new)
Wa-ra-at-te-e
s. of [....]-*ya*?/-*e*?, (4)(13) *JEN* 693:2, 14, [18], 20, 22, 24

WARD-ILIŠU

ÌR-DINGIR-*šu*
s. of BÀD-LUGAL (=Dûr-šarru), *JEN* 691:31; 704:22, 30; 717:10; 767:13; *Du-ur-šar-ru*, *JEN* 727:10, 20; BÀD-LUGAL -*ru*? and BÀD-LUGAL, *JEN* 683:29, 35; *Du-ur*-LUGAL, *JEN* 768:10
JEN 738:18; 755:13

WAŠ?....

WA-*aš*?-[....]
JEN 754:2

WATWA

Wa-at-wa
s. of ^{d}XXX-*na*-⌜*x*⌝-[(*x*-)*a-nu*?], *JEN* 721:12; ⌜*Sí*⌝?-[*in*?-*n*]*a*?-*a-nu*?, *JEN* 726:13

WIRRAḪḪE

Wi-ir-ra-aḫ-ḫe, var. (3) *Wi-ra-aḫ-ḫe*
s. of *At-ti*$_4$-*la-am-mu*, (3) *JEN* 721:14; 726:16
s. of *Ḫa*-[....], *JEN* 702:32, 38

WUNNUKIYA

Wu-un-nu-ki-ya
s. of *Tar-mi-ya*, *JEN* 709:24

WUR-TURUK

Wu-ur-tù-ru-uk
s. of *Ma-li-ya*, *JEN* 686:17; 707:28; 710:18; 716:21; 728:16

Z

ṢALMU

Ṣa-al-mu
s. of *A-a-ba-aš*, *JEN* 747:21

ZAZIYA

Za-zi-ya
s. of [*Ḫa*?-*ši*?-*pa*?-*a*?-*pu*?], *JEN* 726:1, 7, 9, 10, 31
f. of *Mi-na-aš-šúk*, *JEN* 699:10

ZENNI

Ze-en-ni
s. of *Ḫa-ma-an-na*, *JEN* 703:27; [*Ḫa*?-*ma*?-*an*?-*na*?], *JEN* 750:30; [*Ḫa*?-*ma*?-*an*?]-*na*?, *JEN* 770:[24?]

ZETU

Ze-e-tu$_4$
s. of *I-ri-iš-a-bi*, *JEN* 693:35; *I-ri-ša-bi*, *JEN* 769:7, 18

ZI?....

Zi?-[....]
name of a *dimtu*, *JEN* 746:10

ZI?....AYA

Z[i]/K[é]-....-a-a

f. of *E-te-eš-še-ni*, *JEN* 675:5

ZIKAYA

Zi-ka$_4$-a-a, var. (2) *Zi-kà-a-a*, (3) *Zi-ka-a-a*

s. of *El-ḫi-ip*-LUGAL, *JEN* 688:14; 693:31, 42; 723:27; *Éḫ-li-ip*-LUGAL, (2) *JEN* 729:21; *Eḫ-li-<ip>*-LUGAL, (3) *JEN* 762:18; *Él-ḫi-ip*-LUGAL, (2) *JEN* 768:12

s. of *Ku-tùk-ka$_4$*, *JEN* 703:28; *Ku?-tùk?-ka$_4$*, *JEN* 770:25?

f. of *Ak-ku-le-en-ni*, *JEN* 747:29

JEN 691:27, 33

ZIKE

Zi-ké, var. (2) *Zi-ke*

s. of *Ak-ku-ya*, br. of *Na-ḫi-šal-mu*, *JEN* 737:1, 18 (probably the same person)

s. of *Ḫu-pa-pè-e*, *JEN* 724:29

s. of *Iš-ka$_4$-ar-pa*, *JEN* 724:24, 32

s. of *Ka$_4$-ku-zi*, *JEN* 769:11

s. of *Še-ka$_4$-rù*, *JEN* 693:32; (2) 715:24

s. of *Ta-mar-ta-e*, br. of *Ḫu-ti-ya*, [*Ar-te-ya*], [*A-ta-a-a*], and *Ki-pí-ya*, *JEN* 699:3

f. of *Ut-ḫap-ta-e*, *JEN* 681:21; (2) 715:20; *Ut-ḫa-ap-ta-e*, *JEN* 741:37; 744:32; *Ut-ḫáp-ta-e*, *JEN* 693:28; 751:27

name of a *dimtu*, *JEN* 746:10 (see second note to this line)

ZILI-ḪARPA

var. (2) *Zi-li-ḫar-pè*

f. of *Ḫu-ti-ya*, (2) *JEN* 699:44

ZILIP-APU

var. (2) *Zi-li-ip-a-pu*, (3) *Zi-li-pa-a-pu*

s. of *Ip-ša-ḫa-lu*, (2) see note to *JEN* 703:5-6

s. of *Na-al-tù-ya*, *JEN* 719:33, 38

ZILIP-KANARI

Zi-li-ip-ka$_4$-na-ri

f. of *Túr-še-en-ni*, *JEN* 703:4

ZILIP-ŠARRI

Zi-li-ip-LUGAL

s. of *E-en-na-mil-ki*, *JEN* 687:29, 34

ZILIP-TILLA

Zi-li-ip-til-la

s. of *E[n-....]*, *JEN* 697:26?

ZILIYA

Zi-li-ya, var. (2) MI.NI-*ya*

s. of *A-ri-ip-a-pu*, *JEN* 774:12

s. of *Ḫé-el?-la-kál?*, *JEN* 721:13; *Ḫé-el?-la-kál* 726:15

s. of *Te-ḫi-ip*-LUGAL, (2) *JEN* 705:28

s. of *Te-en-te-ya*, *JEN* 682:1; 769:9

s. of *Tu-up-ki-ya*, (1)(2) *JEN* 750:37, 42?

f. of *A-ri-ka$_4$-ma-ri*, *JEN* 756:14

f. of *Še-eḫ-li-ya*, *JEN* 725:26

ZIL-TEŠUP

var. (3) *Zi-il-te-eš-šup*, (5) *Zi-il$_5$-te-eš-šu-up*

s. of *Ar-te-eš-šu-up*, (5) *JEN* 735:14

s. of *Te-eš-šu-ya*, (3) *JEN* 731:17; (3) 759:17

ZIL-TEYA

Zi-il-te-ya, var. (4) *Zi-il$_5$-te-ya*

s. of *Ta-ú-ka$_4$*, *JEN* 701:24; (4) 758:19; (4) 763:21

sassukku, s. of *Ta-ú-ka$_4$*, *JEN* 739:21, 24; 759:20, 23

sassukku, (4) *JEN* 718:22, 34; 731:23

ZINI

Zi-ni
JEN 737:20

ZINIYA

Zi-ni-ya, var. (2) ^{d}XXX-*né-e*
f. of ^{d}*Iškur-an-dùl*, *JEN* 702:37; (2) 743:33; 750:40; (2) 772:39

ZIRRI

Zi-ir-ri
f. of *Mu-uš-te-ya*, *JEN* 755:12

ZIRIRAŠ

Zi-ri-ra, var. (2) *Zi-ri-ra-aš*
f. of *Te-tu-a-e*, (1)(2), *JEN* 762:17 (1), 23 (2)
f. of [...-*y*]*a*?/-⸢*e*⸣?, *JEN* 691:29 (wr. *Zi*!(=GI)-*ri-ra*)

ZIZZIYA

Zi-zi-ya
s. of *Pur-na-pu*, *JEN* 694:23; 723:21

ZUME

Zu-me, var. (2) *Zu-ú-me*, (4) *Zu-mé*
f. of *Ḫé-šal-la*, (2) *JEN* 699:37; *Ḫe-šal-la*, 722:27; 723:38; 724:19; *Ḫe-ša-al-la*, *JEN* 692:28; (2) 745:22; *Ḫé-ša-al-la*, *JEN* 715:22
f. of ŠU-^{d}IM, *JEN* 695:15; 697:23; (2) 699:34; *Gi*$_5$-*mi-la-dá*, *JEN* 694:32; *Gi*$_5$-*mil-li*-^{d}IM, (2) *JEN* 729:19; *Gi-mil*-^{d}IM, (4) *JEN* 768:18
f. of *Še-éḫ-li-ya*, *JEN* 748:[24]

ZUZU

Zu-zu
f. of *Še-eḫ-li-ya*, *JEN* 683:27

GEOGRAPHICAL NAMES

In this index, where geographical names correspond to personal names, *NPN* forms are followed. Otherwise, forms followed by Fisher (1959) are adopted for the most part.

This list does not include land/fields (i.e., A.ŠÀ(.MEŠ) identified by personal name only, for example, "the land of Ar-tešup [son of] Ipša-ḫalu" (*JEN* 747:6).

dimtus

AKAWATIL

A-ka_4*-wa-til*

JEN 703:10; 709:7; 736:7; 743:5-6; 751:7; 761:7; 770:7

ANITA

var. (2) *A-ni-i-ta*

JEN 697:9

APLIYA

Ap-li-a

JEN 709:6

ARIK-KANI

var. (2) *A-ri-*ka_4*-ni*

Implied in note to *JEN* 755:5-6.

AWĪLU

See second note to *JEN* 746:10.

ENIYA

E-ni-ya

JEN 742:7

INB-ILIŠU

Im-bi-li-šu

JEN 743:7

(IPḪUŠŠE: see note to *JEN* 743:8)

KI-X-....-X-....-X-MA?

KI-⸢*x*⸣-[....]-⸢x⸣-[....]-⸢*x*⸣-*ma*?

JEN 773:9

KIPANTIL

var. (2) *Ki-pá-an-til*

(2) *JEN* 727:4

KIP-TEŠUP

Kip-te-šup

JEN 706:9

KUNATU

Ku-na-tù

JEN 674:7; 679:5

MAḪAZI

ma-ḫa-ZI

JEN 771:5, 11 (discussion in note to 771:5)

NANIYA

Na-ni-ya

JEN 683:6

PIRŠANNI

pí-ir-ša-an-ni

JEN 692:5-6

PIRŠANNI ŠA TEḪIP-TILLA

pí-ir-ša-an-ni ša ^{m}*Te-ḫi-ip-til-la*

JEN 752:5-6; 768:3-4

SULAE

Sú-la-e

JEN 677:6; 678:5

ŠAKRUŠŠE

Šá-ak-ru-uš-še, var. (3; new) *Ša-ak-ru-uš-še*, (4; new) *Šá-ak-ru-uš-še-e*, (5; new) *Šá-ar-ku-uš-še*$_{20}$

(3) *JEN* 739:5?; (4) 758:7 (with ^{m}); (5) 763:6; 764:7 (with ^{m}); 765:8 (with ^{m})

ŠULMIYA

Šu-ul-mi-ya

JEN 675:10?; 676:6; 680:6

ŠUMAŠŠAWALLI

Šu-ma-ša-wa-al-li, var. (2) *Šu-ma-ša-wa-al-ḫi*

JEN 710:1, 5 (both without *dimtu*); (2) 746:9

ŠURKUM-ATAL

Šur-ku-ma-tal

JEN 700:5?

TANNA-TAŠŠI

Ta-an-na-taš-ši

JEN 681:6; 683:7 (probably a *dimtu* name)

TEḪIP-TILLA

Te-ḫi-ip-til-la, var. (5; new) *Te-ḫi-ip-til-a*

(5) *JEN* 717:4-5; 744:5

UKIN-ZAḪ

Ú-ki-in-za-aḫ

JEN 698:6, 7

ULŪLIYA

Ú-lu-li-ya

JEN 694:6 (probably); 736:8; 742:9; 744:7; 770:9

UMPIN-API

Um-pí-na-pí

JEN 703:12

UT?-ḪUŠŠE

UD-*ḫu-uš-še*

JEN 743:8

ZI?....

Zi?-[....]

JEN 746:10

ZIKE

See second note to *JEN* 746:10.

....-X-TAYA

[....?]-˹*x*˺-*ta-ya*

JEN 751:6

....?-X-....-X-UR?-ŠENNI

[....?]-˹x˺-[....]-˹*x*˺-*ur?-še-en-ni*

JEN 772:7

TOWNS

AKIP-APU

var. (2) *A-ki-pá-pu*, (3) *A-ki-pa-pu*

(2) or (3) *JEN* 757:3 [poss.: [*-wa*]]; (3) 761:8 [poss.: [*-wa*]]

ANZUGALLI

var. (2) *An-zu-gal-li*, (3) *An-zu-gal-lì*

(2) *JEN* 722:7; (3) 740:8

APENA

var. (2) *A-pè-na-aš*

(2) *JEN* 674:37, 41; (2) 675:11, 48 (twice); (2) 676:6, 34, 41 (twice); (2) 677:6, 40; (2) 678:6, 34, 40 (twice); (2) 679:6, 41; (2) 680:6, 34, 41 (twice); (2) 684:29?; (2) 685:30; (2) ; 691:9

ARRAPḪE

Ar-ra-ap-ḫe

JEN 726:5

ARTIḪI

Ar-ti$_4$-ḫi, var. (2) *Ar-ti-ḫi*

JEN 687:6; 700:6; (2) 702:5; 710:7

ATAKKAL

var. (2) *A-ta-kal*

(2) *JEN* 738:2

DÛR-UBLA

Du-ru-ub-la

JEN 705:6

ERIŠPA

E-ri-iš-pa

JEN 719:11

ḪULUMENI

Ḫu-lu-me-ni-wa

JEN 704:6

ḪURĀṢINA-ṢEḪRU

var. (2) *Ḫu-ra-ṣí-na-*TUR

(2) *JEN* 735:6

KARANNA ŠA PUḪI-ŠENNI

Kà-ra-an-na ša Pu-ḫi-še-en-ni

JEN 733:7

LUPTI

var. (2) *Lu-up-ti$_4$*

JEN 716:6

NAŠMUR

var. (2) *Na-aš-mur*

JEN 718:5

NUḪ....

Nu-uḫ-[....]

JEN 724:5 (see also NUZI)

NUZI

Nu-zi

JEN 674:27; 678:24; 682:6?; 688:2; 693:13, 47; see note to 724:5; 730:5; 737:5?; 740:8; 746:8; 748:5, [7]; 750:5; 753:5?; 756:10; 762:5

PURULLI

var. (2) *Pu-ru-li-wa*, (3) *Pu-ru-ul-li-wa*

(3) *JEN* 760:6; (2) 767:6

ŠININA

Ši-ni-na

JEN 684:7; 685:6; 766:2, 20

TARKULLI

var. (2) *Ta-ar-ku-ul-li*

JEN 699:14

TURŠA

Tù-ur-[*šá*?/*ša*?] [(3) or (6)]

(3) or (6) *JEN* 741:6

ULAMME

Ú-lam-me

JEN 693:12; 714:6

UNAP-ŠE

var. (2) *Ú-na-ap-še-wa*, (5) *Ú-nap-še-wa*, (6) *Ú-náp-še-wa*, (7;new) *Ú-náp-še*

(6) *JEN* 694:8; (5) 703:6; (5) 709:8; (2) 736:5; 747:5; (2) 749:7; (2) 756:18; (2) 757:6 ([-*wa*?]); (2) 761:6; (7) 770:8

X....

⌜X⌝-[....]

JEN 725:6

CANALS

AKIP-TAŠENNI

A-kip-ta-še-en-ni

JEN 692:6-7

KILLI

Ki-il-li

JEN 707:[6]

NIRAŠŠI

Ni-ra-aš-ši, var. (2) *Ni-ri-iš-ši*

JEN 699:11; (note to *JEN* 728:4); (2) 753:4

OTHER

MALAŠU (stream; also a *dimtu*: *EN*, 9/1, 183:5)

(discussion: notes to *JEN* 698:7, 8; cf. note to *JEN* 723:1)

YARRU (watercourse?; road?)

I-a-ar-ru

JEN 686:5; 720:5

ZILIP-KEWAR(?), (Tīl?)

Zi-li-ip!-ke-már

JEN 710:7

ZILURKI(?), (Tīl?)

Zi-lu-ur-k[*i*]?, var. (2) *Zi-li-*UR-*ki+i*

JEN 687:6; 710:7

OCCUPATIONS

The following tasks are omitted from this list as *ad hoc* functions, not true occupations: *šibu*: *JEN* 718, 739, 758, 763, 773; *mušelmû* and *lāmû*: *passim*; and, therefore, *peniḫuru*: *JEN* 763 (cf. *JEN* 49, 836).

dayyānu

JEN 682:4 (cf. ll. 18-19 for I.Ds: Tarmi-tešup s. of Eḫli-tešup and Tarmiya s. of Unap-tae); 706:4 (cf. ll. 20-21, after 22 for I.D.s of T. s. E. & T. s. U.); (711:10-13 would apply if "*dayyānu*" were preserved at start of text); 713:4 (cf. ll. 10-14 for I.D.s:...-tešup(?), ...ir-..., Ḫaši-..., Teššuya son of the king); 740:3 (cf. ll. 22, 25-26 for I.D.s of T. s. U. & T. s. E.); 753:[2] (cf. ll. 18-21 for I.D.s of T. s. U.,Teššuya s. king; T. s. E.)

ḫalṣuḫlu

JEN 682:3 (cf. ll. 20-21 for I.D.: Teḫip-tilla s. of Puḫi-šenni); 706:3 (cf. l. 22 for I.D.: T. s. P.); 740:3 (cf. ll. 23-24 for I.D.: T. s. P.)

ḫazannu (or the like)

Itḫ-apu s. of *Še-ri-*⌜*x*⌝-[(?)], *JEN* 760:19,27

Kušši-ḫarpe, *JEN* 693:46-47

itinnu (=ŠITIM)

Turari, *JEN* 729:22

(*mār šarri* not included. See, in name list, Partasua and Teššuya.)

naggāru

Ariya, *JEN* 722:8

nuaru

Mannu-kī-bêliya, *JEN* 735:24-25

Punniya, *JEN* 734:19

n. ša LUGAL, Igārš(u)-êmi(d), *JEN* 735:20-21

sasinnu

Teḫiya s. of Aku-šenni, *JEN* 689:21-22

sassukku

Zil-teya son of Tauka, *JEN* 739:21-22, 24-25; 759:20,23-24

Zil-teya, *JEN* 718:22; 731:23

ṭupšarru

Ak(ka)dingirra, *JEN* 740:21

Artašenni s. of Apil-sin, *JEN* 729:24-25, 26; 748: 27-28,32

Artašenni, *JEN* 730:25, 26; 762:20

Ar-Tešup s. of Taya, *JEN* 745:25, 29

[E?-/Še?-ḫe?-el?]-tešup s. of Sin-ibnī, *JEN* 749:28; [E?-/

Še?-ḫe]-el-tešup 757:29; (see note to *JEN* 761:41)
Enna-mati, *JEN* 758:35 (*JEN* 763:39 [no DUB.SAR]; see note to this line); (764:22 [no DUB.SAR]); (765:31 [no DUB. SAR]; see note to *JEN* 765:30)
Erwi-šarri, *JEN* 731:20-21? (see note to *JEN* 718:22); 759:25
Ḫamanna, *JEN* 760:23
Ḫutiya s. of ᵈUTU-ma.an.sì, *JEN* 701:26 (, 27: unlikely)
Ila-nîšū s. of Sin-napšir, *JEN* 691:30, 35
Iluya, *JEN* 741:40, 46; 744:37, [41]
Iniya s. of Kiannipu, *JEN* 699:52-53 ("ŠU")
Iškur-andul s. of Ziniya, *JEN* 702:36-37, 41; 743:33, 43; 750:39-40; 772:38-39
Itḫ-apiḫe s. of Taya, *JEN* 686:31,(38); 694:34, 40; 710:32; 716:34; 720:23; 721:22-23, 27; 722:30 (patronymic possible), 37; 723:31; 725:32, 36; 726:24-25; (see note to *JEN* 767:15); (re 770, see Lacheman and Maidman [1989, 32, n. 26])
Itḫ-apiḫe, *JEN* 687:30, 35; 700:27, [33]; 705:31 (see also note to *JEN* 705:26); 711:14; 714:24; 717:19; 719:35; 724:25, 35; 769:16
Nanna-mansi s. of Taya, *JEN* 715:32-33, 37?
Naniya s. of Lu-Nanna, *JEN* 733:22, 23
Balṭu-kašid s. of Apil-sin, *JEN* 682:17
Balṭu-kašid, *JEN* 735:22-23; 755:11; 774:17-18
Sin-iqîša, *JEN* 698:26
[E?-/Še?-ḫe?-el?]-tešup s. of Sin-ibnī, *JEN* 749:28
Šamaš-ilu-ina-mâti?, *JEN* 718:31
Šumu-libšī s. of Taya, *JEN* 694:29, 40; 751:31, 36
Taya s. of Apil-sin, *JEN* 674:36; 680:33, 39; 683:34, 39;684:30, 35; 688:22, 25; 689:27; 692:32, 34; 693:39, 43; 695:19, 22-23; 696:[20], 21; 697:24, 30; 703:36, 45; 704:28; 756:9; 766:21([T.] s. of A.); (re 770, see Lacheman and Maidman [1989, 32, n. 26])
Taya f. of Waqar-bêli, *JEN* 768:19
Taya, *JEN* 675:41; 676:34, 39; 677:38; 678:33, 38; 679:34; 681:28, 33; 685:31, 39; 690:28; 708:23; 709:30; 746:35, 38
Urḫiya s. of Keliya, *JEN* 747:30
Uta-andul s. of Taya, JEN 742:36, 45; 752:36, 40
Waqar-bêli s. of Taya, *JEN* 768:19

wardu

Antaya (slave of Teḫip-tilla), *JEN* 737:3-4
Abutteya (into slavehood to Teḫip-tilla), *JEN* 769:2-3, 4

TERMS TREATED

All terms noted in this list are treated in the notes, albeit sometimes briefly. (Yet, mere reference in the notes to the dictionaries or to Maidman [1976] is not sufficient for a term to appear in this list.) Since not all significant terms have been treated in the notes, neither do they appear in this list. On the other hand, notes on two *topics* (rather than terms) have been included: "scribal errors and peculiarities" and "seal usage."

All references to notes to the lines and citations are given only for main explanatory entries. Cross-references are usually ignored.

alupatḫi
JEN 687:6 (first note)

A.ŠÀ (*eqlu*)
JEN 715:5; 757:13

awiḫaru
JEN 675:9

BÁN
JEN 705:8

ellet
JEN 698:5

erēšu
JEN 688:10

GIŠ.ŠAR
JEN 715:5

ḫararnu
JEN 764:5 (second note)

"ipḫušše"
JEN 743:8

irbu
JEN 746:23-24

kurkizzi-... .
JEN 728:4, 5 (third note)

KÙ.BABBAR (*kaspu*)
JEN 687:23; 715:27; 772:33

kumānu
JEN 764:5 (second note)

-ma
JEN 742:2

*maḫa*ZI
JEN 771:5

ma-QA-*ḫu*
JEN 757:4

nabalkutu
JEN 760:11-12

"Niraššī"
JEN 699:11

paiḫu
JEN 715:5. *NB*: In *JEN* 816 this type of land is built up.

pāqirāna
JEN 759:10; 768: comments

peniḫuru
JEN 763:34
qinnatu
JEN 700:5
qīštu (as a text type)
JEN 688: comments
sassukku
JEN 718:22
(scribal errors and peculiarities)
JEN 675:29, 45-48; 676:7, 34; 679:36; 682:2 (second note); 684:25; 685:33; 686:5-6, 32, 33-34; 692:13, 14-15; 693: comments; 694:29; 698:39; 699: comments, 1 (second note), 2, 3 (second note), 4 (second note); 701:9; 702:5, 6; 703:6; 704:2; 705:8 (first note), 12; 707:6; 708:5 (first note), 6-7, 9 (second note), 20, 24 (both notes); 710:7 (first note); 714:11 (first note); 715:16-17, 32 (first note); 716:3; 717:1, 4-5, 8-9; 718: comments, 12; 719:21; 720: comments, 17-19; 721:28-29; 722: comments, 6-7, 18 (both notes), 30 (second note), 33 (second note); 724:5; 725:29-32; 726:21 (first note), 28, 29 (second note); 728:7 (second note); 730:5-12, 11-12, 12; 733: comments, 12; 735:25; 736:15; 737:comments; 738: comments; 739: comments, 9; 742: comments, 31; 746:25; 748:3; 750: comments, 15, 19; 751:12; 753:7, 18-21; 754: comments; 755:10, 13; 756:16, 19; 757:13-15, 23 (second note); 758:5-7, 11, 12 (second note), 13, 17 (first note), 19, 26; 759:10; 761:43-45; 763:6, 7, 24, 32; 765:30; 767: comments, 5 (second note); 768: comments; 769:17; 770:19; 771:10, 17; 772:10-12; 773: comments; 774:4 (both notes), 4b-7, 7 (second note), 9
(seal usage)
JEN 675:45-48; 676:38, 40; 717:21; 752:37-38; 753:18-21; 762:22-23; 768:22
SILA$_3$
JEN 687:8
sipsiwana
JEN 728:4
SU
See above, Introduction, p. 6.
sutit
JEN 698:5; 699:14
ṣērītu, ṣēru
JEN 729:4
šaptu
Notes to JEN 686:5 (first note); 722:7
ša-qú-ú
JEN 701:6
tabrû
JEN 750:8
ugāru
JEN 682:6; 685:5; 725:4
URU
JEN 761:6
utari
JEN 697:13
Ú-*ti*
JEN 697:13
Yarru
JEN 686:5
ZAG
JEN 761:11

WITNESS SEQUENCES

This list identifies stable (or nearly so) series of witnesses identified with a given town or pair of towns or other toponyms. The place where a witness sequence is discussed is given as well as a list of all texts where the witness sequence can be identified. Unless otherwise indicated, all texts are real estate *mārūtus*.

Arrapḫa?

See note to *JEN* 721:11. The texts of this group are *JEN* 721, 726.

Artiḫi

See first note to *JEN* 686:5. The texts of this group are *JEN* 419, 686, 710, 716, 728.

See note to *JEN* 700:19. The texts of this group are *JEN* 4, 30, 34, 45, 54, 425, 700, *JENu* 973a+1077f(+)973b, 1163, 1183.

See note to *JEN* 705:15. The texts of this group are *JEN* 15, 37, 687, 705. (*JEN* 37 and 687 are especially close.)

See comments to *JEN* 720. The texts of this group are *JEN* 22, 409, 720.

Nuzi

See note to *JEN* 715:9. The texts of this group are *not* a cluster but do have marked similarities. These texts are: *JEN* 213, 259, 693, 715.

See note to *JEN* 748:3. The texts of this group are, strictly speaking, a cluster since, probably, only a single transaction is involved. These texts are: *JEN* 266, 748.

See note to *JEN* 693:37. The texts of this group are *JEN* 46, 693. (Perhaps not a true sequence: the order is not the same.)

Nuzi - Apena

See note to *JEN* 674:23. Cf. note to *JEN* 675:47. The texts of this group are: *JEN* 5, 71, 81, 94, 96, 202, 418, 580, 674-680, and *LG* 1.

Nuzi? - Ḫulumeni?.

See first note to *JEN* 704:5. The texts of this group are *JEN* 41, 43, 704. (The order is not the same.)

Nuzi - Šinina

See note to *JEN* 684:18. The texts of this group are: *JEN* 21, 74, 684, 685, and 766.

Nuzi - Unap-še

See note to *JEN* 690:18. The texts of this group are: *JEN* 44, 51, 58, 70, 408, 581, 582, 690, 756, *JENu* 140a, 716a(+)716d, *SMN* 1721? (=Maidman [1987c]).

See comments to *JEN* 736. The texts of this group are *JEN* 92, 598?, 736, *JENu* 62a. (The order may be: Unap-še - Nuzi.)

(*Nuzi*?-)*Zizza*?

See first note to *JEN* 729:4. The texts of this group are *JEN* 77, 729.

See comments to *JEN* 768. The texts of this group are *JEN* 215, 768.

Šakrušše (*dimtu* of,)

See note to *JEN* 758:5-7. The texts of this group are *JEN* 40, 49, 401, 614, 758, 763, 764, 765. (The order is not stable although the identities of the witnesses mostly are.)

Unap-še (solely?)

See first note to *JEN* 741:28. The texts of this "group" are: *JEN* 38, 91, 741, 743, 744, 751, 841. Some of these are closer to each other than are others. (*JEN* 741 and 744 are close to each other; *JEN* 91 and 751 are very close to each other.)

See second note to *JEN* 743:3. The texts of this group are *JEN* 743, 772.

Unknown locus

See note to *JEN* 718:22. The texts of this group are *JEN* 731, 759.

See comments to *JEN* 733. The texts of this group are *JEN* 578, 733.

See comments to *JEN* 734. The texts of this group are *JEN* 566, 734.

OTHERS

Nuzi? and *Zizza*?

See note to *JEN* 697:18. A rough sequence of three *šupe''ultu* texts: *JEN* 223, 238, 697.

Nuzi?

Slave texts. See comments to *JEN* 769. The texts of this group are *JEN* 611, 769.

CATALOGUE OF INTERRELATED TEXTS

The following list defines texts in *THNT* which are related to other texts. Texts may be interrelated in several ways. They may (a) involve the same principal party (or parties); or (b) document either different phases of the same transaction or different stages in the history of a single object; or (c) mention the same individual now as a principal party, now as the owner (sometimes erstwhile) of land.

These various types of interrelationship are indicated below as follows:

(a) #: ,$\#_2$

(b) #: # - $\#_2$ (in chronological order where this is possible to determine)

#: # ? $\#_2$ (where the direct relationship or the order of the texts is questionable)

(c) #: $\#_2$ (g) (one of these texts contains the PN as a GN, the other as a principal PN)

Further regarding (b), the genres of the texts of each text complex and the sequence of events indicated are briefly indicated.

JEN

674: , *JEN* 532? (According to both, a Kuššiya of Apena apparently has ceded land to the Teḫip-tilla Family.)

675: *JEN* 675 (*mārūtu*) ? 658 (trial; same land?)
, *JEN* 367

681: , *JEN* 683 (Note, however, that the patronym of the adopter is lacking in *JEN* 681.)

682: , *JEN* 69
, *JEN* 791 (g)

683: , *JEN* 681 (*q.v.*)

687[1] , *JEN* 419

[1] Other, formal similarities between *JEN* 687 and *JEN* 37 are discussed in Weeks (1972, 205-6).

697: *JEN* 697 (*šupe''ultu*) ? 544[2] (Possible record of payment of Ú-*ti* of *JEN* 697:12-13.)

699: *JEN* 467 (*tamgurtu*) - 699 (declaration; same land) - 508 (list of cocontracters of *JEN* 467, 699, and of other PNs)

, *JEN* 268

, *JEN* 759?

, *HSS*, XIX, 1

702: , *JEN* 262 (g)[3]

703: *JEN* 703 (*mārūtu*) - 651 (trial; same land) ? 384 (settlement of suit)

, *JEN* 770 - 652 - 365 ? 631 ? 384

, *JEN* 586

, *JEN* 423?

, *JEN* 744

, *JEN* 38

, *JEN* 52

707: *JEN* 707 (*mārūtu*) ? 400 (*mārūtu*) ? 206 (*mārūtu*) - 521 (receipt for tablets).[4]

708: , *JEN* 516? (personnel list)

709: , *JEN* 38?

, *JEN* 52?

716: *JEN* 716 (*mārūtu*) ? 521 (receipt for tablets)[5]

717: *JEN* 717 (*mārūtu*) ? 641 (list of fields)[6]

---

[2] I have collated *JEN* 544. It is essentially correct as copied.

[3] Cf. also *JEN* 583. Weeks (1972, 115-16) suggests that *JEN* 583 and 702 are antecedents to *JEN* 262, an attractive possibility. Cf. also *JEN* 54 for associated real estate.

[4] The complex, *JEN* 400 - 206 - 521 is noted by H. Lewy (1942, 221, nn. 1, 2).

[5] One is tempted to link the Tulpi-šenni son of Turari, adopter in *JEN* 716 (a text witnessed by characteristic Artiḫi witnesses), to the "ḪAP-še-ti" son of Turari of *JEN* 521 (ll. 6-7). (So *NPN*, 55b, *sub voce*; 159b *sub* TURARI 51).) As *JEN* 716 has strong Artiḫi links, so too does *JEN* 521; e.g., cf. l. 4 with *JEN* 30; l. 5 with *JEN* 425. On the connection of *JEN* 521 with other Artiḫi texts, see already H. Lewy (1942, 221 with nn. 1, 2).

Collation of *JEN* 521 itself proved impossible. A slightly indistinct cast of that tablet suggests that ll. 6-7 are probably correct as copied.

[6] More specifically, *JEN* 641:4. The land obtained in *JEN* 717 is less than one homer and is located in Zizza. The land described in *JEN* 641:4 is probably less than one homer and is located in the same area in Zizza. If the Elḫip-... of *JEN* 717 is the Elḫip-šarri son of Turru of *JEN* 641, then *JEN* 641:4 may abstract the transaction recorded in *JEN* 717.

, *JEN* 159?[7]
, *JEN* 745?[7]
, *JEN* 217?[8]
, *JEN* 277(g)?[9]
, *JEN* 778??[10]

723: , *JEN* 742?[11]
, *JEN* 808?[11]
, *JEN* 747 (g)?[11]

737[12]

739: *JEN* 739 (*mārūtu*) ? 545 (receipt)
, *JEN* 411?
, *JEN* 650

741: *JEN* 741 (*mārūtu*) - 656 (trial; same land?)

742: , *JEN* 808
, *JEN* 723?
, *JEN* 747 (g)

744: , *JEN* 38
, *JEN* 52
, *JEN* 703 (*mārūtu*) - 651 (trial; same land) ? 384 (settlement of suit)

745: *JEN* 745 (*mārūtu*) - 641[13] (catalogue of fields)
, *JEN* 159
, *JEN* 217
, *JEN* 717?
, *JEN* 778?

---

7 The principal party is Elḫip-šarri son of Turru. See immediately preceding note.

8 A principal party is possibly Elḫip-šarri.

9 A GN, Elḫip-šarri, in Zizza, is mentioned.

10 A principal party is Elḫip-šarri. This linkage is doubtful. The connection was suggested by Lacheman.

11 The grounds for this possible interrelationship are explicated in the comment to *JEN* 723:1.

12 *JEN* 737 is a Teḫip-tilla Family context. One or both of the brothers who cede real estate in this text appear as principals in the following *non*-Teḫip-tilla contexts: *HSS*, V, 7, 46, 51, 58, 60, 67, 71, 72, 73; IX, 117, 118; XIX, 18.

13 *JEN* 641:1, to be precise.

, *JEN* 277 (g)[10]

746: , *JEN* 140[14]

747: , *JEN* 208 (*mārūtu*) - 369 (trial; same land)
, *JEN* 723 (g)?[15]
, *JEN* 742 (g)
, *JEN* 808 (g)

748: *JEN* 266 (*šupe''ultu*) ? 748 (*šupe''ultu*) ? 131 (declaration of *šupe''ultu*)

750: , *JEN* 259

752: , *JEN* 159

753: , *JEN* 805

755: , *JEN* 562[16]

759: , *JEN* 467? (*tamgurtu*) - 699? (*mārūtu*)

763: , *JEN* 780?

769: , *JEN* 62?
, *JEN* 795?

770: *JEN* 770 (*mārūtu*) - 652 (trial; same land, most likely) - 365 (trial memorandum; same land most likely) ? 631 (declaration possibly pertaining to same land) ? 384 (settlement of suit)
, *JEN* 703 - 651 ? 384
, *JEN* 586
, *JEN* 423?

771: , *JEN* 426 (g)[17]
, *JEN* 3 (g)[17]
JEN 3 (*mārūtu*) - 771[18] (account text)
JEN 771[19] (account text) - 521[20] (catalogue)

---

14 *JEN* 140 may be directly pertinent to *JEN* 746 as a prior record dealing with the same real property.

15 On the connection of these two texts, see note to *JEN* 723:1.

16 More explicitly, *JEN* 562:32-35?.

17 The relationship bears, specifically, on *JEN* 771:1-5.

18 Specifically, *JEN* 771:6-10a.

19 Specifically, ll. 12-13.

20 Specifically, ll. 8-11.

, *JEN* 654[21]

, *JEN* 29 (g)?; 526 (g)?[22]

, *JEN* 346 (g)?[23]

772: , *JEN* 191 or 408 or 399 (cf. 668) or 98 (cf. 107) or none of these.[24]

774: *JEN* 289 (*tidennūtu*) - 517 (receipt) ? 774 (*mārūtu*)

---

21 In specific terms, *JEN* 654:20-22 relates to *JEN* 771:12-14.

22 These two texts (*JEN* 526:18 in the second instance) would relate specifically to *JEN* 771:15.

23 Relating specifically to *JEN* 771:16-17.

24 See *JEN* 772:comments for a discussion of texts possibly connected to *JEN* 772 and for specific references within those texts.

APPENDIX

ADDITIONS TO JEN VII

Presented here for convenience is additional text from *JEN* 775-881, cited in Lacheman and Maidman (1989) as "additional text, see *THNT*." Full details are to be published in the second part of *THNT*.

JEN 776

OBVERSE

(two lines missing after line 11)

12 ⸢*a-na* ^{m}*E*⸣[*n-na-ma-ti*]

16 10 MA.NA AN.[NA.ME]Š? *ù* 1 TÚG [(?)]
17 *an-nu-tù* ^{m}*E*[*n-na*]-*ma-ti*
18 *ki-ma* NÍG.⸢BA⸣ [x (x)] ⸢*a*⸣-*na* ^{m}*Ḫi-iš-me-y*[*a*]
19 ⸢*šum*⸣-*ma* A.Š[À x x x x] x *pa-qí-ra-na* [ ]

LOWER EDGE

20 [^{m}]⸢*Ḫi*⸣-*iš-m*[*e-ya ú-z*]*a*-⸢*ak-ka*$_4$⸣-*ma*
21 [*a-na* ^{m}*En-n*]*a-m*[*a-ti*]

REVERSE

35 (trace)

JEN 779

REVERSE

36 IGI X-[DUMU *Te*]-*eš*-⸢*šu*⸣-[*y*]*a*

JEN 792

REVERSE

23 [ ]x x[ ]

24 [ ]-RI

JEN 827

REVERSE

21 [ ]-⸢*te?-šup*⸣?

24 [ ]-*ti*

UPPER EDGE

S.I.

25 NA$_4$ KIŠIB ^{m}*Ḫu-i-te* x

JEN 846

OBVERSE

17 ⸢*it*⸣-[*ta-du-uš*]

JEN 858

REVERSE

25 (trace)

26 (trace)

(The last line of the copy should be preceded by "[line] 30." Between lines 30 and 31 appears a seal impression.)

JEN 878

OBVERSE

2 (trace)

4 (trace)

BIBLIOGRAPHY OF WORKS CITED

Astour, M.C.

1968 "Mesopotamian and Transtigridian Place Names in the Medinet Habu Lists of Ramses III." *JAOS* 88:733-52.

1970 "Ma'ḫadu, the Harbor of Ugarit." *JESHO* 13:113-27.

1981 "Toponymic Parallels Between the Nuzi Area and Northern Syria." In *SCCNH* [vol. 1,] *In Honor of Ernest R. Lacheman*, ed. M.A. Morrison and D.I. Owen, 11-26. Winona Lake, Ind.: Eisenbrauns.

Borger, R.

1967 *Handbuch der Keilschriftliteratur*. Vol. 1, *Repertorium der sumerischen und akkadischen Texte*. Berlin: Walter de Gruyter & Co.

Brinkman, J., and V. Donbaz.

1977 "A Nuzi Type *Tidennūtu* Tablet Involving Real Estate." *OA* 16:99-104 + 3 plates.

Bush, F.W.

1964 *A Grammar of the Hurrian Language* (Ph.D. diss., Brandeis U.). Ann Arbor, Mich.: University Microfilms.

Cassin, E.

1938 *L'Adoption à Nuzi*. Paris: Adrien Maisonneuve.

1958 "Quelques remarques à propos des archives administratives de Nuzi." *RA* 52: 16-28.

1982 "Heur et malheur du *ḪAZANNU* (Nuzi)." In *Les Pouvoirs locaux en Mésopotamie et dans les régions adjacentes*, ed. A. Finet. Pp. 98-117. Brussels: Institute des hautes études de Belgique.

Cassin, E., and J.-J. Glassner.

1977 *Anthroponymie et Anthropologie de Nuzi*. Vol. 1, *Les Anthroponymes*. Malibu, Calif.: Undena.

Chiera, E.

1927 *JEN*. Vol. 1, *Inheritance Texts*. Paris: Paul Geuthner.

1929 *EN*. Vol. 1, *Texts of Varied Contents*. HSS, 5. Cambridge, Mass.: Harvard U. Press.

1930 *JEN*. Vol. 2, *Declarations in Court*. Paris: Paul Geuthner.

1931 *JEN*. Vol. 3, *Exchange and Security Documents*. Paris: Paul Geuthner.

1934a *JEN*. Vol. 4, *Proceedings in Court*. Philadelphia, Pa.: U. of Pennsylvania Press.

1934b *JEN*. Vol. 5, *Mixed Texts*. Philadelphia, Pa.: U. of Pennsylvania Press.

1938 *They Wrote on Clay*. Chicago, Ill.: U. of Chicago Press.

Chiera, E., and E.A. Speiser.

1927 "Selected 'Kirkuk' Documents." *JAOS*, 47:36-60.

Cohen, H.R.

1978 *Biblical Hapax Legomena in the Light of Akkadian and Ugaritic*. Society for Biblical Literature Dissertation Series, 37. Missoula, Mont.: Scholars Press.

Cogan, M.

1974 *Imperialism and Religion: Assyria, Judah and Israel in the Eighth and Seventh Centuries* B.C.E. Missoula, Mont.: Society of Biblical Literature and Scholars Press.

Contenau, G.

1931 "Textes et Monuments: Tablettes de Kerkouk au Musée du Louvre." *RA* 28:27-39.

Cooper, J.

1974 "*māḫāzu* and ki-šu-peš$_{(5/6/x)}$." *OrNS* 43:83-86.

Cross, D.

1937 *Movable Property in the Nuzi Documents*. AOS, 10. New Haven, Conn.: American Oriental Society.

Dietrich, M., O. Loretz, and W. Mayer.

1972 *Nuzi-Bibliographie*. AOAT, 11. Kevelaer: Butzon & Bercker.

Delitzsch, F.

1920 *Die Lese- und Schreibfehler im alten Testament*. Berlin: Walter de Gruyter.

Dosch, G., and K. Deller.

1981 "Die Familie Kizzuk[:] Sieben Kassitengenerationen in Temtena und ḫuriniwe." In *SCCNH* [vol. 1,] *In Honor of Ernest R. Lacheman*, ed. M.A. Morrison and D.I. Owen, 91-113. Winona Lake, Ind.: Eisenbrauns.

Eichler, B.

1973 *Indenture at Nuzi*. YNER, 5. New Haven, Conn.: Yale U. Press.

Ellis, M.

1976 *Agriculture and State in Ancient Mesopotamia*. Occasional Publications of the Babylonian Fund, 1. Philadelphia, Pa.: Occasional Publications of the Babylonian Fund.

Eph'al, I.

1982 *The Ancient Arabs*. Jerusalem: Magnes Press.

Fadhil, A.

1972 "Rechtsurkunden und Administrative Texte aus Kurruḫanni." Master's thesis, U. of Heidelberg.

1983 *Studien zur Topographie und Prosopographie der Provinzstädte des Königreichs Arrapḫe*. Baghdader Forschungen, 6. Mainz am Rhein: Philipp von Zabern.

Fisher, L.

1959 "Nuzu Geographical Names." Ph.D. diss., Brandeis U.

Frame, G.

1982 "Another Babylonian Eponym." *RA* 76:157-66.

Friberg, J.

1990 "Mathematik." *RLA* 7:531-85.

Gadd, C.J.

1926 "Tablets from Kirkuk." *RA* 23:49-161.

Gelb, I.J.

1941 "Additional Akkadian Values." *AJSL* 53:34-44.

1967 "Approaches to the Study of Ancient Society." *JAOS* 87:1-8.

Gelb, I.J., P.M Purves, and A.A. MacRae.

1943 *Nuzi Personal Names*. OIP, 57. Chicago, Ill.: U. of Chicago Press.

Goetze, A.

1940 (Review of Lacheman [1939b]). *Language* 16: 168-71.

1953 "An Old Babylonian Itinerary." *JCS* 7:51-72.

1956 *The Laws of Eshnunna*. AASOR, 31. New Haven: Department of Antiquities of the Government of Iraq and the American Schools of Oriental Research.

Gordon, C.

1936 "Nouns in the Nuzi Tablets." *Babyloniaca* 16:1-153.

1938 "The Dialect of the Nuzu Tablets." *OrNS* 7:32-63, 215-32.

Grayson, A.K.

1991 "Old and Middle Assyrian Royal inscriptions—Marginalia." In *Ah, Assyria…* . Scripta Hierosolymitana, 33 (Tadmor anniversary volume), ed. M. Cogan, and I. Eph'al, 264-66. Jerusalem: Magnes Press.

Grosz, K.

1988 *The Archive of the Wullu Family*. The Carsten Niebuhr Institute of Ancient Near Eastern Studies, Publications, 5. Copenhagen: Museum Tusculanum.

Hayden, R.

1962 *Court Procedure at Nuzu* (Ph.D. diss., Brandeis U.). Ann Arbor, Mich.: University Microfilms.

Kendall T.

1981 "*gurpisu ša awīli*: The Helmets of the Warriors at Nuzi." In *SCCNH* [vol. 1,] *In Honor of Ernest R. Lacheman*, ed. M.A. Morrison and D.I. Owen, 201-31. Winona Lake, Ind.: Eisenbrauns.

Koschaker, P.

1928 *Neue keilschriftliche Rechtsurkunden aus der el-Amarna-Zeit*. ASAW, 39. Leipzig: S. Hirzel.

1936 (Review of Chiera [1931, 1934a, 1934b]). *OLZ* 39: cols. 151-56.

1944a "Drei Rechtsurkunden aus Arrapḫa." *ZA* 48:161-221.

1944b (Review of Lacheman [1939b] and Nuziana II [*RA* 36]). *OLZ* 47:cols. 98-106.

Kutscher, R.

1969-70 "The Sumerian Equivalents of Akkadian *māḫāzu*" [Hebrew; English summary on sixth page of English appendix]. *Leshonenu* 34:267-69.

Kutscher, Y.

1937 "On Lexical Questions" [Hebrew]. *Leshonenu* 8:136-45.

Lacheman, E.R.

1937 "SU = Šiqlu." *JAOS* 57:181-84.

1939a "Epigraphic Evidences of the Material Culture of the Nuzians." In *Nuzi: Report on the Excavations at Yorghan Tepa*, I, *Text* by R.F.S. Starr, 528-44. Cambridge, Mass.: Harvard U. Press.

1939b *JEN*. Vol. 6, *Miscellaneous Texts*. New Haven, Conn.: American Schools of Oriental Research.

1950 *EN*. Vol. 5, *Miscellaneous Texts from Nuzi, Part II: The Palace and Temple Archives*. HSS, 5. Cambridge, Mass.: Harvard U. Press.

1955 *EN*. Vol. 6, *The Administrative Archives*. HSS, 15. Cambridge, Mass.: Harvard U. Press.

1958 *EN*. Vol. 7, *Economic and Social Documents*. HSS, 16. Cambridge, Mass.: Harvard U. Press.

1962 *EN*. Vol. 8, *Family Law Documents*. HSS, 19. Cambridge, Mass.: Harvard U. Press.

1967 "Les Tablettes de Kerkouk au Musée d'Art et d'Histoire de Genève." *Genava* 15:5-23.

Lacheman, E.R., and M.P. Maidman.

1989 *Joint Expedition with the Iraq Museum at Nuzi, VII: Miscellaneous Texts*. *SCCNH*, vol. 3. Winona Lake, Ind.: Eisenbrauns.

Lacheman, E.R., and D.I. Owen.

1981 "Texts from Arrapḫa and from Nuzi in the Yale Babylonian Collection." In *SCCNH* [vol. 1,] *In Honor of Ernest R. Lacheman*, ed. M.A. Morrison and D.I. Owen, 377-432. Winona Lake, Ind.: Eisenbrauns.

Lacheman, E.R., D.I. Owen, M. Morrison, *et al.*

1987 "Texts in the Harvard Semitic Museum: Excavations at Nuzi 9/1." In *SCCNH*, vol. 2, *General Studies and Excavations at Nuzi 9/1*, ed. D.I. Owen and M.A. Morrison, 355-702. Winona Lake, Ind.: Eisenbrauns.

Leemans, W.F.

1950 *The Old Babylonian Merchant: His Business and Social Position*. Leiden: E.J. Brill.

Lewy, H.

1942 "The Nuzian Feudal System." *OrNS* 11:1-40, 209 -250, 297-349.

1949 "Origin and Development of the Sexagesimal System of Numeration." *JAOS* 69:1-11.

1964 "Notes on the Political Organization of Asia Minor at the Time of the Old Assyrian Texts." *OrNS* 33: 181-98.

1968 "A Contribution to the Historical Geography of the Nuzi Texts." *JAOS*, 88 (= Speiser memorial volume): 150-62.

Lewy, J.

1940 "A New Parallel between ḪĀBĪRU and Hebrews." *HUCA* 15:47-58.

Maidman, M.P.

1976 *A Socio-economic Analysis of a Nuzi Family Archive* (Ph.D. diss., Pennsylvania). Ann Arbor, Mich.: University Microfilms.

1979 "A Nuzi Private Archive: Morphological Considerations." *Assur* 1:179-86.

1981 "The Office of *ḫalṣuḫlu* in the Nuzi Texts." In *SCCNH* [vol. 1,] *In Honor of Ernest R. Lacheman*, ed. M.A. Morrison and D.I. Owen, 233-46. Winona Lake, Ind.: Eisenbrauns.

1987a "*JEN* VII 812: an Unusual Personnel Text from Nuzi." In *SCCNH*, vol. 2, *General Studies and Excavations at Nuzi 9/1*, ed. D.I. Owen and M.A. Morrison, 157-66. Winona Lake, Ind.: Eisenbrauns.

1987b "Royal Inscriptions from Nuzi." In *Assyrian Rulers of the Third and Second Millennia BC (to 1115 BC)* by A.K. Grayson, 331-35. Royal Inscriptions of Mesopotamia: Assyrian Periods, vol. 1. Toronto: U. of Toronto Press.

1987c "A Second Teḫip-Tilla Fragment at Harvard." In *SCCNH*, vol. 2, *General Studies and Excavations at Nuzi 9/1*, ed. D.I. Owen and M.A. Morrison, 349. Winona Lake, Ind.: Eisenbrauns.

1989 "A Revised Publication of a Unique Nuzi Text." In *DUMU-E_2-DUB-BA-A: Studies in Honor of Åke W. Sjöberg*, ed. H. Behrens, *et al.*, 371-81. Occasional Publications of the Samuel Noah Kramer Fund, 11. Philadelphia, Pa.: Occasional Publications of the Samuel Noah Kramer Fund.

1990 "Joins to Five Published Nuzi Texts." *JCS* 42:71-85.

1993 "Some Late Bronze Age Legal Tablets from the British Museum: Problems of Context and Meaning." In *Law, Politics and Society in the Ancient Mediterranean World*, ed. Baruch Halpern and Deborah W. Hobson, 42-89. Sheffield: Sheffield Academic Press.

forthcoming *The Nuzi Texts of the Oriental Institute of the University of Chicago*.

Mayer, W.

1978 *Nuzi-Studien I: Die Archive des Palastes und die Prosopographie der Berufe*. AOAT 205/1. Kevelaer: Butzon & Bercker.

Morrison, M.A.

1987 "The Southwest Archives at Nuzi." In *SCCNH*, vol. 2, *General Studies and Excavations at Nuzi 9/1*, ed. D.I. Owen and M.A. Morrison, 167-201. Winona Lake, Ind.: Eisenbrauns.

1993 "The Eastern Archives at Nuzi." In *SCCNH*, vol. 4, *The Eastern Archives of Nuzi ... and Excavations at Nuzi 9/2*, ed. D.I. Owen and M.A. Morrison, 3-130. Winona Lake, Ind.: Eisenbrauns.

Oppenheim, A.L.

1938 "Étude sur la topographie de Nuzi." *RA* 35:136-55.1939-41 (Review of E. Cassin, *L'Adoption à Nuzi*). *AfO* 13: 74-77.

1964 *Ancient Mesopotamia*. Chicago, Ill.: U. of Chicago Press.

Pfeiffer, R.H.

1932 *EN*. Vol. 2, *The Archives of Shilwateshub Son of the King*. HSS, 9. Cambridge, Mass.: Harvard U. Press.

Pfeiffer, R.H., and E.R. Lacheman.

1942 *EN*. Vol. 4, *Miscellaneous Texts from Nuzi, Part I*. HSS, 13. Cambridge, Mass.: Harvard U. Press.

Pfeiffer, R.H., and E.A. Speiser.

1936 *One Hundred New Selected Nuzi Texts*. AASOR, 16. New Haven, Conn.: American Schools of Oriental Research.

Porada, E.

1947 *Seal Impressions of Nuzi*. AASOR, 24. New Haven, Conn.: American Schools of Oriental Research.

Postgate, J.N.

1973 *The Governor's Palace Archive*. CTN, 2. n.p.: British School of Archaeology in Iraq.

1976 *Fifty Neo-Assyrian Legal Documents*. Warminster: Aris & Phillips.

1989a *The Archive of Urad-Šerūa and His Family: A Middle Assyrian Household in Government Service*. Rome: Roberte Denicola Editore.

1989b "The Ownership and Exploitation of Land in Assyria in the 1st Millennium B.C." In *Reflets des deux fleuves: Volume de mélanges offerts à André Finet*, ed. Marc Lebeau and Philippe Talon, 141-52. Akkadica Supplementum, VI. Leuven: Peeters.

Powell, M.A.

1989-90 "Masse und Gewichte." *RLA* 7:457-517.

Purves, P.M.

1940 "The Early Scribes of Nuzi." *AJSL* 57:162-87.

1945 Commentary on Nuzi Real Property in the Light of Recent Studies. *JNES* 4:68-86.

al-Rawi, F.N.H.

1977 "Studies in the Commercial Life of an Administrative Area of Eastern Assyria in the Fifteenth Century B.C., Based on Published and Unpublished Cuneiform Texts." Ph.D. diss., U. of Wales.

1980 "Two Tidennutu Documents from Tell al-Fahar." *Sumer* 36:133-38.

Von Soden, W.

1965-81 *Akkadisches Handwörterbuch*. Wiesbaden: Otto Harrassowitz.

Von Soden, W., and W. Röllig.

1976 *Das akkadische Syllabar*. 3d ed. AnOr 42. Rome: Pontifical Biblical Institute.

Speiser, E.A.

1941 *Introduction to Hurrian*. AASOR, 20. New Haven: American Schools of Oriental Research.

Steele, F.R.

1943 *Nuzi Real Estate Transactions*. AOS, 25. New Haven: American Oriental Society.

Stein, D.L.

1987 "Seal Impressions on Texts from Arrapḫa and Nuzi in the Yale Babylonian Collection". In *SCCNH*, vol. 2, *General Studies and Excavations at Nuzi 9/1*, ed. D.I. Owen and M.A. Morrison, 225-320. Winona Lake, Ind.: Eisenbrauns.

Tadmor, H.

1961 "Que and Muṣri." *IEJ* 11:143-50.

Weeks, N.K.

1972 *The Real Estate Interests of a Nuzi Family* (Ph.D. diss., Brandeis U.). Ann Arbor, Mich.: University Microfilms.

Wilhelm, G.

1974 "Goldstandard in Nuzi." *Baghdader Mitteilungen* 7:205-8.1980 *Das Archiv des Šilwa-Teššup*, vol. 2: *Rationenlisten*. Wiesbaden: Otto Harrassowitz.

1983 (Review of C. Zaccagnini, *The Rural Landscape of the Land of Arraphe*). *OA* 22:311-13.

1985 *Das Archiv des Šilwa-Teššup*, vol. 3: *Rationenlisten II*. Wiesbaden: Otto Harrassowitz.

n.d. "Gedanken zur Frühgeschichte der Hurriter und zum hurritisch-urartäischen Sprachvergleich." In *Hurriter und Hurritisch*, ed. Volkert Haas, 43-67. Konstanzer Altorientalische Symposien, II = Xenia: Konstanzer Althistorische Vorträge und Forschungen, Heft 21. Konstanz: Universitätsverlag.

Young, G.D.

1973 "Nuzu Texts in the Free Library of Philadelphia." In *Orient and Occident: Essays Presented to Cyrus H. Gordon on the Occasion of his Sixty-fifth Birthday*, ed. H.A. Hoffner, Jr., 223-33. AOAT, 22. Kevelaer: Butzon & Bercker.

Zaccagnini, C.

1975 "The Yield of the Fields at Nuzi." *OA* 14:181-225.

1977a "The Merchant at Nuzi." *Iraq* 39:171-89.

1977b "Pferde und Streitwagen in Nuzi, Bemerkungen zur Technologie." *Jahresbericht des Instituts für Vorgeschichte der Universität Frankfurt a. M.* 1977: 21-38.

1979a "Notes on the Nuzi Surface Measures." *UF* 11:849-56.

1979b "Les Rapports entre Nuzi et Ḫanigalbat." *Assur* 2:1 -27.

1979c *The Rural Landscape of the Land of Arrapḫe*. Quaderni di geografia storica. Rome: U. of Rome.

1981 "A Note on Nuzi Textiles." In *SCCNH* [vol. 1,] *In Honor of Ernest R. Lacheman*, ed. M.A. Morrison and D.I. Owen, 349-61. Winona Lake, Ind.: Eisenbrauns.

1984 "Land Tenure and Transfer of Land at Nuzi (XV-XIV Century B.C." In *Land Tenure and Social Transformation in the Middle East*, ed. by Tarif Khalidi, 79-94. [Beirut:] American University of Beirut.

1989 "Markt." *RLA* 7:421-26.

Zawadzki, S.

1987 "Errors in the Neo-Babylonian Business and Administrative Documents and Problems of Their Deletion." *Papers on Asia Past and Present*. Orientalia Varsoviensia, 1. pp. 15-21. Warsaw: Wydawnictwa Uniwersytetu Warszawskiego.

Studies on the Civilization and Culture of NUZI AND THE HURRIANS

Volume 1. *In Honor of Ernest R. Lacheman on His Seventy-fifth Birthday, April 29, 1981*. Edited by M. A. Morrison and D. I. Owen. Winona Lake: Eisenbrauns, 1982. Pp. xxi + 496. ISBN 0-931464-08-0.

Volume 2. *General Studies and Excavations at Nuzi 9/1*. Edited by D. I. Owen and M. A. Morrison. Winona Lake: Eisenbrauns, 1987. Pp. ix + 723 + 1 foldout. ISBN 0-931464-37-4.

Volume 3. *Joint Expedition with the Iraq Museum at Nuzi VII: Miscellaneous Texts*. By E. R. Lacheman and M. P. Maidman. Edited by D. I. Owen and M. A. Morrison. Winona Lake: Eisenbrauns, 1989. Pp. xii + 307. ISBN 0-931464-45-5.

Volume 4. *The Eastern Archives of Nuzi and Excavations at Nuzi 9/2*. Edited by D. I. Owen and M. A. Morrison. Winona Lake: Eisenbrauns, 1993. Pp. xii + 152 + 244 plates. ISBN 0-931464-64-1.

Volume 5. *General Studies and Excavations at Nuzi 9/3*. Edited by D. I. Owen. Winona Lake: Eisenbrauns, 1994 (in press). Pp. ca. 400. ISBN 0-931464-67-6.

Volume 6. *Two Hundred Nuzi Texts from the Oriental Institute of the University of Chicago*. By M. P. Maidman. Edited by D. I. Owen. Bethesda: CDL Press. Pp. xvi + 443. ISBN 1-883053-05-6.

Volume 7. *Studies on the Civilization and Culture of Nuzi and the Hurrians*. Edited by D. I. Owen and G. Wilhelm. Bethesda: CDL Press, 1995 (in preparation). Pp. ca. 175. ISBN 1-883053-07-2.